Business Analytics

Methods and Cases for Data-Driven Decisions

Business Analytics is about leveraging data analysis and analytical modeling methods to better achieve business objectives. This book is intended for undergraduate and graduate business students with special interest in data science, data science students with special interest in business, and other students with interest in both. It sits at the sweet spot between a cursory survey of business-oriented data science concepts and an in-depth study of statistical learning theory. Methods and cases are presented by appealing to intuition and their business applications, backed up by an appropriate level of mathematical rigor, making the material accessible to students with a broad range of backgrounds: those looking for "So that's how it works!", those looking for "So that's what it's for!", and those looking for "So that's how to do it!" Students will come away well positioned and well differentiated for their future industry, consulting, academic, and government roles as data-savvy business practitioners.

Dr. Richard Huntsinger is an author, professor, expert witness, Silicon Valley entrepreneur, Fortune 500 R&D executive, and management consultant with broad international experience leading programs in data analytics, process automation, and enterprise software development. He has led development and commercialization of more than 20 high-tech products, and has served on the management teams of several venture-backed start-ups from build-out to IPO and acquisition. He now serves as Faculty Director and Distinguished Teaching Fellow at the University of California–Berkeley, where he lectures and oversees research on data science applied to law, business and public policy. He is a strategy and technology advisor to several companies and a frequent guest speaker in industry, academia, and government.

Business Analytics

Methods and Cases for Data-Driven Decisions

Richard Huntsinger
University of California–Berkeley

Shaftesbury Road, Cambridge CB2 8EA, United Kingdom

One Liberty Plaza, 20th Floor, New York, NY 10006, USA

477 Williamstown Road, Port Melbourne, VIC 3207, Australia

314–321, 3rd Floor, Plot 3, Splendor Forum, Jasola District Centre, New Delhi – 110025, India

103 Penang Road, #05–06/07, Visioncrest Commercial, Singapore 238467

Cambridge University Press is part of Cambridge University Press & Assessment, a department of the University of Cambridge.

We share the University's mission to contribute to society through the pursuit of education, learning and research at the highest international levels of excellence.

www.cambridge.org
Information on this title: www.cambridge.org/highereducation/isbn/9781316512159

DOI: 10.1017/9781009057820

When citing this work, please include a reference to the DOI 10.1017/9781009057820

First published 2025

Printed in the United Kingdom by TJ Books Limited, Padstow Cornwall

A catalogue record for this publication is available from the British Library.

A Cataloging-in-Publication data record for this book is available from the Library of Congress.

ISBN 978-1-316-51215-9 Hardback
ISBN 978-1-009-06079-0 Paperback

For Orlando, my mentor

Choices are the hinges of destiny. —Pythagoras

Contents

Detailed Contents

About the Author

Dr. Richard Huntsinger is a professor, expert witness, Silicon Valley entrepreneur, Fortune 500 executive, and management consultant with broad international experience leading programs in operational excellence, data analytics, internet-based and agent-based customer service, process automation, and enterprise software development at organizations such as Hewlett-Packard, AT&T, Symantec, Hitachi, Curtiss-Wright, Bank of America, and US Department of Energy. He has led development and market introduction of more than 20 commercial process automation/data analytics products and customer-facing IT systems. He has served on the management teams of several venture-backed high-tech start-ups from build-out to IPO and acquisition. He now serves as Faculty Director and Distinguished Teaching Fellow at the University of California–Berkeley, where he lectures and oversees research on data strategy and data science applied to law, business, and public policy. He is a strategy and technology advisor to several companies and a frequent guest speaker in industry, academia, and government.

Dr. Huntsinger earned his PhD in Engineering & Public Policy from Carnegie Mellon University; MBA degrees from University of California–Berkeley and Columbia University, honors; and MSc and BSc degrees in Computer Science from California State University, honors. He holds ASQ Six Sigma Black Belt and PMI Project Management Professional certifications.

Preface

Business Analytics: Methods and Cases for Data-Driven Decisions is about leveraging data analysis and analytical modeling methods to better achieve business objectives. Successful business analysts, managers, and executives are increasingly required to leverage newly available data sources – voluminous and varied – to inform their decisions about how to best run their businesses. This book presents a practical data-to-decision process, a rigorous study of 43 data analysis and analytical modeling methods, 14 business cases, and a practicum on implementation skills. It introduces and delves into exploratory data analysis based on statistics and data visualization, descriptive and predictive modeling based on machine learning, and data-driven decision making based on decision science principles and model evaluation. Discussions and examples guide students through how these methods work, expose their individual strengths and weaknesses, and show how to apply them for better business results. The business cases, all based on real industry data, underscore their usefulness.

This book is intended for undergraduate and graduate business students with special interest in data science, data science students with special interest in business, and other students with interest in both. It sits at the sweet spot between a cursory survey of business-oriented data science concepts and an in-depth study of statistical learning theory. Methods are presented by appealing to intuition and their business applications, backed up by an appropriate level of mathematical rigor, making the material accessible to students with a broad range of backgrounds: those looking for "So that's how it works!", those looking for "So that's what it's for!", and those looking for "So that's how to do it!". Students will come away well-positioned and well-differentiated for their future industry, consulting, academic, and government roles as data-savvy business practitioners.

Key Features

Designed for the business-oriented and data-savvy. Methods are explained largely through demonstration, independent of specific technology and always with an eye to how they can be used to inform business decisions. Concepts are developed both bottom-up, building upon simple principles, and top-down, deconstructing complex structures. Details relevant to business decisions, like what assumptions go into the methods and how they perform in various scenarios, are covered rigorously, while other theoretical aspects are covered to an appropriate degree. Copious data tables and data visualizations support the discourse.

Analytical methods with a purpose. In practice, methods are useful only when they are applied to analyses for which they are well-suited. Through copious examples, guidance is provided about how to choose the right methods and data, or combinations of methods and data, to best address a wide variety of business decisions.

Comprehensive collection of analytical methods. A wide array of well-established and leading-edge methods from the exploratory data analysis and machine learning repertoires is represented. The data-to-decision process serves as a context, clarifying how each method fits into the bigger picture. Method presentations are sequenced logically according to the process, but written to also serve later as stand-alone references.

Professional-grade business cases based on real industry data. Several robust business cases complement the method presentations, representing a variety of business functions and industries. All datasets, large and small, are sourced from real industry operations. Only minimal pre-processing is performed on the datasets, so as to provide students practice dealing with the kinds of data-sourcing issues they will likely encounter in their future business roles.

Downloadable reference of method implementations in R. A downloadable reference of over 50 examples of method implementations in R code accompanies this book, along with a library of custom R utility functions and links to select open source libraries of other useful R functions, that demonstrate exactly how to realize the methods and apply them in professional analyses.

Complete course package. A rich set of additional online resources accompanies this book, so that instructors can conveniently stand up new course offerings and enhance existing ones built around the methods and business cases, leveraging classroom-tested lesson plans, homework and exam questions, and other administrative materials. For course offerings that will include coding-based analysis, instructors and students have access to primers, lab work, software tools, guest speaker videos, and examples in interactive Jupyter notebooks running R code.

Experience

The material in this book has been used successfully in several offerings of Advanced Business Analytics, a popular one-semester, upper-division course in the globally top-10 ranked business analytics program at the Haas School of Business, University of California–Berkeley. The course has been attended by students with a variety of backgrounds – not only Business and Data Science majors, but also Economics, Mathematics, Statistics, Computer Science, Operations Research, Engineering, Public Policy, and other Letters & Science majors. The material has also been used in offerings of Applied Machine Learning, a one-semester graduate course in the globally top-ranked data science program at the Graduate School of Information, University of California–Berkeley.

Topics

This book is organized into an executive overview and 11 chapters, each comprising lessons on related methods and business cases.

Executive Overview

We start by setting expectations with a concise overview of everything you will learn about business analytics.

Data & Decisions

We set the stage with an introduction to an end-to-end data-to-decision process that will serve as context and show the relationships between the variety of specific methods that we will cover. Also, we describe how to construct decision models using influence diagrams to analyze decision performance sensitivity to business parameters. This material appears early to help keep our subsequent lessons on more technical material expressed in ways relevant to making business decisions.

Introduction • Data-to-Decision Process Model • Decision Models • Sensitivity Analysis

Data Analysis | Data Preparation, Data Exploration, & Data Transformation

We start our discourse in Chapters 2 through 4 with methods for data analysis and associated cases demonstrating their business application. These methods enable us to get the right part of the data, expose patterns by examining the data from a variety of perspectives, expose the underlying process that may have generated the data, and change the representation of the data to suit a variety of data analysis approaches.

Data Objects • Selection • Amalgamation • Synthetic Variables • Normalization • Dummy Variables • Descriptive Statistics • Similarity • Cross-Tabulation • Data Visualization • Kernel Density Estimation • Balance • Imputation • Alignment • Principal Component Analysis

Predictive Modeling | Classification, Regression, & Ensemble Assembly

We proceed in Chapters 5 through 9 to methods for predictive modeling. We overview how to build models to predict binary categorical results and evaluate quantitatively how much they could help our business. We look into several specific binary classifier construction methods: k-nearest neighbors based on similarities between various parts of the data, logistic regression based on a mathematical function approximated by the data, decision tree based on probabilities inferred from the data, naive Bayes based on probabilities inferred from the data in another way, support vector machine based on boundaries inferred from the data, and perceptron and neural network inspired by how biological neural networks work. Each of these methods can be enhanced to produce multinomial categorical results. Following this, we overview how to build models to predict numerical results and evaluate quantitatively how much they could help our business, and look into linear regression and regression forms of the classifier construction methods. Regression is treated as a variation on classification, with several concepts introduced in the lessons on classification carrying over to regression. Ultimately, we see how to combine predictive models using bagging, boosting, and stacking ensemble assembly methods. For both classification and regression, we see how to systematically tune predictive models to most help our business.

Classification Methodology • Classifier Evaluation • k-Nearest Neighbors • Logistic Regression • Decision Tree • Naive Bayes • Support Vector Machine • Neural Network • Multinomial Classification • Regression Methodology • Regressor Evaluation • Linear Regression • Regression Versions • Bagging • Boosting • Stacking

Descriptive Modeling | Cluster Analysis

In Chapter 10, we introduce methods for cluster analysis that can enable us to discover how customers and other entities are similar to and dissimilar from each other. We start with an overview of cluster analysis and then proceed to look deeper into three methods to cluster the data, each using its own unique approach.

Cluster Analysis Methodology • Cluster Model Evaluation • k-Means • Hierarchical Agglomeration • Gaussian Mixture

Special Data Types

The lessons on modeling methods have so far assumed the availability of data in cross-sectional form. In Chapter 11, we extend the applicability of these methods and introduce new methods to deal with text data, time series data, and network data represented in other forms.

Text Data • Time Series Data • Network Data • PageRank for Network Data • Collaborative Filtering for Network Data

Business Cases

Several robust business cases complement the method presentations, representing a variety of business functions and industries.

High-Tech Stocks: Data preparation with selection, amalgamation, and synthetic variables to discover relationships among companies' financial performance in the high-tech industry.

Fundraising Strategies: Data exploration with descriptive statistics, synthetic variables, cross-tabulation, and data visualization to discover effective fundraising strategies from a historical US presidential campaign.

Iowa Liquor Sales: Data exploration with descriptive statistics, data visualization, and kernel density estimation to discover historical sales patterns that could influence future product management strategies in the beverage industry.

Loan Portfolio: Data transformation with kernel density estimation and principal component analysis to discover relationships predictive of loan defaults in the banking industry.

Loan Portfolio Revisited: Predictive modeling with principal component analysis and k-nearest neighbors to inform loan purchase decisions in the banking industry.

Telecom Customer Churn: Predictive modeling with balance, naive Bayes, cross-validation, and sensitivity analysis to inform a new customer churn reduction strategy in the telecommunications industry.

Truck Fleet Maintenance: Predictive modeling (IIoT industrial internet of things) with balance, principal component analysis, support vector machine, classifier cutoff tuning, and custom test data to inform a new adaptive truck fleet maintenance schedule in the logistics industry.

Facial Recognition: Predictive modeling with principal component analysis and multinomial support vector machine to recognize people in photographs in the gaming industry.

Credit Card Fraud: Comparison of predictive modeling methods to inform a credit card fraud reduction strategy in the financial services industry.

Call Center Scheduling: Predictive modeling with linear regression to inform a partnership agreement between a large retail pet supply client and a business process outsourcing provider.

Fortune 500 Diversity: Cluster analysis to expose race and gender diversity in Fortune 500 companies.

Music Market Segmentation: Cluster analysis with principal component analysis and sensitivity analysis to segment a market for new bands in the music industry.

Deceptive Hotel Reviews: Predictive modeling on text data to detect fraudulent customer surveys and inform a customer service improvement strategy in the hospitality industry.

Targeted Marketing: Network analysis with descriptive statistics for network data to simulate market adoption and inform a marketing strategy in the enterprise software industry.

Online Resources

A rich set of online resources accompanies this book, so that instructors can conveniently stand up new course offerings and enhance existing ones built around the methods and business cases presented in the text.

For Instructors & Students

These resources are available to instructors and students:

Primers: Primers introducing key concepts and coding skills around using Jupyter interactive notebooks, the R language for data analysis, special functions for text and table presentation, functions for data object type manipulation, ggplot2 functions for data visualization, and rgl functions for interactive 3-dimensional data visualization.

Method Implementations: Example implementations of all methods in R, which collectively serve as a comprehensive reference guide and can be leveraged for lab work and project work.

Lab Assignments: Sample lab assignments in R, which can be incorporated into a course offering. Each lab provides students with practice implementing and exploring a specific method.

Project Assignment: A sample term project assignment in R, which can be incorporated into a course offering. The project objective is to recommend a portfolio of equity investments informed by original predictive models based on real financial fundamentals data from thousands of public companies. The project includes sections focusing on data exploration, data transformation, classification and model tuning, regression and model tuning, and model deployment, which can be assigned piecemeal over a term. The project provides students practice implementing the full data-to-decision process. Students have fun pitting their original predictive models against each other, culminating in a friendly contest for the best-performing portfolio.

Function Library: A library of custom R functions to facilitate lessons, labs, and the project.

Datasets: Source data for the business cases and project in csv format.

More Business Cases: Additional business cases, created and available on an ongoing basis, which can be incorporated into a course offering.

Guest Speakers: Video recordings of the author interviewing business practitioners on business analytics applied in real industry settings, created and available on an ongoing basis, which can be incorporated into a course offering.

For Instructors

More resources are available only to instructors.

Syllabi: Sample syllabi for terms of various lengths.

Lesson Plans: Sample lesson plans for terms of various lengths, detailing pace of topic coverage.

Exam Questions & Solutions: Sample exam questions and their solutions.

Lab Solutions: Solutions for the sample lab assignments.

Project Solutions & Reporting Tool: Solutions for the sample term project and a tool to report on students' submissions. Students have fun viewing the report together to see how their recommended portfolios stand up to each other.

Acknowledgements

Thank you to Cambridge University Press and the University of California–Berkeley for providing a supportive environment in which to write this book.

Special thanks are due to professors Paul Fischbeck and Eduard Hovy, and to Jay Stowsky. My work on machine learning and decision theory at Carnegie Mellon University under Paul and Ed's guidance and encouragement led directly to the material realized in this book. Jay, as head of instruction at Berkeley's Haas School of Business, sponsored the creation of the Advanced Business Analytics course where the material for this book took form.

And very special thanks to all my delightful students. Their feedback and suggestions, gathered over class discussions and countless office hour meetings, have been invaluable.

And, of course, infinite thanks to Diane.

Richard Huntsinger, PhD
Berkeley, California USA
June 2024

Executive Overview

Executive Overview

What you'll learn about business analytics for data-driven decisions.

Business Analytics for Data-Driven Decisions

When making a business decision, you can theorize about what happened in the past, is happening now, or will happen in the future. You can then decide what to do based on your best estimates, which will consequently lead to a business result. You might assume that when your estimates are based on patterns you detect in some relevant data, then your estimates will be better, and so your decisions will be better, and so the business result will be better. Indeed, this is often the case. Challenges arise, however, when the patterns in the data are difficult to detect.

Business analytics combine contributions from statistics, computer science, and other fields to detect non-obvious patterns in the data, so that you can make good estimates, so that you can make good decisions, so that you will get good business results more often.

Business analytics enable you to find and quantify answers to questions like these:

- What are the patterns in the data?
- What estimates can be made from these patterns?
- What are the probabilities that the estimates are right or wrong, and what are the probabilities that the estimates are wrong in any of several different ways?
- What decision best leverages the estimates and the probabilities?
- What is the probability that a decision will lead to a good business result, and what are the probabilities that it will lead to any of several other business results?

Data Landscape

Here are a few key terms with definitions that we will adopt in our discourse:

Decision modeling is about exploring the effects of data-informed decisions.

Intuition is about discerning patterns from experience. **Statistical analysis** is about discerning patterns in data. It comprises **descriptive statistics** for summarizing data, **statistical inference** for inferring implications of data samples, and other methods.

Data science comprises **data management** for retrieving and curating data, **data engineering** for designing data pipelines, **statistical analysis**, **computational statistics** for computationally intensive statistical analysis, **data analysis**, and **analytical modeling**. Data engineering involves **cluster computing**, **stream computing**, and **cloud computing** focusing on the parallel processing, incremental availability, and remote access aspects of computing, respectively. Data analysis comprises **descriptive statistics**, **data visualization**, and other methods for representing data, summarizing data with numbers, and summarizing data with graphics. Analytical modeling comprises **machine learning** and other methods to construct models from data. Machine learning comprises **descriptive modeling** to organize data, **predictive modeling** to predict the unknown from data, and **network analysis** to study data about relationships. Machine learning methods improve automatically with increasing exposure to data, without being explicitly programmed to do so.

Computational statistics is also known as **data analytics** or **data mining**. Machine learning is also known as **statistical learning**. Descriptive modeling is also known as **unsupervised learning** or **cluster analysis**. Predictive modeling is also known as **supervised learning**.

Business analytics is about applying data science and other sciences to business problems. **Business intelligence** is about applying data analysis to business situational awareness.

Artifical intelligence is about methods performed by machine that result in actions historically considered doable only by human intellect. Machine learning is a sub-field of artificial intelligence.

Data-to-Decision Process Model

The **data-to-decision process model** prescribes a way to make data-informed decisions by iteratively working through four stages:

- **Decision modeling** involves exploring the effects of data-informed decisions.
- **Data retrieval** involves retrieving data for use in decision making.
- **Data analysis** involves preparing, exploring, and transforming data in various ways to expose patterns that could lead to non-obvious insights useful in decision making.
- **Analytical modeling** involves constructing models that further expose patterns in data by estimating the underlying processes responsible for generating the data. Such models can make predictions or suggest ways to organize data to reveal non-obvious insights useful in decision making.

Decision Model

A **decision model** estimates business results that would come about from various decisions as informed by a business model, business parameter values, and decision method.

A **business model** describes how a business converts products and services into money or other benefits. The business model is a component of the decision model.

Business parameters detail and quantify various aspects of a business's operating environment.

Sensitivity analysis explores the relationship between decision performance, business parameter values, and business results. It exposes and quantifies how much potential changes in decision performance and business parameter values would affect the business results.

A decision model can be conveniently expressed as an **influence diagram**, useful for communicating assumptions upon which the model is based.

Analytical Model

An **analytical model** is a formula or algorithm with inputs and outputs, perhaps simple or perhaps complex, that can act directly as a decision method or indirectly as a tool to inform decision making. Machine learning methods, guided by patterns they detect in data, have proved to be an effective and popular way to construct useful analytical models. Model construction is also known as **training** a model or **fitting** a model.

One kind of analytical model predicts as-yet unobserved examples not explicitly reflected in data. This is a **predictive model**. It could be constructed using a **predictive modeling method**, also known as a **supervised learning method**, so called because the method makes use of examples of correct predictions. A predictive model that predicts categorical values is called a **classifier**, the categorical values it predicts are called **classes**, and a method to construct it is called a **classifier construction method**. A predictive model that predicts numerical values is called a **regressor**, the numerical values it predicts are called **outcomes**, and a method to construct it is called a **regressor construction method**.

Another kind of analytical model organizes data into clusters. This is a **cluster model**. It could be constructed using a **descriptive modeling method**, also known as a **cluster analysis method**, also known as an **unsupervised learning method**, so called because the method does not make use of examples of correct organizations.

Another kind of analytical model considers relationships between entities. This is a **network**.

A model comprising a combination of several other models working in concert is called an **ensemble model**, and is constructed by an **ensemble assembly method**.

Any particular model construction method is defined by its general approach and its specific **hyper-parameter** values. Any particular model, constructed by such a method, is defined by its general form and its specific **parameter** values.

Data Analysis Methods

Data analysis makes use of methods for data preparation, data exploration, and data transformation.

Data Preparation

After data are retrieved, and perhaps in response to data exploration, it is often necessary to adjust their representation, without introducing new information beyond the original data. This is **data preparation**. Here are some popular data preparation methods:

- **Selection and amalgamation** involve slicing and dicing data to get at just a subset of interest, which could include a subset of observations and/or a subset of variables, arranged in various ways.
- **Synthesis** adds new variables whose values are constructed based only on information already captured in the original data.

Data Exploration

After data are retrieved, and perhaps in response to preparing or transforming their representation, it might be useful to to look for patterns in the data that can produce insights and inform decisions. This is **data exploration**.

A **descriptive statistic** is a number that conveniently summarizes some data, specifically one or more variable distributions. Popular descriptive statistics include size, probability, arithmetic mean, geometric mean, median, mode, weighted average, variance, standard deviation, percentile, and correlation coefficient.

A **cross-table** is a table that conveniently summarizes some data, organized by rows and columns that correspond to variable values, and aggregated by various functions like mean, sum, or count.

A **data visualization** is a graphic representation of some data, specifically one or more variable distributions. Here are some popular data visualizations:

- A **scatterplot** shows distributions of some numerical variables represented by points positioned along axes, and perhaps distributions of other categorical variables represented by color, size, shape, or pattern.
- A **scatterplot projection** is a scatterplot with 3 axes, projected onto a flat surface.
- An **animation** or **trellis** shows the distribution of a variable, often indicating time, represented by a sequence of other data visualizations.
- A **lineplot** shows distributions of some numerical variables represented by points positioned along axes, and further relationships between data represented by line segments connecting the points, and perhaps distributions of other categorical variables represented by color, size, shape, or pattern.
- A **bar chart** shows the distribution of a categorical variable represented by heights of adjacently positioned bars, and perhaps distributions of other categorical variables represented by color or pattern.
- A **histogram** shows counts of particular ranges of values in the distribution of a numerical variable represented by heights of adjacently positioned bars.
- A **density plot** shows an estimated proportion of values within any range of a numerical variable represented by the area under a curve. The **kernel density estimation** method is one way to produce a density plot.
- Other data visualizations include **stepplot**, **pathplot**, **pie chart**, **violinplot**, **boxplot**, **heat map**, and **conditional format**.

Data Transformation

After a dataset is retrieved and perhaps in response to preparing or exploring it, it might be useful to transform its representation, perhaps even introducing new information beyond the original data, so that various methods can be applied or made more effective. This is **data transformation**. Here are some popular data transformation methods:

- **Balance** duplicates or removes observations to make a particular categorical variable distribution reflect equal numbers of each possible value.
- **Imputation** fills in missing values with synthetic values, often derived from descriptive statistics.

- **Alignment** expands or contracts observations to make a particular variable distribution match another dataset's particular variable distribution, often indicating time.
- **Principal component analysis** synthesizes a set of new variables, called **principal components**, that capture in entirety the same relationships between observations as do the original variables, but concentrate variance disproportionately in just the first few of the new variables.

Data Transformation of Special Data Types

Many data analysis and analytical modeling methods cannot be applied directly to text, time series, or network data because of their special representations. Often, though, these methods can be applied to such data when transformed to an appropriate alternative representation.

- **Text data** can be transformed to **document-term matrix** form, where observations correspond to documents and variables correspond to occurrences of words. Data analysis and analytical modeling methods can then be applied as usual.
- **Time series data** can be transformed to **cross-sectional data**, where observations correspond to points in time and include variables with information about points in time past called **lookbacks** and points in time future called **lookaheads**. Data analysis and analytical modeling methods can then be applied to forecast by **direct prediction** some number of timesteps ahead of a **viewpoint**, or by **recursive prediction** one timestep ahead of previous predictions.
- **Network data** are often represented in a special form such as an **adjacency matrix** or **link list**, and data analysis on them requires special descriptive statistics, like **PageRank**. **Recommender systems** based on **collaborative filtering** operate on **bipartite graphs**, a special kind of network data.

Analytical Modeling Methods

Analytical modeling makes use of methods for model construction, model evaluation, and model tuning that rely on data.

Model Construction Methods

Analytical modeling methods include methods to produce binary classifiers, multinomial classifiers, regressors, ensemble models, and cluster models.

Predictive Model Construction: Binary Classifiers A **binary classifier construction method** examines data to construct a predictive model capable of estimating the probabilities that new unclassified observations should be classified as one class or another class. From these probabilities, taken along with some chosen **cutoff** threshold, you can predict a new observation's class. Such a predictive model is called a **binary classifier**, or often just a **classifier**.

Here are some popular binary classifier construction methods:

- The **k-nearest neighbors (kNN)** method (classification version) constructs predictive models based on how similar observations are to each other. Hyper-parameters include number of nearest neighbors and others. Measures of dissimilarity can be Manhattan distance, Euclidean distance, cosine distance, or others.

- The **logistic regression** method constructs predictive models based on the optimal S-shaped hyper-curve through observations in variable space.
- The **decision tree (DT)** method (classification version) constructs predictive models based on the optimal splitting of the data into progressively smaller subsets of data. Hyper-parameters include maximum depth of tree, maximum number of nodes, and others.
- The **naive Bayes** method constructs predictive models based on probabilities and conditional probabilities of values appearing in the data. **LaPlace smoothing** is a technique incorporated into the naive Bayes method that may improve its models' predictions. Hyper-parameters include LaPlace smoothing factor and others.
- The **support vector machine (SVM)** method constructs predictive models based on an optimal separation of observations in variable space. Hyper-parameters include cost, kernel, and others.
- The **neural network** method (classification version) constructs predictive models based on how values appearing in the data can be combined as they propagate throughout a network structure. This method is inspired by, but different from, how biological brain neurons communicate with each other. Hyper-parameters include number of levels, number of nodes in each level, and others. The **perceptron** method is a simplified version of the neural network method. **Deep learning** refers to constructing models using the neural network method.

Predictive Model Construction: Multinomial Classifiers A **multinomial classifier construction method** is a generalization of a binary classifier construction method, which constructs a predictive model capable of estimating the probabilities that new observations should be classified as any of several classes. Such a predictive model is called a **multinomial classifier**, or often just a **classifier**.

Here are some popular classifier construction methods that have both binary and multinomial forms:

- k-nearest neighbors
- decision tree
- naive Bayes
- neural network

Any binary classifier can be converted to a multinomial classifier by applying either of two binary-to-multinomial conversion approaches:

- The **one vs. one** approach reorganizes a dataset into several other datasets, one for each class versus all other classes treated as a single other class. Models are constructed based on all these datasets, and predictions are made by majority rule or cutoff among the models.
- The **one vs. rest** approach reorganizes a dataset into several other datasets, one for each pair of classes, excluding the other classes. Models are then constructed based on these datasets, and predictions are made by a round robin tournament among the models.

Predictive Model Construction: Regressors A **regressor construction method** examines data to construct a predictive model capable of predicting numerical values associated with new unknown-outcome observations. Such a predictive model is called a **regressor**.

Here are some popular regressor construction methods:

- The **k-nearest neighbors (kNN)** method (regression version) constructs predictive models based on how similar observations are to each other. Hyper-parameters include number of nearest neighbors and others. Measures of dissimilarity can be Manhattan distance, Euclidean distance, cosine distance, or others.
- The **decision tree (DT)** method (regression version) constructs predictive models based on the optimal splitting of the data into progressively smaller subsets of data. Hyper-parameters include maximum depth of tree, maximum number of nodes, and others.
- The **support vector regression (SVR)** method constructs predictive models based on an optimal separation of observations in variable space. Hyper-parameters include cost, kernel, and others.
- The **neural network** method (regression version) constructs predictive models based on how values appearing in the data can be combined as they propagate throughout a network structure. This method is inspired by, but different from, how biological brain neurons communicate with each other. Hyper-parameters include number of levels and number of nodes in each level. **Deep learning** refers to constructing models using the neural network method.
- The **linear regression** method constructs predictive models based on the optimal line, plane, or hyper-plane fitted through observations in variable space.

Some regressor construction methods involve finding optimal solutions to various formulae, using search algorithms such as **gradient descent** or others.

Predictive Model Construction: Ensemble Models An **ensemble assembly method** combines several component predictive models, constructed by component methods, working in concert to construct a new predictive model with benefits derived from all the component models.

Here are some popular ensemble assembly methods:

- The **bootstrap aggregating (bagging)** ensemble assembly method produces a set of predictive models, each constructed by a common model construction method, but based on different random subsets of a reference dataset. You can think of the resulting model as a committee of experts.
- The **boosting** ensemble assembly method produces a set of predictive models, each constructed by a common model construction method, based on a single component method, but based on different random subsets of a reference dataset, where each subset includes disproportionately more observations predicted incorrectly by previously constructed models. You can think of the resulting set of predictive models as a committee of experts, with each expert having increasingly specialized knowledge.
- The **stacking** ensemble assembly method constructs predictive models based on several component methods, and on the predictions made by models constructed using those component methods. You can think of the resulting model as a committee of experts on other experts.
- The **random forest** method is a variation on bootstrap aggregating. It uses decision tree as the single component method, uses several random subsets of data, and also uses several randomly selected variables.

Descriptive Model Construction: Cluster Models A **cluster analysis method** examines data and organizes observations into several clusters. Such an organization is called a **cluster model**, and can be useful for informing decisions involving market segmentation and other business applications.

Here are some popular cluster analysis methods:

- **k-means** constructs cluster models by tentatively organizing observations into several clusters and then iteratively improving the organization based on the observations' similarity to other observations.
- **Hierarchical agglomeration** constructs cluster models by agglomerating observations into clusters based on the observations' similarity to other observations.
- **Gaussian mixture** constructs cluster models by assigning observations partial membership in all possible clusters and then iteratively concentrating membership in the most expected assignments.

Popular ways to measure dissimilarity between observations include **Manhattan distance**, **Euclidean distance**, **cosine distance**, and others. Measures of dissimilarity between clusters are calculated assuming some **linkage**, which can be **single**, **complete**, **centroid**, or **average** linkage.

Model Evaluation Methods

Model evaluation is about quantifying the performance of models so that you can compare their likely usefulness. For predictive models, we are interested in how well they predict. For descriptive models, we are interested in how well they organize.

Predictive Model Evaluation You can quantify a predictive model's performance by constructing it based on **training** data, and then seeing how well it predicts something about **testing** data. Here are three popular methods to evaluate a predictive model's performance: **in-sample** performance evalaution, **out-of-sample** performance evaluation, and **cross-validation** performance evaluation. Each has its own particular way of dealing with training and testing data.

In-sample performance evaluation of a model constructed from all the data works like this: Use the model to predict the classes/outcomes of the data, and compare those predictions with the known actual classes/outcomes measured per some performance metric. This method has the advantage that the model is constructed from all the data, but has the disadvantage that predictions are about data already known to the model.

Out-of-Sample performance evaluation of a model constructed from all the data works like this: Construct a new model from a subset of all the data (referred to as **training data**) to predict the classes/outcomes of the remaining data (referred to as **testing data**), and then compare those predictions with the known actual classes/outcomes per some performance metric. The new model is constructed using the same method and hyper-parameter values as those for the model to be evaluated, but using different data. Assume that the new model has performance closely approximating that of the model to be evaluated. This method is also known as **holdout** performance evaluation, and the testing data are also known as the holdout data. This method has the disadvantage that the new model is constructed from only some of the data, but has the advantage that predictions are about data not known to the model.

Cross-validation performance evaluation of a model constructed from all the data works like this: Partition the data into subsets called **folds**. For each fold, construct a model from data not in that fold and use it to make predictions about data that are in that fold. Evaluate the out-of-sample performance of each of these models, and average the results. Assume that the models on average have performance closely approximating that of the model to be evaluated. This method has the advantage that the models taken together are constructed from all the data, and further has the advantage that predictions made by any particular model are about data not known to that model.

When evaluating a **classifier**, the **confusion matrix** for some model, testing dataset, and cutoff threshold indicate the relationship between how the model would predict classes and the known actual classes. For a binary classifier, the confusion matrix is a 2×2 matrix comprising four counts of predictions: predicted positive class observations that are actually positive class observations, predicted positive class observations that are actually negative class observations, predicted negative class observations that are actually positive class observations, and predicted negative class observations that are actually negative class observations.

Classifier performance metrics are calculated from values in a confusion matrix. Here are some popular classifier performance metrics:

- accuracy (also known as correct prediction rate)
- true positive rate (also known as sensitivity or recall)
- true negative rate (also known as specificity)
- false positive rate
- false negative rate
- positive predictive value (also known as precision)
- negative predictive value
- f1 score
- business result, calculated per a decision model

When evaluating a **regressor**, the **error table** for some model and testing dataset indicates the relationship between how the model would predict outcomes and the known actual outcomes.

Regressor performance metrics are calculated from values in an error table. Here are some popular regressor performance metrics:

- root mean square error (RMSE)
- mean absolute percent error (MAPE)
- business result, calculated per a decision model

Descriptive Model Evaluation Popular cluster model performance metrics include **dispersion ratio**, **Bayes information criterion (BIC)**, **Akaike information criterion (AIC)**, and others. Each of these reflects the average dissimilarity between observations within a cluster and the average dissimilarity between clusters.

Model Tuning Methods

Model tuning is about systematically optimizing the choice of model construction method, variables, hyper-parameter settings, and/or cutoff settings to produce a well- or best-performing analytical model.

Here are three popular approaches to model tuning:

- **Forward feature selection** evaluates the effect of using each variable individually, keeping the best variable, and then proceeding to evaluate the effects including additional variables.
- **Backward feature selection** evaluates the effect of using each combination of all variables less one, keeping the best combination, and then proceeding to evaluate the effects removing variables.
- **Exhaustive feature selection** evaluates the effect of each possible combination of variables.

Principal component analysis is often used in combination with forward feature selection to reduce the number of variables.

Technology

R and Python are popular open-source computer programming languages often used for data analysis and analytical modeling. Both languages can be used within special interactive development environments (IDE) or within Jupyter notebooks running on a local machine or JupyterHub server.

SQL is a popular query language often used for data selection, data amalgamation, and other aspects of data management and data analysis.

Copious commercial software applications are available for data management, data analysis, and analytical modeling, too.

1 | Data and Decisions

Learning Objectives

Terms

Know the terms:

- Data-to-decision process model
- Process diagram
- Analytical modeling
- Decision model
- Influence diagram
- Sensitivity

Use the Methods

Know how to use the methods:

- Interpret the data-to-decision process model expressed as a process diagram.
- Construct a decision model to map a decision to a business result.
- Construct a decision model to map a decision method to a business result.
- Express a decision model as an influence diagram.
- Interpret a decision model expressed as an influence diagram.
- Estimate a business result using a decision model.
- Analyze a decision model to show how adjustments in decision method performance can affect a business result.
- Analyze a decision model to show how adjustments in business parameter values can affect a business result.

1.1 Introduction

1.1.1 Let's Make a Deal

Here is the game. You are presented with 3 doors. You can't see what is behind them, but you have been truthfully told that behind 1 door is a fabulous luxury car, which you want. Behind the other 2 doors are goats, which you don't want. You get to choose any 1 of the doors and receive the prize behind it.

Which door should you choose? Your intuition and basic statistics tell you that each door has the same $\frac{1}{3}$ probability of fronting the car. It seems that any choice is equally likely to win you the car, so perhaps you randomly choose door 1.

But now things get more interesting. You are shown a goat behind 1 of the doors that you didn't choose, say door 2, and offered a chance to choose a different door. Should you change your choice to door 3 or stay with your initial choice of door 1? What does your intuition tell you? What does basic statistics tell you? Perhaps it seems that either choice of door 1 or door 3 is still equally likely to win you the car, so neither choice would give you any advantage. Based on this reasoning, perhaps you discard the new information about door 2 as useless and randomly decide to stay with door 1. It turns out that the car is actually behind door 3, so you don't win, but you can console yourself with the knowledge that this result is just a coincidence. The car could easily have been behind door 1.

	situation			change strategy			stay strategy		
	prize	initial	shown	final	win	win.cumulative	final	win	win.cumulative
1	3	1	2	3	1	1	1	0	0

Indeed, if you were to play this game 10 times and always stay with your initial choice, perhaps you would expect to win about half of the time. Here is a record of someone doing just that. See that the player wins 5 out of 10 times with an always-stay strategy.

	situation			change strategy			stay strategy		
	prize	initial	shown	final	win	win.cumulative	final	win	win.cumulative
1	3	1	2	3	1	1	1	0	0
2	3	1	2	3	1	2	1	0	0
3	3	2	1	3	1	3	2	0	0
4	3	3	1	2	0	3	3	1	1
5	3	3	1	2	0	3	3	1	2
6	2	3	1	2	1	4	3	0	2
7	1	1	2	3	0	4	1	1	3
8	2	2	3	1	0	4	2	1	4
9	3	3	1	2	0	4	3	1	5
10	2	1	3	2	1	5	1	0	5

However, play the game 10 more times, and see that by the 20th iteration, an always-change strategy wins more often than an always-stay strategy.

	situation			change strategy			stay strategy		
	prize	initial	shown	final	win	win.cumulative	final	win	win.cumulative
11	2	2	3	1	0	5	2	1	6
12	2	1	3	2	1	6	1	0	6
13	2	3	1	2	1	7	3	0	6
14	1	1	3	2	0	7	1	1	7
15	3	2	1	3	1	8	2	0	7
16	3	3	2	1	0	8	3	1	8
17	3	1	2	3	1	9	1	0	8
18	3	1	2	3	1	10	1	0	8
19	1	2	3	1	1	11	2	0	8
20	1	2	3	1	1	12	2	0	8

Play the game 1,000 times and a clear pattern in the data emerges. By the 1,000th iteration, an always-change strategy wins about twice as often.

	situation			change strategy			stay strategy		
	prize	initial	shown	final	win	win.cumulative	final	win	win.cumulative
991	2	3	1	2	1	673	3	0	318
992	1	1	3	2	0	673	1	1	319
993	1	1	3	2	0	673	1	1	320
994	3	3	2	1	0	673	3	1	321
995	3	2	1	3	1	674	2	0	321
996	1	1	3	2	0	674	1	1	322
997	3	1	2	3	1	675	1	0	322
998	2	3	1	2	1	676	3	0	322
999	3	3	1	2	0	676	3	1	323
1000	1	2	3	1	1	677	2	0	323

Although it might go against your intuition, the revelation of a goat behind 1 of the doors that you don't initially choose is not useless information. Before your initial choice, each door has a $\frac{1}{3}$ probability of fronting the car. That means the 2 doors that you don't choose have a $\frac{2}{3}$ probability of fronting the car. When the goat is revealed, those 2 doors still have a $\frac{2}{3}$ probability of fronting the car. So, you can choose 1 of those 2 doors with $\frac{2}{3}$ probability of winning – just be sure not to choose the door that you now know comes with a goat. The $\frac{2}{3}$ probability of winning with a new choice is double the $\frac{1}{3}$ probability of winning with the initial choice.

The lesson here is that sometimes insights discerned from patterns in data can usefully inform a business decision. It's important to ***understand what the data are telling you***.

1.1.2 Let's Make Another Deal

Here is another game. You and a group of other businesspeople are presented with 1 door. You can't see what is behind it, but you have been truthfully told it fronts a gem worth between \$1 and \$1,000,000. The sight-unseen gem goes up for auction and you get to bid any amount.

How much should you bid? Perhaps you are risk-averse and decide to not bid at all. Perhaps you are risk-prone and decide to bid some amount, but not close to \$1,000,000.

But now things get more interesting. You are truthfully told that there is a 99% probability that the gem behind the door is worth \$1,000,000. Should you change your mind and bid at least a small amount? How about bidding \$500,000, half the gem's anticipated worth? How about bidding \$990,000, the expected value of the gem's worth? What does your intuition tell you? What does basic statistics tell you? Perhaps it seems like an opportunity too good to pass up.

Although it might go against your intuition, the revelation of a 99% probability of high worth is useless information. Probability is a statistic to summarize data, but here we don't know which data. It turns out that before the auction, a \$1,000,000 gem was placed behind the door. Then it was removed. Then it was replaced. That happened 99 times. Then some gem, which could have been a \$1,000,000 gem or any other gem, was placed behind the door. For 99 out of 100 times, that is to say with 99% probability, the gem behind the door is worth \$1,000,000. For 1 out of 100 times, that is to say with 1% probability, the gem behind the door is worth some unknown amount. But that gem is the only one relevant to the decision, and it's the only one we don't know anything about.

The lesson here is that sometimes insights discerned from patterns in data are irrelevant to a business decision. It's important to ***understand what the data are telling you and what they're not telling you***.

1.1.3 Data Landscape

W. Edwards Deming famously cautioned us, "Without data, you're just another person with an opinion." As we set out for ways to better understand data to better inform our business decisions, we enter an exciting, active landscape of research and practice. Here is a taxonomy of methods in the field.

Decision modeling is about exploring the effects of data-informed decisions.

- Decision Modeling *(effects of decisions)*

Intuition is about discerning patterns from experience. **Statistical analysis** is about discerning patterns in data. It comprises **descriptive statistics** for summarizing data, **statistical inference** for inferring implications of data samples, and other methods.

- Intuition *(patterns discerned from experience)*
- Statistical Analysis *(patterns discerned from data)*
  - Descriptive Statistics *(summarize data)*
  - Statistical Inference *(hypothesis testing)*
  - Other methods

Data science comprises **data management** for retrieving and curating data, **data engineering** for designing data pipelines, **statistical analysis**, **computational statistics** for computationally intensive statistical analysis, **data analysis**, and **analytical modeling**. Data engineering involves **cluster computing**, **stream computing**, and **cloud computing** focusing on the parallel processing, incremental availability, and remote access aspects of computing, respectively. Data analysis comprises **descriptive statistics**, **data visualization**, and other methods for representing data, summarizing data with numbers, and summarizing data with graphics. Analytical modeling comprises **machine learning** and other methods to construct models from data. Machine learning comprises **descriptive modeling** to organize data, **predictive modeling** to predict the unknown from data, and **network analysis** to study data about relationships. Machine learning methods improve automatically with increasing exposure to data, without being explicitly programmed to do so.

Computational statistics is also known as **data analytics** or **data mining**. Machine learning is also known as **statistical learning**. Descriptive modeling is also known as **unsupervised learning** or **cluster analysis**. Predictive modeling is also known as **supervised learning**.

- Data Science
  - Data Management *(retrieve and curate data)*
  - Data Engineering *(design data pipeline)*
  - Statistical Analysis *(patterns discerned from data)*
  - Computational Statistics
    (statistics + computer science, patterns discerned from data by machine, also known as Data Analytics or Data Mining)
    - Data Analysis
    - Machine Learning *(also known as Statistical Learning)*
      - Descriptive Modeling *(also known as Unsupervised Learning or Cluster Analysis)*
      - Predictive Modeling *(also known as Supervised Learning)*
      - Network Analysis
    - Other analytical modeling methods

Business Analytics is about applying data science and other sciences to business problems.

- Business Analytics
  - Descriptive Statistics applied to business problems
  - Data Visualization applied to business problems
  - Descriptive Modeling applied to business problems
  - Predictive Modeling applied to business problems
  - Stochastic Modeling applied to business problems *(also known as Simulation)*
  - Prescriptive Analytics applied to business problems *(also known as Optimization)*
  - Other methods

Business intelligence is about applying data analysis to business situational awareness.

- Business Intelligence
  - Descriptive Statistics applied to business situational awareness
  - Data Visualization applied to business situational awareness
  - Other methods

Artifical intelligence is about methods performed by machine that result in actions historically considered doable only by human intellect. Machine learning is a sub-field of artificial intelligence.

- Artifical Intelligence
  - Rule-Based Systems *(rules/heuristics specified, also known as Expert Systems)*
  - Machine Learning *(rules/heuristics discerned from data)*
  - Other methods

Because data science comprises contributions from several fields, much of its terminology is not universally agreed upon. In some business, academic, and popular circles, you can expect to hear some of these terms used with redundant, ambiguous, or even contradictory meanings.

1.2 Data-to-Decision Process Model

Adopt a data-to-decision process model to guide data-informed decision making.

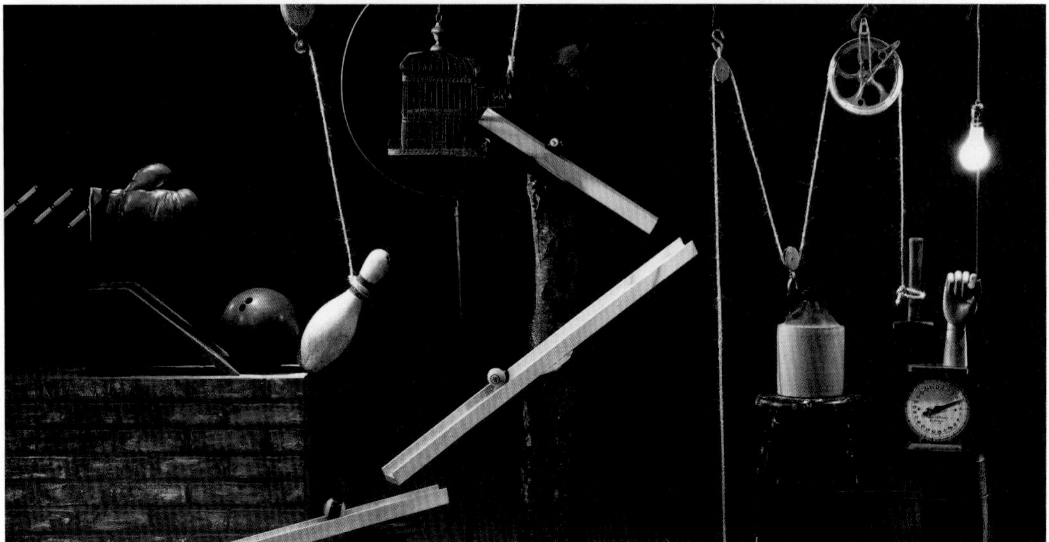

1.2.1 Introduction

How do you bring together the cornucopia of data methods to go from receiving data to making a decision? In our discourse, we adopt an end-to-end data-to-decision process model to guide us through a logical sequence of analysis activities, feeding the outputs of the various methods as inputs to other methods along the way, to ultimately reach a decision.

1.2.2 From Data to Decision

The **data-to-decision process model** prescribes a way to make data-informed decisions by iteratively working through four stages: decision modeling, data retrieval, data analysis, and analytical modeling.

1.2.2.1 Decision Modeling

Decision modeling involves exploring the effects of data-informed decisions. Construct a decision model to show how a decision or decision method leads to a business result. The decision model can be described informally when the path to a business result is simple, or formally when it involves complex relationships and calculations. Assume business parameters for the model, determined by data analysis or provided by business management. Analyze how sensitive the model is to changes in the decision method or business parameters. Based on sensitivity, you might want to revise the model, the decision method, or the business parameters. You can use the decision model to inform your business decision or use as input to machine learning methods.

1.2.2.2 Data Retrieval

Data retrieval involves retrieving data for use in decision making. Receive data via an interface to a data store. We assume that any data management methods required to produce the data are beyond the interface.

1.2.2.3 Data Analysis

Data analysis involves preparing, exploring, and transforming data in various ways to expose patterns that could lead to non-obvious insights useful in decision making. Explore the data, searching for patterns that offer useful insights. Try representing the data in different ways, as evoked by your findings, to better expose any still non-obvious patterns. Continue exploring and changing representations. You can use the insights you gather to inform your business decision or as inputs to machine learning methods.

1.2.2.4 Analytical Modeling

Analytical modeling involves constructing models that further expose patterns in data by estimating the underlying processes responsible for generating the data. Fortify the insights gleaned from data analysis with cluster, predictive, and network models constructed by machine learning methods. Provide data to cluster model construction methods, evaluate the resulting cluster models for quality as measured by a decision model, and repeat as appropriate to tune the cluster models for best quality. Similarly, construct predictive models based on the provided data, evaluate their performance as measured by a decision model, and repeat as appropriate to tune for best performance. Typically, text data and time series data must be represented in cross-sectional form for use with predictive model construction methods. Also construct network models based on the provided data, which typically must be represented in special form appropriate for network analysis. The cluster, predictive, and network models might lead you to further explore the data, or you can use the models to inform your business decision.

1.2.3 Process Diagram

Here is the data-to-decision process model visualized as a **process diagram**. Categories of methods are shown as bubbles. Data and key outputs are shown as blocks sprouting from dashed arrows. Solid arrows indicate flow-through activities and method outputs, allowing for cycles of activity and ultimately informing a decision.

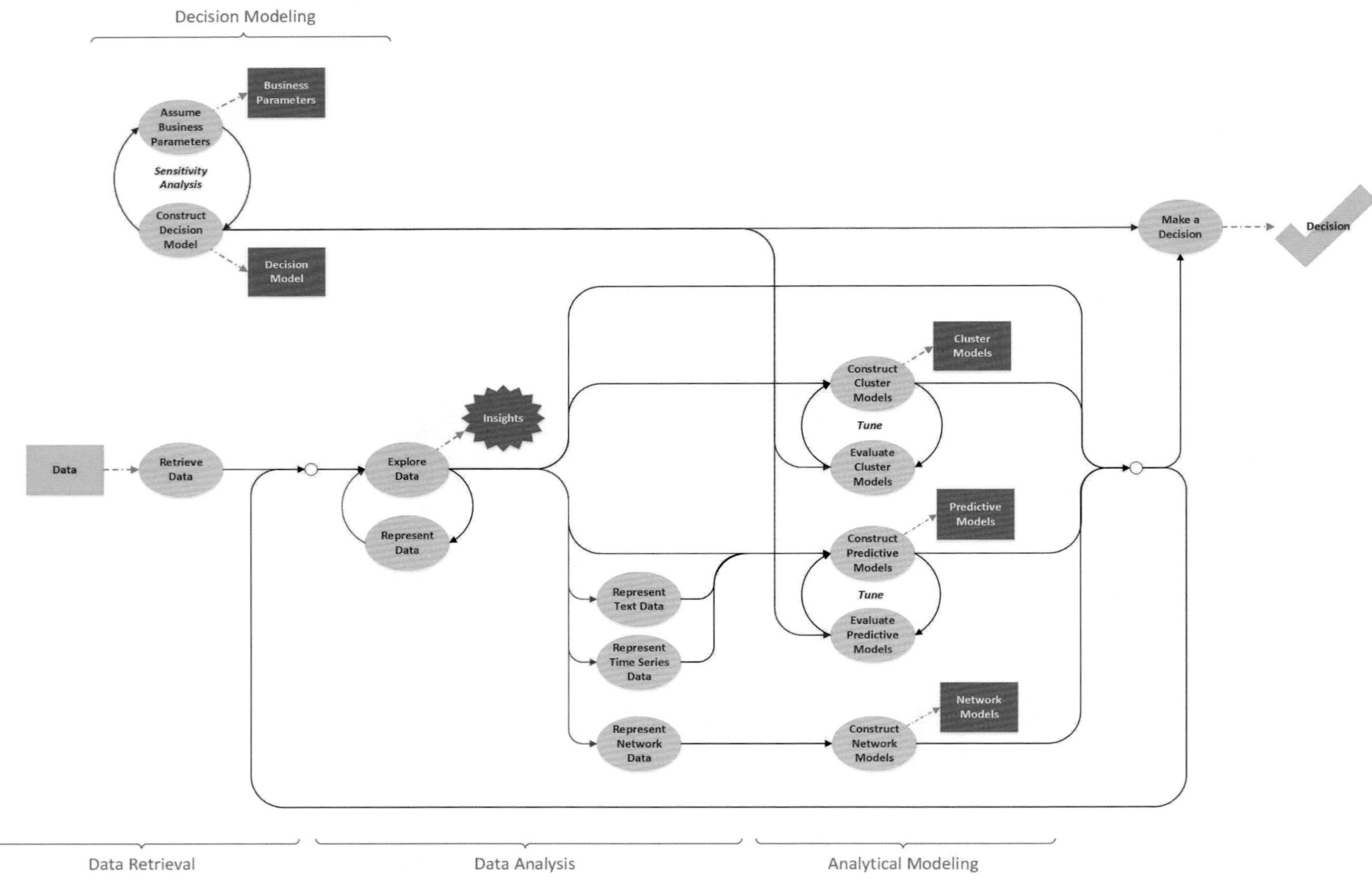
Data-to-Decison Process Model
Decision Modeling
Assume Business Parameters
Business Parameters
Sensitivity Analysis
Construct Decision Model
Decision Model
Make a Decision
Decision
Cluster Models
Construct Cluster Models
Tune
Evaluate Cluster Models
Insights
Data
Retrieve Data
Explore Data
Represent Data
Predictive Models
Construct Predictive Models
Tune
Evaluate Predictive Models
Represent Text Data
Represent Time Series Data
Network Models
Represent Network Data
Construct Network Models
Data Retrieval
Data Analysis
Analytical Modeling

1.3 Decision Models

Construct a decision model to show how a decision or decision method leads to a business result.

1.3.1 Introduction

What happens to your business when you make a decision? A decision model estimates the business results that would come about from various decisions informed by a business model, business parameter values, and decision method. Typically, you directly control the decision or decision method, but are ultimately interested in the business result. The decision model translates from the language of decisions to the language of business.

1.3.2 About Decision Models

A **decision model** is essentially a map that links a decision or decision method to an estimated business result via intermediary inter-dependent calculations. You can think of it as simply a formula, or as a decision or decision method propagating through a feed-forward network of calculating machines.

1.3.2.1 Elements of Decision Models

Robust, expressive decision models can be constructed from these elements:

- **Decision:** Specify the decision or decisions to be made.
  Typical examples: which product to produce, how to organize customers, how much to invest
- **Decision Method:** If interested in the effect of a decision method (rather than the effect of a decision), then indicate so.
- **Decision Method Performance:** If modeling the effect of a decision method (rather than the effect of a decision), then identify which calculated values are measures of decision method performance.

- **Business Parameters:** Specify exogenous values determined by data analysis or provided by business management.
  Typical examples: market size, product price, employee pay rate, equipment failure rate
- **Dependencies:** For each calculated value, specify which decision, business parameters, and other calculated values it depends on.
  Typical examples: variable cost is dependent on product unit cost and product volume, total cost is dependent on fixed cost and variable cost
- **Calculated Values:** Specify the various intermediary inter-dependent calculations.
  Typical examples: variable cost, total cost, number of satisfied customers
- **Business Result:** Indicate which calculated value is a measure of the business result.
  Typical examples: profit, revenue, cost savings, customer satisfaction level

1.3.2.2 Influence Diagram

It can be useful to visualize a decision model as an **influence diagram**, with elements shown as nodes and arrows. In our discourse, we'll show the decision as a violet square node, bounded by a light violet box, if necessary, to indicate that we're interested in the effect of a decision method. Calculated values are blue square nodes except for the business result, which is a green hexagon node bounded by a light green box. Any calculated values that are measures of decision quality or decision method performance are bounded by a light blue box. Business parameters are red maraschino cherry nodes. Dependencies are arrows that connect nodes, pointing from the influencer node to the dependent calculated value node.

Elements of Decision Model for Visualization as Influence Diagram

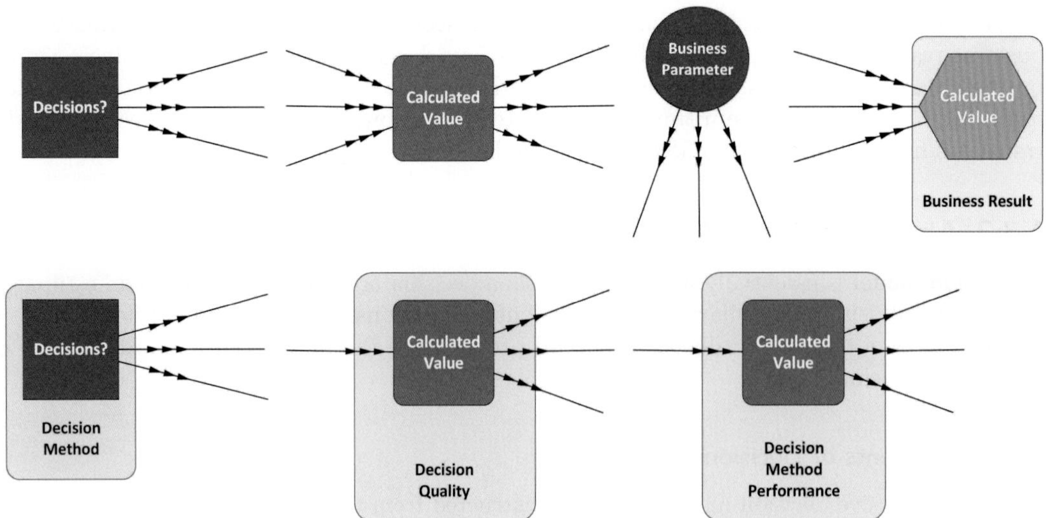

Here is an example of a decision model visualized as an influence diagram.

Example of Decision Model Visualized as Influence Diagram

Influence diagrams are especially useful for communicating what assumptions are built into a decision model. It is common for an influence diagram to invoke healthy debate and discussion among business stakeholders, leading to model adjustments and higher confidence in estimated business results.

1.3.2.3 Decision to Business Result

A decision model to map a decision to a business result starts with a decision, describes intermediary calculated values dependent on the decision, business parameters, and other calculated values, and ends with a calculated business result.

Here is a sketch of an example decision model to map a categorical decision to a business result. In this type of decision model, the decision involves picking 1 categorical value, such as A, B, or C.

Categorical Decision to Business Result

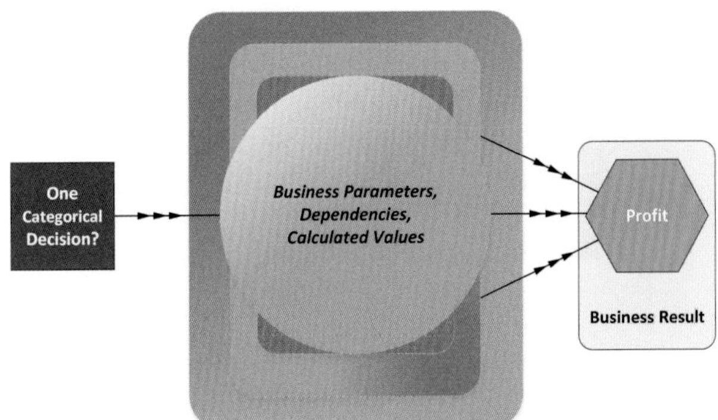

Here is a sketch of an example decision model to map a numerical decision to a business result. In this type of decision model, the decision involves picking 1 numerical value, such as any number between 0 and 10.

Numerical Decision to Business Result

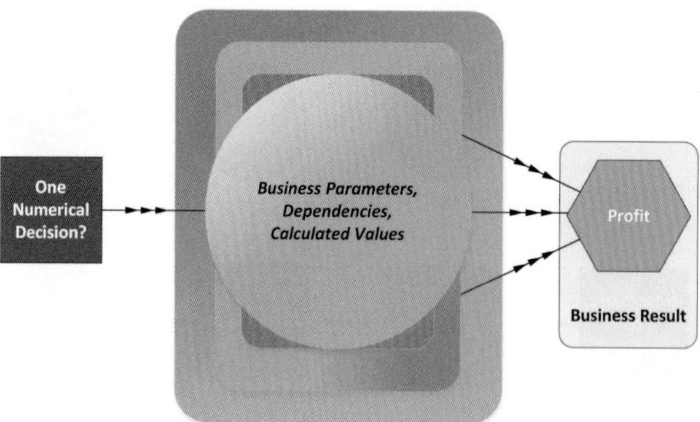

Here is a sketch of an example decision model to map an organization decision to a business result. In this type of decision model, the decision involves picking many categorical values that act as labels as a way to organize cases. Perhaps the names are account managers A, B, and C; the cases are customers; and the decision is about how to assign account managers to customers. Note that the calculated values nearest the decision typically involve measures of decision quality.

Organization Decision to Business Result

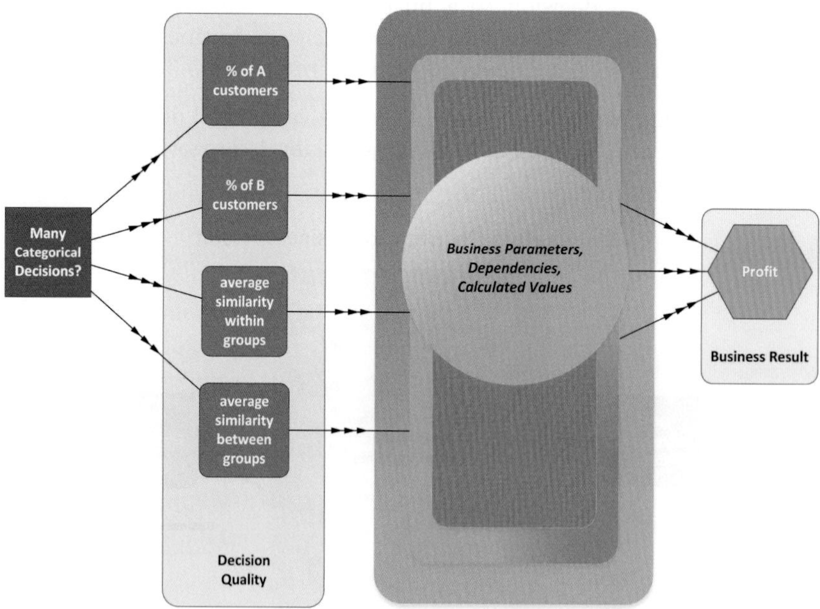

1.3.2.4 Decision Method to Business Result

A decision model to map a decision method to a business result is similar to one for mapping a decision, but it also describes calculated values dependent on decision method performance.

Here is a sketch of an example decision model to map a categorical decision method to a business result. In this type of model, the decision involves picking many categorical values for various cases, each of which could fall into any of several performance categories. Perhaps the categorical values are products A and B; the performance categories are (1) decided A and customer prefers A, (2) decided A but customer prefers B, (3) decided B but customer prefers A, and (4) decided B and customer prefers B; the cases are customers; and the decision is about which products to market to which customers. Note that the calculated values nearest the decision typically involve measures of decision method performance.

Categorical Decision Method to Business Result

Here is a sketch of an example decision model to map a numerical decision method to a business result. In this type of model, the decision involves picking many numerical values for various cases, each of which could be measured by several performance metrics. Perhaps the numerical values are auction bids between $1 and $10,000,000; the performance metrics are the difference and percent difference between an offered bid and the winning bid; the cases are properties up for auction; and the decision is about how much to bid for the properties.

Numerical Decision Method to Business Result

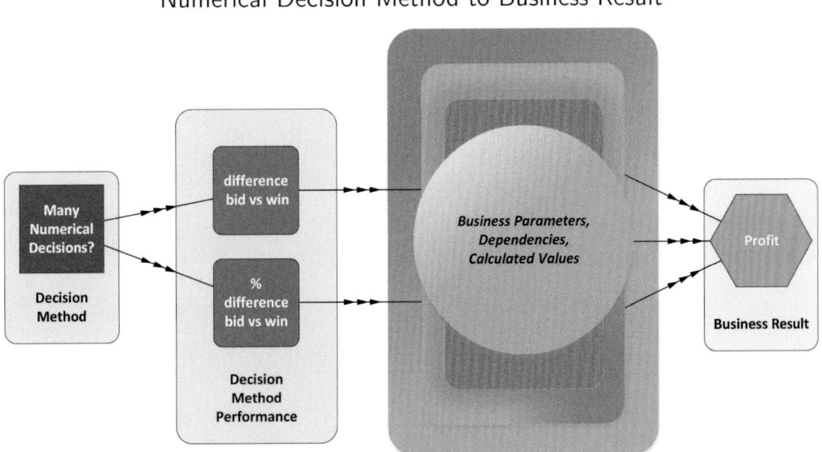

1.3.3 Decision Model

Consider this business opportunity to purchase land, some of which could produce gold. We like land with gold, and we don't like land without gold, but we're not sure in advance where the gold is. There are 100 sites for sale. From geology studies, we estimate that each has a 10% chance of producing gold. To decide which sites to purchase, we can use a complex decision method that accounts for various site characteristics, which was developed based on our experience with other opportunities over many years. Because we've used this decision method so often, we have a good idea of how well it works.

What business result can we expect if we use this decision method? Let's construct a decision model to show how the decision method leads to a business result.

1.3.3.1 Construct Decision Model

A decision model to map a categorical decision method to a business result comprises a decision, decision method, decision method performance, business parameters, dependencies, calculated values, and business result.

Decision: We need to decide which sites to purchase. That's one categorical decision – purchase or pass – for each of many sites.

Decision Method: Assume that we'll use the decision method that we've used in the past. Although it's complex and accounts for various site characteristics, we need not concern ourselves about the details. What matters to us is how well it performs.

Decision Method Performance: How many gold-producing sites can we expect our decision method to choose, and how many dud sites, which don't produce gold, will it choose? We need an estimate of how well the decision method works, which we can infer from how well it worked in the past. Our records show that of all the sites under consideration that we later learned actually could produce gold, we decided at the time to purchase only 80% of them. Our decision method missed the opportunity to purchase the other 20% of actual gold-producing sites. Also, of all the sites that actually could not produce gold, we unfortunately purchased 60% of them. Our decision method did, however, avoid the other 40% of actual dud sites.

decision method performance

prop_gold_sites_purchased	prop_dud_sites_purchased
0.8	0.6

example of decisions made for another opportunity

site	actual	decision
1	gold	purchase
2	gold	purchase
3	gold	purchase
4	gold	purchase
5	gold	pass
6	dud	purchase
7	dud	purchase
8	dud	purchase
9	dud	pass
10	dud	pass

Note that in this example, the proportion of gold sites purchased is not the complement of the proportion of dud sites purchased. Rather, the 80% proportion of gold sites purchased and the

20% proportion of gold sites not purchased sum to 100% of the gold sites, regardless of the proportion of dud sites purchased. Similarly, the 60% proportion of dud sites purchased and the 40% proportion of dud sites not purchased sum to 100% of the dud sites, regardless of the proportion of gold sites purchased. The quantitative relationship between proportion of gold sites purchased and proportion of dud sites purchased can be determined only when the actual number of gold sites and dud sites is known.

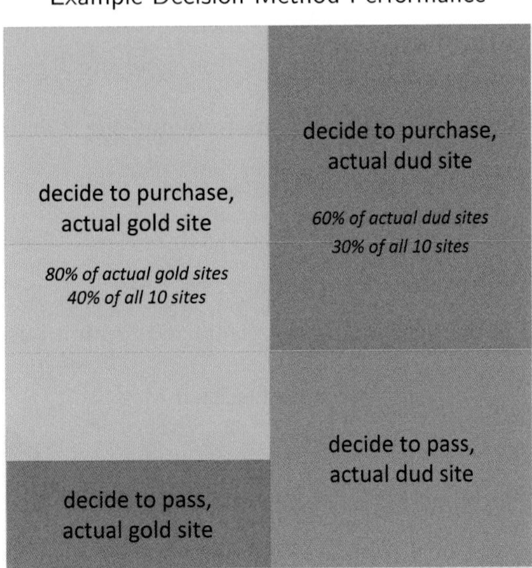

Business Parameters: There are 100 sites for sale, each with a 10% chance of producing gold. We need to know how much a site is worth. Our records show that a gold-producing site typically produces about $8,000,000 profit, after subtracting purchase price and other operational expenses. A dud site typically reduces profit by about $1,000,000 due to purchase price and operational expenses.

business parameters

sites	prob_gold	gold_profit_per_site	dud_profit_per_site
100	0.1	8,000,000	-1,000,000

Dependencies, Calculated Values, and Business Result: The number of gold sites we purchase depends on how well the decision method picks gold sites, and on how many gold sites there are, which in turn depends on the probability of gold at any site and the total number of sites. Similarly, the number of dud sites we purchase depends on how well the decision method avoids dud sites, and how many dud sites there are. Note that how well the decision method picks sites is the decision method performance that we quantified earlier. The probability of gold and the number of sites are business parameters.

The profit from purchased gold sites depends on the number of gold sites we purchased and the profit per site. Similarly, the (negative) profit from purchased dud sites depends on the number of dud sites we purchased and the (negative) profit per site. The profits per site are business parameters.

Ultimately, profit depends on profit from gold sites and the profit from dud sites. Profit is the business result.

$$
\begin{aligned}
\text{gold sites purchased} &= \mathit{round}\left(\begin{array}{c}\text{proportion of gold sites purchased} \times \\ \text{probability of gold} \times \text{sites}\end{array}\right) \\
\text{dud sites purchased} &= \mathit{round}\left(\begin{array}{c}\text{proportion of dud sites purchased} \times \\ (1 - \text{probability of gold}) \times \text{sites}\end{array}\right) \\
\text{profit from gold sites} &= \text{profit per site from gold site} \times \text{gold sites purchased} \\
\text{profit from dud sites} &= \text{profit per site from dud site} \times \text{dud sites purchased} \\
\text{profit} &= \text{profit from gold sites} + \text{profit from dud sites}
\end{aligned}
$$

Influence Diagram: Here is the decision model visualized as an influence diagram.

Site Purchase Decision Model

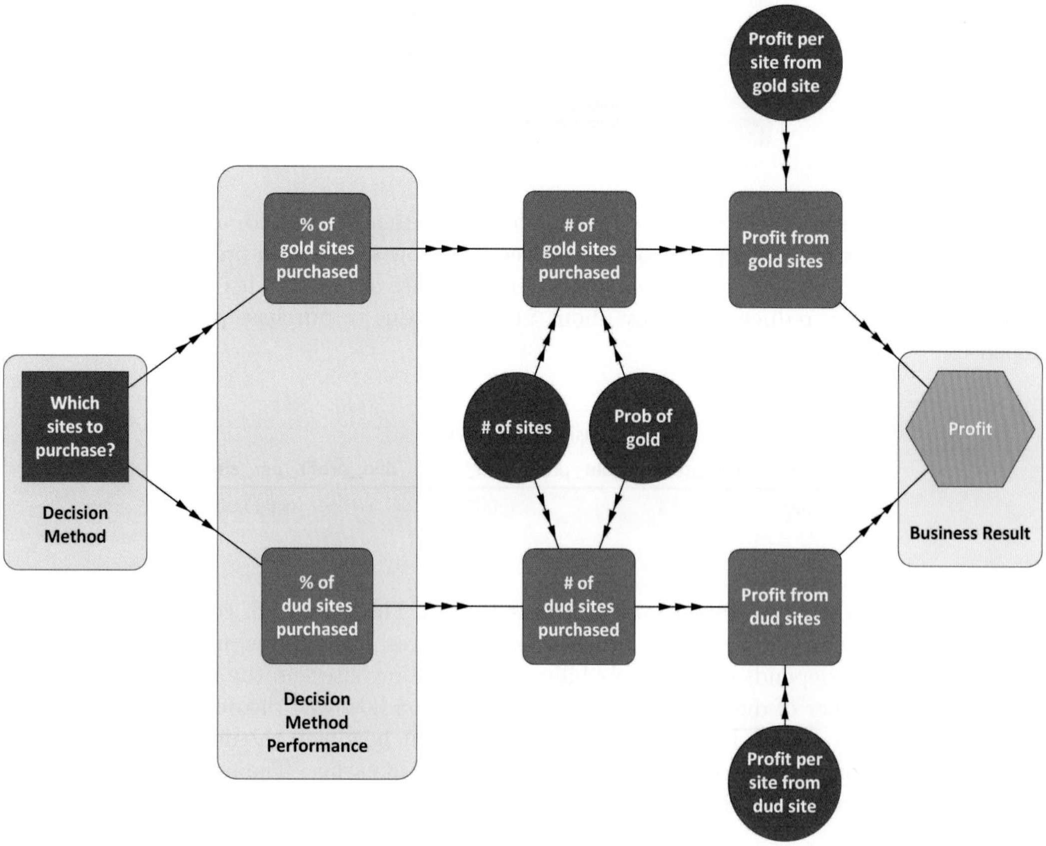

Profit per site from gold site
% of gold sites purchased
# of gold sites purchased
Profit from gold sites
Which sites to purchase?
Decision Method
# of sites
Prob of gold
Profit
Business Result
% of dud sites purchased
# of dud sites purchased
Profit from dud sites
Decision Method Performance
Profit per site from dud site

1.3.3.2 Estimate Business Result

Equipped with a decision model, we can see how the decision method leads to a business result.

$$\begin{aligned}
\text{gold sites purchased} &= \mathit{round}(0.8 \times 0.1 \times 100) &&= 8\\
\text{dud sites purchased} &= \mathit{round}(0.6 \times (1 - 0.1) \times 100) &&= 54
\end{aligned}$$

$$\begin{aligned}
\text{profit from gold sites} &= 8{,}000{,}000 \times 8 &&= 64{,}000{,}000\\
\text{profit from dud sites} &= -1{,}000{,}000 \times 54 &&= -54{,}000{,}000
\end{aligned}$$

$$\text{profit} = 64{,}000{,}000 + -54{,}00{,}000 = 10{,}000{,}000$$

gold_sites_purchased	dud_sites_purchased
8	54

gold_profit	dud_profit
64,000,000	-54,000,000

profit
10,000,000

The decision model tells us that if we use our decision method to pick sites in this new opportunity, then we can expect about \$10,000,000 profit.

1.4 Sensitivity Analysis

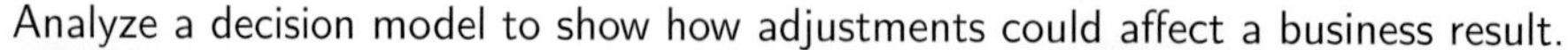
Analyze a decision model to show how adjustments could affect a business result.

1.4.1 Introduction

The vice president of marketing is considering funding a new set of targeted advertising campaigns. An algorithm will identify to what degree individual prospective customers are receptive to the campaign alternatives. A decision model shows that if the algorithm identifies prospects correctly, then he can expect high profit. However, the vice president has some prudent questions about the **sensitivity** of the model. If the algorithm is wrong for 1% of prospects, then how much would estimated profit differ? If a 1% decrease in algorithm performance would change estimated profit by 90%, then the vice president will have to very carefully weigh the potential high profit against the high risk of failure. Perhaps he will suggest more work on the decision model in order to be more confident about the estimated profit. Perhaps he will suggest more work on the algorithm to be more confident about its performance. Perhaps he will accept the model and the algorithm, but change the product launch strategy.

Also, the vice president has been asked to approve new product pricing. His staff is justifying the pricing recommendation by a decision model that shows it leading to high profit. But again, the vice president has questions. If pricing differed by 1%, then how much would estimated profit differ? Maybe profit would decrease by 1%, in which case it wouldn't matter that pricing was not set precisely. Maybe profit would decrease by 90%, which would be disastrous for the company. Perhaps the vice president will suggest more work on the model. Perhaps he will accept the model, but change the product launch strategy to reduce risk.

Sensitivity analysis is about finding how a decision model is sensitive to changes in decision method performance and business parameter values.

1.4.2 About Sensitivity Analysis

To find how a decision model is sensitive to changes in decision method performance, systematically iterate through different measures of performance and note the estimated business results. Similarly, to find the effects of changes in business parameter values, systematically iterate through different business parameter values and note the estimated business results.

1.4.3 Sensitivity to Decision Method Performance

Consider again the business opportunity to purchase gold-producing land. Recall that we estimated the decision method performance to be 80% correct about choosing gold-producing sites and 60% wrong about avoiding dud sites. That led to an estimated profit of $10,000,000.

decision method performance

prop_gold_sites_purchased	prop_dud_sites_purchased
0.8	0.6

calculated values & business result

gold_sites_purchased	dud_sites_purchased	gold_profit	dud_profit	profit
8	54	64,000,000	-54,000,000	10,000,000

How sure are we about decision method performance? What if it actually works slightly better? What if it actually works slightly worse? Let's analyze the model's sensitivity to decision method performance.

First assume that the performance is slightly better, say 90% correct about choosing gold-producing sites and 50% wrong about avoiding dud sites. That would lead to a much higher estimated profit of $27,000,000.

decision method performance

prop_gold_sites_purchased	prop_dud_sites_purchased
0.9	0.5

$$
\begin{aligned}
\text{gold sites purchased} &= \mathit{round}(0.9 \times 0.1 \times 100) &&= 9 \\
\text{dud sites purchased} &= \mathit{round}(0.5 \times (1 - 0.1) \times 100) &&= 45 \\
\text{profit from gold sites} &= 8{,}000{,}000 \times 9 &&= 72{,}000{,}000 \\
\text{profit from dud sites} &= -1{,}000{,}000 \times 45 &&= -45{,}000{,}000 \\
\text{profit} &= 72{,}000{,}000 + -45{,}00{,}000 &&= 27{,}000{,}000
\end{aligned}
$$

calculated values & business result

gold_sites_purchased	dud_sites_purchased	gold_profit	dud_profit	profit
9	45	72,000,000	-45,000,000	27,000,000

Then assume that the performance is slightly worse, say 70% correct about choosing gold-producing sites and 70% wrong about avoiding dud sites. That would lead to a substantial loss of $7,000,000.

decision method performance

prop_gold_sites_purchased	prop_dud_sites_purchased
0.7	0.7

$$\begin{aligned}
\text{gold sites purchased} &= \mathit{round}(0.7 \times 0.1 \times 100) &= 7 \\
\text{dud sites purchased} &= \mathit{round}(0.7 \times (1 - 0.1) \times 100) &= 63 \\
\text{profit from gold sites} &= 8{,}000{,}000 \times 7 &= 56{,}000{,}000 \\
\text{profit from dud sites} &= -1{,}000{,}000 \times 63 &= -63{,}000{,}000 \\
\text{profit} &= 56{,}000{,}000 + -63{,}00{,}000 &= -7{,}000{,}000
\end{aligned}$$

calculated values & business result

gold_sites_purchased	dud_sites_purchased	gold_profit	dud_profit	profit
7	63	56,000,000	-63,000,000	-7,000,000

See that even a small amount of uncertainty about the decision method performance corresponds to a $34,000,000 swing in estimated profit, anywhere from plus $27,000,000 to minus $7,000,000. It would be prudent to …

- enhance the decision model by accounting for additional business parameters, calculated values, and dependencies, to make it less sensitive to decision method performance, or
- analyze the decision method further to gain more confidence about its performance, or
- both of the above, or
- use the decision method anyway, but with full awareness of the risk.

1.4.4 Sensitivity to Business Parameter Values

Still considering the business opportunity to purchase gold-producing land, recall that we estimated a 10% probability that a site would produce gold. That led to an estimated profit of $10,000,000.

business parameters

sites	prob_gold	gold_profit_per_site	dud_profit_per_site
100	0.1	8,000,000	-1,000,000

calculated values & business result

gold_sites_purchased	dud_sites_purchased	gold_profit	dud_profit	profit
8	54	64,000,000	-54,000,000	10,000,000

How sure are you about the probability of finding gold? What if a slightly higher proportion of sites would actually produce gold? What if a slightly lower proportion would? Let's analyze the model's sensitivity to the probability of gold business parameter.

First, assume that the probability is slightly higher, say 12% of sites would produce gold. That would lead to a profit of \$27,000,000.

business parameters

sites	prob_gold	gold_profit_per_site	dud_profit_per_site
100	0.12	8,000,000	-1,000,000

$$\begin{aligned}
\text{gold sites purchased} &= \mathit{round}(0.8 \times 0.12 \times 100) &&= 10 \\
\text{dud sites purchased} &= \mathit{round}(0.6 \times (1 - 0.12) \times 100) &&= 53 \\
\text{profit from gold sites} &= 8{,}000{,}000 \times 10 &&= 80{,}000{,}000 \\
\text{profit from dud sites} &= -1{,}000{,}000 \times 53 &&= -53{,}000{,}000 \\
\text{profit} &= 80{,}000{,}000 + -53{,}00{,}000 &&= 27{,}000{,}000
\end{aligned}$$

calculated values & business result

gold_sites_purchased	dud_sites_purchased	gold_profit	dud_profit	profit
10	53	80,000,000	-53,000,000	27,000,000

Then, assume that the probability of finding gold is slightly lower, say 8% of sites would produce gold. That would lead to a loss of \$7,000,000.

business parameters

sites	prob_gold	gold_profit_per_site	dud_profit_per_site
100	0.08	8,000,000	-1,000,000

$$\begin{aligned}
\text{gold sites purchased} &= \mathit{round}(0.8 \times 0.08 \times 100) &&= 6 \\
\text{dud sites purchased} &= \mathit{round}(0.6 \times (1 - 0.08) \times 100) &&= 55 \\
\text{profit from gold sites} &= 8{,}000{,}000 \times 6 &&= 48{,}000{,}000 \\
\text{profit from dud sites} &= -1{,}000{,}000 \times 56 &&= -55{,}000{,}000 \\
\text{profit} &= 48{,}000{,}000 + -55{,}00{,}000 &&= -7{,}000{,}000
\end{aligned}$$

calculated values & business result

gold_sites_purchased	dud_sites_purchased	gold_profit	dud_profit	profit
6	55	48,000,000	-55,000,000	-7,000,000

See that even a small amount of uncertainty about the probability of finding gold corresponds to a $34,000,000 swing in estimated profit, anywhere from plus $27,000,000 to minus $7,000,000. It would be prudent to ...

- enhance the decision model to make it less sensitive to business parameter values, or
- conduct more geological research to gain more confidence about the probability of finding gold, or
- both of the above, or
- use the decision method anyway, but with full awareness of the risk.

2 | Data Preparation

Learning Objectives

Terms

Know the terms:

- Data object
- Categorical
- Numerical
- String
- Logical (or Boolean)
- Table (or dataframe)
- Matrix
- Vector
- Value
- List
- Function
- Dataset
- Observation
- Variable
- Index-based selection
- Name-based selection
- Criterion-based selection
- Row-wise concatenation
- Column-wise concatenation
- Join
- Synthetic variable
- Unit conversion
- Linear recombination
- Non-linear recombination
- Descriptive statistic
- Lag
- Normalization
- Dummy variable

Use the Methods

Know how to use the methods:

- Use values of different types in combination.
- Select any part of interest from a dataset.
- Append a dataset to another dataset, by rows or columns.
- Insert a dataset into another dataset, by rows or columns.
- Join datasets.
- Compute a synthetic variable by units conversion.
- Compute a synthetic variable by linear or non-linear recombination.
- Compute a synthetic variable by descriptive statistic.
- Compute a synthetic variable by lag.
- Covert a dataset to normalized representation.
- Convert a dataset represented by categorical variables to dummy variable representation.
- Convert a new observation to match a dataset in dummy variable representation.

2.1 Data Objects

Store and organize a dataset.

2.1.1 Introduction

For her New Year's resolution, Gaowen has determined to finally get organized. She puts up shelves and racks, adds new filing cabinets, cupboards, a desk, and assorted bins, and sets about putting her electronics equipment, clothes, dishes, books, keys, and everything else all in their proper places. You can think of data objects as containers to help you get organized.

Data objects are about storing and organizing datasets.

2.1.2 About Data Objects

A **data object** is a construct to hold a collection of values.

In data analysis and analytical modeling, it's most often useful to restrict values to be of specific value types:

- **Numerical:** The domain of possible numerical values is the infinite set of all real numbers.
- **String:** The domain of possible string values is the infinite set of all sequences of characters.
- **Categorical:** There are an infinite number of categorical value types. For any specific categorical value type, the domain of possible categorical values is specified to be a finite set of labels, and depends on the context in which values are being used. Categorical is also referred to as factor.
- **Logical:** The domain of possible logical values is the finite set TRUE, FALSE. Note that the logical value type is a specific categorical value type. Logical is also referred to as Boolean.

There are a variety of useful data object types to hold collections of values in various ways.

- **Table:** Holds a collection of values in a 2-dimensional grid, indexed by row and column. Each row has a row number and optionally a row name. Each column has a column number and name. All values in a single column must be of the same type, but any specific column need not have values of the same type as any other column.
- **Matrix:** Holds a collection of values in a 2-dimensional grid, indexed by row and column. Each row has a row number and optionally a row name. Each column has a column number and optionally a name. All values in the matrix must be of the same type. Note that a matrix is like a table in which all columns hold values of the same type.
- **Vector:** Holds a collection of values in 1-dimensional grid, indexed by position. Each position has a position number. All values in a vector must be of the same type. Note that a vector is like a table column.
- **Value:** Holds a single value. Note that a value is like a vector of length 1.
- **List:** Holds a sequence of data objects, which can be of any type and not necessarily all the same. This is the least restrictive type of data object.

Functions operate on data objects to extract information and insights from them.

- **Function:** Generates a data object, called the result, given several other data objects that it employs to calculate the result, called the arguments.

2.1.3 Anatomy of a Dataset

A **dataset** is a collection of **observations**, with each observation described by **variables**. In our discourse, we usually store datasets as tables, though not always. Each row of a table corresponds to an observation. Each column of a table corresponds to a variable.

Nomenclature around datasets varies widely, depending on the scientific, engineering, or business field involved. You can expect to hear different terms used for the same concept, and to hear the same term used for different concepts.

Here is a synopsis of dataset elements, terms commonly used as synonyms, and examples.

dataset
also_known_as
table
database
population
dataframe

example				
	x1	x2	x3	x4
1	A	C	100	205
2	B	D	102	204
3	A	E	101	200
4	B	C	103	201
5	A	D	105	202
6	B	E	104	203

observation #
also_known_as
row #
record #
instance #
example #
measurement #
case #

example				
	x1	x2	x3	x4
1	A	C	100	205
2	B	D	102	204
3	A	E	101	200
4	B	C	103	201
5	A	D	105	202
6	B	E	104	203

observation also_known_as
row
record
instance
example
measurement
datapoint
case
slice

example	x1	x2	x3	x4
1	A	C	100	205
2	B	D	102	204
3	A	E	101	200
4	B	C	103	201
5	A	D	105	202
6	B	E	104	203

variable name also_known_as
column name
field name
random variable name
feature name
attribute name
dimension name

example	x1	x2	x3	x4
1	A	C	100	205
2	B	D	102	204
3	A	E	101	200
4	B	C	103	201
5	A	D	105	202
6	B	E	104	203

variable also_known_as
variable values
vector
column
array
distribution
slice

example	x1	x2	x3	x4
1	A	C	100	205
2	B	D	102	204
3	A	E	101	200
4	B	C	103	201
5	A	D	105	202
6	B	E	104	203

value also_known_as
cell
datum
item

example	x1	x2	x3	x4
1	A	C	100	205
2	B	D	102	204
3	A	E	101	200
4	B	C	103	201
5	A	D	105	202
6	B	E	104	203

sample also_known_as
subset
slice

example	x1	x2	x3	x4
1	A	C	100	205
2	B	D	102	204
3	A	E	101	200
4	B	C	103	201
5	A	D	105	202
6	B	E	104	203

vector

also_known_as
array
distribution
slice

example

	x1	x2	x3	x4
1	A	C	100	205
2	B	D	102	204
3	A	E	101	200
4	B	C	103	201
5	A	D	105	202
6	B	E	104	203

2.1.4 Respecting Value Types

Careful assignment of value types to data makes for effective data analysis and analytical modeling, but take care to respect when you can and when you cannot use different value types in combination.

Consider the following 2 datasets: **data.1** and **data.2**. Here **data.1**'s variables and **data.2**'s variables all contain numerical values. **data.1.revised** is an attempt to revise **data.1** by replacing its first x_1 value with **data.2**'s first x_1 value. Because those values are of the same type, the number 2.3 can easily be replaced by the number 3.3.

data.1

x1	x2
2.3	3
0.4	2
-2.1	1
9.0	4
4.5	5

data.2

x1	x2
3.3	3
9.4	0
7.1	0
-2.0	7
1.5	5

data.1 value counts

	1	2	3	4	5
-2.1	1	0	0	0	0
0.4	0	1	0	0	0
2.3	0	0	1	0	0
4.5	0	0	0	0	1
9	0	0	0	1	0

data.2 value counts

	0	3	5	7
-2	0	0	0	1
1.5	0	0	1	0
3.3	0	1	0	0
7.1	1	0	0	0
9.4	1	0	0	0

data.1.revised

x1	x2
3.3	3
0.4	2
-2.1	1
9.0	4
4.5	5

Consider the following 2 datasets: **data.1** and **data.2**. Here **data.1**'s variables and **data.2**'s variables all contain string values. **data.1.revised** is an attempt to revise **data.1** by replacing its first x_1 value with **data.2**'s first x_1 value. Because those values are of the same type, the string "A" can easily be replaced by the string "B".

data.1

x1	x2
A	D
C	E
C	D
A	H
A	G

data.2

x1	x2
B	D
A	F
A	F
B	D
B	D

data.1 value counts

	D	E	G	H
A	1	0	1	1
C	1	1	0	0

data.2 value counts

	D	F
A	0	2
B	3	0

data.1.revised

x1	x2
B	D
C	E
C	D
A	H
A	G

Consider the following 2 datasets: **data.1** and **data.2**. Here **data.1**'s variables contain string values and **data.2**'s variables contain numerical values. **data.1.revised** is an attempt to revise

data.1 by replacing its first x_1 value with **data.2**'s first x_1 value. Because those values are of different types, the number 3.3 must be coerced into the string "3.3", and then can replace the string "A". Note that **data.1.revised**'s x_1 still contains only string values. It would be nonsensical, for example, to attempt to add a number to the string "3.3".

data.1

x1	x2
A	D
C	E
C	D
A	H
A	G

data.2

x1	x2
3.3	3
9.4	0
7.1	0
-2.0	7
1.5	5

data.1 value counts

	D	E	G	H
A	1	0	1	1
C	1	1	0	0

data.2 value counts

	0	3	5	7
-2	0	0	0	1
1.5	0	0	1	0
3.3	0	1	0	0
7.1	1	0	0	0
9.4	1	0	0	0

data.1.revised

x1	x2
3.3	D
C	E
C	D
A	H
A	G

Consider the following 2 datasets: **data.1** and **data.2**. Here **data.1**'s x_1 variable and **data.2**'s x_1 variable both contain categorical values from the domain A, B, C. **data.1.revised** is an attempt to revise **data.1** by replacing its first x_1 value with **data.2**'s first x_1 value. Because those values are of the same type, the label A can easily be replaced by the label B.

data.1

x1	x2
A	D
C	E
C	D
A	H
A	G

data.2

x1	x2
B	D
A	F
A	F
B	D
B	D

data.1 value counts

	D	E	F	G	H
A	1	0	0	1	1
B	0	0	0	0	0
C	1	1	0	0	0

data.2 value counts

	D	E	F	G	H
A	0	0	2	0	0
B	3	0	0	0	0
C	0	0	0	0	0

data.1.revised

x1	x2
B	D
C	E
C	D
A	H
A	G

Consider the following 2 datasets: **data.1** and **data.2**. Here **data.1**'s variables contain categorical values and **data.2**'s variables contain numerical values. **data.1.revised** is an attempt to revise **data.1** by replacing its first x_1 value with **data.2**'s first x_1 value. Because those values are of different types, the label A cannot be replaced by the number 3.3.

data.1

x1	x2
A	D
C	E
C	D
A	H
A	G

data.2

x1	x2
3.3	3
9.4	0
7.1	0
-2.0	7
1.5	5

data.1 value counts

	D	E	F	G	H
A	1	0	0	1	1
B	0	0	0	0	0
C	1	1	0	0	0

data.2 value counts

	0	3	5	7
-2	0	0	0	1
1.5	0	0	1	0
3.3	0	1	0	0
7.1	1	0	0	0
9.4	1	0	0	0

data.1.revised

x1	x2
NA	D
C	E
C	D
A	H
A	G

Consider the following 2 datasets: **data.1** and **data.2**. Here **data.1**'s x_1 variable and **data.2**'s x_1 variable both contain categorical values, but from different domains. **data.1**'s x_1 variable values are from the domain A, C. **data.2**'s x_1 variable values are from the domain A, B. **data.1.revised** is an attempt to revise **data.1** by replacing its first x_1 value with **data.2**'s first x_1 value. Because those values are of the different types, the label A cannot be replaced by the label B.

data.1

x1	x2
A	D
C	E
C	D
A	H
A	G

data.2

x1	x2
B	D
A	F
A	F
B	D
B	D

data.1 value counts

	D	E	G	H
A	1	0	1	1
C	1	1	0	0

data.2 value counts

	D	F
A	0	2
B	3	0

data.1.revised

x1	x2
NA	D
C	E
C	D
A	H
A	G

2.2 Selection

Select part of a dataset.

2.2.1 Introduction

A virtuoso chef envisions the evening's meal to come, pondering how best to prepare the assortment of fine produce laid out before her. With expert knife skills, she swiftly and gracefully slices and dices the ingredients to assemble just the right pieces for her culinary masterpiece. You can think of data selection as slicing and dicing.

Various data analysis and analytical modeling methods work on various parts of datasets, depending on your analysis objectives. Data selection is about selecting the part of a dataset that you want.

2.2.2 About Selection

Data selection is accomplished by specifying vectors for rows and columns of interest.

- **Index-based selection** involves specifying vectors of row numbers for rows and column numbers for columns.
- **Name-based selection** involves specifying vectors of column names for columns.
- **Criterion-based selection** involves specifying logical criteria for rows and columns.

2.2.3 Index-Based Selection | Rows

We can select part of a dataset by specifying a vector of row numbers for rows, or a single row number for just 1 row.

- We get a new dataset comprising values from the specified rows.

Here are some examples:

dataset (select row 1)

	x1	x2	x3	x4
1	**A**	**C**	**100**	**205**
2	B	D	102	204
3	A	E	101	200
4	B	C	103	201
5	A	D	105	202
6	B	E	104	203

row #

1

new dataset

	x1	x2	x3	x4
1	A	C	100	205

dataset (select row 5)

	x1	x2	x3	x4
1	A	C	100	205
2	B	D	102	204
3	A	E	101	200
4	B	C	103	201
5	**A**	**D**	**105**	**202**
6	B	E	104	203

row #

5

new dataset

	x1	x2	x3	x4
1	A	D	105	202

dataset (select rows 1,2,3)

	x1	x2	x3	x4
1	**A**	**C**	**100**	**205**
2	**B**	**D**	**102**	**204**
3	**A**	**E**	**101**	**200**
4	B	C	103	201
5	A	D	105	202
6	B	E	104	203

vector of row #

1
2
3

new dataset

	x1	x2	x3	x4
1	A	C	100	205
2	B	D	102	204
3	A	E	101	200

dataset (select rows 2,3,4)

	x1	x2	x3	x4
1	A	C	100	205
2	**B**	**D**	**102**	**204**
3	**A**	**E**	**101**	**200**
4	**B**	**C**	**103**	**201**
5	A	D	105	202
6	B	E	104	203

vector of row #

2
3
4

new dataset

	x1	x2	x3	x4
1	B	D	102	204
2	A	E	101	200
3	B	C	103	201

dataset (select rows 2,3,5)

	x1	x2	x3	x4
1	A	C	100	205
2	**B**	**D**	**102**	**204**
3	**A**	**E**	**101**	**200**
4	B	C	103	201
5	**A**	**D**	**105**	**202**
6	B	E	104	203

vector of row #

2
3
5

new dataset

	x1	x2	x3	x4
1	B	D	102	204
2	A	E	101	200
3	A	D	105	202

2.2.4 Index-Based Selection | Columns

We can select part of a dataset by specifying a vector of column numbers for columns, or a single column number for just 1 column.

- If we specify 1 column, then we get a new vector comprising the values from the specified column.
- If we specify multiple columns, then we get a new dataset comprising values from the specified columns.

Here are some examples:

data (select column 1)

	x1	x2	x3	x4
1	A	C	100	205
2	B	D	102	204
3	A	E	101	200
4	B	C	103	201
5	A	D	105	202
6	B	E	104	203

column #

1

new vector

A
B
A
B
A
B

dataset (select column 3)

	x1	x2	x3	x4
1	A	C	100	205
2	B	D	102	204
3	A	E	101	200
4	B	C	103	201
5	A	D	105	202
6	B	E	104	203

column #

3

new vector

100
102
101
103
105
104

dataset (select columns 2,4)

	x1	x2	x3	x4
1	A	C	100	205
2	B	D	102	204
3	A	E	101	200
4	B	C	103	201
5	A	D	105	202
6	B	E	104	203

vector of column #

2
4

new datatset

	x2	x4
1	C	205
2	D	204
3	E	200
4	C	201
5	D	202
6	E	203

2.2.5 Index-Based Selection | Rows & Columns

We can select part of a dataset by specifying a vector of row numbers for rows and a vector of column numbers for columns, or a single row number for just 1 row, or a single column number for just 1 column.

- If we specify 1 row and 1 column, then we get a value from the intersection of the specified row and column.
- If we specify multiple rows and 1 column, then we get a new vector comprising values from the specified rows at their intersection with the specified column.
- If we specify 1 or multiple rows and multiple columns, then we get a new dataset comprising values from the intersections of the specified rows and columns.

Here are some examples:

dataset (select row 2, column 2)

	x1	x2	x3	x4
1	A	C	100	205
2	B	D	102	204
3	A	E	101	200
4	B	C	103	201
5	A	D	105	202
6	B	E	104	203

row #
2

column #
2

new value
D

dataset (select row 2, columns 2,3,4)

	x1	x2	x3	x4
1	A	C	100	205
2	B	D	102	204
3	A	E	101	200
4	B	C	103	201
5	A	D	105	202
6	B	E	104	203

row #
2

vector of column #
2
3
4

new dataset

	x2	x3	x4
1	D	102	204

dataset (select row 2, columns 1,3,4)

	x1	x2	x3	x4
1	A	C	100	205
2	B	D	102	204
3	A	E	101	200
4	B	C	103	201
5	A	D	105	202
6	B	E	104	203

row #
2

vector of column #
1
3
4

new dataset

	x1	x3	x4
1	B	102	204

dataset (select rows 2,3,4, column 3)

	x1	x2	x3	x4
1	A	C	100	205
2	B	D	102	204
3	A	E	101	200
4	B	C	103	201
5	A	D	105	202
6	B	E	104	203

vector of row #
2
3
4

column #
3

new vector
102
101
103

dataset (select rows 1,3,4, column 3)

	x1	x2	x3	x4
1	A	C	100	205
2	B	D	102	204
3	A	E	101	200
4	B	C	103	201
5	A	D	105	202
6	B	E	104	203

vector of row #

1
3
4

column #

3

new vector

100
101
103

dataset (select rows 2,3,4, columns 1,2,3)

	x1	x2	x3	x4
1	A	C	100	205
2	B	D	102	204
3	A	E	101	200
4	B	C	103	201
5	A	D	105	202
6	B	E	104	203

vector of row #

2
3
4

vector of column #

1
2
3

new dataset

	x1	x2	x3
1	B	D	102
2	A	E	101
3	B	C	103

dataset (select rows 2,4,5, columns 1,2,4)

	x1	x2	x3	x4
1	A	C	100	205
2	B	D	102	204
3	A	E	101	200
4	B	C	103	201
5	A	D	105	202
6	B	E	104	203

vector of row #

2
4
5

vector of column #

1
2
4

new dataset

	x1	x2	x4
1	B	D	204
2	B	C	201
3	A	D	202

2.2.6 Name-Based Selection | One Column

We can select part of a dataset by specifying a vector of row numbers for rows and a column name for a column, or a single row number for just 1 row.

- If we specify 1 row and 1 column, then we get a value from the intersection of the specified row and column.
- If we specify multiple rows and 1 column, then we get a new vector comprising values from the specified rows at their intersections with the specified column.

Here are some examples:

dataset (select row 2, column x2)

	x1	x2	x3	x4
1	A	C	100	205
2	B	D	102	204
3	A	E	101	200
4	B	C	103	201
5	A	D	105	202
6	B	E	104	203

row #	column name	new value
2	x2	D

dataset (select rows 1,3,4 column x3)

	x1	x2	x3	x4
1	A	C	100	205
2	B	D	102	204
3	A	E	101	200
4	B	C	103	201
5	A	D	105	202
6	B	E	104	203

vector of row #	column name	new vector
1	x3	100
3		101
4		103

2.2.7 Name-Based Selection | Columns

We can select part of a dataset by specifying a vector of row numbers for rows and a vector of column names for columns, or a single row number for just 1 row.

- If we specify 1 or multiple rows and multiple columns, then we get a new dataset comprising values from the intersections of the specified rows and columns.

Here are some examples:

dataset (select row 1, columns x1,x2,x3)

	x1	x2	x3	x4
1	A	C	100	205
2	B	D	102	204
3	A	E	101	200
4	B	C	103	201
5	A	D	105	202
6	B	E	104	203

row #	vector of column name
1	x1
	x2
	x3

new dataset

	x1	x2	x3
1	A	C	100

dataset (select row 1, columns x1,x2,x4)

	x1	x2	x3	x4
1	A	C	100	205
2	B	D	102	204
3	A	E	101	200
4	B	C	103	201
5	A	D	105	202
6	B	E	104	203

row #	vector of column name
1	x1
	x2
	x4

new dataset

	x1	x2	x4
1	A	C	205

dataset (select rows 2,4,5 columns x1,x2,x4)

	x1	x2	x3	x4
1	A	C	100	205
2	B	D	102	204
3	A	E	101	200
4	B	C	103	201
5	A	D	105	202
6	B	E	104	203

vector of row #

2
4
5

vector of column name

x1
x2
x4

new dataset

	x1	x2	x4
1	B	D	204
2	B	C	201
3	A	D	202

2.2.8 Selection with Reorder

We can select part of a dataset by specifying a vector of row numbers for rows and a vector of column numbers for columns, and reordering the rows and columns.

- We get a new dataset comprising values from the intersections of the specified rows and columns, in the appropriate order.

Here are some examples:

dataset (select rows 2,4,5, columns 1,2,4)

	x1	x2	x3	x4
1	A	C	100	205
2	B	D	102	204
3	A	E	101	200
4	B	C	103	201
5	A	D	105	202
6	B	E	104	203

vector of row # (reordered)

4
5
2

vector of column #

1
2
4

new dataset

	x1	x2	x4
1	B	C	201
2	A	D	202
3	B	D	204

dataset (select rows 2,4,5, columns 1,2,4)

	x1	x2	x3	x4
1	A	C	100	205
2	B	D	102	204
3	A	E	101	200
4	B	C	103	201
5	A	D	105	202
6	B	E	104	203

vector of row #

2
4
5

vector of column # (reordered)

4
1
2

new dataset

	x4	x1	x2
1	204	B	D
2	201	B	C
3	202	A	D

dataset (select rows 2,4,5, columns 1,2,4)

	x1	x2	x3	x4
1	A	C	100	205
2	B	D	102	204
3	A	E	101	200
4	B	C	103	201
5	A	D	105	202
6	B	E	104	203

vector of row # (reordered)

4
5
2

vector of column # (reordered)

4
2
1

new dataset

	x4	x2	x1
1	201	C	B
2	202	D	A
3	204	D	B

2.2.9 Selection with Random Reorder | Rows

We can select part of a dataset by specifying a vector of row numbers chosen at random for rows.

- If we specify all rows, then this effectively ***scrambles*** the observations in the dataset.
- If we specify fewer than all rows, then this effectively ***takes a random sample*** of observations from the dataset.

Here are some examples:

dataset (all rows)

	x1	x2	x3	x4
1	A	C	100	205
2	B	D	102	204
3	A	E	101	200
4	B	C	103	201
5	A	D	105	202
6	B	E	104	203

vector of random row #

6
1
4
3
5
2

new dataset

	x1	x2	x3	x4
1	B	E	104	203
2	A	C	100	205
3	B	C	103	201
4	A	E	101	200
5	A	D	105	202
6	B	D	102	204

dataset (rows 1,4,3,6)

	x1	x2	x3	x4
1	A	C	100	205
2	B	D	102	204
3	A	E	101	200
4	B	C	103	201
5	A	D	105	202
6	B	E	104	203

vector of random row #

1
4
3
6

new dataset

	x1	x2	x3	x4
1	A	C	100	205
2	B	C	103	201
3	A	E	101	200
4	B	E	104	203

2.2.10 Criterion-Based Selection | Rows

An especially powerful way to select part of a dataset is to specify a logical criterion for rows. Set the criterion to be an expression or function of the variables that evaluates to TRUE or FALSE. Apply the criterion to each observation, one at a time, to produce a vector of TRUE/FALSE values that indicate which observations should appear in the new dataset. Note that we are using ***variables*** (i.e., columns) to specify ***observations*** (i.e., rows).

- We get a new dataset comprising values from only those rows that satisfy the criterion.

Here is an example where we set the logical criterion to $x_3 \leq 101$. The criterion applied to observation 1 evaluates to TRUE because (x_1=A, x_2=C, x_3=100, x_4=205) satisfies $x_3 \leq 101$, so observation 1 should appear in the new dataset. The criterion applied to observation 2 evaluates to FALSE because (x_1=B, x_2=D, $x_3 = 102$, x_4=204) doesn't satisfy $x_3 \leq 101$, so observation 2 should not appear in the new dataset. Similarly, apply the criterion to the remaining observations. See that the result is a new dataset comprising the original dataset's observation 1 as its first observation, and the original dataset's observation 3 as its second observation.

dataset

	x1	x2	x3	x4
1	A	C	100	205
2	B	D	102	204
3	A	E	101	200
4	B	C	103	201
5	A	D	105	202
6	B	E	104	203

vector of x3 $\leq$ 101

1	TRUE
2	FALSE
3	TRUE
4	FALSE
5	FALSE
6	FALSE

new dataset

	x1	x2	x3	x4
1	A	C	100	205
2	A	E	101	200

Here are some more examples:

dataset

	x1	x2	x3	x4
1	A	C	100	205
2	B	D	102	204
3	A	E	101	200
4	B	C	103	201
5	A	D	105	202
6	B	E	104	203

vector of (x3 > 101) and (x3 $\leq$ 104)

1	FALSE
2	TRUE
3	FALSE
4	TRUE
5	FALSE
6	TRUE

new dataset

	x1	x2	x3	x4
1	B	D	102	204
2	B	C	103	201
3	B	E	104	203

dataset

	x1	x2	x3	x4
1	A	C	100	205
2	B	D	102	204
3	A	E	101	200
4	B	C	103	201
5	A	D	105	202
6	B	E	104	203

vector of not ((x3 $\leq$ 101) or (x3 > 104))

1	FALSE
2	TRUE
3	FALSE
4	TRUE
5	FALSE
6	TRUE

new dataset

	x1	x2	x3	x4
1	B	D	102	204
2	B	C	103	201
3	B	E	104	203

dataset

	x1	x2	x3	x4
1	A	C	100	205
2	B	D	102	204
3	A	E	101	200
4	B	C	103	201
5	A	D	105	202
6	B	E	104	203

vector of (x3 > 101) and (x4 $\leq$ 203) and (x1 = B)

1	FALSE
2	FALSE
3	FALSE
4	TRUE
5	FALSE
6	TRUE

new dataset

	x1	x2	x3	x4
1	B	C	103	201
2	B	E	104	203

2.2.11 Criterion-Based Selection | Columns

We can filter in or filter out variables by specifying a logical criterion for columns. Set the criterion to be an expression or function of the observations that evaluates to TRUE or FALSE. Apply the criterion to each variable, one at a time, to produce a vector of TRUE/FALSE values that indicates which variables should appear in the new dataset. Note that we are using ***observations*** (i.e., rows) to specify ***variables*** (i.e., columns).

- We get a new dataset comprising values from only those columns that satisfy the criterion.

Here is an example where we set the logical criterion to *unique values* ≥ 3. The criterion applied to the x_1 variable evaluates to FALSE because that variable includes only 2 values, A and B, so x_1 should not appear in the new dataset. The criterion applied to the x_2 variable evaluates to TRUE because it includes 3 values, C, D, and E, so x_2 should appear in the new dataset. Similarly, apply the criterion to the remaining variables. See that the result is a new dataset comprising the original dataset's second variable x_2 as its first variable, the original dataset's third variable x_3 as its second variable, and the original dataset's fourth variable x_4 as its third variable.

dataset

	x1	x2	x3	x4
1	A	C	100	205
2	B	D	102	204
3	A	E	101	200
4	B	C	103	201
5	A	D	105	202
6	B	E	104	203

vector of unique values $\geq$ 3

x1	FALSE
x2	TRUE
x3	TRUE
x4	TRUE

new dataset

	x2	x3	x4
1	C	100	205
2	D	102	204
3	E	101	200
4	C	103	201
5	D	105	202
6	E	104	203

Here are some more examples:

dataset

	x1	x2	x3	x4
1	A	C	100	205
2	B	D	102	204
3	A	E	101	200
4	B	C	103	201
5	A	D	105	202
6	B	E	104	203

vector of numerical

x1	FALSE
x2	FALSE
x3	TRUE
x4	TRUE

new dataset

	x3	x4
1	100	205
2	102	204
3	101	200
4	103	201
5	105	202
6	104	203

dataset

	x1	x2	x3	x4
1	A	C	100	205
2	B	D	102	204
3	A	E	101	200
4	B	C	103	201
5	A	D	105	202
6	B	E	104	203

vector of categorical

x1	TRUE
x2	TRUE
x3	FALSE
x4	FALSE

new dataset

	x1	x2
1	A	C
2	B	D
3	A	E
4	B	C
5	A	D
6	B	E

dataset

	x1	x2	x3	x4
1	A	C	100	205
2	B	D	102	204
3	A	E	101	200
4	B	C	103	201
5	A	D	105	202
6	B	E	104	203

vector of (categorical and max < C) or (numerical and max < 150)

x1	TRUE
x2	FALSE
x3	TRUE
x4	FALSE

new dataset

	x1	x3
1	A	100
2	B	102
3	A	101
4	B	103
5	A	105
6	B	104

2.3 Amalgamation

Combine multiple datasets into one dataset.

2.3.1 Introduction

Various data analysis and analytical modeling methods work on the assumption that all relevant information is contained in one provided dataset. However, relevant information is often spread across multiple datasets. Amalgamation addresses this problem by combining multiple datasets into one dataset.

2.3.2 About Amalgamation

Amalgamation is accomplished by **concatenation** or **join**. The term "concatenation" has its usual colloquial meaning: attach something onto the end of something else. The term join refers to a specific method for selecting and combining observations.

- **Row-wise concatenation** is useful for appending or inserting when datasets have corresponding variables.
- **Column-wise concatenation** is useful for appending or inserting when datasets have corresponding observations ordered in the same way.
- **Join** is useful when datasets describe the same kind of events, but employ different variables or include observations about different specific events.

2.3.3 Row-Wise Concatenation

Consider this current dataset **data** and new dataset **new**. Each comprises the same number and types of variables.

data

	x1	x2	x3	x4
1	A	C	100	205
2	B	D	102	204
3	A	E	101	200
4	B	C	103	201
5	A	D	105	202
6	B	E	104	203

new

	x1	x2	x3	x4
1	A	D	106	207
2	B	E	104	203

2.3.3.1 Append New Data | Row-Wise

To append the new dataset **new** to the current dataset **data**, row-wise concatenate **data** and **new**.

data enhanced

	x1	x2	x3	x4
1	A	C	100	205
2	B	D	102	204
3	A	E	101	200
4	B	C	103	201
5	A	D	105	202
6	B	E	104	203
7	A	D	106	207
8	B	E	104	203

2.3.3.2 Insert New Data | Row-Wise

To insert the new dataset **new** into the current dataset **data**, do this: Select the rows from **data** that are to precede the insertion; call this **data.1**. Select the rows from **data** that are to follow the insertion; call this **data.2**. Row-wise concatenate **data.1**, **new**, and **data.2**.

data.1

	x1	x2	x3	x4
1	A	C	100	205
2	B	D	102	204

new

	x1	x2	x3	x4
1	A	D	106	207
2	B	E	104	203

data.2

	x1	x2	x3	x4
1	A	E	101	200
2	B	C	103	201
3	A	D	105	202
4	B	E	104	203

data enhanced

	x1	x2	x3	x4
1	A	C	100	205
2	B	D	102	204
3	A	D	106	207
4	B	E	104	203
5	A	E	101	200
6	B	C	103	201
7	A	D	105	202
8	B	E	104	203

2.3.4 Column-Wise Concatenation

Consider this current dataset **data** and new dataset **new**. Each comprises the same number of observations.

data

	x1	x2	x3	x4
1	A	C	100	205
2	B	D	102	204
3	A	E	101	200
4	B	C	103	201
5	A	D	105	202
6	B	E	104	203

new

	x5	x6
1	300	3
2	304	2
3	315	4
4	307	7
5	295	8
6	301	6

2.3.4.1 Append New Data | Column-Wise

To append the new dataset **new** to the current dataset **data**, column-wise concatenate **data** and **new**.

data enhanced

x1	x2	x3	x4	x5	x6
A	C	100	205	300	3
B	D	102	204	304	2
A	E	101	200	315	4
B	C	103	201	307	7
A	D	105	202	295	8
B	E	104	203	301	6

2.3.4.2 Insert New Data | Column-Wise

To insert the new dataset **new** into the current dataset **data**, do this: Select the columns from **data** that are to precede the insertion; call this **data.1**. Select the columns from **data** that are to follow the insertion; call this **data.2**. Column-wise concatenate **data.1**, **new**, and **data.2**.

data.1

	x1	x2
1	A	C
2	B	D
3	A	E
4	B	C
5	A	D
6	B	E

new

	x5	x6
1	300	3
2	304	2
3	315	4
4	307	7
5	295	8
6	301	6

data.2

	x3	x4
1	100	205
2	102	204
3	101	200
4	103	201
5	105	202
6	104	203

data enhanced

	x1	x2	x5	x6	x3	x4
1	A	C	300	3	100	205
2	B	D	304	2	102	204
3	A	E	315	4	101	200
4	B	C	307	7	103	201
5	A	D	295	8	105	202
6	B	E	301	6	104	203

Alternatively, do this instead: Column-wise concatenate **data** and **new**. Select all columns reordered from the resulting dataset.

data enhanced
(column-wise concatenate)

	x1	x2	x3	x4	x5	x6
1	A	C	100	205	300	3
2	B	D	102	204	304	2
3	A	E	101	200	315	4
4	B	C	103	201	307	7
5	A	D	105	202	295	8
6	B	E	104	203	301	6

data enhanced
(select with reorder)

	x1	x2	x5	x6	x3	x4
1	A	C	300	3	100	205
2	B	D	304	2	102	204
3	A	E	315	4	101	200
4	B	C	307	7	103	201
5	A	D	295	8	105	202
6	B	E	301	6	104	203

2.3.5 Join by One Variable

Consider these 2 current datasets, **data.1** and **data.2**, comprising observations about some events, but employing different variables to do so. **data.1** describes events in terms of x_1, x_2, x_3, and x_4 variables. **data.2** also describes events in terms of the x_1 variable, but not the others, though it does describe additional information in terms of x_5 and x_6 variables. The datasets do not each comprise the same number of observations. The observations are necessarily ordered in a way so that we can tell which observations refer to the same event.

data.1

x1	x2	x3	x4
A	X	100	204
B	Y	102	200
C	X	101	201
D	X	103	202
E	Y	105	203

data.2

x1	x5	x6
D	300	3
A	304	2
B	315	4
B	303	1

To join **data.1** to **data.2**, do this: Determine which variable the datasets have in common, and treat this variable as an event identifier. We'll treat x_1 as the identifier variable. In this way, each event is uniquely identified by an x_1 value, and we'll know which observations describe which events. For each 4-variable observation in **data.1**, check it against every 3-variable observation in **data.2**. Where the identifier variable value is the same in both datasets, construct new 6-variable observations comprising variables from both datasets. Compile all of the new 6-variable observations into a new dataset.

See that the first observation in **data.1**, which is (x_1=A, x_2=X, x_3=100, x_4=204), checks with the second observation in **data.2**, which is (x_1=A, x_5=304, x_6=2). This is because the identifier variable x_1 is A in both datasets. So, we construct a new observation comprising variables from both datasets, namely (x_1=A, x_2=X, x_3=100, x_4=204, x_5=304, x_6=2). Note that each identifier variable appears only once in the new observation; it's not duplicated. The new observation becomes an observation in our new dataset.

The second observation in **data.1**, which is (x_1=B, x_2=Y, x_3=102, x_4=200), checks with both the third and fourth observations in **data.2**, because the identifier variable x_1 is B in both datasets. So, we construct 2 new observations: one from **data.1**'s second observation and **data.2**'s third observation, and one from **data.1**'s second observation and **data.2**'s fourth observation. These 2 new observations become observations in our new dataset.

Similarly for the remaining observations to produce the new 4-observation, 6-variable dataset.

data enhanced (joined by x1)

x1	x2	x3	x4	x5	x6
A	X	100	204	304	2
B	Y	102	200	315	4
B	Y	102	200	303	1
D	X	103	202	300	3

Here is an example of joining datasets where the identifier variable x_1 includes duplicate values in both datasets.

data.1

x1	x2	x3	x4
A	C	100	205
B	D	102	204
A	E	101	200
B	C	103	201
A	D	105	202
B	E	104	203

data.2

x1	x5	x6
A	300	3
B	304	2
A	315	4

data enhanced (joined by x1)

x1	x2	x3	x4	x5	x6
A	C	100	205	300	3
A	C	100	205	315	4
A	E	101	200	300	3
A	E	101	200	315	4
A	D	105	202	300	3
A	D	105	202	315	4
B	D	102	204	304	2
B	C	103	201	304	2
B	E	104	203	304	2

Here is an example of joining datasets where 2 different variables use the same name. In this case, x_2 in **data.1** describes something other than what x_2 in **data.2** does. When we join the datasets, we'll give those variables different names, namely $x2.x$ and x2.y.

data.1

x1	x2	x3	x4
A	C	100	205
B	D	102	204
A	E	101	200
B	C	103	201
A	D	105	202
B	E	104	203

data.2

x1	x2	x5	x6
A	E	300	3
B	C	304	2
A	D	315	4

data enhanced (joined by x1)

x1	x2.x	x3	x4	x2.y	x5	x6
A	C	100	205	E	300	3
A	C	100	205	D	315	4
A	E	101	200	E	300	3
A	E	101	200	D	315	4
A	D	105	202	E	300	3
A	D	105	202	D	315	4
B	D	102	204	C	304	2
B	C	103	201	C	304	2
B	E	104	203	C	304	2

2.3.6 Join by Many Variables

Consider these 2 current datasets, **data.1** and **data.2**, comprising observations about some events, but employing different variables to do so. The datasets do not each comprise the same number of observations. The observations are necessarily ordered in a way so that we can tell which observations refer to the same event.

data.1

x1	x2	x3	x4
A	C	100	205
B	D	102	204
A	E	101	200
B	C	103	201
A	D	105	202
B	E	104	203

data.2

x1	x2	x5	x6
A	D	300	3
B	C	304	2
A	E	315	4

The datasets have 2 variables in common, x_1 and x_2, which together we'll treat as an event identifier. In this way, each event is uniquely identified by a combination of x_1 and x_2 values, and we'll know which observations are describing which events.

Join **data.1** to **data.2** by identifier variables x_1 and x_2. See that the first and second observations in **data.1** do not check with any observations in **data.2**. The combination x_1=A and x_2=C never appears in **data.2**. Nor does the combination x_1=B and x_2=D. However, **data.1**'s third observation does check with **data.2**'s third observation, because x_1=A and x_2=E in both datasets. So, we construct a new observation comprising variables from both datasets, namely (x_1=A, x_2=E, x_3=101, x_4=200, x_5=315, x_6=4), which becomes an observation in our new dataset. Similarly for the remaining observations to produce a new 3-observation, 6-variable dataset.

data enhanced (joined by x1,x2)

x1	x2	x3	x4	x5	x6
A	D	105	202	300	3
A	E	101	200	315	4
B	C	103	201	304	2

2.4 Synthetic Variables

Add a variable to represent a dataset in some more useful form, without adding or removing information.

2.4.1 Introduction

Synthetic variables are about representing a dataset in some more useful form, without adding or removing information.

2.4.2 About Synthetic Variables

Synthetic variables are defined in terms of other already existing variables. Adding synthetic variables does not transform a dataset by adding or removing information. Rather, it preserves information, but represents it in a different way that might be more useful.

Here are some ways to construct synthetic variables:

- **Unit conversion:** Define the synthetic variable as $cx + d$, where x is an already existing variable, c is a conversion rate, and d is a zero or non-zero conversion shift.
- **Linear recombination:** Define a synthetic variable as $c_1x_1 + c_2x_2 + \cdots + c_nx_n + d$, where x_1, x_2, …, x_n are already existing variables, c_1, c_2, …, c_n are coefficients not expressed in terms of variables, and d is a zero or non-zero constant not expressed in terms of variables. Unit conversion is a special case of linear recombination.
- **Non-linear recombination:** Define a synthetic variable as a formula involving already existing variables. Linear combination is a special case of non-linear recombination.
- **Descriptive statistic:** Define a synthetic variable as a descriptive statistic function. Descriptive statistic is a special case of linear or non-linear recombination.
- **Lag:** Define a synthetic variable such that the value at any observation is a formula involving already existing variable values at **other** observations.

2.4.3 Synthetic Variables by Unit Conversion

Consider this 1-variable dataset describing distances measured in units of miles. Perhaps it would be more useful to have this information measured in units of kilometers. Add a synthetic variable to do so.

$$\text{distance.km} = 1.609 \text{ kilometers per mile} \times \text{distance.mi}$$

data		data enhanced	
distance.mi		distance.mi	distance.km
1.7		1.7	2.735
2.3		2.3	3.701
3.1		3.1	4.988
4.6		4.6	7.401
26.1		26.1	41.995

2.4.4 Synthetic Variables by Linear Recombination

A marketing department has developed a formula based on research to predict how much a customer will like the company's new product. Higher score indicates higher acceptance. Age is measured in years. Student status is measured as 1 when customers are students and 0 when they are not.

$$\text{score} = (0.5 \times (100 - \text{age})) + (50 \times \text{student})$$

Consider this 2-variable dataset of customer information. Will these customers like the new product?

Add a synthetic variable *student.01* defined as 1 if *student* = TRUE and 0 if *student* = FALSE. Then add a synthetic variable *score* defined by the formula. Note that the *score* synthetic variable is a linear recombination of the *age* and *student.01* variables.

data		student.01	score	data enhanced			
age	student			age	student	student.01	score
45	FALSE	0	27.5	45	FALSE	0	27.5
47	TRUE	1	76.5	47	TRUE	1	76.5
55	FALSE	0	22.5	55	FALSE	0	22.5
18	TRUE	1	91.0	18	TRUE	1	91.0
22	TRUE	1	89.0	22	TRUE	1	89.0

2.4.5 Synthetic Variables by Non-Linear Recombination

Consider this 2-variable dataset describing the relationship between the x and y variables. We can represent the relationship in many different ways, which might expose a pattern or make subsequent analysis easier.

Add synthetic variables for x^2, y^2, $x \times y$, $log(x)$, $log(y)$, and $sin(x)$. Note that these synthetic variables are non-linear recombinations of the x and y variables.

data

x	y
3	25
4	42
5	53
4	47
5	51
5	65

data enhanced

x	y	square.x	square.y	xy	ln.x	ln.y	sin.x
3	25	9	625	75	1.099	3.219	0.1411
4	42	16	1,764	168	1.386	3.738	-0.7568
5	53	25	2,809	265	1.609	3.970	-0.9589
4	47	16	2,209	188	1.386	3.850	-0.7568
5	51	25	2,601	255	1.609	3.932	-0.9589
5	65	25	4,225	325	1.609	4.174	-0.9589

2.4.6 Synthetic Variables by Descriptive Statistic

Consider this 5-variable dataset. We can summarize the variables with a descriptive statistic, which might expose a pattern or make subsequent analysis easier.

Add a synthetic variable *mean* defined as the mean of x_1, x_2, x_3, x_4, and x_5. Note that, like many descriptive statistics, the mean function operates on a vector of numerical values. So, for each observation, the mean takes as input a vector constructed from values across a collection of variables, not from a vector made up of values within a single variable.

data

x1	x2	x3	x4	x5
3	4	5	3	4
4	2	4	4	6
2	3	5	3	5
3	1	6	2	3
4	2	7	1	2
5	3	6	2	1

data enhanced

x1	x2	x3	x4	x5	mean
3	4	5	3	4	3.8
4	2	4	4	6	4.0
2	3	5	3	5	3.6
3	1	6	2	3	3.0
4	2	7	1	2	3.2
5	3	6	2	1	3.4

2.4.7 Synthetic Variables by Lag

Consider this 2-variable, 11-observation times series dataset. The *timestep* variable names a timestep. The *start* variable indicates the quantity of something at the beginning of a timestep. How does the quantity change from one timestep to the next timestep?

Select rows 2 to 11 at the *start* column to get a 10-element vector; call it *offset*. Append a missing value indicator to *offset* to get an 11-element vector. Add a synthetic variable *end* and assign the 11-element vector to it.

Now each observation has values for quantity at both the start and end of its timestep. Add a synthetic variable *change* defined as $end - start$.

data	
timestep	start
1	100.00
2	77.90
3	100.26
4	111.19
5	116.63
6	135.06
7	142.49
8	89.77
9	113.56
10	130.70
11	133.45

offset
77.90
100.26
111.19
116.63
135.06
142.49
89.77
113.56
130.70
133.45

offset, append NA
77.90
100.26
111.19
116.63
135.06
142.49
89.77
113.56
130.70
133.45
NA

data enhanced			
timestep	start	end	change
1	100.00	77.90	-22.10
2	77.90	100.26	22.36
3	100.26	111.19	10.93
4	111.19	116.63	5.44
5	116.63	135.06	18.43
6	135.06	142.49	7.43
7	142.49	89.77	-52.72
8	89.77	113.56	23.79
9	113.56	130.70	17.14
10	130.70	133.45	2.75
11	133.45	NA	NA

2.5 Normalization

Re-scale variables to standard units.

2.5.1 Introduction

A business operations manager based at headquarters is scheduling visits to his company's field offices. One field office is 200 miles from headquarters. Is that far away or close by? That depends on the units used to measure distance. If distance is measured in miles, does the number 200 seem large or small? If distance is measured in angstroms, as is typically done for measuring atomic particles, perhaps the large number 3.219×10^{15} makes the office seem far away. If distance is measured in light-years, as is typically done for measuring supernovae, perhaps the small number 3.402×10^{-11} makes it seem close by. Alternatively, the manger could assess proximity by how the distance to the office compares with the distances to other offices, regardless of units. Perhaps that's a better way.

Some data analysis and analytic methods can produce distorted results with information measured in arbitrarily chosen units. Normalization addresses this problem.

2.5.2 About Normalization

Normalization transforms a dataset measured in any units into a similar dataset with all variables scaled to standard units that account for mean and standard deviation of variables. New normalized variable values are calculated like this:

$$x_{1i}' = \frac{x_{1i} - \mu_{x_1}}{\sigma_{x_1}} \quad x_{2i}' = \frac{x_{2i} - \mu_{x_2}}{\sigma_{x_2}} \quad \ldots \quad x_{mi}' = \frac{x_{mi} - \mu_{x_m}}{\sigma_{x_m}}$$

where ...

- m is the number of variables
- x_{1i}, x_{2i}, ..., x_{mi} are the ith observation's first, second, ..., and m^{th} variable values
- μ_{x_1}, μ_{x_2}, ..., μ_{x_m} are the means of the first, second, ..., and m^{th} variables
- σ_{x_1}, σ_{x_2}, ..., σ_{x_m} are the standard deviations of the first, second, ..., and m^{th} variables
- x_{1i}', x_{2i}', ..., x_{mi}' are the ith observation's first, second, ..., and m^{th} normalized variable values

Normalization does not cause loss or addition of information to the dataset, except for information specific to the units, which can often facilitate useful data analysis and analytical modeling.

2.5.3 Normalization

Consider this 2-variable dataset. The x_1 variable measures costs of product components in units of US dollars. The x_2 variable measures corresponding length of product component in units of inches. As it stands, see that component 1 is relatively distinguished from the other components – its cost and length are both much lower. Components 2 and 3 are similar to each other – their costs and lengths are about the same. Components 4 and 5 are even more similar to each other.

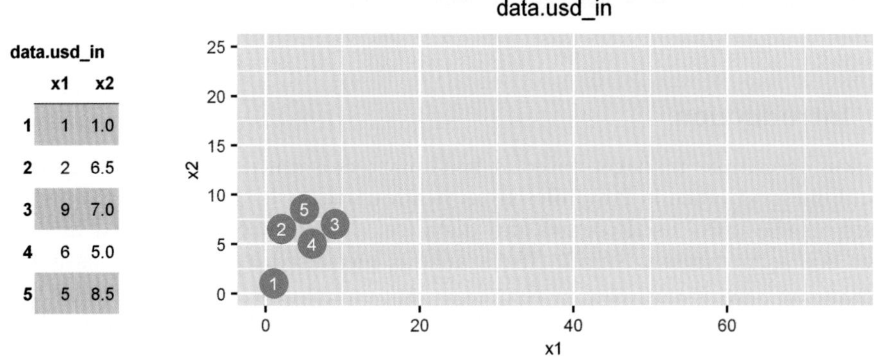

data.usd_in

	x1	x2
1	1	1.0
2	2	6.5
3	9	7.0
4	6	5.0
5	5	8.5

However, the choice of x_2 variable units was arbitrary. Length could just as easily be measured in units of centimeters. If so, see that components 2 and 3 don't appear as similar to each other as they did. Components 4 and 5 now appear less similar to each other than components 2 and 3 do to each other.

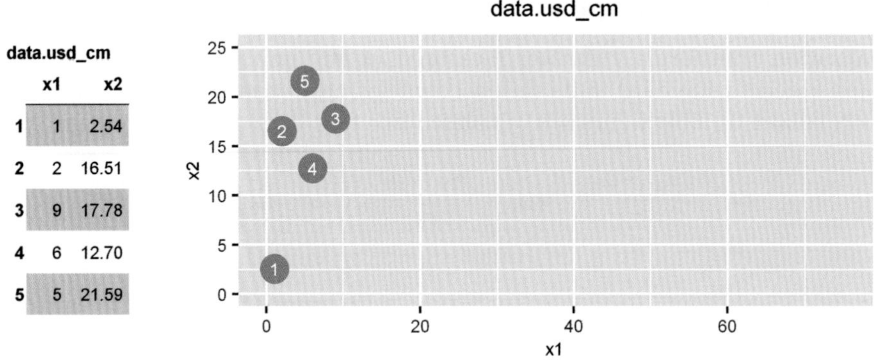

data.usd_cm

	x1	x2
1	1	2.54
2	2	16.51
3	9	17.78
4	6	12.70
5	5	21.59

The choice of x_1 variable units was likewise arbitrary. Cost could just as easily be measured in Bolivian bolivianos. If so, see that components 2 and 3 no longer appear similar to each other. Component 1 appears more similar to component 2 than any other component does.

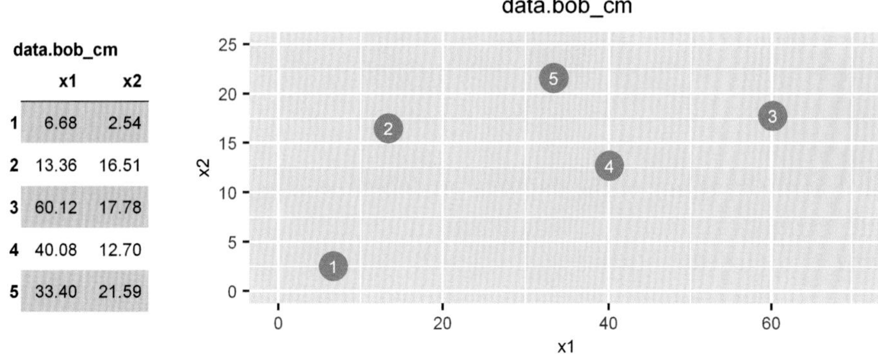

data.bob_cm

	x1	x2
1	6.68	2.54
2	13.36	16.51
3	60.12	17.78
4	40.08	12.70
5	33.40	21.59

Let's avoid this confusion by normalizing the dataset, which scales all variables to standard units, effectively removing the influence of units altogether. First calculate the means and standard deviations of the variables.

usd_in

	x1	x2
mean	4.600	5.600
sd	3.209	2.859

usd_cm

	x1	x2
mean	4.600	14.224
sd	3.209	7.262

bob_cm

	x1	x2
mean	30.73	14.224
sd	21.44	7.262

Then calculate normalized variable values from the dataset in which x_1 is measured in US dollars and x_2 is measured in inches.

$$\begin{array}{lll} \text{observation 1:} & {x_1}' = \dfrac{1-4.6}{3.209} = -1.1217 & {x_2}' = \dfrac{1-5.6}{2.8959} = -1.6088 \\ \text{observation 2:} & {x_1}' = \dfrac{2-4.6}{3.209} = -0.8101 & {x_2}' = \dfrac{6.5-5.6}{2.8959} = 0.3148 \\ \vdots & \vdots & \vdots \end{array}$$

Or calculate normalized variable values from the dataset in which x_1 is measured in US dollars and x_2 is measured in centimeters.

$$\begin{array}{lll} \text{observation 1:} & {x_1}' = \dfrac{1-4.6}{3.209} = -1.1217 & {x_2}' = \dfrac{2.54-14.224}{7.262} = -1.6088 \\ \text{observation 2:} & {x_1}' = \dfrac{2-4.6}{3.209} = -0.8101 & {x_2}' = \dfrac{16.51-14.224}{7.262} = 0.3148 \\ \vdots & \vdots & \vdots \end{array}$$

Or calculate normalized variable values from the dataset in which x_1 is measured in Bolivian bolivianos and x_2 is measured in centimeters.

$$\begin{array}{llll}
\text{observation 1:} & x_1{}' = \dfrac{6.68 - 30.73}{21.44} = -1.1217 & x_2{}' = \dfrac{2.54 - 14.224}{7.262} = -1.6088 \\
\text{observation 2:} & x_1{}' = \dfrac{13.36 - 30.73}{21.44} = -0.8101 & x_2{}' = \dfrac{16.51 - 14.224}{7.262} = 0.3148 \\
\vdots & \vdots & \vdots
\end{array}$$

Note that normalizing any of the datasets produces the same result, regardless of which units they start with.

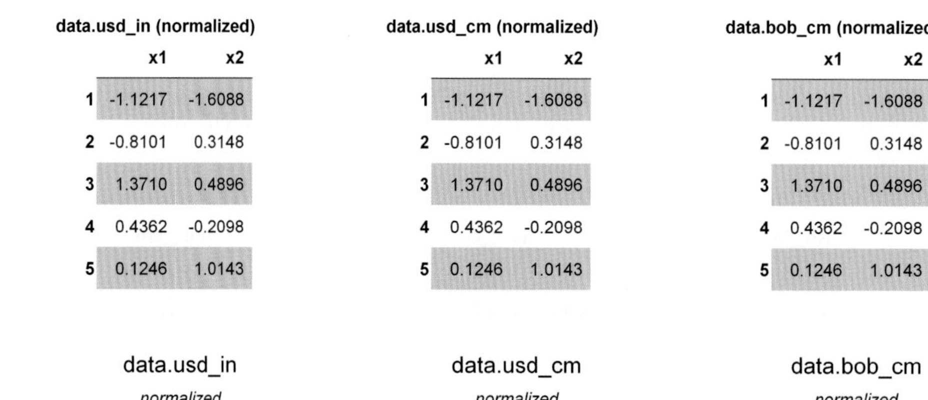

data.usd_in (normalized)

	x1	x2
1	-1.1217	-1.6088
2	-0.8101	0.3148
3	1.3710	0.4896
4	0.4362	-0.2098
5	0.1246	1.0143

data.usd_cm (normalized)

	x1	x2
1	-1.1217	-1.6088
2	-0.8101	0.3148
3	1.3710	0.4896
4	0.4362	-0.2098
5	0.1246	1.0143

data.bob_cm (normalized)

	x1	x2
1	-1.1217	-1.6088
2	-0.8101	0.3148
3	1.3710	0.4896
4	0.4362	-0.2098
5	0.1246	1.0143

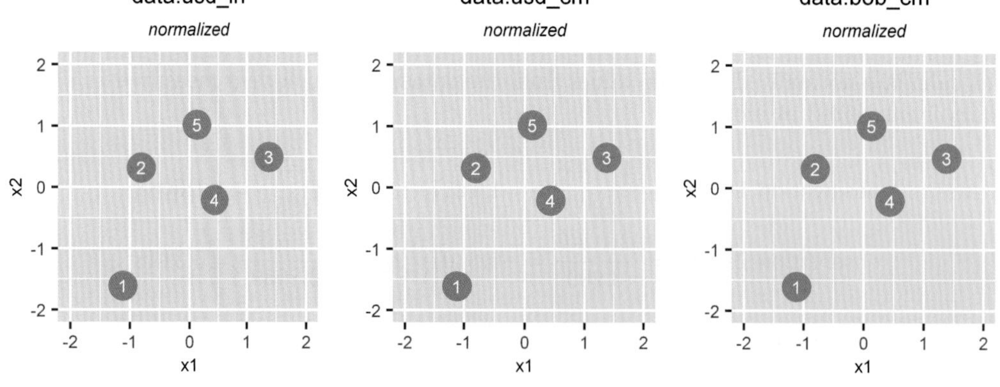

2.6 Dummy Variables

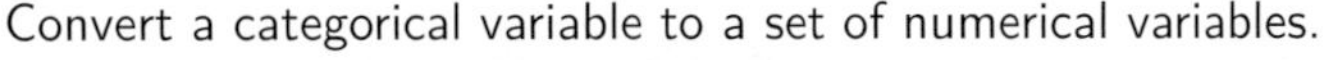

Convert a categorical variable to a set of numerical variables.

2.6.1 Introduction

Some data analysis and analytical modeling methods work on datasets represented only by numerical variables. However, datasets are often represented by combinations of numerical and categorical variables. Dummy variables address this problem by converting a categorical variable to a set of numerical variables without adding or removing information.

2.6.2 About Dummy Variables

Converting a categorical variable to a set of numerical variables works like this:

- For each value of the categorical variable's domain, create a new numerical variable, called a **dummy variable**.
- For each observation, assign dummy variables.
- For each observation, assign each dummy variable to be 1 if it corresponds to the categorical variable value; otherwise, assign it to be 0.
- Discard the categorical variable.
- Discard one of the dummy variables, because the remaining dummy variables are enough to preserve all information that was in the categorical variable.

2.6.3 Categorical to Dummy in a Dataset

Consider this 3-variable classified dataset. The x_1 variable is numerical. The x_2 variable is categorical with domain A, B, C. The x_3 class variable is also categorical, but can take on different values. Let's convert the x_2 variable to a set of dummy variables.

data

x1	x2	class
1.0	A	D
2.0	B	D
3.0	C	D
4.0	A	E
6.0	A	E
6.5	B	D
7.0	C	D
9.0	C	E

Replace the x_2 variable with new dummy variables x_{2A}, x_{2B}, and x_{2C}, corresponding to values in the x_2 domain. For each observation, assign x_{2A} to be 1 if x_2 is A; otherwise, assign it to be 0. Similarly for the remaining dummy variables. See that the first observation's x_2 value was A, so that observation's x_{2A} value is 1, its x_{2B} value is 0, and its x_{2C} value is 0. The dummy variables capture exactly as much information as the categorical variable did.

data enhanced (dummified)

x1	x2_A	x2_B	x2_C	class
1.0	1	0	0	D
2.0	0	1	0	D
3.0	0	0	1	D
4.0	1	0	0	E
6.0	1	0	0	E
6.5	0	1	0	D
7.0	0	0	1	D
9.0	0	0	1	E

Only 2 of the 3 dummy variables are necessary to capture all the information from the categorical variable. Any 2 dummy variables assigned 0 imply that the other dummy variable must be assigned 1.

$$\begin{bmatrix} x_{2A}{=}0, x_{2B}{=}0 \Rightarrow x_{2C}{=}1 \\ x_{2A}{=}1, x_{2B}{=}0 \Rightarrow x_{2C}{=}0 \\ x_{2A}{=}0, x_{2B}{=}1 \Rightarrow x_{2C}{=}0 \end{bmatrix} \quad \begin{bmatrix} x_{2A}{=}0, x_{2C}{=}0 \Rightarrow x_{2B}{=}1 \\ x_{2A}{=}1, x_{2C}{=}0 \Rightarrow x_{2B}{=}0 \\ x_{2A}{=}0, x_{2C}{=}1 \Rightarrow x_{2B}{=}0 \end{bmatrix} \quad \begin{bmatrix} x_{2B}{=}0, x_{2C}{=}0 \Rightarrow x_{2A}{=}1 \\ x_{2B}{=}1, x_{2C}{=}0 \Rightarrow x_{2A}{=}0 \\ x_{2B}{=}0, x_{2C}{=}1 \Rightarrow x_{2A}{=}0 \end{bmatrix}$$

In general, for a categorical variable with domain of any size, we'll need 1 fewer dummy variable than there are values in the domain. So, let's discard 1 of the dummy variables. By convention, we typically discard the first dummy variable.

data enhanced (dummified, first discarded)

x1	x2_B	x2_C	class
1.0	0	0	D
2.0	1	0	D
3.0	0	1	D
4.0	0	0	E
6.0	0	0	E
6.5	1	0	D
7.0	0	1	D
9.0	0	1	E

2.6.4 Categorical to Dummy in a New Observation

Consider this unclassified new observation. Let's convert the x_2 variable to a set of dummy variables.

new

x1	x2
5	B

Converting only makes sense when we know the categorical variable's domain. Here we know that the dataset and new observation are describing the same kind of events, so the new observation's x_2 domain is A, B, C.

Replace the x_2 variable with new dummy variables x_{2A}, x_{2B}, and x_{2C}, and discard the x_{2A} variable.

new enhanced (dummified)

x1	x2_A	x2_B	x2_C
5	0	1	0

new enhanced (dummified, first discarded)

x1	x2_B	x2_C
5	1	0

2.7 CASE | High-Tech Stocks

Data preparation with selection, amalgamation, and synthetic variables to discover relationships among companies' financial performance in the high-tech industry.

2.7.1 Business Situation

A hedge fund manager is considering investing in certain high-tech companies, and is interested in the historical performance of their stocks.

- **Role:** Hedge Fund Manager
- **Decision:** Invest in certain high-tech stocks?
- **Approach:** Use data preparation to answer a few questions about historical performance.

2.7.2 Data

Retrieve a dataset describing S&P 500 returns and Apple and IBM stock prices from 2001 to 2023. Each observation is a snapshot at the end of the day on the last day of the month. There are 5 variables.

- *Date* is the decimal date of the month, where the integer portion is the year, and the fractional portion is the elapsed fraction of a year to the middle of the month. For example, 2,001.04 indicates January 2001 because the integer portion is year 2000, and the fractional portion is $(31 \div 2) \div 365 = 0.04$ of the way into 2000.
- *SP500.Return* is the S&P 500 return rate from the beginning to the end of the month.
- *Apple.Price* is the stock price of Apple at the end of the month.
- *IBM.Price* is the stock price of IBM at the end of the month.
- *Calendar.Date* is the calendar date expressed as 8 digits. The first 4 digits are the year. The next 2 digits are the month number. The last 2 digits are the day of the month.

data *size 276×5, first few observations shown*

Date	SP500.Return	Apple.Price	IBM.Price	Calendar.Date
2,001.04	0.0346	0.386161	107.0746	20010131
2,001.12	-0.0923	0.325893	95.5067	20010228
2,001.21	-0.0642	0.394107	91.9503	20010331
2,001.29	0.0768	0.455179	110.0765	20010430
2,001.38	0.0051	0.356250	106.8834	20010531
2,001.46	-0.0250	0.415179	108.5086	20010630

2.7.3 Index-Based Selection | Rows

Let's answer some questions using index-based selection of rows.

What were S&P 500 return and company stock prices at the end of January 2001?

select row 1

Date	SP500.Return	Apple.Price	IBM.Price	Calendar.Date
2,001.04	0.0346	0.386161	107.075	20010131

What were S&P 500 return and company stock prices 12 months later?

select row 13

Date	SP500.Return	Apple.Price	IBM.Price	Calendar.Date
2,002.04	-0.0156	0.441429	103.145	20020131

What were S&P 500 returns and company stock prices in 2001?

select rows 1 to 12

Date	SP500.Return	Apple.Price	IBM.Price	Calendar.Date
2,001.04	0.0346	0.386161	107.0746	20010131
2,001.12	-0.0923	0.325893	95.5067	20010228
2,001.21	-0.0642	0.394107	91.9503	20010331
2,001.29	0.0768	0.455179	110.0765	20010430
2,001.38	0.0051	0.356250	106.8834	20010531
2,001.46	-0.0250	0.415179	108.5086	20010630
2,001.54	-0.0108	0.335536	100.5832	20010731
2,001.63	-0.0641	0.331250	95.5545	20010831
2,001.71	-0.0817	0.276964	87.6864	20010930
2,001.79	0.0181	0.313571	103.3174	20011031
2,001.87	0.0752	0.380357	110.5067	20011130
2,001.96	0.0076	0.391071	115.6405	20011231

What were S&P 500 returns and company stock prices in 2002?

select rows 13 to 24

Date	SP500.Return	Apple.Price	IBM.Price	Calendar.Date
2,002.04	-0.0156	0.441429	103.1453	20020131
2,002.12	-0.0208	0.387500	93.8050	20020228
2,002.21	0.0367	0.422679	99.4264	20020331
2,002.29	-0.0614	0.433393	80.0765	20020430
2,002.38	-0.0091	0.416071	76.9120	20020531
2,002.46	-0.0725	0.316429	68.8336	20020630
2,002.54	-0.0790	0.272500	67.3040	20020731
2,002.63	0.0049	0.263393	72.0650	20020831
2,002.71	-0.1100	0.258929	55.7457	20020930
2,002.79	0.0864	0.286964	75.4685	20021031
2,002.87	0.0571	0.276786	83.0975	20021130
2,002.96	-0.0603	0.255893	74.0918	20021231

What were S&P 500 returns and company stock prices at end of first month in each 6-month period in 2001 and 2002?

select rows 1,7,13,19

Date	SP500.Return	Apple.Price	IBM.Price	Calendar.Date
2,001.04	0.0346	0.386161	107.075	20010131
2,001.54	-0.0108	0.335536	100.583	20010731
2,002.04	-0.0156	0.441429	103.145	20020131
2,002.54	-0.0790	0.272500	67.304	20020731

2.7.4 Index-Based Selection | Rows & Columns

Let's answer some questions using index-based selection of rows and columns.

What was S&P 500 return at end of January 2001?

select row 1, column 2

0.0346

What were company stock prices at end of January 2001?

select row 1, columns 3,4

Apple.Price	IBM.Price
0.386161	107.075

What were company stock prices at end of January in 2001 and 2002?

select rows 1,13, columns 1,3,4

Date	Apple.Price	IBM.Price
2,001.04	0.386161	107.075
2,002.04	0.441429	103.145

What were company stock prices in 2001?

select rows 1 to 12, columns 1,3,4

Date	Apple.Price	IBM.Price
2,001.04	0.386161	107.0746
2,001.12	0.325893	95.5067
2,001.21	0.394107	91.9503
2,001.29	0.455179	110.0765
2,001.38	0.356250	106.8834
2,001.46	0.415179	108.5086
2,001.54	0.335536	100.5832
2,001.63	0.331250	95.5545
2,001.71	0.276964	87.6864
2,001.79	0.313571	103.3174
2,001.87	0.380357	110.5067
2,001.96	0.391071	115.6405

What were S&P 500 returns and company stock prices in 2001? Show calendar date first, hide decimal date.

select rows 1 to 12, columns 5, 2 to 4

Calendar.Date	SP500.Return	Apple.Price	IBM.Price
20010131	0.0346	0.386161	107.0746
20010228	-0.0923	0.325893	95.5067
20010331	-0.0642	0.394107	91.9503
20010430	0.0768	0.455179	110.0765
20010531	0.0051	0.356250	106.8834
20010630	-0.0250	0.415179	108.5086
20010731	-0.0108	0.335536	100.5832
20010831	-0.0641	0.331250	95.5545
20010930	-0.0817	0.276964	87.6864
20011031	0.0181	0.313571	103.3174
20011130	0.0752	0.380357	110.5067
20011231	0.0076	0.391071	115.6405

2.7.5 Name-Based Selection | Rows & One Column

Let's answer some questions using name-based selection of 1 column.

What was S&P 500 return at end of January 2001?

select row 1, column SP500.Return

0.0346

What were S&P 500 returns in 2001?

select rows 1 to 12, column SP500.Return

0.0346
-0.0923
-0.0642
0.0768
0.0051
-0.0250
-0.0108
-0.0641
-0.0817
0.0181
0.0752
0.0076

What were S&P 500 returns at end of first month of each quarter in 2001?

select rows 1,4,7,10, column SP500.Return

0.0346
0.0768
-0.0108
0.0181

2.7.6 Name-Based Selection | Rows & Columns

Let's answer some questions using name-based selection of columns.

What was S&P 500 return at end of January 2001?

select row 1, column SP500.Return

0.0346

What were company stock prices at end of January 2001? Show calendar date first, hide decimal date.

select row 1, columns Calendar.Date, Apple.Price, IBM.Price

Calendar.Date	Apple.Price	IBM.Price
20010131	0.386161	107.075

What were company stock prices at end of January 2001 and 2002? Show calendar date first, hide decimal date.

select rows 1,13, columns Calendar.Date, Apple.Price, IBM.Price

Calendar.Date	Apple.Price	IBM.Price
20010131	0.386161	107.075
20020131	0.441429	103.145

2.7.7 Selection with Random Reorder | Rows

Let's take a random sample of S&P 500 returns and company stock prices.

select 6 rows at random

Date	SP500.Return	Apple.Price	IBM.Price	Calendar.Date
2,014.87	0.0245	29.73250	155.038	20141130
2,011.71	-0.0719	13.61857	167.180	20110930
2,023.46	0.0639	193.97000	133.810	20230630
2,016.54	0.0354	26.05250	153.556	20160731
2,008.04	-0.0609	4.83429	102.400	20080131
2,022.87	0.0457	148.03000	148.900	20221130

2.7.8 Criterion-Based Selection | Rows

Let's answer some questions using criterion-based selection of rows.

What were S&P 500 returns and company stock prices in 2001?

select rows where Date < 2002

Date	SP500.Return	Apple.Price	IBM.Price	Calendar.Date
2,001.04	0.0346	0.386161	107.0746	20010131
2,001.12	-0.0923	0.325893	95.5067	20010228
2,001.21	-0.0642	0.394107	91.9503	20010331
2,001.29	0.0768	0.455179	110.0765	20010430
2,001.38	0.0051	0.356250	106.8834	20010531
2,001.46	-0.0250	0.415179	108.5086	20010630
2,001.54	-0.0108	0.335536	100.5832	20010731
2,001.63	-0.0641	0.331250	95.5545	20010831
2,001.71	-0.0817	0.276964	87.6864	20010930
2,001.79	0.0181	0.313571	103.3174	20011031
2,001.87	0.0752	0.380357	110.5067	20011130
2,001.96	0.0076	0.391071	115.6405	20011231

What were S&P 500 returns and company stock prices in 2002?

select rows where Date ≥ 2002 and Date < 2003

Date	SP500.Return	Apple.Price	IBM.Price	Calendar.Date
2,002.04	-0.0156	0.441429	103.1453	20020131
2,002.12	-0.0208	0.387500	93.8050	20020228
2,002.21	0.0367	0.422679	99.4264	20020331
2,002.29	-0.0614	0.433393	80.0765	20020430
2,002.38	-0.0091	0.416071	76.9120	20020531
2,002.46	-0.0725	0.316429	68.8336	20020630
2,002.54	-0.0790	0.272500	67.3040	20020731
2,002.63	0.0049	0.263393	72.0650	20020831
2,002.71	-0.1100	0.258929	55.7457	20020930
2,002.79	0.0864	0.286964	75.4685	20021031
2,002.87	0.0571	0.276786	83.0975	20021130
2,002.96	-0.0603	0.255893	74.0918	20021231

What were S&P 500 returns and company stock prices in 2002? Alternatively, we could answer the question this way.

select rows where not (Date < 2002 or Date ≥ 2003)

Date	SP500.Return	Apple.Price	IBM.Price	Calendar.Date
2,002.04	-0.0156	0.441429	103.1453	20020131
2,002.12	-0.0208	0.387500	93.8050	20020228
2,002.21	0.0367	0.422679	99.4264	20020331
2,002.29	-0.0614	0.433393	80.0765	20020430
2,002.38	-0.0091	0.416071	76.9120	20020531
2,002.46	-0.0725	0.316429	68.8336	20020630
2,002.54	-0.0790	0.272500	67.3040	20020731
2,002.63	0.0049	0.263393	72.0650	20020831
2,002.71	-0.1100	0.258929	55.7457	20020930
2,002.79	0.0864	0.286964	75.4685	20021031
2,002.87	0.0571	0.276786	83.0975	20021130
2,002.96	-0.0603	0.255893	74.0918	20021231

What were S&P 500 returns in 2002? Show calendar date first, hide decimal date.

select
rows where Date ≥ 2002 and Date < 2003,
columns Calendar.Date, SP500.Return

Calendar.Date	SP500.Return
20020131	-0.0156
20020228	-0.0208
20020331	0.0367
20020430	-0.0614
20020531	-0.0091
20020630	-0.0725
20020731	-0.0790
20020831	0.0049
20020930	-0.1100
20021031	0.0864
20021130	0.0571
20021231	-0.0603

2.7.9 Row-Wise Concatenation

A new dataset called **data.2000.a** has become available. It describes S&P 500 returns and company stock prices for the first 10 months of 2000. Observations are represented by the same variables as in our dataset, and they are in chronological order.

data.2000.a

Date	SP500.Return	Apple.Price	IBM.Price	Calendar.Date
2,000.04	-0.0509	0.926339	107.3136	20000131
2,000.12	-0.0201	1.023438	98.2314	20000229
2,000.21	0.0967	1.212612	113.1692	20000331
2,000.29	-0.0308	1.107701	106.5966	20000430
2,000.38	-0.0219	0.750000	102.5932	20000531
2,000.46	0.0239	0.935268	104.7443	20000630
2,000.54	-0.0163	0.907366	107.3136	20000731
2,000.63	0.0607	1.088170	126.2100	20000831
2,000.71	-0.0535	0.459821	107.6721	20000930
2,000.79	-0.0050	0.349330	94.1683	20001031

Let's enhance our dataset to include information about 2000. Keep observations in chronological order. We can do this by row-wise concatenating **data.2000.a** to our dataset.

data enhanced *size 286×5, first few observations shown*

Date	SP500.Return	Apple.Price	IBM.Price	Calendar.Date
2,000.04	-0.0509	0.926339	107.3136	20000131
2,000.12	-0.0201	1.023438	98.2314	20000229
2,000.21	0.0967	1.212612	113.1692	20000331
2,000.29	-0.0308	1.107701	106.5966	20000430
2,000.38	-0.0219	0.750000	102.5932	20000531
2,000.46	0.0239	0.935268	104.7443	20000630
2,000.54	-0.0163	0.907366	107.3136	20000731
2,000.63	0.0607	1.088170	126.2100	20000831
2,000.71	-0.0535	0.459821	107.6721	20000930
2,000.79	-0.0050	0.349330	94.1683	20001031
2,001.04	0.0346	0.386161	107.0746	20010131
2,001.12	-0.0923	0.325893	95.5067	20010228
2,001.21	-0.0642	0.394107	91.9503	20010331
2,001.29	0.0768	0.455179	110.0765	20010430
2,001.38	0.0051	0.356250	106.8834	20010531
2,001.46	-0.0250	0.415179	108.5086	20010630
2,001.54	-0.0108	0.335536	100.5832	20010731
2,001.63	-0.0641	0.331250	95.5545	20010831

Another new dataset called **data.2000.b** has become available. It describes S&P 500 returns and company stock prices for the last 2 months of 2000. Observations are represented by the same variables as in our dataset, and they are in chronological order.

data.2000.b

Date	SP500.Return	Apple.Price	IBM.Price	Calendar.Date
2,000.87	-0.0801	0.294643	89.3881	20001130
2,000.96	0.0041	0.265625	81.2619	20001231

Let's enhance our dataset to include the additional information about 2000. Keep observations in chronological order. We can effectively insert observations into their appropriate positions by row-wise concatenation. First, select the first 10 rows of our dataset; call this **data.1**. Second, select all rows beyond row 10 of our dataset; call this **data.2**. Third, row-wise concatenate **data.1** to **data.2000.b**. Fourth, row-wise concatenate the resulting dataset to **data.2**.

data.1
(by selecting rows 1 to 10 of data)

Date	SP500.Return	Apple.Price	IBM.Price	Calendar.Date
2,000.04	-0.0509	0.926339	107.3136	20000131
2,000.12	-0.0201	1.023438	98.2314	20000229
2,000.21	0.0967	1.212612	113.1692	20000331
2,000.29	-0.0308	1.107701	106.5966	20000430
2,000.38	-0.0219	0.750000	102.5932	20000531
2,000.46	0.0239	0.935268	104.7443	20000630
2,000.54	-0.0163	0.907366	107.3136	20000731
2,000.63	0.0607	1.088170	126.2100	20000831
2,000.71	-0.0535	0.459821	107.6721	20000930
2,000.79	-0.0050	0.349330	94.1683	20001031

data.2
(by selecting rows 11 to last row of data)
first few observations shown

Date	SP500.Return	Apple.Price	IBM.Price	Calendar.Date
2,001.04	0.0346	0.386161	107.0746	20010131
2,001.12	-0.0923	0.325893	95.5067	20010228
2,001.21	-0.0642	0.394107	91.9503	20010331
2,001.29	0.0768	0.455179	110.0765	20010430
2,001.38	0.0051	0.356250	106.8834	20010531
2,001.46	-0.0250	0.415179	108.5086	20010630

data enhanced *size 288×5, first few observations shown*

Date	SP500.Return	Apple.Price	IBM.Price	Calendar.Date
2,000.04	-0.0509	0.926339	107.3136	20000131
2,000.12	-0.0201	1.023438	98.2314	20000229
2,000.21	0.0967	1.212612	113.1692	20000331
2,000.29	-0.0308	1.107701	106.5966	20000430
2,000.38	-0.0219	0.750000	102.5932	20000531
2,000.46	0.0239	0.935268	104.7443	20000630
2,000.54	-0.0163	0.907366	107.3136	20000731
2,000.63	0.0607	1.088170	126.2100	20000831
2,000.71	-0.0535	0.459821	107.6721	20000930
2,000.79	-0.0050	0.349330	94.1683	20001031
2,000.87	-0.0801	0.294643	89.3881	20001130
2,000.96	0.0041	0.265625	81.2619	20001231
2,001.04	0.0346	0.386161	107.0746	20010131
2,001.12	-0.0923	0.325893	95.5067	20010228
2,001.21	-0.0642	0.394107	91.9503	20010331
2,001.29	0.0768	0.455179	110.0765	20010430
2,001.38	0.0051	0.356250	106.8834	20010531
2,001.46	-0.0250	0.415179	108.5086	20010630

2.7.10 Column-Wise Concatenation

A new dataset called **data.microsoft** has become available. It describes Microsoft stock prices in 2000 to 2023. Observations are represented by decimal date, price, and calendar date variables, and they are in chronological order corresponding to observations in our dataset.

data.microsoft *size 288×3, first few observations shown*

Date	Microsoft.Price	Calendar.Date
2,000.04	48.9375	20000131
2,000.12	44.6875	20000229
2,000.21	53.1250	20000331
2,000.29	34.8750	20000430
2,000.38	31.2812	20000531
2,000.46	40.0000	20000630

Let's enhance our dataset to include information about Microsoft. We can do this by column-wise concatenating our dataset to **data.microsoft**. First, select the first 4 columns of our dataset; call this **data.1**. Second, select columns 2 and 3 of **data.microsoft**; call this **data.2**. Third, column-wise concatenate **data.1** to **data.2**.

data.1
(by selecting columns 1 to 4 of data)
first few observations shown

Date	SP500.Return	Apple.Price	IBM.Price
2,000.04	-0.0509	0.926339	107.3136
2,000.12	-0.0201	1.023438	98.2314
2,000.21	0.0967	1.212612	113.1692
2,000.29	-0.0308	1.107701	106.5966
2,000.38	-0.0219	0.750000	102.5932
2,000.46	0.0239	0.935268	104.7443

data.2
(by selecting columns 2,3 of data.microsoft)
first few observations shown

Microsoft.Price	Calendar.Date
48.9375	20000131
44.6875	20000229
53.1250	20000331
34.8750	20000430
31.2812	20000531
40.0000	20000630

data enhanced *size 288×6, first few observations shown*

Date	SP500.Return	Apple.Price	IBM.Price	Microsoft.Price	Calendar.Date
2,000.04	-0.0509	0.926339	107.3136	48.9375	20000131
2,000.12	-0.0201	1.023438	98.2314	44.6875	20000229
2,000.21	0.0967	1.212612	113.1692	53.1250	20000331
2,000.29	-0.0308	1.107701	106.5966	34.8750	20000430
2,000.38	-0.0219	0.750000	102.5932	31.2812	20000531
2,000.46	0.0239	0.935268	104.7443	40.0000	20000630

2.7.11 Join

A new dataset called **data.dell** has become available. It describes Dell stock prices for only some months in 2017 to 2023. Observations are represented by decimal date, price, and calendar date variables.

data.dell *size 84×3, first few observations shown*

Date	Dell.Price	Calendar.Date
2,017.04	17.6777	20170131
2,017.12	17.8181	20170228
2,017.21	17.9836	20170331
2,017.29	18.8340	20170430
2,017.38	19.4739	20170531
2,017.46	17.1501	20170630

Let's enhance our dataset to include information about Dell. Keep only observations that completely describe Apple, IBM, Microsoft, and Dell prices, not any observations that describe only some of these company prices. We can do this by joining our dataset to **data.dell** on the *Date* variable (or on the *Calendar.Date* variable, or on both the *Date* and *Calendar.Date* variables). Note that our dataset's observations do not correspond one-to-one with **data.dell**'s observations, so it would be nonsensical to try to column-wise concatenate the datasets.

data enhanced
(by joining data,data.dell on Date,Calendar.Date)
size 84×7, first few observations shown

Date	Calendar.Date	SP500.Return	Apple.Price	IBM.Price	Microsoft.Price	Dell.Price
2,017.04	20170131	0.0121	30.3375	166.845	64.65	17.6777
2,017.12	20170228	0.0341	34.2475	171.912	63.98	17.8181
2,017.21	20170331	-0.0073	35.9150	166.482	65.86	17.9836
2,017.29	20170430	0.0093	35.9125	153.241	68.46	18.8340
2,017.38	20170531	0.0098	38.1900	145.918	69.84	19.4739
2,017.46	20170630	0.0032	36.0050	147.065	68.93	17.1501

2.7.12 Synthetic Variables by Descriptive Statistic

What are the average company stock prices in each month for which we have data? Add a synthetic variable *Mean.Price* defined as the mean of the four price variables.

data *first few observations shown, Date variable not shown*

Calendar.Date	SP500.Return	Apple.Price	IBM.Price	Microsoft.Price	Dell.Price	Mean.Price
20170131	0.0121	30.3375	166.845	64.65	17.6777	69.8776
20170228	0.0341	34.2475	171.912	63.98	17.8181	71.9894
20170331	-0.0073	35.9150	166.482	65.86	17.9836	71.5601
20170430	0.0093	35.9125	153.241	68.46	18.8340	69.1119
20170531	0.0098	38.1900	145.918	69.84	19.4739	68.3554
20170630	0.0032	36.0050	147.065	68.93	17.1501	67.2875

2.7.13 Synthetic Variables by Lag

What was the average monthly return rate on an investment in Apple stock in 2019? By average monthly return rate, we mean the fixed interest rate compounded monthly that some other investment would have to pay to be equally valuable.

See that rows 24 to 36 from our dataset contain information about 2019. This includes the observation about December 2018 because the price at the end of December 2018 is the price at the beginning of January 2019.

data (select rows 24 to 36) *Date variable not shown*

Calendar.Date	SP500.Return	Apple.Price	IBM.Price	Microsoft.Price	Dell.Price	Mean.Price
20181231	-0.1016	39.4350	108.671	101.57	24.7694	68.6114
20190131	0.0917	41.6100	128.509	104.43	24.6275	74.7940
20190228	0.0304	43.2875	132.055	112.03	28.2919	78.9162
20190331	0.0129	47.4875	134.895	117.94	29.7466	82.5172
20190430	0.0341	50.1675	134.101	130.60	34.1662	87.2588
20190531	-0.0678	43.7675	121.405	123.68	30.1825	79.7588
20190630	0.0691	49.4800	131.836	133.96	25.7476	85.2558
20190731	0.0030	53.2600	141.721	136.27	29.2651	90.1290
20190831	-0.0181	52.1850	129.570	137.86	26.1176	86.4331
20190930	0.0233	55.9925	139.025	139.03	26.2848	90.0831
20191031	0.0181	62.1900	127.849	143.37	26.8069	90.0540
20191130	0.0296	66.8125	128.537	151.38	24.5768	92.8266
20191231	0.0277	73.4125	128.145	157.70	26.0466	96.3261

To find the average monthly return rate, it will be useful to create a new dataset that will make our calculations easier. So, create a new 12-observation dataset called **data.apple2019** with variables *month* and *start stock price*. Assign a vector of month names to the *month* variable. Select rows 24 to 35 at the *Apple.Price* column in our dataset and assign the resulting vector to the *start stock price* variable in the **data.apple2019** dataset.

data.apple2019

month	start_stock_price
January	39.4350
February	41.6100
March	43.2875
April	47.4875
May	50.1675
June	43.7675
July	49.4800
August	53.2600
September	52.1850
October	55.9925
November	62.1900
December	66.8125

We need to have available both the start stock price and end stock price for each month to calculate return rate and growth rate for each month. Add a synthetic variable *end stock price* to the **data.apple2019** dataset, defined as *start stock price* at the next row, except for the last row where it's the price at the end of December 2019.

Here is how to do that. Select rows 2 to 12 at the *start stock price* column in the **data.apple2019** dataset to get an 11-element vector. Select row 36 at the *Apple.Price* column in our dataset to get a value. Concatenate the 11-element vector with this value to get a 12-element vector, and assign it to the *end stock price* variable.

data.apple2019

month	start_stock_price	end_stock_price
January	39.4350	41.6100
February	41.6100	43.2875
March	43.2875	47.4875
April	47.4875	50.1675
May	50.1675	43.7675
June	43.7675	49.4800
July	49.4800	53.2600
August	53.2600	52.1850
September	52.1850	55.9925
October	55.9925	62.1900
November	62.1900	66.8125
December	66.8125	73.4125

Add synthetic variables to the **data.apple2019** dataset, defined like this:

$$\text{return rate} = \frac{\text{end stock price} - \text{start stock price}}{\text{start stock price}}$$

$$\text{growth factor} = 1 + \text{return rate}$$

data.apple2019

month	start_stock_price	end_stock_price	return_rate	growth_factor
January	39.4350	41.6100	0.055154	1.055154
February	41.6100	43.2875	0.040315	1.040315
March	43.2875	47.4875	0.097026	1.097026
April	47.4875	50.1675	0.056436	1.056436
May	50.1675	43.7675	-0.127573	0.872427
June	43.7675	49.4800	0.130519	1.130519
July	49.4800	53.2600	0.076394	1.076394
August	53.2600	52.1850	-0.020184	0.979816
September	52.1850	55.9925	0.072962	1.072962
October	55.9925	62.1900	0.110684	1.110684
November	62.1900	66.8125	0.074329	1.074329
December	66.8125	73.4125	0.098784	1.098784

Equipped with the **data.apple2019** dataset, we can conveniently calculate average monthly return rate:

$$\text{average monthly return rate} = geomean(\text{growth factor}) - 1 = 5.31\%$$

Note that to calculate average monthly return rate, we used the geometric mean applied to the growth factor variable, not the arithmetic mean applied to the return rate variable. That would have incorrectly led us to believe that the average monthly return rate was 5.54%, which is nonsense and not very useful. To see this clearly, try calculating monthly stock prices assuming both a 5.54% monthly return rate and a 5.31% monthly return rate. Under the 5.54% assumption, stock price at the end of 2019 would have reached \$75.32 per share, which does not fit reality. Under the 5.31% assumption, stock price reaches \$73.41 per share, which is indeed as it should be.

$$\text{nonsense rate} = \textit{mean}(\text{return rate}) = 5.54\%$$

$$\text{average monthly return rate} = \textit{geomean}(\text{growth factor}) - 1 = 5.31\%$$

nonsense_rate	avg_monthly_return_rate
0.055404	0.053151

assume 5.54% | wrong

month	start	return_rate	end
January	39.4350	0.055404	41.6199
February	41.6199	0.055404	43.9258
March	43.9258	0.055404	46.3594
April	46.3594	0.055404	48.9279
May	48.9279	0.055404	51.6387
June	51.6387	0.055404	54.4997
July	54.4997	0.055404	57.5192
August	57.5192	0.055404	60.7059
September	60.7059	0.055404	64.0693
October	64.0693	0.055404	67.6190
November	67.6190	0.055404	71.3653
December	71.3653	0.055404	75.3192

assume 5.31% | right

month	start	return_rate	end
January	39.4350	0.053151	41.5310
February	41.5310	0.053151	43.7384
March	43.7384	0.053151	46.0632
April	46.0632	0.053151	48.5115
May	48.5115	0.053151	51.0899
June	51.0899	0.053151	53.8054
July	53.8054	0.053151	56.6652
August	56.6652	0.053151	59.6770
September	59.6770	0.053151	62.8489
October	62.8489	0.053151	66.1894
November	66.1894	0.053151	69.7075
December	69.7075	0.053151	73.4125

3 | Data Exploration

Learning Objectives

Terms

Know the terms:

- Frequency table
- Relative frequency table
- Mean
- Median
- Mode
- Minimum
- Maximum
- Range
- Variance
- Standard deviation
- Interquartile range
- Quartile
- Percentile
- Pairwise minimum
- Pairwise maximum
- Covariance
- Correlation
- Similarity
- Dissimilarity
- Euclidean distance
- Manhattan distance
- Maximum distance
- Canberra distance
- Simple Matching Coefficient distance (or SMC)
- Jaccard Coefficient distance
- Aggregation method
- Aggregate table
- Long table
- Cross-tabulation method
- Cross-table
- Identifier variables
- Measure variables
- Scatterplot
- Bubbleplot
- Trellis
- Lineplot
- Stepplot
- Pathplot
- Bar chart
- Histogram
- Pie chart
- Violinplot
- Boxplot
- Heat map
- Conditional format
- Underlying process
- Probabilistic model
- Probability distribution
- Probability density function
- Kernel density estimation (or KDE)
- Kernel
- Bandwidth
- Gaussian function
- Bi-variate Gaussian function

Effects of Assumptions

Know the effects of assumptions:

- Effect of bandwidth on a probability density function
- Effect of using two 1-variable kernel density estimates vs. one 2-variable kernel density estimate on a probability density function

Use the Methods

Know how to use the methods:

- Compute various descriptive statistics applied to 1-variable data.
- Compute various descriptive statistics applied to 2-variable data.
- Compute the Euclidean distance between observations.
- Compute an aggregate table.
- Compute a cross-table.
- Compute a data visualization using any of a variety of methods.
- Compute a 1-variable probability density function using the kernel density estimation method.
- Compute a 1-variable probability density function visualization.
- Compute a 2-variable probability density function using the kernel density estimation method.
- Compute a 2-variable probability density function visualization as a heat map.
- Interpret a 2-variable probability density function visualization.
- Compute the probability density of an observation at specific variable values, given a probability density function.
- Compute the probability of generating values within a specific range, given a probability density function.

3.1 Descriptive Statistics

Summarize a dataset with just a few numbers.

3.1.1 Introduction

Blackjack is a game of chance providing a player with a 42.22% probability of winning a bet. That 42.44% summarizes a vast number of possible outcomes succinctly in just one useful number.

Francis Galton, the nineteenth-century polymath who made numerous contributions to statistics and other dubious fields of inquiry, described statistics in 1883 this way: "The object of statistical science is to discover methods of condensing information concerning large groups of allied facts into brief and compendious expressions suitable for discussion."

3.1.2 About Descriptive Statistics

A descriptive statistic summarizes a dataset in just a few numbers, often just 1 number. Many descriptive statistics operate on 1 variable at a time, others operate on 2 or more. Each is defined in its own way to summarize a specific aspect of a dataset.

3.1.3 Data

Consider this dataset. Let's summarize it with descriptive statistics in a variety of ways.

data

x1	x2	x3	x4
5	53	41	C
4	47	NA	A
5	51	51	B
5	65	41	C
8	81	89	B
7	47	NA	C

3.1.4 Descriptive Statistics of One Variable

Here we summarize each variable by count, count of unique values, and list of unique values.

count.x1
6

count.x2
6

count.x3
6

count.x4
6

count_unique.x1
4

count_unique.x2
5

count_unique.x3
4

count_unique.x4
3

unique.x1
4
5
7
8

unique.x2
47
51
53
65
81

unique.x3
41
51
89
NA

unique.x4
A
B
C

Here we summarize the x_4 variable by a **frequency table** and a **relative frequency table**. The tables show a list of the unique values of the variable along with the value counts or probabilities.

freq.x4

value	count
A	1
B	2
C	3

rfreq.x4

value	probability
A	0.1667
B	0.3333
C	0.5000

freq.B_in_x4
2

rfreq.B_in_x4
0.3333

Here we summarize each variable by its central tendency, using **mean**, **median**, and **mode**, where applicable. Note that mean and median are not defined for categorical variables like x_4.

mean.x1
5.667

mean.x2
57.33

mean.x3
55.5

median.x1
5

median.x2
52

median.x3
46

mode.x1
5

mode.x2
47

mode.x3
41

mode.x4
C

Here we summarize each variable by its dispersion, using **minimum**, **maximum**, **range**, **variance**, **standard deviation**, **interquartile range**, list of **quartile** boundaries, and list of 10 **percentile** boundaries.

min.x1
4

min.x2
47

min.x3
41

max.x1
8

max.x2
81

max.x3
89

range.x1
4

range.x2
34

range.x3
NA

var.x1
2.267

var.x2
178.3

var.x3
521

sd.x1
1.506

sd.x2
13.35

sd.x3
22.83

interquartile_range.x1
1.5

interquartile_range.x2
14

interquartile_range.x3
19.5

	quartile.x1
0%	4.0
25%	5.0
50%	5.0
75%	6.5
100%	8.0

	quartile.x2
0%	47
25%	48
50%	52
75%	62
100%	81

	quartile.x3
0%	41.0
25%	41.0
50%	46.0
75%	60.5
100%	89.0

	percentile.x1
10%	4.5
20%	5.0
30%	5.0
40%	5.0
50%	5.0
60%	5.0
70%	6.0
80%	7.0
90%	7.5
100%	8.0

	percentile.x2
10%	47
20%	47
30%	49
40%	51
50%	52
60%	53
70%	59
80%	65
90%	73
100%	81

	percentile.x3
10%	41.0
20%	41.0
30%	41.0
40%	43.0
50%	46.0
60%	49.0
70%	54.8
80%	66.2
90%	77.6
100%	89.0

3.1.5 Descriptive Statistics of Two Variables

Here we summarize each pair of variables by pairwise relationship, using **pairwise minimum** and **pairwise maximum**.

pairwise_min.x1_x2
5
4
5
5
8
7

pairwise_min.x1_x3
5
NA
5
5
8
NA

pairwise_min.x2_x3
41
NA
51
41
81
NA

pairwise_max.x1_x2
53
47
51
65
81
47

pairwise_max.x1_x3
41
NA
51
41
89
NA

pairwise_max.x2_x3
53
NA
51
65
89
NA

Here we summarize each pair of variables by relationship, using **covariance** and **correlation**. It's often convenient to organize such statistics into tables accounting for all possible pairs of variables. Note that covariance and correlation are defined only for pairs of variables with no missing data.

cov.x1_x2
12.13

cov.x1_x3
NA

cov.x2_x3
NA

cor.x1_x2
0.6036

cor.x1_x3
NA

cor.x2_x3
NA

cov.x1_x2_x3

	x1	x2	x3
x1	2.267	12.13	NA
x2	12.133	178.27	NA
x3	NA	NA	NA

cor.x1_x2_x3

	x1	x2	x3
x1	1.0000	0.6036	NA
x2	0.6036	1.0000	NA
x3	NA	NA	1

Although some observations could be missing data, it might still be useful to summarize variables accounting for just the observations without missing data.

Here we summarize the relationship between x_1 and x_3 using covariance and correlation, but ignoring observations with missing data. To do this, we construct a vector to identify which observations are missing data ***in either of*** the variables, and apply criterion-based selection to get the appropriate variable parts. Then we apply the statistic to the pair of appropriate variable parts.

	x1
1	5
2	4
3	5
4	5
5	8
6	7

	x3
1	41
2	NA
3	51
4	41
5	89
6	NA

	ok
1	TRUE
2	FALSE
3	TRUE
4	TRUE
5	TRUE
6	FALSE

x1.clip
5
5
5
8

x3.clip
41
51
41
89

cov.x1_x3
33.5

cor.x1_x3
0.9784

3.2 Similarity

Summarize a dataset by assessing how similar observations are to each other.

3.2.1 Introduction

A sales manager looks over a demographics report on his customers. Some are much alike. Some are very different from each other. What is it about them that makes customers look alike or different?

Similarity is about measuring how alike observations are.

3.2.2 About Similarity

To determine how similar one observation is to another observation, use some specification for inter-observation distance that can be calculated given the two observations. Treat the distance between the observations as a measure of their **dissimilarity**, or the inverse distance as a measure of their **similarity**. Long distance indicates very dissimilar, short distance indicates very similar.

In practice, the terms "distance" and "dissimilarity" are often used interchangeably because we treat distance as a measure of dissimilarity.

We typically calculate distances based on normalized variables because they are expressed without units, and therefore cannot distort distance calculations the way non-normalized variables can. Imagine calculating the distance to a spot along a straight street. You could just as easily measure the distance in units of feet, meters, inches, centimeters, or even light-years. However, imagine calculating the distance to a spot on a flat field. You could measure going east in units of centimeters and measure going north in units of light-years. The east component of distance would be a relatively large number and the north component would be a relatively small number. Even if the spot is close in the east direction and far in the north direction, calculating distance based on these numbers could make it incorrectly seem that the spot is farther east. Now imagine calculating distance to a spot on a flat field at some point in time.

This situation is even more awkward since units could be in, say, centimeters, light-years, and hours. So, it's best to avoid the problem of different units by representing east, north, and time without any units at all. That's what normalizing variables does. It represents each variable as the number of standard deviations from the mean, which is unitless.

Euclidean distance is typically an appropriate way to specify distance, but for some special applications others might work better. Here are some popular specifications for inter-observation distance:

- **Euclidean Distance** specifies inter-observation distance to be the square root of the sum of squared differences across all variables.
- **Manhattan Distance** specifies inter-observation distance to be the sum of absolute differences across all variables.
- **Maximum Distance** specifies inter-observation distance to be the largest difference in any variable.
- **Canberra** specifies inter-observation distance to be the sum of a series of fraction differences between variables.
- **Simple Matching Coefficient Distance (SMC)** specifies inter-observation distance to be the fraction of matching values across all categorical variables.
- **Jaccard Coefficient Distance**, also known as Jaccard Index or Tanimoto Index or Critical Success Index, specifies inter-observation distance to be the fraction of positive-class matching values across all categorical variables.

3.2.3 Euclidean Distance

Consider these two 3-variable unclassified observations **a** and **b** from a dataset in normalized representation. How similar are they to each other? Let's use Euclidean distance to determine the similarity.

data

	x1	x2	x3
a	-1.356	-0.6628	0.7167
b	-1.208	0.8721	0.4918

The Euclidean distance based on 1 variable between 2 observations is the absolute value of the difference between variable values.

$$distance = |\,\mathbf{b}_{x_1} - \mathbf{a}_{x_1}|$$

Here the distance based on only x_1 between observations **a** and **b** is $|-1.208 - -1.356| = 0.1486$.

distance_a_b
0.1486

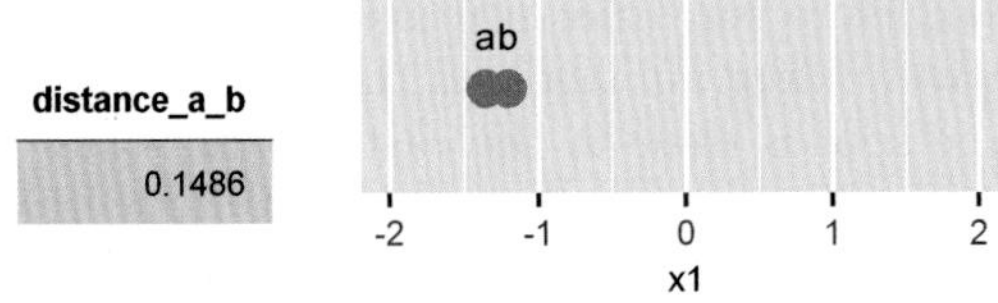

The Euclidean distance based on 2 variables between 2 observations is derived from the familiar Pythagorean Theorem.

$$distance = \sqrt{(\mathbf{b}_{x1} - \mathbf{a}_{x1})^2 + (\mathbf{b}_{x2} - \mathbf{a}_{x2})^2}$$

Here the distance based on x_1 and x_2 between observations named **a** and **b** is $\sqrt{(-1.208 - -1.356)^2 + (0.8721 - -0.6628)^2} = 1.542$.

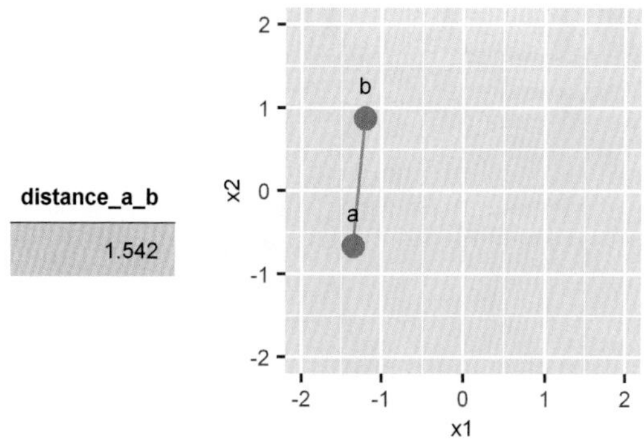

The Euclidean distance based on 3 variables between 2 observations is derived from an extension of the Pythagorean Theorem into 3 dimensions.

$$distance = \sqrt{(\mathbf{b}_{x1} - \mathbf{a}_{x1})^2 + (\mathbf{b}_{x2} - \mathbf{a}_{x2})^2 + (\mathbf{b}_{x3} - \mathbf{a}_{x3})^2}$$

Here the distance based on x_1, x_2, and x_3 between the 2 observations named **a** and **b** is $\sqrt{(-1.208 - -1.356)^2 + (0.8721 - -0.6628)^2 + (0.4918 - 0.7176)^2} = 1.558$. So, the dissimilarity between observations **a** and **b** is 1.558.

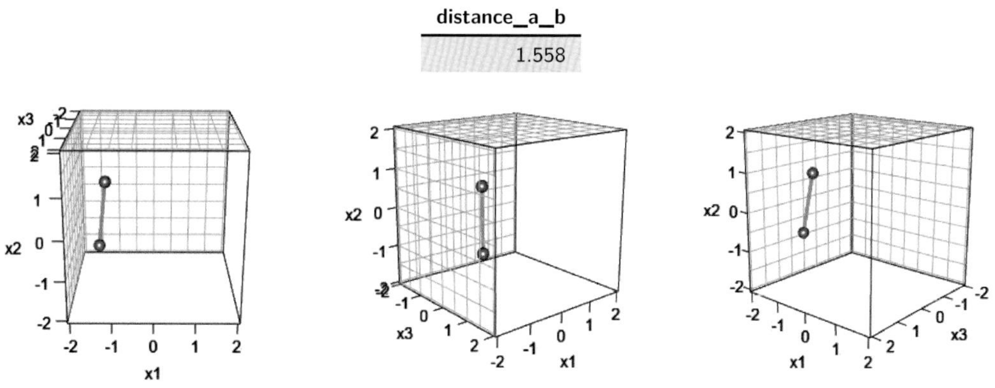

In general, the Euclidean distance based on multiple variables is derived from an extension of the Pythagorean Theorem into multiple dimensions. It may be difficult (and not very useful) to picture what 4- or 5- or higher-dimensional distances look like, but it is easy enough to calculate them.

$$distance = \sqrt{(\mathbf{b}_{x1} - \mathbf{a}_{x1})^2 + (\mathbf{b}_{x2} - \mathbf{a}_{x2})^2 + \ldots + (\mathbf{b}_{xn} - \mathbf{a}_{xn})^2}$$

3.3 Cross-Tabulation

Summarize a dataset with a small table.

3.3.1 Introduction

An operations manager looks over the record of defects in products coming off the assembly line. She's concerned that the defect rate on Mondays might average higher than on other days. Or perhaps the average on Mondays and Fridays is higher. Or perhaps there's a problem on Mondays in the first week of the month. To assess whether there really is a problem, and if so where, it would certainly be useful to have a small table of average defect rates organized in a way that clearly exposes what's happening on days of the week and parts of the month.

3.3.2 About Cross-Tabulation

Cross-tabulation is about summarizing a dataset with a small table, which might be more convenient to use or might expose otherwise obscured patterns in the data.

The **aggregation method** constructs a small table, called an **aggregate table**, that summarizes a dataset. Here is how it works:

- Choose 1 or more variables by which to group observations. Call these the group-by variables.
- Choose a variable to aggregate. Call this the aggregate variable.
- Choose an aggregation function.
- Put observations into groups according to the group-by variables' values.
- For each group, apply the aggregation function to the aggregate variable.
- Compile the results into a table: 1 row for each group, 1 or more variables for components of group names, 1 variable for aggregated aggregate variable values.

Observations typically include variables to identify themselves and variables to report some measurements. For example, the observation ($date$=2023-01-01, $sales$=1,000,000) includes a *date* variable to identify itself as the observation made on 2023-01-01, and a *sales* variable to report on what it measured. **Long table** representation of a dataset keeps the **identifier variables**, but replaces the **measure variables** with 2 new variables: 1 for the names of measure variables, and 1 for the values of measurements themselves. The names of measure variables are duplicated as necessary to preserve all values of measurements. Note that what were measure variable names become a new variable's values. The resulting table comprises fewer columns, but more rows. Converting a dataset to long table representation is especially useful as an intermediary step on the way to constructing cross-tables.

The **cross-tabulation method** is a generalized version of the aggregation method. It constructs a small table, called a **cross-table**, that summarizes a dataset. The cross-table's rows and columns are named after the dataset's variable values and variable names. Here is how it works:

- Convert the dataset to long table representation.
  - Which variables have ***values*** that might be used as row names or column names in the cross-table? Treat these as identifier variables.
  - Which variables have ***names*** that might be used as row names or column names in the cross-table? Treat these as measure variables.
- Specify rows and columns of the cross-table.
  - Which long table variables have values that will be used as row names in the cross-table? Treat these as the row specification.
  - Which long table variables have values that will be used as column names in the cross-table? Treat these as the column specifications.
- Choose an aggregration function to aggregate measure values when necessary.
- Construct a table with rows and columns as specified.
- Populate the table with the appropriate measure values, aggregated whenever there are multiple measure values corresponding to a single cross-table value.

3.3.3 Data

Consider the following dataset. It comprises 3 weeks of observations made 3 times per week. The *date*, *month*, and day-of-week *dow* variables identify when an observation was made. The x_1, x_2, and x_3 record what was measured.

data

date	month	dow	x1	x2	x3
2020-12-21	December	Monday	2.5	9.0	9.0
2020-12-23	December	Wednesday	3.0	9.5	11.0
2020-12-25	December	Friday	2.5	9.0	9.0
2020-12-28	December	Monday	2.0	9.6	10.0
2020-12-30	December	Wednesday	9.0	10.3	1.0
2021-01-01	January	Friday	6.5	11.0	2.0
2021-01-04	January	Monday	8.0	2.5	1.5
2021-01-06	January	Wednesday	4.0	8.5	10.5
2021-01-08	January	Friday	7.2	8.0	10.7

3.3.4 Aggregate Table

Let's aggregate the dataset in a variety of ways.

Here we group observations by *month*, and then for each group we calculate the mean of x_1.

aggregate x1 by month | mean

month	x1
January	6.425
December	3.800

Here we group observations by *dow*, and then for each group we calculate the mean of x_1.

aggregate x1 by dow | mean

dow	x1
Monday	4.167
Wednesday	5.333
Friday	5.400

Here we group observations by combinations of *month* and *dow*, and then for each group we calculate the mean of x_1. We can sort by *month* within *dow*.

aggregate x1 by month,dow | mean

month	dow	x1
January	Monday	8.00
December	Monday	2.25
January	Wednesday	4.00
December	Wednesday	6.00
January	Friday	6.85
December	Friday	2.50

Or we can sort by *dow* within *month*.

aggregate x1 by dow,month | mean

dow	month	x1
Monday	January	8.00
Wednesday	January	4.00
Friday	January	6.85
Monday	December	2.25
Wednesday	December	6.00
Friday	December	2.50

3.3.5 Long Table

Let's represent the dataset as a long table from which we can later construct various cross-tables. Ignore the *date* variable because we don't want to use it in a cross-table. Set *month* and *dow* to be ***identifier variables*** because we might want to use their **values** as row names or column names of a cross-table. Set x_1, x_2, and x_3 to be ***measure variables*** because we might want to use their ***names*** as row names or column names of a cross-table. See that the long table comprises observations for each pair of *month* value and *dow* value combined with the name x1, x2, or x3. All of the x_1, x_2, and x_3 values are preserved.

data.long *size 27×4, rows 1-14 shown*

	month	dow	variable	value
1	December	Monday	x1	2.5
2	December	Wednesday	x1	3.0
3	December	Friday	x1	2.5
4	December	Monday	x1	2.0
5	December	Wednesday	x1	9.0
6	January	Friday	x1	6.5
7	January	Monday	x1	8.0
8	January	Wednesday	x1	4.0
9	January	Friday	x1	7.2
10	December	Monday	x2	9.0
11	December	Wednesday	x2	9.5
12	December	Friday	x2	9.0
13	December	Monday	x2	9.6
14	December	Wednesday	x2	10.3

data.long *size 27×4, rows 15-27 shown*

	month	dow	variable	value
15	January	Friday	x2	11.0
16	January	Monday	x2	2.5
17	January	Wednesday	x2	8.5
18	January	Friday	x2	8.0
19	December	Monday	x3	9.0
20	December	Wednesday	x3	11.0
21	December	Friday	x3	9.0
22	December	Monday	x3	10.0
23	December	Wednesday	x3	1.0
24	January	Friday	x3	2.0
25	January	Monday	x3	1.5
26	January	Wednesday	x3	10.5
27	January	Friday	x3	10.7

3.3.6 Cross-Table

Let's cross-tabulate the dataset in a variety of ways.

Specify row names to come from the long table's *dow* variable, which has values of Monday, Wednesday, Friday. Specify column names to come from the long table's *variable* variable, which has values x1, x2, and x3. Specify that the long table's *value* variable should be aggregated when necessary by the mean function. See that the average of x_1 values across all observations with *dow*=Monday is 4.167. Similarly, the other cross-table values convey other useful averages.

cross-tabulate dow by variable | mean

dow	x1	x2	x3
Monday	4.167	7.033	6.833
Wednesday	5.333	9.433	7.500
Friday	5.400	9.333	7.233

We can swap the specifications for rows and columns.

cross-tabulate variable by dow | mean

variable	Monday	Wednesday	Friday
x1	4.167	5.333	5.400
x2	7.033	9.433	9.333
x3	6.833	7.500	7.233

We can specify rows to come from the combination of *month* and *dow* variables, sorted by *month* then *dow*.

cross-tabulate month,dow by variable | mean

month	dow	x1	x2	x3
January	Monday	8.00	2.5	1.50
January	Wednesday	4.00	8.5	10.50
January	Friday	6.85	9.5	6.35
December	Monday	2.25	9.3	9.50
December	Wednesday	6.00	9.9	6.00
December	Friday	2.50	9.0	9.00

Or we can sort by *dow* then *month*.

cross-tabulate dow,month by variable | mean

dow	month	x1	x2	x3
Monday	January	8.00	2.5	1.50
Monday	December	2.25	9.3	9.50
Wednesday	January	4.00	8.5	10.50
Wednesday	December	6.00	9.9	6.00
Friday	January	6.85	9.5	6.35
Friday	December	2.50	9.0	9.00

We can specify columns to come from the combination of *month* and *dow* variables, sorted by *month* then *day*.

cross-tabulate variable by month,dow | mean

first few variables shown

variable	January_Monday	January_Wednesday	January_Friday	December_Monday
x1	8.0	4.0	6.85	2.25
x2	2.5	8.5	9.50	9.30
x3	1.5	10.5	6.35	9.50

Or we can sort by *dow* then *month*.

cross-tabulate variable by dow,month | mean
first few variables shown

variable	Monday_January	Monday_December	Wednesday_January	Wednesday_December
x1	8.0	2.25	4.0	6.0
x2	2.5	9.30	8.5	9.9
x3	1.5	9.50	10.5	6.0

We can specify column names to come from the combination of *dow* and *variable* variables, sorted by *dow* then *variable*.

cross-tabulate month by dow,variable | mean
first few variables shown

month	Monday_x1	Monday_x2	Monday_x3	Wednesday_x1	Wednesday_x2	Wednesday_x3
January	8.00	2.5	1.5	4	8.5	10.5
December	2.25	9.3	9.5	6	9.9	6.0

Or we can sort by *variable* then *dow*:

cross-tabulate month by variable,dow | mean
first few variables shown

month	x1_Monday	x1_Wednesday	x1_Friday	x2_Monday	x2_Wednesday	x2_Friday
January	8.00	4	6.85	2.5	8.5	9.5
December	2.25	6	2.50	9.3	9.9	9.0

3.4 Data Visualization

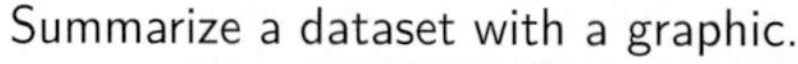

3.4.1 Introduction

It's ubiquitous today, but there was a time recently when data visualization was a new thing. Here are a few notable examples of early data visualizations.

Nineteenth-century Scottish engineer, economist, and secret agent William Playfair invented several data visualization methods that we still depend on today, including the lineplot, bar chart, and pie chart. His 1821 visualization of economic data compares the price of wheat with worker wages under various monarchs.

Prices, Wages, & Monarchs in Great Britain, by William Playfair in 1821

In 1854, London suffered a devastating and poorly understood cholera outbreak. John Snow visualized data he collected on the locations of victims by positioning bars with lengths corresponding to number of victims onto a city map, revealing the heaviest concentrations of illness near public water pumps. This quickly led to the realization that contaminated water was the source of the scourge and to the public policy to deal with it.

Cholera in London 1854, by John Snow in 1854

The business of war can be the business of unimaginable loss until revealed by data visualization. French civil engineer Charles Joseph Minard is famous for his 1869 depiction of Napolean's Russian campaign of 1812–13, with 6 types of data cleverly represented in 1 chart.

1. Size of army is indicated by width of band.
2. Location of army, latitude, is indicated by vertical position of band.
3. Location of army, longitude, is indicated by horizontal position of band.
4. Temperature on return is indicated by vertical position of line.
5. Direction of travel is indicated by color.
6. Date is indicated by label.

Napolean's Russia Campaign 1812–13, by Charles Joseph Minard in 1861

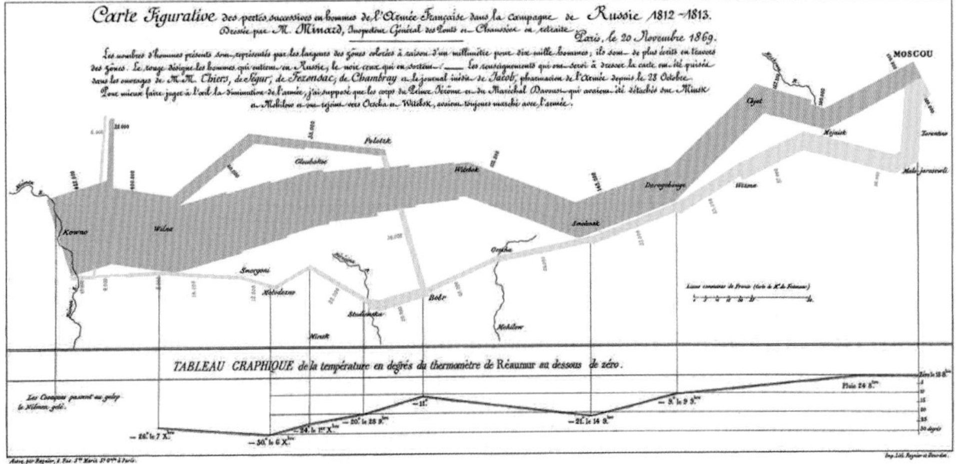

In 1858, statistician, founder of modern nursing, and all-around positive role model Florence Nightingale presented data on the state of the Crimean War to the British Parliament, visualized in what came to be known as a rose chart. Whereas the data represented as tables obscured evidence of unnecessary mortality, the graphic clearly revealed the significant effect of poor sanitation. Her work led to major social reforms and public health policy in Britain, India, and beyond.

Causes of Mortality in the Army in the East 1854–56, by Florence Nightingale in 1858

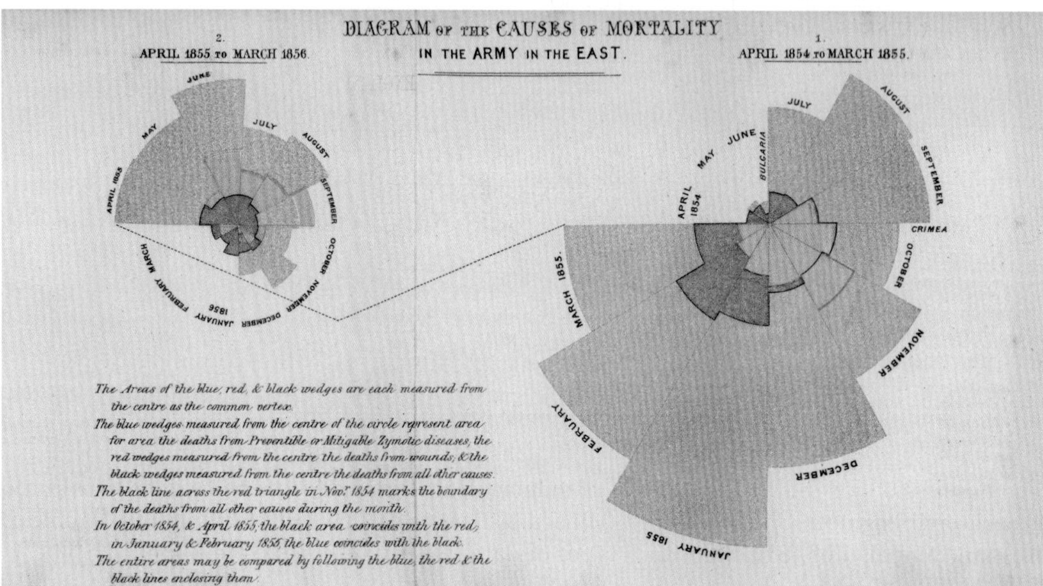

3.4.2 About Data Visualization

Data visualization is about summarizing a dataset using a graphic. Here are some popular data visualization methods: 1-axis scatterplot, 2-axis scatterplot, trellis of scatterplots, 3-axis scatterplot projection, lineplot, stepplot, pathplot, bar chart, histogram, pie chart, violinplot, boxplot, heat map, conditional format.

3.4.3 Data

Consider this dataset. Let's visualize it in a variety of ways.

data

x1	x2	x3	x4	x5	x6	x7	x8
3	3	B	A	B	1	4	A
2	2	D	B	C	2	5	A
1	1	A	D	C	2	3	A
4	5	E	C	D	4	6	B
5	4	D	E	A	3	2	B
0	1	C	C	B	4	5	B

3.4.4 One-Axis Scatterplot

A **1-axis scatterplot** maps 1 variable to positions on an axis. Draw points at the positions. Other variables can map to various other attributes of those points. A **trellis** of scatterplots lays out multiple scatterplots in a grid according to some variable.

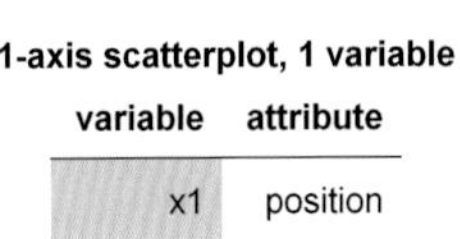

1-axis scatterplot, 1 variable

variable	attribute
x1	position

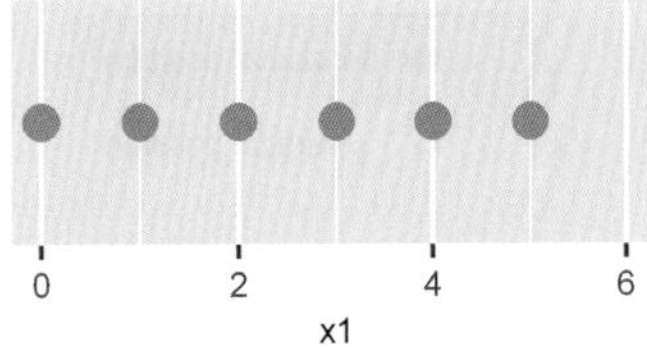

1-axis scatterplot, 5 variables

variable	attribute
x1	position
x3	color
x4	size
x5	shape
x8	label

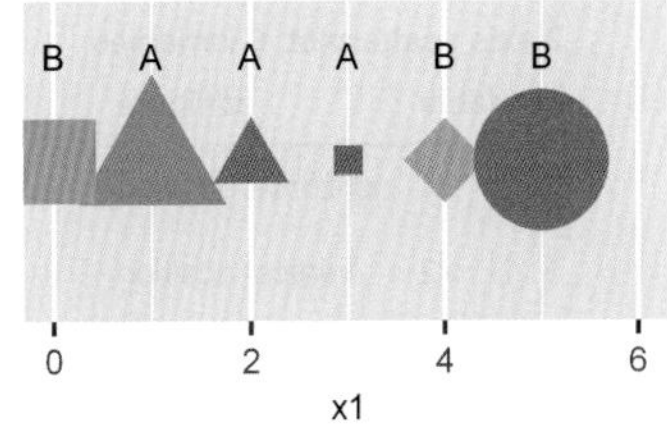

1-axis scatterplots as trellis, 6 variables

variable	attribute
x1	position
x3	color
x4	size
x5	shape
x8	label
x6	panel

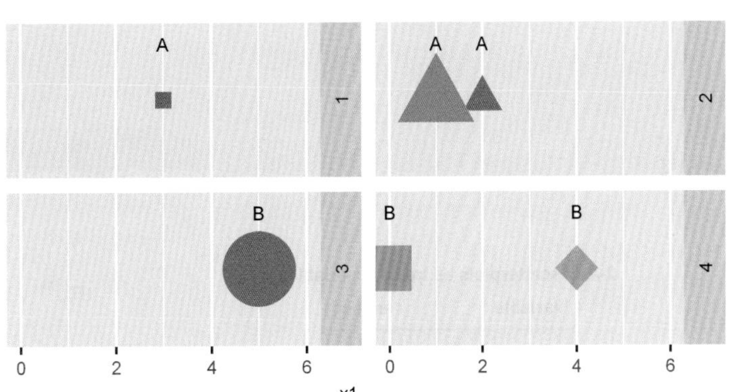

3.4.5 Two-Axis Scatterplot

A **2-axis scatterplot** maps 1 variable to positions on a horizontal axis, and a second variable to positions on a vertical axis. Draw points at the intersections of the horizontal and vertical positions. Other variables can map to various other attributes of those points. A scatterplot that maps a varibale to size is called a **bubbleplot**. A **trellis** of scatterplots lays out multiple scatterplots in a grid according to some variable.

2-axis scatterplot, 2 variables

variable	attribute
x1	horizontal position
x2	vertical position

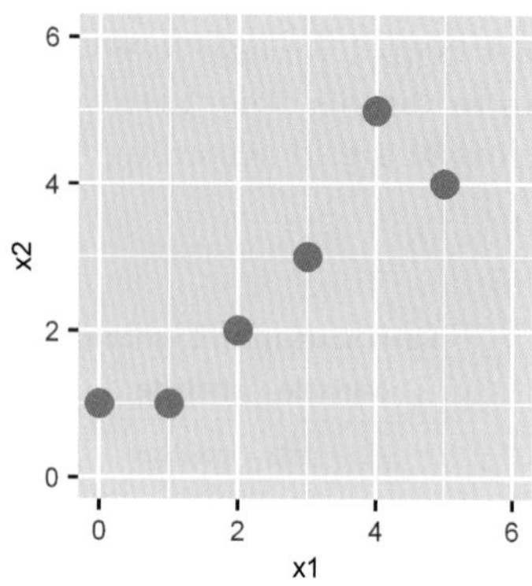

2-axis scatterplot, 6 variables

variable	attribute
x1	horizontal position
x2	vertical position
x3	color
x4	size
x5	shape
x8	label

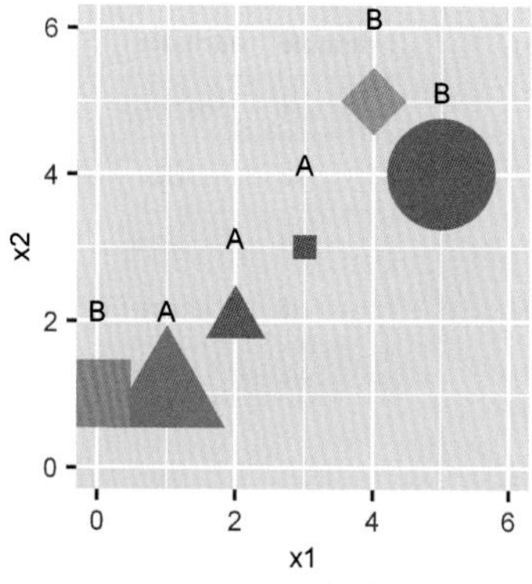

2-axis scatterplots as trellis, 7 variables

variable	aspect
x1	horizontal position
x2	vertical position
x3	color
x4	size
x5	shape
x8	label
x6	panel

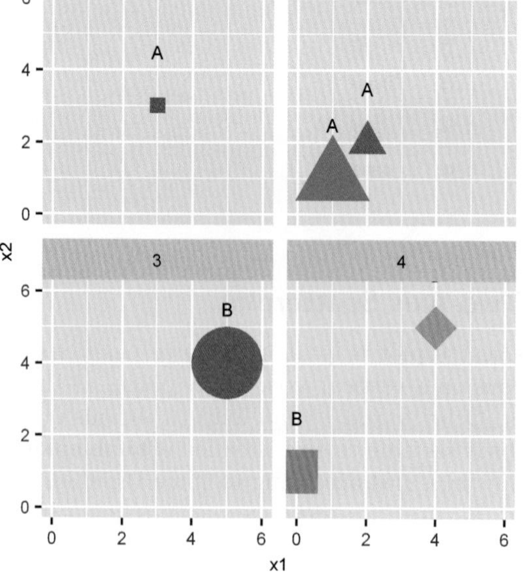

3.4.6 Three-Axis Scatterplot Projection

A **3-axis scatterplot projection** maps 1 variable to positions on a horizontal axis, a second variable to positions on a vertical axis, and a third variable to positions on a depth axis. Draw points at the intersections of the horizontal, vertical, and depth positions. Other variables can map to various other attributes of those points. Then project into 2-dimensional space.

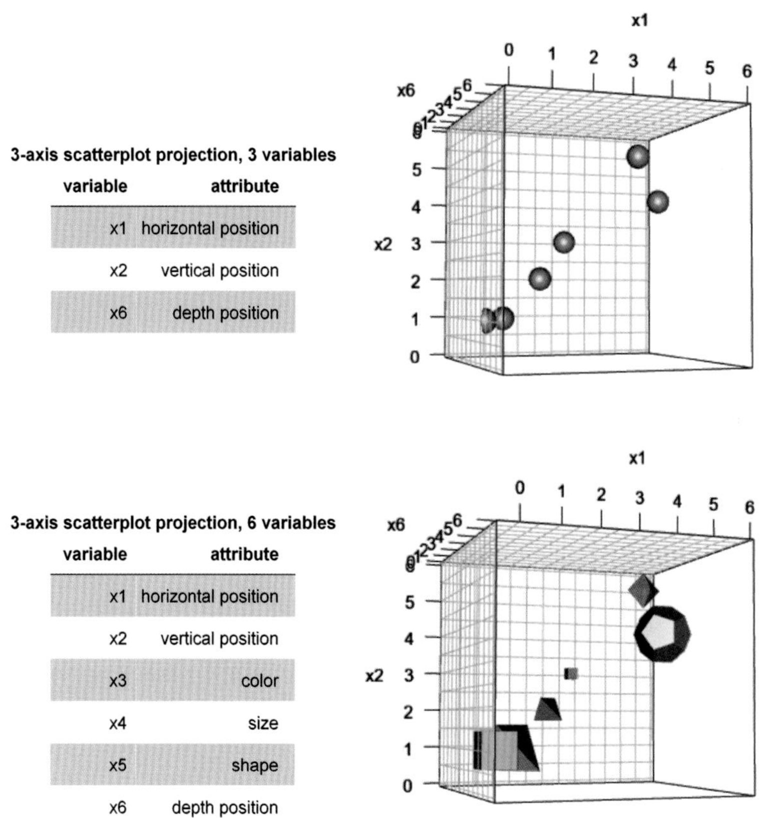

3.4.7 Lineplot

A **lineplot** maps 1 variable to positions on a horizontal axis, and a second variable to positions on a vertical axis. Call the first variable the control variable. Draw points at the intersections of the horizontal and vertical positions, and connect the points by line segments going left to right along the horizontal axis. For a third variable, use the same control variable positions on the horizontal axis, and map the third variable to positions on the vertical axis. Draw points at the intersections of the horizontal and vertical positions, and connect the points by line segments going left to right along the horizontal axis. Make these line segments a different color or shape to distinguish which variable they go with. Similarly for any additional variables. Note that colors or patterns indicate which variable, not variable values. Also note that a single observation is thereby represented by points on many lines lines at 1 horizontal position.

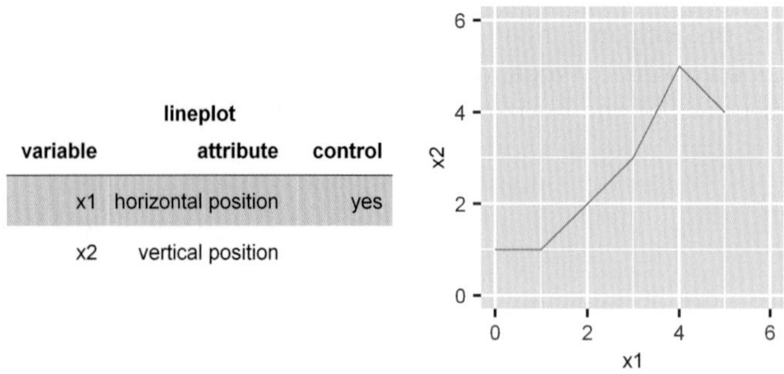

lineplot

variable	attribute	control
x1	horizontal position	yes
x2	vertical position	

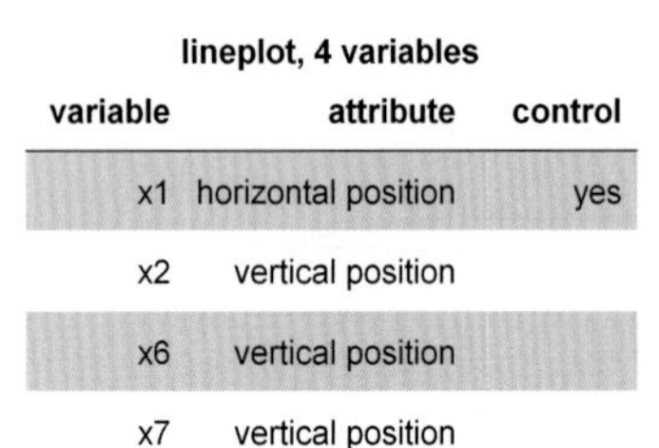

lineplot, 4 variables

variable	attribute	control
x1	horizontal position	yes
x2	vertical position	
x6	vertical position	
x7	vertical position	

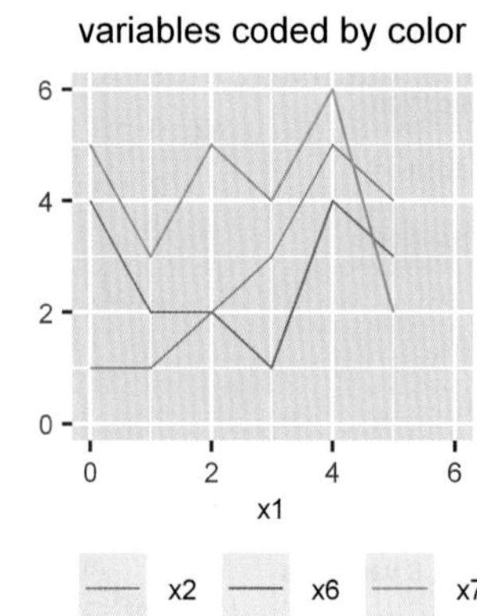

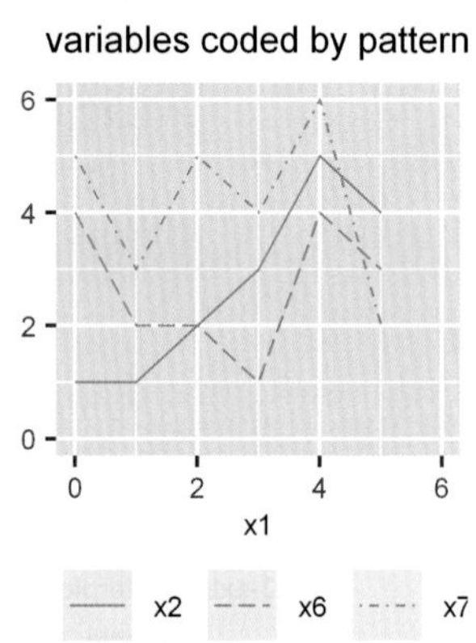

lineplot, 2 variables

variable	attribute	control	type
x4	horizontal position	yes	categorical
x2	vertical position		numerical

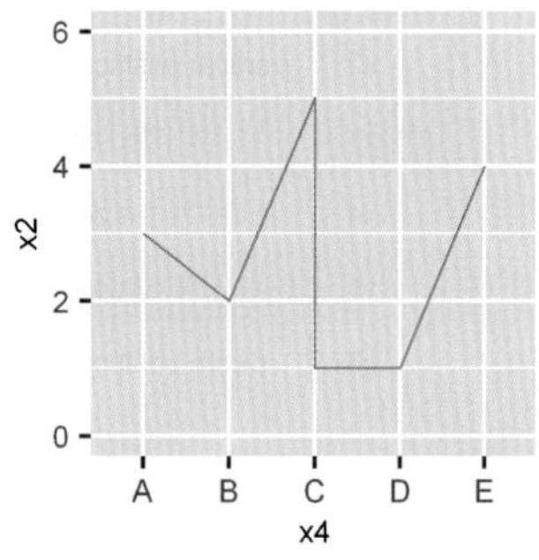

lineplot, 4 variables

variable	attribute	control	type
x4	horizontal position	yes	categorical
x2	vertical position		numerical
x6	vertical position		numerical
x7	vertical position		numerical

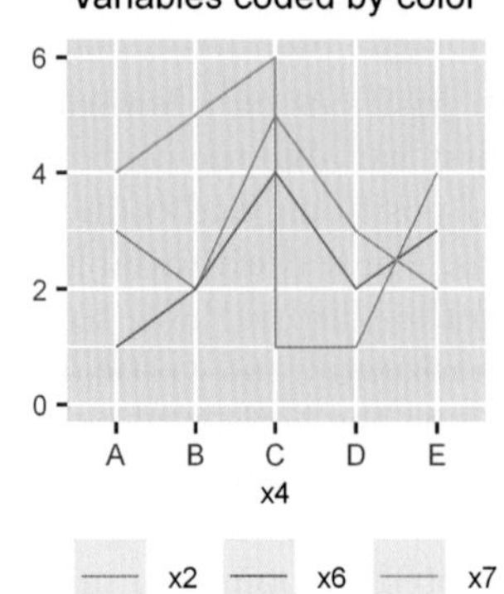

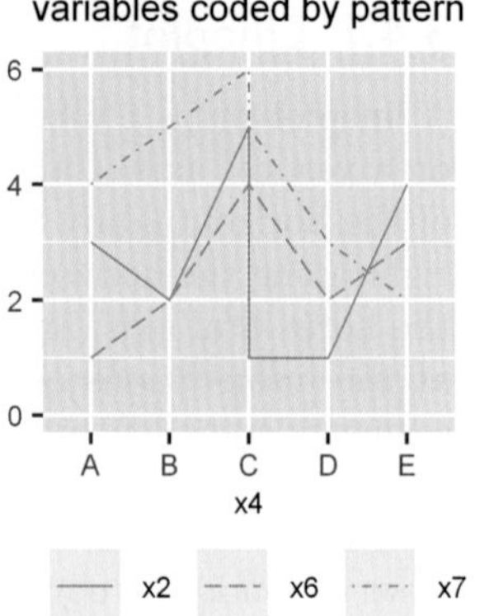

3.4.8 Stepplot

A **stepplot** is like a lineplot, except that points are connected by steps rather than line segments.

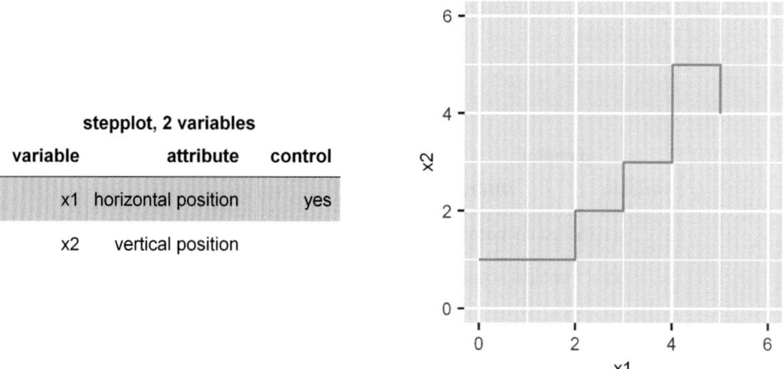

stepplot, 2 variables

variable	attribute	control
x1	horizontal position	yes
x2	vertical position	

Nudge steps just a bit to expose the otherwise hidden steps.

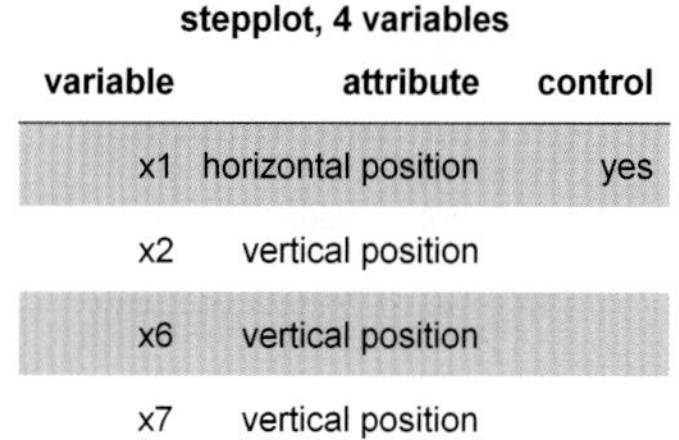

stepplot, 4 variables

variable	attribute	control
x1	horizontal position	yes
x2	vertical position	
x6	vertical position	
x7	vertical position	

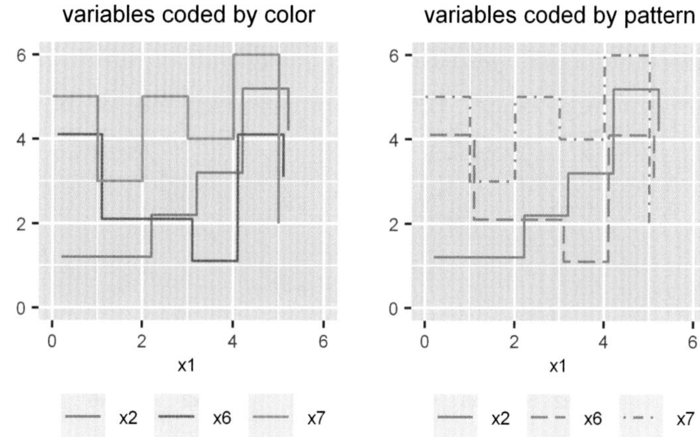

3.4.9 Pathplot

A **pathplot** is like a lineplot, except that points are connected going in the order that observations appear in the dataset, rather than going left to right along the horizontal axis.

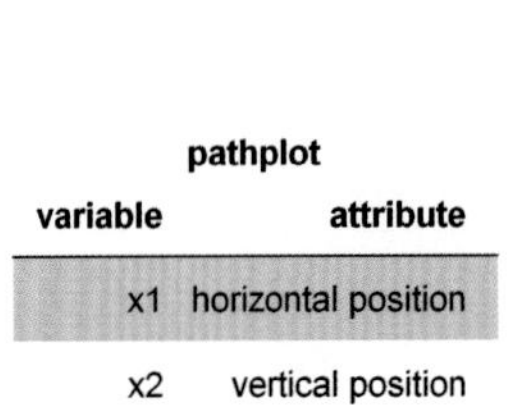

pathplot

variable	attribute
x1	horizontal position
x2	vertical position

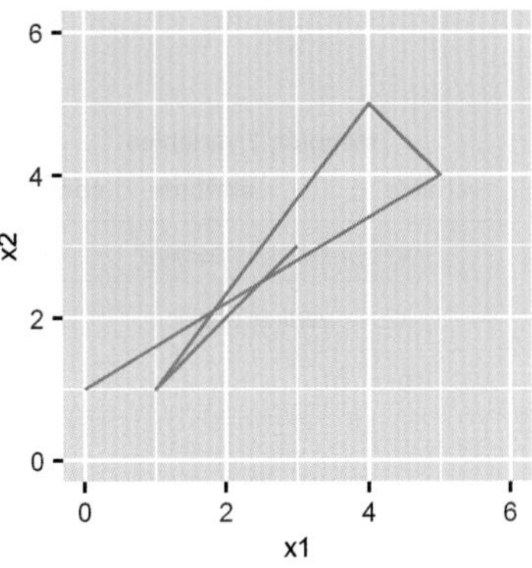

pathplot, 4 variables

variable	attribute
x1	horizontal position
x2	vertical position
x6	vertical position
x7	vertical position

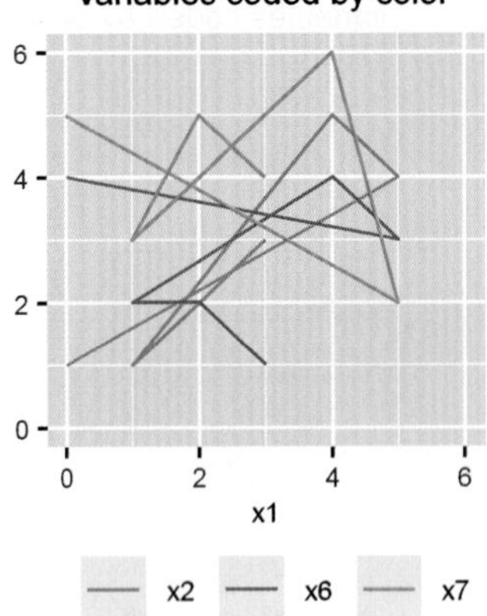

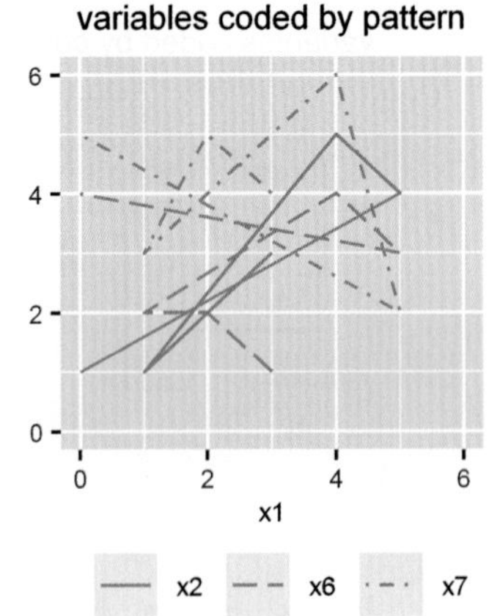

3.4.10 Bar Chart

A **bar chart** maps 1 variable to positions on a horizontal axis, and another variable to positions on a vertical axis. Mark points at the intersections of the horizontal and vertical positions. Draw bars from the points straight down to the bottom of the vertical axis. If more convenient, the horizontal and vertical axes can be swapped.

barplot, 3 variables

variable	attribute	type
x5	horizontal position	categorical
x6	vertical position	numerical
x3	color	categorical

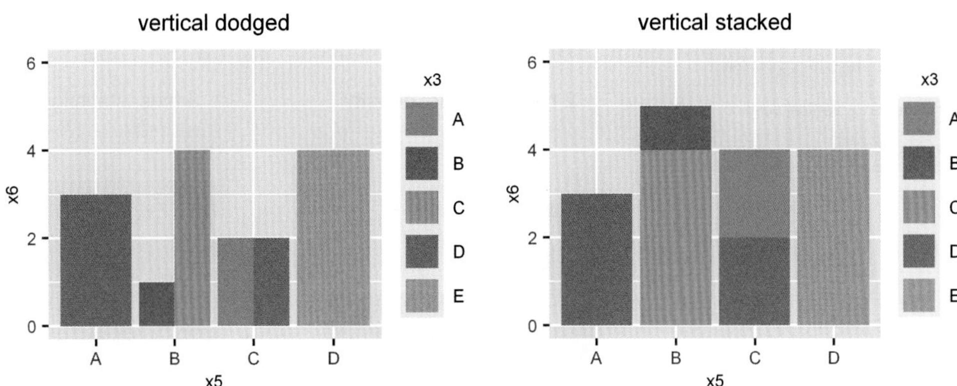

barplot, 3 variables

variable	attribute	type
x6	horizontal position	numerical
x5	vertical position	categorical
x3	color	categorical

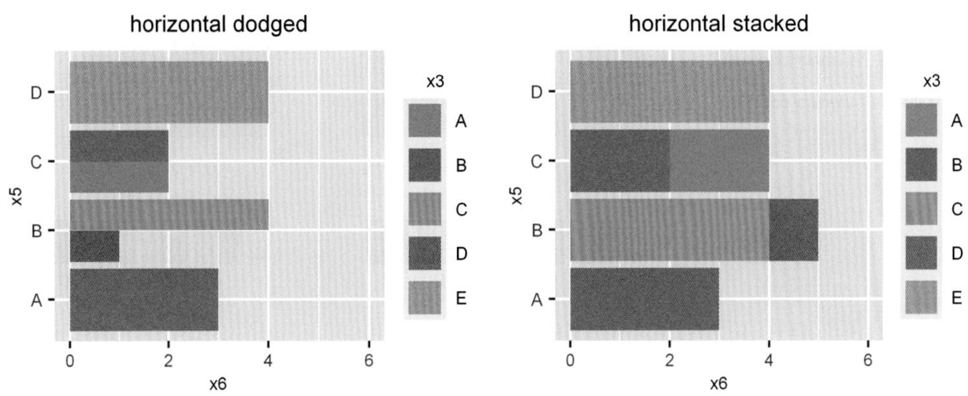

3.4.11 Histogram

A **histogram** is a special bar chart to visualize the dispersion of 1 variable. Each bar corresponds to a range of values. Bar height corresponds to the count or probability of values in that range present in the variable.

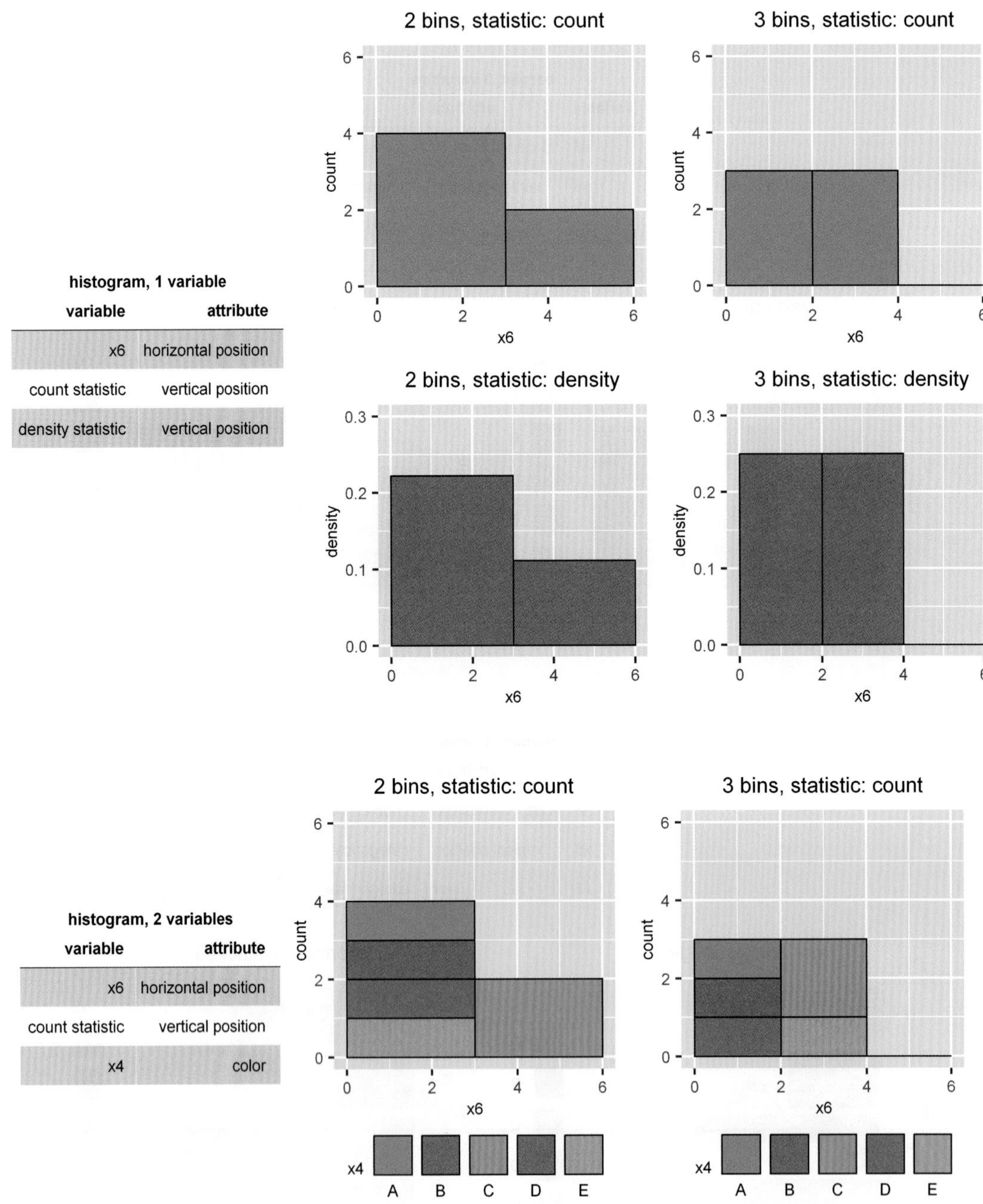

3.4.12 Pie Chart

A **pie chart** maps 1 variable to areas swept around a circle. A second variable can map to colors of those areas.

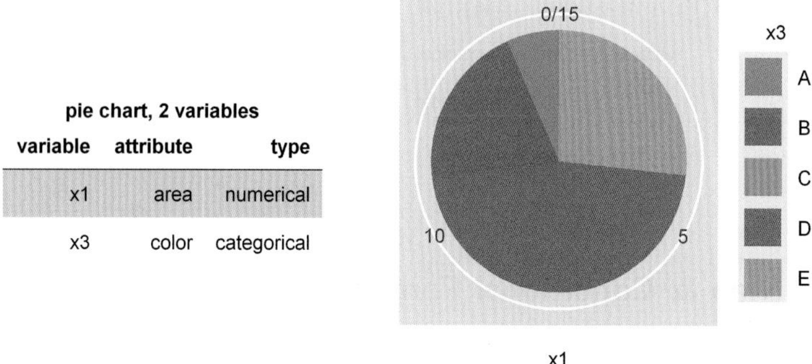

pie chart, 2 variables

variable	attribute	type
x1	area	numerical
x3	color	categorical

3.4.13 Violinplot

A **violinplot** maps 1 variable to positions on an axis. Mark points at the positions. Draw a shape around the points with width at each position proportional to the concentration of points near that position. This is especially useful comparing for variable dispersions.

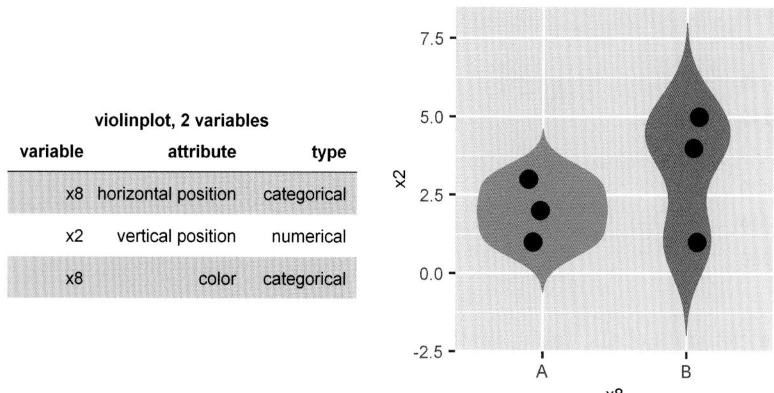

violinplot, 2 variables

variable	attribute	type
x8	horizontal position	categorical
x2	vertical position	numerical
x8	color	categorical

3.4.14 Boxplot

A **boxplot** maps the quartile boundaries of 1 variable to positions on an axis. Draw a box spread out along the axis, with one end at the first/second quartile boundary and the other end at the third/fourth quartile boundary. Draw a line segment through the middle of the box at the second/third quartile boundary. Draw a line segment extending from the lower end of the box to the minimum value. Draw a line segment extending from the upper end of the box to the maximum value.

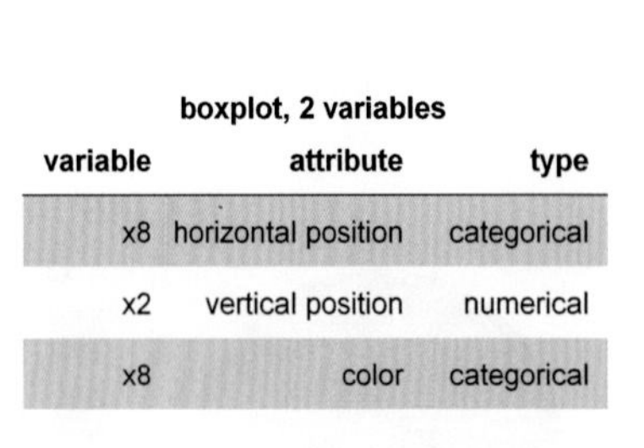

boxplot, 2 variables

variable	attribute	type
x8	horizontal position	categorical
x2	vertical position	numerical
x8	color	categorical

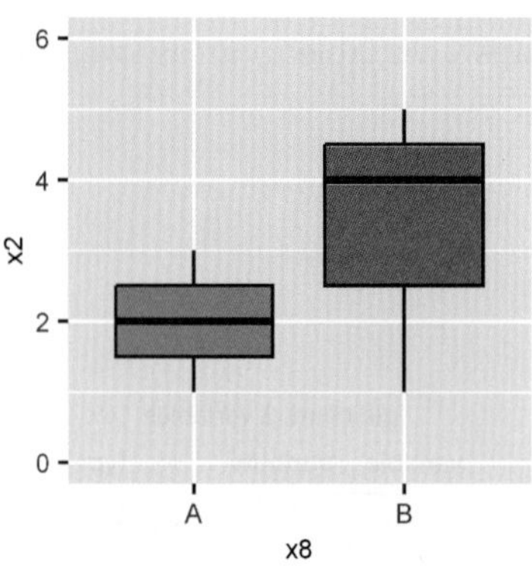

3.4.15 Heat Map & Conditional Format

A **heat map** is a dataset represented as a table, with elements color-coded according to how values correspond to a continuous spectrum of color shades. Often, the spectrum used goes from blue through white to red, so low values are color-coded shades of blue, medium values are color-coded white, and high values are color-coded red.

A **conditional format** is a dataset represented as a table, with elements color-coded according to how values correspond to some arbitrary scheme of discrete colors.

Consider this dataset produced by the Mandelbrot function at 8×8 step resolution.

data

	-2.0000	-1.5714	-1.1429	-0.7143	-0.2857	0.1429	0.5714	1.0000
1.5000	1	1	1	1	1	1	1	1
1.0714	1	2	3	5	5	3	2	1
0.6429	2	3	3	50	50	3	3	2
0.2143	2	3	6	50	50	6	3	2
-0.2143	2	5	50	50	50	50	5	2
-0.6429	2	4	35	50	50	35	4	2
-1.0714	2	2	3	4	4	3	2	2
-1.5000	2	2	2	2	2	2	2	2

To color-code elements of the table, first change it to long table representation.

size(data.long)

observations	variables
64	3

data.long (first few observations)

x2	x1	k
1.5000	-2.000	1
1.0714	-2.000	1
0.6429	-2.000	2
0.2143	-2.000	2
-0.2143	-2.000	2
-0.6429	-2.000	2
-1.0714	-2.000	2
-1.5000	-2.000	2
1.5000	-1.571	1
1.0714	-1.571	2

Then show as a scatterplot, with large square-shaped points color-coded by shades of blue or by arbitrary discrete colors.

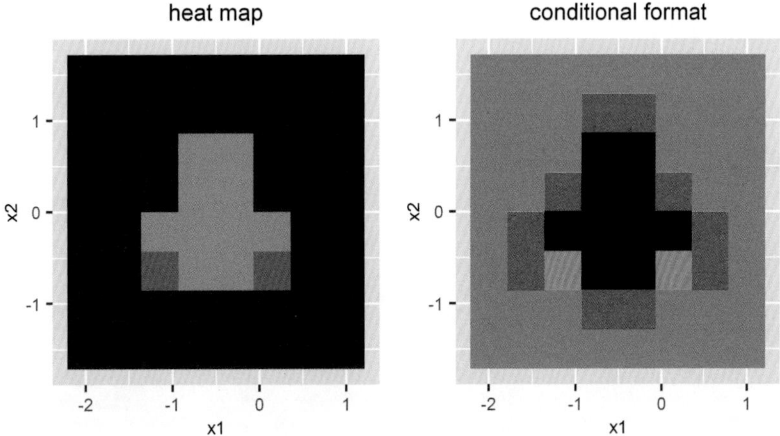

Here are some more heat maps and conditional formats of larger size, higher resolution datasets:

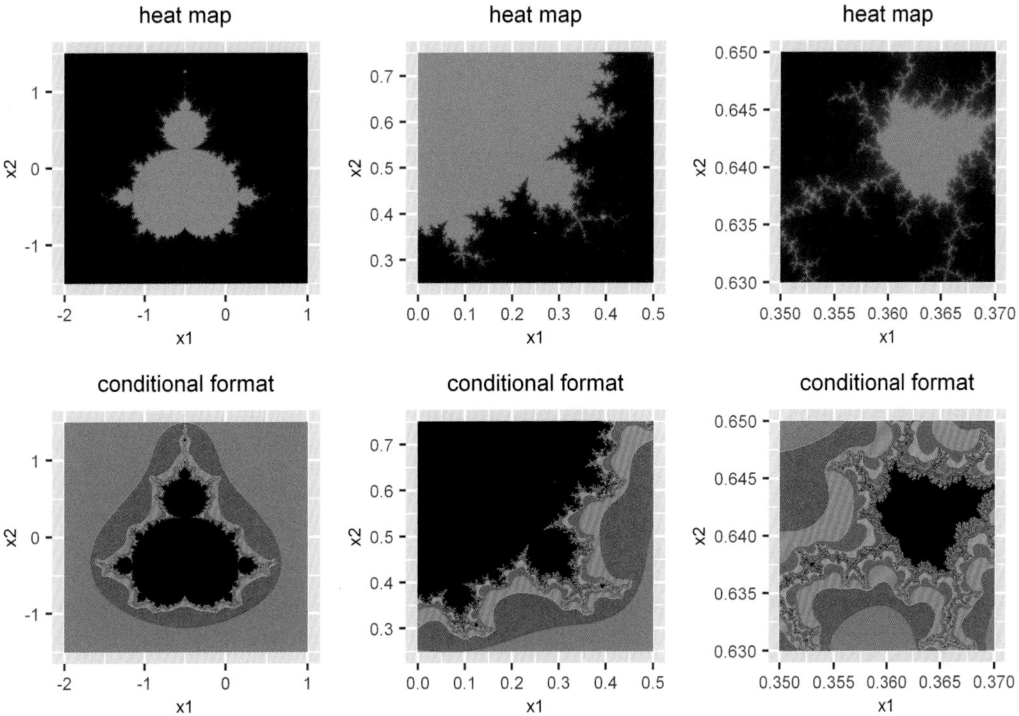

3.5 Kernel Density Estimation

Characterize the underlying process that generated a dataset.

3.5.1 Introduction

A sales manager is reviewing sales transactions of enterprise software over the past year. One transaction involved a premium functionality version licensed for 1,000 users with 24 × 7 × 365 support sold for $2,500,000 to an agriculture company. Another transaction involved a standard functionality version licensed for 500 users with 8 × 5 × 260 support sold for $1,000,000 to a toy company. Other transactions involved other configurations. The process leading to the various configurations is complex, involving the interplay of account managers, sales training, sales budgets, customer relationships, government regulations, competitors' products, the economy, and many other factors. Yet, the manager thinks of the process as a simple machine, generating some configurations with certain probabilities, and other configurations with other probabilities. That's enough for him to make reasonably good guesses about what the next few transactions will look like.

3.5.2 About Kernel Density Estimation

Kernel density estimation is a method to guess about the underlying process that generates a dataset. Specifically, it constructs a probability density function that approximates the underlying process.

- An **underlying process** is the actual process that generates a dataset. Typically, an underlying process is too complex to fully understand it.
- A **probabilistic model** is a simplified approximation of an underlying process, in which various values get generated with various probabilities.
- A **probability distribution** is a kind of probabilistic model. It's a set of probabilities, one for each value that could possibly be generated.

- A **probability density function** is another kind of probabilistic model. It's a function where the area under the curve between any 2 points corresponds to the probability of generating a value between those 2 points.

The kernel density estimation method works like this:

> *Choose a kernel and bandwidth(s)*
> *For each observation in space ...*
>   *Place the kernel in space, centered about the observation's value(s)*
> *For every point in space ...*
>   *Sum the kernels*
> *Interpret the result as a probability density function*

Bandwidth(s) controls how much kernels overlap. Higher bandwidth causes more overlap, which results in a flatter probability density function. Lower bandwidth causes less overlap, which results in a spikier probability density function.

To find the probability of generating a value between 2 points, integrate the probability density function between those points.

3.5.3 Guess the Underlying Process

We can make a reasonable guess about an underlying process by reviewing which values it has already generated, provided that we have a large enough sample.

3.5.3.1 A Simple Underlying Process

Consider this 1-variable, 10-observation dataset, visualized as a jittered scatterplot and bar chart. 7 observations are (x_1=1) and 3 observations are (x_1=2). From these 10 observations, try to guess the underlying process that's generating values. Does it generate 1's with 70% probability, and 2's with 30% probability? Perhaps we don't have enough observations to be very sure.

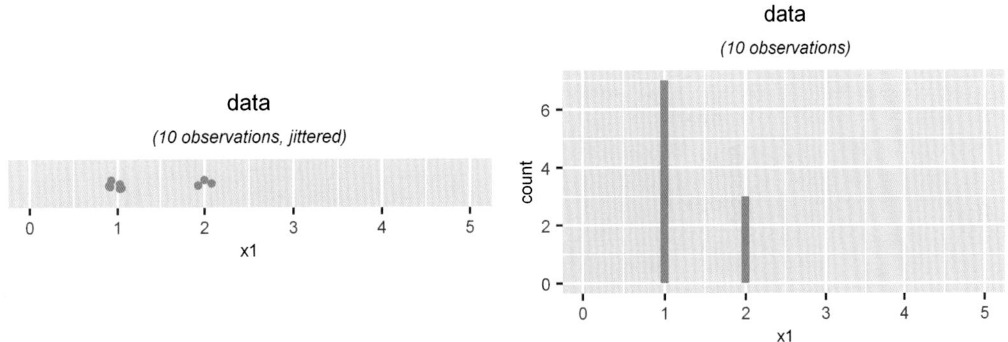

Gather 10 more observations. Now the dataset comprises 20 observations: 13 observations are (x_1=1) and 7 observations are (x_1=2). Does this change your guess about the underlying process? Perhaps we still don't have enough observations.

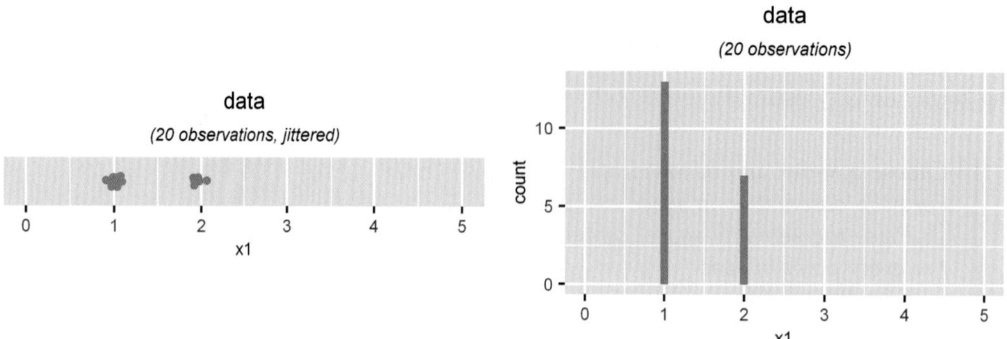

Gather many more observations. Eventually, the dataset comprises roughly equal numbers of observations with values 1 and 2. Do we finally have enough observations to make a good guess about the underlying process?

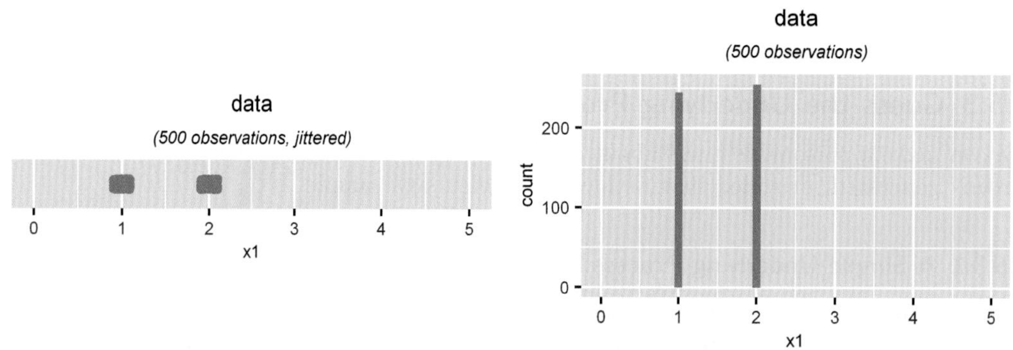

It turns out that the underlying process, called Mystery Process A, actually generates 1's with 50% probability and 2's with 50% probability. With a dataset of 500 observations, we were able to make a reasonably good guess about the underlying process.

3.5.3.2 A Complex Underlying Process

Consider another 1-variable, 10-observation dataset, and try to guess the underlying process. From these observations, it seems that values are being generated with highest probability around 4, with modest probability around 17, and almost never around 12. However, we don't have many observations to go by.

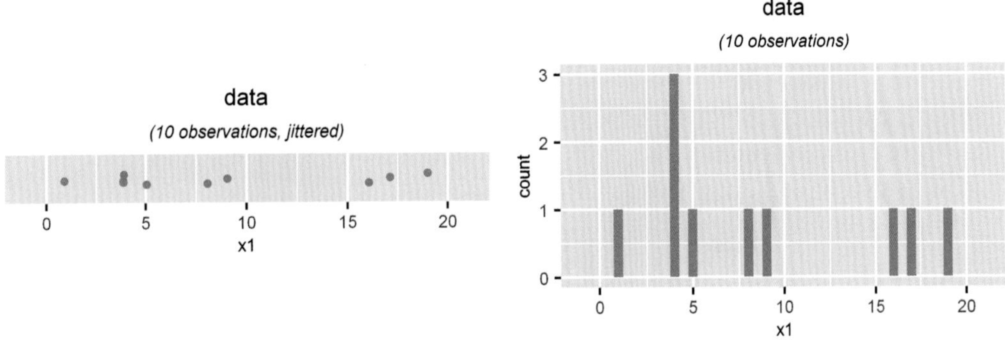

Gather 10 more observations. With twice as many observations, the probability distribution looks about the same, supporting our initial guess about the underlying process. However, the guess is still based on only a few observations.

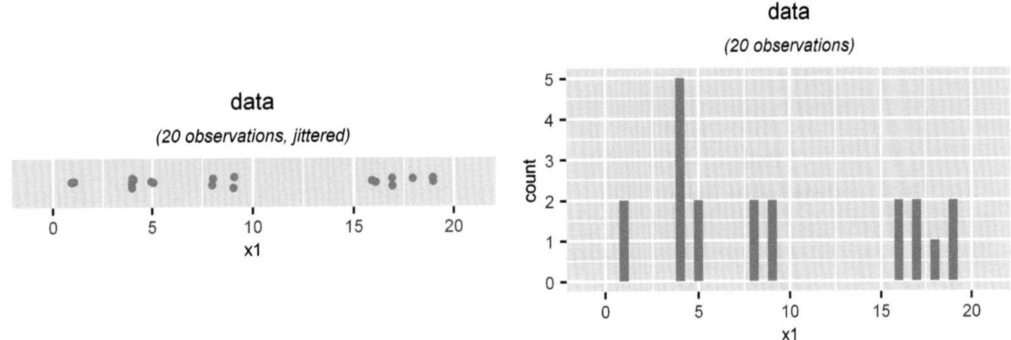

Gather many more observations. Now the probability distribution looks different. It seems that values are being generated with highest probability around 19, with modest probability around 1 and 9, and almost never around 13. Try to guess the underlying process now.

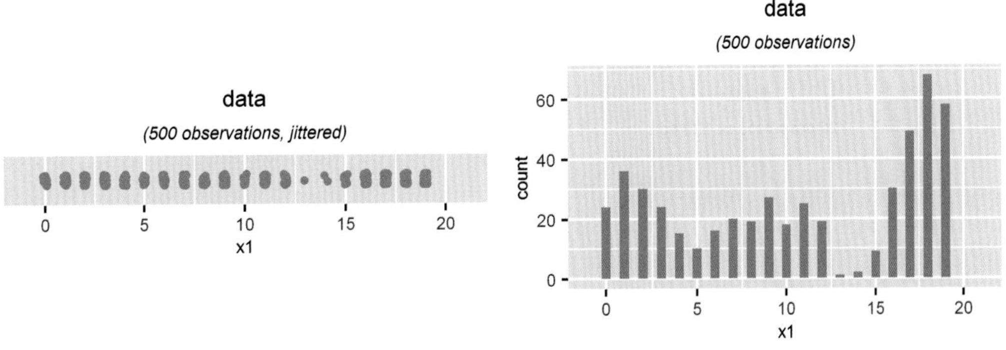

It turns out that the underlying process, called Mystery Process B, actually generates integer values between 0 and 19 according to a complex probability distribution. Again, with a dataset of 500 observations, we were able to make a reasonably good guess about the underlying process.

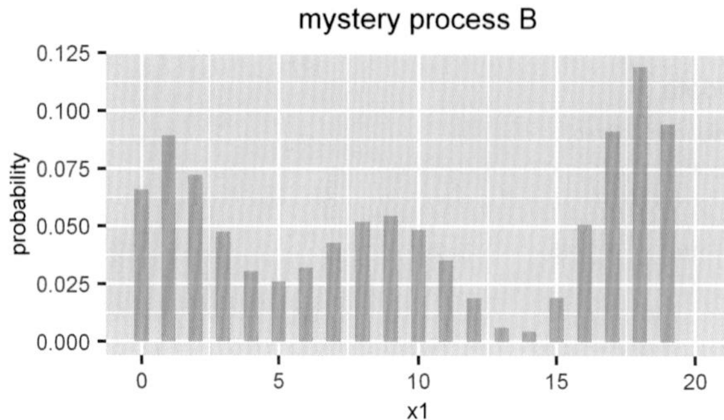

3.5.3.3 Another Complex Underlying Process

Consider yet another 1-variable, 10-observation dataset, and try to guess the underlying process. This time, we see non-integer values.

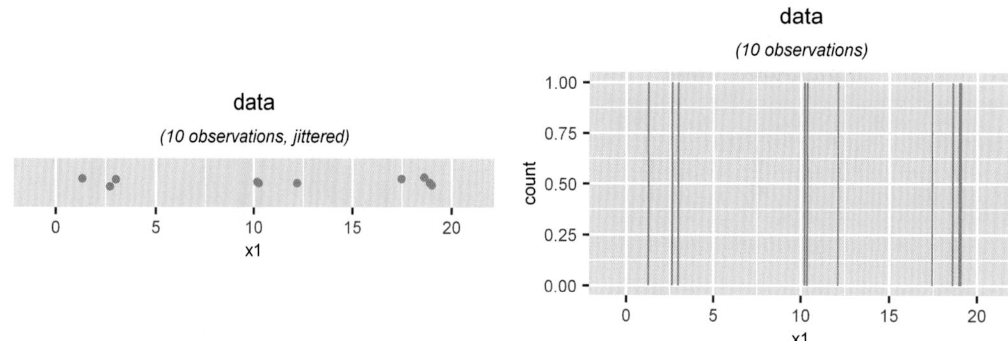

Gather 10 more observations and try to guess again.

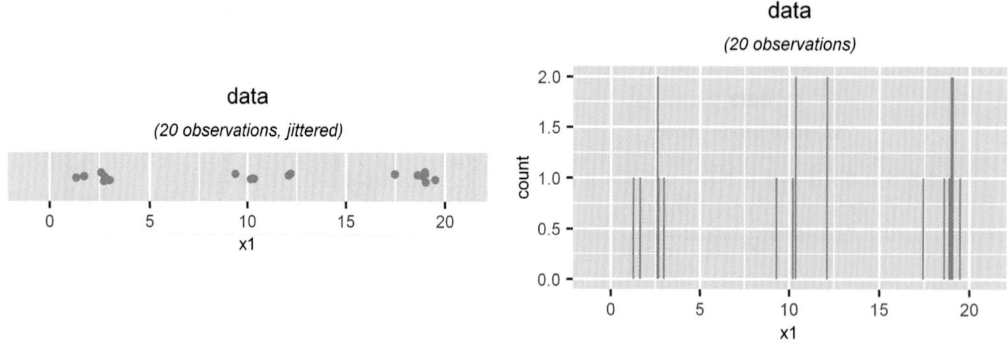

Gather many more observations. The bar chart shows many spikes with discrete heights of 1, 2, 3, or 4, separated by a variety of small and large gaps. Is that a good guess about the underlying process?

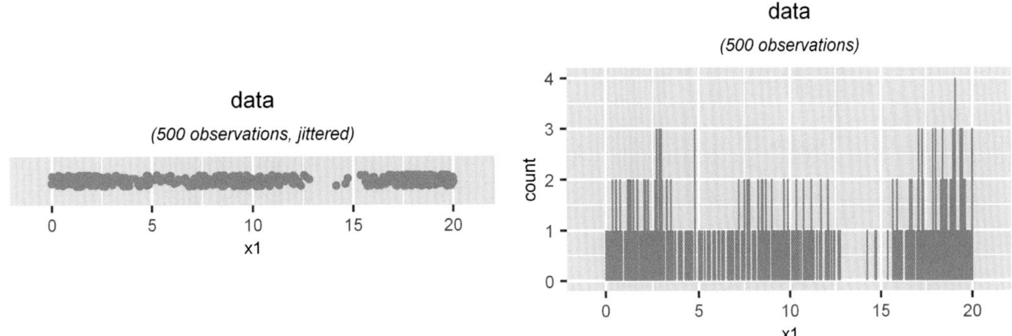

It turns out that the underlying process, called Mystery Process C, actually generates real number values anywhere between 0 and 20 according to a complex probability density function. For any range of values, the area under the curve indicates the probability of generating a value within that range.

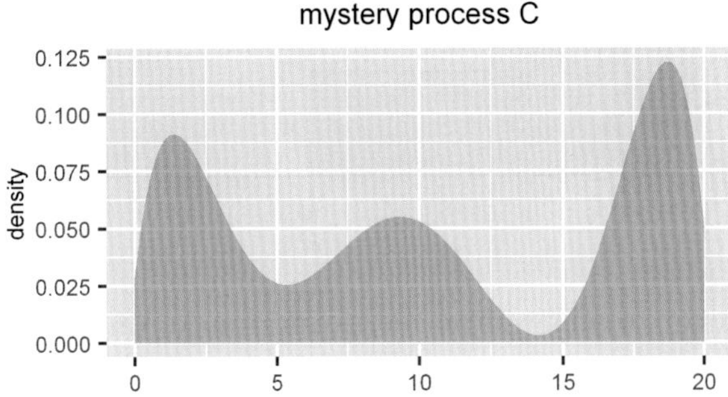

3.5.4 Histogram Density Estimation | One Variable

Consider this new 1-variable, 11-observation dataset, and try to guess the underlying process. This time, more typical of real business situations, we can't gather any more observations because it would be too expensive, take too long, or be prohibitive for some other reason. We know roughly what the underlying process is doing, but want to have at least a good guess of a more nuanced understanding. With only a few observations, what's your best guess about the underlying process?

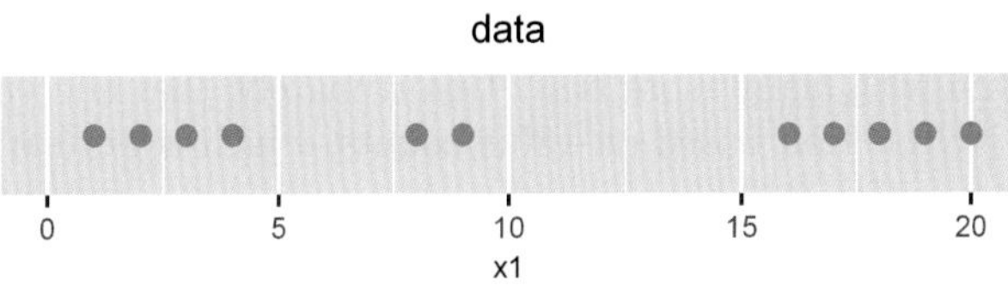

Here is a probability density function based on the distribution of the value counts. Perhaps this doesn't feel like a satisfying guess of the underlying process.

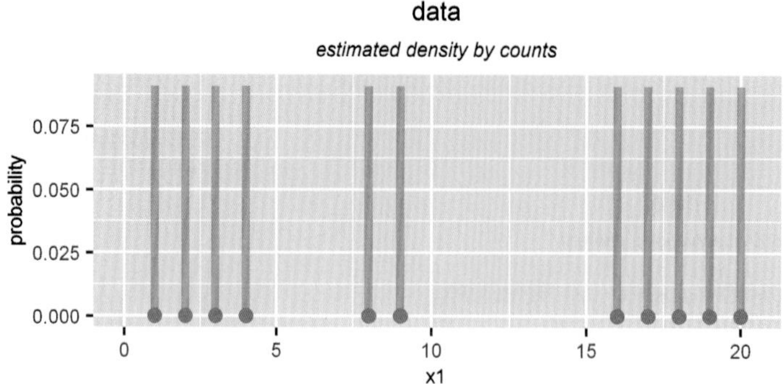

Here is a probability density function based on a histogram of the values. Perhaps this doesn't feel much better.

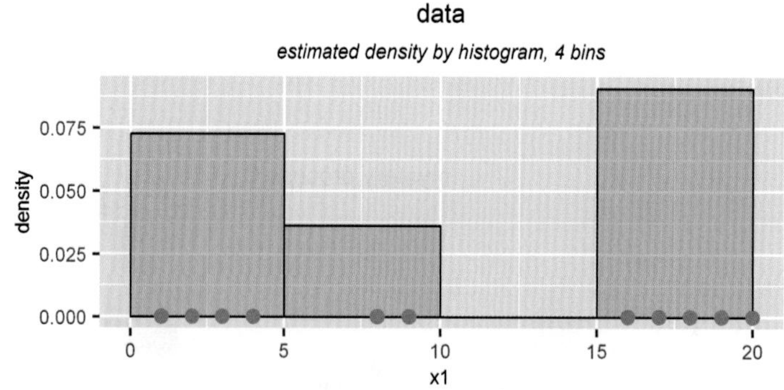

Let's try a histogram with a few more bins. Perhaps this is looking better, but not good enough.

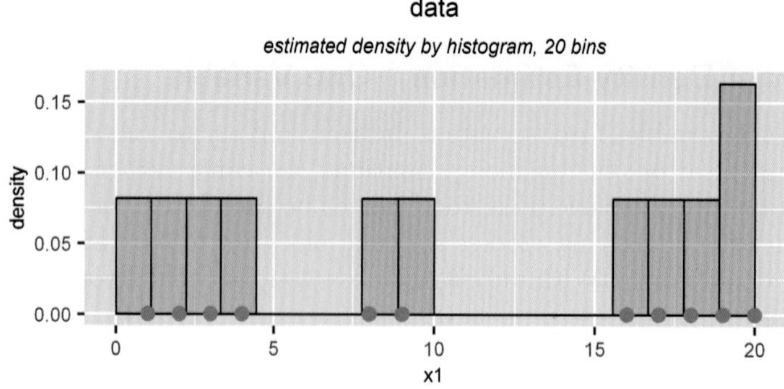

So, let's try a histogram with many more bins. Unfortunately, that effectively just takes us back to a probability density function based on value counts, which is not satisfying at all.

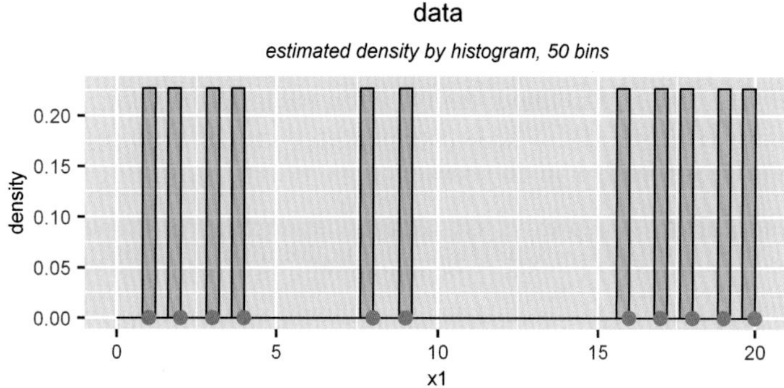

While any of the functions based on counts or histograms could be the actual underlying process that generated the dataset, they might not fit our rough understanding of what the process is doing, and so they just don't feel likely to be right. Instead, a probability density function something like this would perhaps be more satisfying. Here, probabilities peak where most values actually occur, gently sloping into deep valleys in between.

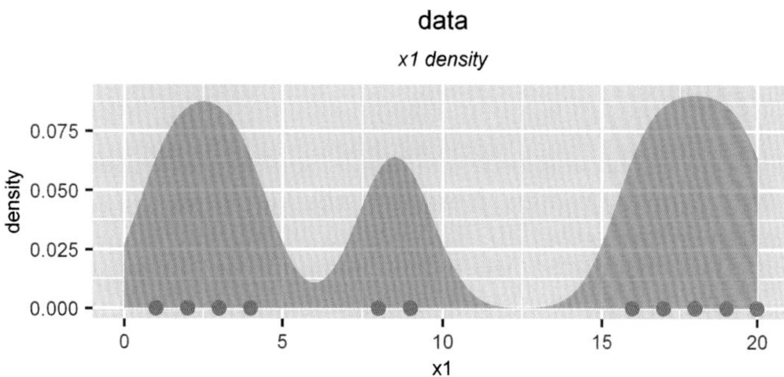

3.5.5 Kernel Density Estimation | One Variable

Consider again this 1-variable, 11-observation dataset. Let's guess the underlying process using kernel density estimation.

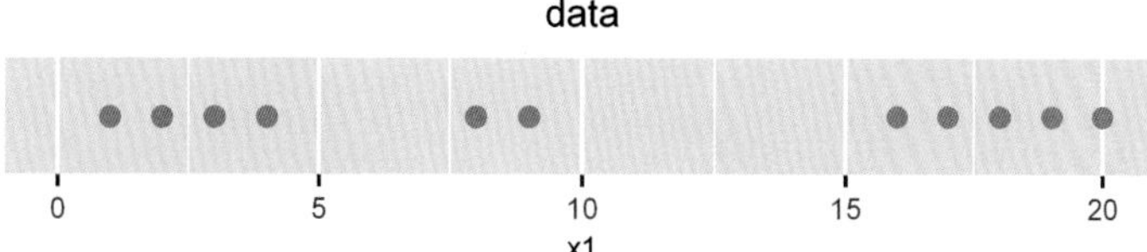

3.5.5.1 Rectangle Function as Kernel

Set the **kernel** to be a rectangle function. Set the **bandwidth** to 1.

A rectangle function is 0, except where it abruptly jumps up over some range of values. It's further defined by width, height, and point. Our rectangle function's width is calculated as $2 \times \text{bandwidth} = 2 \times 1 = 2$. Height is calculated such that $\text{width} \times \text{height} = 1 \div 11 = 0.0909$, because there are 11 observations. That makes height $0.0909 \div 2 = 0.0454$. Point is where the function is centered. You can think of a rectangle function as placing a rectangle shape on top of a point on a straight line.

Now that our kernel is set and defined, center it on each observation, one at a time, starting with the first observation (x_1=1). The kernel centered on the first observation is 0.0454 over the range of values 0 to 2, with 1 in the center.

Once the kernel is in place, sweep from left to right, summing the kernels at every point on the line. There's only been 1 kernel placed so far, so summing the kernels at every point is trivially just the kernel at every point.

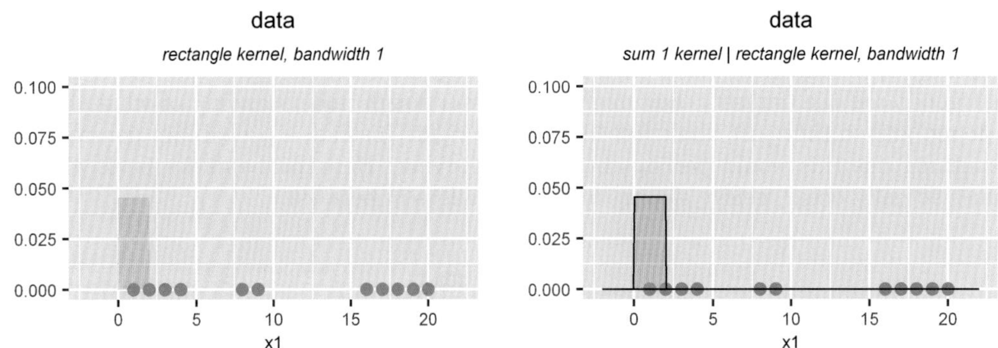

Center our kernel on the second observation, (x_1=2), so that the kernel is 0.0454 over the range of values 1 to 3, with 2 in the center. Note that the kernel on the first observation and the kernel on the second observation overlap. Sweep from left to right, summing the kernels at every point on the line. From values 0 to 1, the first kernel at every point is 0.0454. From values 1 to 2, because the 2 kernels overlap, the sum of kernels at every point is $0.0454 + 0.0454 = 0.0909$. From 2 to 3, the second kernel at every point is 0.0454. See that this traces out a peak from values 1 to 2, tapering off on either side.

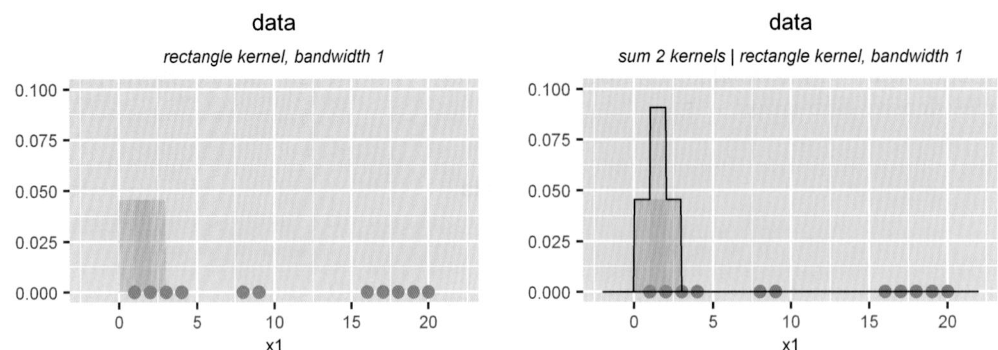

Similarly for the remaining observations. Where kernels overlap over ranges with high concentrations of values, we traced out peaks. Where they don't overlap, we traced out valleys. Interpreting the overall shape as a probability density function, this is a reasonable guess about the underlying process that generated the dataset. Note that the area under the curve is 1 because of the way we defined kernel height, as it should be for a probability density function.

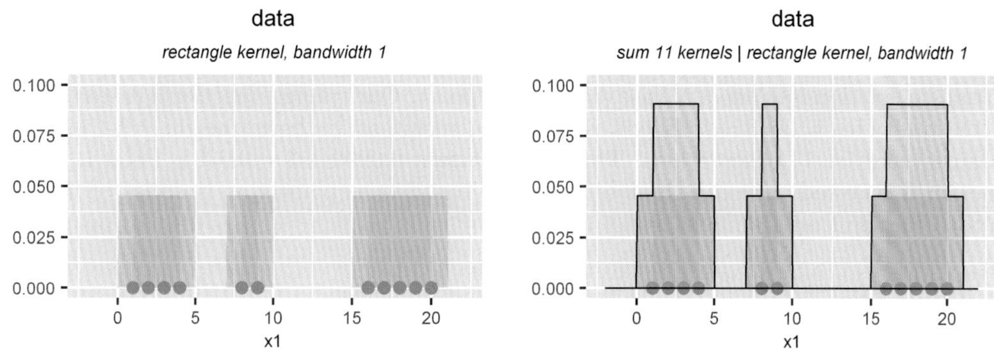

For a different guess, try setting bandwidth to 5. The shorter, wider kernels overlap more, so summing them involves more kernels at most points. The larger bandwidth results in a flatter overall shape. Interpreting this shape as a probability density function, it's also a reasonable guess about the underlying process.

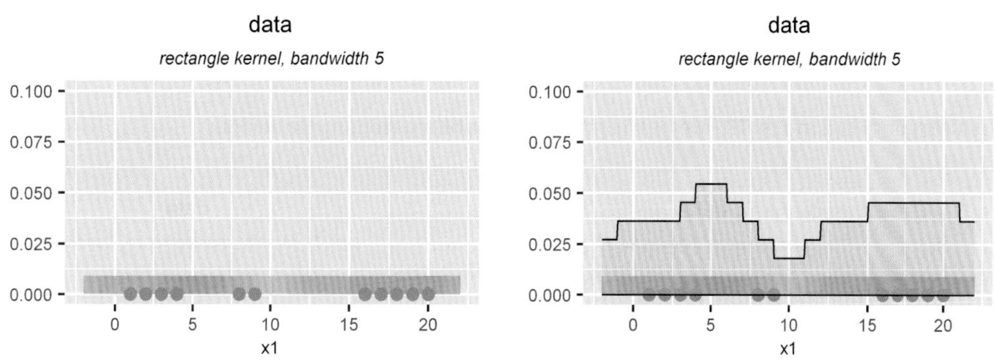

Here is what we get by setting bandwidth to 0.5. As the bandwidth gets smaller, the overall shape gets spikier.

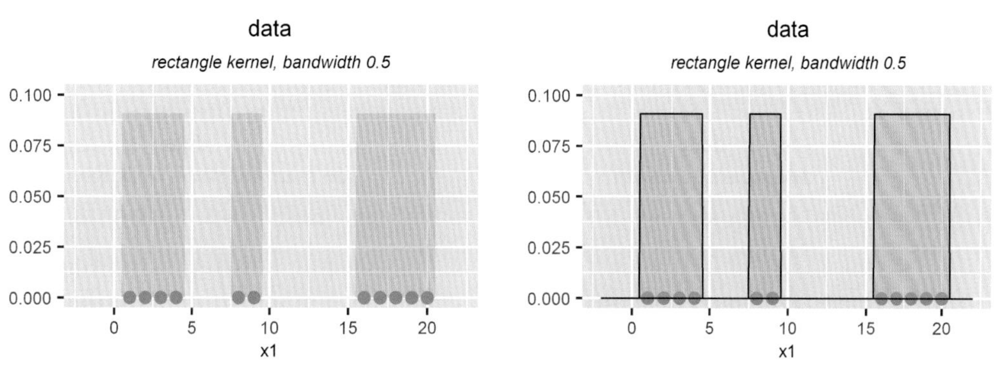

3.5.5.2 Triangle Function as Kernel

We can smooth the probability density function produced by kernel density estimation by setting the kernel to be a smoother function. Set kernel to be a triangle function and bandwidth to be 3. A triangle function is defined by base, height, and point. Our triangle function's base is calculated as $2 \times \text{bandwidth} = 2 \times 3 = 6$. Height is calculated such that $\frac{1}{2} \times \text{base} \times \text{height} = 1 \div 11 = 0.0909$, because there are 11 observations. That makes height $0.0909 \div 3 = 0.0303$. Point is where the function is centered. You can think of a triangle function as placing an isosceles triangle shape on top of a point on a straight line.

Here is the resulting probability density function:

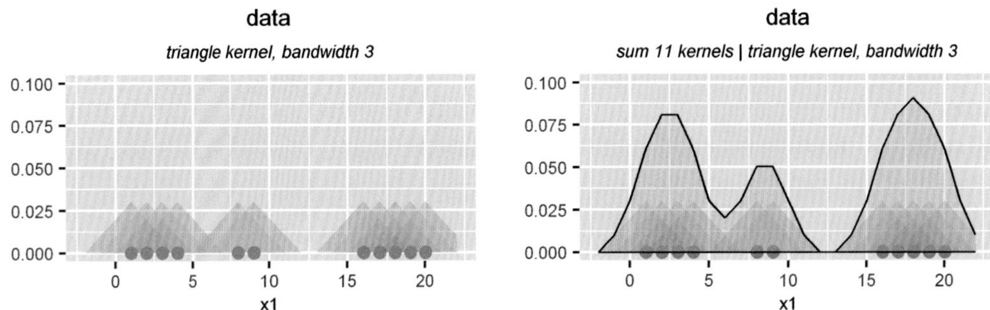

With larger bandwidth 10, we get a flatter probability density function:

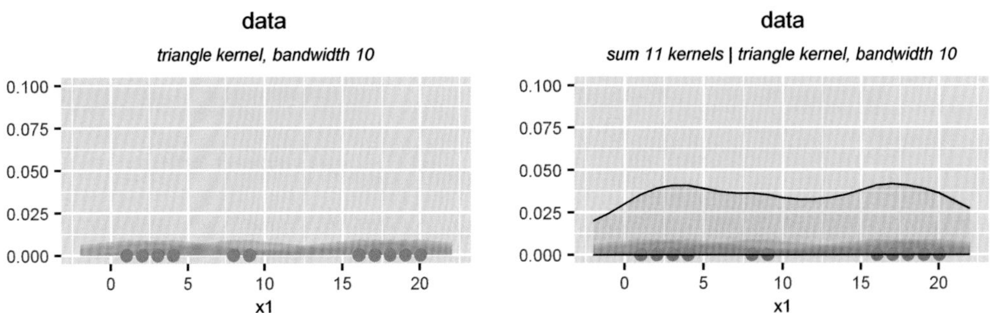

With smaller bandwidth 1, we get a spikier probability density function:

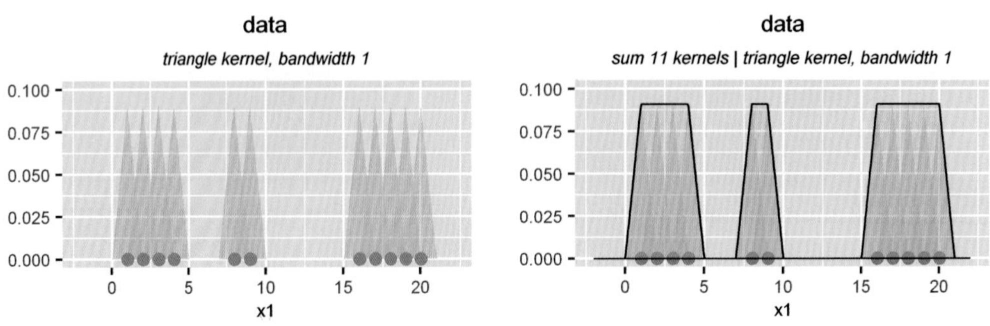

3.5.5.3 Gaussian Function as Kernel

We can smooth the probability density function produced by kernel density estimation even more by setting the kernel to be a **Gaussian function**, defined by mean, standard deviation, and size. A Gaussian function traces out a bell-shaped curve, centered at some point and symmetrically drifting down to near 0 on either side.

$$\text{Gaussian function: } g(x) = k\frac{1}{\sigma\sqrt{2\pi}}e^{-\frac{1}{2}\left(\frac{x-\mu}{\sigma}\right)^2}$$

where ...

- $g(x)$ is the Gaussian function evaluated at x
- μ is some mean to adjust the center point
- σ is some standard deviation to adjust the spread
- k is some factor to adjust the size

Set kernel to be a Gaussian function and bandwidth to be 1. Our Gaussian function's standard deviation is bandwidth 1. Size is calculated such that the area under the bell curve is $1 \div 11 = 0.0909$, because there are 11 observations. Mean is where the function is centered. You can think of a Gaussian function as placing a bell on top of a point on a straight line.

Here is the resulting probability density function:

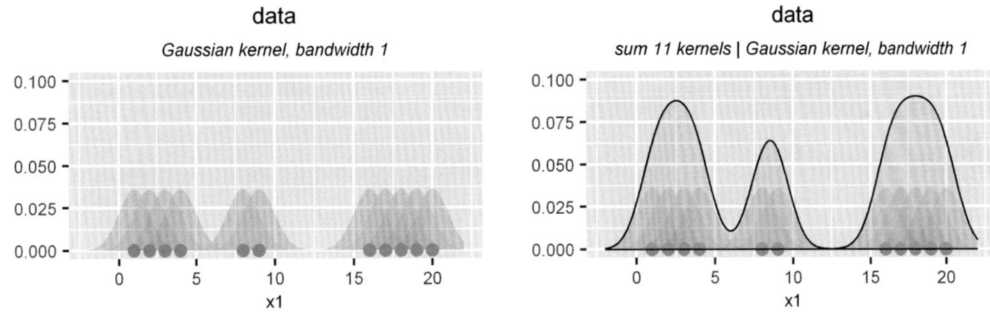

With larger bandwidth 2, we get a flatter probability density function:

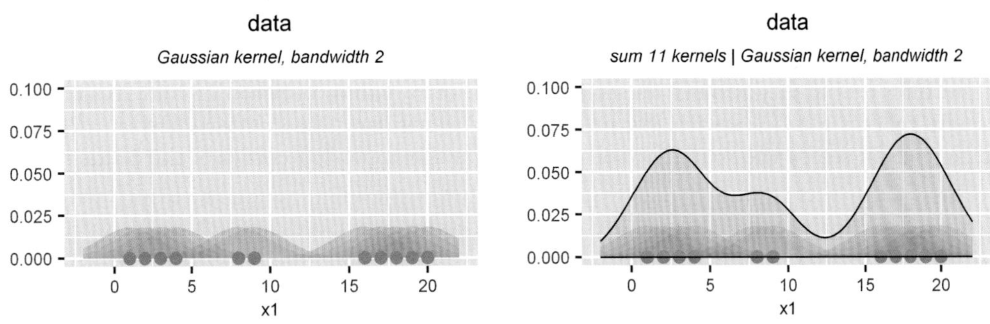

With smaller bandwidth 0.5, we get a spikier probability density function:

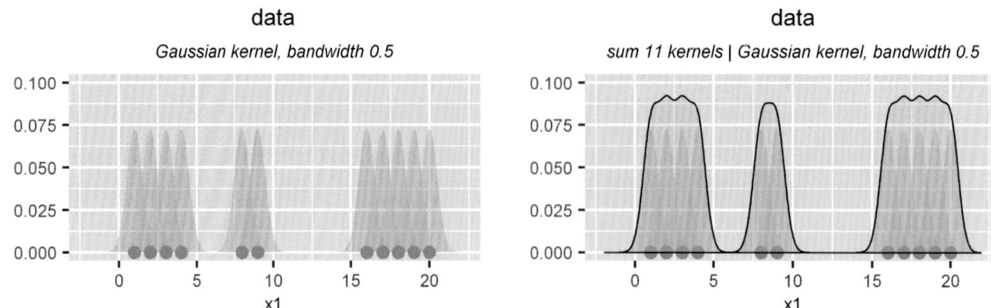

3.5.6 Kernel Density Estimation | Two Variables

Consider this 2-variable, 11-observation dataset. What is the underlying process that generated this dataset?

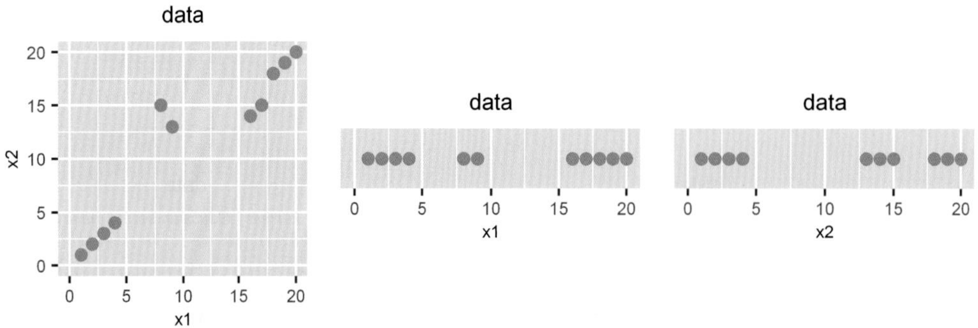

3.5.6.1 Variable Independence Assumption

If the variables were independent of each other, we could guess the underlying process using kernel density estimation on each variable. The process would then have 2 components: a probability density function that generates x_1 values, and a different probability density function that generates x_2 values. However, the variables are not independent, and assuming independence could lead to guessing an unlikely process. To see how, consider that such a process would have a high probability of generating an observation like $(x_1{=}2.5, x_2{=}19)$ because the probability density functions would indicate high probability around the concentration of x_1 values between 1 and 4, and high probability around the concentration of x_2 values between 18 and 20. The dataset, though, reflects a process with low probability of generating observations like $(x_1{=}2.5, x_2{=}19)$, which you can see by the sparsity of observations in the upper-left corner of the 2-axis scatterplot.

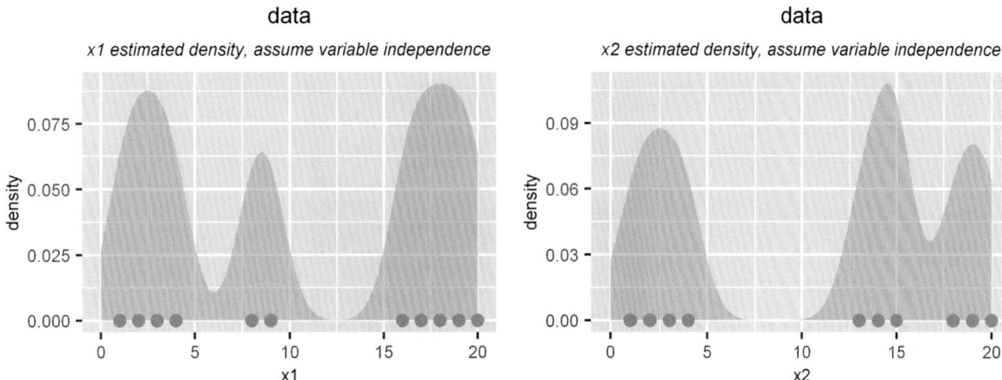

3.5.6.2 Variable Dependence Assumption

Rather than assume variable independence, let's guess the underlying process using kernel density estimation on both variables taken together. The resulting probability density function will be a contour rippling over a surface.

We'll use a **bi-variate Gaussian function** for our kernel, defined by 2 means, 2 standard deviations, and size. It traces out a mound-shaped contour, centered at some point in 2-dimensional space and symmetrically drifting down to near 0 all around. There are 2 means because 2 numbers are needed to specify a center point in 2-dimensional space. There are 2 standard deviations because 2 numbers are needed to specify how the function spreads out in 2-dimensional space.

Set kernel to be a bi-variate Gaussian function, and bandwidths to be 10 and 10. Standard deviations along the x_1 and x_2 axes are bandwidths 10 and 10. Size is calculated such that the volume under the mound contour is $1 \div 11 = 0.0909$, because there are 11 observations. Means indicate where the function is centered. You can think of a bi-variate Gaussian function as placing a 3-dimensional mound on top of a point on a 2-dimensional surface.

Now that our kernel is set and defined, center it on each observation, one at a time. Sum the kernels at every point in x_1,x_2 space and interpret the overall shape as a probability density function. This is a reasonable guess about the underlying process that generated the dataset. Note that the volume under the contour is 1 because of the way we defined kernel size, as it should be for a probability density function.

Here is the probability density function visualized as a heat map. Observations are shown as blue points. Shades of red indicate points where probability density is low. Shades of yellow indicate points where probability density is high. Black lines indicate points of equal probability density. See that yellow peaks and red valleys correspond to high and low concentrations of observations.

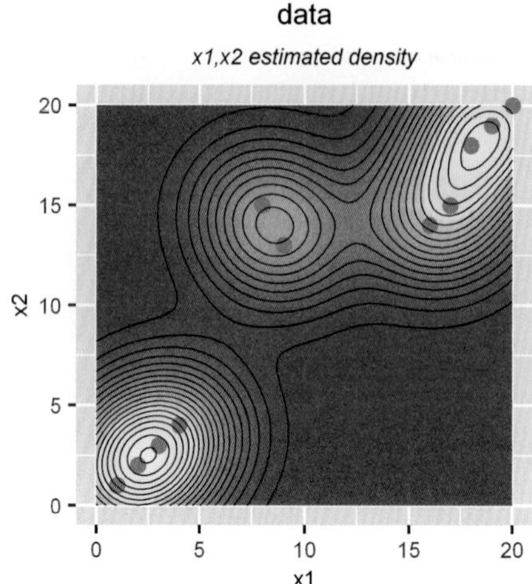

Here is the probability density function visualized as a 3-axis scatterplot projection:

data (x1,x2 estimated density)

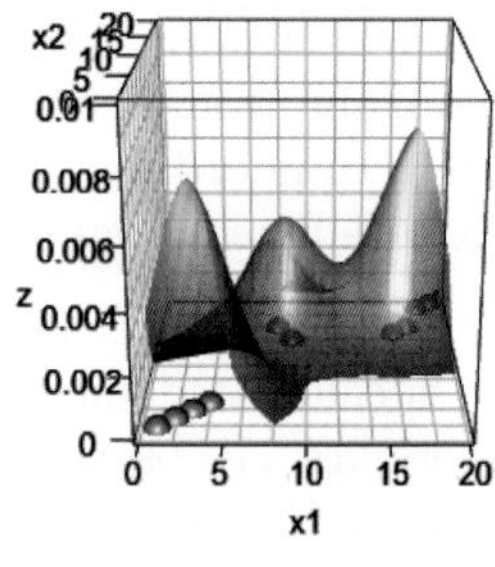

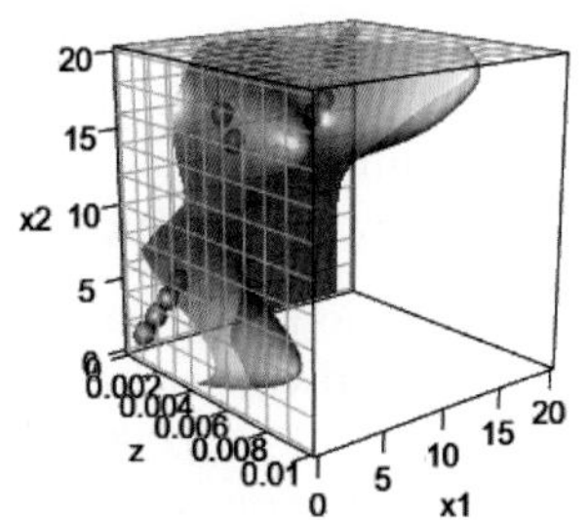

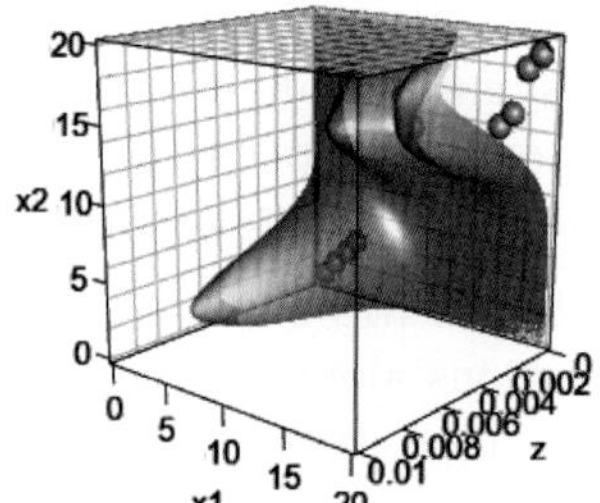

3.5.7 Probability from Kernel Density Estimate

Consider this 1-variable, 11-observation dataset and a good guess about its underlying process, which is expressed as a probability density function derived by kernel density estimation using a Gaussian function kernel. From such a process, we can estimate the probabilities of generating new values. What is the probability that this underlying process will generate a new value between 4 and 7?

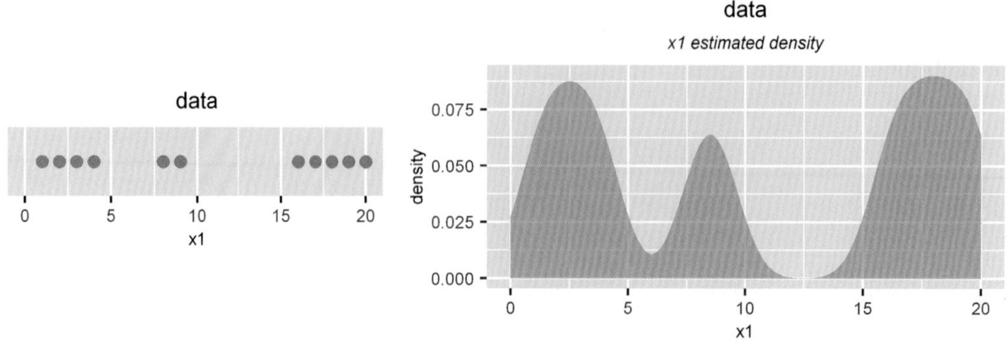

The probability density at x_1=4 is 0.0636. The probability density at x_1=7 is 0.0274. These numbers by themselves don't tell us anything directly about the probability we want.

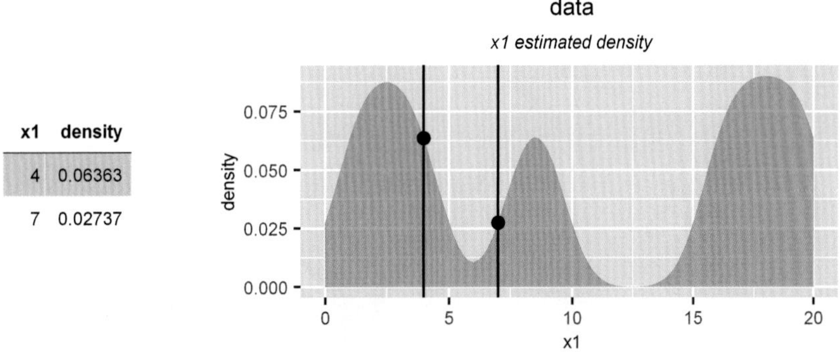

Integrate the probability density function from x_1=4 to x_1=7. We typically integrate using some implementation of the Riemann sum algorithm, so it doesn't matter how complex the function is. This gives us area under the curve 0.0786, which we interpret as there being a 7.86% probability that the underlying process will generate a new value between 4 and 7. Note that integrating from 0 to 20, the range of actual values in the dataset, gives us area under the curve 0.9221, which is less than 1. This is because kernel density estimation used kernels spanning negative to positive infinity, and the sums of overlapping kernels at every point on the straight line are non-zero. Integrating from negative to positive infinity would give us area under the curve 1.

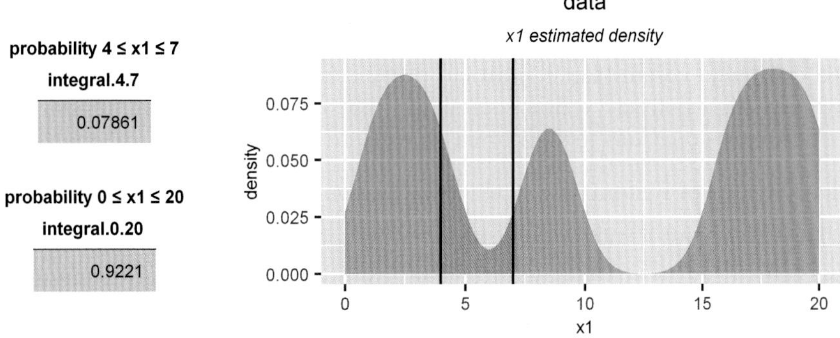

3.6 CASE | Fundraising Strategy

Data exploration with descriptive statistics, synthetic variables, cross-tabulation, and data visualization to discover effective fundraising strategies from a historical US presidential campaign.

3.6.1 Business Situation

A new candidate for US president has hired a political campaign expert to help with fundraising in the early stage of her campaign. In the US, donations can be made directly to a candidate's authorized campaign committee, a political party committee, a labor organization's separate segregated fund, or a political action committee. The expert will initially focus the fundraising strategy on driving donations in California directly to the candidate's campaign committee.

- **Role:** Director of Fundraising, California Region, for a US presidential candidate.
- **Business Decision:** Target whom, target where, target when?
- **Approach:** Explore the history of donations made to authorized campaign committees in California, specifically those made during January to September 2019. Compare with donations made in Texas to get a sense for how unique or common state environments are. Use insights about what strategies seemed to be effective for past campaigns to inform decisions about a strategy for the new campaign.

3.6.2 Data

Three relevant datasets are publicly available: a register of candidates, a register of authorized campaign committees, and a register of individual donations.

Retrieve the register of candidates. The variable names are available in a separate file, so retrieve that file, too, and set the dataset's variable names accordingly. The dataset describes 6,064 candidates for various offices in various election years, each identified by a candidate ID number.

size of data.cn	
observations	variables
6,064	15

data.cn__variables

CAND_ID, CAND_NAME, CAND_PTY_AFFILIATION, CAND_ELECTION_YR, CAND_OFFICE_ST, CAND_OFFICE, CAND_OFFICE_DISTRICT, CAND_ICI, CAND_STATUS, CAND_PCC, CAND_ST1, CAND_ST2, CAND_CITY, CAND_ST, CAND_ZIP

Select only the 2020 presidential candidates, indicated by *CAND OFFICE*=P and *CAND ELECTION YR*=2020. For convenience, rename *CAND PTY AFFILIATION* to be *PARTY*. See that there are 1,015 candidates for president affiliated with 51 political parties. One candidate, for some reason, has 2 candidate ID numbers.

size of data.cn	
observations	variables
1,016	15

# of candidates
1,015

# of parties
51

data.cn__PARTY_values

NNE, IND, DEM, OTH, REP, NPA, GRE, UN, CRV, LBL, HRP, FHB, IAP, W, KSP, , CIT, AIP, LIB, PPY, GWP, UNK, N/A, AMP, NON, IDP, ICD, FED, GRN, DFL, APF, COM, VET, UST, RTL, NAP, SUS, PRO, CON, AKI, NIC, SWP, SLP, ACE, POP, PAF, REF, EAS, SOC, AIC, NP

Retrieve the register of authorized campaign committees. The variable names are available in a separate file, so retrieve that file, too, and set the dataset's variable names accordingly. The dataset describes 5,843 committees. Note that each committee is identified by a committee ID number and is associated with a specific candidate ID number.

size of data.link	
observations	variables
5,843	7

data.link__variables

CAND_ID, CAND_ELECTION_YR, FEC_ELECTION_YR, CMTE_ID, CMTE_TP, CMTE_DSGN, LINKAGE_ID

Retrieve the register of California donations made from January to September 2019. The variable names are available in a separate file, so retrieve that file, too, and set the dataset's variable names accordingly. The dataset describes 1,244,098 donations. For convenience, rename *TRANSACTION DT* to be *DATE*, and rename *TRANSACTION AMT* to be *AMOUNT*. Change the *DATE* variable type from character string to special date type, in anticipation of later using it in a time series visualization. For convenience, fill in missing *OCCUPATION* values with "blank". Note that each donation is a record of the donor name, donor occupation, date of donation, and amount of donation. Also note, each donation is associated with a specific authorized campaign committee.

size of data.x	
observations	**variables**
1,244,098	9

data.x__variables
CMTE_ID, NAME, CITY, STATE, ZIP_CODE, EMPLOYER, OCCUPATION, DATE, AMOUNT

Join the 3 datasets into 1 dataset, like this. Join the candidate dataset and committee dataset by the *CAND ID* and *CAND ELECTION YR* variables. Then join the resulting dataset and donation dataset by the *CMTE ID* variable. That leaves 271,464 donations made to 48 candidates. The excluded candidates either didn't have authorized campaign committees or didn't have any donations. The excluded donations were those made to committees of candidates seeking other offices. Select the *CAND NAME*, *PARTY*, *NAME*, *CITY*, *OCCUPATION*, *DATE*, and *AMOUNT* variables.

size of data	
observations	**variables**
271,464	7

# of candidates with committees & donations
48

data__variables
CAND_NAME, PARTY, NAME, CITY, OCCUPATION, DATE, AMOUNT

Add a synthetic variable *tier* to coarsen the donation amounts:

- low indicates donation amount \$0 to \$99.99
- mid indicates donation amount \$100 to \$999.99
- high indicates donation amount \$1,000 or more
- other indicates donation amount less than \$0, which can refer to loans to campaigns being repaid

Some candidates donate to themselves, in 1 case \$15,000,000. Such donations are not relevant to crafting a fundraising strategy, so filter them out by selecting only observations where *CAND NAME* of candidate does not equal *NAME* of donor.

The **data** dataset ultimately comprises information about 270,823 donations, each described by 8 variables, made from January to September 2019.

data *size 270823×8, first few observations shown, first 3 variables shown*

	CAND_NAME	PARTY	NAME
1	SANFORD, MARSHALL HON	REP	CARATAN, PATRICK
2	SANFORD, MARSHALL HON	REP	PARROTT, IDA
3	SANFORD, MARSHALL HON	REP	HUEBSCHER, FRED
4	SANFORD, MARSHALL HON	REP	MURPHY, MIKE
5	DELANEY, JOHN K.	DEM	ELVERUM, JAMIE
6	DELANEY, JOHN K.	DEM	FLYNN, GREG
7	DELANEY, JOHN K.	DEM	SAUNDERS, MARSHALL L
8	DELANEY, JOHN K.	DEM	HOLMSTROM, RICK
9	DELANEY, JOHN K.	DEM	COWAN, GEOFFREY
10	DELANEY, JOHN K.	DEM	BECKER, DAVID
11	DELANEY, JOHN K.	DEM	ELVERUM, JAMIE
12	DELANEY, JOHN K.	DEM	THACHER, JOHN
13	DELANEY, JOHN K.	DEM	ELVERUM, JAMIE
14	DELANEY, JOHN K.	DEM	ELVERUM, JAMIE
15	DELANEY, JOHN K.	DEM	ROGOVIN, JOHN
16	DELANEY, JOHN K.	DEM	ELVERUM, JAMIE
17	DELANEY, JOHN K.	DEM	MIHALKE, MICHAEL

data *size 270823×8, first few observations shown, last 5 variables shown*

	CITY	OCCUPATION	DATE	AMOUNT	tier
1	BAKERSFIELD	blank	2019-09-08	400	mid
2	FRESNO	RETIRED	2019-09-09	500	mid
3	HERMOSA BEACH	CONSULTANT	2019-09-08	1,000	high
4	LOS ANGELES	CONSULTANT	2019-09-08	1,000	high
5	CARMICHAEL	SALES MANAGER	2019-07-14	25	low
6	SAN FRANCISCO	blank	2019-03-31	1,000	high
7	CORONADO	RETIRED	2019-07-08	1,000	high
8	WOODSIDE	blank	2019-06-20	200	mid
9	LOS ANGELES	PROFESSOR	2019-04-10	20	low
10	KENTFIELD	EXECUTIVE	2019-07-07	2,800	high
11	CARMICHAEL	SALES MANAGER	2019-07-28	25	low
12	SAINT HELENA	blank	2019-03-25	1,000	high
13	CARMICHAEL	SALES MANAGER	2019-08-20	5	low
14	CARMICHAEL	SALES MANAGER	2019-09-28	25	low
15	LOS ANGELES	GENERAL COUNSEL	2019-09-17	2,000	high
16	CARMICHAEL	SALES MANAGER	2019-08-28	25	low
17	SANTA MONICA	blank	2019-02-14	2,700	high

3.6.3 Donations

Let's look into candidate and party performance. Which candidates raised the most money, from how many donors, in what quantities? Which parties raised the most money, from how many donors, in what quantities?

Construct a dataset to summarize donations by candidate, called **data.cand**, like this:

- With **data**, aggregate *AMOUNT* by count, grouped by *CAND NAME* and *PARTY*. For clarity, rename *AMOUNT* to be *count*.
- With **data**, aggregate *AMOUNT* by sum, grouped by *CAND NAME* and *PARTY*. Join the resulting aggregate table and the previous table by *CAND NAME* and *PARTY*. For clarity, rename *AMOUNT* to be *sum*.
- With **data**, aggregate *AMOUNT* by mean, grouped by *CAND NAME* and *PARTY*. Join the resulting aggregate table and the previous table by *CAND NAME* and *PARTY*. For clarity, rename *AMOUNT* to be *mean*.

Some candidates received only a few donations. Such candidates are not relevant to crafting a fundraising strategy, so filter them out of **data.cand** by selecting only observations where *count* exceeds 100 donors. Note that this collaterally filters out all but the Democratic and Republican parties.

Revise **data** for the remainder of the analysis to include only candidates with more than 100 donations. To do this, select the *CAND NAME* variable from **data.cand** and keep it as a dataset rather than reduce it to a vector. Then join **data** and the resulting dataset by *CAND NAME*. This effectively removes any candidates from **data** that do not appear in **data.cand**.

Construct a dataset to summarize donations by party, called **data.party**, like this:

- With **data**, aggregate *AMOUNT* by count, grouped by *PARTY*. For clarity, rename *AMOUNT* to be *count*.
- With **data**, aggregate *AMOUNT* by sum, grouped by *PARTY*. Join the resulting aggregate table and the previous table by *PARTY*. For clarity, rename *AMOUNT* to be *sum*.
- With **data**, aggregate *AMOUNT* by mean, grouped by *PARTY*. Join the resulting aggregate table and the previous table by *PARTY*. For clarity, rename *AMOUNT* to be *mean*.

Here are **data.cand** and **data.party**, summarizing candidate and party performance by count, sum, and mean. See that 24 candidates each received more than 100 donations. They collectively received a total of $42,041,742 in donations, averaging $155.40 per donation. With that kind of money expected to come in again in future elections, it's certainly worthwhile to have a fundraising strategy that can extract a big piece of it for our own candidate.

size of data	
observations	variables
270,532	8

donations			
candidates	count	sum	mean
24	270,532	42,041,742	155.4

donations by candidate

CAND_NAME	PARTY	count	sum	mean
BENNET, MICHAEL F.	DEM	1,097	612,003	557.89
BIDEN, JOSEPH R JR	DEM	12,979	4,836,782	372.66
BOOKER, CORY A.	DEM	6,322	2,540,229	401.81
BULLOCK, STEVE	DEM	507	366,892	723.65
BUTTIGIEG, PETE	DEM	45,252	9,223,713	203.83
CASTRO, JULIAN	DEM	228	167,837	736.13
DELANEY, JOHN K.	DEM	167	105,163	629.72
GABBARD, TULSI	DEM	1,245	429,401	344.90
GILLIBRAND, KIRSTEN	DEM	1,196	752,071	628.82
HARRIS, KAMALA D.	DEM	17,552	7,478,362	426.07
HICKENLOOPER, JOHN W.	DEM	385	297,517	772.77
INSLEE, JAY R	DEM	1,579	521,332	330.17
KLOBUCHAR, AMY J.	DEM	4,931	1,117,414	226.61
MOULTON, SETH	DEM	216	165,724	767.24
O'ROURKE, ROBERT BETO	DEM	1,239	396,741	320.21
RYAN, TIMOTHY J.	DEM	219	101,521	463.57
SANDERS, BERNARD	DEM	94,172	4,593,227	48.77
STEYER, TOM	DEM	507	313,842	619.02
SWALWELL, ERIC MICHAEL	DEM	643	324,962	505.38
TRUMP, DONALD J.	REP	13,255	1,205,931	90.98
WARREN, ELIZABETH	DEM	48,699	4,219,663	86.65
WELD, WILLIAM FLOYD (BILL)	REP	225	70,579	313.68
WILLIAMSON, MARIANNE	DEM	4,791	726,239	151.58
YANG, ANDREW MR.	DEM	13,126	1,474,597	112.34

donations by party

PARTY	count	sum	mean
DEM	257,052	40,765,232	158.6
REP	13,480	1,276,510	94.7

Here is **data.cand** visualized as a set of bar charts. See that performance was very different depending on which descriptive statistic we're considering. Sanders looks best by far when considering donation counts, but Buttigieg and Harris pulled in much more money with fewer donations. None of the top-performing candidates by count or sum received big donations, on average. Should our fundraising strategy try to attract the most donors or the biggest donors?

donations

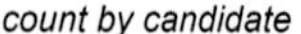
count by candidate

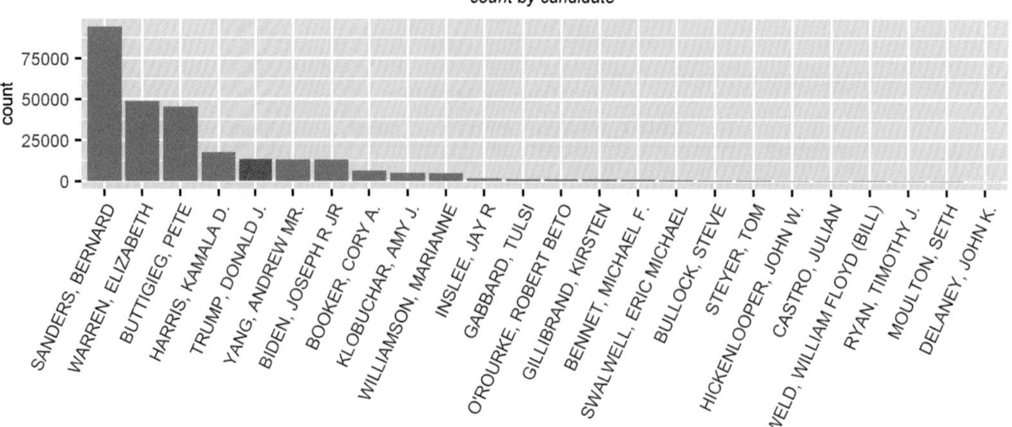
count
75000
50000
25000
0
SANDERS, BERNARD
WARREN, ELIZABETH
BUTTIGIEG, PETE
HARRIS, KAMALA D.
TRUMP, DONALD J.
YANG, ANDREW MR.
BIDEN, JOSEPH R JR
BOOKER, CORY A.
KLOBUCHAR, AMY J.
WILLIAMSON, MARIANNE
INSLEE, JAY R
GABBARD, TULSI
O'ROURKE, ROBERT BETO
GILLIBRAND, KIRSTEN
BENNET, MICHAEL F.
SWALWELL, ERIC MICHAEL
BULLOCK, STEVE
STEYER, TOM
HICKENLOOPER, JOHN W.
CASTRO, JULIAN
WELD, WILLIAM FLOYD (BILL)
RYAN, TIMOTHY J.
MOULTON, SETH
DELANEY, JOHN K.

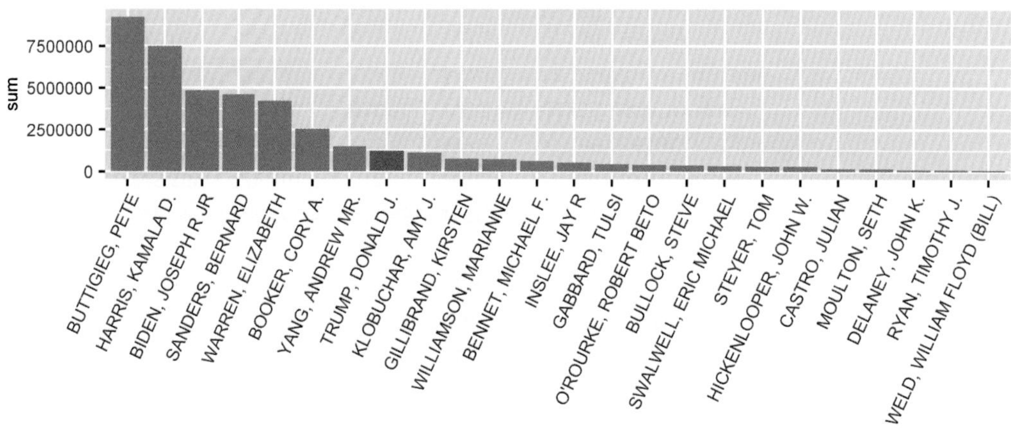
donations
sum by candidate
sum
7500000
5000000
2500000
0
BUTTIGIEG, PETE
HARRIS, KAMALA D.
BIDEN, JOSEPH R JR
SANDERS, BERNARD
WARREN, ELIZABETH
BOOKER, CORY A.
YANG, ANDREW MR.
TRUMP, DONALD J.
KLOBUCHAR, AMY J.
GILLIBRAND, KIRSTEN
WILLIAMSON, MARIANNE
BENNET, MICHAEL F.
INSLEE, JAY R
GABBARD, TULSI
O'ROURKE, ROBERT BETO
BULLOCK, STEVE
SWALWELL, ERIC MICHAEL
STEYER, TOM
HICKENLOOPER, JOHN W.
CASTRO, JULIAN
MOULTON, SETH
DELANEY, JOHN K.
RYAN, TIMOTHY J.
WELD, WILLIAM FLOYD (BILL)

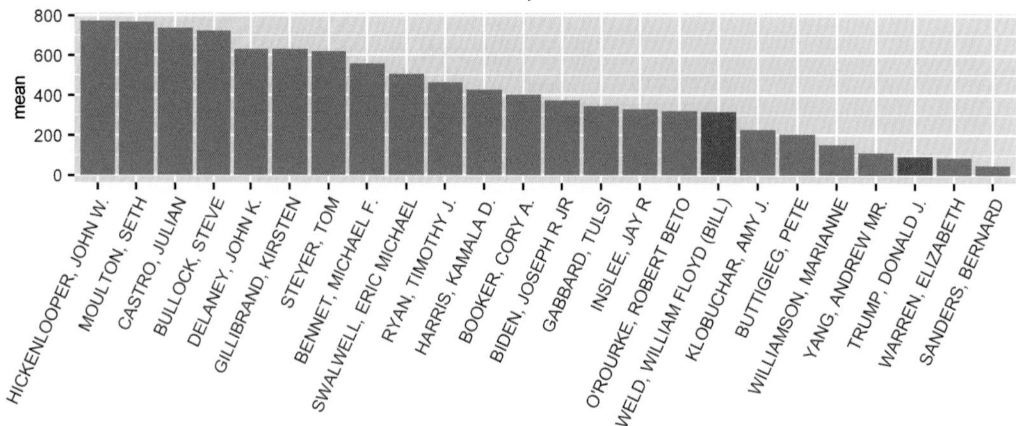
donations
mean by candidate
mean
800
600
400
200
0
HICKENLOOPER, JOHN W.
MOULTON, SETH
CASTRO, JULIAN
BULLOCK, STEVE
DELANEY, JOHN K.
GILLIBRAND, KIRSTEN
STEYER, TOM
BENNET, MICHAEL F.
SWALWELL, ERIC MICHAEL
RYAN, TIMOTHY J.
HARRIS, KAMALA D.
BOOKER, CORY A.
BIDEN, JOSEPH R JR
GABBARD, TULSI
INSLEE, JAY R
O'ROURKE, ROBERT BETO
WELD, WILLIAM FLOYD (BILL)
KLOBUCHAR, AMY J.
BUTTIGIEG, PETE
WILLIAMSON, MARIANNE
YANG, ANDREW MR.
TRUMP, DONALD J.
WARREN, ELIZABETH
SANDERS, BERNARD

Take a closer look at candidate performance by sum, like this:

- With **data**, aggregate *AMOUNT* by sum, grouped by *CAND NAME* and *tier*. For clarity, rename *AMOUNT* to be *sum*. Call the resulting dataset **data.agg.**
- From **data.agg**, select the observations where *tier* is high, re-order them by *sum*, and select *CAND NAME*. Call the resulting vector **sort_by_high_donor**.
- Visualize **data.agg** as a bar chart, one bar for each candidate, bar heights set to *sum*, laid out in order of **sort_by_high_donor**, bars stacked and color-coded by *tier*.

Similarly to visualize mid- and low-tier donations.

Buttigieg and Harris received about the same amount of money from high-tier donors, but Buttigieg received more money from mid- and low-tier donors. Warren and Sanders received almost as much money from mid- and low-tier donors, but much less from high-tier donors. So, while having the most donors or biggest donors did not result in the most money, it looks like it's still good to have plenty of relatively big donors.

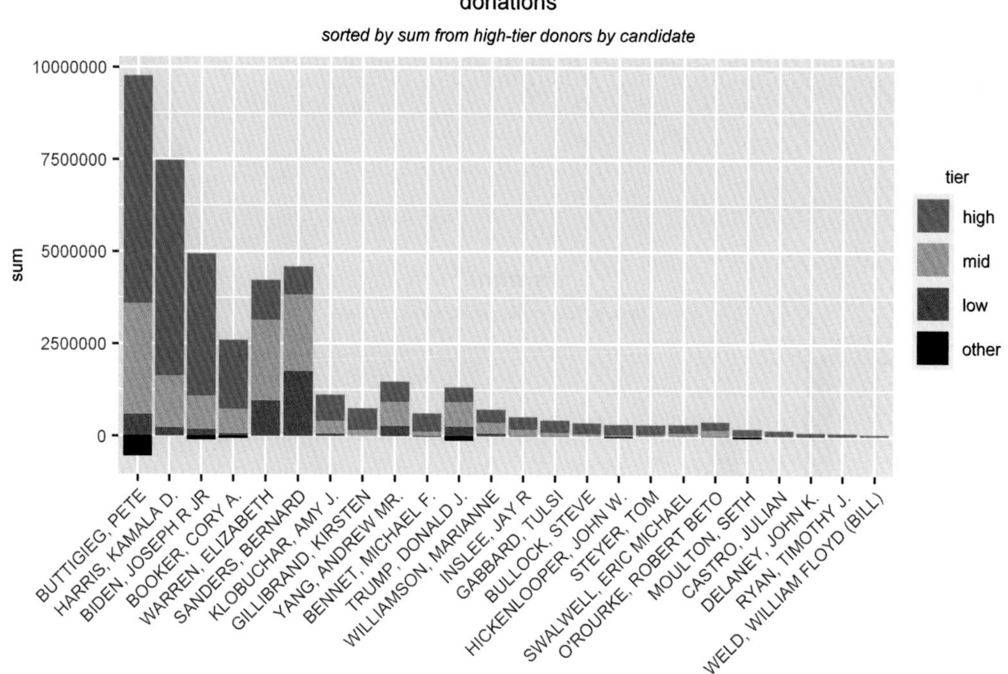

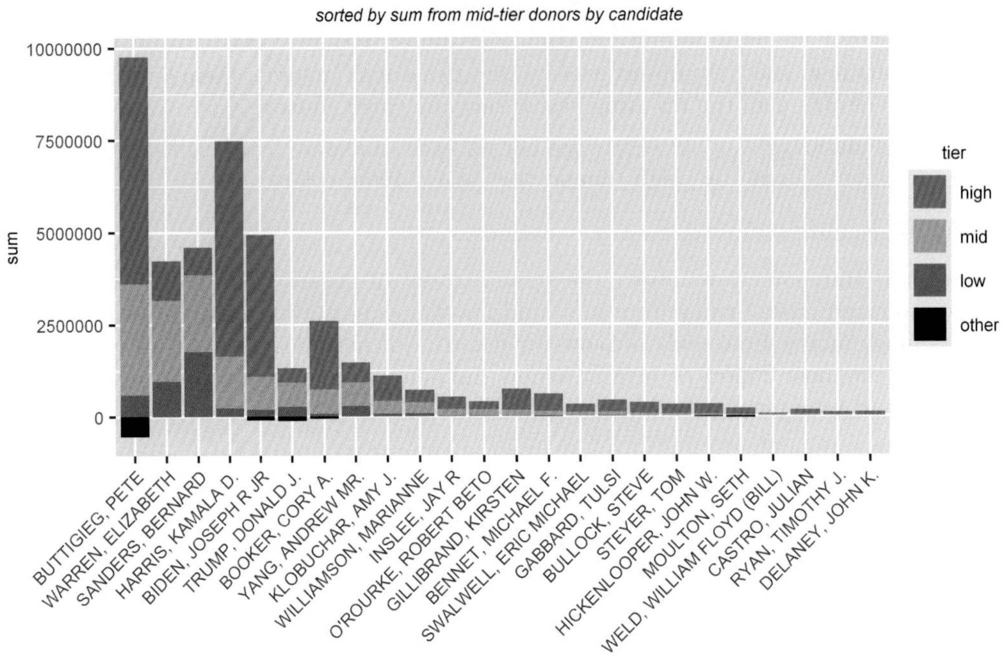
donations
sorted by sum from mid-tier donors by candidate
10000000
7500000
5000000
2500000
0
sum
tier
high
mid
low
other
BUTTIGIEG, PETE
WARREN, ELIZABETH
SANDERS, BERNARD
HARRIS, KAMALA D.
BIDEN, JOSEPH R JR
TRUMP, DONALD J.
BOOKER, CORY A.
YANG, ANDREW MR.
KLOBUCHAR, AMY J.
WILLIAMSON, MARIANNE
INSLEE, JAY R
O'ROURKE, ROBERT BETO
GILLIBRAND, KIRSTEN
BENNET, MICHAEL F.
SWALWELL, ERIC MICHAEL
GABBARD, TULSI
BULLOCK, STEVE
STEYER, TOM
HICKENLOOPER, JOHN W.
MOULTON, SETH
WELD, WILLIAM FLOYD (BILL)
CASTRO, JULIAN
RYAN, TIMOTHY J.
DELANEY, JOHN K.

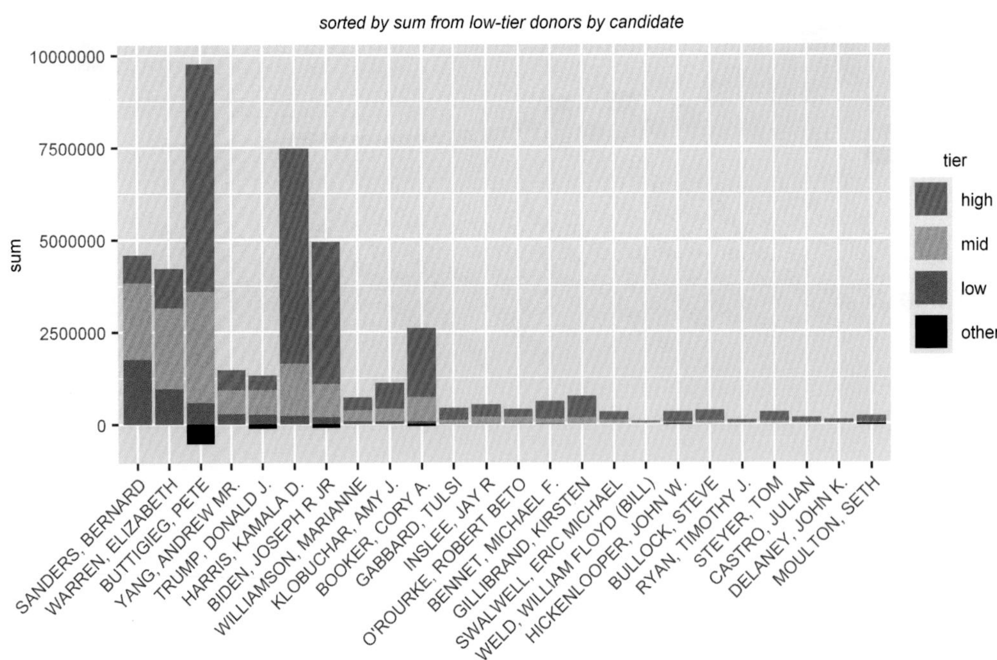
donations
sorted by sum from low-tier donors by candidate
10000000
7500000
5000000
2500000
0
sum
tier
high
mid
low
other
SANDERS, BERNARD
WARREN, ELIZABETH
BUTTIGIEG, PETE
YANG, ANDREW MR.
TRUMP, DONALD J.
HARRIS, KAMALA D.
BIDEN, JOSEPH R JR
WILLIAMSON, MARIANNE
KLOBUCHAR, AMY J.
BOOKER, CORY A.
GABBARD, TULSI
INSLEE, JAY R
O'ROURKE, ROBERT BETO
BENNET, MICHAEL F.
GILLIBRAND, KIRSTEN
SWALWELL, ERIC MICHAEL
WELD, WILLIAM FLOYD (BILL)
HICKENLOOPER, JOHN W.
BULLOCK, STEVE
RYAN, TIMOTHY J.
STEYER, TOM
CASTRO, JULIAN
DELANEY, JOHN K.
MOULTON, SETH

Here is **data.party** visualized as a set of bar charts. See that more donors and more money went to Democratic campaigns than to Republican campaigns. We should account for that in our fundraising strategy, as the potential share of total money received seems to depend on the candidate's party.

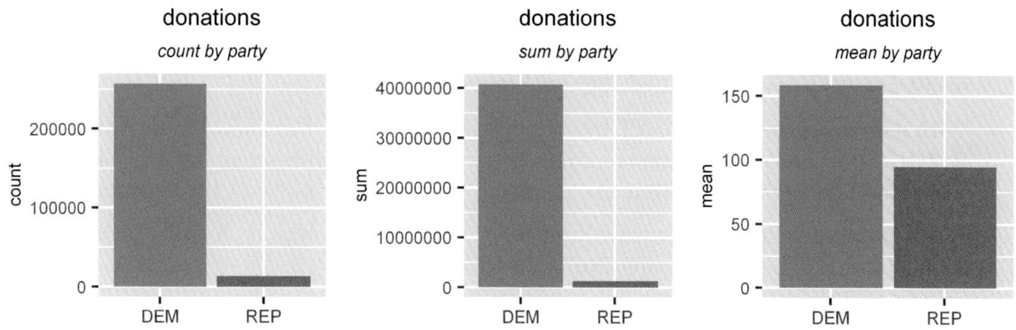

It might be easier to compare candidate performance if we could see all 3 descriptive statistics in just 1 graphic. Visualize **data.cand** as a 2-axis scatterplot, *CAND NAME* on the horizontal axis, *sum* on the vertical axis, and *PARTY*, *count*, and *mean* shown as color, point size, and color intensity. Note that we can lay out categorical values on the horizontal axis.

variable	attribute
candidate	horizontal position
party	color
$ donated	vertical position
# donated	size
average $ donated	color intensity

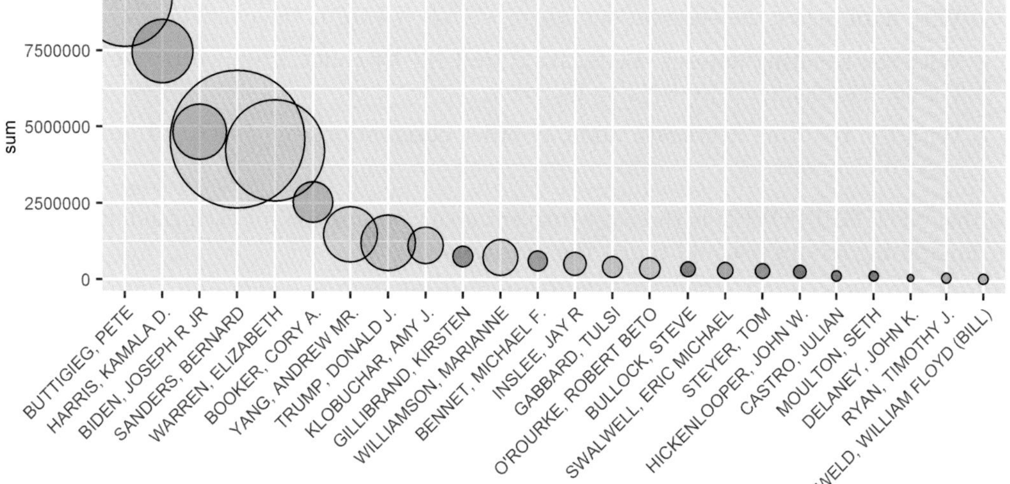

3.6.4 Donor Occupations

Let's look into the donors. Who is making donations? What are their occupations? By law, donors must self-report their occupations.

Focus on the few candidates with the highest sum donations and the few most frequent occupations:

- With **data.cand**, re-order observations by *sum*, and select the first 4 elements from the resulting vector to get a list of top candidates.
- With **data**, aggregate *AMOUNT* by count, grouped by *OCCUPATION*. For clarity, rename *AMOUNT* to be *count*. Then re-order observations by *count*, select *OCCUPATION*, and select the first 4 elements from the resulting vector to get a list of top occupations.
- With **data**, select the observations where *CAND NAME* is a top candidate and *OCCUPATION* is a top occupation. Call this **data.f**.
- Convert **data.f** to long table representation, with *CAND NAME* and *OCCUPATION* as identifier variables, and *AMOUNT* as a measure variable. Call this **data.long**.
- With **data.long**, cross-tabulate *CAND NAME* and *OCCUPATION* by count.

See that NOT EMPLOYED is among the most frequent donor occupations. Sanders and Buttigieg especially received many donations from the unemployed.

count by candidate,occupation

CAND_NAME	ATTORNEY	NOT EMPLOYED	RETIRED	SOFTWARE ENGINEER
BIDEN, JOSEPH R JR	729	4,934	516	35
BUTTIGIEG, PETE	1,403	14,895	1,011	386
HARRIS, KAMALA D.	1,183	3,460	2,562	230
SANDERS, BERNARD	887	23,112	1,016	2,511

Try viewing occupations another way. Construct an aggregate table for each top candidate, like this:

- With **data**, select the observations where *CAND NAME* is the candidate.
- With the resulting dataset, aggregate *AMOUNT* by count, grouped by *OCCUPATION*. For clarity, rename *AMOUNT* to be *count*.
- With the resulting aggregate table, re-order observations by *AMOUNT*, and select the first 10 observations.

See that NOT EMPLOYED is the most frequent donor occupation for each candidate. Perhaps our fundraising strategy should target the unemployed.

BUTTIGIEG, PETE

OCCUPATION	count
NOT EMPLOYED	14,895
ATTORNEY	1,403
RETIRED	1,011
TEACHER	766
PHYSICIAN	743
CONSULTANT	629
ENGINEER	602
WRITER	583
blank	533
CEO	447

HARRIS, KAMALA D.

OCCUPATION	count
NOT EMPLOYED	3,460
RETIRED	2,562
ATTORNEY	1,183
PHYSICIAN	335
CONSULTANT	271
SOFTWARE ENGINEER	230
TEACHER	225
EXECUTIVE	218
WRITER	217
CEO	215

BIDEN, JOSEPH R JR

OCCUPATION	count
NOT EMPLOYED	4,934
ATTORNEY	729
RETIRED	516
blank	309
CONSULTANT	233
PHYSICIAN	230
CEO	224
LAWYER	211
EXECUTIVE	199
TEACHER	179

SANDERS, BERNARD

OCCUPATION	count
NOT EMPLOYED	23,112
NONE	2,885
TEACHER	2,879
SOFTWARE ENGINEER	2,511
ENGINEER	1,973
SALES	1,123
RETIRED	1,016
blank	940
ATTORNEY	887
PHYSICIAN	820

Perhaps you suspect that CEOs are especially active donors. Indeed, CEOs are among the 10 most frequent kind of donor for 3 of the top 4 candidates. Look into CEO donations for all the candidates, like this:

- With **data**, select the observations where *OCCUPATION* is CEO.
- With the resulting dataset, aggregate *AMOUNT* by count, grouped by *CAND NAME* and *PARTY*. For clarity, rename *AMOUNT* to be *count*.
- Visualize as a bar chart, one bar for each candidate, bar heights set to *count*, laid out in order of *count*, bars color-coded by *PARTY*.

See that CEOs were frequent donors to a variety of candidates. Note that Sanders had so many donations from other kinds of donors that CEO was not among his top 10 donor occupations, though he did get more CEO donations than almost any other candidate did.

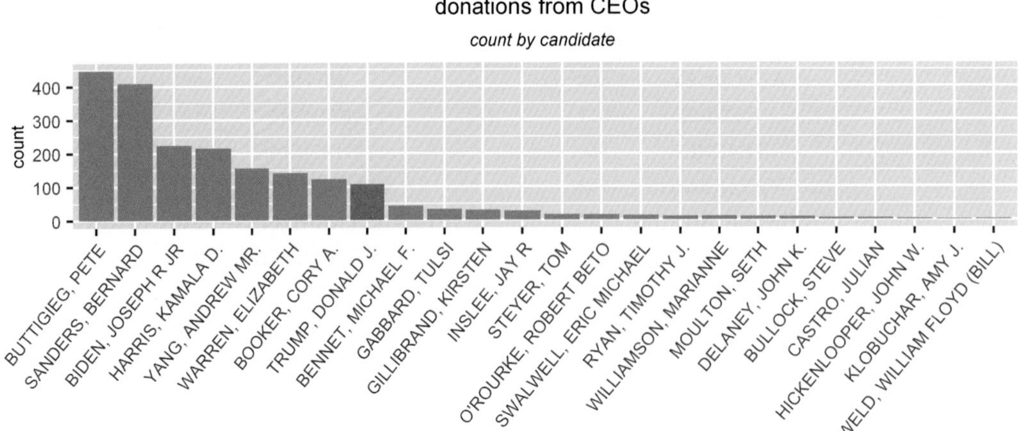

3.6.5 Donor Cities

Let's look into where donations are coming from. Which cities are donations coming from?

Focus on the few cities with the highest sum donations:

- With **data**, aggregate *AMOUNT* by sum, grouped by *CITY*. For clarity, rename *AMOUNT* to be *sum*.
- With the resulting aggregate table, re-order the observations by *sum*, and select the first 20 observations to get a dataset of the top cities.
- Visualize as a bar chart, one bar for each city, bar heights set to *sum*, laid out in order of *sum*.

See that Los Angeles and San Francisco are where most of the money is coming from. Of course, these cities have large populations, but look at Beverly Hills, Santa Monica, Pacific Palisades, West Hollywood, Pasedena, and Encino. These cities with modest-sized populations are all adjacent to Los Angeles. Similarly, Oakland, Palo Alto, Berkeley, San Jose, Menlo Park, Atherton, Mill Valley, Hillsborough, and Los Altos are all located in the San Francisco Bay Area. Perhaps our fundraising strategy should focus on these cities.

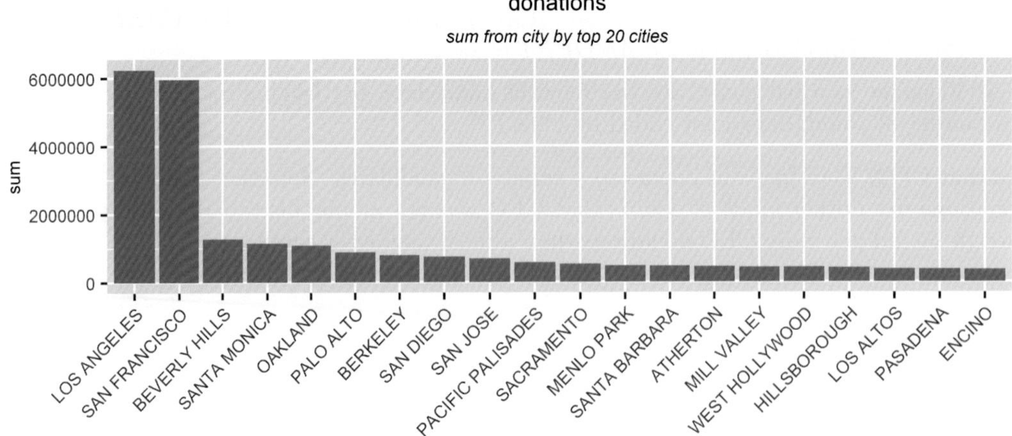

Try viewing cities through a party lens, like this:

- With **data**, select the observations where *PARTY* is the party.
- With the resulting dataset, aggregate *AMOUNT* by sum, grouped by *CITY*. For clarity, rename *AMOUNT* to be *sum*.
- With the resulting aggregate table, re-order the observations by *sum*, and select the first 20 observations to get a dataset of the top cities.
- Visualize as a bar chart, one bar for each city, bar heights set to *sum*, laid out in order of *sum*.

Los Angeles and San Francisco are still the richest sources of donations to both Democratic and Republican candidates. However, other cities favor one party over the other. Santa Monica, Oakland, and others are good cities for Democratic candidates, while Huntington Beach, Irvine, and others are good cities for Republican candidates. Note the different vertical axis scales used in these graphics.

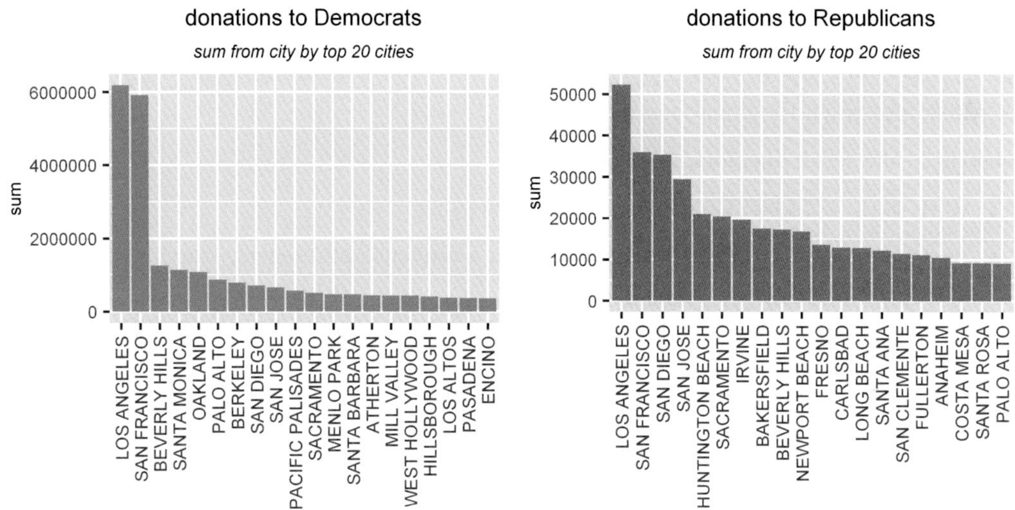

Try viewing specific cities through a candidate lens, like this:

- With **data**, select the observations where *CITY* is Berkeley.
- Aggregate *AMOUNT* by sum, grouped by *CAND NAME* and *PARTY*. For clarity, rename *AMOUNT* to be *sum*.
- Visualize as a bar chart, one bar for each candidate, bar heights set to *sum*, laid out in order of *sum*, bars color-coded by *PARTY*.

See that professor emerita Warren brought in the most money. The top 4 candidates brought in much more than all other candidates combined.

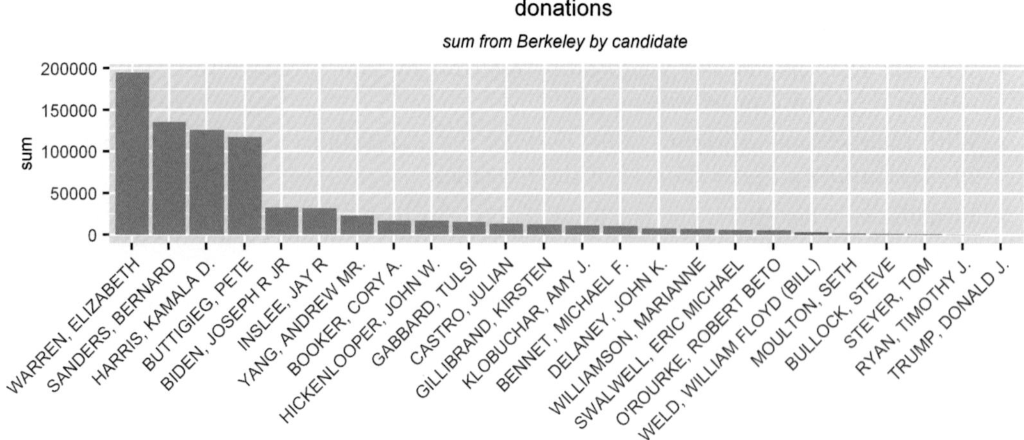

3.6.6 Timing

Let's look into when the donations were made.

Construct time series lineplots, like this:

- With **data**, re-order the observations by *DATE*.
- Add a synthetic variable *cumcount*. Assign a sequence of integers, starting at value 1, to *cumcount*.
- Add a synthetic variable *cumsum*. Apply the cumulative sum function to *AMOUNT*, and assign the resulting vector to *cumsum*.
- For cumulative count, visualize as a lineplot, with *DATE* on the horizontal axis, and *cumcount* on the vertical axis.
- For cumulative sum, visualize as a lineplot, with *DATE* on the horizontal axis, and *cumsum* on the vertical axis.

See that the pace of donations increased over time, but total money increased relatively linearly. As campaigns proceeded, ever more people made donations, but on average the donations tended to get smaller.

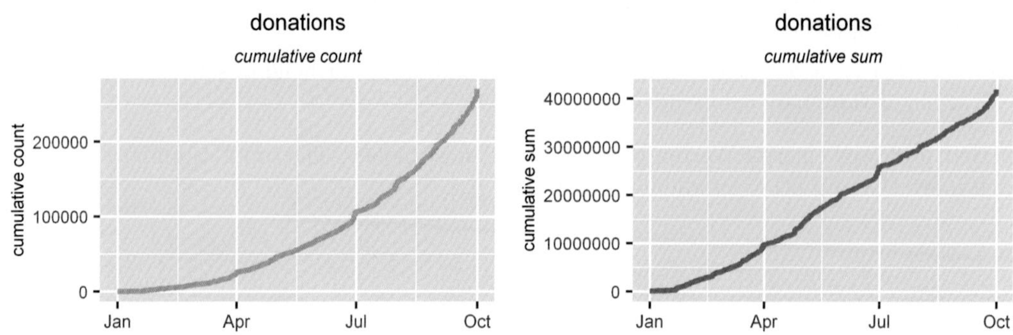

Take a closer look at timing, with lineplots similarly constructed for the top 4 candidates. See that Sanders's and Buttigieg's rate of donations accelerated as their campaigns proceeded, while Harris's and Biden's stayed relatively steady throughout. Should our fundraising strategy count on the rate of donations accelerating or staying steady?

Regarding total money received, Harris experienced big jumps around March and June, just before she pulled out of the race. Biden started late in May with a big jump, followed by modest growth, and another big jump in September. Buttigieg started slow, but then took off around April. Should our fundraising strategy try for an early, slow start; a late, fast start; bursts of progress; regular progress; or something else?

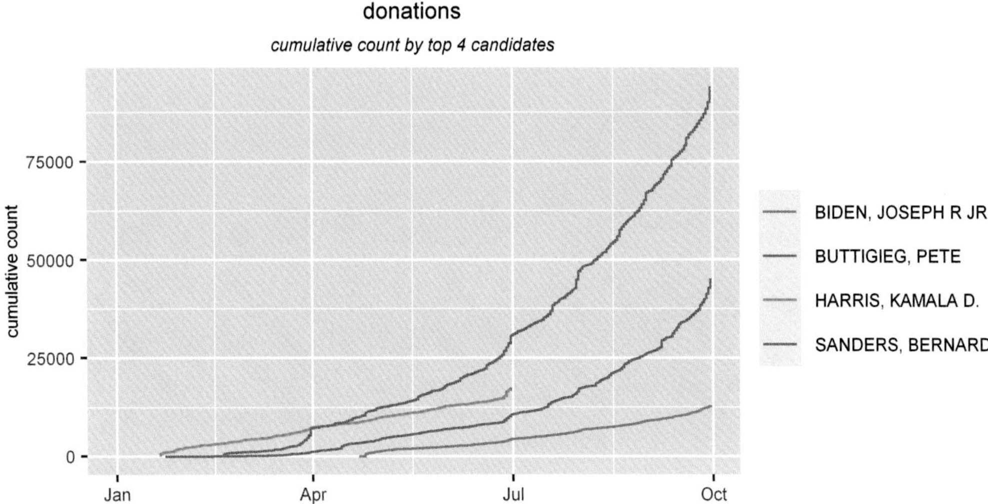

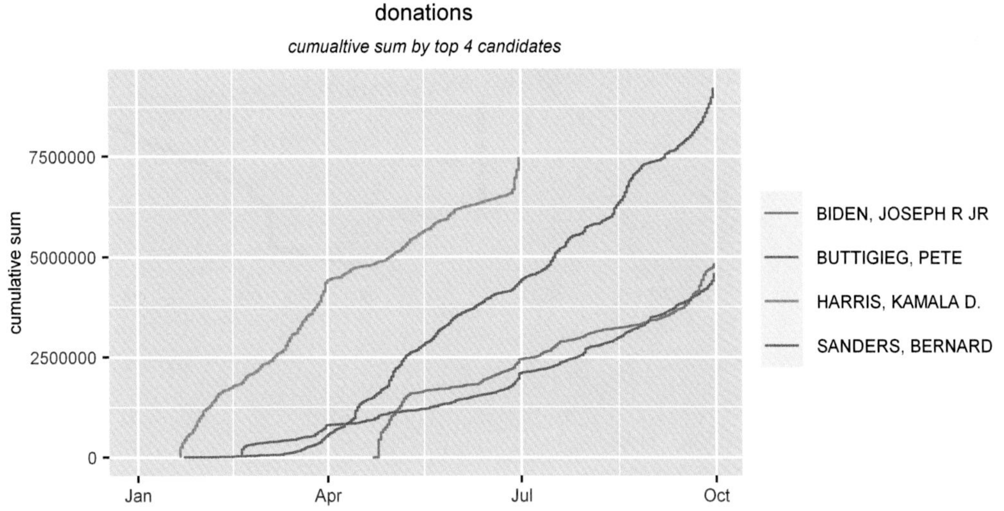

3.6.7 Comparative Analysis

As a check on our analysis, it's useful to compare what happened in California with what happened in another state, say in Texas, to get a feel for how unusual or typical California is. Here are some performance and timing summaries for Texas. What do the states have in common? How are they different from each other?

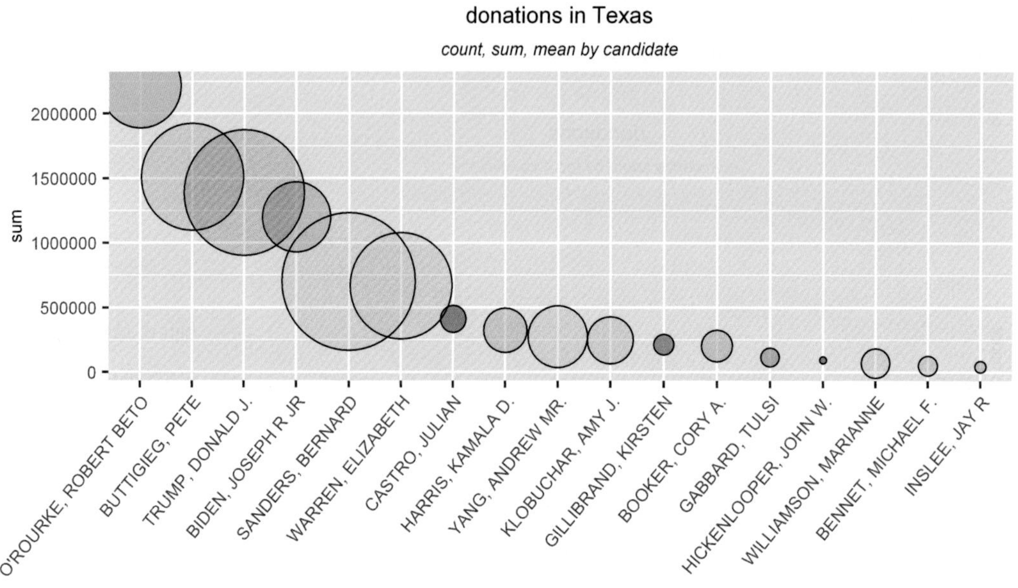

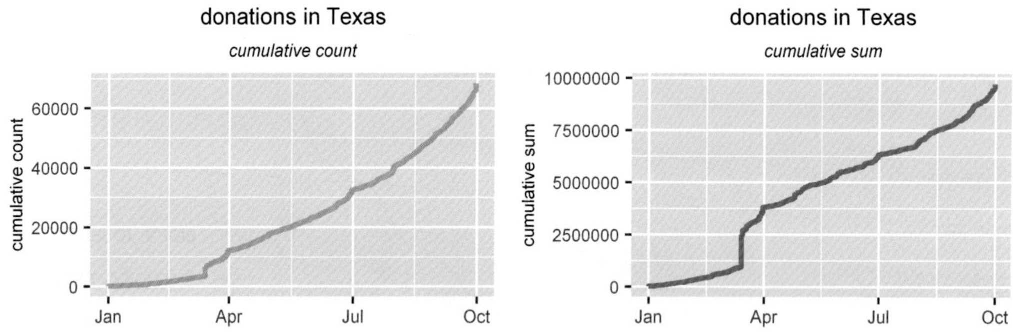

3.7 CASE | Iowa Liquor Sales

Data exploration with descriptive statistics, data visualization, and kernel density estimation to discover historical sales patterns that could influence future product management strategies in the beverage industry.

3.7.1 Business Situation

A product manager for a beverage wholesale company is looking over the Iowa retail liquor market and thinking about pricing his products next year. Customers purchase liquor from retail distributors in transactions of various amounts. If he bundles and prices his products consistent with transaction amounts that customers expect, the product manager reasons, then customers will feel more comfortable purchasing his products than a competitor's.

- **Role:** Product manager for a beverage wholesale company, especially interested in the Iowa retail liquor market.
- **Business Decision:** How to bundle and price products next year?
- **Approach:** Use kernel density estimation to model the underlying processes for Iowa retail liquor sales in 2013, 2014, 2015, and 2016, and inform decisions with insights about customers' expectations.

3.7.2 Data

Retrieve datasets of all retail liquor transactions in Iowa in 2013, 2014, 2015, and 2016. Each transaction is described by 7 variables. The *sales.dollars* variable indicates sale amount.

data.2013.all *size 2063763×7, first few observations shown*

store_ID	store_name	sale.dollars	volume.gallons	year	month	day
4,794	Smokin' Joe's #17 Tobacco and Liquor	130.00	0.79	2,013	2	20
3,908	County Market #214 / Fort Madison	135.00	3.17	2,013	7	8
3,929	Liquor And Tobacco Outlet	51.00	0.21	2,013	5	21
2,551	Hy-Vee Food Store / Chariton	98.82	1.19	2,013	11	26

data.2014.all *size 2097796×7, first few observations shown*

store_ID	store_name	sale.dollars	volume.gallons	year	month	day
2,614	Hy-Vee #3 Food and Drugstore	78.00	0.79	2,014	2	26
2,603	Hy-Vee Wine and Spirits / Bettendorf	98.94	2.77	2,014	4	7
4,819	Super Stop 2 / Altoona	62.28	2.77	2,014	6	12
2,515	Hy-Vee Food Store #1 / Mason City	66.22	0.40	2,014	5	23

data.2015.all *size 2184483×7, first few observations shown*

store_ID	store_name	sale.dollars	volume.gallons	year	month	day
2,191	Keokuk Spirits	162.8	1.19	2,015	11	20
2,205	Ding's Honk And Holler	325.7	2.38	2,015	11	21
3,549	Quicker Liquor Store	19.2	0.08	2,015	11	16
2,513	Hy-Vee Food Store #2 / Iowa City	160.0	1.39	2,015	11	4

data.2016.all *size 2279879×7, first few observations shown*

store_ID	store_name	sale.dollars	volume.gallons	year	month	day
3,621	Jensen Liquors, Ltd.	32.25	0.20	2,016	1	26
2,552	Hy-Vee Food Store #3 / Cedar Rapids	58.74	0.40	2,016	1	12
2,513	Hy-Vee Food Store #2 / Iowa City	352.44	2.38	2,016	1	13
3,869	Bootleggin' Barzini's Fin	88.11	0.59	2,016	1	13

Here are the sales by year visualized as distinct histograms. They're mostly empty because the interesting details are obscured by the scales, though we can see that most sales are relatively small and at least a few are very large.

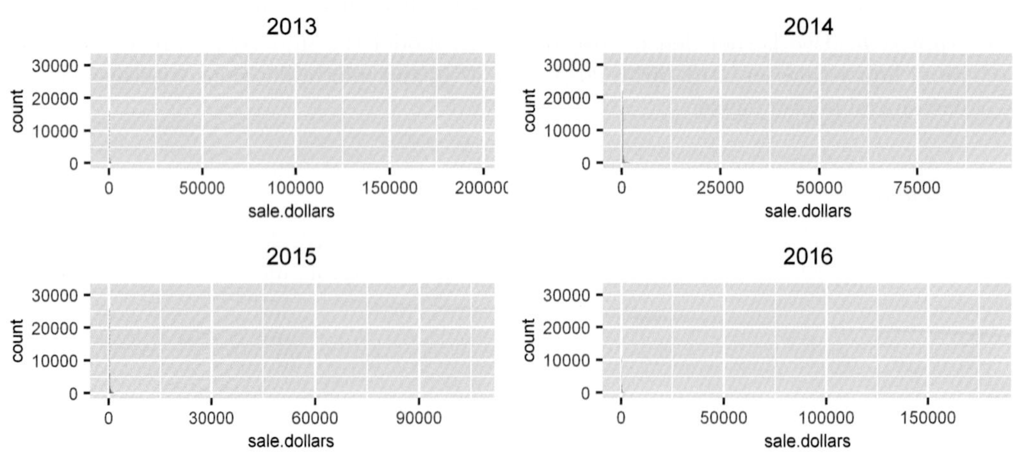

Here are the smallest and largest sales by year. See that each year the largest sale was made at one specific store. See also that such large sales were not typical. Only 2.25% of sales were over $500.

some descriptive statistics

year	min_sale	max_sale	number_over_500	fraction_over_500
2013	0.00	196,005	48,505	0.0235
2014	1.46	94,591	52,498	0.0250
2015	1.34	106,326	56,214	0.0257
2016	0.00	181,962	37,209	0.0163
all 4 years	0.00	196,005	194,426	0.0225

largest sales

store_ID	store_name	sale.dollars	volume.gallons	year	month	day
2,633	Hy-Vee #3 / BDI / Des Moines	196,005	2,939	2,013	6	24
2,633	Hy-Vee #3 / BDI / Des Moines	94,591	913	2,014	6	27
2,633	Hy-Vee #3 / BDI / Des Moines	106,326	1,046	2,015	3	9
2,633	Hy-Vee #3 / BDI / Des Moines	181,962	1,744	2,016	4	25

We'll treat the few atypical large sales as not relevant to our business decision, and restrict our analysis to the transactions with sales under $500.

size of data.2013

observations	variables
2,015,258	7

size of data.2014

observations	variables
2,045,298	7

size of data.2015

observations	variables
2,128,269	7

size of data.2013

observations	variables
2,242,670	7

Here are the sales under $500 by year visualized as distinct histograms, and also visualized overlaid in 1 histogram.

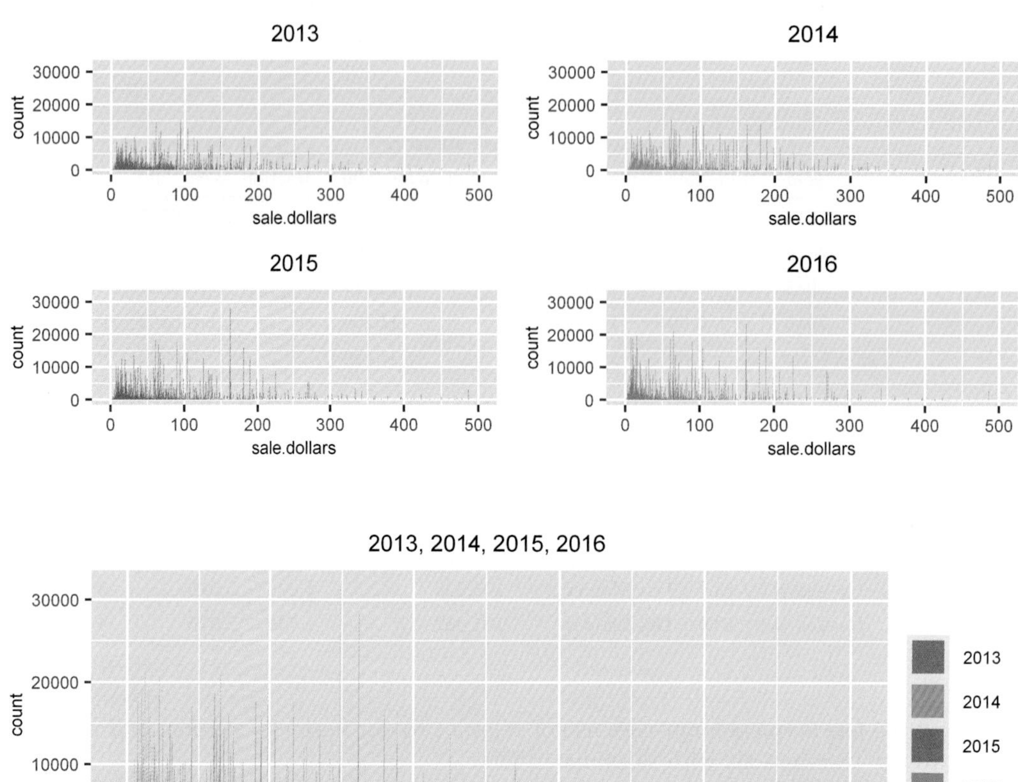

3.7.3 High-Level Trend Analysis

Let's explore the sales trends. Here are lineplots of transaction count and total sales by year. See that customers made increasingly more transactions each successive year. The relative count increase in 2016 was about the same as in 2015, which in turn was a bit more than in 2014. However, something striking happened in 2016 regarding total sales. Even though more transactions were made in 2016 than in 2015, total sales went down in 2016.

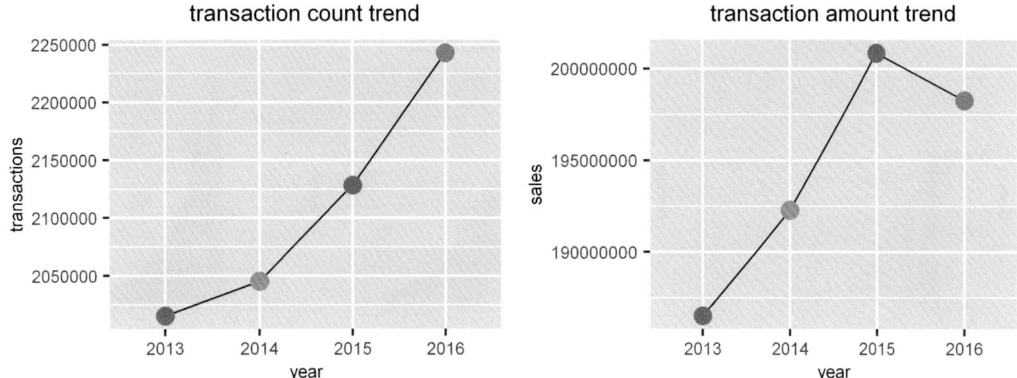

3.7.4 Low-Level Trend Analysis

Our product manager should be concerned about the anomalous dip in total sales. Larger transaction count and lower total sales indicate that customer behavior changed, with customers abruptly making smaller sales on average. That's enough insight to inform how to bundle and price products, but a deeper understanding might prove even more useful. We can get a deeper understanding with a model of the underlying processes that generate the transactions.

Model the underlying processes for each year's sales with probability density functions, using kernel density estimation with Gaussian kernel. It might not be clear at first which bandwidth will be most useful, so try several. Here are results for bandwidths 0.01, 100, and 10. Each function represents a guess about an underlying process. The functions based on bandwidth 0.01 are spiky. The functions based on bandwidth 100 are flat. The functions based on bandwidth 10 are in between.

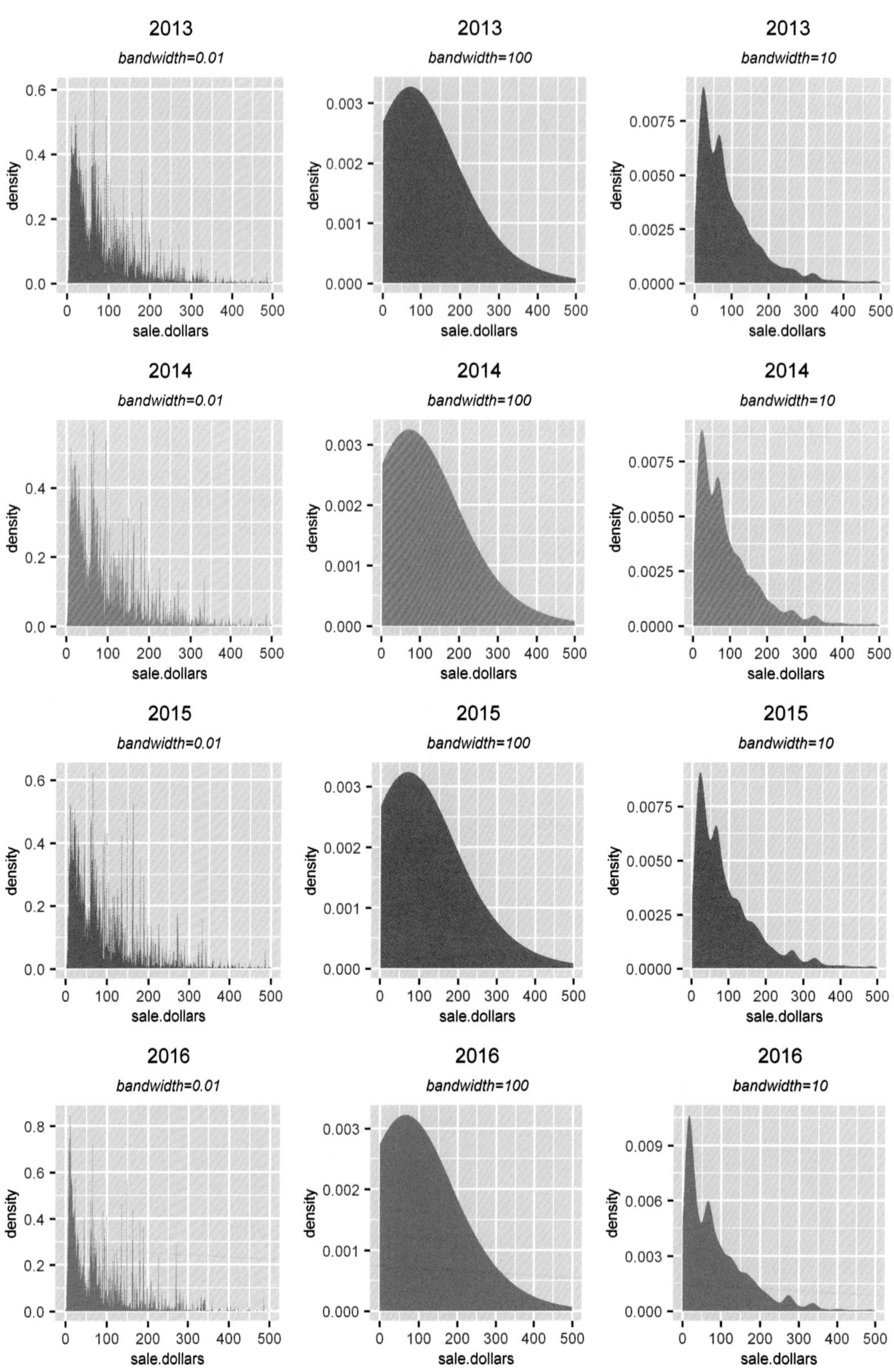
2013
bandwidth=0.01
2013
bandwidth=100
2013
bandwidth=10
2014
bandwidth=0.01
2014
bandwidth=100
2014
bandwidth=10
2015
bandwidth=0.01
2015
bandwidth=100
2015
bandwidth=10
2016
bandwidth=0.01
2016
bandwidth=100
2016
bandwidth=10
density
sale.dollars

Here are the year-to-year differences in sales visualized by overlaying probability density functions, assuming a guess about the underlying processes based on bandwidth 0.01. It's so spiky that the differences are not very clear.

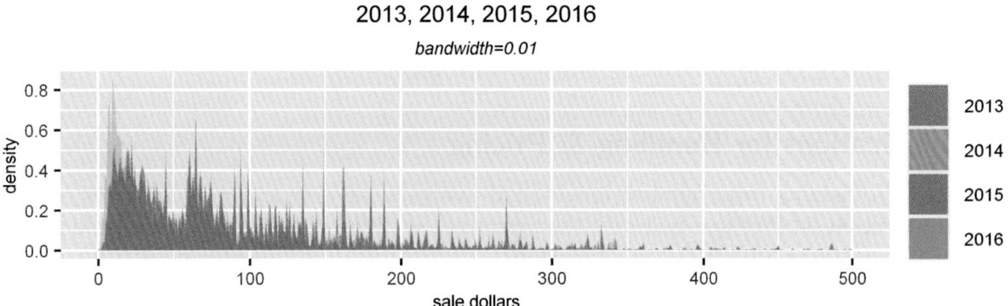

Here are sales visualized assuming a guess based on bandwidth 100. See that 2013, 2014, and 2015 densities at all amounts coincide almost exactly. Customer behavior appears to have been consistent in these years. By contrast, sales in 2016 under about $50 are slightly more probable than in previous years, as indicated by the small blue area between the 2016 function and the other years' functions. Further, sales over about $50 are slightly less probable, with roughly equal difference in probability at any amount, as indicated by the small purple/green/red area above the 2016 function.

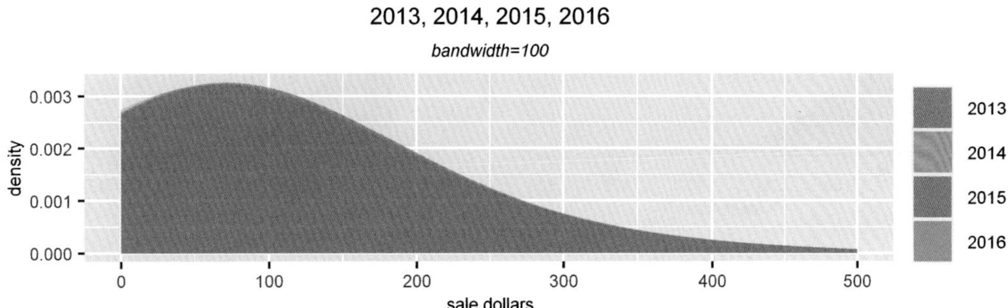

Here are sales assuming a guess based on bandwidth 10. See clearly that in 2016, sales under about $20 are much more probable, sales $20 to $70 are much less probable, and sales $70 and $150 are slightly less probable. Further, sales $275 to $300, and $325 to $350, are more probable.

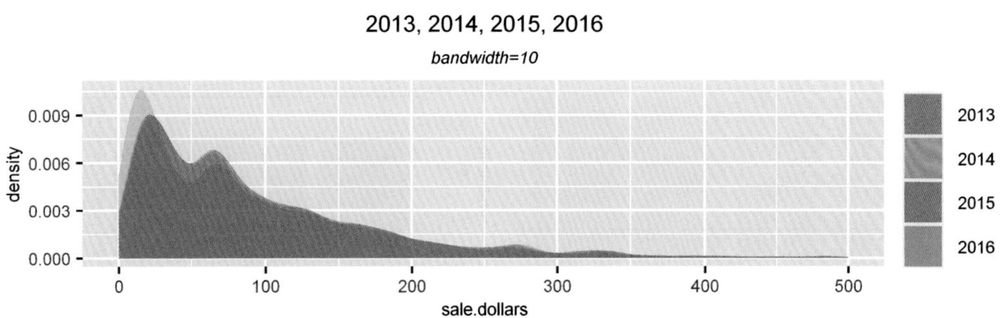

The underlying processes guessed by bandwidth 100 confirm that customers, on average, undertook smaller sales in 2016. The underlying processes guessed by bandwidth 10 provide us a more nuanced understanding: customers started making more of the smallest sales, but also started making more of the larger sales. Perhaps the market started to bifurcate for some reason, with some customers in the middle downgrading to the cheap stuff, and others moving up to the more expensive stuff. It is still not clear why this happened, but it is more clear now what actually did happen.

3.7.5 Implications for Bundling & Pricing

Equipped with insights from our low-level trend analysis, we now know which sales ranges to focus our attention on. We can quantify the year-to-year differences in sales over various ranges by integrating the probability density functions.

Transactions \$0 to \$20 accounted for about 13% of all transactions in 2013, 2014, and 2015, but accounted for 18.09% of them in 2016. Perhaps we should decrease prices of our low-end products to be consistent with customers' expectations. Perhaps we should produce new product bundles with lower prices. Perhaps 2016 is just a one-time anomaly and shouldn't affect our bundling and pricing. Perhaps the market changes every fourth year due to Iowa presidential primaries, Olympic Games broadcasts, or some other reason, and our bundling and pricing should reflect that.

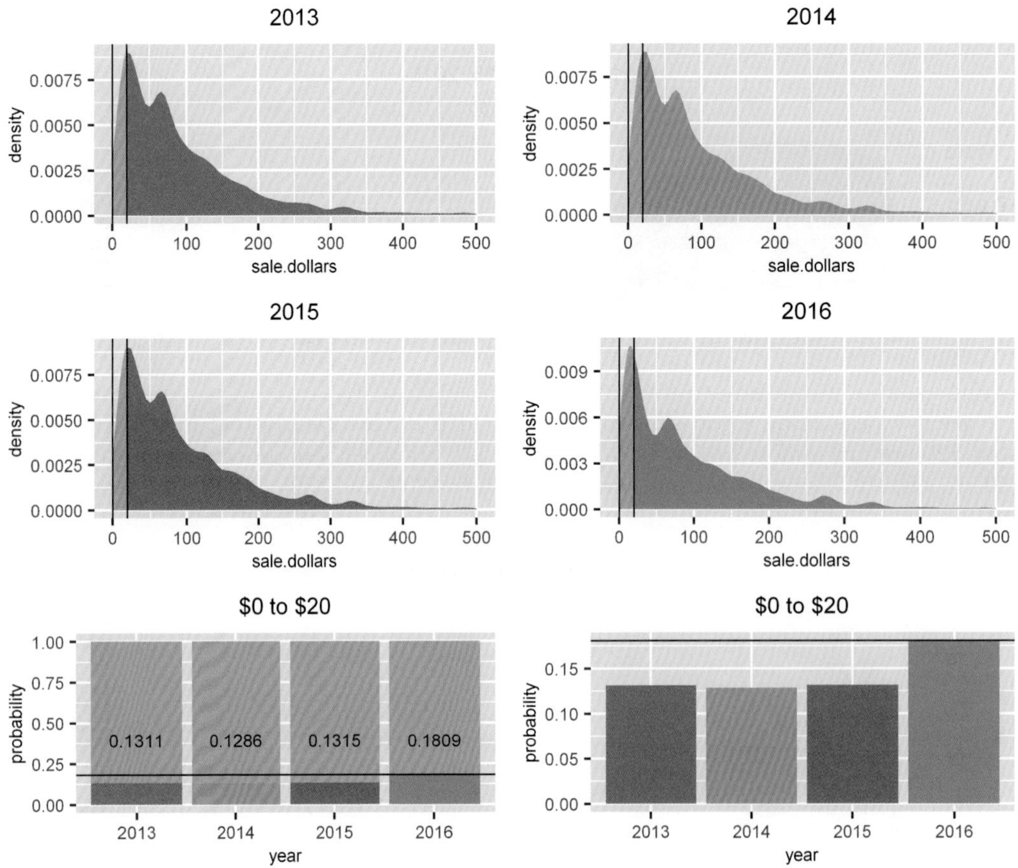

Transactions \$275 to \$300 steadily increased from 1.02% of all transactions in 2013 to 1.47% of them in 2016, going up about 15% per year. Perhaps we should increase the price of our high-end products by 15%.

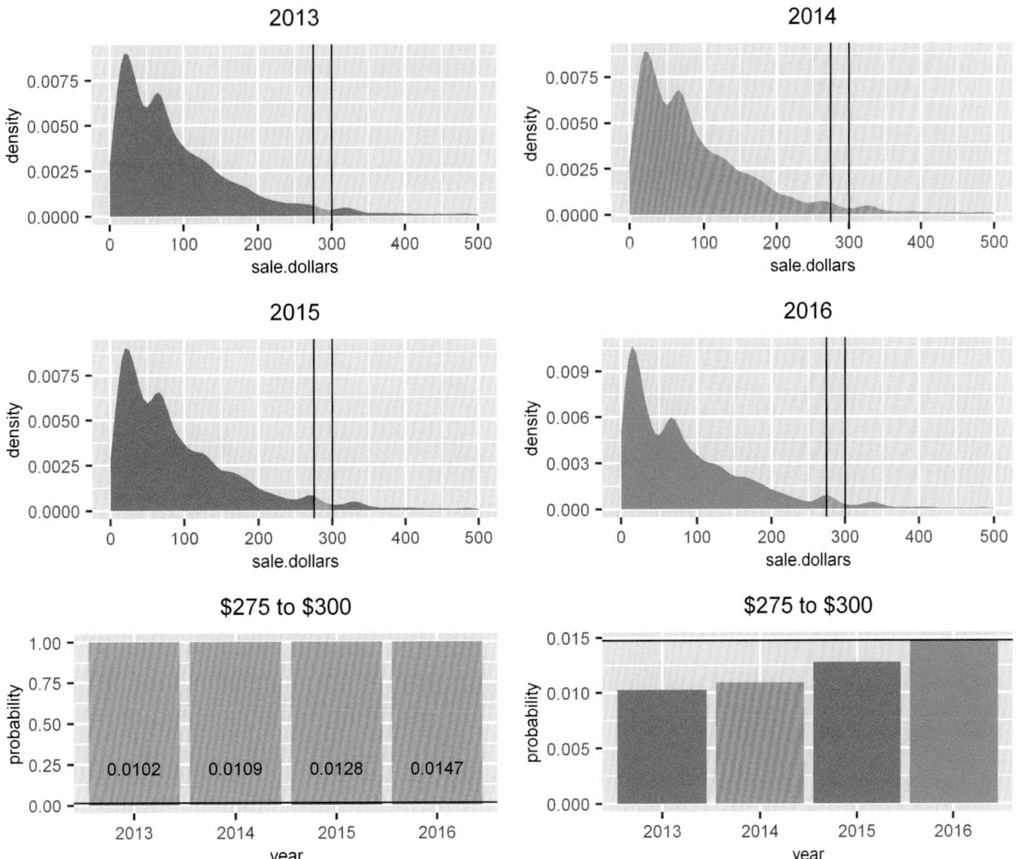

4 | Data Transformation

Learning Objectives

Terms

Know the terms:

- Balanced dataset
- Unbalanced dataset
- Majority class
- Minority class
- Downsample
- Bootstrap
- Trimming
- Imputation
- Linear interpolation
- Alignment
- Coarse resolution
- Fine resolution
- Contraction
- Expansion
- Principal component analysis
- Principal components
- Scree chart

Effects of Assumptions

Know the effects of assumptions:

- Effect of balance by downsample on the information contained in a transformed dataset
- Effect of balance by bootstrap on the information contained in a transformed dataset
- Effect of the choice of trimming method on a transformed dataset
- Effect of the choice of imputation method on a transformed dataset
- Effect of normalizing a dataset prior to transforming it to principal component representation

Use the Methods

Know how to use the methods:

- Compute a balanced dataset using balance by downsample.
- Compute a balanced dataset using balance by bootstrap.
- Compute a balanced dataset using balance by downsample and bootstrap.
- Compute a dataset without any missing values using any of various trimming or imputation methods.
- Compute an aligned dataset by contraction.
- Compute an aligned dataset by expansion.
- Compute scree information and visualize data statistics as a scree chart.
- Compute the centroid and weight matrix needed to transform a dataset to principal component representation.
- Transform a dataset to principal component representation.
- Transform a new observation to principal component representation, based on a previously computed centroid and weight matrix.

4.1 Balance

Transform a dataset into a similar one with an equal number of observations in each class.

4.1.1 Introduction

A company solicits feedback about its products from its customers. Most customers are pleased with the products, but they don't bother to respond. Few customers are displeased with the products, but of those few, many of them let the company know about it. The information collected is unbalanced, in the sense that there are fewer observations of pleased customers than of displeased customers. The company already knows the proportions of customers that like or don't like its products, but wants to better understand what distinguishes a pleased customer from a displeased customer.

Another company successfully defends its computer systems from a ransomware attack. A forensic analysis of system log files uncovers a few corrupted registry events among millions of appropriate events. The information collected is unbalanced, in the sense that there are fewer observations of corrupted events than of appropriate events. The company already knows the proportions of corrupted events and appropriate events, but wants to better understand what distinguishes them.

Some data analysis and analytical modeling methods don't work well with unbalanced information, but could otherwise be useful to you. Balance addresses this problem.

4.1.2 About Balance

A **balanced dataset** comprises an approximately equal number of observations for every possible class value. An **unbalanced dataset** doesn't. **Balance** transforms a classified, unbalanced dataset into a similar, but balanced dataset.

In the case of an unbalanced dataset with binary class variable, where there are 2 possible class values, we call one class value the majority class and the other the minority class.

- The **majority class** is the class value that the majority of the observations have.
- The **minority class** is the class value that the minority of the observations have.

We say that an observation is in the majority class if its class value is the majority class. We say an observation is in the minority class if its class value is the minority class.

There are several popular balance methods, including these:

- **Balance by downsample:** Discard some observations from the majority class.
- **Balance by bootstrap:** Add some observations by duplicating some observations from the minority class.
- **Balance by downsample and bootstrap:** Discard some observations from the majority class and add some observations by duplicating some observations from the minority class.

Balance causes loss and/or addition of information to the dataset, but that can often facilitate useful data analysis and analytical modeling.

4.1.3 Balance by Downsample

Consider this 8-observation, 3-variable dataset with class variable *class*. See that the dataset is unbalanced: 5 observations are in the majority class A, 3 observations are in the minority class B. Let's transform it into a balanced dataset by downsampling the majority class observations.

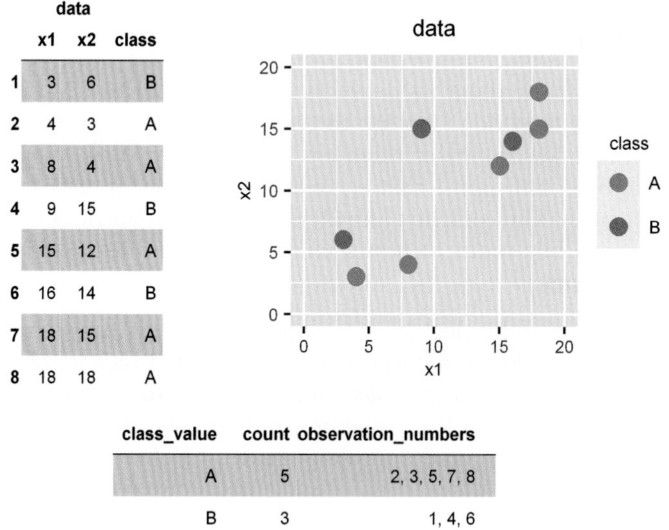
data

	x1	x2	class
1	3	6	B
2	4	3	A
3	8	4	A
4	9	15	B
5	15	12	A
6	16	14	B
7	18	15	A
8	18	18	A

class_value	count	observation_numbers
A	5	2, 3, 5, 7, 8
B	3	1, 4, 6

The minority class B contains 3 observations. Keep these, and add to them a random sample without replacement of 3 observations from majority class A. The transformed dataset comprises 6 observations and the same 3 variables. Some information has been lost from the original dataset.

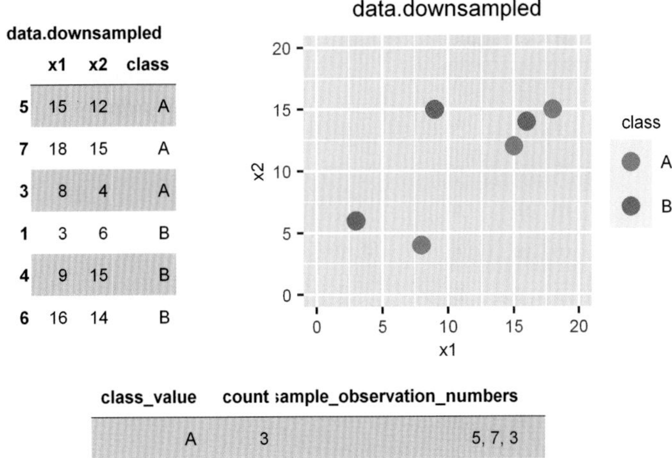

data.downsampled

	x1	x2	class
5	15	12	A
7	18	15	A
3	8	4	A
1	3	6	B
4	9	15	B
6	16	14	B

class_value	count	sample_observation_numbers
A	3	5, 7, 3

4.1.4 Balance by Bootstrap

Consider again the unbalanced 8-observation, 3-variable dataset with class variable *class*. Let's transform it into a balanced dataset by bootstrapping the minority class observations.

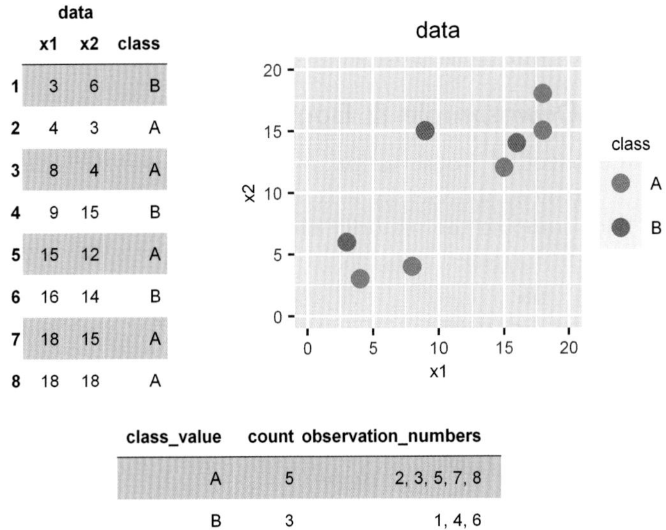

data

	x1	x2	class
1	3	6	B
2	4	3	A
3	8	4	A
4	9	15	B
5	15	12	A
6	16	14	B
7	18	15	A
8	18	18	A

class_value	count	observation_numbers
A	5	2, 3, 5, 7, 8
B	3	1, 4, 6

The majority class A contains 5 observations. Keep these, and add to them a random sample with replacement of 5 observations from minority class B. The transformed dataset comprises 10 observations and the same 3 variables. Some information has been added to the original dataset.

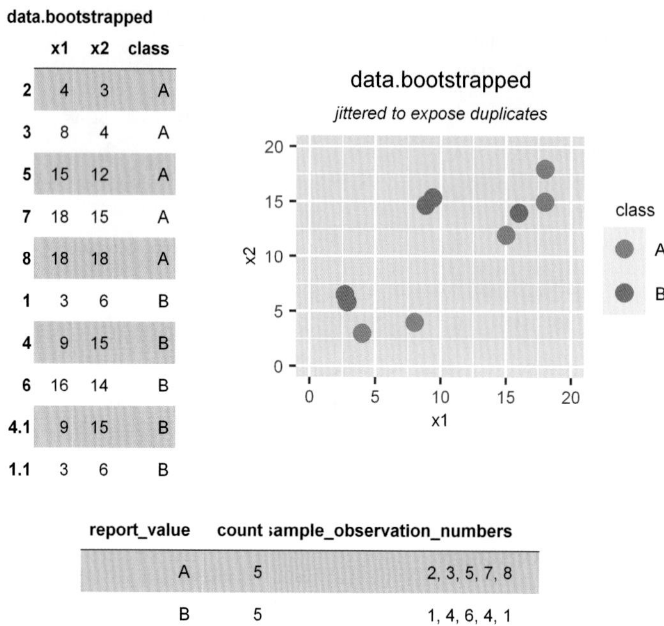

data.bootstrapped

	x1	x2	class
2	4	3	A
3	8	4	A
5	15	12	A
7	18	15	A
8	18	18	A
1	3	6	B
4	9	15	B
6	16	14	B
4.1	9	15	B
1.1	3	6	B

report_value	count	sample_observation_numbers
A	5	2, 3, 5, 7, 8
B	5	1, 4, 6, 4, 1

4.1.5 Balance by Downsample & Bootstrap

Consider again the unbalanced 8-observation, 3-variable dataset with class variable *class*. Let's transform it into a balanced dataset by a combination of downsampling the majority class observations and bootstrapping the minority class observations.

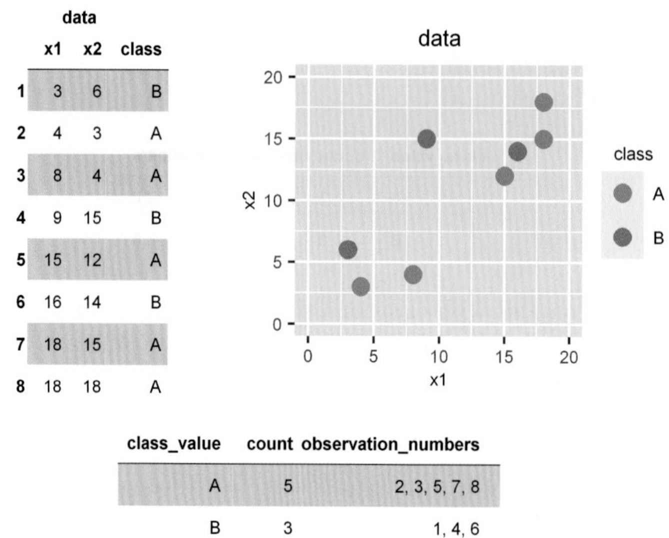

data

	x1	x2	class
1	3	6	B
2	4	3	A
3	8	4	A
4	9	15	B
5	15	12	A
6	16	14	B
7	18	15	A
8	18	18	A

class_value	count	observation_numbers
A	5	2, 3, 5, 7, 8
B	3	1, 4, 6

The majority class A contains 5 observations. The minority class B contains 3 observations.

Choose some number of observations in between, say 4. Take a random sample without replacement of 4 observations from majority class A. Add to these a random sample with replacement of 4 observations from minority class B. The transformed dataset comprises 8 observations and the same 3 variables. Some information has been lost from the original dataset and some information has been added to the original dataset.

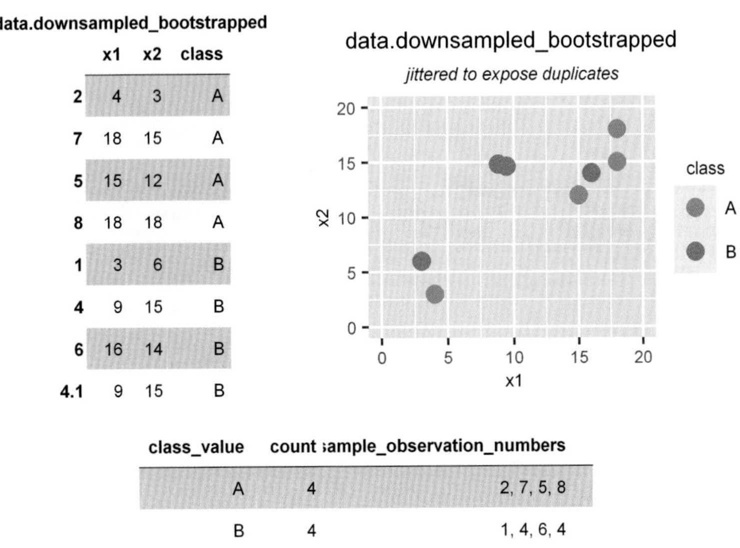

data.downsampled_bootstrapped

	x1	x2	class
2	4	3	A
7	18	15	A
5	15	12	A
8	18	18	A
1	3	6	B
4	9	15	B
6	16	14	B
4.1	9	15	B

class_value	count	sample_observation_numbers
A	4	2, 7, 5, 8
B	4	1, 4, 6, 4

4.2 Imputation

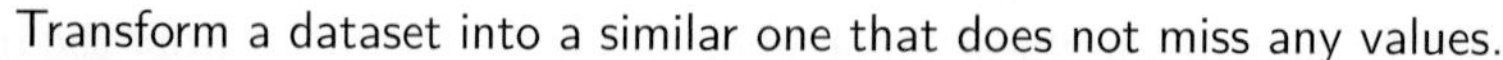
Transform a dataset into a similar one that does not miss any values.

4.2.1 Introduction

A government agency has a report due soon on the effectiveness of a recently implemented public health policy. With limited budget, limited time, and unreliable data collection resources, the staff within the agency complains that the report will have to be based on incomplete information. That's unfortunate, but the report is still due, so based on incomplete information it will have to be. How often in business do you have to work with incomplete information? Some would say very nearly always.

Some data analysis and analytical modeling methods don't work well with missing information, but could otherwise be useful to you. Trimming and imputation address this problem.

4.2.2 About Imputation

Trimming transforms a dataset with missing values into a dataset without any missing values. It does so by simply discarding incomplete or unusable parts of the dataset. **Imputation** also transforms a dataset with missing values into a similar dataset without any missing values. It does so by replacing missing values with new synthesized values.

There are several popular trimming and imputation methods, including these:

- **Remove observations with missing values**
- **Remove variables with missing values**
- **Impute by variable mean:** Within a variable, replace missing values with the variable mean.
- **Impute by neighbor mean:** Within a variable, replace missing values with the mean of the nearest non-missing values.

- **Impute by linear interpolation:** Within a variable, replace missing values with the linear interpolation of the nearest non-missing values.

Neighbor mean and linear interpolation are applicable only for time series datasets, where the notion of nearest values makes sense.

Trimming causes loss of information from the dataset, and imputation causes addition of information to the dataset, but that can often facilitate useful data analysis and analytic modeling.

4.2.3 Data

Consider this 6-observation, 3-variable dataset with missing values. Let's explore addressing the missing values in various ways.

data

	date	x1	x2
1	2017-12-30	2.5	9.0
2	2017-12-31	2.0	NA
3	2018-01-01	9.0	NA
4	2018-01-02	6.5	14.0
5	2018-01-03	8.0	2.5
6	2018-01-04	4.0	8.5

4.2.4 Remove Observations with Missing Values

Remove observations with missing values. Observations 2 and 3 are missing x_2 values, so discard those observations. This effectively produces a new 4-observation, 3-variable dataset.

data.remove_observations

	date	x1	x2
1	2017-12-30	2.5	9.0
4	2018-01-02	6.5	14.0
5	2018-01-03	8.0	2.5
6	2018-01-04	4.0	8.5

4.2.5 Remove Variables with Missing Values

Remove variables with missing values. Variable x_2 is missing the second and third values, so discard this variable. This effectively produces a new 6-observation, 2-variable dataset.

data.remove_variables

	date	x1
1	2017-12-30	2.5
2	2017-12-31	2.0
3	2018-01-01	9.0
4	2018-01-02	6.5
5	2018-01-03	8.0
6	2018-01-04	4.0

4.2.6 Impute by Variable Mean

Within a variable, replace missing values with the variable mean. The mean of the x_2 variable's non-missing values is 8.5, so replace the missing values with 8.5.

imputed_value
8.5

data.impute_by_variable_mean

	date	x1	x2
1	2017-12-30	2.5	9.0
2	2017-12-31	2.0	**8.5**
3	2018-01-01	9.0	**8.5**
4	2018-01-02	6.5	14.0
5	2018-01-03	8.0	2.5
6	2018-01-04	4.0	8.5

4.2.7 Impute by Neighbor Mean

Within a variable, replace missing values with the mean of the nearest non-missing values. If the dataset is treated as time series, in the sense that observation order is meaningful, then x_2's first value 9 and fourth value 14 are nearest the missing values. The mean of 9 and 14 is 11.5, so replace missing values with 11.5.

imputed_value
11.5

data.impute_by_neighbor_mean

	date	x1	x2
1	2017-12-30	2.5	9.0
2	2017-12-31	2.0	**11.5**
3	2018-01-01	9.0	**11.5**
4	2018-01-02	6.5	14.0
5	2018-01-03	8.0	2.5
6	2018-01-04	4.0	8.5

4.2.8 Impute by Linear Interpolation

Within a variable, replace missing values with the linear interpolation of the nearest non-missing values. If the dataset is treated as a time series, in the sense that observation order is meaningful, then there are 2 missing values between the nearest non-missing values 9 and 14. That makes 3 steps across a gap of $14 - 9 = 5$ to get from 9 to 14. Replace the first missing value with a new value one-third of the way from 9 to 14, which is 10.67. Replace the second missing value with a new value two-thirds of the way from 9 to 14, which is 12.33.

gap	steps	step_size	imputed_value.1	imputed_value.2
5	3	1.667	10.67	12.33

data.impute_by_linear_interpolation

	date	x1	x2
1	2017-12-30	2.5	9.00
2	2017-12-31	2.0	**10.67**
3	2018-01-01	9.0	**12.33**
4	2018-01-02	6.5	14.00
5	2018-01-03	8.0	2.50
6	2018-01-04	4.0	8.50

4.2.9 Compare Imputation Methods

Here is a comparison of the datasets resulting from the various methods, visualized as line plots.

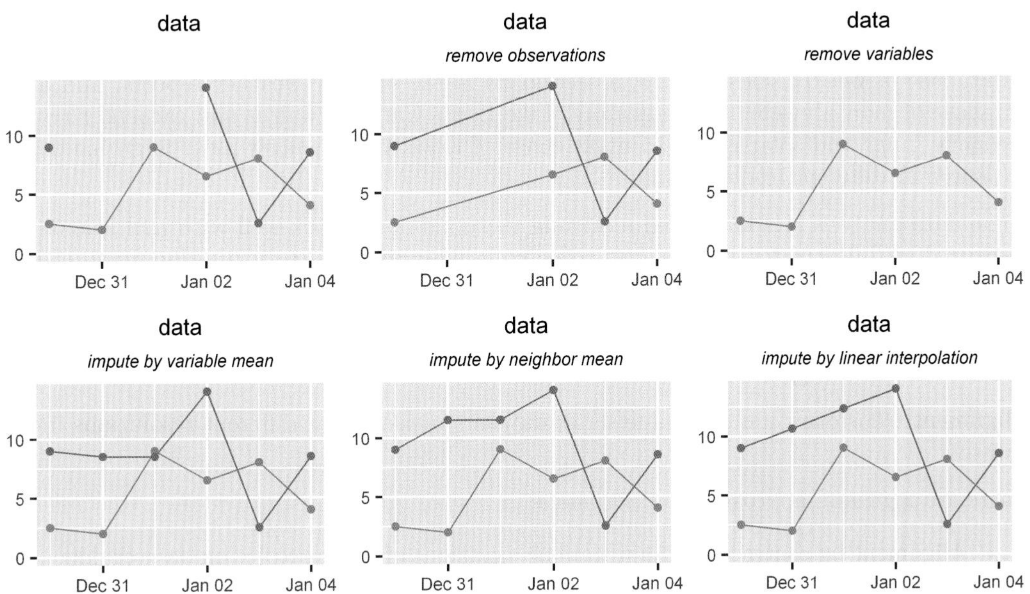

4.3 Alignment

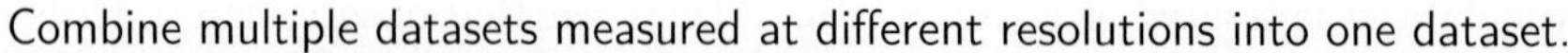

Combine multiple datasets measured at different resolutions into one dataset.

4.3.1 Introduction

A grocery chain sales operations manager is interested in how sales of various foods have increased or decreased along with changes in the economy and the weather. He has access to a database of weekly sales reports, a second database of daily weather reports, and a third database of monthly economic indicators. Like Lewis Carroll's walrus and carpenter trying to reconcile lunar and solar cycles to make sense of tides, the manager must align his datasets measured at different resolutions.

Some data analysis and analytical modeling methods don't work well with multiple datasets measured at different resolutions, but could otherwise be useful to you. Alignment addresses this problem.

4.3.2 About Alignment

Alignment transforms multiple time series datasets measured at different resolutions into one dataset.

There are 2 general approaches to alignment:

- **Alignment by contraction:** Aggregate observations of a fine resolution dataset down to the size of a **coarse resolution** dataset, and then join the datasets.
- **Alignment by expansion:** Duplicate observations of a coarse resolution dataset up to the size of a **fine resolution** dataset, disaggregate the duplicated observations, and then join the datasets.

With alignment by contraction, the choice of aggregation function should make sense for the variable being aggregated. For example, if you're interested in total sales at the end of the year, you could aggregate observations of daily sales by sum. Or if you're interested in mean sales at the end of the year, you could aggregate observations of daily sales by mean.

With alignment by expansion, the choice of disaggregation function should similarly make sense for the variable being disaggregated. For example, if you're interested in total sales at the end of the year, and you have daily costs but only weekly sales, you could disaggregate observations of weekly sales by dividing by the number of days in a week.

Contraction causes loss of information from the datasets, and expansion causes addition of information to the datasets, but that can often facilitate useful data analysis and analytical modeling.

4.3.3 Data

Consider these time series datasets. Variables x_1 and x_2 are not aligned at the same resolution. The x_1 variable is relatively coarse resolution at 1 observation per day. The x_2 variable is relatively fine resolution at 1 observation per half-day. Let's combine them first by contraction, then by expansion.

data.1

date	x1
2017-12-30	1,000
2017-12-31	1,100
2018-01-01	900
2018-01-02	950
2018-01-03	800
2018-01-04	1,050

data.2

date	x2
2017-12-30 00:00:00	72
2017-12-30 12:00:00	56
2017-12-31 00:00:00	86
2017-12-31 12:00:00	60
2018-01-01 00:00:00	76
2018-01-01 12:00:00	63
2018-01-02 00:00:00	80
2018-01-02 12:00:00	68
2018-01-03 00:00:00	82
2018-01-03 12:00:00	59
2018-01-04 00:00:00	74
2018-01-04 12:00:00	61

4.3.4 Alignment by Contraction

Add a synthetic variable *step* to both datasets to mark observations with step numbers. The fine resolution dataset should adopt the coarse resolution dataset's step numbers, repeating as necessary.

data.1 (with steps)

date	x1	step
2017-12-30	1,000	1
2017-12-31	1,100	2
2018-01-01	900	3
2018-01-02	950	4
2018-01-03	800	5
2018-01-04	1,050	6

data.2 (with doublesteps)

date	x2	step
2017-12-30 00:00:00	72	1
2017-12-30 12:00:00	56	1
2017-12-31 00:00:00	86	2
2017-12-31 12:00:00	60	2
2018-01-01 00:00:00	76	3
2018-01-01 12:00:00	63	3
2018-01-02 00:00:00	80	4
2018-01-02 12:00:00	68	4
2018-01-03 00:00:00	82	5
2018-01-03 12:00:00	59	5
2018-01-04 00:00:00	74	6
2018-01-04 12:00:00	61	6

Then aggregate by *step* so that the number of fine resolution observations matches the number of coarse resolution observations, using a function that makes sense for the x_1 and x_2 variable meanings. Here we aggregate by mean.

data.1

date	x1	step
2017-12-30	1,000	1
2017-12-31	1,100	2
2018-01-01	900	3
2018-01-02	950	4
2018-01-03	800	5
2018-01-04	1,050	6

data.2.aggregated

step	x2
1	64.0
2	73.0
3	69.5
4	74.0
5	70.5
6	67.5

Then join the datasets by *step*. Note that this is done using a join operation, not a column-wise concatenation operation. Discard the *step* variable when no longer needed.

data.aligned_by_contraction

date	x1	x2
2017-12-30	1,000	64.0
2017-12-31	1,100	73.0
2018-01-01	900	69.5
2018-01-02	950	74.0
2018-01-03	800	70.5
2018-01-04	1,050	67.5

4.3.5 Alignment by Expansion

Duplicate the coarse resolution observations as necessary so that the number of coarse observations matches the number of fine resolution observations.

data.1.duplicated

date	x1
2017-12-30	1,000
2017-12-30	1,000
2017-12-31	1,100
2017-12-31	1,100
2018-01-01	900
2018-01-01	900
2018-01-02	950
2018-01-02	950
2018-01-03	800
2018-01-03	800
2018-01-04	1,050
2018-01-04	1,050

data.2

date	x2
2017-12-30 00:00:00	72
2017-12-30 12:00:00	56
2017-12-31 00:00:00	86
2017-12-31 12:00:00	60
2018-01-01 00:00:00	76
2018-01-01 12:00:00	63
2018-01-02 00:00:00	80
2018-01-02 12:00:00	68
2018-01-03 00:00:00	82
2018-01-03 12:00:00	59
2018-01-04 00:00:00	74
2018-01-04 12:00:00	61

Add a synthetic variable *step* to both datasets to mark observations with step numbers. The coarse resolution dataset should adopt the fine resolution dataset's step numbers.

data.1.duplicated (with steps)

date	x1	step
2017-12-30	1,000	1
2017-12-30	1,000	2
2017-12-31	1,100	3
2017-12-31	1,100	4
2018-01-01	900	5
2018-01-01	900	6
2018-01-02	950	7
2018-01-02	950	8
2018-01-03	800	9
2018-01-03	800	10
2018-01-04	1,050	11
2018-01-04	1,050	12

data.2 (with steps)

date	x2	step
2017-12-30 00:00:00	72	1
2017-12-30 12:00:00	56	2
2017-12-31 00:00:00	86	3
2017-12-31 12:00:00	60	4
2018-01-01 00:00:00	76	5
2018-01-01 12:00:00	63	6
2018-01-02 00:00:00	80	7
2018-01-02 12:00:00	68	8
2018-01-03 00:00:00	82	9
2018-01-03 12:00:00	59	10
2018-01-04 00:00:00	74	11
2018-01-04 12:00:00	61	12

Then disaggregate the x_1 variable of the coarse dataset, using a function that makes sense for the x_1 variable meaning. Here we disaggregate by dividing by 2.

data.1.disaggregated

date	x1	step
2017-12-30	500	1
2017-12-30	500	2
2017-12-31	550	3
2017-12-31	550	4
2018-01-01	450	5
2018-01-01	450	6
2018-01-02	475	7
2018-01-02	475	8
2018-01-03	400	9
2018-01-03	400	10
2018-01-04	525	11
2018-01-04	525	12

data.2 (with steps)

date	x2	step
2017-12-30 00:00:00	72	1
2017-12-30 12:00:00	56	2
2017-12-31 00:00:00	86	3
2017-12-31 12:00:00	60	4
2018-01-01 00:00:00	76	5
2018-01-01 12:00:00	63	6
2018-01-02 00:00:00	80	7
2018-01-02 12:00:00	68	8
2018-01-03 00:00:00	82	9
2018-01-03 12:00:00	59	10
2018-01-04 00:00:00	74	11
2018-01-04 12:00:00	61	12

Then join the datasets by *step*. Note that this is done using a join operation, not a column-wise concatenation operation. Discard the *step* variable when no longer needed.

data.aligned_by_expansion

date	x1	x2
2017-12-30 00:00:00	500	72
2017-12-30 12:00:00	500	56
2017-12-31 00:00:00	550	86
2017-12-31 12:00:00	550	60
2018-01-01 00:00:00	450	76
2018-01-01 12:00:00	450	63
2018-01-02 00:00:00	475	80
2018-01-02 12:00:00	475	68
2018-01-03 00:00:00	400	82
2018-01-03 12:00:00	400	59
2018-01-04 00:00:00	525	74
2018-01-04 12:00:00	525	61

4.4 Principal Component Analysis

Transform a dataset into a similar one that concentrates variance into just a few variables.

4.4.1 Introduction

In 246 BCE, Chinese emperor Qin Shi Huang began constructing a massive mausoleum that would ultimately house more than 8,000 life-size terracotta statues to guard the tomb. Amazingly, each statue depicts a unique soldier with its own distinctive features. Some have long faces, some have round faces. Some are tall, some are short. Some wear mustaches, some wear beards, some wear both or neither. They wear different hair styles. They wear different uniforms. If you had to distinguish the statues from each other based on just a few features, how would you choose the features? You could try the features that vary most among the statues. Or, perhaps better, you could make up some new features, cleverly defined as combinations of the other features, which vary even more among the statues. You can think of principal component analysis as making up new features from combinations of other features, so as to get a few features that vary widely across a dataset.

Restricting data analysis or analytical modeling to just a few high-variation variables from among all variables available is called variable selection, or dimensionality reduction, or feature engineering. There are several reasons that it might be useful to do this:

- Too many variables might obscure insights that would otherwise be obvious from just a few variables.
- Some methods work only on datasets represented by just a few variables.
- Some methods work better on datasets represented by just a few variables.
- Some methods work faster on datasets represented by just a few variables.

Principal component analysis is often a good approach to variable selection. It is considered by many the best way to convert "big data to tiny data".

4.4.2 About Principal Component Analysis

Principal component analysis transforms a dataset represented by a set of variables to a dataset represented by a new set of variables. All of the information and variance contained in the original dataset is still present in the transformed dataset, but most of the variance in the transformed dataset is concentrated in just the first few new variables. So, many of the new variables can be discarded without sacrificing much loss of variance. We'll call the variables in the original dataset the native variables. **Principal components** are the new variables and, equivalently, the axes used to calculate the new variable values.

- Think of principal components as new variables: Each principal component variable's values are weighted sums of all of the native variables' values, possibly shifted by some amount.
- Think of principal components as axes: The principal component axes are an alternative set of orthogonal axes, each going through the centroid of the dataset. The values spread along the first principal component axis have the maximum variance possible as compared with any other orthogonal axis, the values along the second principal component axis have the next most variance, and so on.

Principal component analysis works like this:

Optionally, normalize the dataset.
Calculate the centroid of the dataset.
Calculate the weight matrix for the dataset (use a principal component analysis function).
For each observation ...
   Calculate principal component values
   (use centroid, weight matrix, and observation variable values).

Principal component analysis typically produces more useful results when the dataset is first normalized. This is because the weight matrix will incorporate some information about distance between observations in multivariate space. Unitless variables won't distort the weight matrix.

Calculate the centroid of the dataset as the set of all variable means. In the case of a normalized dataset, trivially calculate the centroid to be the zero origin, since the mean of any normalized variable is zero.

$$c = (x_1{=}mean(x_1),\ x_2{=}mean(x_2),\ \ldots,\ x_m{=}mean(x_m)) \qquad \text{for any dataset}$$

$$c = (x_1{=}0,\ x_2{=}0,\ \ldots,\ x_m{=}0) \qquad \text{for a normalized dataset}$$

where ...

- c is the dataset centroid
- m is the number of variables
- $x_1, x_2, \ldots, x_m$ are the first, second, ..., and m^{th} variables

Calculate the weight matrix for the dataset using a principal component analysis function, which incorporates a search algorithm to find lines of optimal variance in multivariate space. The weight matrix will comprise rows for all native variables and columns for all principal component variables.

Equipped with centroid and weight matrix, apply the principal component formula to each observation to calculate the corresponding principal component representation of the observation.

For an observation represented by 2 native variables, the principal component formula specifies values for 2 corresponding principal component variables.

$$\begin{bmatrix} x_1 \\ x_2 \end{bmatrix} \rightarrow \begin{bmatrix} PC_1 = (w_{x1,PC_1} \times (x_1 - c_{x_1})) + (w_{x2,PC_1} \times (x_2 - c_{x2})) \\ PC_2 = (w_{x1,PC_2} \times (x_1 - c_{x_1})) + (w_{x2,PC_2} \times (x_2 - c_{x2})) \end{bmatrix}$$

where ...

- x_1 is the observation's first variable value
- x_2 is the observation's second variable value
- c_{x_1} is the dataset centroid's first variable value
- c_{x_2} is the dataset centroid's second variable value
- $w_{x_1 PC_1}$ is the weight matrix's value for the first variable and the first principal component
- $w_{x_1 PC_2}$ is the weight matrix's value for the first variable and the second principal component
- $w_{x_2 PC_1}$ is the weight matrix's value for the second variable and the first principal component
- $w_{x_2 PC_2}$ is the weight matrix's value for the second variable and the second principal component
- PC_1 is the observation's first principal component value
- PC_2 is the observation's second principal component value

More generally, an observation represented by any number of native variables can be converted to an observation represented by the same number of principal component variables.

$$\begin{bmatrix} x_1 \\ x_2 \\ \vdots \\ x_m \end{bmatrix} \rightarrow \begin{bmatrix} PC_1 = (w_{x_1,PC_1} \times (x_1 - c_{x_1})) + \cdots + \cdots + (w_{x_m,PC_1} \times (x_m - c_{x_m})) \\ PC_2 = (w_{x_1,PC_2} \times (x_1 - c_{x_1})) + \cdots + \cdots + (w_{x_m,PC_2} \times (x_m - c_{x_m})) \\ \vdots \\ PC_m = (w_{x_1,PC_m} \times (x_1 - c_{x_1})) + \cdots + \cdots + (w_{x_m,PC_m} \times (x_m - c_{x_m})) \end{bmatrix}$$

where ...

- x_i is the observation's i^{th} variable value
- PC_j is the observation's j^{th} principal component value
- m is the number of variables, which is also the number of principal components
- c_{x_i} is the dataset centroid's i^{th} variable value
- $w_{x_i PC_j}$ is the weight matrix's value for the ith variable and the jth principal component

Note that the principal component formula does not generate any new observations. Rather, it merely changes the representation of the existing observations, leveraging information (stored in the centroid and weight matrix) found in all observations. However, in contrast, each principal component variable is a new variable, and does not correspond to any one native variable. Rather, each principal component variable is calculated from information found in ***all*** native variables.

4.4.3 Principal Component Analysis | Two Variables

Consider this 2-variable dataset. Which variable distinguishes observations better?

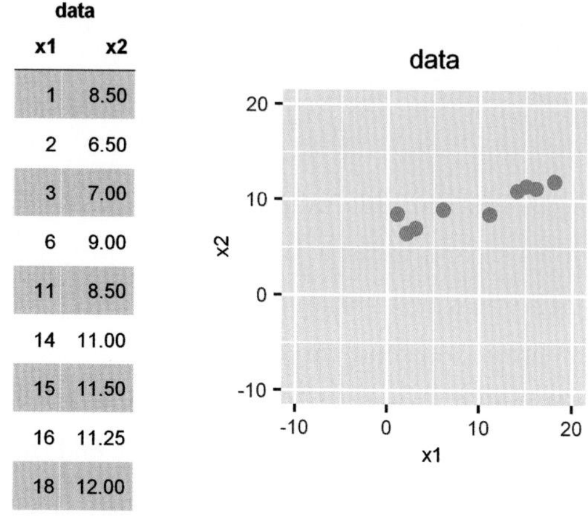

data

x1	x2
1	8.50
2	6.50
3	7.00
6	9.00
11	8.50
14	11.00
15	11.50
16	11.25
18	12.00

4.4.3.1 Variance in Native Representation

There is more variance in the x_1 variable than in the x_2 variable. We can see this clearly in 1-axis scatterplots, which effectively show the projections of observations into 1 dimension at a time. Observations along the x_1-axis are spread out. Observations along the x_2-axis are huddled together.

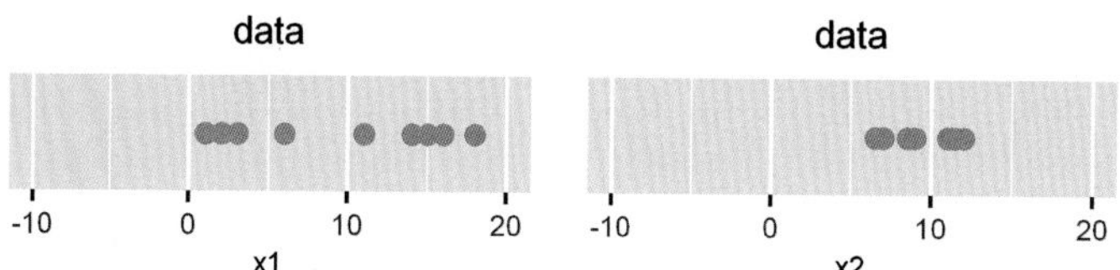

Specifically, variance in the x_1 variable is 43.778, variance in the x_2 variable is 4.132. Total variance in the dataset is $43.778 + 4.132 = 47.91$. Expressed in terms of relative variance, the x_1 variable accounts for $43.778 \div 47.91 = 91.38\%$ of the total variance. The x_2 variable accounts for $4.132 \div 47.91 = 8.62\%$ of the total variance. A bar chart of relative variance across variables is called a **scree chart**.

scree of data

variable	standard_deviation	variance	cum_variance	relative_variance	cum_relative_variance
x1	6.617	43.778	43.78	0.9138	0.9138
x2	2.033	4.132	47.91	0.0862	1.0000

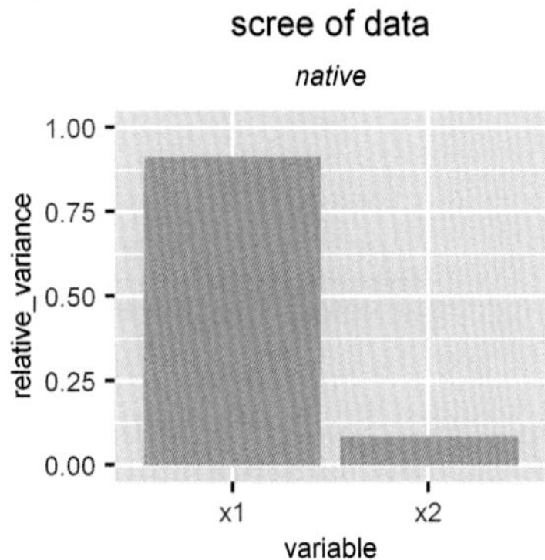

As it stands, the x_1 variable, because it has more variance, distinguishes observations better than the x_2 variable does.

4.4.3.2 Transform to Principal Component Representation

Can we concoct new variables that distinguish observations even better? Let's transform the dataset to principal component representation and look at how that affects variance.

Determine the centroid, shown here as a black dot. Find the line through the maximum variation, shown here in blue. Determine the line through the centroid and orthogonal to the first line, shown here in red. Store information about the lines in a weight matrix. Shift the centroid to the origin (x_1=0, x_2=0) and drag the observations along. Rotate the lines and observations around the origin until the lines align with the x_1- and x_2-axes, using the weight matrix to do so. Rename the axes as PC_1 and PC_2.

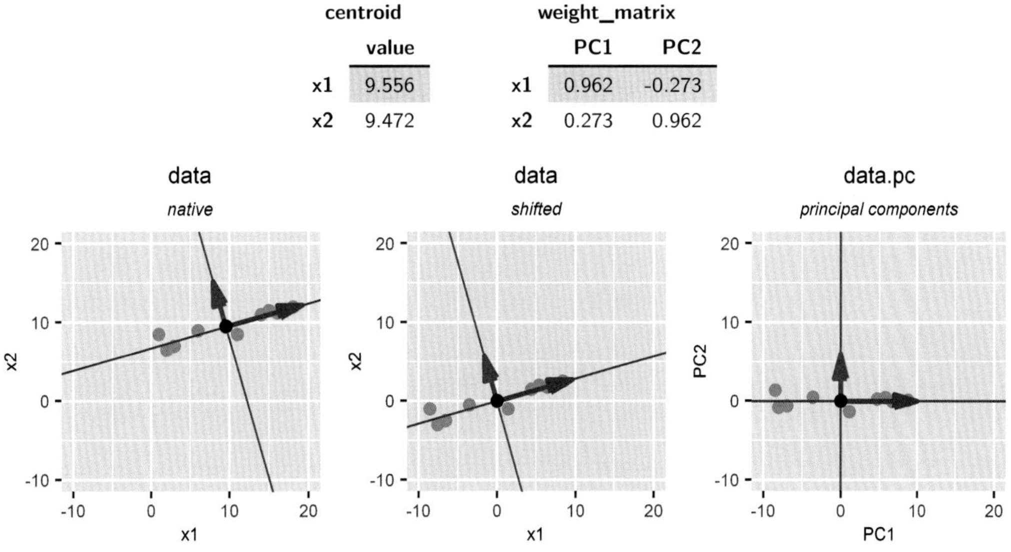

centroid

	value
x1	9.556
x2	9.472

weight_matrix

	PC1	PC2
x1	0.962	-0.273
x2	0.273	0.962

Let's look more closely at how the observations get dragged and rotated. In native representation, the first observation is (x_1=1, x_2=8.5). In principal component representation, the first observation is (PC_1=−8.496, PC_2=1.400), calculated as prescribed by the principal component formula.

$$\begin{bmatrix} x_1 = 1 \\ x_2 = 8.5 \end{bmatrix} \rightarrow \begin{bmatrix} PC_1 = (0.962 \times (1 - 9.556)) + (0.273 \times (8.5 - 9.472)) = -8.496 \\ PC_2 = (-0.273 \times (1 - 9.556)) + (0.962 \times (8.5 - 9.472)) = 1.400 \end{bmatrix}$$

data.pc
first observation shown

PC1	PC2
-8.496	1.4

Note that the first observation's PC_1 and PC_2 values are calculated based on the first observation's x_1 and x_2 values, ***and*** the centroid and weight matrix, which are themselves calculated based on ***all*** observations. Effectively, each one observation's principal component values are calculated based on all observations' variable values.

Similarly, apply the principal component formula to the other observations, too.

data

x1	x2
1	8.50
2	6.50
3	7.00
6	9.00
11	8.50
14	11.00
15	11.50
16	11.25
18	12.00

data.pc

PC1	PC2
-8.496	1.4004
-8.080	-0.7966
-6.981	-0.5886
-3.549	0.5164
1.124	-1.3296
4.693	0.2564
5.791	0.4644
6.685	-0.0491
8.814	0.1264

4.4.3.3 Variance in Principal Component Representation

With the dataset in principal component representation, there is more variance in the PC_1 variable than in the PC_2 variable. Indeed, there is much more variance.

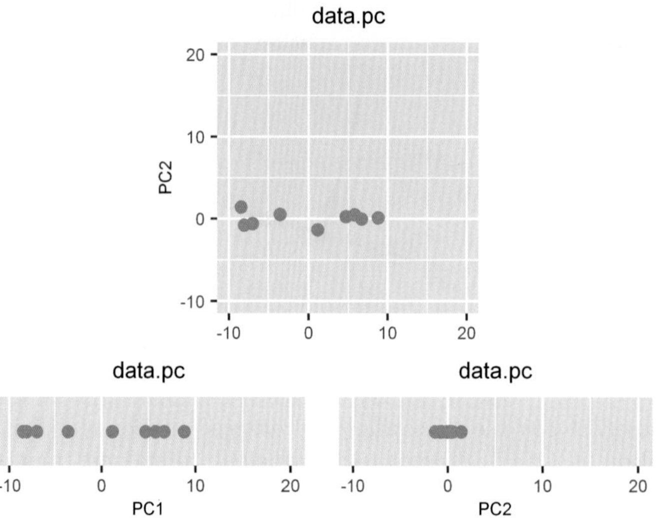

Specifically, variance in the PC_1 variable is 47.2501; variance in the PC_2 variable is 0.6596. Total variance in the dataset is still 47.91. Expressed in terms of relative variance, the PC_1 variable accounts for $47.2501 \div 47.91 = 98.62\%$ of the total variance. The PC_2 variable accounts for $0.6596 \div 47.91 = 1.38\%$ of the total variance. Here are the scree charts for the dataset in native and principal component representations:

scree of data

variable	standard_deviation	variance	cum_variance	relative_variance	cum_relative_variance
x1	6.617	43.778	43.78	0.9138	0.9138
x2	2.033	4.132	47.91	0.0862	1.0000

scree of data.pc

variable	standard_deviation	variance	cum_variance	relative_variance	cum_relative_variance
PC1	6.8739	47.2501	47.25	0.9862	0.9862
PC2	0.8121	0.6596	47.91	0.0138	1.0000

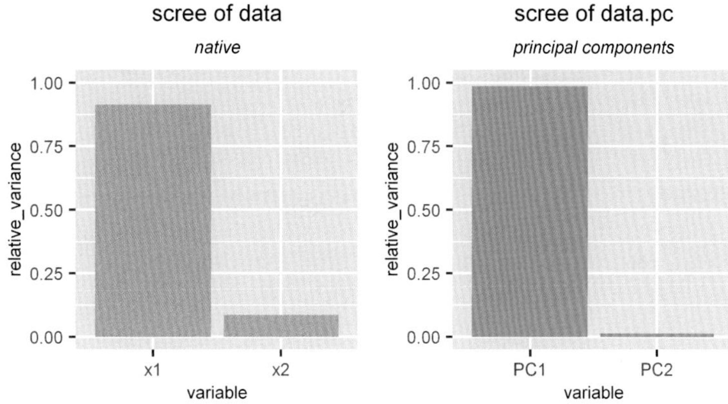

Note that the variance difference between principal component variables is greater than the variance difference between native variables. Also, the PC_1 variable has more variance than the x_1 variables does. The PC_2 variable distinguishes observations better than the x_1 variable does.

4.4.4 Principal Component Analysis | Two Normalized Variables

Consider again the 2-variable dataset, this time normalized. It might be that the variables were measured in units that could distort the weight matrix. Depending on which units were used, we'd get different weight matrices, and potentially very different variances in any principal component variables. By normalizing the dataset, we remove units altogether and thereby avoid distorting the weight matrix.

data

x1	x2
1	8.50
2	6.50
3	7.00
6	9.00
11	8.50
14	11.00
15	11.50
16	11.25
18	12.00

data.norm

x1	x2
-1.2931	-0.4783
-1.1419	-1.4622
-0.9908	-1.2162
-0.5374	-0.2323
0.2183	-0.4783
0.6717	0.7516
0.8229	0.9976
0.9740	0.8746
1.2763	1.2435

4.4.4.1 Variance in Normalized Representation

Normalizing the dataset divides total variance evenly among the variables.

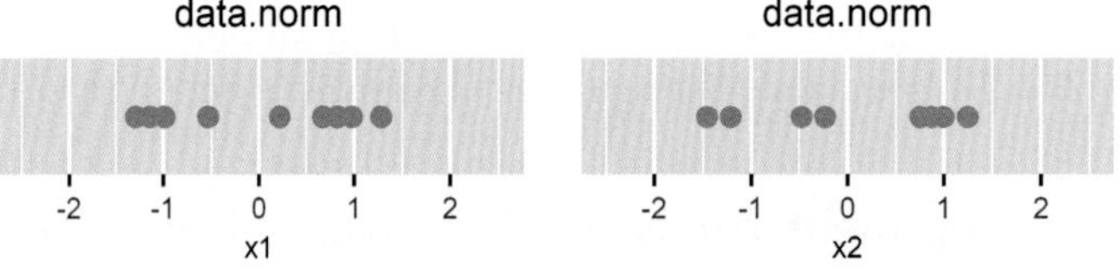

Variance in the x_1 variable is 1, variance in the x_2 variable is 1. Total variance is 2. The x_1 variable accounts for $1 \div 2 = 50\%$ of the total variance. The x_2 variable accounts for $1 \div 2 = 50\%$ of the total variance. Here is the scree chart:

scree of data.norm

variable	standard_deviation	variance	cum_variance	relative_variance	cum_relative_variance
x1	1	1	1	0.5	0.5
x2	1	1	2	0.5	1.0

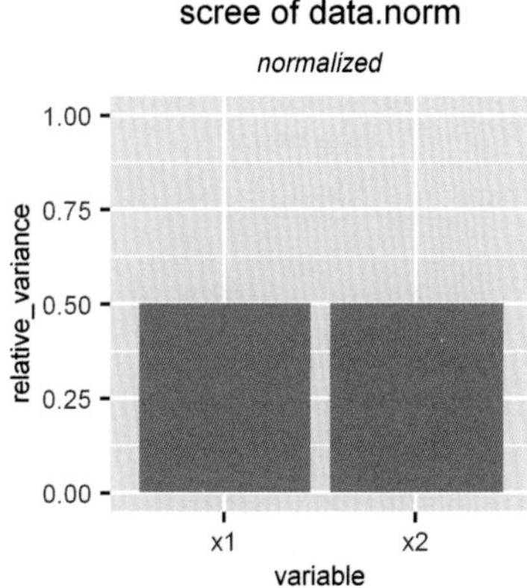

As it stands, neither variable distinguishes observations better than the other, and both variables distinguish observations worse than the x_1 variable did before it was normalized.

4.4.4.2 Transform to Principal Component Representation

Let's transform the normalized dataset to principal component representation and look at how that affects variance.

The centroid is at the origin (x_1=0, x_2=0), shown here as a black dot. The line through maximum variation is the positive-sloped diagonal running through the origin, shown here in blue. Orthogonal to that is the negative-sloped diagonal running through the origin, shown here in red. Store information about the lines in a weight matrix. There is no need to drag observations anywhere because the centroid is already at the origin. Rotate the lines and observations 45 degrees around the origin, using the weight matrix to do so. Rename the axes as PC_1 and PC_2.

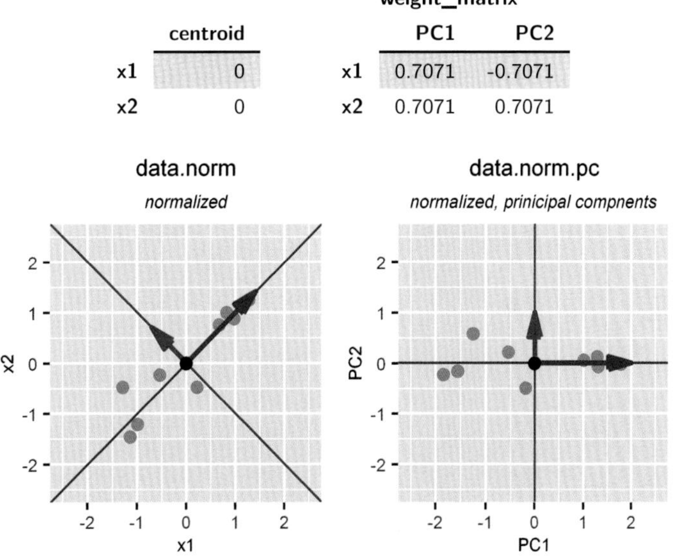

centroid

	centroid
x1	0
x2	0

weight_matrix

	PC1	PC2
x1	0.7071	-0.7071
x2	0.7071	0.7071

Here is the dataset transformed first to normalized representation and then on to principal components representation:

data		data.norm		data.norm.pc	
x1	x2	x1	x2	PC1	PC2
1	8.50	-1.2931	-0.4783	-1.2525	0.5761
2	6.50	-1.1419	-1.4622	-1.8414	-0.2265
3	7.00	-0.9908	-1.2162	-1.5606	-0.1594
6	9.00	-0.5374	-0.2323	-0.5443	0.2157
11	8.50	0.2183	-0.4783	-0.1838	-0.4926
14	11.00	0.6717	0.7516	1.0064	0.0565
15	11.50	0.8229	0.9976	1.2872	0.1235
16	11.25	0.9740	0.8746	1.3071	-0.0703
18	12.00	1.2763	1.2435	1.7818	-0.0231

4.4.4.3 Variance in Principal Component Representation

With the normalized dataset in principal component representation, there is much more variance in the PC_1 variable than in the PC_2 variable:

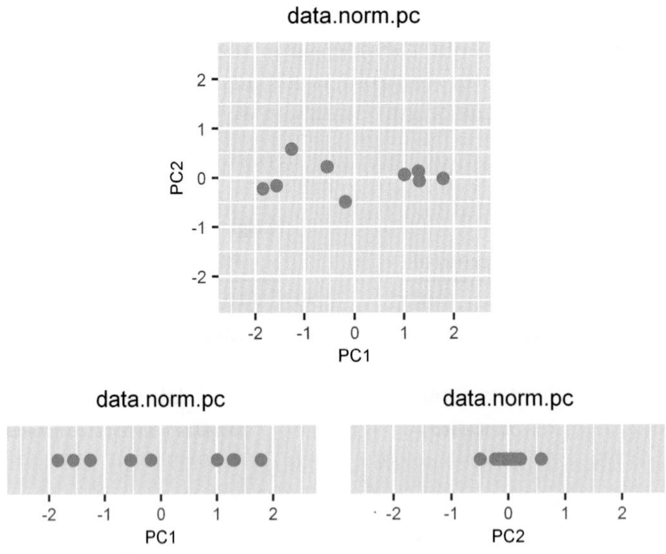

Specifically, variance in the PC_1 variable is 1.9098, variance in the PC_2 variable is 0.0902. Total variance in the dataset is still 2. Expressed in terms of relative variance, the PC_1 variable accounts for $1.9098 \div 2 = 95.49\%$ of the total variance. The PC_2 variable accounts for $0.0902 \div 2 = 4.51\%$ of the total variance. Here are the scree charts for the dataset in native, normalized, and principal component representations:

scree of data

variable	standard_deviation	variance	cum_variance	relative_variance	cum_relative_variance
x1	6.617	43.778	43.78	0.9138	0.9138
x2	2.033	4.132	47.91	0.0862	1.0000

scree of data.pc

variable	standard_deviation	variance	cum_variance	relative_variance	cum_relative_variance
PC1	6.8739	47.2501	47.25	0.9862	0.9862
PC2	0.8121	0.6596	47.91	0.0138	1.0000

scree of data.norm.pc

variable	standard_deviation	variance	cum_variance	relative_variance	cum_relative_variance
PC1	1.3820	1.9098	1.91	0.9549	0.9549
PC2	0.3004	0.0902	2.00	0.0451	1.0000

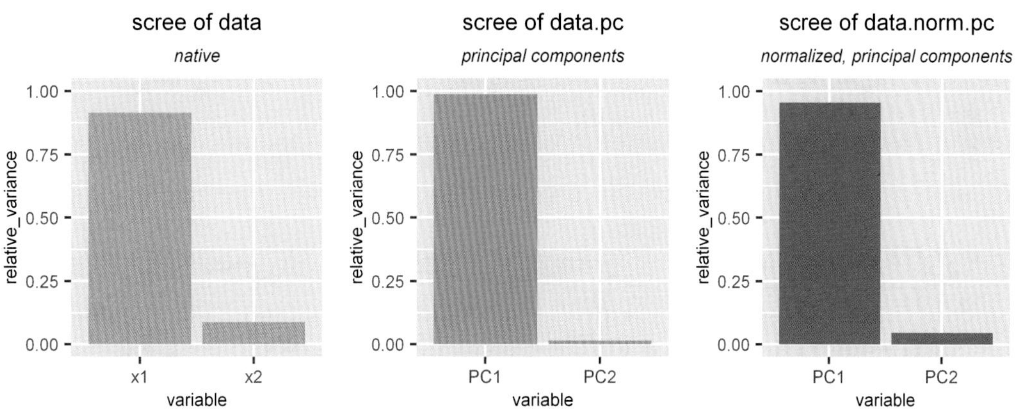

Note that the PC_1 variable with normalization has less variance than the PC_1 variable without normalization. However, the PC_1 variable with normalization is a better candidate for distinguishing observations because it has more variance than the x_1 variable does while avoiding any issues that might arise from units.

4.4.5 Principal Component Analysis | Three Normalized Variables

Consider this 3-variable dataset, in native and normalized representations:

data			data.norm		
x1	x2	x3	x1	x2	x3
1	8.50	1	-1.2931	-0.4783	-1.3224
2	6.50	2	-1.1419	-1.4622	-1.1421
3	7.00	10	-0.9908	-1.2162	0.3006
6	9.00	13	-0.5374	-0.2323	0.8416
11	8.50	16	0.2183	-0.4783	1.3826
14	11.00	15	0.6717	0.7516	1.2022
15	11.50	4	0.8229	0.9976	-0.7814
16	11.25	8	0.9740	0.8746	-0.0601
18	12.00	6	1.2763	1.2435	-0.4208

data

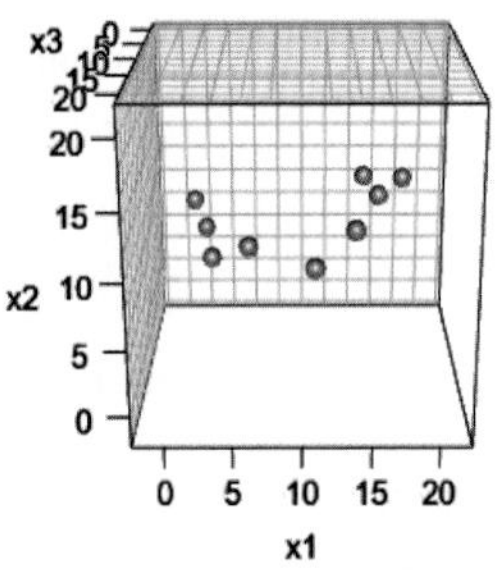

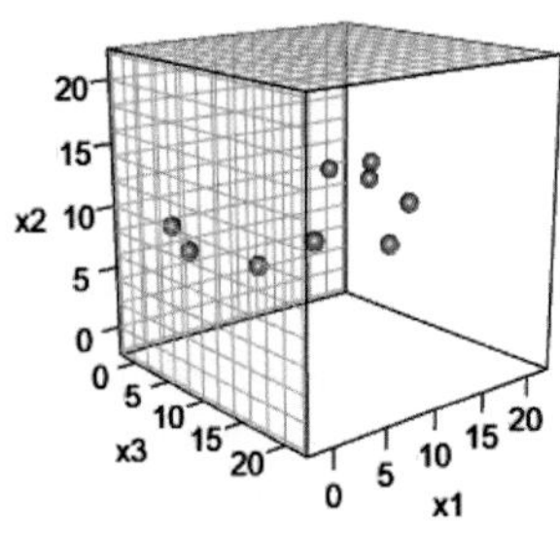

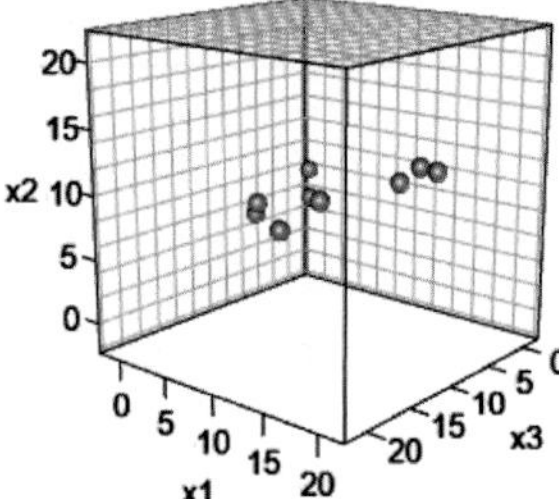

data.norm

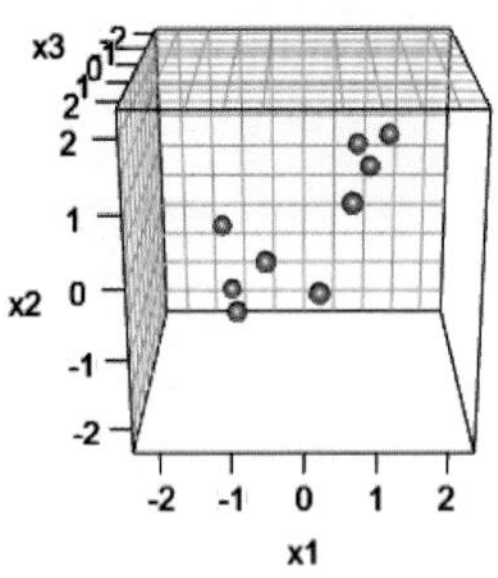

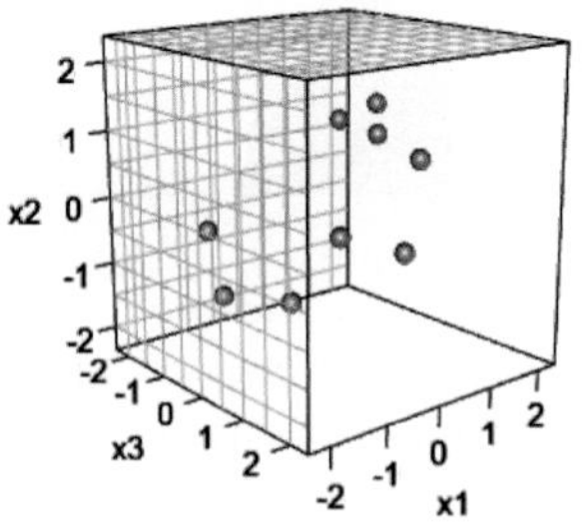

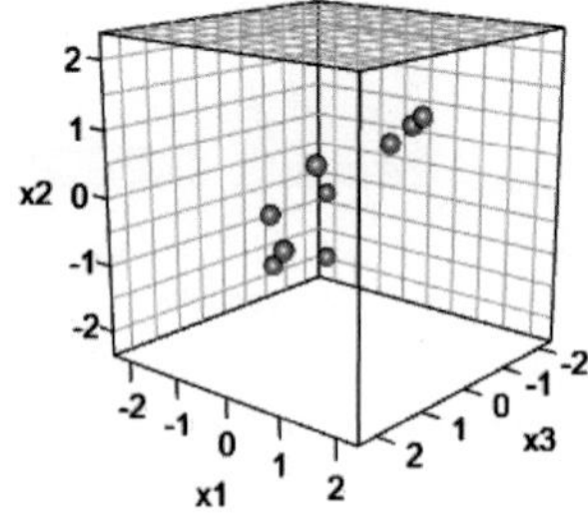

4.4.5.1 Variance in Normalized Representation

Normalizing the dataset divides total variance evenly among the variables:

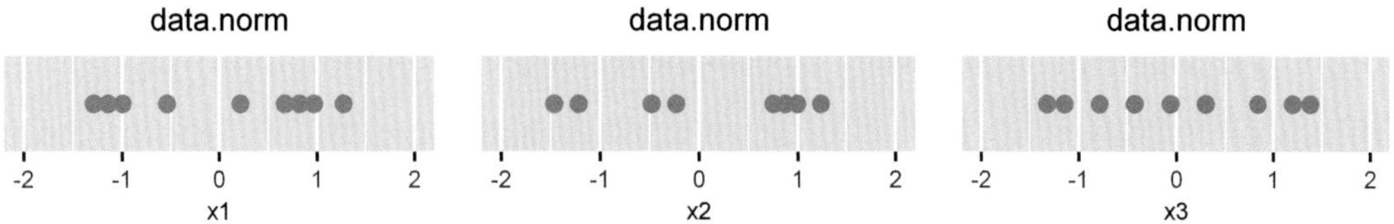

Variance in the x_1 variable is 1, variance in the x_2 variable is 1, variance in the x_3 is 1. Total variance is 3. Each variable accounts for $1 \div 3 = 33.33\%$ of the total variance. Here is the scree chart:

scree of data.norm

variable	standard_deviation	variance	cum_variance	relative_variance	cum_relative_variance
x1	1	1	1	0.3333	0.3333
x2	1	1	2	0.3333	0.6667
x3	1	1	3	0.3333	1.0000

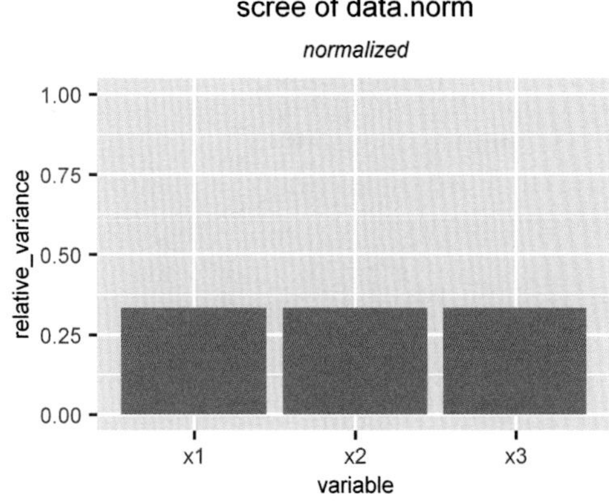

4.4.5.2 Transform to Principal Component Representation

Let's transform the normalized dataset to principal component representation and look at how that affects variance.

The centroid is at the origin (x_1=0, x_2=0, x_3=0), shown here as a black sphere. The line through the maximum variation, shown here in blue. Find a second line through the origin, orthogonal to the first line, and through as much variation as possible under such constraints, shown here in red. Determine a third line through the origin and orthogonal to both the first and second lines, shown here in violet. Store information about the lines in a weight matrix. Rotate the lines and observations around the origin until lines align with the x_1-, x_2-, and x_3-axes, using the weight matrix to do so. Rename the axes as PC_1, PC_2, and PC_3.

centroid	value
x1	0
x2	0
x3	0

weight_matrix	PC1	PC2	PC3
x1	0.6976	-0.0698	0.7131
x2	0.6730	-0.2778	-0.6855
x3	0.2460	0.9581	-0.1468

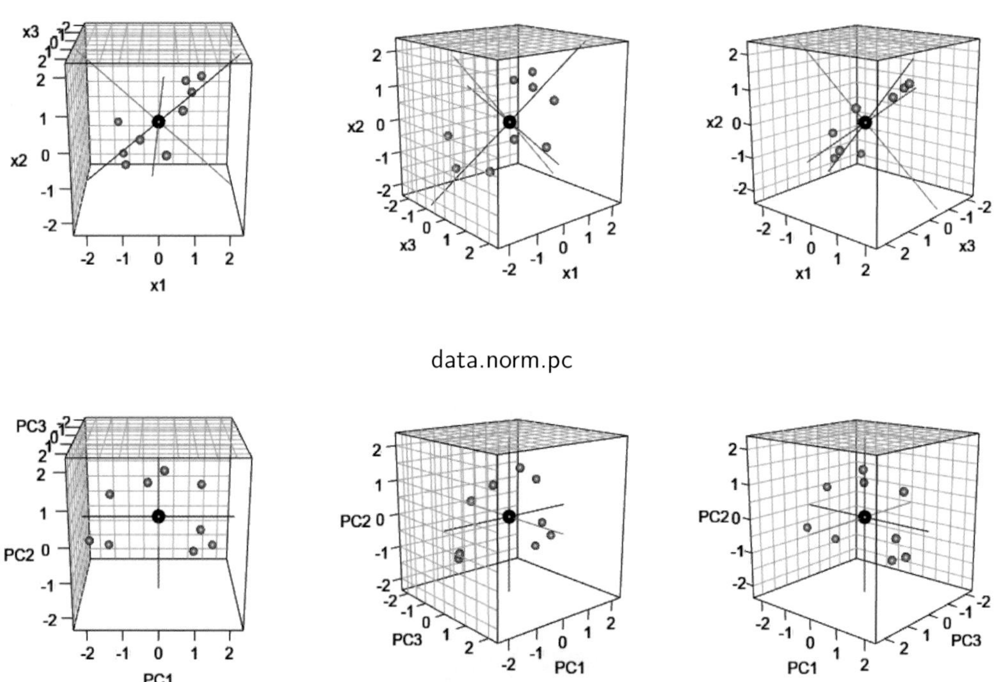

Here is the dataset transformed first to normalized representation and then on to principal components representation:

data x1	x2	x3	data.norm x1	x2	x3	data.norm.pc PC1	PC2	PC3
1	8.50	1	-1.2931	-0.4783	-1.3224	-1.5492	-1.0439	-0.4001
2	6.50	2	-1.1419	-1.4622	-1.1421	-2.0615	-0.6083	0.3557
3	7.00	10	-0.9908	-1.2162	0.3006	-1.4357	0.6950	0.0831
6	9.00	13	-0.5374	-0.2323	0.8416	-0.3242	0.9084	-0.3475
11	8.50	16	0.2183	-0.4783	1.3826	0.1705	1.4423	0.2806
14	11.00	15	0.6717	0.7516	1.2022	1.2701	0.8961	-0.2127
15	11.50	4	0.8229	0.9976	-0.7814	1.0531	-1.0833	0.0176
16	11.25	8	0.9740	0.8746	-0.0601	1.2532	-0.3686	0.1038
18	12.00	6	1.2763	1.2435	-0.4208	1.6237	-0.8377	0.1194

4.4.5.3 Variance in Principal Component Representation

With the normalized dataset in principal component representation and looking at the variables in order, each variable has more variance than as any variables that follow it:

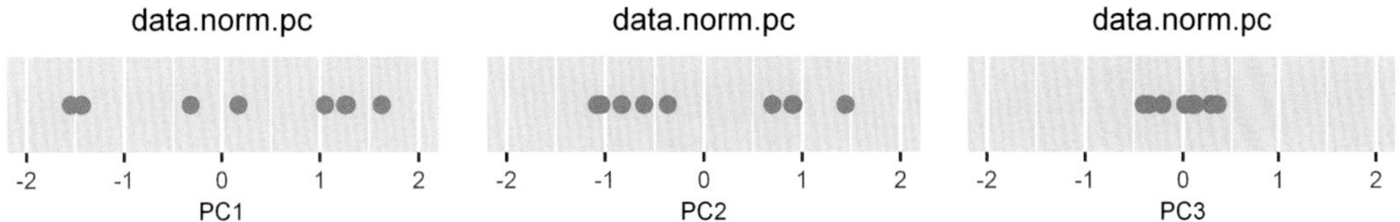

Specifically, variance in the PC_1 variable is 1.9718, variance in the PC_2 variable is 0.9578, and variance in the PC_3 variable is 0.704. Total variance in the dataset is still 3. Expressed in terms of relative variance, the PC_1 variable accounts for $1.9718 \div 3 = 65.73\%$ of the total variance. The PC_2 variable accounts for $0.9578 \div 3 = 31.93\%$ of the total variance. The PC_3 variable accounts for $0.0704 \div 3 = 2.35\%$ of the total variance. Here is the scree chart for the dataset in principal component representation:

scree of data.norm.pc

variable	standard_deviation	variance	cum_variance	relative_variance	cum_relative_variance
PC1	1.4042	1.9718	1.972	0.6573	0.6573
PC2	0.9787	0.9578	2.930	0.3193	0.9765
PC3	0.2654	0.0704	3.000	0.0235	1.0000

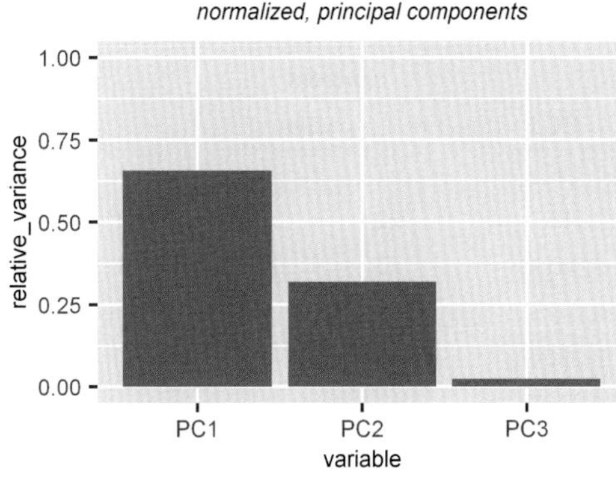

If you were restricted to use just one variable to distinguish observations, you could expect the PC_1 variable to be the most useful. If you were restricted to use just 2 variables to distinguish observations, you could expect the PC_1 and PC_2 variable combination to be the most useful.

4.4.6 Transform a New Observation to Principal Component Representation

Consider this 3-variable dataset, its transformation to normalized representation, and transformation onto principal component representation. See that transformation to normalized representation involved calculating mean and standard deviation for each variable. Also, see that transformation to principal component representation involved calculating the dataset's centroid and weight matrix.

data

x1	x2	x3
1	8.50	1
2	6.50	2
3	7.00	10
6	9.00	13
11	8.50	16
14	11.00	15
15	11.50	4
16	11.25	8
18	12.00	6

data.norm

x1	x2	x3
-1.2931	-0.4783	-1.3224
-1.1419	-1.4622	-1.1421
-0.9908	-1.2162	0.3006
-0.5374	-0.2323	0.8416
0.2183	-0.4783	1.3826
0.6717	0.7516	1.2022
0.8229	0.9976	-0.7814
0.9740	0.8746	-0.0601
1.2763	1.2435	-0.4208

normalization arguments

	x1	x2	x3
mean	9.556	9.472	8.333
standard deviation	6.617	2.033	5.545

data.norm.pc

PC1	PC2	PC3
-1.5492	-1.0439	-0.4001
-2.0615	-0.6083	0.3557
-1.4357	0.6950	0.0831
-0.3242	0.9084	-0.3475
0.1705	1.4423	0.2806
1.2701	0.8961	-0.2127
1.0531	-1.0833	0.0176
1.2532	-0.3686	0.1038
1.6237	-0.8377	0.1194

centroid

	value
x1	0
x2	0
x3	0

weight matrix

	PC1	PC2	PC3
x1	0.6976	-0.0698	0.7131
x2	0.6730	-0.2778	-0.6855
x3	0.2460	0.9581	-0.1468

Also consider this new observation. Perhaps there's been some data analysis or analytical modeling done with the dataset in principal component representation. To apply any resulting insights or models to the new observation, it would have to be in principal component representation, too. Let's convert the new observation to principal component representation.

new

x1	x2	x3
5	10	7

Express the new observation in the same unitless representation as the normalized dataset, using the normalization arguments calculated earlier. Note that the normalization arguments – the means and standard deviations – come from the dataset, not from the new observation.

$$x_1 = \frac{5 - 9.556}{6.617} = -0.6885$$

$$x_2 = \frac{10 - 9.472}{2.033} = 0.2596$$

$$x_3 = \frac{7 - 8.333}{5.545} = -0.2404$$

new.norm

x1	x2	x3
-0.6885	0.2596	-0.2404

normalization arguments

	x1	x2	x3
mean	9.556	9.472	8.333
standard deviation	6.617	2.033	5.545

Calculate principal component values, using the principal component formula applied to the new observation with the centroid and weight matrix.

$$PC_1 = \begin{pmatrix} (0.6976 \times (-0.6885{-}0)) + \\ (0.6730 \times (0.2596{-}0)) + \\ (0.2460 \times (-0.2404{-}0)) \end{pmatrix} = -0.3647$$

$$PC_2 = \begin{pmatrix} (-0.0698 \times (-0.6885{-}0)) + \\ (-0.2778 \times (0.2596{-}0)) + \\ (0.9581 \times (-0.2404{-}0)) \end{pmatrix} = -0.2544$$

$$PC_3 = \begin{pmatrix} (0.7131 \times (-0.6885{-}0)) + \\ (-0.6855 \times (0.2596{-}0)) + \\ (-0.1468 \times (-0.2404{-}0)) \end{pmatrix} = -0.6337$$

new.norm.pc

PC1	PC2	PC3
-0.3647	-0.2544	-0.6337

centroid

	value
x1	0
x2	0
x3	0

weight matrix

	PC1	PC2	PC3
x1	0.6976	-0.0698	0.7131
x2	0.6730	-0.2778	-0.6855
x3	0.2460	0.9581	-0.1468

The new observation can be expressed in principal component representation as ($PC_1 = -0.3647, PC_2 = -0.2544, PC_3 = -0.6337$).

4.4.7 An Analogy for Principal Component Analysis

You can think of finding principal component axes as building a mechanical machine. The axes are 3 rods, the centroid is a bearing fixed in space and connecting the rods at their centers, and observations are marbles fixed in space. Attach each marble to the first rod by an elastic string, which will cause the rod to spin around the bearing until eventually coming to rest where the tug of the strings in all directions balances. Fix the rod in this position and proceed to the second rod. The bearing keeps the second rod orthogonal to the first rod, but allows it to spin in a plane. Fix a wall right alongside the plane. Move the marbles to their shadows on the plane and attach each marble to the second rod by an elastic string, which will cause the rod to spin around the bearing until eventually coming to rest where the tug of the strings in all directions balances. Fix the rod in this position. The bearing keeps the third rod orthogonal to the first and second rods.

4.5 CASE | Loan Portfolio

Data transformation with principal component analysis to discover relationships predictive of loan defaults in the banking industry.

4.5.1 Business Situation

A financial institution is considering purchasing a batch of loans from a bank, each of which comes with documentation about the terms of the loan, the status of the loan, the background of the lendee, and other relevant information. Company management is interested leveraging any detectable patterns in the documentation to distinguish loans likely to be paid back from those likely to default, and thereby inform its decision about which loans to purchase.

- **Role:** Loan Acquisition Manager
- **Decision:** Which loans to purchase?
- **Approach:** Use kernel density estimation and principal component analysis to look for features that distinguish known good loans from known bad loans, and use that insight to inform the decision about which loans to purchase.

4.5.2 Data

Retrieve raw data, prepare the data, and transform the data to ready it for analysis.

4.5.2.1 Raw Data

Retrieve a reference classified dataset of loan documentation. Each of 85,000 observations describes a unique loan. There are 74 variables that represent predictors of loan performance and results of loan performance. The *loan_status* variable indicates whether a loan has been fully paid back, has defaulted, or is still active.

data.raw__variables

id, member_id, loan_amnt, funded_amnt, funded_amnt_inv, term, int_rate, installment, grade, sub_grade, emp_title, emp_length, home_ownership, annual_inc, verification_status, issue_d, loan_status, pymnt_plan, url, desc, purpose, title, zip_code, addr_state, dti, delinq_2yrs, earliest_cr_line, inq_last_6mths, mths_since_last_delinq, mths_since_last_record, open_acc, pub_rec, revol_bal, revol_util, total_acc, initial_list_status, out_prncp, out_prncp_inv, total_pymnt, total_pymnt_inv, total_rec_prncp, total_rec_int, total_rec_late_fee, recoveries, collection_recovery_fee, last_pymnt_d, last_pymnt_amnt, next_pymnt_d, last_credit_pull_d, collections_12_mths_ex_med, mths_since_last_major_derog, policy_code, application_type, annual_inc_joint, dti_joint, verification_status_joint, acc_now_delinq, tot_coll_amt, tot_cur_bal, open_acc_6m, open_il_6m, open_il_12m, open_il_24m, mths_since_rcnt_il, total_bal_il, il_util, open_rv_12m, open_rv_24m, max_bal_bc, all_util, total_rev_hi_lim, inq_fi, total_cu_tl, inq_last_12m

data.raw *size 85000×74, first few observations shown, a few variables shown*

id	loan_amnt	term	int_rate	grade	sub_grade	emp_length
1,077,501	5,000	36 months	10.65	B	B2	10+ years
1,077,430	2,500	60 months	15.27	C	C4	< 1 year
1,077,175	2,400	36 months	15.96	C	C5	10+ years
1,076,863	10,000	36 months	13.49	C	C1	10+ years

data.raw *size 85000×74, first few observations shown, a few variables shown*

home_ownership	loan_status	desc	purpose
RENT	Fully Paid	Borrower added on 12/22/11 > I need to upgrade my business technologies. 	credit_card
RENT	Charged Off	Borrower added on 12/22/11 > I plan to use this money to finance the motorcycle i am looking at. I plan to have it paid off as soon as possible/when i sell my old bike.I only need this money because the deal im looking at is to good to pass up. I have finished college with an associates degree in business and its takingmeplaces 	car
RENT	Fully Paid		small_business
RENT	Fully Paid	Borrower added on 12/21/11 > to pay for property tax (borrow from friend, need to pay back) and central A/C need to be replace. I'm very sorry to let my loan expired last time. 	other

4.5.2.2 Prepare Data

Prepare the dataset for analysis.

Our analysis will require a class variable to distinguish good loans from bad loans. We can derive that from the detailed loan status described by the *loan_status* variable.

loan_status__values

Charged Off, Current, Default, Does not meet the credit policy. Status:Charged Off, Does not meet the credit policy. Status:Fully Paid, Fully Paid, In Grace Period, Late (16-30 days), Late (31-120 days)

Add a synthetic variable *class*, derived from variable *loan_status*, like this:

- Assign *class* to good if *loan_status* is Fully Paid or Does not meet the credit policy. Status:Fully Paid.
- Assign *class* to bad if *loan_status* is Default, Charged Off, or Does not meet the credit policy. Status:Charged Off.

Our analysis will require that each loan's class is known. Filter in only inactive loans for which class is known, which are those loans with a *loan_status* value mapped to class good or bad. Other *loan_status* values indicate that a loan is still active.

Our analysis will require variables to be in numerical representation, though the dataset includes potentially useful information in categorical representation.

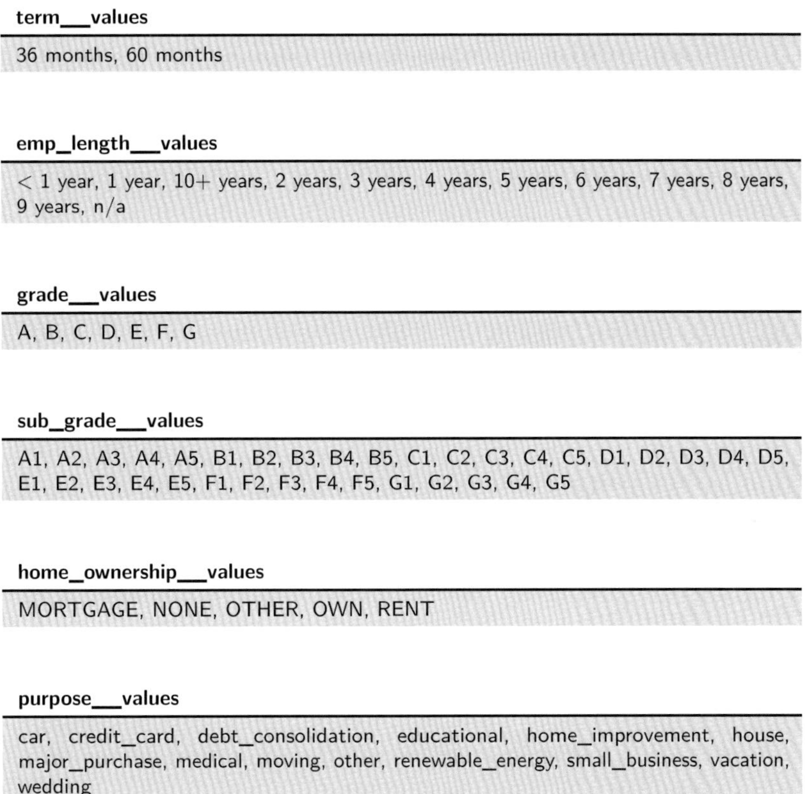

term__values
36 months, 60 months

emp_length__values
< 1 year, 1 year, 10+ years, 2 years, 3 years, 4 years, 5 years, 6 years, 7 years, 8 years, 9 years, n/a

grade__values
A, B, C, D, E, F, G

sub_grade__values
A1, A2, A3, A4, A5, B1, B2, B3, B4, B5, C1, C2, C3, C4, C5, D1, D2, D3, D4, D5, E1, E2, E3, E4, E5, F1, F2, F3, F4, F5, G1, G2, G3, G4, G5

home_ownership__values
MORTGAGE, NONE, OTHER, OWN, RENT

purpose__values
car, credit_card, debt_consolidation, educational, home_improvement, house, major_purchase, medical, moving, other, renewable_energy, small_business, vacation, wedding

Convert categorical variables to numerical representation, like this:

- *term* from categorical to numerical, remove "months"
- *emp_length* from categorical to numerical, remove "years", change "<1" to 0, change "10+" to 10, change "n/a" to missing data indicator
- *grade* from categorical to numerical by index coding
- *sub_grade* from categorical to numerical by index coding
- *home_ownership* from categorical to numerical by index coding
- *purpose* from categorical to numerical by index coding

data *size 59835×74, first few observations shown, a few variables shown*

class	id	loan_amnt	term	int_rate	grade	sub_grade	emp_length
good	1,077,501	5,000	36	10.65	2	7	10
bad	1,077,430	2,500	60	15.27	3	14	0
good	1,077,175	2,400	36	15.96	3	15	10
good	1,076,863	10,000	36	13.49	3	11	10

data *size 59835×74, first few observations shown, a few variables shown*

home_ownership	desc	purpose
5	Borrower added on 12/22/11 > I need to upgrade my business technologies. 	2
5	Borrower added on 12/22/11 > I plan to use this money to finance the motorcycle i am looking at. I plan to have it paid off as soon as possible/when i sell my old bike.I only need this money because the deal im looking at is to good to pass up. I have finished college with an associates degree in business and its takingmeplaces 	1
5		12
5	Borrower added on 12/21/11 > to pay for property tax (borrow from friend, need to pay back) and central A/C need to be replace. I'm very sorry to let my loan expired last time. 	10

4.5.2.3 Transform Data

Transform the dataset for analysis.

Filter out some of the variables, like this:

- Identification variables, like ID number *id* and account number *member_id*, are not predictive, so don't include them.
- Leaky variables are those that contain information that could only be known when the class is already known. Since we're ultimately interested in predicting class before class can actually be known, don't include the leaky variables *recoveries*, *collection_recovery_fee*, or *collections_12_mths_ex_med*.
- Empty variables are missing any information at all, so don't include them.
- No-variance variables are missing any information at all, so don't include them.
- Sparse variables, those with more than half of their values missing, might be too difficult to sensibly impute, so don't include them.

Also, for convenience, don't include non-numerical variables, except for the class variable.

Impute by simply substituting zeros for missing values.

data__variables
class, loan_amnt, funded_amnt, funded_amnt_inv, term, int_rate, installment, grade, sub_grade, emp_length, home_ownership, annual_inc, purpose, dti, delinq_2yrs, inq_last_6mths, open_acc, pub_rec, revol_bal, revol_util, total_acc, out_prncp, out_prncp_inv, total_pymnt, total_pymnt_inv, total_rec_prncp, total_rec_int, total_rec_late_fee, last_pymnt_amnt, acc_now_delinq

data *size 59835×30, first few observations shown, a few variables shown*

class	loan_amnt	funded_amnt	funded_amnt_inv	term	int_rate	installment	grade	sub_grade
good	5,000	5,000	4,975	36	10.65	162.87	2	7
bad	2,500	2,500	2,500	60	15.27	59.83	3	14
good	2,400	2,400	2,400	36	15.96	84.33	3	15
good	10,000	10,000	10,000	36	13.49	339.31	3	11

4.5.3 Data Exploration

With the dataset ready for analysis, we could start exploring any of myriad aspects. Perhaps we suspect that loan amount and interest rate are related to whether loans get paid back, so we'll start there. Here is the dataset visualized as a scatterplot: each point represents a unique loan positioned horizontally by loan amount and vertically by interest rate. See that loans are concentrated in the lower-left corner, indicating that most loans are for relatively small amounts and at relatively low interest rates. So far, we can't infer much more than that.

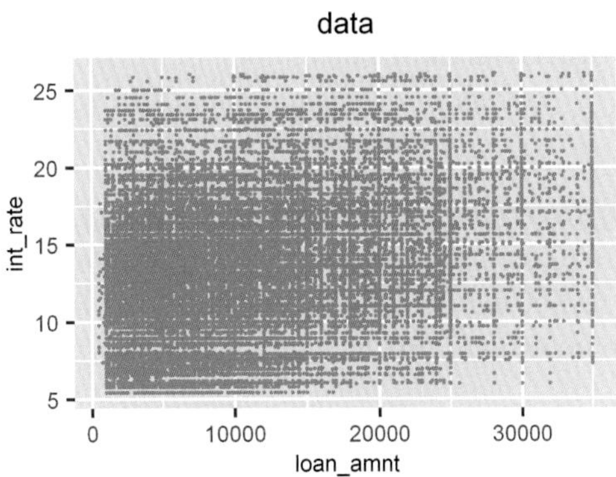

We can gain more insight by visualizing the probability density of each variable separately. Here we use kernel density estimation to estimate the probability densities, which does indeed provide us a more nuanced understanding of the distribution of loan amounts and interest rates. See that the loan amount probability density is highest around amounts of \$5,000 to \$10,000, indicating many loans with amounts in this range. The number of loans steadily decreases as amount increases, until reaching very few loans with amounts above \$30,000. In contrast, interest rate probability density is high from rates around 8% to 15%, except for 9%, falling off sharply on both sides at lower and higher rates.

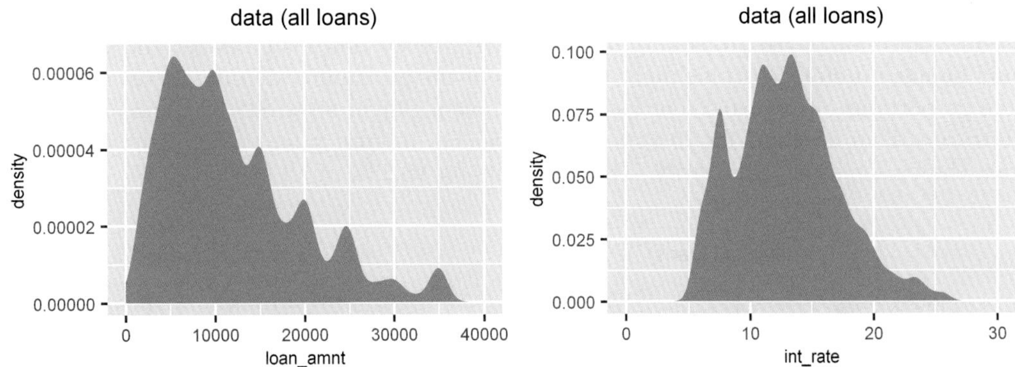

4.5.4 Try to Distinguish Observations

Are the loan amount and interest rate variables enough to distinguish good loans from bad loans?

Here is the dataset visualized as a scatterplot, color-coded by class. See that it's difficult to make out anything that might distinguish good loans from bad loans.

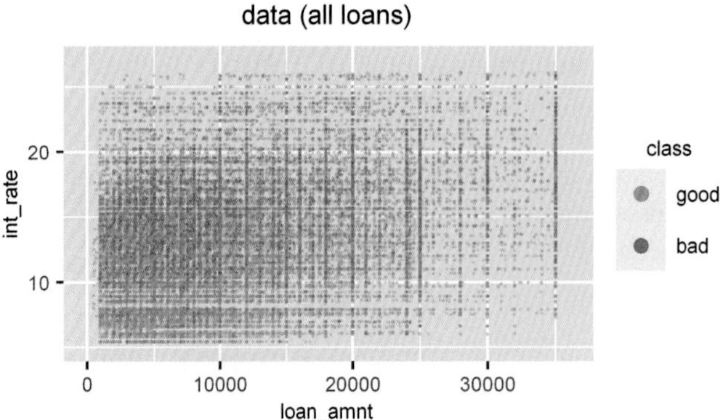

Here are data visualizations as scatterplots with data separated into good loan and bad loan subsets. We can just barely make out how loan amount and interest rate can distinguish good loans from bad loans, albeit not distinguish very well. Good loans appear to be slightly more concentrated at low loan amounts and slightly less concentrated at mid interest rates.

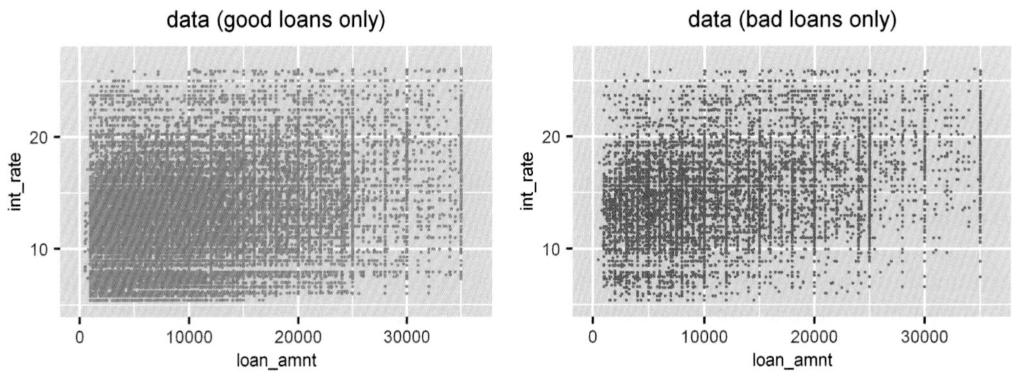

Careful inspection of the probability densities might reveal how loan amount and interest rate could be more useful. First, highlight the ranges of the probability density curves representing large proportions of the loans. For loan amount, we highlight \$0 to \$18,000, chosen somewhat arbitrarily. That accounts for 79.12% of all loans. For interest rate, we highlight 10% to 20%, again chosen somewhat arbitrarily. That accounts for 68.23% of all loans.

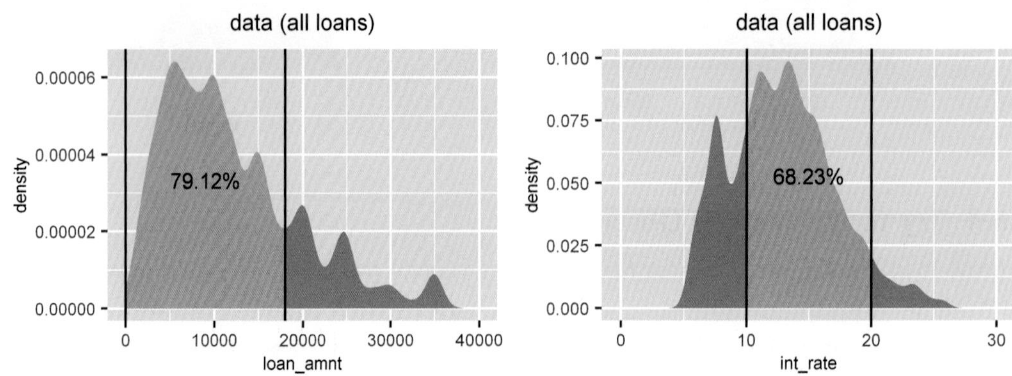

Next, separate the known good loans from the known bad loans. Use kernel density estimation to estimate the loan amount probability density and interest rate probability density for these subsets. See that the probability density curves don't look quite the same as those for all loans. See that 80.23% of good loans have amounts between \$0 and \$18,000, while 73.75% of bad loans do. The probability that a good loan would be in that range is slightly higher than the probability that a bad loan would be in that range. From this you could reason that a new loan in that range – good or bad being unknown – is slightly more likely to be good than bad. For interest rate, it's the other way around: 66.43% of good loans have rates between 10% and 20%, while 76.91% of bad loans do. You could reason that a new loan with an interest rate in that range is slightly more likely to be bad than good.

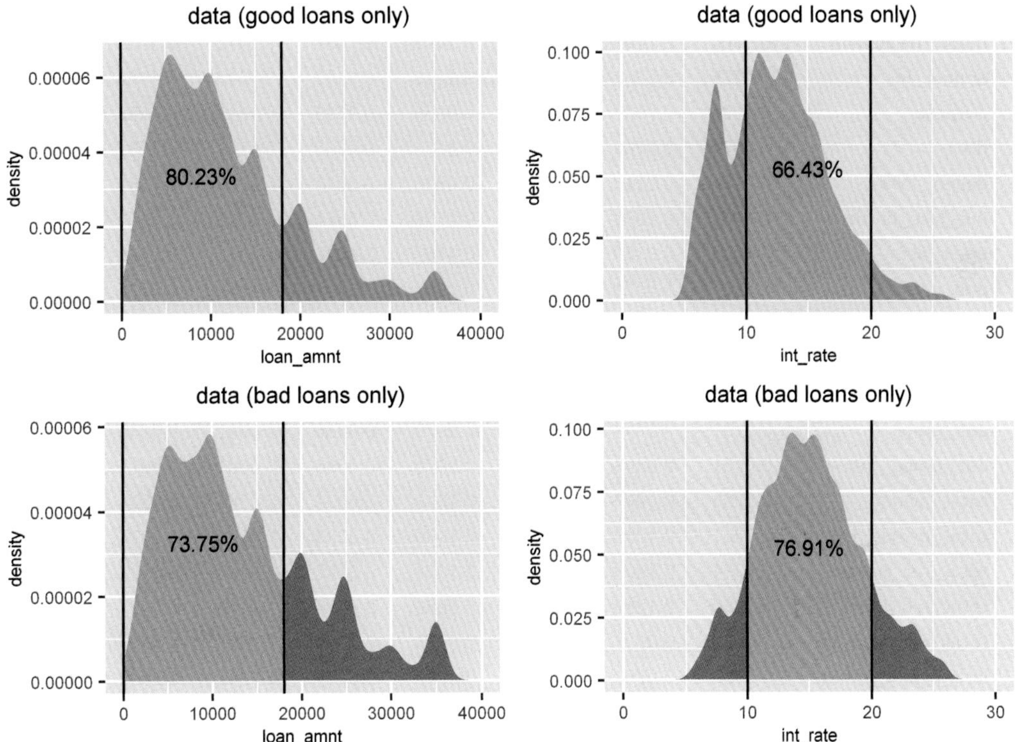

4.5.5 Principal Component Analysis

Our analysis so far focused on the loan amount and interest rate variables, which we chose only because we suspected that they could help us distinguish good loans from bad loans. Perhaps other variables would prove even more useful. There are 536,870,911 multivariate combinations, so even at a swift processing speed of 1 per second it would take an impractical 17 years to try them all. We could instead restrict ourselves to just the 29 variables, 1 at a time, or the 406 2-variable combinations, and hope that we get lucky.

However, we can improve our chances by transforming the dataset further to principal component representation. Then, with the dataset's overall variance concentrated in the first few principal component variables, we can reasonably expect that those first few will prove most useful.

Here is the weight matrix to transform the dataset to principal component representation. All 29 rows and 8 of the 29 columns are shown.

weight matrix *all rows shown, first few columns shown*

	PC1	PC2	PC3	PC4	PC5	PC6	PC7	PC8
loan_amnt	0.3286	0.0644	-0.0185	0.0685	-0.0117	0.0151	-0.0522	-0.0016
funded_amnt	0.3308	0.0662	-0.0188	0.0709	-0.0042	0.0131	-0.0544	0.0047
funded_amnt_inv	0.3262	0.0740	-0.0177	0.0739	0.0226	-0.0187	-0.0251	0.0045
term	0.1369	-0.2115	-0.0057	0.0087	-0.1019	-0.2428	0.1301	-0.2070
int_rate	0.1413	-0.4717	-0.0105	-0.0509	-0.0143	-0.0482	0.0416	0.0115
installment	0.3157	0.0801	-0.0182	0.0619	0.0212	0.0806	-0.0900	0.0659
grade	0.1221	-0.4929	-0.0257	-0.0432	-0.0729	0.0059	-0.0059	-0.0069
sub_grade	0.1249	-0.4960	-0.0253	-0.0421	-0.0716	0.0070	-0.0078	-0.0080
emp_length	0.0733	0.0470	0.0876	-0.1672	-0.0587	0.0101	0.5643	-0.0233
home_ownership	-0.0806	-0.1148	-0.1118	0.2493	0.2437	-0.0571	-0.3629	0.1025
annual_inc	0.1225	0.0881	0.0527	-0.1216	-0.3147	0.4243	0.1499	0.0773
purpose	-0.0696	-0.0525	-0.0510	0.0865	-0.4333	0.1311	-0.1258	-0.0672
dti	0.0574	-0.0786	0.1482	-0.3032	0.4833	-0.1117	-0.1785	-0.0150
delinq_2yrs	0.0164	-0.0718	0.0650	-0.0838	-0.2047	-0.2057	0.0251	0.6164
inq_last_6mths	0.0001	-0.1334	0.0400	-0.1537	-0.3571	-0.0225	-0.2622	-0.2284
open_acc	0.1014	0.0769	0.2278	-0.4763	-0.0040	-0.1606	-0.2695	-0.0555
pub_rec	-0.0107	-0.0724	0.0114	-0.0509	-0.0249	-0.2156	0.3729	-0.1471
revol_bal	0.1123	0.0353	0.1054	-0.2426	0.0860	0.5454	0.0369	0.0380
revol_util	0.0698	-0.2529	0.0080	-0.0557	0.4279	0.3641	0.1803	0.1099
total_acc	0.1174	0.1201	0.2279	-0.4778	-0.0875	-0.1332	-0.1292	-0.0278
out_prncp	0.0101	-0.0398	0.6378	0.2976	-0.0066	-0.0001	0.0077	-0.0156
out_prncp_inv	0.0101	-0.0398	0.6378	0.2976	-0.0066	-0.0001	0.0077	-0.0156
total_pymnt	0.3256	0.0972	-0.0620	0.1042	-0.0006	-0.0286	-0.0320	-0.0040
total_pymnt_inv	0.3221	0.1030	-0.0595	0.1040	0.0203	-0.0520	-0.0074	-0.0051
total_rec_prncp	0.3054	0.1608	-0.0673	0.1022	0.0137	-0.0443	-0.0202	0.0089
total_rec_int	0.2760	-0.1289	-0.0268	0.0886	-0.0414	0.0144	-0.0464	-0.0513
total_rec_late_fee	0.0057	-0.0731	0.0047	0.0325	-0.1347	0.2853	-0.3116	0.1005
last_pymnt_amnt	0.2257	0.0788	-0.0463	0.0222	0.0275	-0.2246	0.1092	-0.0158
acc_now_delinq	0.0074	-0.0192	0.0154	-0.0390	-0.0716	-0.1338	0.0461	0.6679

Here is the principal component constituents table corresponding to the weight matrix. All of the rows and 5 of the 29 columns are shown. Each column corresponds to 1 principal component variable, listing the original variables in order of decreasing weight for that principal component variable. Note that each principal component variable gets contributions from ***all*** of the original variables, but weighting them in its own specific way.

principal component constituents *first few columns shown*

PC1	PC2	PC3	PC4	PC5
funded_amnt	sub_grade	out_prncp	total_acc	dti
loan_amnt	grade	out_prncp_inv	open_acc	purpose
funded_amnt_inv	int_rate	total_acc	dti	revol_util
total_pymnt	revol_util	open_acc	out_prncp	inq_last_6mths
total_pymnt_inv	term	dti	out_prncp_inv	annual_inc
installment	total_rec_prncp	home_ownership	home_ownership	home_ownership
total_rec_prncp	inq_last_6mths	revol_bal	revol_bal	delinq_2yrs
total_rec_int	total_rec_int	emp_length	emp_length	total_rec_late_fee
last_pymnt_amnt	total_acc	total_rec_prncp	inq_last_6mths	term
int_rate	home_ownership	delinq_2yrs	annual_inc	total_acc
term	total_pymnt_inv	total_pymnt	total_pymnt	revol_bal
sub_grade	total_pymnt	total_pymnt_inv	total_pymnt_inv	grade
annual_inc	annual_inc	annual_inc	total_rec_prncp	acc_now_delinq
grade	installment	purpose	total_rec_int	sub_grade
total_acc	last_pymnt_amnt	last_pymnt_amnt	purpose	emp_length
revol_bal	dti	inq_last_6mths	delinq_2yrs	total_rec_int
open_acc	open_acc	total_rec_int	funded_amnt_inv	last_pymnt_amnt
home_ownership	funded_amnt_inv	grade	funded_amnt	pub_rec
emp_length	total_rec_late_fee	sub_grade	loan_amnt	funded_amnt_inv
revol_util	pub_rec	funded_amnt	installment	installment
purpose	delinq_2yrs	loan_amnt	revol_util	total_pymnt_inv
dti	funded_amnt	installment	int_rate	int_rate
delinq_2yrs	loan_amnt	funded_amnt_inv	pub_rec	total_rec_prncp
pub_rec	purpose	acc_now_delinq	grade	loan_amnt
out_prncp	emp_length	pub_rec	sub_grade	out_prncp
out_prncp_inv	out_prncp_inv	int_rate	acc_now_delinq	out_prncp_inv
acc_now_delinq	out_prncp	revol_util	total_rec_late_fee	funded_amnt
total_rec_late_fee	revol_bal	term	last_pymnt_amnt	open_acc
inq_last_6mths	acc_now_delinq	total_rec_late_fee	term	total_pymnt

Here is the dataset in principal component representation:

data.pc__variables

class, PC1, PC2, PC3, PC4, PC5, PC6, PC7, PC8, PC9, PC10, PC11, PC12, PC13, PC14, PC15, PC16, PC17, PC18, PC19, PC20, PC21, PC22, PC23, PC24, PC25, PC26, PC27, PC28, PC29

data.pc *size 59835×30, first few observations shown, first few variables shown*

class	PC1	PC2	PC3	PC4	PC5	PC6	PC7	PC8	PC9	PC10
good	-2.5514	-0.2817	-0.1229	0.3203	2.4678	0.5139	0.8548	0.1885	0.1314	0.5912
bad	-3.5842	-2.0119	-0.8824	1.5122	-1.6591	-0.9939	-0.6945	-1.1367	-0.0093	-0.5752
good	-3.3290	-2.2414	-0.7090	1.1091	-0.3551	1.0261	0.9848	-0.1318	0.4629	-0.2186
good	-0.5087	-0.0898	0.2137	-0.3828	-0.9308	0.1807	-1.3018	-0.0943	0.0156	2.1246

Here are the variance-related statistics and a scree chart for the dataset in principal component representation. As must be, most of the dataset's overall variance is concentrated in the first few principal component variables.

scree of data.pc

variable	sdev	variance	cum_variance	relative_variance	cum_relative_variance
PC1	2.8647	8.2064	8.206	0.2830	0.2830
PC2	1.8099	3.2756	11.482	0.1130	0.3959
PC3	1.4166	2.0068	13.489	0.0692	0.4651
PC4	1.4064	1.9778	15.467	0.0682	0.5333
PC5	1.1781	1.3879	16.855	0.0479	0.5812
PC6	1.0849	1.1771	18.032	0.0406	0.6218
PC7	1.0626	1.1291	19.161	0.0389	0.6607
PC8	1.0403	1.0823	20.243	0.0373	0.6980
PC9	1.0061	1.0123	21.255	0.0349	0.7329
PC10	0.9888	0.9778	22.233	0.0337	0.7667
PC11	0.9574	0.9165	23.150	0.0316	0.7983
PC12	0.9305	0.8659	24.015	0.0299	0.8281
PC13	0.9087	0.8257	24.841	0.0285	0.8566
PC14	0.8515	0.7251	25.566	0.0250	0.8816
PC15	0.8337	0.6950	26.261	0.0240	0.9056
PC16	0.7999	0.6399	26.901	0.0221	0.9276
PC17	0.7442	0.5538	27.455	0.0191	0.9467
PC18	0.6973	0.4862	27.941	0.0168	0.9635
PC19	0.6639	0.4408	28.382	0.0152	0.9787
PC20	0.5250	0.2757	28.658	0.0095	0.9882
PC21	0.3632	0.1319	28.790	0.0045	0.9927
PC22	0.3197	0.1022	28.892	0.0035	0.9963
PC23	0.2385	0.0569	28.949	0.0020	0.9982
PC24	0.1398	0.0195	28.968	0.0007	0.9989
PC25	0.1338	0.0179	28.986	0.0006	0.9995
PC26	0.0892	0.0080	28.994	0.0003	0.9998
PC27	0.0634	0.0040	28.998	0.0001	0.9999
PC28	0.0429	0.0018	29.000	0.0001	1.0000
PC29	0.0007	0.0000	29.000	0.0000	1.0000

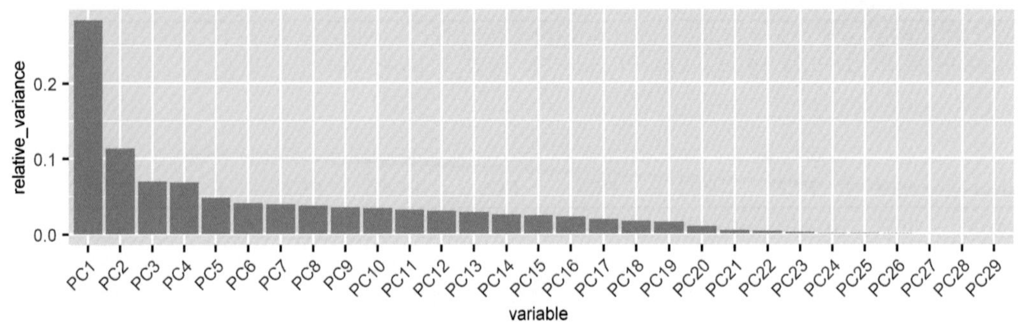

4.5.6 Try Again to Distinguish Observations

With the dataset in principal component representation, let's turn our attention to the first 2 principal component variables. Are the PC_1 and PC_2 variables enough to distinguish good loans from bad loans?

Here is the dataset visualized as a scatterplot, color-coded by class. See that most of the good loans appear farther to the upper-left than the bad loans do.

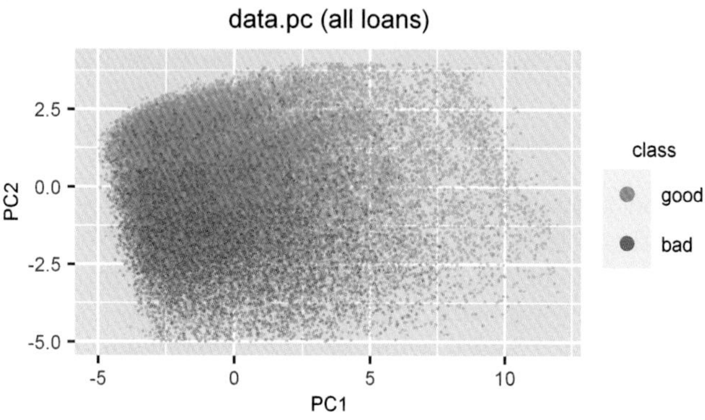

Here are data visualizations as scatterplots with data separated into good loan and bad loan subsets. We can make out more clearly now how at least some good loans look different from bad loans.

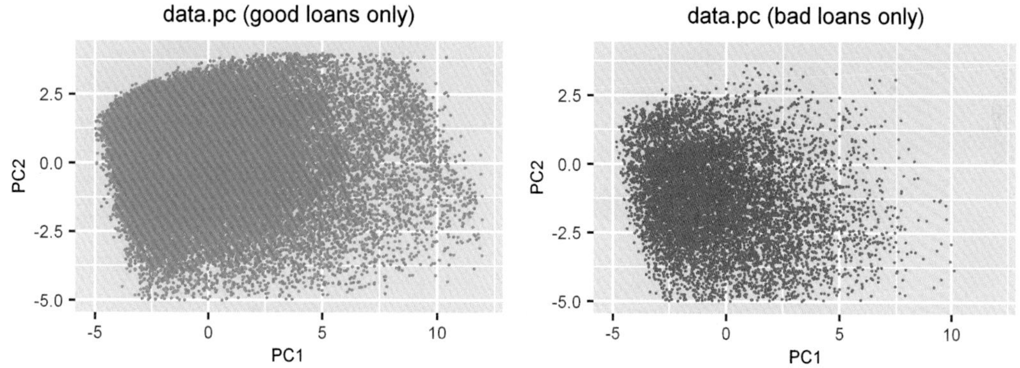

Again, this time with the dataset in principal component representation, use kernel density estimation to estimate probability densities, and highlight ranges of the probability density curves. For PC_1, we highlight values 1 to 6, chosen somewhat arbitrarily. That accounts for 25.55% of all loans. For PC_2, we highlight -5.5 to 0, again chosen somewhat arbitrarily. That accounts for 47.17% of all loans.

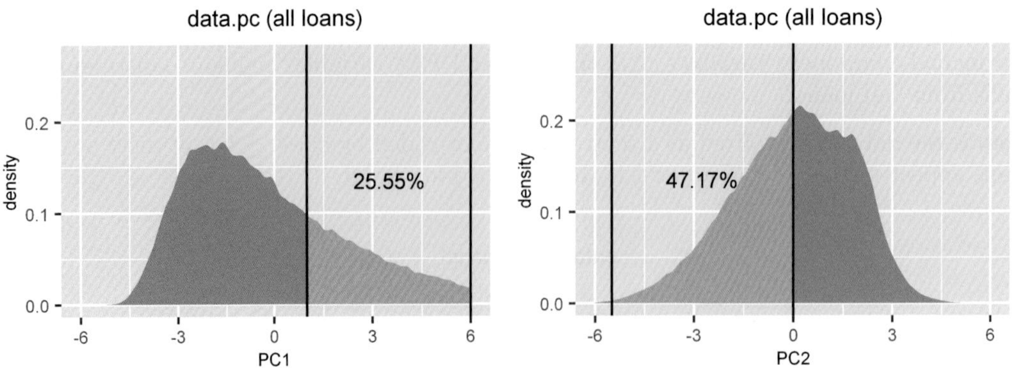

Separate the known good loans from the known bad loans. Use kernel density estimation to estimate the probability densities for these subsets. See that the PC_1 probability density curves do look quite the same as the one for all loans, as does the PC_2 probability density curve for good loans, but not so for PC_2 probability density curve for bad loans. The 26.01% of good loans have PC_1 values between 1 and 6, while 23.33% of bad loans do, which is very close to the same. For PC_2, 41.55% of good loans have values between -5.5 and 0, very close to the same as for all loans. However, 74.28% of bad loans have values in that range. You could reason that a new loan with a PC_2 value in that range is much more likely to be bad than good.

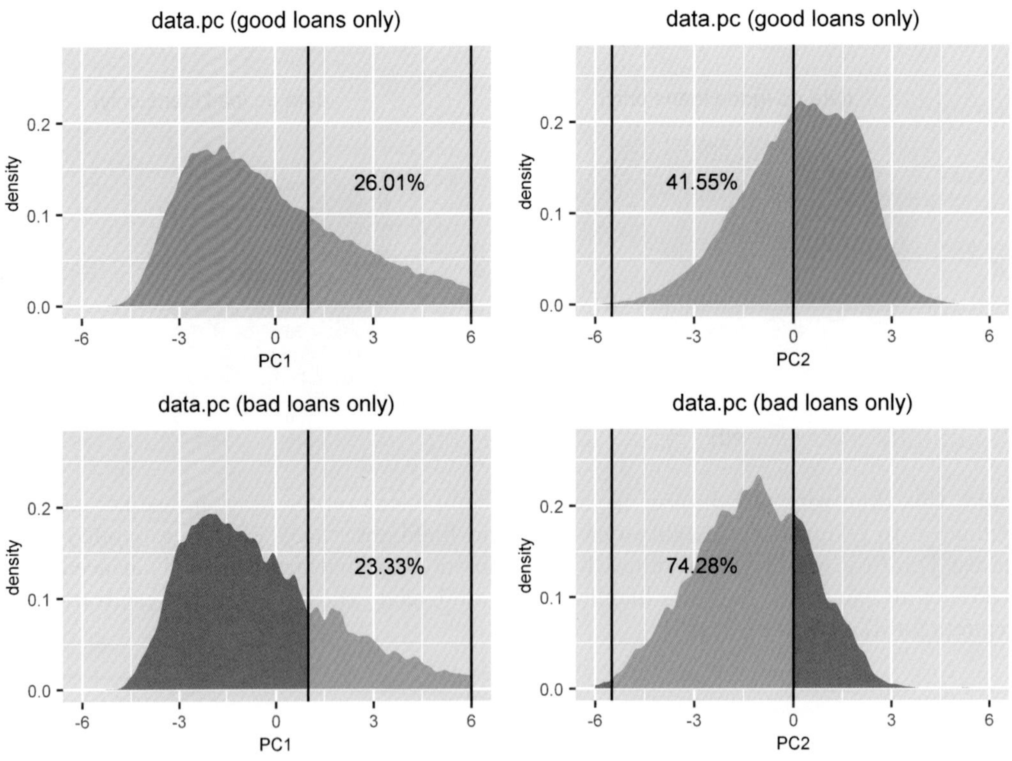

4.5.7 Decision about a New Loan

Equipped with an imperfect but tenable criterion to distinguish good loans from bad loans, we can now decide whether we want to purchase a specific new loan, like this one here. It's described in terms of the 29 variables we'll need to assess it.

	value		value		value
loan_amnt	5,000.00	annual_inc	24,000.00	out_prncp	0.0
funded_amnt	5,000.00	purpose	2.00	out_prncp_inv	0.0
funded_amnt_inv	4,975.00	dti	27.65	total_pymnt	5,861.1
term	36.00	delinq_2yrs	0.00	total_pymnt_inv	5,831.8
int_rate	10.65	inq_last_6mths	1.00	total_rec_prncp	5,000.0
installment	162.87	open_acc	3.00	total_rec_int	861.1
grade	2.00	pub_rec	0.00	total_rec_late_fee	0.0
sub_grade	6.00	revol_bal	13,648.00	last_pymnt_amnt	171.6
emp_length	10.00	revol_util	83.70	acc_now_delinq	0.0
home_ownership	5.00	total_acc	9.00		

Use the weight matrix calculated earlier in the analysis to convert the new loan description to principal component representation. Note that we do not calculate a new weight matrix for this 1 new loan description.

	value		value		value
PC1	-2.5696	PC11	0.0671	PC21	-0.0117
PC2	-0.2095	PC12	1.0222	PC22	-0.0098
PC3	-0.1192	PC13	-1.2524	PC23	-0.0053
PC4	0.3265	PC14	-0.6994	PC24	-0.1491
PC5	2.4782	PC15	-0.0578	PC25	0.1698
PC6	0.5129	PC16	0.8341	PC26	0.0017
PC7	0.8560	PC17	1.0882	PC27	0.0061
PC8	0.1897	PC18	-0.1249	PC28	0.0039
PC9	0.1320	PC19	0.3569	PC29	0.0000
PC10	0.5999	PC20	-0.1605		

The new loan's PC_2 value is -0.2095, which is in the range -5.5 to 0. Note that this 1 value, -0.2095, incorporates information about the new loan described by **all** the original variables. Our criterion suggests that a loan with such a PC_2 value is more likely bad than good. So, we decide to not purchase the new loan.

5 | Classification I

Learning Objectives

Terms

Know the terms:

- Classification
- Classifier
- Construction
- Prediction
- Evaluation
- Reference classified dataset
- New unclassified dataset
- Predictor variable
- Class variable
- Hyper-parameter
- Parameter
- Confusion matrix
- Performance metric
- Accuracy
- True positive rate (or sensitivity or recall)
- True negative rate (or specificity)
- False positive rate
- False negative rate
- Positive predictive value (or precision)
- Negative predictive value
- F1 score
- Training data
- Testing data
- In-sample performance
- Out-of-sample performance
- Holdin data
- Holdout data
- Cross-validation performance
- Fold
- k-nearest neighbors method
- Euclidean distance
- Logistic regression method
- Sigmoid function
- Vector sigmoid function
- Logistic function
- Decision tree method
- Decision tree model (or decision tree)
- Split
- Root node
- Leaf node (or terminal node)
- Entropy function
- Information gain
- Pruning

Effects of Assumptions

Know the effects of assumptions:

- Effect of using in-sample vs. out-of-sample vs. cross-validation evaluation on a model's performance metric value
- Effect of normalizing a reference dataset prior to applying the k-nearest neighbors method
- Effect of the number of neighbors on a k-nearest neighbors model's predictions
- Effects of various hyper-parameters on a decision tree model and its predictions

Use the Methods

Know how to use the methods:

- Frame your thinking about classification based on the classification methodology.
- Compute the confusion matrix for a model with respect to a test dataset by in-sample evaluation.
- Compute the confusion matrix for a model with respect to a test dataset by out-of-sample evaluation.
- Compute the confusion matrix for a model with respect to a test dataset by cross-validation evaluation.
- Compute a performance metric value for a model by confusion matrix analysis.
- Compute a k-nearest neighbors model.
- Compute a prediction using a k-nearest neighbors model.
- Compute a logistic regression model.
- Compute a prediction using a logistic regression model.
- Compute a decision tree model.
- Compute a decision tree model visualization.
- Compute a prediction using a decision tree model.

5.1 Classification Methodology

Construct a classifier, use it to predict, and evaluate its performance.

5.1.1 Introduction

The legend goes that Alexander of Macedonia, before embarking on a campaign of world conquest, first visited the Oracle of Delphi, known for her ability to predict the future. Alexander asked the oracle how the campaign would fare, but she replied that such a prediction could not be made with certainty. Unsatisfied, Alexander pressured her until she predicted, "You are invincible, my son!" Then satisfied, Alexander concluded, "Now I have my answer," and decided to proceed with the campaign.

Classifier construction methods construct classifiers that can make predictions. They do so by detecting patterns in some reference classified dataset, where classified here means a dataset that includes some ***categorical*** variable with known values that indicates the class of each observation. The classifiers constructed by these methods then leverage the patterns to predict, with some level of certainty, the class of each observation in some new unclassified dataset.

Classifiers are useful in a variety of business applications, notably any time it is advantageous to have categorical predictions about the future based on what happened in the past, which is pretty much all the time. For example, you may want to predict whether a project will be successful based on what kinds of projects were successful in the past, or predict whether a machine part will fail within a certain time period based on how machine parts failed in the past, or predict whether customers will like a new product based on what kind of products they liked in the past, or predict whether a new credit card transaction will turn out to be fraudulent based on circumstances around fraudulent credit card transactions in the past. Classifiers are also useful for making predictions about the past, present, or future based on the past, present, or future, in general. For example, you may want to predict whether a competitor is currently a threat to your business based on past demand for products, present supply chain structure, and projected future raw material prices.

Let's consider more carefully how we might predict whether a machine part will fail within a certain time period – say, within a month. Repairing a part that won't fail soon is an unnecessary expense, repairing a part just before it fails is a modest expense, and repairing an already failed part is a large expense. Operating conditions of parts throughout our factory are continuously monitored by copious sensors, which once per minute report their pressure and temperature measurements to a central computer via wireless internet connection. Technicians report information about failed parts whenever they make repairs, which is sent to the same central computer and aligned with the pressure and temperature data. The combined data are transformed into a representation in which each observation corresponds to a part, the pressures and temperatures of the part over a month, the pressures and temperatures of other parts over a month, and a status indicating whether the part had to be repaired at the end of the month. A classifier construction method is applied to the data weekly, which finds patterns that distinguish parts about to fail from parts that aren't, and constructs a classifier to predict that. The classifier is applied to new data as the data are updated over the week, predicts which parts are likely to fail within a month, and generates notifications to technicians to preemptively investigate and repair those parts before they fail, avoiding significant expense.

There are several popular classifier construction methods, including k-nearest neighbors, logistic regression, decision tree, naive Bayes, support vector machine, and neural network.

5.1.2 About Classification Methodology

The **classification** methodology comprises three parts:

- **construction** of a classifier, using some classifier construction method and some reference classified dataset
- **prediction** of **class variable** values, using a classifier applied to some new unclassified dataset
- **evaluation** of classifier performance, which estimates the quality of a classifier's predictions

5.1.2.1 Construction

In **construction**, a classifier construction method takes as input some reference classified dataset and hyper-parameter settings. The job of the classifier construction method is to detect patterns in the **reference classified dataset** that distinguish observations of different classes, and output a classifier with knowledge of those patterns built into it. The resulting classifier is defined by its form and parameter settings, both determined by the classifier construction method. Note that we have here a method that is constructing a method – the constructed classifier is not a set of predictions, but rather is a method to estimate class probabilities with which to make predictions.

Hyper-parameters are provided by a classifier construction method as a way to configure its specific behavior. Each particular classifier construction method provides its own set of hyper-parameters. You can think of hyper-parameters as switches and dials to set the operating conditions of a classifier construction machine. Hyper-parameters allow for several variations of any particular classifier construction method, effectively expanding the set of methods available for classifier construction.

Parameters, in contrast to hyper-parameters, are components of a classifier, set by a classifier construction method. You can think of parameters as switches and dials to set the operating conditions of a classifier machine.

Construction is also known as supervised learning, supervised machine learning, training, modeling, model building, model fitting, or predictive data analytics. A classifier is also known as a classification model, predictive analytical model, or just a model.

Here we see a reference classified dataset with five observations and nine variables. Eight of the variables are treated as **predictor variables** and one categorical variable is treated as the **class variable**, which can take on values of A or B. The classifier construction method is configured to specific behavior when you set the hyper-parameters. The method outputs a classifier that will accept a new unclassified dataset with eight predictor variables as input and estimate class value probabilities as output.

Construct a Classifier

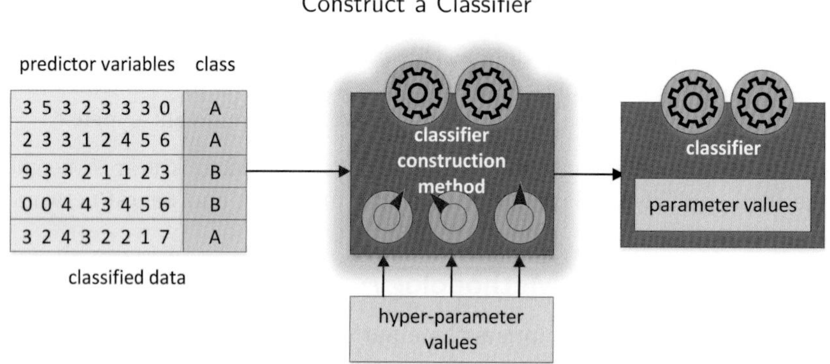

5.1.2.2 Prediction

In prediction, a classifier takes as input some new unclassified dataset. The job of the classifier is then to use its built-in knowledge of patterns in a reference classified dataset to estimate probabilities of class values for the new unclassified dataset. Each observation in the new unclassified dataset gets assigned its own class value probability. Arbitrarily treat one class value as the positive class and the other class value as the negative class. Then, to make a prediction, an observation's class value probability for the positive class can be compared with some cutoff. If the class value probability is equal to or exceeds the cutoff, then predict the observation to be of the positive class. If the class probability does not exceed the cutoff, then predict the observation to be of the negative class. Note that we have here a method constructed by a method – the classifier is the output of a classifier construction method, and the classifier is itself a method to estimate class value probabilities that can be used to make predictions.

Often you set the cutoff to 0.50, so that observations with class value probabilities equal to or exceeding 0.50 are classified one way and all other observations are classified another way. But the cutoff doesn't have to be set to 0.50. Rather, the cutoff can be set to any number in the range 0 to 1, depending on the business situation. When the cutoff is set higher than 0.50, it means that the classifier must be even more sure about how observations should be classified before making conclusions. Imagine predicting whether an extremely expensive project will succeed – you may want to be much more than 50% sure that it will succeed before concluding that it will succeed and proceeding with funding it. When the cutoff is set lower than 0.50, it means that the classifier can be less sure. Imagine predicting whether an inexpensive project with a high potential return will succeed – you may be comfortable funding it even if less than 50% sure that it will succeed.

Prediction, in this context, is also known as classification.

Below we see a new unclassified dataset with five observations and eight predictor variables. The classifier accepts the dataset as input and outputs class value probabilities for the positive class. The classifier estimates a 40% probability that the first observation should be classified as A, and therefore a 60% probability that the first observation should be classified as B. You earlier set the cutoff to 0.5, and since the probability estimated for the first observation does not exceed the cutoff, you can conclude that the first observation should be classified as B. Similarly for the other observations.

Use a Classifier to Make Predictions

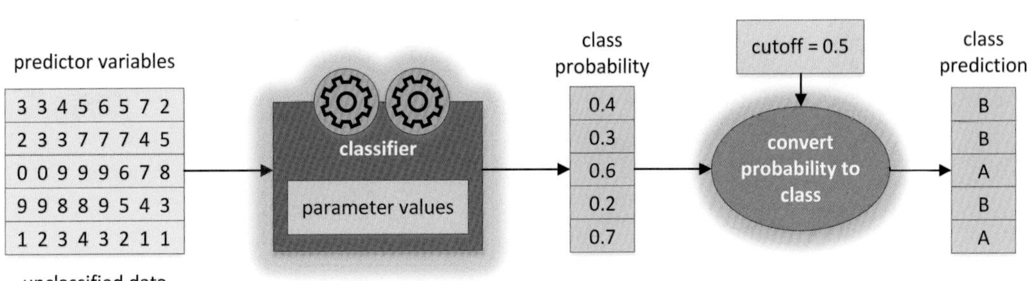

5.1.2.3 Evaluation

In evaluation, we usually estimate the quality of a classifier's predictions by examining not the classifier directly, but rather by examining 1 or more other similar classifiers. We'll call the classifier we're evaluating the prime classifier and call the other similar classifiers the evaluation classifiers. The evaluation classifiers are constructed using the same classifier construction method and hyper-parameter settings as for the prime classifier, but using only subsets of the reference classified dataset as inputs. Because the evaluation classifiers are constructed in almost the same way as the prime classifier, we make the assumption that their performance will be similar to that of the prime classifier. We can then take estimates of the evaluation classifiers' performance as an estimate of the prime classifier's performance. The reason that we usually do not examine a prime classifier directly, but rather examine evaluation classifiers, is so that we can leverage reference classified data in various useful ways.

Note that evaluation classifiers are required only for estimating the prime classifier's performance. We can discard the evaluation classifiers after the prime classifier's performance has been estimated. Their job will have been done.

Evaluation is also known as validation or testing.

Below we see a classifier being evaluated. The reference classified dataset used to construct the prime classifier is provided to a process that partitions the dataset into subsets as necessary. The dataset subsets are input to a classifier construction method that constructs evaluation classifiers. **Performance metric** values are calculated for the evaluation classifiers based on how well they back-predict. A single performance metric value for the prime classifier, here accuracy 0.5, is derived from the collection of performance metric values across the evaluation classifiers.

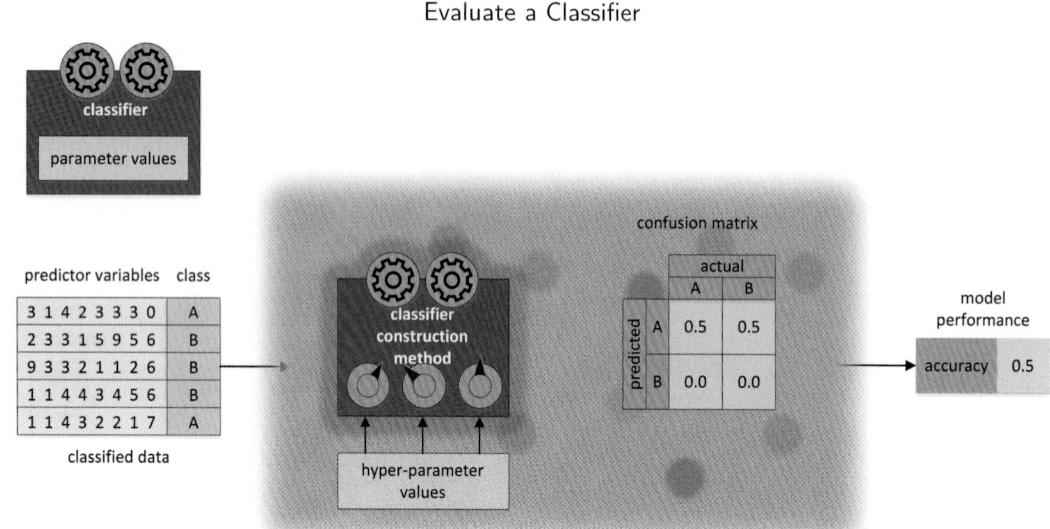

5.1.3 Construction

Construction involves applying a classifier construction method to a reference classified dataset to calculate classifier parameter values.

Consider this reference classified dataset. Note that the class variable is categorical and indicates each observation's known class.

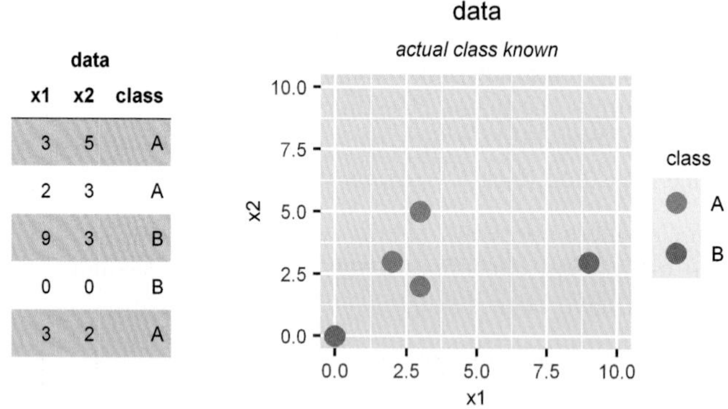

Use a classifier construction method to construct a classifier. Here we use the "My Special Method" method, with its 1 hyper-parameter set to 0.7, applied to the reference classified dataset. The resulting classifier has a form that is not completely transparent to us, but we do see that it is defined by parameter settings 0.35 and 3.4, will accept as input new unclassified datasets with 2 predictor variables, x_1 and x_2, and will output class value probabilities for classes A and B. Note that the hyper-parameter setting is not present in the classifier, although it is reflected in how the parameter settings were determined.

model

method	vars	parameter_1	parameter_2	classes
My Special Method	x1, x2	0.35	3.4	A, B

5.1.4 Prediction

Prediction involves applying a classifier to a new unclassified observation or dataset to calculate class probabilities, then comparing those probabilities with a cutoff to calculate class values.

Consider this new unclassified dataset:

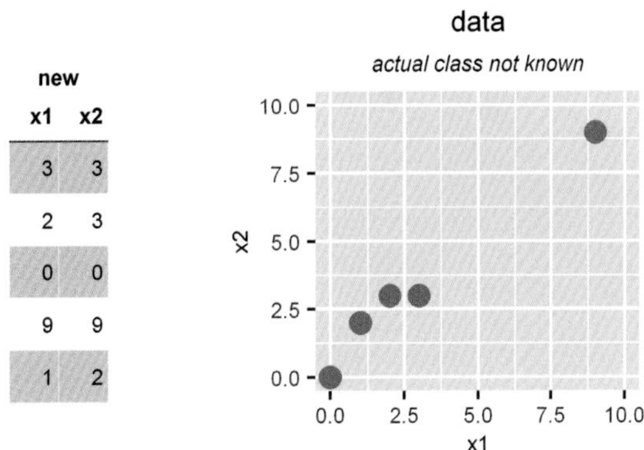

new

x1	x2
3	3
2	3
0	0
9	9
1	2

Use the classifier applied to the new unclassified dataset to estimate class value probabilities:

prob

A	B
0.6176	0.3824
0.4118	0.5882
0.0000	1.0000
1.0000	0.0000
0.2059	0.7941

new

x1	x2	prob.A
3	3	0.6176
2	3	0.4118
0	0	0.0000
9	9	1.0000
1	2	0.2059

Use the class value probabilities and a cutoff to calculate class values and thereby classify the new unclassified dataset. Here the cutoff is set to 0.5 and we are treating class A as the positive class, so we can conclude that the dataset should be classified accordingly.

cutoff
0.5

new

x1	x2	prob.A	class.predicted
3	3	0.6176	A
2	3	0.4118	B
0	0	0.0000	B
9	9	1.0000	A
1	2	0.2059	B

Here is the reference classified dataset compared with the new unclassified dataset as the classifier would have it classified:

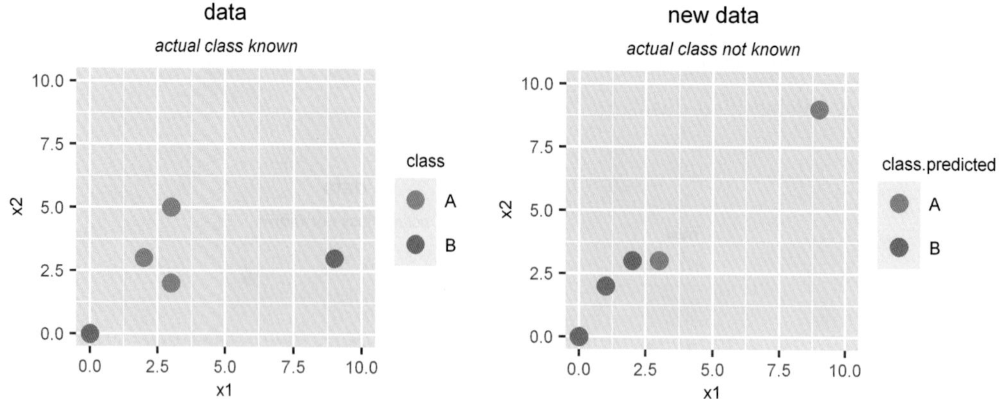

5.1.5 Evaluation

Evaluation involves back-predicting a classified dataset and comparing predicted class values to known class values.

5.1.5.1 Back-Prediction

We can know if a classifier predicts correctly or incorrectly only when we can compare predicted class values to known class values. Back-prediction involves using a classifier to predict class values of already classified observations, but in a way that the known class values are hidden from the classifier. Then the classifier's predicted class values can be compared with the known class values. Back-prediction can be applied to the reference classified dataset that was used to construct the classifier, or applied to a subset of that dataset, or applied to a completely different dataset.

Here we apply back-prediction to the reference classified dataset with the known class values hidden:

data

x1	x2	class
3	5	A
2	3	A
9	3	B
0	0	B
3	2	A

data (known class is hidden)

x1	x2
3	5
2	3
9	3
0	0
3	2

Use the classifier (previously constructed) to estimate class value probabilities.

prob			data (known class is hidden)		
A	B		x1	x2	prob.A
0.6176	0.3824		3	5	0.6176
0.4118	0.5882		2	3	0.4118
1.0000	0.0000		9	3	1.0000
0.0000	1.0000		0	0	0.0000
0.6176	0.3824		3	2	0.6176

Use class value probabilities and a cutoff to classify the dataset. The predicted class values might be different from the known class values.

cutoff
0.5

data (known class is hidden)			
x1	x2	prob.A	class.predicted
3	5	0.6176	A
2	3	0.4118	B
9	3	1.0000	A
0	0	0.0000	B
3	2	0.6176	A

5.1.5.2 Comparison

Compare the predicted class values to the known class values. Mark each observation as a hit if it was correctly classified or as a miss if it was incorrectly classified.

data		
x1	x2	class
3	5	A
2	3	A
9	3	B
0	0	B
3	2	A

data (known class is hidden)				
x1	x2	prob.A	class.predicted	hit
3	5	0.6176	A	TRUE
2	3	0.4118	B	FALSE
9	3	1.0000	A	FALSE
0	0	0.0000	B	TRUE
3	2	0.6176	A	TRUE

Here is a visualization of the dataset showing how specific observations have been correctly or incorrectly classified:

- The first observation (x_1=3, x_2=5) is known to be of class A and it was correctly predicted to be of class A.
- The second observation (x_1=2, x_2=3) is known to be of class A and it was incorrectly predicted to be of class B.
- The third observation (x_1=9, x_2=3) is known to be of class B and it was incorrectly predicted to be of class A.
- The fourth observation (x_1=0, x_2=0) is known to be of class B and it was correctly predicted to be of class B.

- The fifth observation (x_1=3, x_2=2) is known to be of class A and it was correctly predicted to be of class A.

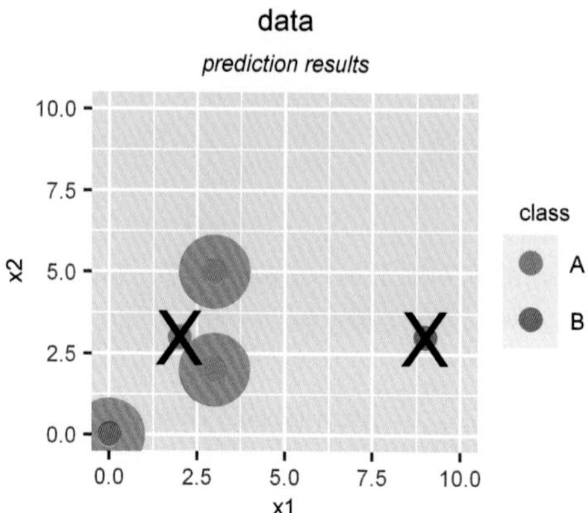

Calculate some performance metric based on the prediction hits and misses. Here we calculate the proportion of correct predictions. This is our estimate of our classifier's performance.

proportion.of.correct.predictions
0.6

5.2 Classifier Evaluation

More about evaluating a classifier's performance.

5.2.1 Introduction

When a classifier construction method produces a classifier, that classifier might or might not make good predictions. If we think that it will make good predictions, then perhaps we should use it to inform our business decisions. If we think that it won't, then perhaps we should discard it as useless. We don't know in advance how good the predictions will be, but we can estimate that. Let's look further into estimating how good a classifier's predictions will be.

5.2.2 Confusion Matrix

Consider this reference classified dataset. Note that the class variable is categorical and indicates each observation's known class.

data

x1	x2	class
3	5	A
2	3	A
9	3	B
0	0	B
3	2	A

A **confusion matrix** summarizes how a classifier and cutoff correctly or incorrectly back-predict class values, and provides a convenient way from which to calculate performance metrics. Usually it is structured as a 2×2 matrix, rows corresponding to predicted class values, columns corresponding to known class values, with the arbitrarily chosen positive class positioned before the negative class. In other contexts, it may represented as a 2×2 matrix with the sense of the rows and columns switched, or as frequency table.

The four values contained in a confusion matrix can indicate absolute numbers of observations or relative numbers of observations. By convention, we title a confusion matrix with uppercase letters if it contains absolute numbers and with lowercase letters if it contains relative numbers.

How to interpret a confusion matrix:

- row 1, column 1: how many observations are predicted to be positive class and known to be positive class
- row 2, column 1: how many observations are predicted to be negative class but known to be positive class
- row 1, column 2: how many observations are predicted to be positive class but known to be negative class
- row 2, column 2: how many observations are predicted to be negative class and known to be negative class

Here we see absolute and relative confusion matrices (in usual and frequency table forms) for a previously constructed classifier and cutoff 0.5 applied to back-predict the reference classified dataset:

CM

	A	B
A	2	1
B	1	1

CM (as frequency table)

Prediction	Reference	Freq
A	A	2
B	A	1
A	B	1
B	B	1

cm

	A	B
A	0.4	0.2
B	0.2	0.2

cm (as frequency table)

Prediction	Reference	Freq
A	A	0.4
B	A	0.2
A	B	0.2
B	B	0.2

Interpretation of the confusion matrix:

- 2 observations (40%) are predicted to be of class A and known to be of class A (upper-left part of confusion matrix).
- 1 observation (20%) is predicted to be of class B but known to be of class A (lower-left part of confusion matrix).
- 1 observation (20%) is predicted to be of class A but known to be of class B (upper-right part of confusion matrix).
- 1 observation (20%) is predicted to be of class B and known to be of class B (lower-right part of confusion matrix).

5.2.3 Performance Metrics

From a confusion matrix, we can calculate any of several useful classifier performance metrics.

Essential classifier performance metrics:

- **accuracy:** $\frac{\text{correct predictions}}{\text{total predictions}}$
- **true positive rate (also known as sensitivity or recall):** $\frac{\text{correct positive predictions}}{\text{positive actuals}}$
- **true negative rate (also known as specificity):** $\frac{\text{correct negative predictions}}{\text{negative actuals}}$
- **false positive rate:** $\frac{\text{incorrect positive predictions}}{\text{negative actuals}}$
- **false negative rate:** $\frac{\text{incorrect negative predictions}}{\text{positive actuals}}$
- **positive predictive value (also known as precision):** $\frac{\text{correct positive predictions}}{\text{positive predictions}}$
- **negative predictive value:** $\frac{\text{correct negative predictions}}{\text{negative predictions}}$
- **F1 score:** $\frac{(2 \times \text{correct positive predictions})}{\left(\begin{array}{c}(2 \times \text{correct positive predictions}) + \\ \text{incorrect positive predictions} + \text{incorrect negative predictions}\end{array}\right)}$

Here we see a confusion matrix and the corresponding essential performance metric values.

cm

	A	B
A	0.4	0.2
B	0.2	0.2

accuracy	tpr	tnr	fpr	fnr	ppv	npv	f1
0.6	0.6667	0.5	0.5	0.3333	0.6667	0.5	0.6667

Calculations based on the confusion matrix:

- Accuracy is 60% (sum of diagonal divided by sum of all).
- True positive rate is 67% (upper-left divided by sum of all left).
- True negative rate is 50% (lower-right divided by sum of all right).
- False positive rate is 50% (upper-right divided by sum of all right).
- False negative rate is 33% (lower-left divided by sum of all left).
- Positive predictive value is 67% (upper-left divided by all upper).
- Negative predictive value is 50% (lower-right divided by all lower).
- F1 score is 67% (2 $\times$ upper-left divided by sum of 2 $\times$ upper-left, lower-left, upper-right).

5.2.4 Evaluation by In-Sample Performance

Evaluation by **in-sample performance** is 1 of 3 popular versions of evaluation. It uses all of the reference classified dataset, referred to in this context as **training data**, to construct 1 evaluation classifier. It uses all of the same reference classified dataset, referred to in this context as **testing data**, to predict and compare classes.

Here we see evaluation by in-sample performance of a classifier.

Use the "My Special Method" method applied to the 5-observation reference classified dataset to construct the prime classifier.

data

x1	x2	class
3	5	A
2	3	A
9	3	B
0	0	B
3	2	A

model.prime

method	vars	parameter_1	parameter_2	classes
My Special Method	x1, x2	0.35	3.4	A, B

Use the same "My Special Method" method applied to the reference classified dataset to construct an evaluation classifier, which in this case is exactly the same as the prime classifier.

data.train

x1	x2	class
3	5	A
2	3	A
9	3	B
0	0	B
3	2	A

model.evaluation

method	vars	parameter_1	parameter_2	classes
My Special Method	x1, x2	0.35	3.4	A, B

Input the same reference dataset with the class variable hidden to the evaluation classifier to produce class value probabilities. Set cutoff to 0.5 and predict 5 class values, which in turn compare with the 5 known class values. From there, construct a confusion matrix and use it to compute a performance metric, in this example accuracy 0.60, which is an estimate of the prime classifier's performance.

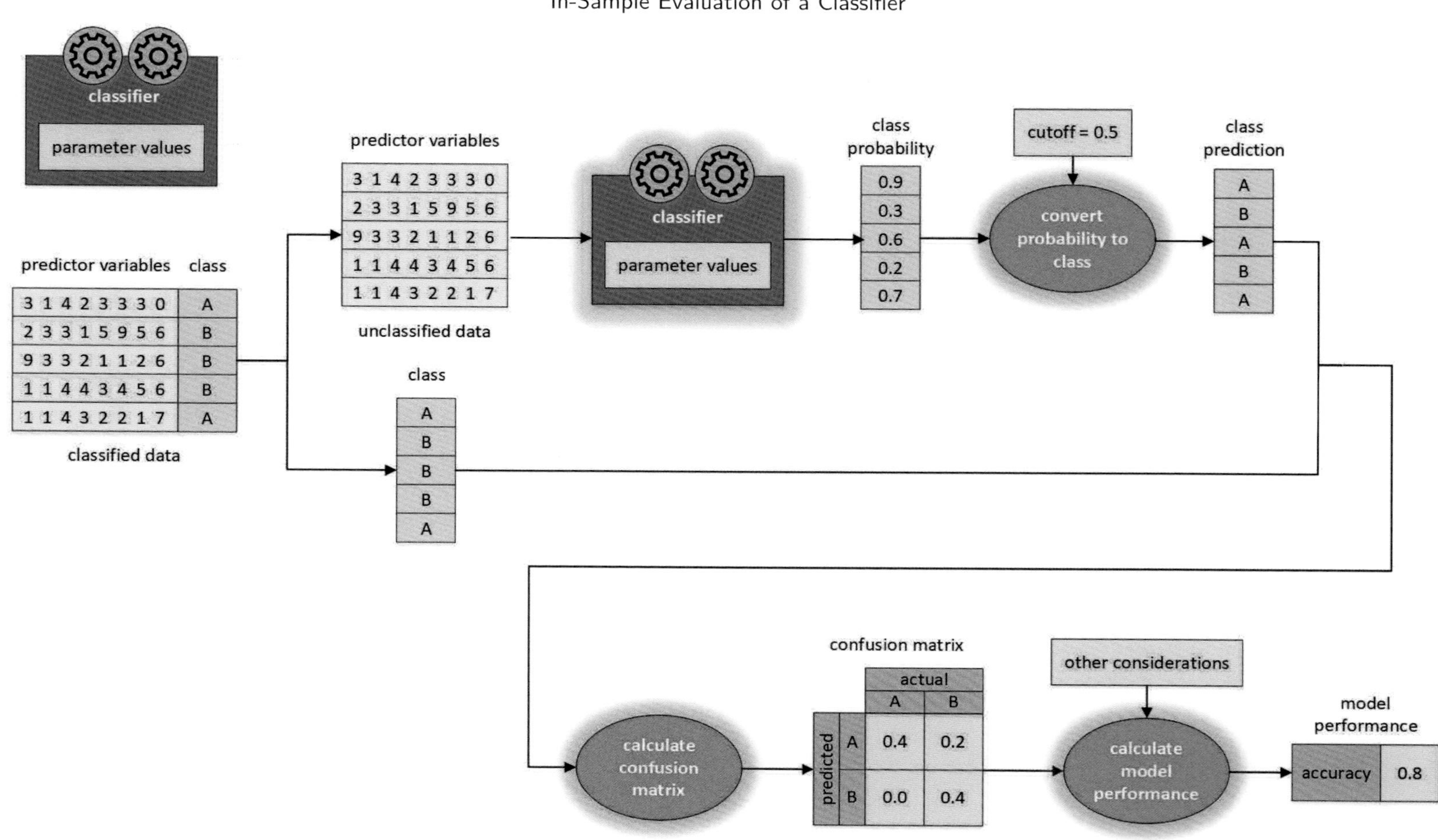
In-Sample Evaluation of a Classifier
classifier
parameter values
predictor variables
class
3 1 4 2 3 3 3 0 A
2 3 3 1 5 9 5 6 B
9 3 3 2 1 1 2 6 B
1 1 4 4 3 4 5 6 B
1 1 4 3 2 2 1 7 A
classified data
predictor variables
3 1 4 2 3 3 3 0
2 3 3 1 5 9 5 6
9 3 3 2 1 1 2 6
1 1 4 4 3 4 5 6
1 1 4 3 2 2 1 7
unclassified data
class
A
B
B
B
A
classifier
parameter values
class probability
0.9
0.3
0.6
0.2
0.7
cutoff = 0.5
convert probability to class
class prediction
A
B
A
B
A
calculate confusion matrix
confusion matrix
actual
A B
predicted
A 0.4 0.2
B 0.0 0.4
other considerations
calculate model performance
model performance
accuracy 0.8

data.test

x1	x2	class
3	5	A
2	3	A
9	3	B
0	0	B
3	2	A

cutoff
0.5

data.test (known class is hidden)

x1	x2	prob.A	class.predicted	hit
3	5	0.6176	A	TRUE
2	3	0.4118	B	FALSE
9	3	1.0000	A	FALSE
0	0	0.0000	B	TRUE
3	2	0.6176	A	TRUE

cm

	A	B
A	0.4	0.2
B	0.2	0.2

accuracy
0.6

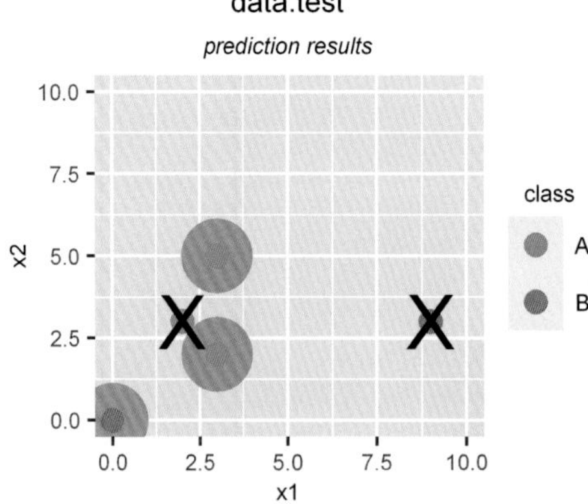

An inherent problem with evaluation by in-sample performance is that its estimate of a classifier's performance is based on how well it classifies a dataset with a classifier that already has built-in knowledge of that dataset. Imagine a student who studies the answers to certain questions and then is tested on only those questions. The test results might overstate how the student would perform when tested on other questions. In a business situation, imagine a classifier that is constructed from a certain dataset and then back-predicts that dataset. The results might overstate how the classifier would perform when classifying another dataset.

5.2.5 Evaluation by Out-of-Sample Performance

Evaluation by **out-of-sample performance** is another 1 of 3 popular versions of evaluation. It uses some of the reference classified dataset, referred to in this context as **holdin** data, to construct an evaluation classifier. It uses the rest of the reference classified dataset, referred to in this context as **holdout data**, to predict and compare class values.

Out-of-sample performance is also known as holdout performance.

Here we see evaluation by out-of-sample performance of a classifier.

Use the "My Special Method" method applied to the 5-observation reference classified dataset to construct the prime classifier.

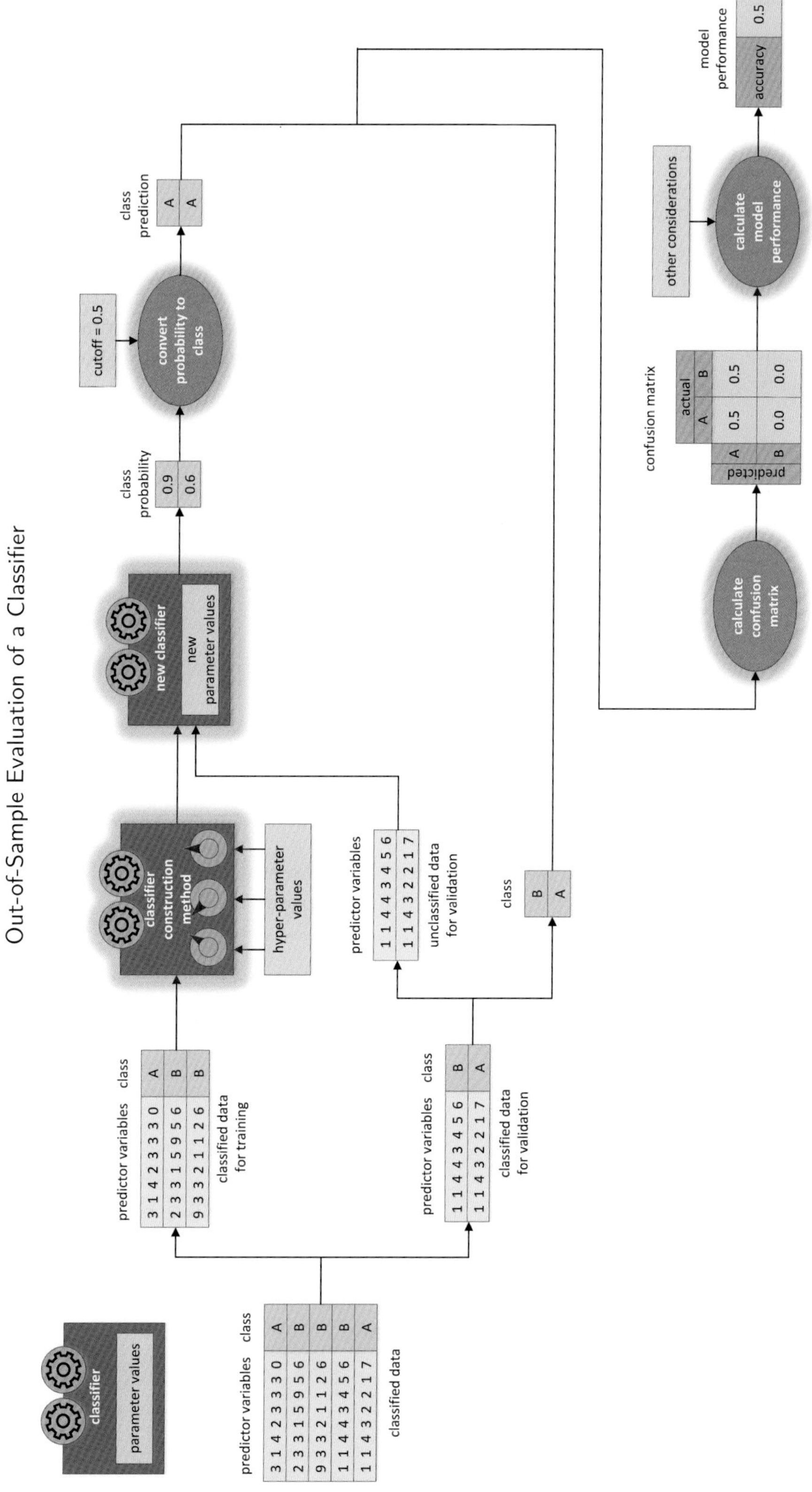
Out-of-Sample Evaluation of a Classifier
classifier
parameter values
predictor variables
class
3 1 4 2 3 3 3 0 A
2 3 3 1 5 9 5 6 B
9 3 3 2 1 1 2 6 B
1 1 4 4 3 4 5 6 B
1 1 4 3 2 2 1 7 A
classified data
predictor variables
class
3 1 4 2 3 3 3 0 A
2 3 3 1 5 9 5 6 B
9 3 3 2 1 1 2 6 B
classified data for training
predictor variables
class
1 1 4 4 3 4 5 6 B
1 1 4 3 2 2 1 7 A
classified data for validation
classifier construction method
hyper-parameter values
predictor variables
1 1 4 4 3 4 5 6
1 1 4 3 2 2 1 7
unclassified data for validation
class
B
A
new classifier
new parameter values
class probability
0.9
0.6
cutoff = 0.5
convert probability to class
class prediction
A
A
calculate confusion matrix
confusion matrix
actual
A
B
predicted
A
0.5
0.5
B
0.0
0.0
other considerations
calculate model performance
model performance
accuracy
0.5

data

x1	x2	class
3	5	A
2	3	A
9	3	B
0	0	B
3	2	A

model.prime

method	vars	parameter_1	parameter_2	classes
My Special Method	x1, x2	0.35	3.4	A, B

Partition the reference classified dataset into a holdin part for training and a holdout part for testing. Here we choose to tag 40% of the dataset's observations, sampled at random, as holdout for testing: observations 1 and 3. We tag the remaining 60% of the dataset as holdin for training: observations 2, 4, and 5.

holdin
2
4
5

data.train

x1	x2	class
2	3	A
0	0	B
3	2	A

holdout
1
3

data.test

x1	x2	class
3	5	A
9	3	B

Use the "My Special Method" method applied to the 3-observation holdin dataset to construct an evaluation classifier, which will be different from the prime classifier.

data.train

x1	x2	class
2	3	A
0	0	B
3	2	A

model.evaluation

method	vars	parameter_1	parameter_2	classes
My Special Method	x1, x2	0.35	1.667	A, B

Input the 2-observation holdout dataset to the evaluation classifier to produce class value probabilities. Set cutoff to 0.5 and predict 2 class values, and in turn compare with the 2 known class values. From there, construct a confusion matrix and use it to compute a performance metric, in this example accuracy 0.50, which is an estimate of the prime classifier's performance. At this point, we can discard the evaluation classifier.

data.test

x1	x2	class
3	5	A
9	3	B

cutoff
0.5

data.test (known class is hidden)

x1	x2	prob.A	class.predicted	hit
3	5	1	A	TRUE
9	3	1	A	FALSE

cm

	A	B
A	0.5	0.5
B	0.0	0.0

accuracy
0.5

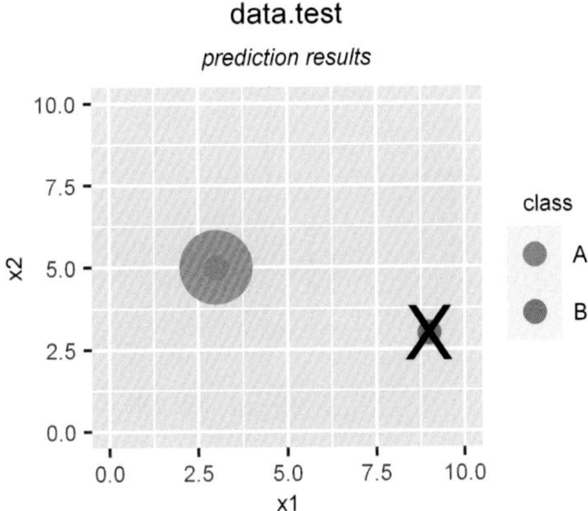

Evaluation by out-of-sample performance is considered to produce better estimates of classifier performance than evaluation by in-sample performance. It avoids the problem of using the same dataset for both training and testing. However, it has its own inherent problem in that it uses only some of the reference classified dataset to train and only some of it to test. Imagine a student who studies the answers to certain questions and then is tested on other questions, but not tested on any of the questions for which she studied. Had she studied the answers to those other questions she might have performed better. The results might understate or overstate how the student would perform on other tests. In a business situation, imagine a classifier that is constructed from a certain dataset and then back-predicts another dataset. The results might understate or overstate how the classifier would perform classifying other datasets.

5.2.6 Evaluation by Cross-Validation Performance

Evaluation by **cross-validation performance** is yet another one of three popular versions of evaluation. It works by organizing a reference classified dataset into several approximately equally sized **folds**, where each fold comprises a subset of the dataset for training and the rest of the dataset for testing. It uses all of the reference classified dataset, but only one subset at a time, to construct several evaluation classifiers. It uses all of the reference classified dataset, but only one subset at a time, to predict and compare class values.

Here we see evaluation by cross-validation performance of a classifier.

Use the “My Special Method” method applied to the 5-observation reference classified dataset to construct the prime classifier.

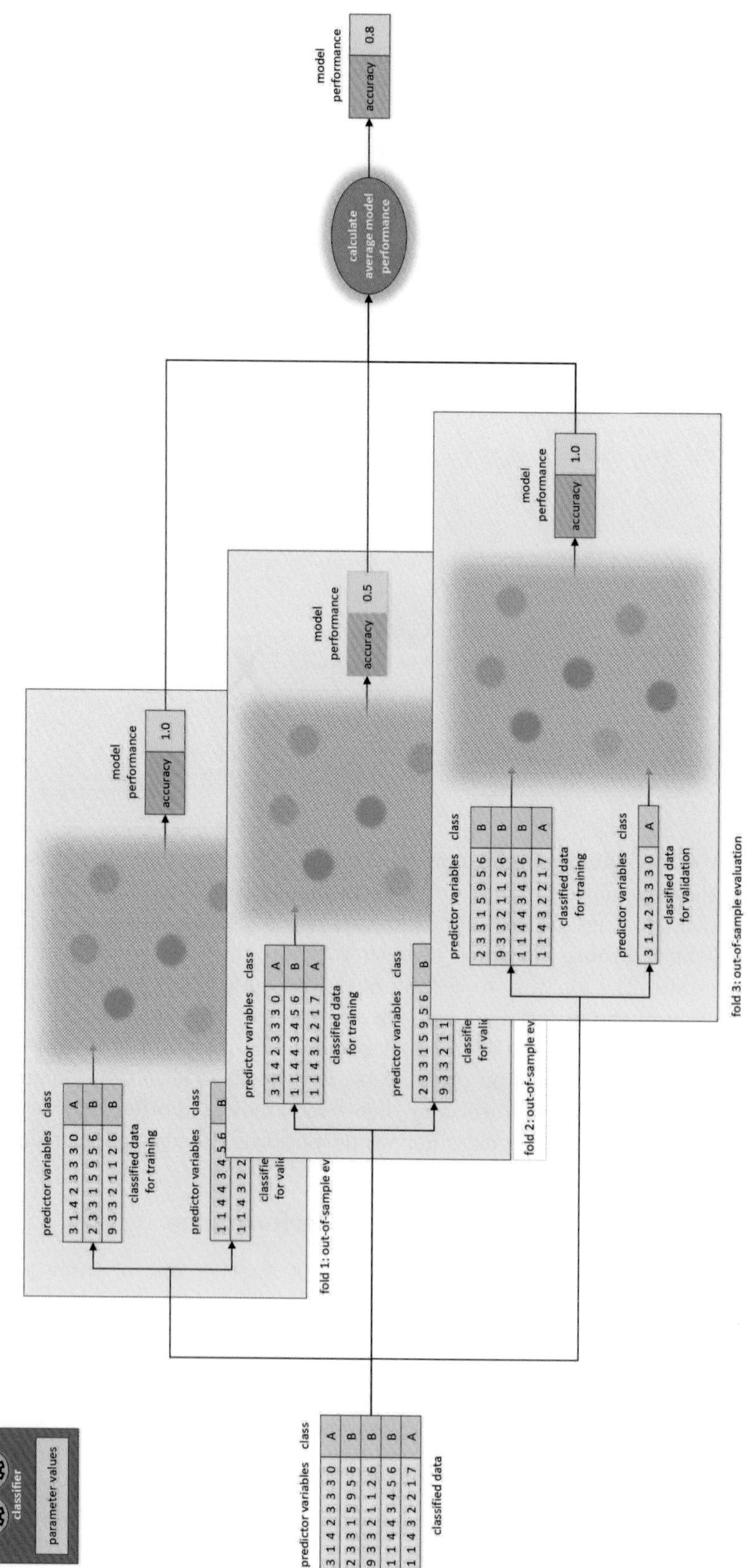

Cross-Validation Evaluation of a Classifier
classifier
parameter values
predictor variables class
3 1 4 2 3 3 3 0 A
2 3 3 1 5 9 5 6 B
9 3 3 2 1 1 2 6 B
1 1 4 4 3 4 5 6 B
1 1 4 3 2 2 1 7 A
classified data
classified data for training
classified data for validation
model performance
accuracy 1.0
accuracy 0.5
accuracy 1.0
fold 1: out-of-sample evaluation
fold 2: out-of-sample evaluation
fold 3: out-of-sample evaluation
calculate average model performance
accuracy 0.8

data

x1	x2	class
3	5	A
2	3	A
9	3	B
0	0	B
3	2	A

model.prime

method	vars	parameter_1	parameter_2	classes
My Special Method	x1, x2	0.35	3.4	A, B

Organize the reference classified dataset into several approximately equally sized folds. Do this by first partitioning the dataset into approximately equally sized subsets, sampling at random. Here we choose to organize as 3 folds, and so partition into 3 subsets: observations 4 and 5; observation 2; and observations 1 and 3.

Fold1	Fold2	Fold3
4, 5	2	1, 3

For each fold, assign the reference datatset subset to be its testing dataset. Then for each fold, assign the part of the reference dataset not used for testing in that fold to be its training dataset. Here the first fold comprises a 3-observation dataset for training and a 2-observation dataset for testing. The dataset for training comprises observations 1, 2, and 3. The dataset for testing comprises observations 4 and 5. Similarly for folds 2 and 3.

Note that some observations used for training will be duplicated across folds, but no observations used for testing will be duplicated across folds. Also note that each fold uses all of the reference dataset, some for training and the rest for testing.

data_1.train

x1	x2	class
3	5	A
2	3	A
9	3	B

data_2.train

x1	x2	class
3	5	A
9	3	B
0	0	B
3	2	A

data_3.train

x1	x2	class
2	3	A
0	0	B
3	2	A

data_1.test

x1	x2	class
0	0	B
3	2	A

data_2.test

x1	x2	class
2	3	A

data_3.test

x1	x2	class
3	5	A
9	3	B

For each fold, input its dataset for training to the "Special Classifier Construction Method" to construct an evaluation classifier, and input its dataset for testing to that classifier to produce class value probabilities, predict class values, construct a confusion matrix, and compute a performance metric. Note that we construct 3 different evaluation classifiers and compute 3 different performance metrics. Here the first fold performance metric is accuracy 0.50, the second fold performance metric is accuracy 0.00, and the third fold performance metric is accuracy 0.50.

Fold 1: Here are the results for fold 1. Note that the fold 1 evaluation classifier's performance is accuracy 0.5.

data_1.train

x1	x2	class
3	5	A
2	3	A
9	3	B

model_1.evaluation

method	vars	parameter_1	parameter_2	classes
My Special Method	x1, x2	0.35	4.667	A, B

data_1.test

x1	x2	class
0	0	B
3	2	A

cutoff
0.5

data_1.test (known class is hidden)

x1	x2	prob.A	class.predicted	hit
0	0	0.00	B	TRUE
3	2	0.45	B	FALSE

cm_1

	A	B
A	0.0	0.0
B	0.5	0.5

accuracy_1
0.5

Fold 2: Here are the results for fold 2. Note that the fold 2 evaluation classifier's performance is accuracy 0.

data_2.train

x1	x2	class
3	5	A
9	3	B
0	0	B
3	2	A

model_2.evaluation

method	vars	parameter_1	parameter_2	classes
My Special Method	x1, x2	0.35	3.75	A, B

data_2.test

x1	x2	class
2	3	A

cutoff
0.5

data_2.test (known class is hidden)

x1	x2	prob.A	class.predicted	hit
2	3	0.3733	B	FALSE

cm_2

	A	B
A	0	0
B	1	0

accuracy_2
0

Fold 3: Here are the results for fold 3. Note that the fold 3 evaluation classifier's performance is accuracy 0.5.

data_3.train

x1	x2	class
2	3	A
0	0	B
3	2	A

mdoel_3.evaluation

method	vars	parameter_1	parameter_2	classes
My Special Method	x1, x2	0.35	1.667	A, B

data_3.test

x1	x2	class
3	5	A
9	3	B

cutoff
0.5

data_3.test (known class is hidden)

x1	x2	prob.A	class.predicted	hit
3	5	1	A	TRUE
9	3	1	A	FALSE

cm_3

	A	B
A	0.5	0.5
B	0.0	0.0

accuracy_3
0.5

Here is a comparison of the prediction results across the 3 folds:

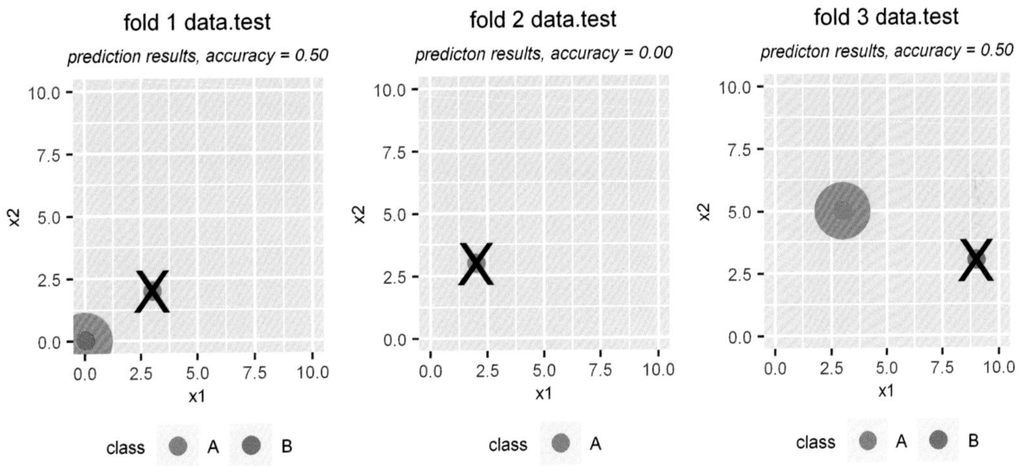

Compute the average of the 3 performance metrics, in this example accuracy 0.33, which is an estimate of the prime classifier's performance. At this point, we can discard all 3 of the evaluation classifiers.

fold	accuracy
1	0.5
2	0.0
3	0.5

accuracy.cv
0.3333

Evaluation by cross-validation performance is considered to produce better estimates of classifier performance than either evaluation by in-sample or out-of-sample performance. It avoids the problem of using the same dataset for both training and testing. It also avoids the problem of using only some of the reference classified data to train and only some to test.

In practice, evaluation by cross-validation performance is often done using 5 or 10 folds.

5.3 k-Nearest Neighbors

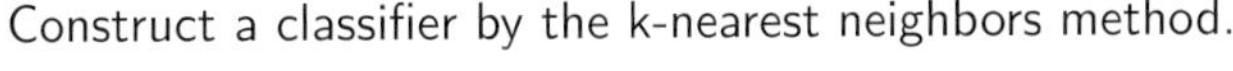
Construct a classifier by the k-nearest neighbors method.

5.3.1 Introduction

Jigokudani Monkey Park is the location of a prestigious, beautiful country club and spa ... for monkeys. Japanese macaques relax in its hot springs, with the highest ranking members congregating in the best spots. When a new monkey joins in, perhaps you can distinguish whether it's from the upper class or lower class by which other monkeys it approaches.

The k-nearest neighbors method treats a reference classified dataset as a classifier, which can be used to classify new observations based on how close they are to a subset of observations in the dataset.

5.3.2 About k-Nearest Neighbors

The **k-nearest neighbors method** involves computing distances (dissimilarities) between observations.

5.3.2.1 How to Construct a Classifier

Constructing a k-nearest neighbors classifier based on a reference classified dataset is trivial. The reference classified dataset **is** the classifier. It effectively serves as a lookup table.

5.3.2.2 How to Predict

Use the k-nearest neighbors classifier to predict the class of a new unclassified observation:

- Set the number of neighbors to consider, k.
- Set how distance (dissimilarity) between observations is to be measured.

- Normalize the reference classified dataset (optional).
- Find distances (dissimilarities) from the new observation to all observations in the reference classified dataset, ignoring the class variable.
- Identify the k observations with shortest distances (least dissimilarity).
- Calculate the mean of the class dummy of the k identified observations; 1 is positive class and 0 is negative class.
- Interpret the resulting number as the probability that the new unclassified observation is in the positive class.
- Predict the new unclassified observation's class based on probability.

5.3.2.3 Measures of Distance

There are several ways to measure distance (dissimilarity) between observations, including Manhattan distance, **Euclidean distance**, extensions to Euclidean distance, or any way we devise that makes sense for our application. Typically, Euclidean distance is used in the absence of a compelling reason to use anything else.

5.3.2.4 Other Considerations

Typically, the number of neighbors to consider, k, is set to a number in the range 1 to 20.

The reference classified dataset can (should) be normalized when predictor variables are expressed in units of very different scales. This effectively puts all predictor variables on the same unitless scale and so avoids any distance distortions across variables.

Note that constructing a k-nearest neighbors classifier requires zero compute-time. However, predicting can be very compute-time intensive when the reference classified dataset is large. Any prediction requires distance calculations for every observation in the dataset.

5.3.3 k-Nearest Neighbors

The k-nearest neighbors method can be applied to datasets with many predictor variables where distance (dissimilarity) between observations can be computed.

5.3.3.1 Data

Consider this reference classified dataset and new unclassified observation. Should the new observation be classified as A or B?

data

x1	x2	class
49	38	A
671	26	A
772	47	A
136	48	A
123	40	A
36	29	B
192	31	B
6,574	35	B
2,200	58	B
2,100	30	B

new

x1	x2
800	32

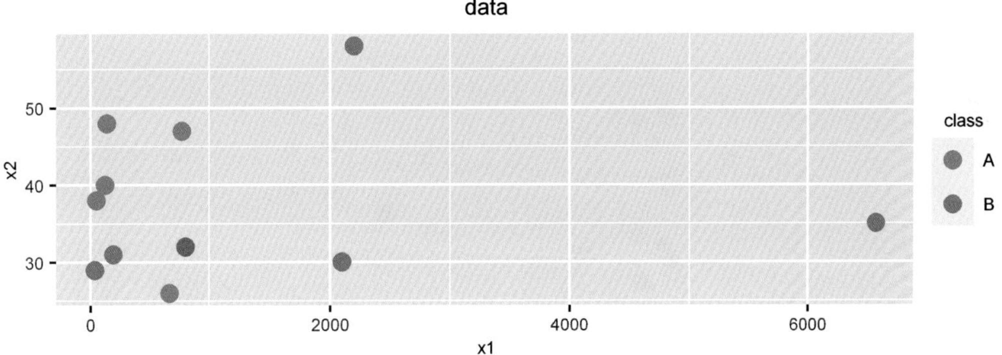

5.3.3.2 Normalization

The new observation (x_1=800, x_2=32) might at first appear closest to (x_1=671, x_2=26), (x_1=36, x_2=29), and (x_1=192, x_2=31), but x_1 and x_2 are on very different scales. The x_1 values range from 36 all the way to 6574, while x_2 values are all within the relatively small range 26 to 58. The observations are all relatively close to each other along the x_2 axis, but spread out along the x_1 axis. This is an artifact of the units in which x_1 and x_2 are expressed. If x_2 were expressed in smaller units (resulting in larger numbers, say 26,000 to 58,000) and x_1 were expressed in larger units (resulting in smaller numbers, say 0.036 to 6.574), then the observations would instead be relatively far from each other along the x_1 axis and close along the x_1 axis.

To avoid this undesirable situation, normalize the dataset and new observation to effectively express x_1 and x_2 without units. The reference dataset should be normalized per the means and standard deviations of its predictor variables. The new observation should be normalized per the same means and standard deviations of the reference dataset's predictor variables.

data.norm

x1	x2	class
-0.6092	-0.0197	A
-0.3027	-1.1991	A
-0.2529	0.8649	A
-0.5663	0.9632	A
-0.5727	0.1769	A
-0.6156	-0.9043	B
-0.5387	-0.7077	B
2.6060	-0.3145	B
0.4507	1.9461	B
0.4014	-0.8060	B

new.norm

x1	x2
-0.2391	-0.6094

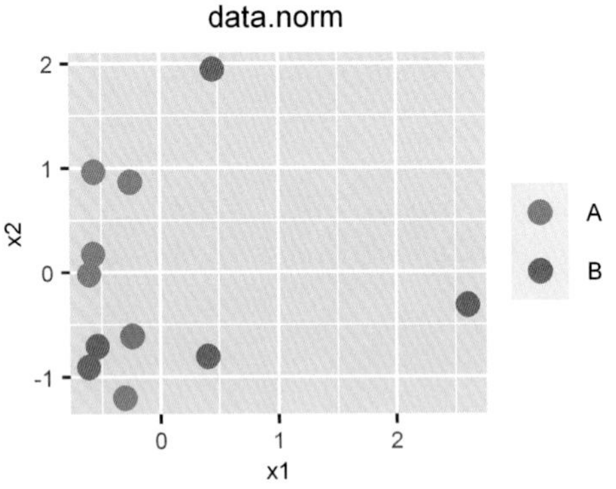

Note that following normalization, 1 of the 3 observations closest to the new observation is of class A and the other 2 are of class B.

5.3.3.3 Prediction

Set the number of neighbors to consider, k, to 3. Measure distance (dissimilarity) as Euclidean distance. Calculate distances from the new observation to all other observations in the dataset. Identify the 3 nearest.

data.norm

x1	x2	class	distance_to_new	nearest_3_check
-0.6092	-0.0197	A	0.6962	FALSE
-0.3027	-1.1991	A	0.5932	TRUE
-0.2529	0.8649	A	1.4744	FALSE
-0.5663	0.9632	A	1.6063	FALSE
-0.5727	0.1769	A	0.8542	FALSE
-0.6156	-0.9043	B	0.4782	TRUE
-0.5387	-0.7077	B	0.3153	TRUE
2.6060	-0.3145	B	2.8603	FALSE
0.4507	1.9461	B	2.6470	FALSE
0.4014	-0.8060	B	0.6701	FALSE

Calculate the probability of positive class as the mean of the class dummies of the 3 nearest observations.

data.nearest_3

x1	x2	class	class.dummy
-0.3027	-1.1991	A	1
-0.6156	-0.9043	B	0
-0.5387	-0.7077	B	0

prob

A	B
0.3333	0.6667

Set cutoff to 0.5. Predict that the new observation should be in class B because the probability 0.33 for class A does not exceed cutoff 0.5.

new

x1	x2	class.predicted
800	32	B

5.4 Logistic Regression

Construct a classifier by the logistic regression method.

5.4.1 Introduction

What is most striking about a flamboyance of flamingos? Pink feathers? Spindly legs? Bent beaks? Or sinuous neck twisted into a characteristic S-shaped curve?

The logistic regression method constructs a classifier by searching for an S-shaped curve that best approximates a reference classified dataset.

5.4.2 About Logistic Regression

The **logistic regression method** involves finding an appropriate vector sigmoid function. The form of the classifier it constructs is the set of coefficients of a sigmoid or vector sigmoid function.

5.4.2.1 How to Construct a Classifier

Construct a logistic regression classifier:

- Start with a reference classified dataset.
- Treat the predictor variables as arguments to a vector sigmoid function.
- Treat the class dummy as the outcome of a vector sigmoid function, where 0 is positive class and 1 is negative class.
- Find the *vector sigmoid function* that best approximates the dataset. Leverage a search algorithm and some best-fit criterion to do this.

5.4.2.2 How to Predict

Use the logistic regression classifier to predict the class of a new unclassified observation:

- Apply the *vector sigmoid function* to the new unclassified observation's predictor variable values.
- Interpret the resulting number as the probability that the new unclassified observation is in the negative class.
- Predict the new unclassified observation's class based on probability.

5.4.2.3 Sigmoid and Vector Sigmoid Functions

A **sigmoid function** rescales any numerical value into range 0 to 1.

$$sigmoid(x) = \frac{1}{(1 + e^{-x})} \quad \text{where } 0 < sigmoid(x) < 1, \text{ for any } x$$

$$sigmoid_{\beta_0\beta_1}(x) = \frac{1}{1 + e^{-(\beta_0+\beta_1 x)}} \quad \text{where } 0 < sigmoid_{\beta_0\beta_1}(x) < 1, \text{ for any } x$$

A **vector sigmoid function** rescales any vector of numerical values into range 0 to 1.

$$sigmoid_{\beta_0\beta_1\beta_2\ldots}(x_1, x_2, \ldots) = \frac{1}{1 + e^{-(\beta_0+\beta_1 x_1+\beta_2 x_2+\ldots)}}$$

$$\text{where } 0 < sigmoid_{\beta_0\beta_1\beta_2\ldots}(x_1,x_2,\ldots) < 1, \text{ for any } x$$

The sigmoid function is also known as the **logistic function**.

5.4.3 Logistic Regression with One Predictor Variable

The logistic regression method can be applied to datasets with one predictor variable.

5.4.3.1 Data

Consider this reference classified dataset and new unclassified observation. Should the new observation be classified as A or B?

data

x1	class
-9	B
-5	B
-1	A
0	B
3	A
5	A
9	A

new

x1
1.2

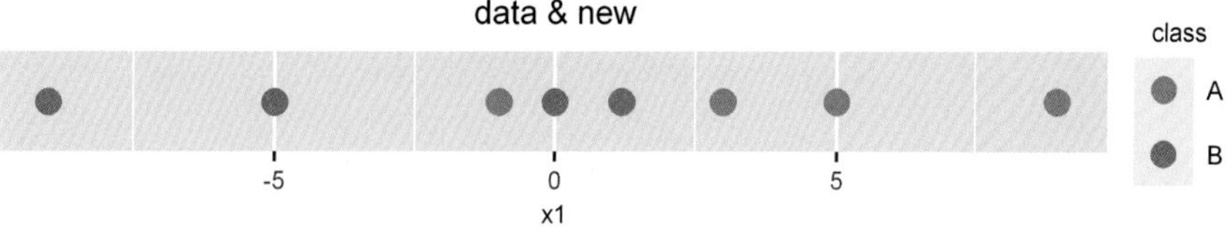

Prepare the dataset by adding a class dummy synthetic variable (0 is A and 1 is B).

data

x1	class	class.bin
-9	B	0
-5	B	0
-1	A	1
0	B	0
3	A	1
5	A	1
9	A	1

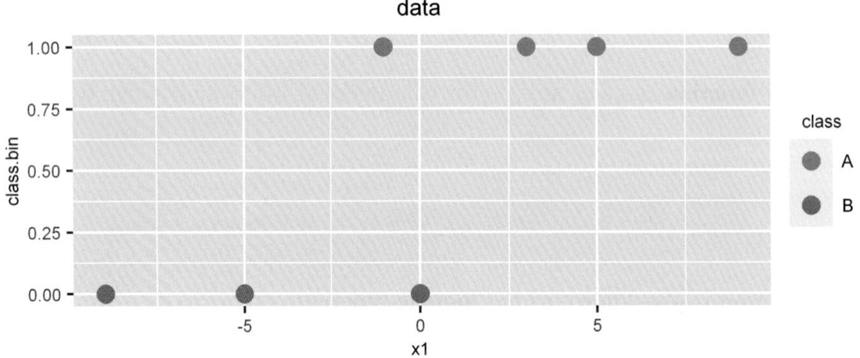

5.4.3.2 Construction

Find the vector sigmoid function that best approximates the dataset. This is the logistic regression classifier.

model

b0	b1
0.4446	0.7041

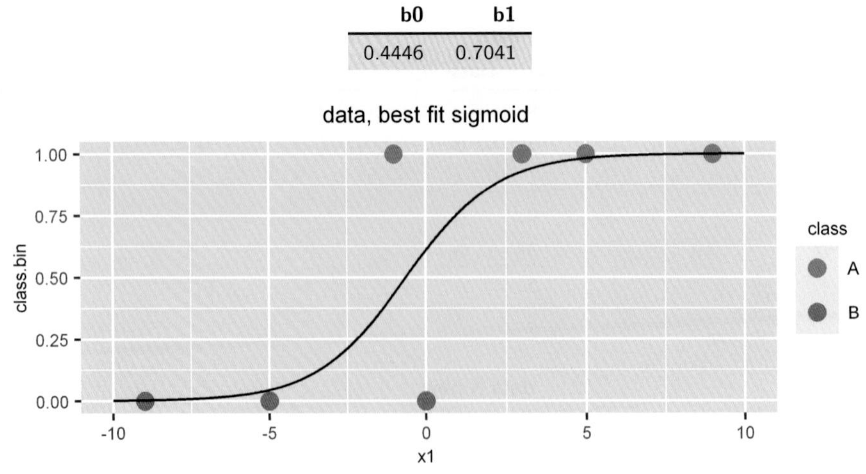

5.4.3.3 Prediction

Calculate probability as the vector sigmoid of the new unclassified observation.

$$probability(\mathsf{A}) = \frac{1}{1 + e^{-(0.44 + 0.70 \times 1.20)}} = 0.78$$

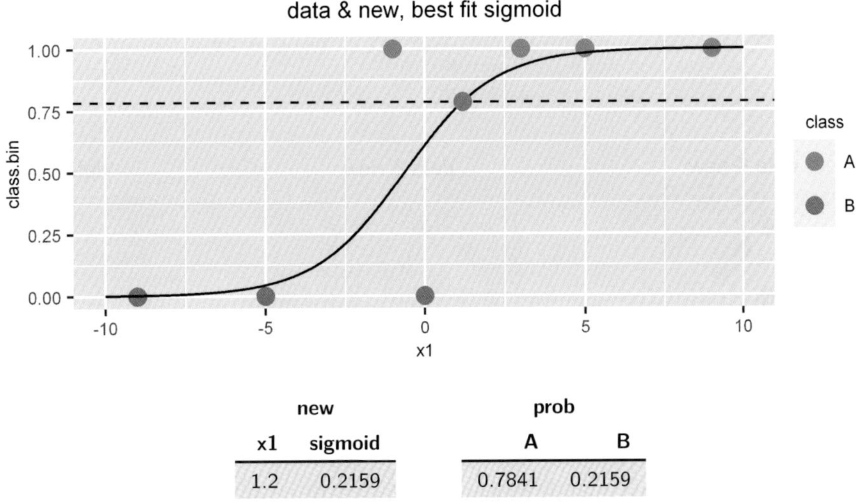

new	
x1	**sigmoid**
1.2	0.2159

prob	
A	**B**
0.7841	0.2159

Set cutoff 0.5. Predict the new unclassified observation to be in class B because probability 0.22 for class A does not exceed cutoff 0.5.

new	
x1	**class.predicted**
1.2	A

5.4.4 Logistic Regression with Many Predictor Variables

The logistic regression method can be applied to datasets with many predictor variables.

5.4.4.1 Data

Consider this reference classified dataset and new unclassified dataset. Should the observations in the new dataset be classified as A or B?

data					new		
x1	x2	x3	class		x1	x2	x3
4	9	9	A		5	8	1
2	7	8	B		6	7	5
3	6	2	A		4	6	2
2	5	2	B		1	1	6
5	4	3	A				
1	8	3	B				
7	2	4	A				
8	1	4	B				

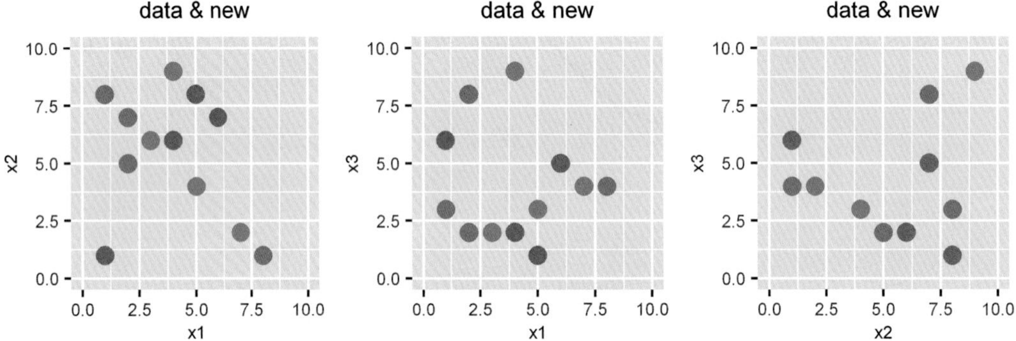

5.4.4.2 Construction

Find the vector sigmoid function that best approximates the dataset. This is the logistic regression classifier.

$$probability(\mathsf{A}) = \frac{1}{1 + e^{-(88.58 - 11.88x_1 - 10.97x_2 + 4.25x_3)}}$$

model			
b0	b1	b2	b3
-88.58	11.88	10.97	-4.249

5.4.4.3 Prediction

Calculate probabilities as the vector sigmoid of the observations in the new unclassified dataset.

new					prob	
x1	x2	x3	sigmoid		A	B
5	8	1	1		1	0
6	7	5	1		1	0
4	6	2	1		1	0
1	1	6	0		0	1

Set cutoff 0.5. Predict the new observations' classes.

new

x1	x2	x3	class.predicted
5	8	1	A
6	7	5	A
4	6	2	A
1	1	6	B

5.5 Decision Tree

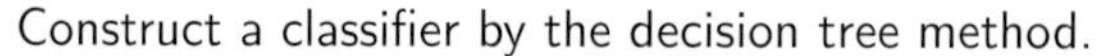

Construct a classifier by the decision tree method.

5.5.1 Introduction

In Lewis Carroll's *Alice's Adventures in Wonderland*, Alice asks, "Would you tell me, please, which way I ought to go from here?" The Cheshire Cat replies, "That depends a good deal on where you want to get to."

The decision tree method constructs a classifier by recursively partitioning a reference classified dataset. The form of the classifier is a decision tree that has branches leading to subsets of the dataset and their associated class probabilities.

5.5.2 Prediction Based on Probabilities

Consider this reference classified dataset and new unclassified observation. Should the new observation be classified as A or B?

data

x1	x2	class
2	5	B
1	2	A
6	4	A
7	5	A
8	1	A
11	2	B
12	5	A
14	2	A
15	1	B
13	1	B

new

x1	x2
8	3

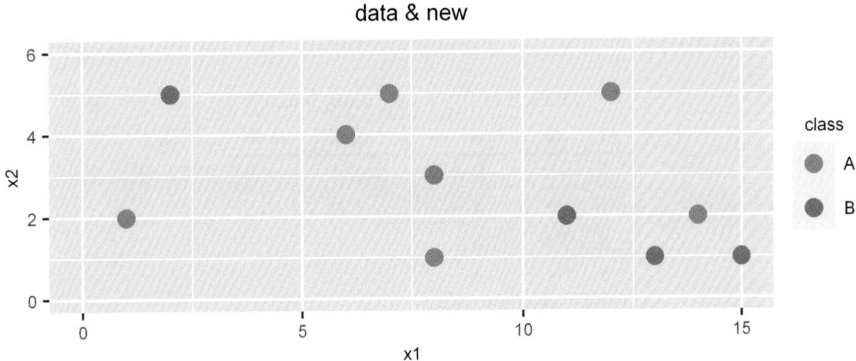

5.5.2.1 Prediction Based on Probabilities from a Full Dataset

We can predict the new observation's class based on probabilities. Doing so, we would predict the class that appears in the dataset with probability that exceeds some cutoff, regardless of the new observation.

Here we see that class A appears with probability 0.60 and class B appears with probability 0.40. Assuming a cutoff 0.50, we predict the new observation is in class A because 0.60 exceeds cutoff 0.50.

prob_info

class	prob
A	0.6
B	0.4

new

x1	x2	class.predicted
8	3	A

5.5.2.2 Prediction Based on Probabilities from a Split Dataset

Alternatively, we can instead first partition the dataset into two subsets – call them the left split and the right split – and then predict the new observation's class based on the probabilities of just one of the splits. To partition the dataset, choose a variable/value pair to serve as the split criterion indicating which observations go in the left split and which go in the right split. To predict, apply the split criterion to the new observation and choose the left or right split accordingly.

Here we choose $x_1 < 9.5$ as our split criterion. The dataset's 5 observations with $x_1 < 9.5$ go in the left split, and the other 5 observations go in the right split. For the left split, class A appears with probability 0.8 and class B appears with probability 0.2. For the right split, class A appears with probability 0.4 and class B appears with probability 0.6.

split_variable	split_value
x1	9.5

data.left

x1	x2	class
2	5	B
1	2	A
6	4	A
7	5	A
8	1	A

prob_info.left

class	prob
A	0.8
B	0.2

data.right

x1	x2	class
11	2	B
12	5	A
14	2	A
15	1	B
13	1	B

prob_info.right

class	prob
A	0.4
B	0.6

We can visualize this arrangement as a tree diagram, which looks somewhat like an upside tree:

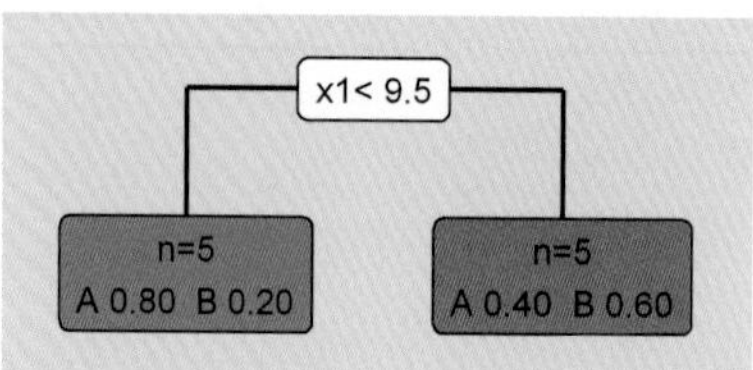

To make a prediction, apply the split criterion $x_1 < 9.5$ to the new observation (x_1=8, x_2=3). We see that $8 < 9.5$ so we consider the left split. Class A appears in the left split with probability 0.80 and class B appears with probability 0.20. Assuming cutoff 0.50, predict that the new observation is in class A because probability 0.80 exceeds cutoff 0.50.

prob_info

class	prob
A	0.8
B	0.2

new

x1	x2	class.predicted
8	3	A

5.5.2.3 Prediction Based on Probabilities from a Recursively Split Dataset

We can extend the notion of splitting the dataset to also split the splits, and split those resulting splits, and keep splitting recursively to the point where each terminal split comprises observations of a single class.

This arrangement is a decision tree classifier. The dataset-level split criterion is called the **root node** of the tree. Subsequent split criteria are called nodes. Terminal splits are called **leaf nodes** or **terminal nodes**.

Here we choose $x_1 < 9.5$ as our dataset-level split criterion. For the left split, we choose $x_1 \geq 4$ as our split criterion. For the right split, we choose $x_2 \geq 1.5$ as our split criterion. We then further split the left and right splits, choosing split criteria along the way, resulting in these 6 terminal splits:

- 3 observations are in class A with $(x_1 < 9.5)$ & $(x_1 \geq 4)$.
- 1 observation is in class A with $(x_1 < 9.5)$ & $(x_1 < 4)$ & $(x_1 < 1.5)$, i.e., $(x_1 < 1.5)$.
- 1 observation is in class B with $(x_1 < 9.5)$ & $(x_1 < 4)$ & $(x_1 \geq 1.5)$, i.e., $(x_1 < 4)$ & $(x_1 \geq 1.5)$.
- 2 observations are in class A with $(x_1 \geq 9.5)$ & $(x_2 \geq 1.5)$ & $(x_1 \geq 11.5)$, i.e., $(x_1 \geq 11.5)$ & $(x_2 \geq 1.5)$.
- 1 observation is in class B with $(x_1 \geq 9.5)$ & $(x_2 \geq 1.5)$ & $(x_1 < 11.5)$.
- 2 observations is in class B with $(x_1 \geq 9.5)$ & $(x_2 < 1.5)$.

Here is the decision tree classifier visualized as a tree diagram:

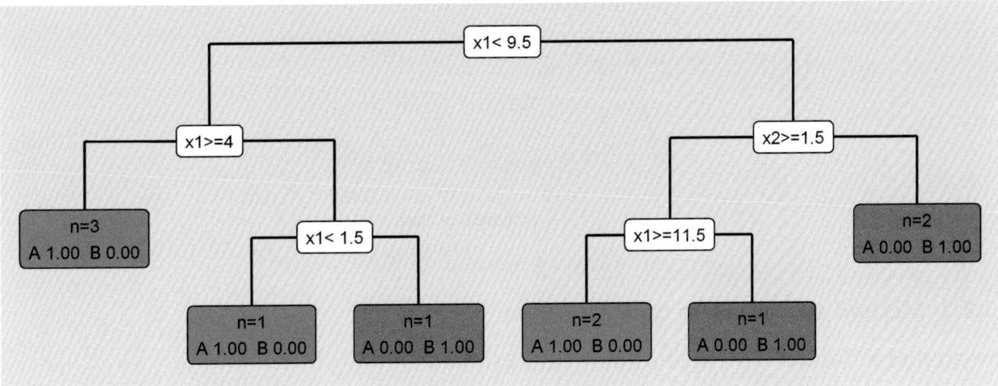

To make a prediction, apply the split criteria to the new observation (x_1=8, x_2=3). We see that $8 < 9.5$ and $8 \geq 4$, so we traverse the decision tree to the first terminal split. Class A appears with probability 100% and class B appears with probability 0%. Assuming cutoff 0.5, predict that the new observation is in class A because probability 1.00 exceeds cutoff 0.50.

new

x1	x2	class.predicted
8	3	A

5.5.3 About Finding Best Splits

So far, we've seen the split criteria chosen arbitrarily. Now let's look more closely at how to find the best split criteria.

5.5.3.1 Entropy

Entropy is a measure of uncertainty in a distribution. The best split criteria are determined based on entropy.

Here is the definition of the **entropy function** H for a distribution of class labels A, B, ... :

$$H = -\big(probability(\mathsf{A}) \times log_2(probability(\mathsf{A})) + probability(\mathsf{B}) \times log_2(probability(\mathsf{B})) + \ldots\big)$$

The entropy function for a distribution of 2 class labels A and B looks like this. Note that maximum entropy corresponds to maximum uncertainty in the distribution, that is, there is a 50% probability that a value in the distribution is A. Minimum entropy corresponds to minimum uncertainty, that is, there is either a 0% or 100% probability that a value in the distribution is A.

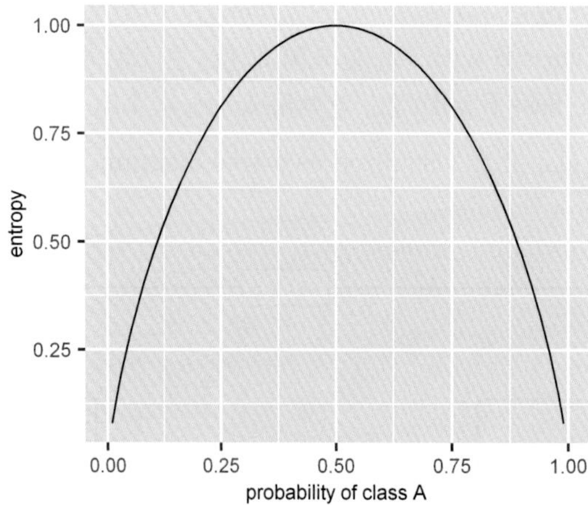

5.5.3.2 Method to Find Best Split Criterion

How to find a dataset's (or split's) best split criterion:

> *Calculate the entropy of the dataset's class distribution*
> *For each candidate split criterion ...*
>   *Determine the two splits*
>   *Calculate the entropy of each split's class distribution*
>   *Calculate the weighted average of split entropies*
>   *Calculate the information gain associated with the candidate split criterion*
> *Pick the split criterion associated with the largest information gain*

Information gain is the difference between the dataset's entropy and the weighted average of split entropies.

The list of candidate split criteria should include all (non-class) variables and values that split the individual variable distributions every possible way.

5.5.4 Finding Best Splits

Consider this reference classified dataset.

The probability of an observation of class A is $6 \div 10 = 0.6$. The probability of an observation of class B is $4 \div 10 = 0.4$.

The entropy of the dataset's class distribution is $-((0.6 \times log_2(0.6)) + (0.4 \times log_2(0.4))) = 0.97$.

data

x1	x2	class
2	5	B
1	2	A
6	4	A
7	5	A
8	1	A
11	2	B
12	5	A
14	2	A
15	1	B
13	1	B

prob_info

class	prob	log2
A	0.6	-0.737
B	0.4	-1.322

entropy.root
0.971

5.5.4.1 Candidate Split Criteria & Associated Entropies

Here are a few candidate split criteria:

A split at $x_1 < 9.5$ would result in weighted average entropy 0.84 and information gain 0.12.

split_variable	split_value	entropy.root	entropy.children	info_gain
x1	9.5	0.971	0.8464	0.1245

data.left

x1	x2	class
2	5	B
1	2	A
6	4	A
7	5	A
8	1	A

prob_info.left

class	prob
A	0.8
B	0.2

entropy_info.left

entropy	weight
0.7219	0.5

data.right

x1	x2	class
11	2	B
12	5	A
14	2	A
15	1	B
13	1	B

prob_info.right

class	prob
A	0.4
B	0.6

entropy_info.right

entropy	weight
0.971	0.5

A split at $x_1 < 7.5$ would result in weighted average entropy 0.92 and information gain 0.046.

split_variable	split_value	entropy.root	entropy.children	info_gain
x1	7.5	0.971	0.9245	0.0464

data.left

x1	x2	class
2	5	B
1	2	A
6	4	A
7	5	A

prob_info.left

class	prob
A	0.75
B	0.25

entropy_info.left

entropy	weight
0.8113	0.4

data.right

x1	x2	class
8	1	A
11	2	B
12	5	A
14	2	A
15	1	B
13	1	B

prob_info.right

class	prob
A	0.5
B	0.5

entropy_info.right

entropy	weight
1	0.6

A split at $x_2 < 4.5$ would result in weighted average entropy 0.97 and information gain 0.0058.

split_variable	split_value	entropy.root	entropy.children	info_gain
x2	4.5	0.971	0.9651	0.0058

data.left

x1	x2	class
1	2	A
6	4	A
8	1	A
11	2	B
14	2	A
15	1	B
13	1	B

prob_info.left

class	prob
A	0.5714
B	0.4286

entropy_info.left

entropy	weight
0.9852	0.7

data.right

x1	x2	class
2	5	B
7	5	A
12	5	A

prob_info.right

class	prob
A	0.6667
B	0.3333

entropy_info.right

entropy	weight
0.9183	0.3

The best split criterion among these 3 candidates and all other candidates is $x_1 < 9.5$ because its associated information gain 0.12 is largest.

information gain			
x1_9.5	x1_7.5	x2_4.5	others
0.1245	0.0464	0.0058	some values

We determine split criteria for the subsequent splits similarly.

5.5.5 Pruning

A decision tree classifier constructed by fully recursively splitting as much as possible tends to overfit. To address this problem, the decision tree classifier construction method provides hyper-parameters to restrict splitting – effectively **pruning** some branches off the tree – leaving terminal splits that comprise not single classes, but rather multiple classes at various probabilities. There are many popular pruning methods, including pruning by maximum depth and pruning by minimum number of observations per node.

5.5.5.1 Pruning by Maximum Depth

Here are two decision tree classifiers. The first was constructed with splits restricted such that the maximum depth is 2 levels of splits. The second was constructed with splits restricted such that the maximum depth is 3 levels of splits.

A Decision Tree Classifier

maximum depth 2

x1< 9.5
n=5
A 0.80 B 0.20
x2>=1.5
n=3
A 0.67 B 0.33
n=2
A 0.00 B 1.00

A Decision Tree Classifier

maximum depth 3

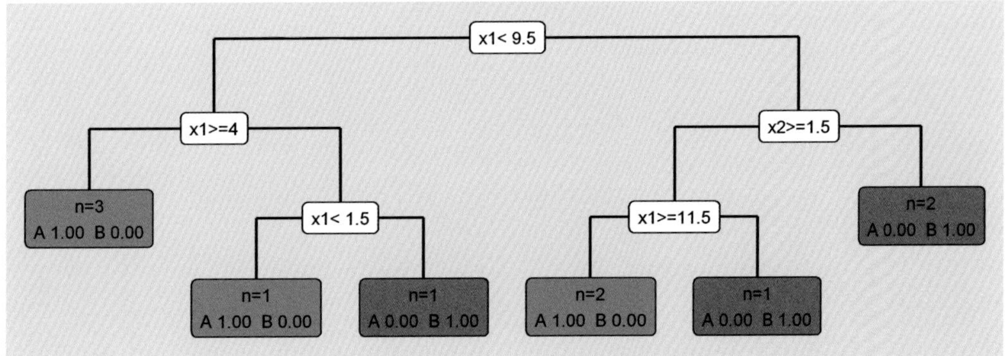

5.5.5.2 Pruning by Minimum Number of Observations per Node

Here are two decision tree classifiers. The first was constructed with splits restricted such that the size of any split is at least 2 observations. The second was constructed with splits restricted such that the size of any split is at least 3 observations.

A Decision Tree Classifier

minimum number of observations per node 2

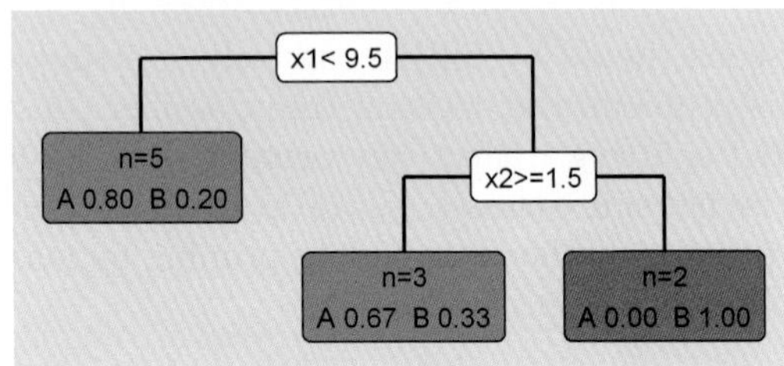

A Decision Tree Classifier

minimum number of observations per node 3

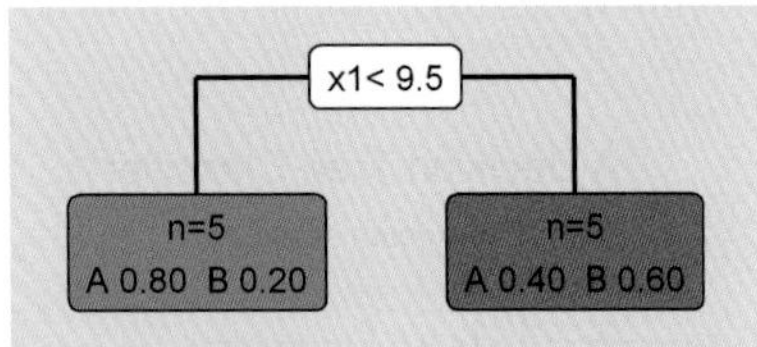

5.6 CASE | Loan Portfolio Revisited

Predictive modeling with principal component analysis and k-nearest neighbors to inform loan purchase decisions in the banking industry.

5.6.1 Business Situation

A financial institution is considering purchasing a batch of loans from a bank, each of which comes with documentation about the terms of loan, the status of the loan, the background of the lendee, and other relevant information. Company management is interested leveraging any detectable patterns in the documentation to distinguish loans likely to be paid back from those likely to default, and thereby inform its decision about which loans to purchase.

- **Role:** Loan Acquisition Manager
- **Decision:** Which loans to purchase?
- **Approach:** Construct a k-nearest neighbors classifier to distinguish good loans from bad loans. Tune the classifier predictor variables and hyper-parameter settings for best expected business result. Use the best performing classifier applied to a set of loans for sale to inform the decision about which loans to purchase.

5.6.2 Decision Model

The decision model starts with a decision method that predicts whether loans will be fully paid back or default. Loans predicted to be fully paid back are purchased. Loans predicted to default are not purchased. The business result of interest is the return on investment measured as the relative value of the purchased loans beyond the cost of the purchased loans.

Business parameters include the following:

- **number of loans (loan_count):** number of loans for sale, a value gathered from the bank that is offering the loans

- **default_rate:** proportion of loans that will default from among all loans, a value derived from the data
- **value per good loan:** average payback amount among loans that are fully paid back, a value derived from the data
- **value per bad loan:** average payback amount among loans that default, a value derived from the data
- **cost per loan:** a value gathered from the bank that is offering the loans

loan_count	default_rate	value_per_good_loan	value_per_bad_loan	cost_per_loan
1,000	to be derived from data	to be derived from data	to be derived from data	11,000

We treat good loans as the positive class. We treat bad loans as the negative class. Possible results of the decision method include the following:

- Correctly predict that some loans are good from among those that are actually good – this proportion is the ***true positive rate***.
- Incorrectly predict that some loans are good from among those that actually are bad – this proportion is the ***false positive rate***.

The absolute numbers of loans in each of these groups depend on the proportions, the (total) number of loans, and the default rate. The value of the purchased good loans depends the value per good loan and how many good loans are purchased. The value of the purchased bad loans depends the value per bad loan and how many bad loans are purchased. The cost of the purchased loans depends on the cost per loan, how many good loans are purchased, and how many bad loans are purchased – although good loans and bad loans each cost the same amount. The return on investment depends on value of the purchased good loans, the value of the purchased bad loans, and the cost of the purchased loans.

Loans that are predicted to be bad, regardless of whether they are actually good or bad, based on the true negative rate and false negative rate, are not reflected in the model because they do not influence return on investment. There is no value or cost for loans that are not purchased.

See the decision model in the influence diagram representation on the next page.

5.6.3 Data

Retrieve raw data, prepare the data, and transform the data to ready it for analysis.

5.6.3.1 Raw Data

Retrieve a reference classified dataset of loan documentation. Each of 85,000 observations describes a unique loan. The 74 variables represent predictors of loan performance and results of loan performance. The *loan_status* variable indicates whether a loan has been fully paid back, has defaulted, or is still active.

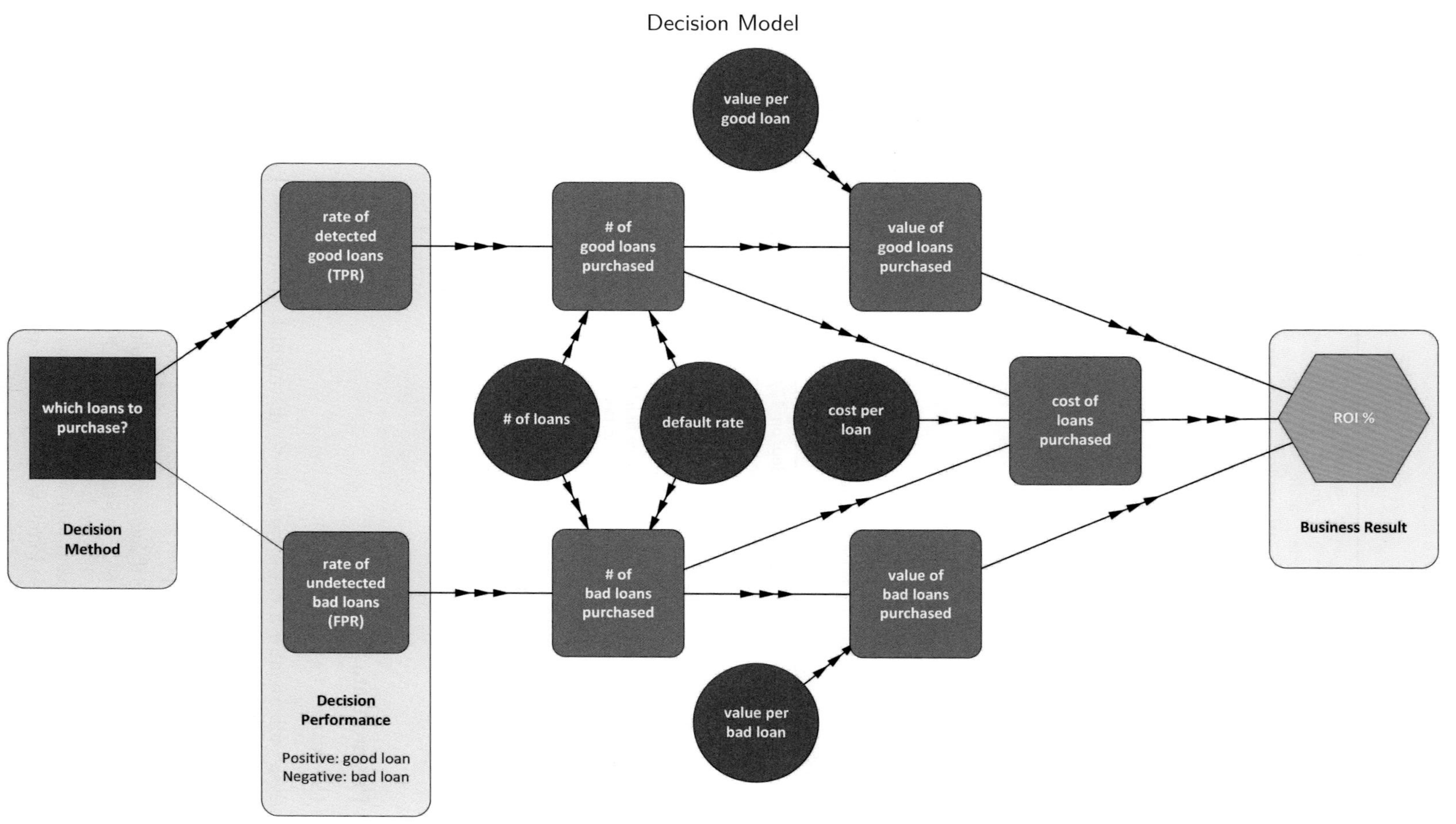
Decision Model
which loans to purchase?
Decision Method
rate of detected good loans (TPR)
rate of undetected bad loans (FPR)
Decision Performance
Positive: good loan
Negative: bad loan
# of good loans purchased
# of bad loans purchased
# of loans
default rate
value per good loan
value of good loans purchased
cost per loan
value of bad loans purchased
value per bad loan
cost of loans purchased
ROI %
Business Result

all variables

all_variables
id, member_id, loan_amnt, funded_amnt, funded_amnt_inv, term, int_rate, installment, grade, sub_grade, emp_title, emp_length, home_ownership, annual_inc, verification_status, issue_d, loan_status, pymnt_plan, url, desc, purpose, title, zip_code, addr_state, dti, delinq_2yrs, earliest_cr_line, inq_last_6mths, mths_since_last_delinq, mths_since_last_record, open_acc, pub_rec, revol_bal, revol_util, total_acc, initial_list_status, out_prncp, out_prncp_inv, total_pymnt, total_pymnt_inv, total_rec_prncp, total_rec_int, total_rec_late_fee, recoveries, collection_recovery_fee, last_pymnt_d, last_pymnt_amnt, next_pymnt_d, last_credit_pull_d, collections_12_mths_ex_med, mths_since_last_major_derog, policy_code, application_type, annual_inc_joint, dti_joint, verification_status_joint, acc_now_delinq, tot_coll_amt, tot_cur_bal, open_acc_6m, open_il_6m, open_il_12m, open_il_24m, mths_since_rcnt_il, total_bal_il, il_util, open_rv_12m, open_rv_24m, max_bal_bc, all_util, total_rev_hi_lim, inq_fi, total_cu_tl, inq_last_12m

data.raw *size 85000×74, first few observations shown, a few variables shown*

id	loan_amnt	term	int_rate	grade	sub_grade	emp_length
1,077,501	5,000	36 months	10.65	B	B2	10+ years
1,077,430	2,500	60 months	15.27	C	C4	< 1 year
1,077,175	2,400	36 months	15.96	C	C5	10+ years
1,076,863	10,000	36 months	13.49	C	C1	10+ years

data.raw *size 85000×74, first few observations shown, a few variables shown*

home_ownership	loan_status	desc	purpose
RENT	Fully Paid	Borrower added on 12/22/11 > I need to upgrade my business technologies. 	credit_card
RENT	Charged Off	Borrower added on 12/22/11 > I plan to use this money to finance the motorcycle i am looking at. I plan to have it paid off as soon as possible/when i sell my old bike.I only need this money because the deal im looking at is to good to pass up. I have finished college with an associates degree in business and its takingmeplaces 	car
RENT	Fully Paid		small_business
RENT	Fully Paid	Borrower added on 12/21/11 > to pay for property tax (borrow from friend, need to pay back) and central A/C need to be replace. I'm very sorry to let my loan expired last time. 	other

5.6.3.2 Prepare Data

Prepare the dataset for analysis.

Our analysis will require a class variable to distinguish good loans from bad loans. Add a synthetic variable *class*, derived from variable *loan_status*.

- Assign *class* to good (pos) if *loan_status* is Fully Paid or Does not meet the credit policy. Status:Fully Paid.
- Assign *class* to bad (neg) if *loan_status* is Default, Charged Off, or Does not meet the credit policy. Status:Charged Off.

Our analysis will require that each loan's class is known. Filter in only inactive loans for which class is known, which are those loans with a *loan_status* value mapped to class good or bad. Other *loan_status* values indicate that a loan is still active.

Convert some of the variables from categorical to numerical representation.

- *term* from categorical to numerical, remove "months"
- *emp_length* from categorical to numerical, remove "years", change "<1" to 0, change "10+" to 10, change "n/a" to missing data indicator
- *grade* from categorical to numerical by index coding
- *sub_grade* from categorical to numerical by index coding
- *home_ownership* from categorical to numerical by index coding
- *purpose* from categorical to numerical by index coding

data *size 59835×74, first few observations shown, a few variables shown*

class	id	loan_amnt	term	int_rate	grade	sub_grade	emp_length
good	1,077,501	5,000	36	10.65	2	7	10
bad	1,077,430	2,500	60	15.27	3	14	0
good	1,077,175	2,400	36	15.96	3	15	10
good	1,076,863	10,000	36	13.49	3	11	10

data *size 59835×74, first few observations shown, a few variables shown*

home_ownership	desc	purpose
5	Borrower added on 12/22/11 > I need to upgrade my business technologies. 	2
5	Borrower added on 12/22/11 > I plan to use this money to finance the motorcycle i am looking at. I plan to have it paid off as soon as possible/when i sell my old bike.I only need this money because the deal im looking at is to good to pass up. I have finished college with an associates degree in business and its takingmeplaces 	1
5		12
5	Borrower added on 12/21/11 > to pay for property tax (borrow from friend, need to pay back) and central A/C need to be replace. I'm very sorry to let my loan expired last time. 	10

5.6.3.3 Business Parameters from Data

With the dataset prepared, the outstanding business parameter values can be calculated.

The estimate for default rate is the proportion of bad loans from among all loans.

The estimate for value per good loan is the mean across good loans of the sum of principal paid, interest paid, and late fees paid.

The estimate for value per bad loan is the mean across bad loans of the sum of principal paid, interest paid, and late fees paid.

loan_count	default_rate	value_per_good_loan	value_per_bad_loan	cost_per_loan
1,000	0.1717	13,605	5,834	11,000

5.6.3.4 Transform Data

With all business parameter values set, transform the dataset for analysis.

Filter out some of the variables.

- Identification variables, like ID number and account number, are not predictive, so we don't include them.
- Leaky variables are those that contain information that could only be known when the class is already known. Since we're ultimately interested in predicting class before class can actually be known, we don't include leaky variables like *recoveries*, *collection_recovery_fee*, or *collections_12_mths_ex_med*.
- Empty variables are missing any information at all, so we don't include them.
- No-variance variables are missing any information at all, so we don't include them.
- Sparse variables, those with say more than half of their values missing, might be too difficult to sensibly impute, so we don't include them.

Also, for convenience, we don't include non-numerical variables.

Impute by simply substituting zeros for missing values.

Convert to principal component representation.

data *size 59835×30, first few observations shown, first few variables shown*

class	PC1	PC2	PC3	PC4	PC5	PC6	PC7	PC8
good	-2.5514	-0.2817	-0.1229	0.3203	2.4678	0.5139	0.8548	0.1885
bad	-3.5842	-2.0119	-0.8824	1.5122	-1.6591	-0.9939	-0.6945	-1.1367
good	-3.3290	-2.2414	-0.7090	1.1091	-0.3551	1.0261	0.9848	-0.1318
good	-0.5087	-0.0898	0.2137	-0.3828	-0.9308	0.1807	-1.3018	-0.0943

Filter out low variance principal components.

data *size 59835×3, first few observations shown*

class	PC1	PC2
good	-2.5514	-0.2817
bad	-3.5842	-2.0119
good	-3.3290	-2.2414
good	-0.5087	-0.0898

5.6.4 Baseline

The baseline business scenario is to purchase all loans. This is equivalent to a decision method that always predicts that loans are good.

baseline

loan_count	loan_purchase_count	value	cost	roi
1,000	1,000	12,270,970	11,000,000	0.1155

$$\begin{aligned}
\text{loan purchase count} &= \text{loan count} \\
\text{value} &= \left(\begin{array}{c} (\text{loan count} \times (1 - \text{default rate}) \times \text{value per good loan}) + \\ (\text{loan count} \times \text{default rate} \times \text{value per bad loan}) \end{array} \right) \\
\text{cost} &= \text{loan purchase count} \times \text{cost per loan} \\
\text{return on investment} &= \frac{\text{value}}{\text{cost}} - 1
\end{aligned}$$

The baseline return on investment is 11.6%. That's the number to beat.

5.6.5 Classifier Construction

Use the dataset as a k-nearest neighbors classifier.

model parameters *first few parameters shown*

class	PC1	PC2
good	-2.5514	-0.2817
bad	-3.5842	-2.0119
good	-3.3290	-2.2414
good	-0.5087	-0.0898
good	-3.3629	0.9651
good	-2.4753	-3.3091
bad	-2.1353	-4.3943
bad	-3.3423	-1.1276
good	-1.3254	-0.9316
good	0.4874	0.8607

5.6.6 Classifier Evaluation by In-Sample Performance

Here are the results of the 1-nearest neighbor classifier applied to the dataset. Note that it predicts perfectly. This is not surprising because it is effectively just looking up the correct prediction for every observation in the dataset. However, we would not expect it to perform this well when classifying new observations.

cm

	good	bad
good	0.8283	0.0000
bad	0.0000	0.1717

performance

accuracy	tpr	fnr	fpr	tnr
1	1	0	0	1

Here are the results of the 5-nearest neighbors classifier applied to the dataset with cutoff 0.5. In-sample true positive rate is 98% and in-sample false positive rate is 52%. These are estimates for the decision performance metrics that will influence the business result.

cm	good	bad
good	0.8130	0.0901
bad	0.0153	0.0816

performance				
accuracy	tpr	fnr	fpr	tnr
0.8946	0.9816	0.0184	0.5248	0.4752

5.6.7 Classifier Evaluation by Cross-Validation Performance

Better estimates of decision performance can be had from cross-validation. Here are the results of the 5-nearest neighbors classifier cross-validated on the dataset. For each of 5 folds, true positive rate and false positive rate are calculated, the number and value of purchased loans are calculated from those numbers, and return on investment is in turn calculated from those numbers. The cross-validation return on investment is the average of the fold returns on investment, 12.8%. That's better than the baseline return on investment of 11.8%. Based on this estimate, using the k-nearest neighbors classifier to pick loans is an improvement over the baseline scenario.

performance

fold	accuracy	tpr	fnr	fpr	tnr	loan_count	value	roi
1	0.7989	0.9239	0.0761	0.8044	0.1956	903.4	11,217,765	0.1288
2	0.7962	0.9216	0.0784	0.8092	0.1908	902.3	11,196,397	0.1281
3	0.8014	0.9291	0.0709	0.8146	0.1854	909.4	11,286,065	0.1282
4	0.7958	0.9212	0.0788	0.8092	0.1908	902.0	11,191,942	0.1280
5	0.7953	0.9208	0.0792	0.8102	0.1898	901.8	11,188,370	0.1279
cross-validation	0.7975	0.9233	0.0767	0.8095	0.1905	903.8	11,216,108	0.1282

business result

method	cutoff	k	variables	loan_count.cv	value.cv	cost	roi.cv
knn	0.5	5	PC1, PC2	903.8	11,216,108	9,941,638	0.1282

5.6.8 Classifier Tuning

Somewhat arbitrarily, we chose to use the 5-nearest neighbors classifier, rather than say 3-, 4-, or 6-nearest neighbors. Similarly, we could have just as easily chosen cutoff to be something other than 0.5. And we assumed that using both predictor variables would result in better performance than using just one or the other. How should we set number of neighbors, cutoff, and predictor variables to provide us the classifier that produces the best business result?

Here are the results of re-running the analysis 24 times, each time setting a different combination of number of neighbors, cutoff, and predictor variables. We try 3, 4, 5, and 6 number of neighbors. We try cutoff 0.33 and 0.50. We try PC_1 alone, PC_2 alone, and PC_1 and PC_2 together as predictor variables.

tune

method	cutoff	k	variables	loan_purchase_count.cv	value.cv	cost	roi.cv
knn	0.33	3	PC1, class	969.6	11,899,963	10,665,596	0.1157
knn	0.33	4	PC1, class	965.1	11,845,519	10,615,592	0.1159
knn	0.33	5	PC1, class	984.5	12,085,579	10,829,949	0.1159
knn	0.33	6	PC1, class	991.5	12,168,870	10,906,426	0.1158
knn	0.33	3	PC2, class	952.9	11,747,100	10,481,940	0.1207
knn	0.33	4	PC2, class	944.2	11,654,285	10,386,528	0.1221
knn	0.33	5	PC2, class	962.9	11,873,658	10,591,511	0.1211
knn	0.33	6	PC2, class	973.3	11,989,244	10,705,859	0.1199
knn	0.33	3	PC1, PC2, class	953.3	11,763,953	10,485,802	0.1219
knn	0.33	4	PC1, PC2, class	944.0	11,665,064	10,383,587	0.1234
knn	0.33	5	PC1, PC2, class	959.2	11,839,381	10,551,616	0.1220
knn	0.33	6	PC1, PC2, class	969.4	11,950,257	10,663,206	0.1207
knn	0.50	3	PC1, class	920.9	11,306,634	10,129,707	0.1162
knn	0.50	4	PC1, class	920.9	11,306,634	10,129,707	0.1162
knn	0.50	5	PC1, class	933.9	11,466,847	10,273,101	0.1162
knn	0.50	6	PC1, class	959.7	11,781,134	10,556,396	0.1160
knn	0.50	3	PC2, class	895.6	11,103,294	9,851,372	0.1271
knn	0.50	4	PC2, class	895.6	11,103,294	9,851,372	0.1271
knn	0.50	5	PC2, class	904.5	11,213,223	9,949,911	0.1270
knn	0.50	6	PC2, class	922.3	11,429,505	10,145,148	0.1266
knn	0.50	3	PC1, PC2, class	827.8	10,295,071	9,105,723	0.1306
knn	0.50	4	PC1, PC2, class	914.8	11,337,833	10,062,420	0.1268
knn	0.50	5	PC1, PC2, class	903.8	11,216,108	9,941,638	0.1282
knn	0.50	6	PC1, PC2, class	914.3	11,339,779	10,057,274	0.1275

We can expect a 13% return on investment from the 3-nearest neighbors classifier with cutoff 0.5 using both PC_1 and PC_2 as predictor variables. That's better than what any of the other options could produce.

best

method	cutoff	k	variables	loan_purchase_count.cv	value.cv	cost	roi.cv
knn	0.5	3	PC1, PC2, class	827.8	10,295,071	9,105,723	0.1306

6 | Classification II

Learning Objectives

Terms

Know the terms:

- Naive Bayes method
- Naive Bayes model
- Prior probability
- Likelihood
- Posterior score
- Relative posterior score
- LaPlace smoothing
- Support vector machine method (or SVM)
- Support vector machine model
- Support vector
- Linearly separable
- Sigmoid function
- Kernel
- Perceptron method
- Perceptron model (or perceptron)
- Neural network method
- Neural network model (or neural network)
- Activation function
- Hidden layer
- Back-propagation algorithm

Effects of Assumptions

Know the effects of assumptions:

- Effect of assuming variable independence on a naive Bayes model and its predictions
- Effect of LaPlace smoothing on a naive Bayes model and its predictions
- Effect of a kernel on a support vector machine model and its predictions
- Effect of a cost penalty on a support vector machine model and its predictions
- Effect of non-linearly separable data on a perceptron model and its predictions
- Effect of hidden layers on a neural network model and its predictions

Use the Methods

Know how to use the methods:

- Compute a naive Bayes model.
- Compute a prediction using a naive Bayes model.
- Calculate prior probabilities, likelihoods, posterior scores, and relative posterior scores within the naive Bayes method.
- Compute a support vector machine model.
- Compute a prediction using a support vector machine model.
- Compute a perceptron model.
- Calculate weights and error at any step within the perceptron method.
- Compute a prediction using a perceptron model.
- Compute a neural network model.

- Compute a neural network model visualization.
- Compute a prediction using a neural network model.
- Calculate the hidden node values used to compute a prediction by a neural network model.

6.1 Naive Bayes

Construct a classifier by the naive Bayes method.

6.1.1 Introduction

There is a criminal trial in progress and the prosecutor tells the jury that the defendant's DNA was found at the crime scene. This, says the prosecutor, is enough to prove that the defendant did commit the crime. In fact, someone's DNA was indeed found at the crime scene, and it could be the defendant's, according to a DNA expert who testifies that there is only a 1 in a million chance that the DNA could be from someone else. Even so, the prosecutor insists, that means there is a 99.99999% chance that the DNA is from the defendant, which is so overwhelmingly conclusive that any reasonable person would agree the DNA must be from the defendant. The prosecutor presses the jury for a conviction.

Is the DNA really from the defendant? We have established that there is a 1 in a million chance that it is from someone else. Is that a lot? How many other people could the DNA be from? There are more than 8 billion people in the world. So, notwithstanding other information to the contrary, the DNA could be from any of 8,000 people. That means that the probability that the DNA is from the defendant is really $1 \div 8{,}000 = 0.0125\%$, which is almost negligible. The DNA evidence by itself indicates that the defendant is extremely unlikely to be the culprit.

The prosecutor's reasoning accounts for the likelihood of 1 in a million, but it does not account for the prior probability of 1 in 8,000. (This kind of reasoning is known as the prosecutor's fallacy and has shown up in several famous real criminal trials, resulting in unfortunate, incorrect convictions.)

The **naive Bayes method** calculates and makes use of likelihoods and prior probabilities from a classified datatset to construct a classifier.

6.1.2 Naive Bayes | One Numerical Predictor Variable

Consider this reference classified dataset and new observation. Note that the predictor variable x_1 is numerical. All the observations of class A are at x_1 less than or equal to 11. Most of the observations of class B are at x_1 greater or equal to 14. There are 5 observations classified as A and 6 observations classified as B. Should the new observation be classified as A or B?

data

x1	class
1.0	A
8.0	A
8.5	A
9.5	A
11.0	A
9.0	B
14.0	B
15.0	B
16.0	B
16.5	B
18.0	B

new

x1
10

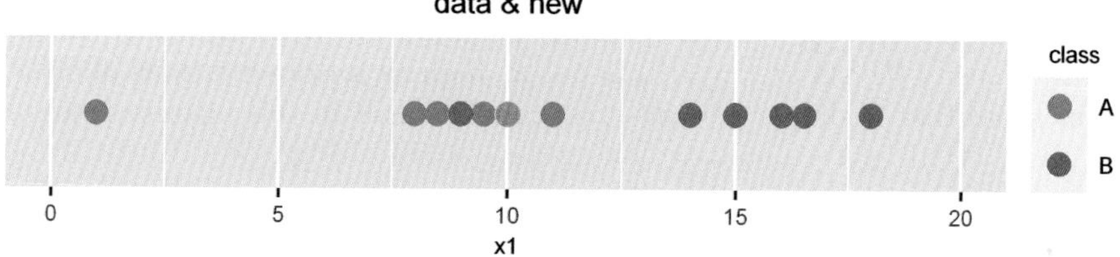

6.1.2.1 Prediction by Likelihood

The new observation is surrounded by observations of class A. There is also 1 observation of class B in the vicinity, but because there is only 1, we might want to overlook it. Accordingly, we might want to classify the new observation as A. This seems like a reasonable option. It incorporates the notion of **likelihood**. Indeed, many (or most) people use this approach often when making their own predictions.

Let's see how taking likelihood into account would play out. Partition the data by class, which effectively conditions our next steps on class. Build 2 probability density functions, 1 for each partition. Recall that you can use the kernel density estimation method to build probability density functions. The probability densities can range from 0 to approaching infinity.

Here is a 1-axis scatterplot of x_1 values color-coded by class overlaid onto plots of the 2 probability density functions.

data.A

x1	class
1.0	A
8.0	A
8.5	A
9.5	A
11.0	A

data.B

x1	class
9.0	B
14.0	B
15.0	B
16.0	B
16.5	B
18.0	B

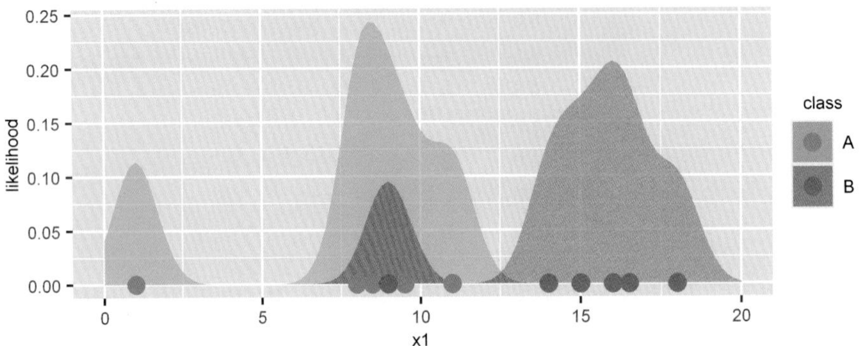

For observations of class A, the high probability density 0.1431 at (x_1=10) quantifies our sense that finding a new observation of class A in this vicinity is likely. For observations of class B, the probability density 0.0344 at (x_1=10) is not as high as for observations of class A, so this quantifies our sense that finding a new observation of class B in this vicinity is less likely.

x1	class	likelihood
10	A	0.1431
10	B	0.0344

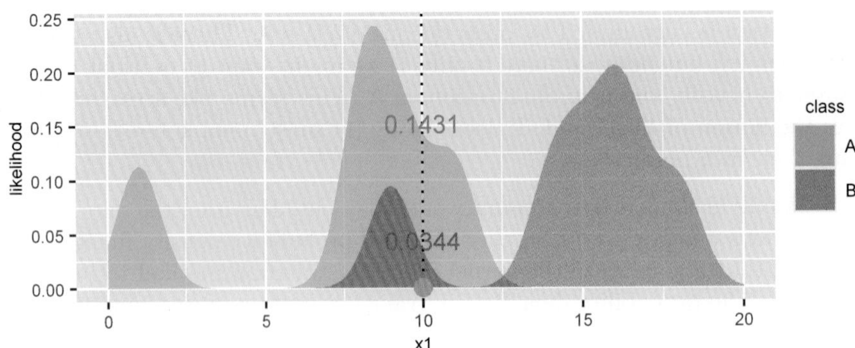

Chances are that a new observation in this vicinity should be classified as A rather than B. Note that to reach this conclusion, we needed 2 likelihoods, 1 for each class.

new

x1	class.predicted
10	A

6.1.2.2 Prediction by Prior Probability

An alternative to predicting based on likelihood is predicting based on prior probability. Notice that the observations are more often than not classified as B. There are 5 observations of class A and 6 observations of class B. Accordingly, we might want to classify the new observation as B to match what we see in the background, regardless of its x_1 value. It incorporates the notion of prior probability. This also seems like a reasonable option, though many (or most) people seldomly use this approach when making their own decisions.

data.A

x1	class
1.0	A
8.0	A
8.5	A
9.5	A
11.0	A

data.B

x1	class
9.0	B
14.0	B
15.0	B
16.0	B
16.5	B
18.0	B

Let's see how taking prior probability into account would play out. There are no probability density functions involved here. We only have to consider the class variable. Build a relative frequency table to calculate class proportions. The proportions can range from 0 to 1.

Here is a bar chart showing that observations of class A comprise 45% of the dataset and observations of class B comprise 55% of the dataset:

class	prior
A	0.4545
B	0.5455

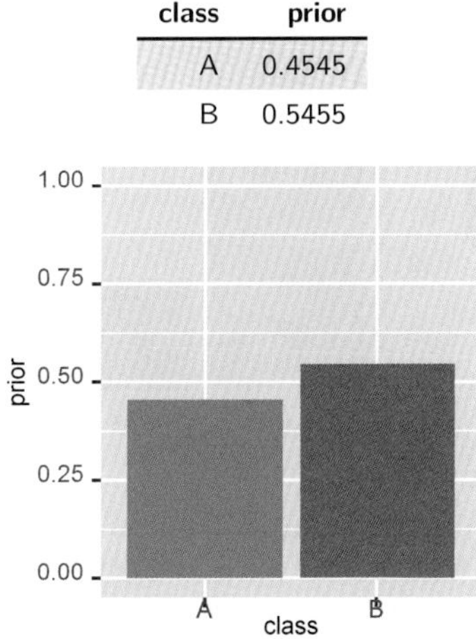

Chances are that a new observation, regardless of vicinity, should be classified as B rather than A. Note that to reach this conclusion, we needed 2 prior probabilities, 1 for each class.

new

x1	class.predicted
10	B

6.1.2.3 Prediction by Relative Posterior Score

Those are the two options: predict by likelihood or predict by prior probability. Each has its merits. But rather than debate which option is better, we can take both likelihood and prior probability into account when classifying a new observation. To do that, we still classify based on single metrics for each class, but those metrics must incorporate information about the likelihoods and prior probabilities. You may be able to think of several different ways to combine likelihoods and prior probabilities. One way is to simply multiply them together to get what we call the **posterior score**, which aligns with our intuition about how such a metric should behave. If the likelihood is a large number, then that will drive the posterior score to be large, which is what we want. If the prior probability is a large number, then that will drive the posterior score to be large, which is what we want. The posterior score is easy to calculate and compared with other approaches simplifies some upcoming math. The **relative posterior score** is the posterior score scaled so that all posterior scores sum to 1.

Let's see how taking the relative posterior score into account would play out. We already have 2 likelihoods, 1 for each class. We already have 2 prior probabilities, 1 for each class. Multiply the likelihood and prior probability for class A together. Multiply the likelihood and prior probability for class B together. That produces 2 posterior scores. Each could potentially range from 0 to approaching infinity. The posterior score for our new observation, if classified as A, is 0.0650. The posterior score for our new observation, if classified as B, is 0.01873.

x1	class	likelihood	prior	posterior
10	A	0.1431	0.4545	0.0650
10	B	0.0344	0.5455	0.0187

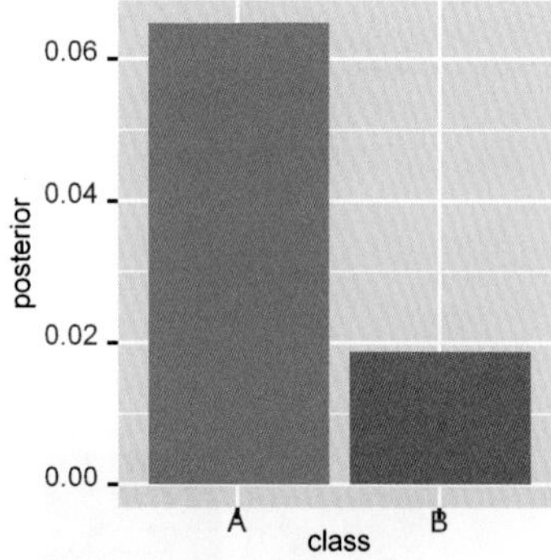

The relative posterior score for our new observation, if classified as A, is 0.7763, because the posterior score for class A is 77.63% of the sum of both posterior scores. Now re-scale these scores. The relative posterior score for our new observation, if classified as B, is 0.2236, because the posterior score for class B is 22.36% of the sum of both posterior scores. The relative posterior scores range from 0 to 1.

x1	class	likelihood	prior	posterior	relative_posterior	probability
10	A	0.1431	0.4545	0.0650	0.7763	0.7763
10	B	0.0344	0.5455	0.0187	0.2237	0.2237

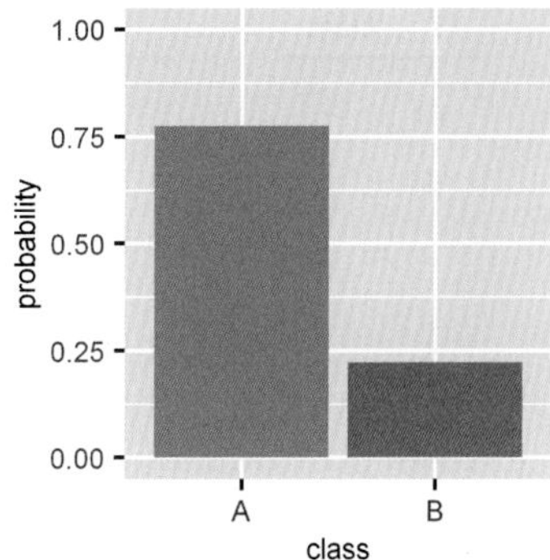

Chances are that a new observation in this vicinity should be classified as A rather than B. Note that to reach this conclusion, we needed 2 relative posterior scores, 1 for each class.

Treat the relative posterior score for a class as the probability that a new observation should be classified that way. Then compare the probability with the cutoff. If it exceeds that cutoff, accordingly classify the new observation as the appropriate class.

The relative posterior score for the new observation (x_1=10), if classified as A, is 77.63%. So, according to the classifier generated by the naive Bayes method, the probability that the new observation is classified as A is 77.63%. Assuming cutoff 0.5, the probability exceeds the cutoff, so the new observation should be classified as A.

new

x1	cutoff	class.predicted
10	0.5	A

6.1.3 Naive Bayes | One Categorical Predictor Variable

Consider this reference classified dataset and new observation. Note that the predictor variable x_1 is categorical. Most of the observations of class A are at x_1 equal to r or s. The observations of class B are more evenly spread out across x_1 equal to q, r, and s. Also, there are 7 observations classified as A and 4 observations classified as B. Should the new observation be classified as A or B?

data

x1	class
q	A
r	B
r	A
r	A
s	A
s	A
s	A
r	A
q	B
q	B
s	B

new

x1
q

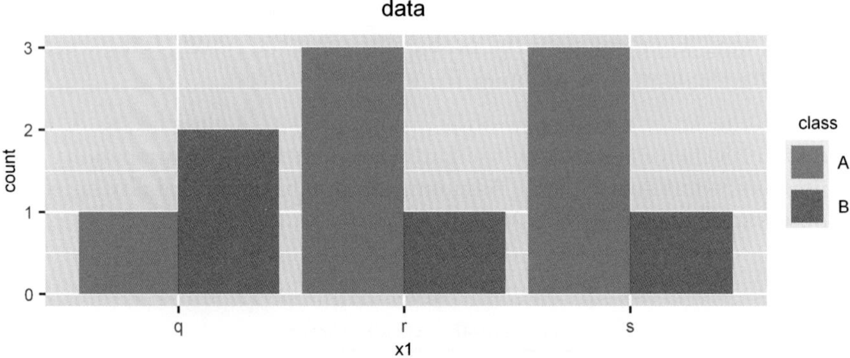

6.1.3.1 Calculate Likelihoods

Again, we can classify based on both likelihoods and prior probabilities. Because the predictor variable is categorical, we use relative frequency tables to find the likelihoods of a new observation, rather than use kernel density estimation.

Partition the data by class, which effectively conditions our next steps on class:

data.A

x1	class
q	A
r	A
r	A
s	A
s	A
s	A
r	A

data.B

x1	class
r	B
q	B
q	B
s	B

Build 2 relative frequency tables, 1 for each partition. The relative frequency for each x_1 value within each table can range from 0 to 1. Treat the relative frequencies as the likelihoods.

info.A

x1	likelihood	class
q	0.1429	A
r	0.4286	A
s	0.4286	A

info.B

x1	likelihood	class
q	0.50	B
r	0.25	B
s	0.25	B

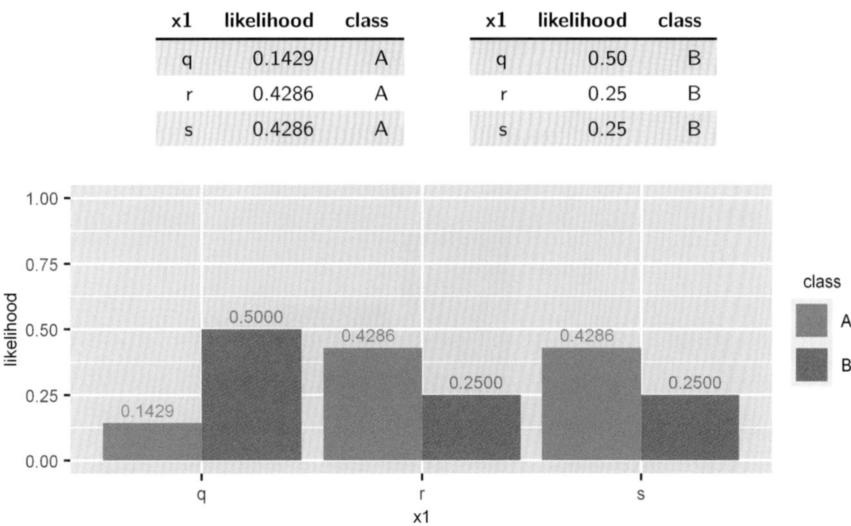

For an observation of class A, the low relative frequency 0.1429 at (x_1=q) quantifies our sense that finding a new observation of class A at (x_1=q) is only somewhat likely. For an observation of class B, the relative frequency 0.5000 at (x_1=q) is almost 5 times higher than for an observation of class A, so this quantifies our sense that finding a new observation of class B at (x_1=q) is more likely. Note that to reach this conclusion, we needed 2 likelihoods, 1 for each class.

x1	likelihood	class
q	0.1429	A
q	0.5000	B

To recap: When the predictor variable is numerical, then the likelihoods are probability densities. When the predictor variable is categorical, then the likelihoods are relative frequencies.

6.1.3.2 Calculate Prior Probabilities

Prior probabilities can be calculated as before since they do not involve the predictor variable.

Here the dataset comprises 7 observations of class A and 4 observations of class B, 11 observations in total. The prior probability of an observation of class A is $7 \div 11 = 63.63\%$. The prior probability of an observation of class B is $4 \div 11 = 36.36\%$.

data.A

x1	class
q	A
r	A
r	A
s	A
s	A
s	A
r	A

data.B

x1	class
r	B
q	B
q	B
s	B

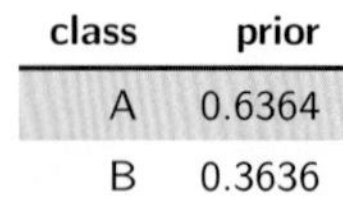

class	prior
A	0.6364
B	0.3636

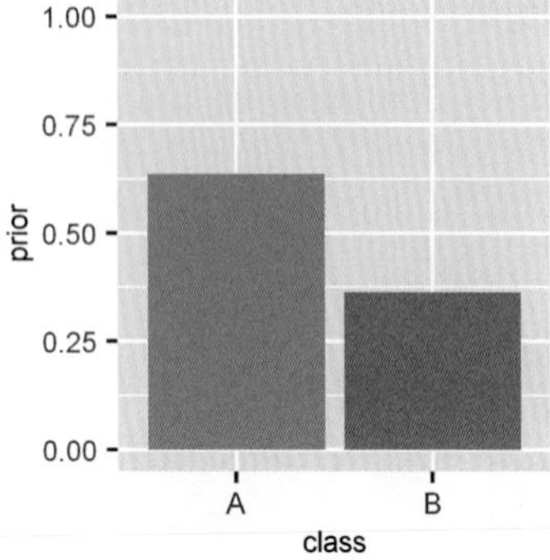

6.1.3.3 Predict by Relative Posterior Score

Now take into account both likelihoods and prior probabilities by multiplying them together to get the posterior scores. The posterior score for a new observation (x_1=q), if classified as A, is $0.1429 \times 0.6363 = 0.0909$. The posterior score for a new observation (x_1=q), if classified as B, is $0.5000 \times 0.3636 = 0.1818$.

x1	class	likelihood	prior	posterior
q	A	0.1429	0.6364	0.0909
q	B	0.5000	0.3636	0.1818

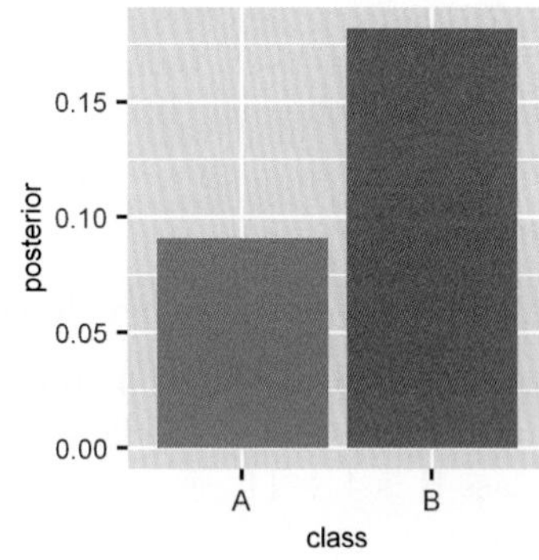

The posterior scores sum to 0.2727. The relative posterior score for a new observation (x_1=q), if classified as A, is $0.0909 \div 0.2727 = 33.33\%$. The relative posterior score for a new observation (x_1=q), if classified as B, is $0.1818 \div 0.2727 = 66.66\%$.

x1	class	likelihood	prior	posterior	relative_posterior	probability
q	A	0.1429	0.6364	0.0909	0.3333	0.3333
q	B	0.5000	0.3636	0.1818	0.6667	0.6667

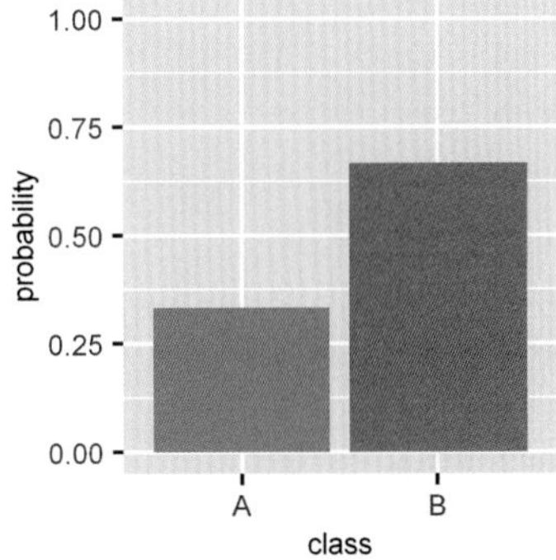

Treat the relative posterior scores as the probabilities that the new observation should be classified as A or B. According to the classifier generated by the naive Bayes method, the probability that the new observation is classified as A is 33.33%. Assuming a cutoff 0.5, that is smaller than the cutoff, so the new observation should be classified as B.

cutoff
0.5

new	
x1	class.predicted
q	B

6.1.4 Naive Bayes | Two Predictor Variables

Consider this reference classified dataset and new observation. Note that there are 2 predictor variables, x_1 and x_2. Both x_1 and x_2 happen to be numerical. A 2-axis scatterplot of x_2 values versus x_1 values color-coded by class exposes some patterns. The observations of class A have relatively low x_1 and x_2 values, so they appear in the lower-left part of the plot. The observations of class B have relatively high x_1 and x_2 values, so they appear in the upper-right part of the plot. Observations of class A and observations of class B both appear in the middle of the plot. Also, there are 5 observations of class A and 6 observations of class B. Should the new observation be classified as A or B?

data

x1	x2	class
1.0	1.0	A
8.0	2.0	A
8.5	3.5	A
9.5	3.0	A
11.0	5.5	A
9.0	5.0	B
14.0	6.5	B
15.0	7.0	B
16.0	6.2	B
16.5	5.7	B
18.0	7.5	B

new

x1	x2
10	4

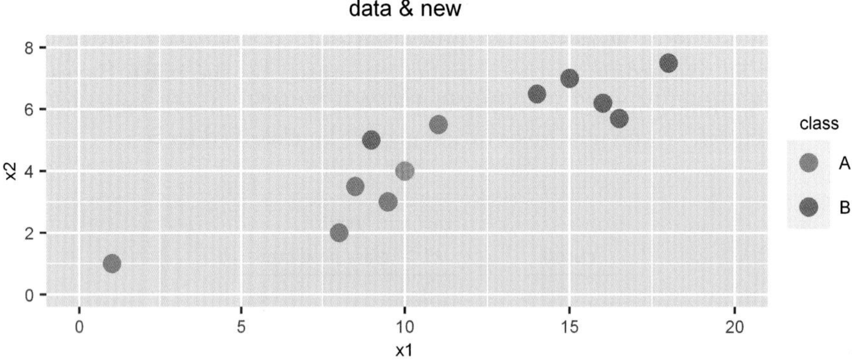

6.1.4.1 Calculate Likelihoods

One way to adjust the likelihood calculation to deal with more than 1 predictor variable, which is not what the naive Bayes method does, would be to find multivariate probability density functions and use those as measures of likelihood. Those would effectively be probability density contours or hyper-contours that account for many variables. Recall that there are versions of the kernel density estimation method that do account for many variables. This approach would be computationally intensive and mathematically complex.

A simpler way to adjust the likelihood calculation, which is what the naive Bayes method does, is to find separate probability density functions for each variable. That is a 1-variable probability density function for each class for each variable. This approach does not account for any interaction there might be between variables, which we will just accept as not necessary to capture.

Let's see how finding separate probability functions for each predictor variable would play out. Partition the data by class, which effectively conditions our next steps on class. For each variable, x_1 and x_2, build 2 probability density functions, 1 for each partition. Recall that you can use the kernel density estimation method to build probability density functions. The probability densities can range from 0 to approaching infinity.

A 1-axis scatterplot of x_1 values color-coded by class overlaid onto plots of the 2 probability density functions exposes some patterns. For observations of class A, the high probability density

0.1431 at (x_1=10) quantifies our sense that finding a new observation classified as A in this vicinity is likely. For observations of class B, the probability density 0.0344 at (x_1=10) is not as high as for those of class A, so this quantifies our sense that finding a new observation of class B in this vicinity is less likely.

x1	class	likelihood
10	A	0.1431
10	B	0.0344

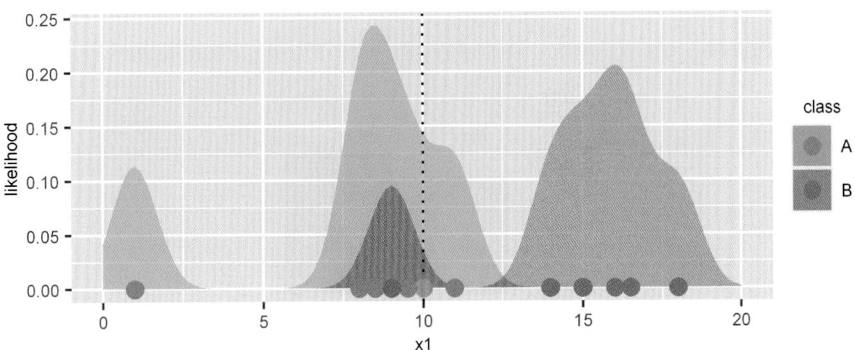

Similarly, a 1-axis scatterplot of x_2 values color-coded by class overlaid onto plots of the 2 probability density functions exposes some other patterns. For observations of class A, the probability density 0.1431 at (x_2=4) quantifies our sense that finding a new observation of class A in this vicinity is somewhat likely. For observations of class B, the probability density 0.0403 at (x_2=4) is much lower, so this quantifies our sense that finding a new observation of class B in this vicinity is less likely.

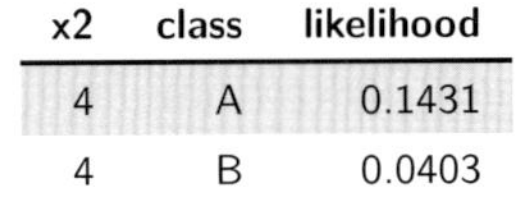

x2	class	likelihood
4	A	0.1431
4	B	0.0403

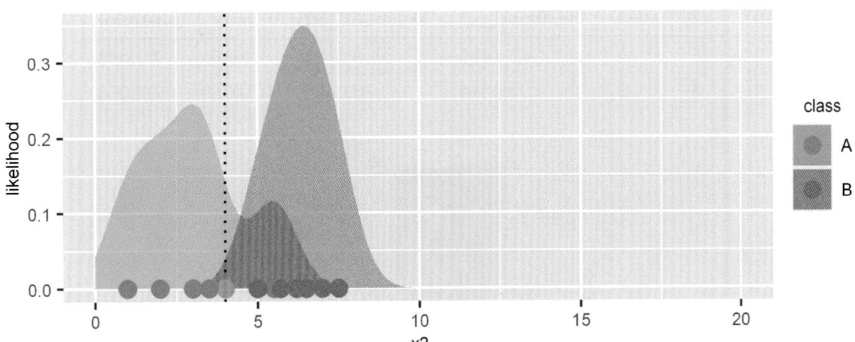

From the perspective of x_1 and the perspective of x_2, chances are that a new observation in this vicinity should be classified as A rather than B. Note that to reach this conclusion, we needed 4 likelihoods, 1 for each class for each variable.

6.1.4.2 Calculate Prior Probabilities

Prior probabilities are calculated as before because they do not depend on predictor variables. The prior probability of an observation of class A is $5 \div 11 = 45\%$. The prior probability of an observation of class B is $6 \div 11 = 55\%$.

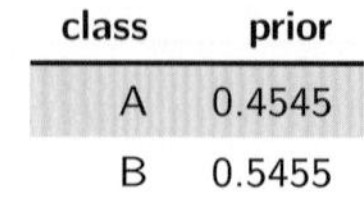

class	prior
A	0.4545
B	0.5455

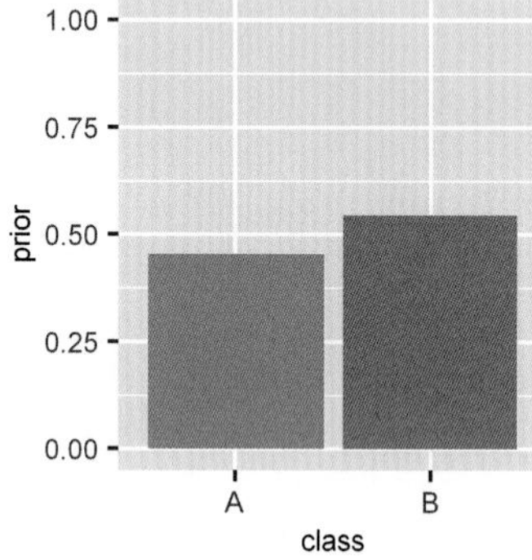

6.1.4.3 Predict by Relative Posterior Score

Now, we want the posterior scores to account for all the likelihoods and the prior probabilities. Each class is associated with not 1, but 2 likelihoods, 1 for x_1 and 1 for x_2. When we worked with 1 predictor variable, we calculated the posterior score for each class as the product of the likelihood and the prior probability. With more than 1 predictor variable, we can calculate the posterior score as the product of all the likelihoods and the prior probability. The posterior score for a new observation (x_1=10, x_2=4), if classified as A, is $0.1431 \times 0.1431 \times 0.4545 = 0.009304$. The posterior score for a new observation (x_1=10, x_2=4), if classified as B, is $0.0344 \times 0.0403 \times 0.5454 = 0.000754$. The posterior scores sum to $0.009304 + 0.000754 = 0.0100$.

x1	x2	class	likelihood_x1	likelihood_x2	prior	posterior
10	4	A	0.1431	0.1431	0.4545	0.0093
10	4	B	0.0344	0.0403	0.5455	0.0008

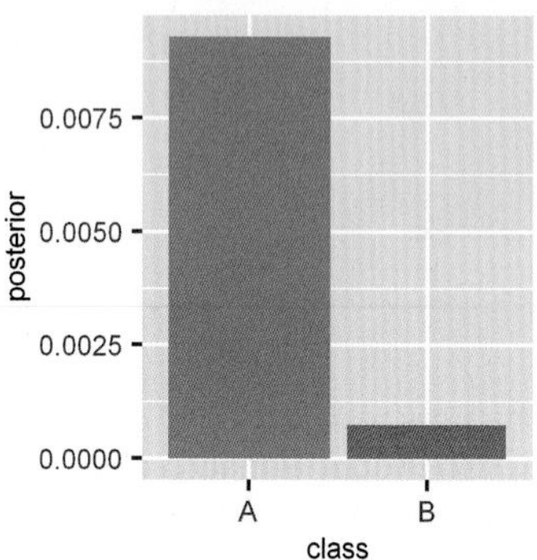

The relative posterior score for a new observation (x_1=10, x_2=4), if classified as A, is 0.009304 ÷ 0.0100 = 0.9249. The relative posterior score for a new observation (x_1=10, x_2=4), if classified as B, is 0.000754 ÷ 0.0100 = 0.0750.

class	likelihood_x1	likelihood_x2	prior	posterior	relative_posterior	probability
A	0.1431	0.1431	0.4545	0.0093	0.925	0.925
B	0.0344	0.0403	0.5455	0.0008	0.075	0.075

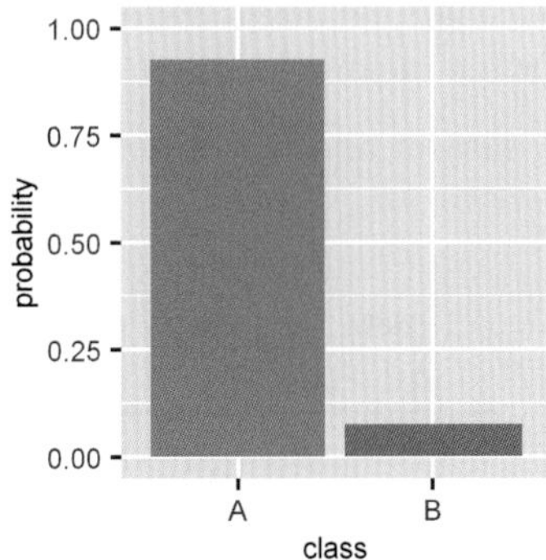

Treat the relative posterior scores as the probabilities that the new observation should be classified as A or B. According to the classifier generated by the naive Bayes method, the probability that the new observation is classified as A is 92.49%. Assuming a cutoff 0.5, that exceeds the cutoff, so the new observation should be classified as A.

cutoff
0.5

new		
x1	x2	class.predicted
10	4	A

See that the posterior score calculated as the product of more than 1 likelihood and a prior probability aligns with our intuition about how such a metric should behave. If any of the likelihoods are a large number, then that will drive the posterior score to be large, which is what we want. If the prior probability is a large number, then that will drive the posterior score to be large, which is what we want. If some of the factors are large and some are small, then there is a competition for which factors overwhelm the others, which is what we want. You may still be concerned that the likelihoods could be extremely large while the prior probabilities will always be less than 1, so that the prior probability's contribution to the posterior scores will too often get overwhelmed. But this will not be a problem for us because ultimately we are concerned only with the relative magnitudes of the posterior scores. Whatever contribution the prior probabilities make to the relative posterior scores will be on the same order of magnitude for both classes.

6.1.5 Naive Bayes | Many Predictor Variables

We can generalize this approach to handle more than 2 predictor variables and handle any combination of numerical and categorical predictor variables. Calculate as many sets of likelihoods as there are predictor variables, using probability density functions for numerical variables and relative frequency tables for categorical variables. Calculate posterior scores for each class as the products of all likelihoods and prior probabilities for that class. Scale the posterior scores to relative posterior scores and treat those as the probabilities that a new observation should be classified as A or B.

6.1.6 Naive Bayes | Gaussian Density Estimation

Here is a popular simplified version of naive Bayes that uses Gaussian density estimation rather than kernel density estimation to find likelihoods for numerical predictor variables. Recall that a Gaussian function generates a bell-shaped curve corresponding to the probability density of a normal distribution of values at some mean and standard deviation.

Consider this reference classified dataset and new observation. Should the new observation be classified as A or B?

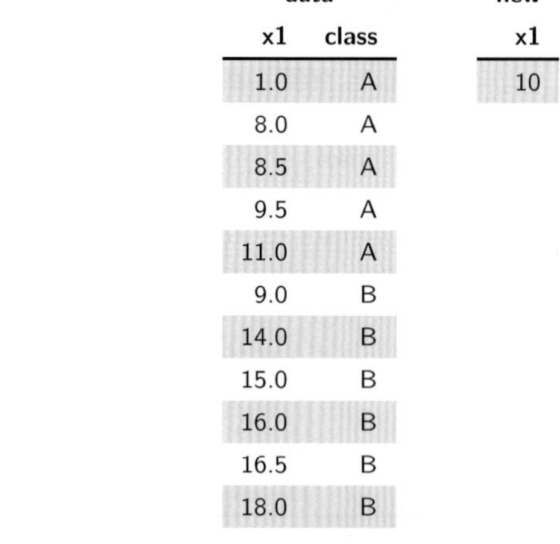

data

x1	class
1.0	A
8.0	A
8.5	A
9.5	A
11.0	A
9.0	B
14.0	B
15.0	B
16.0	B
16.5	B
18.0	B

new

x1
10

data & new

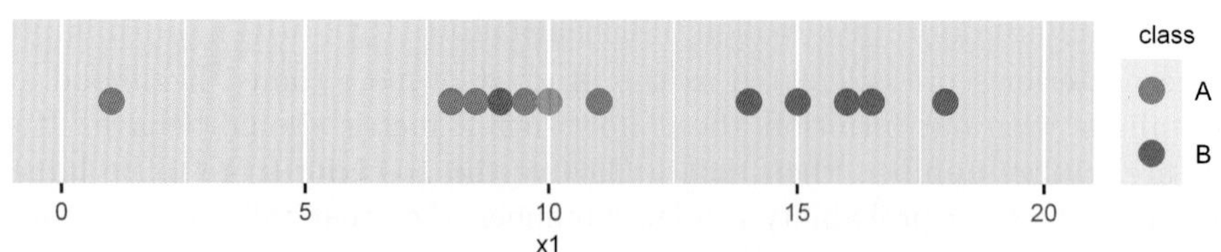

6.1.6.1 Calculate Likelihoods

Let's see how using Gaussian functions to find likelihoods would play out. Partition the data by class, which effectively conditions our next steps on class. Build 2 Gaussian functions, 1 for each partition. To build the Gaussian function for class A, find the mean and standard deviation of x_1 values for observations of class A. The mean is 7.60 and the standard deviation is 3.86. Similarly, to build the Gaussian function for class B, find the mean and standard deviation of x_1 values for observations of class B. The mean is 14.74 and the standard deviation is 3.12. A 1-axis scatterplot of x_1 values color-coded by class overlaid onto plots of the 2 Gaussian functions exposes some patterns.

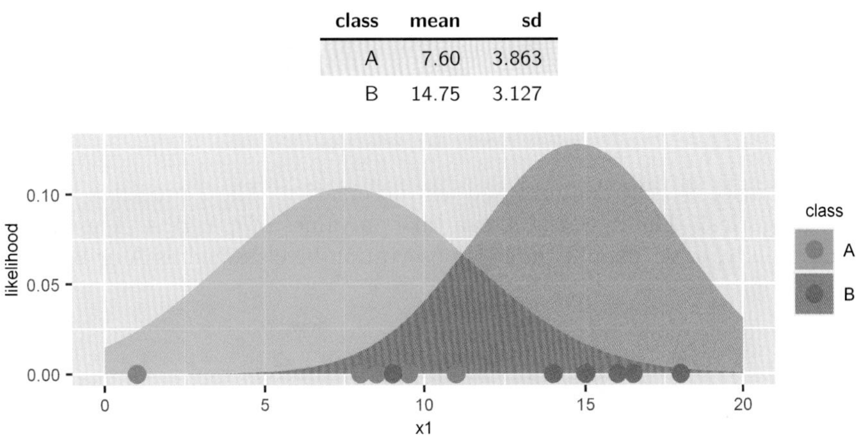

class	mean	sd
A	7.60	3.863
B	14.75	3.127

For observations of class A, the Gaussian high mark is at (x_1=7.60) near the largest concentration of observations of class A. The Gaussian 0.0851 at (x_1=10) quantifies our sense that finding a new observation of class A in this vicinity is likely. For observations of class B, the Gaussian high mark is at (x_1=14.75) near the largest concentration of observations of class B. The Gaussian 0.0402 at (x_1=10) is not as high as for observations of class A, so this quantifies our sense that finding a new observation of class B in this vicinity is less likely.

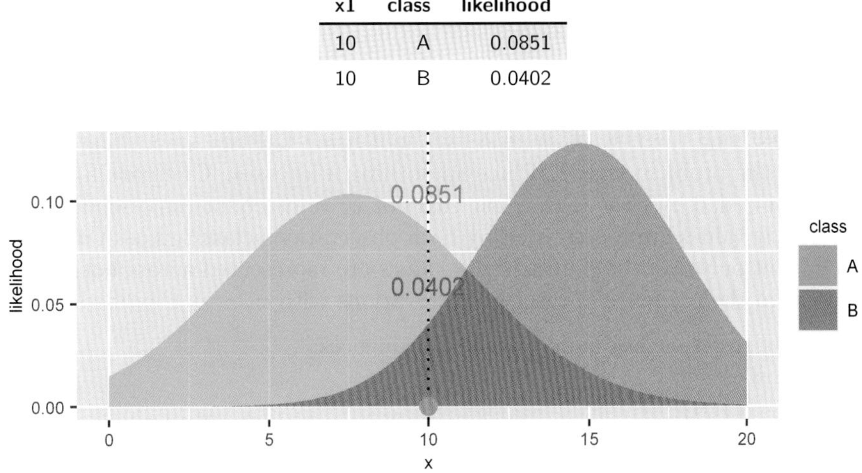

x1	class	likelihood
10	A	0.0851
10	B	0.0402

Note that to construct a classifier that uses Gaussian functions to calculate likelihoods, we need only the mean and standard deviation for each class for each predictor variable, along with the prior probability for each class.

Perhaps surprisingly, this version of the naive Bayes method, where likelihood is calculated from Gaussian density estimation rather than kernel density estimation, tends to produce classifiers that perform very well, even though it ignores much of the detail about the distribution of observations.

6.1.7 LaPlace Smoothing

Here is a popular enhanced version of naive Bayes that adjusts the relative frequency tables to address a problem that can come up when new observations have variable values not present in certain partitions of the reference dataset. This enhancement is called **LaPlace smoothing**. Depending on your perspective, you can think of it as a sophisticated improvement to the method or as a fix to keep the method from breaking. Either way, LaPlace smoothing is quite useful.

Consider this reference classified dataset and new observation. The 2 predictor variables x_1 and x_2 are both categorical. The x_1 variable can take on values of q, r, or s. The x_2 variable can take on values of u, v, or w. Should the new observation be classified as A or B?

data

x1	x2	class
q	w	A
r	u	B
r	v	A
r	v	A
s	v	A
s	v	A
s	u	A
r	u	A
q	u	B
q	v	B
s	u	B

new

x1	x2
q	w

6.1.7.1 An Undesirable Situation

Let's see how classifying the new observation without using LaPlace smoothing would play out. This will expose the problem that LaPlace smoothing addresses. Compare a bar chart of x_1 value counts color-coded by class with a bar chart of x_2 value counts color-coded by class. See that all possible x_1 values are represented by both observations classified as A and observations classified as B. But only 2 of the 3 possible x_2 values are represented across both classes. There are no examples in the reference dataset of observations with $x_2 = \text{w}$ classified as B.

We'll see that this situation has undesirable consequences.

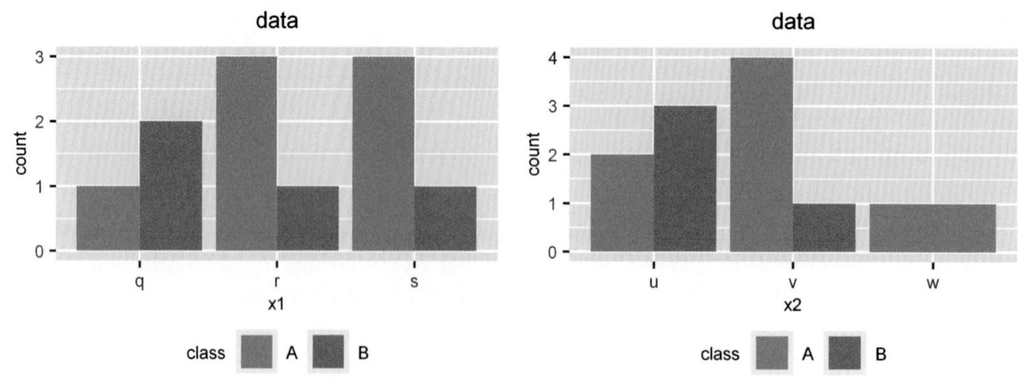

6.1.7.2 Calculate LIkelihoods

Let's see how the situation plays out when we calculate likelihoods and posterior scores.

Partition the data by class, which effectively conditions our next steps on class.

data.A

x1	x2	class
q	w	A
r	v	A
r	v	A
s	v	A
s	v	A
s	u	A
r	u	A

data.B

x1	x2	class
r	u	B
q	u	B
q	v	B
s	u	B

Build a relative frequency table for each class for each variable. There will be 4 tables: x_1 class A, x_1 class B, x_2 class A, and x_2 class B. Pay particular attention to the table for x_2 class B. There are three 3 of 4 observations of class B at $x_2 =$ u, 1 out of 4 at $x_2 =$ v, and none at $x_2 =$ w. The corresponding likelihoods are 0.75 for observations of class B at $x_2 =$ u, 0.25 at $x_2 =$ v, and 0 at $x_2 =$ w.

info.A.x1

x1	count	likelihood	class
q	1	0.1429	A
r	3	0.4286	A
s	3	0.4286	A

info.B.x1

x1	count	likelihood	class
q	2	0.50	B
r	1	0.25	B
s	1	0.25	B

info.A.x2

x2	count	likelihood	class
u	2	0.2857	A
v	4	0.5714	A
w	1	0.1429	A

info.B.x2

x2	count	likelihood	class
u	3	0.75	B
v	1	0.25	B
w	0	0.00	B

From the relative frequency tables, you can then find the four likelihoods of the new observation (x_1=q, x_2=w). Pay particular attention to the likelihood of a new observation, if classified as B, at $x_2 =$ w. It is 0.

info.x1

x1	likelihood	class
q	0.1429	A
q	0.5000	B

info.x2

x2	likelihood	class
w	0.1429	A
w	0.0000	B

The posterior score for the new observation, if classified as B, which is the product of all likelihoods and the prior probability, is then certain to be 0 regardless of any other variable values and prior probability. What is undesirable is that the likelihood for just 1 class for 1 variable cancels out all other potentially useful information about the class. The classifier constructed by this method will always classify any new observation with $x_2 = \text{w}$ as A, without considering anything about x_1 or the prior probability, which is not what we want.

6.1.7.3 Calculate Likelihoods Adjusted by LaPlace Smoothing

We address this problem by inserting LaPlace smoothing into the calculation of likelihoods for categorical predictor variables.

Partition the dataset by class and build relative frequency tables as before. But adjust the frequency tables by adding 1 to each variable value count. The frequency table for x_2 class B goes from 3 counts of u, 1 count of v, 0 counts of w to 4 counts of u, 2 counts of v, and 1 count of w.

info.A.x1

x1	count	class
q	1	A
r	3	A
s	3	A

info.B.x1

x1	count	class
q	2	B
r	1	B
s	1	B

info.A.x2

x2	count	class
u	2	A
v	4	A
w	1	A

info.B.x2

x2	count	class
u	3	B
v	1	B
w	0	B

info.A.x1 smoothed

x1	count.s	class
q	2	A
r	4	A
s	4	A

info.B.x1 smoothed

x1	count.s	class
q	3	B
r	2	B
s	2	B

info.A.x2 smoothed

x2	count.s	class
u	3	A
v	5	A
w	2	A

info.B.x2 smoothed

x2	count.s	class
u	4	B
v	2	B
w	1	B

That makes the relative frequency for an observation of class B at $x_2 = \text{w}$ now $1 \div (4+2+1) = 0.1428$ rather than $0 \div (3+1+0) = 0$. The 3 other relative frequency tables and likelihood calculations are adjusted similarly. From there on, the method proceeds as before.

info.A.x1 smoothed

x1	count.s	likelihood.s	class
q	2	0.2	A
r	4	0.4	A
s	4	0.4	A

info.B.x1 smoothed

x1	count.s	likelihood.s	class
q	3	0.4286	B
r	2	0.2857	B
s	2	0.2857	B

info.A.x2 smoothed

x2	count.s	likelihood.s	class
u	3	0.3	A
v	5	0.5	A
w	2	0.2	A

info.B.x2 smoothed

x2	count.s	likelihood.s	class
u	4	0.5714	B
v	2	0.2857	B
w	1	0.1429	B

The posterior score of a new observation (x_1=q, x_2=w), if classified as B, is calculated as the product of the likelihood 0.4285 of an observation, if classified as B, at x_1 = q, the likelihood 0.1428 of an observation, if classified as B, at x_2 = w, and the prior probability 0.3636 of an observation classified as B. The other posterior scores are calculated similarly.

info.x1		
x1	likelihood.s	class
q	0.2000	A
q	0.4286	B

info.x2		
x2	likelihood.s	class
w	0.2000	A
w	0.1429	B

See that the likelihood calculated from adjusted frequency tables aligns with our intuition about how such a metric should behave. If the reference dataset comprises many observations, then adding 1 to each count will not affect the relative frequency of any particular variable value very much, but it will prevent any relative frequency from being exactly 0. That way, posterior scores always account for at least some information from all variables and prior probabilities.

You can generalize LaPlace smoothing by adding numbers other than 1 to relative frequency tables. Indeed, in some cases some LaPlace smoothing addends result in better performing classifiers than others do.

6.1.7.4 Why It's Called LaPlace Smoothing

A brief digression here on why we name this enhancement after Pierre-Simon LaPlace, the eighteenth-century polymath. LaPlace preceded data science and the naive Bayes method, but he introduced us to the Sunrise Problem. What is the probability that the sun will not rise tomorrow? Based on historical observations about which days the sun did or did not rise, the probability that the sun will not rise tomorrow could be calculated to be 0%. This because every historical observation shows the sun rising on some day, and no observation shows the sun not rising on some day. But it just did not feel right that the probability is really 0 merely because we have never seen anything to the contrary. LaPlace proposed that we instead imagine that we have 1 (or a few) extra observation that shows the sun not rising on some day. With 1 real observation and the imagined extra observation, the probability is 50% that the sun will not rise tomorrow (1 day when the sun did not rise ÷ 2 days total). With 2 real observations the probability is 33%. With 3 real observations the probability is 25%. With many real observations the probability is very small, but never exactly 0. There is always at least a little room left for the possibility that the sun will not rise tomorrow. The naive Bayes method enhanced by LaPlace smoothing harkens back to the Sunrise Problem.

6.1.8 Statistical Formulation of Naive Bayes Method

We have developed the naive Bayes method here largely based on intuition and practicality. Be aware that there is a widely embraced, more theoretical development based on statistics, too.

Start with Bayes rule, discovered or invented by Thomas Bayes in the eighteenth century. It states the relationship between the conditional probability of a class given variable values and the conditional probability of variable values given a class. This is what we are interested in when we classify a new observation. We start knowing a new observation's variable values, but we do not know how it is classified. We want to know what the probabilities are of an observation described by certain variable values being classified as A or B. Note that the relationship also involves the prior probabilities of observations classified as A or B, and the probabilities of observations with certain variable values (regardless of how the observations are classified).

Bayes Rule

$$P(class = \mathsf{A} \mid x_1 = \mathsf{u}, x_2 = \mathsf{v}, \ldots) = \frac{\begin{pmatrix} P(x_1 = \mathsf{u}, x_2 = \mathsf{v}, \ldots \mid class = \mathsf{A}) \times \\ P(class = \mathsf{A}) \end{pmatrix}}{P(x_1 = \mathsf{u}, x_2 = \mathsf{v}, \ldots)}$$

$$P(class = \mathsf{B} \mid x_1 = \mathsf{u}, x_2 = \mathsf{v}, \ldots) = \frac{\begin{pmatrix} P(x_1 = \mathsf{u}, x_2 = \mathsf{v}, \ldots \mid class = \mathsf{B}) \times \\ P(class = \mathsf{B}) \end{pmatrix}}{P(x_1 = \mathsf{u}, x_2 = \mathsf{v}, \ldots)}$$

Calculating the prior probabilities is straightforward. We have seen how this is done several times already. Calculating the conditional probabilities of variable values given a class is trickier. We will deal with this by making an assumption that simplifies things. Calculating the probabilities of certain variable values is pretty much impossible. It turns out that we will not have to explicitly calculate these.

The simplifying assumption we make is that all variables are independent of each other. Under this assumption, the conditional probability of variable values given a class reduces to the product of the conditional probabilities of 1 variable value at a time given a class. Those we know how to calculate. They are the likelihoods. So, we have dealt with how to do that calculation. But pause. You may be uncomfortable with the assumption about variable independence. After all, how often do you get data in the real world where the variables are all independent of each other? Almost never. Or perhaps never ever. But this assumption is still acceptable because it is not our goal to faithfully represent the reference dataset in a Bayes rule-compliant statistical model. Rather, our goal is to construct a classifier that performs well. It turns out that in practice classifiers constructed under the assumption of variable independence do often perform well. The assumption of variable independence is why the method is not called the Bayes method, but rather is called the naive Bayes method. We naively assume variable independence.

$$P(class = \mathsf{A} \mid x_1 = \mathsf{u}, x_2 = \mathsf{v}, \ldots) = \frac{\begin{pmatrix} P(x_1 = \mathsf{u} \mid class = \mathsf{A}) \times \\ P(x_2 = \mathsf{v} \mid class = \mathsf{A}) \times \\ \ldots \times \\ P(class = \mathsf{A}) \end{pmatrix}}{P(x_1 = \mathsf{u}, x_2 = \mathsf{v}, \ldots)}$$

$$P(class = \mathsf{B} \mid x_1 = \mathsf{u}, x_2 = \mathsf{v}, \ldots) = \frac{\begin{pmatrix} P(x_1 = \mathsf{u} \mid class = \mathsf{B}) \times \\ P(x_2 = \mathsf{v} \mid class = \mathsf{B}) \times \\ \ldots \times \\ P(class = \mathsf{B}) \end{pmatrix}}{P(x_1 = \mathsf{u}, x_2 = \mathsf{v}, \ldots)}$$

Regarding the probabilities of certain variable values, as far as we know they could be anything. But whatever they are, they are the same for observations of class A as for observations of class B. This is because the class is not involved at all in the calculation of these probabilities.

Ultimately, we are interested in the relative magnitudes of the conditional probabilities of class given variable values, not the absolute magnitudes. So, we can ignore (or treat as canceled out) the probabilities of certain variable values in the calculation of the relative magnitude of one conditional probability with respect to the other.

$$P(\textit{class} = \mathsf{A} \mid x_1 = \mathsf{u}, x_2 = \mathsf{v}, \ldots) \approx \begin{pmatrix} P(x_1 = \mathsf{u} \mid \textit{class} = \mathsf{A}) \times \\ P(x_2 = \mathsf{v} \mid \textit{class} = \mathsf{A}) \times \\ \ldots \times \\ P(\textit{class} = \mathsf{A}) \end{pmatrix}$$

$$P(\textit{class} = \mathsf{B} \mid x_1 = \mathsf{u}, x_2 = \mathsf{v}, \ldots) \approx \begin{pmatrix} P(x_1 = \mathsf{u} \mid \textit{class} = \mathsf{B}) \times \\ P(x_2 = \mathsf{v} \mid \textit{class} = \mathsf{B}) \times \\ \ldots \times \\ P(\textit{class} = \mathsf{B}) \end{pmatrix}$$

From there, the math quickly converges to a form that exactly matches our earlier development.

$$\text{relative posterior}_{\mathsf{A}} = \frac{\begin{pmatrix} P(x_1 = \mathsf{u} \mid \textit{class} = \mathsf{A}) \times \\ P(x_2 = \mathsf{v} \mid \textit{class} = \mathsf{A}) \times \\ \ldots \times \\ P(\textit{class} = \mathsf{A}) \end{pmatrix}}{\left(\begin{pmatrix} P(x_1 = \mathsf{u} \mid \textit{class} = \mathsf{A}) \times \\ P(x_2 = \mathsf{v} \mid \textit{class} = \mathsf{A}) \times \\ \ldots \times \\ P(\textit{class} = \mathsf{A}) \end{pmatrix} + \begin{pmatrix} P(x_1 = \mathsf{u} \mid \textit{class} = \mathsf{B}) \times \\ P(x_2 = \mathsf{v} \mid \textit{class} = \mathsf{B}) \times \\ \ldots \times \\ P(\textit{class} = \mathsf{B}) \end{pmatrix} \right)}$$

$$\textit{relative posterior}_{\mathsf{B}} = \frac{\begin{pmatrix} P(x_1 = \mathsf{u} \mid \textit{class} = \mathsf{B}) \times \\ P(x_2 = \mathsf{v} \mid \textit{class} = \mathsf{B}) \times \\ \ldots \times \\ P(\textit{class} = \mathsf{B}) \end{pmatrix}}{\left(\begin{pmatrix} P(x_1 = \mathsf{u} \mid \textit{class} = \mathsf{A}) \times \\ P(x_2 = \mathsf{v} \mid \textit{class} = \mathsf{A}) \times \\ \ldots \times \\ P(\textit{class} = \mathsf{A}) \end{pmatrix} + \begin{pmatrix} P(x_1 = \mathsf{u} \mid \textit{class} = \mathsf{B}) \times \\ P(x_2 = \mathsf{v} \mid \textit{class} = \mathsf{B}) \times \\ \ldots \times \\ P(\textit{class} = \mathsf{B}) \end{pmatrix} \right)}$$

$$P(c \mid X) \approx \frac{\left(\prod_{x \in X} P(x \mid c) \right) P(c)}{\sum_{c \in C} \left(\left(\prod_{x \in X} P(x \mid c) \right) P(c) \right)}$$

6.2 Support Vector Machine

Construct a classifier by the support vector machine method.

6.2.1 Introduction

The Great Wall is a series of fortifications built across the historical northern borders of ancient Chinese states and meant to protect against various nomadic groups from the Eurasian Steppe. It separated groups mostly as intended, though in practice several unwelcome groups resided on either side of the boundary at various times.

The **support vector machine method** searches for and makes use of a boundary winding through a classified dataset to construct a classifier. The support vector machine method is often referred to as **SVM**.

6.2.2 Linearly Separable Data

A **linearly separable** dataset is a classified dataset that can be partitioned by its predictor variables in such a way that each subset comprises observations of a single class.

- A linearly separable dataset with 1 predictor variable and a class variable can be partitioned into subsets of a single class by a point.
- A linearly separable dataset with 2 predictor variables and a class variable can be partitioned into subsets of a single class by a line.
- A linearly separable dataset with 3 predictor variables and a class variable can be partitioned into subsets of a single class by a plane.
- A linearly separable dataset with with 4 or more predictor variables and a class variable can be partitioned into subsets of a single class by a hyper-plane.

6.2.3 Support Vector Machine | One Predictor Variable & Linearly Separable Data

Consider this reference classified dataset and new unclassified observation. Note that the dataset is linearly separable. The observations in class A can be separated from the observations in class B by the predictor variable x_1. Any observation between (x_1=6) and (x_1=14) could be used to partition the dataset into a subset comprising only observations of class A and a subset comprising only observations of class B. The new observation is in the space between the observations of different classes, but closer to the observations of class A than to those of class B. Should the new observation be classified as A or B?

data

x1	class
1	A
2	A
3	A
6	A
14	B
15	B
16	B
18	B

new

x1
8

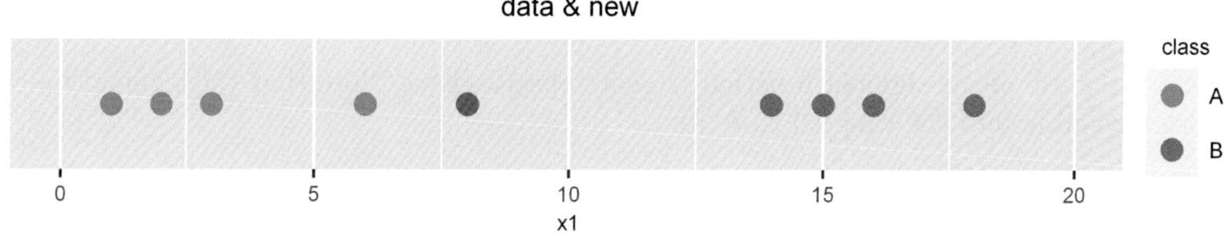

6.2.3.1 Find Support Vectors and Boundary

The **margin** is the space separating observations of different classes. **Support vectors** are those observations at the edges of the margin. The **boundary** is the middle of the margin.

Here we have 2 support vectors, the observations (x_1=6) and (x_1=14). The observation (x_1=6) is the support vector defining the lower edge of the margin. The observation (x_1=14) is the support vector defining the upper edge of the margin. The boundary is point (x_1=10), in the middle of the margin, midway between the two support vectors.

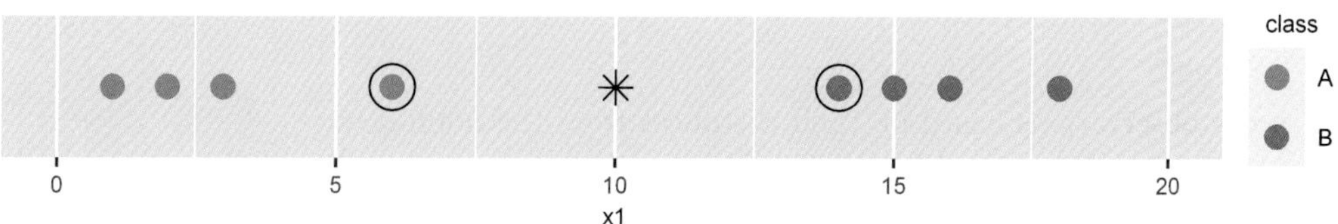

6.2.3.2 Score Observations by Distance

Perhaps observations far from the boundary seem to be very surely in 1 of the classes, while observations close to the boundary seem less so. Both observations (x_1=1) and (x_1=6) seem to be in class A, but (x_1=1) seems more surely to be in class A since it is farther from the boundary than (x_1=6) is. That is, (x_1=1) is relatively farther from all those observations in class B.

Score the observations according to how surely they seem to be in 1 class or the other. One way to do this could be to set scores as simply the distances from observations to the boundary. Here the lower support vector (x_1=6) is distance 4 from the boundary (x_1=10), where we treat 10 minus 6 as positive distance. The upper support vector (x_1=14) is distance −4 from boundary (x_1=10), where we treat 10 minus 14 as negative distance.

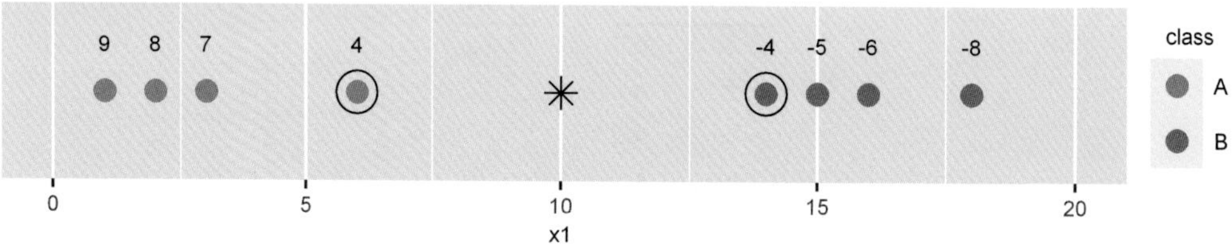

6.2.3.3 Score Observations by Probability

Another way to score observations could be not by distance from boundary, but rather by sigmoid of distance from boundary. Then you interpret the scores as probabilities and classify based on probability and a cutoff.

So, let's make use of the **sigmoid function** to score observations. Note that the sigmoid function rescales any value into the range 0 to 1.

$$sigmoid(x) = \frac{1}{(1 + e^{-x})} \qquad \text{where } 0 < sigmoid(x) < 1, \text{ for any } x$$

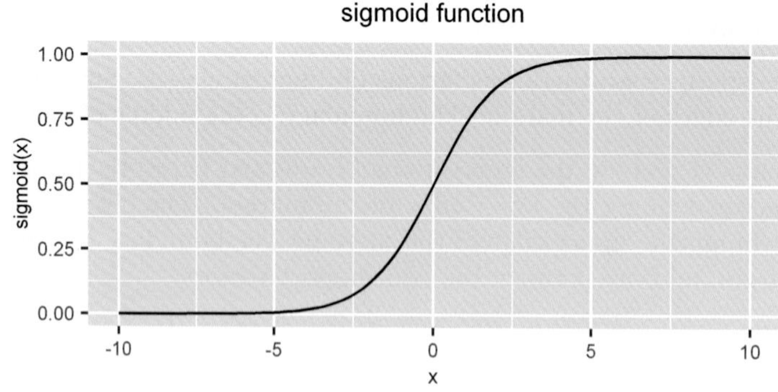

First, score observations based on their distances from the boundary.

Here, as before, the support vector scores are 4 and −4.

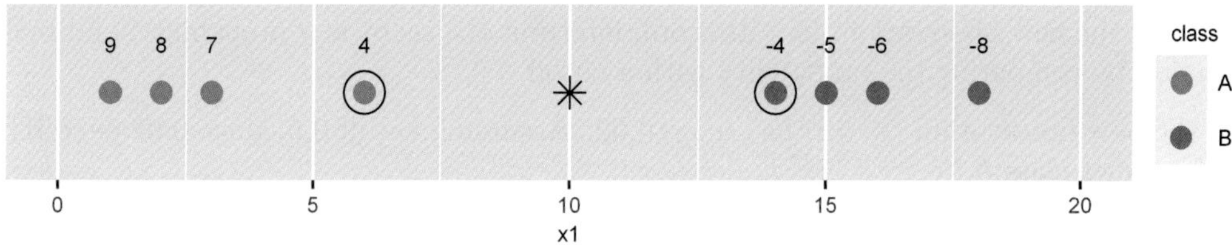

Second, re-scale the scores so that support vectors have score 1 or −1. This step is meant to get scores to be distributed in an intuitive way.

Here support vector (x_1=6) has its score 4 re-scaled to 1 by dividing by 4. Support vector (x_1=14) has its score −4 re-scaled to −1 by dividing by 4. The other observations' scores are similarly divided by 4 to get their re-scaled scores.

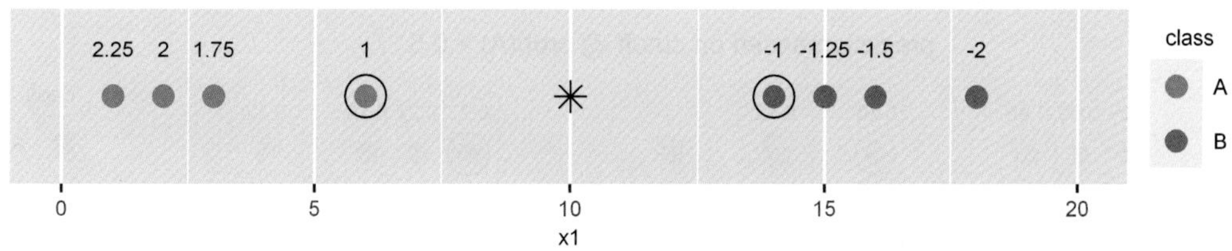

Third, further re-scale the scores to the range 0 to 1. Use the sigmoid function to do this. This step is meant to get scores into a form in which they can be interpreted as probabilities.

Here support vector (x_1=6) has its re-scaled score 1 further re-scaled to 0.73. Support vector (x_1=14) has its re-scaled score −1 further re-scaled to 0.27.

data

x1	distance	rescale_by_divide	sigmoid
1	9	2.25	0.9047
2	8	2.00	0.8808
3	7	1.75	0.8520
6	4	1.00	0.7311
14	-4	-1.00	0.2689
15	-5	-1.25	0.2227
16	-6	-1.50	0.1824
18	-8	-2.00	0.1192

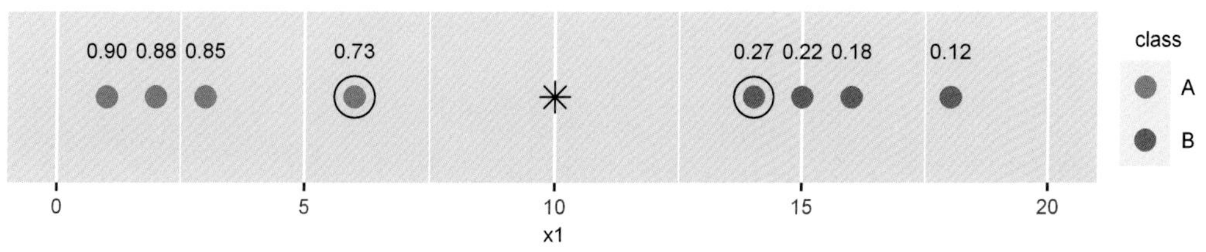

6.2.3.4 Predict

To classify the new observation, find its score, interpret the score as a probability, and make a prediction by comparing the probability with a cutoff.

Here the new observation (x_1=8) has score 0.62. Assuming cutoff 0.5, since 0.62 exceeds the cutoff, predict class A.

In a different situation, you might assume cutoff 0.7. In that situation, since 0.62 does not exceed the cutoff, predict class B.

new

x1	new.score	prob.A	prob.B
8	0.6225	0.6225	0.3775

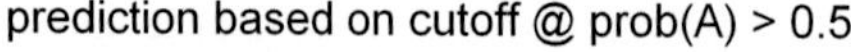

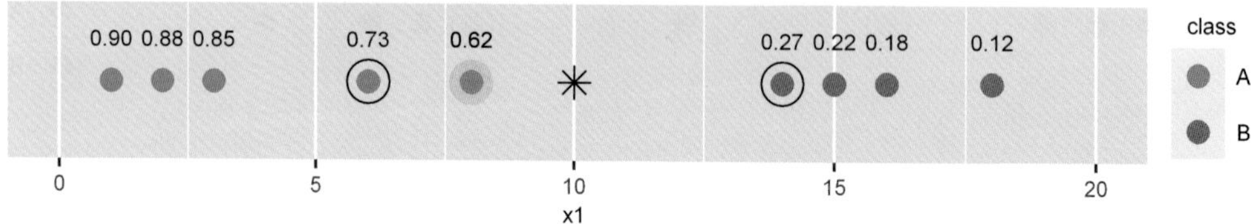

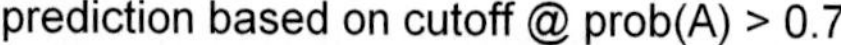

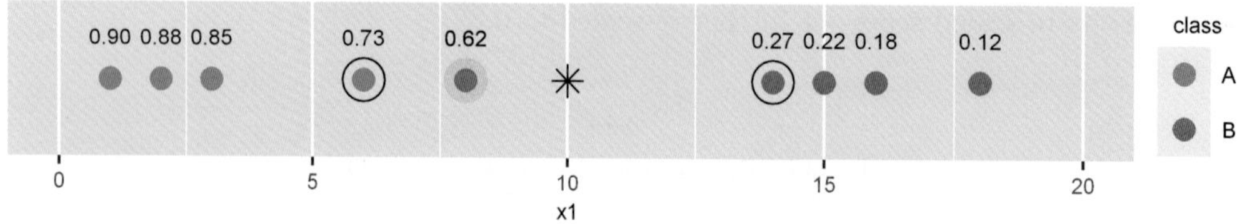

6.2.4 Support Vector Machine | One Predictor Variable & Penalties

A real business dataset is unlikely to be linearly separable. One enhancement to the support vector machine method to deal with non-linearly separable data is to include penalties.

Consider this reference classified dataset and new unclassified observation. Note that this dataset is not linearly separable. There is no point that separates the observations of class A from those of class B. Should the new observation be classified as A or B?

data		new
x1	class	x1
2	A	12
3	A	
4	B	
5	A	
20	B	
21	B	
22	B	
23	B	

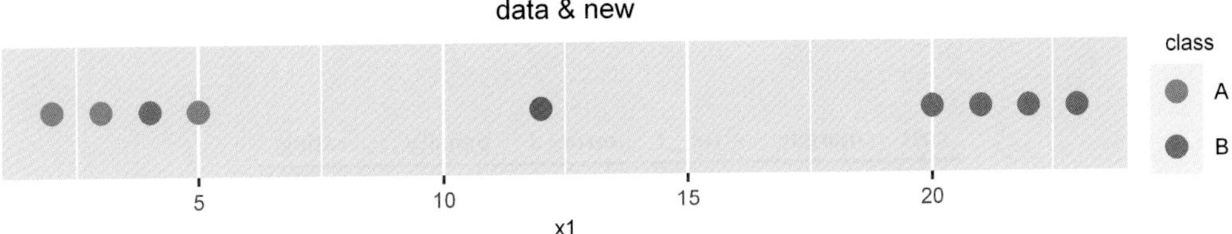

6.2.4.1 Find Support Vectors and Boundary, Assign Penalties

The support vectors are now those observations at the edges of the margin separating the classes and any observations on the wrong side of the boundary. The support vectors are determined so that the margin width is maximized, but subject to a penalty to account for the offending observations. The penalty depends on a cost and the offending observations' distances from the correct edges. You choose the cost.

Which observations are the support vectors? Candidates for support vectors can be rated according the margin between the them adjusted by a penalty for observations being on the wrong side of the boundary. Here is one way to define such a rating.

$$\text{rating} = \left(\frac{2}{\text{margin}}\right) + \left(\text{cost} \times (\text{error}_1 + \text{error}_2 + \ldots)\right)$$

Note that a rating is high when the margin is low and the errors are high. Conversely, a rating is low when the margin is high and the errors are low. So, good candidates for support vectors are those with a low rating.

Consider observations (x_1=5) and (x_1=20) as candidates for the support vectors. The margin between support vectors would be $20 - 5 = 15$, but observation (x_1=4) would be distance 16 on the wrong side of the (x_1=20) edge. If cost is assumed to be 0.1, then the penalty for being on the wrong side would be $cost \times distance = 0.1 \times 16 = 1.6$. The rating would be $(2 \div 15) + (0.1 \times 16) = 1.733$. Similarly, if cost is assumed to be 1 or 10, then the rating would be $(2 \div 15) + (1 \times 16) = 16.133$ or $(2 \div 15) + (10 \times 16) = 160.133$, respectively.

cost	margin	error	penalty	rating
0.1	15	16	1.6	1.733
1.0	15	16	16.0	16.133
10.0	15	16	160.0	160.133

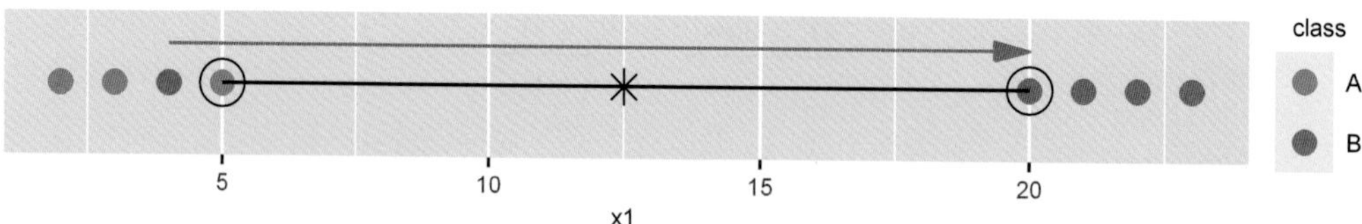

Now, instead, consider observations (x_1=3) and (x_1=20) as candidates for the support vectors. The margin would be $20 - 3 = 17$, but observation (x_1=4) would be distance 16 on the wrong side of the (x_1=20) edge, and observation (x_1=5) would be distance 2 on the wrong side of the (x_1=3) edge. If cost is assumed to be 0.1, then the penalty would be $0.1 \times (16+2) = 1.8$, and so the rating would be $(2 \div 17) + (0.1 \times (16+2)) = 1.918$. Similarly, if cost is assumed to be 1 or 10, then the rating would be $(2 \div 17) + (1 \times (16+2)) = 18.118$ or $(2 \div 17) + (10 \times (16+2)) = 180.118$, respectively.

cost	margin	error_1	error_2	penalty	rating
0.1	17	16	2	1.8	1.918
1.0	17	16	2	18.0	18.118
10.0	17	16	2	180.0	180.118

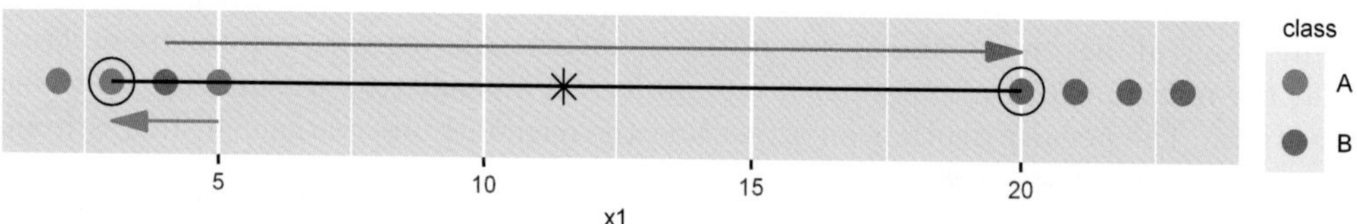

Here, at cost 0.1, observations (x_1=5) and (x_1=20) would be preferred over observations (x_1=3) and (x_1=20) as support vectors because $1.733 < 1.918$. Accordingly, we find the better boundary to be (x_1=12.5), midway between (x_1=5) and (x_1=20).

At cost 10, rating 160.133 beats rating 180.118, so (x_1=12.5) is still the better boundary. However, in general, the assumption about cost influences the determination of the support vectors, which determines the boundary, and so different costs could result in different boundaries.

The support vector machine method relies on an optimization algorithm to search for support vectors that best trade-off maximizing the margin and minimizing the penalty.

6.2.4.2 Predict

To classify the new observation, find its score with respect to the boundary, interpret the score as a probability, and make a prediction by comparing the probability with a cutoff.

Here the new observation (x_1=12) has score 0.52. Assuming cutoff 0.5, since 0.52 exceeds the cutoff, predict class A.

new

x1	new.score	prob.A	prob.B
12	0.5167	0.5167	0.4833

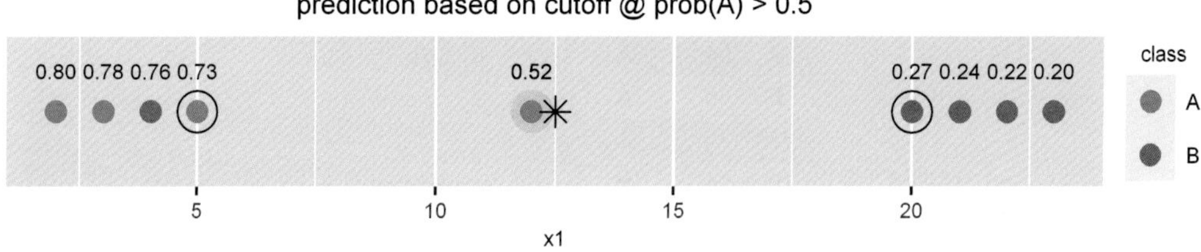

6.2.5 Support Vector Machine | One Predictor Variable & Kernel Trick

A second enhancement to the support vector machine method to deal with non-linearly separable data is the **kernel trick**.

Consider this reference classified dataset and new unclassified observation. Note that the dataset is not linearly separable. Should the new observation be classified as A or B?

data

x1	class
4	A
6	A
7	A
10	B
11	B
12	B
14	B
18	A
19	A
20	A

new

x1
8

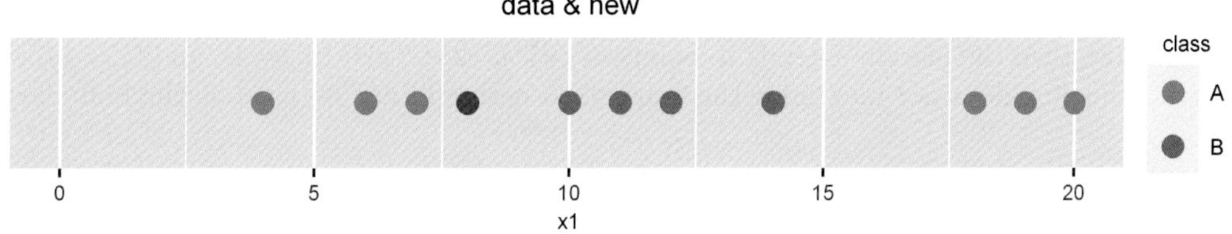

6.2.5.1 Apply Kernel

Add a synthetic variable to the dataset by applying a kernel function. This effectively increases the dimensionality of the dataset. You can think of this as popping the dataset into 2-dimensional space.

Here we apply the kernel function $y = (x_1 - 12)^2$. Note that when viewed from this higher dimension, the dataset is linearly separable. The observations in class A can be separated from the observations in class B by the variables x_1 and y, specifically by some line expressed in terms of x_1 and y.

data				new	
x1	y	class		x1	y
4	64	A		8	16
6	36	A			
7	25	A			
10	4	B			
11	1	B			
12	0	B			
14	4	B			
18	36	A			
19	49	A			
20	64	A			

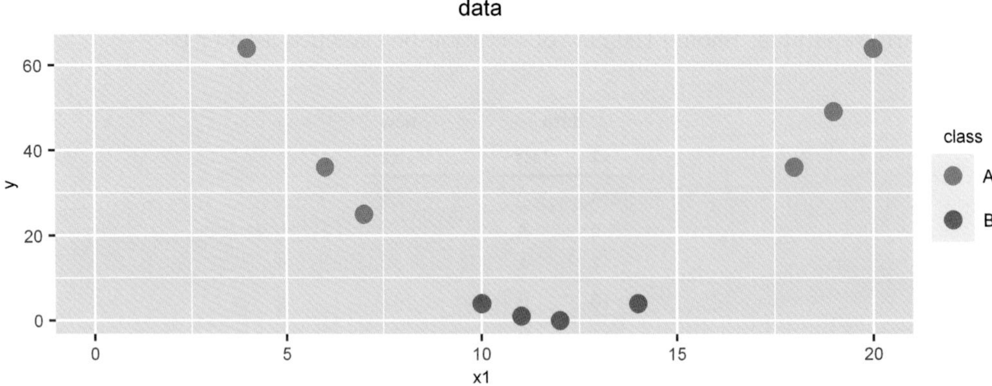

6.2.5.2 Find Support Vectors and Boundary

The support vectors are those observations at the edge of the margin separating the observations of different classes, where the margin is maximized. The boundary is the middle of the margin (a line in 2-dimensional space).

Here is a candidate boundary line that separates observations of different classes. If this line were the boundary, then the margin extends to points (x_1=7, y=25), (x_1=10, y=4), and (x_1=14, y=4). However, this line does not maximize the margin, so it should not be used as the boundary.

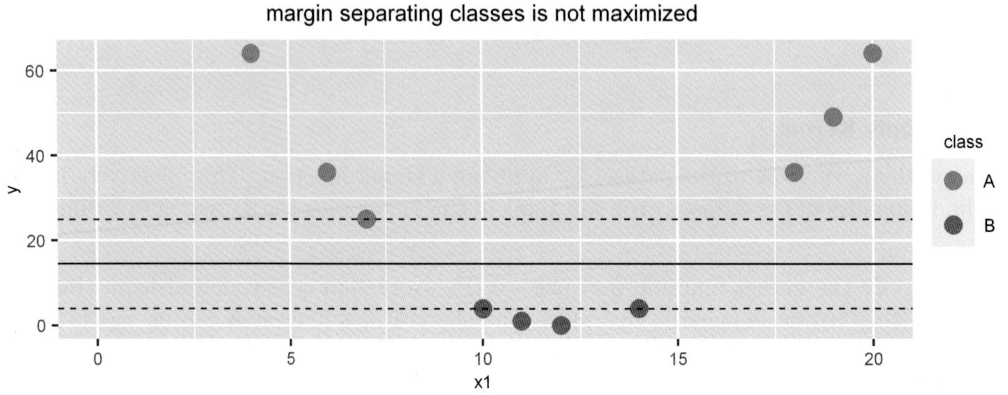

Here is the boundary line that does separate observations of different classes and maximizes the margin. The edges of the margin are lines defined by points $(x_1{=}7), y{=}25)$, $(x_1{=}10, y{=}4)$, and $(x_1{=}18, y{=}36)$, which correspond to support vectors $(x_1{=}7)$, $(x_1{=}10)$, and $(x_1{=}18)$, respectively.

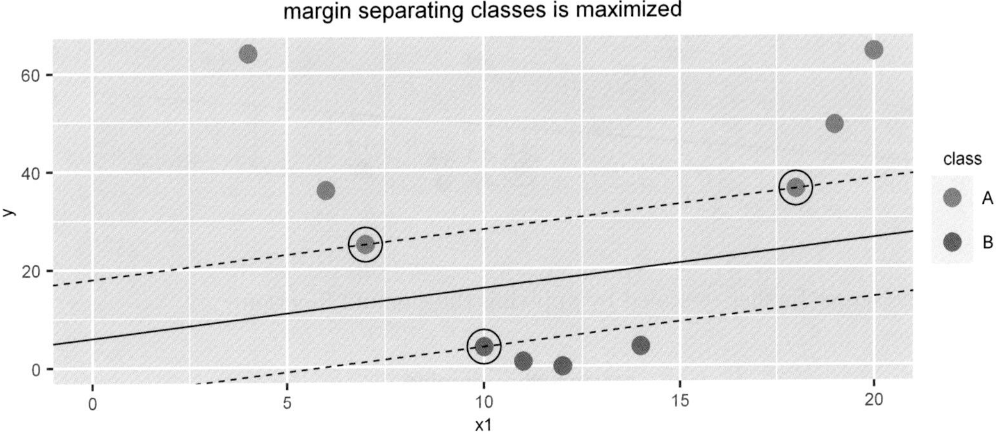

6.2.5.3 Score Observations

Score observations based on their distances from the boundary. Each is a distance orthogonal from a line to a point.

Here the points corresponding to the support vectors $(x_1{=}7)$, $(x_1{=}10)$, and $(x_1{=}18)$ are distances 8.5, -8.5, and 8.5, respectively, from the boundary. The point $(x_1{=}8, y{=}16)$ corresponds to a new observation $(x_1{=}8)$, which is distance 1.4 from the boundary.

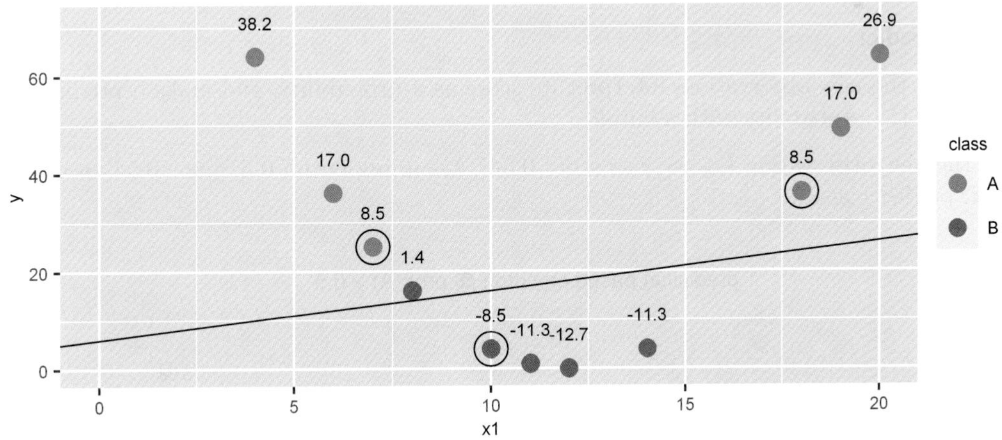

Here are the scores re-scaled by dividing by 8.5 so that scores of the points corresponding to the support vectors are 1 or -1.

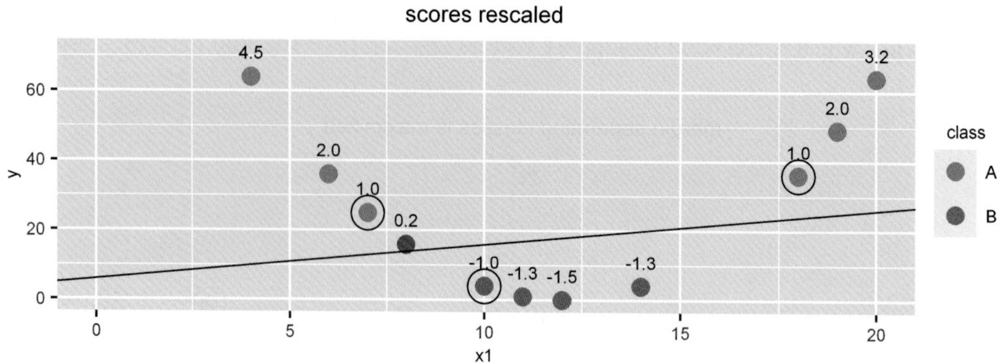

Here are the scores further re-scaled by applying the sigmoid function.

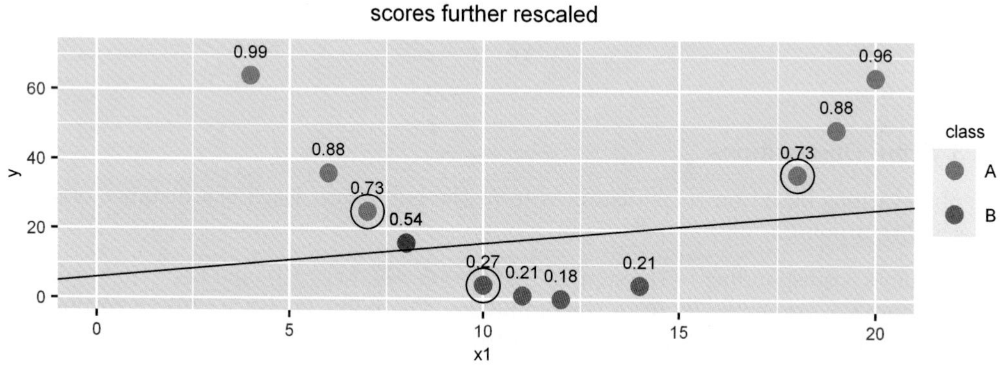

6.2.5.4 Predict

To classify the new observation, interpret its score as a probability, and make a prediction by comparing the probability with a cutoff.

Here the new observation (x_1=8) has score 0.54. Assuming cutoff 0.5, since 0.54 exceeds the cutoff, predict class A.

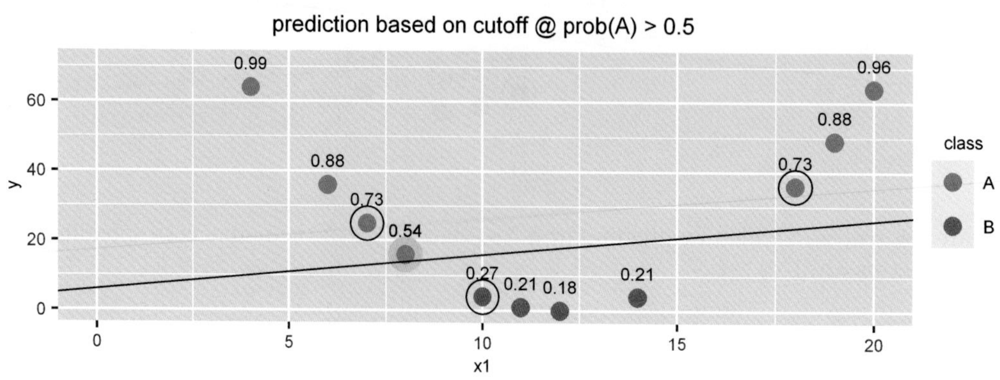

See that the support vector machine method effectively recognizes 2 groups of class A observations and 1 group of class B observations, and constructs a classifier to place the new observation in the group to which it is closest.

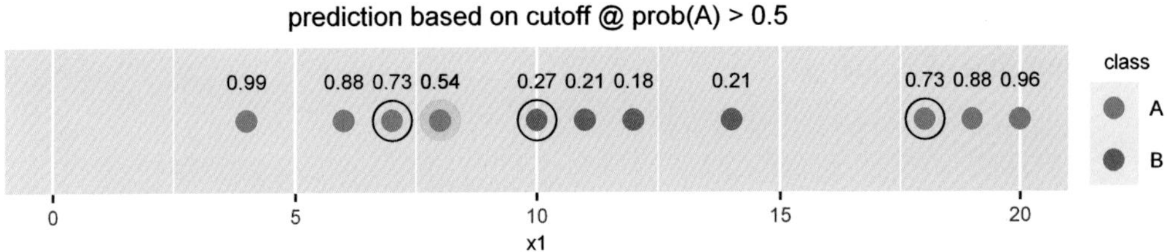

6.2.6 Support Vector Machine | More of One Predictor Variable & Kernel Trick

The support vector machine method can deal with a very non-linearly separable dataset using a carefully chosen kernel function.

Consider this reference classified dataset and new unclassified observation. Note that the dataset is ***very*** non-linearly separable. Should the new observation be classified as A or B?

data

x1	class
1	B
2	B
4	A
6	A
7	A
10	B
11	B
12	B
14	B
18	A
19	A
20	A

new

x1
8

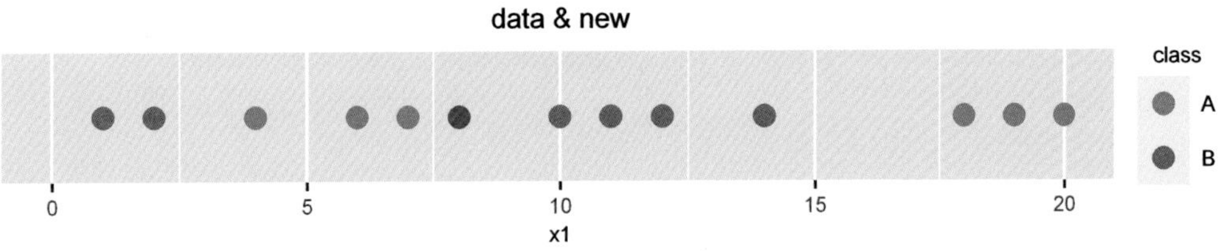

6.2.6.1 Apply Kernel

Add a synthetic variable to the dataset by applying a kernel function.

Here we apply the kernel function $y = -1.8 + 3.0x_1 - 0.4{x_1}^2 + 0.1{x_1}^3$. Note that when viewed from this higher dimension, the dataset is linearly separable. The observations in class A can be separated from the observations in class B by the variables x_1 and y, specifically by some line expressed in terms of x_1 and y.

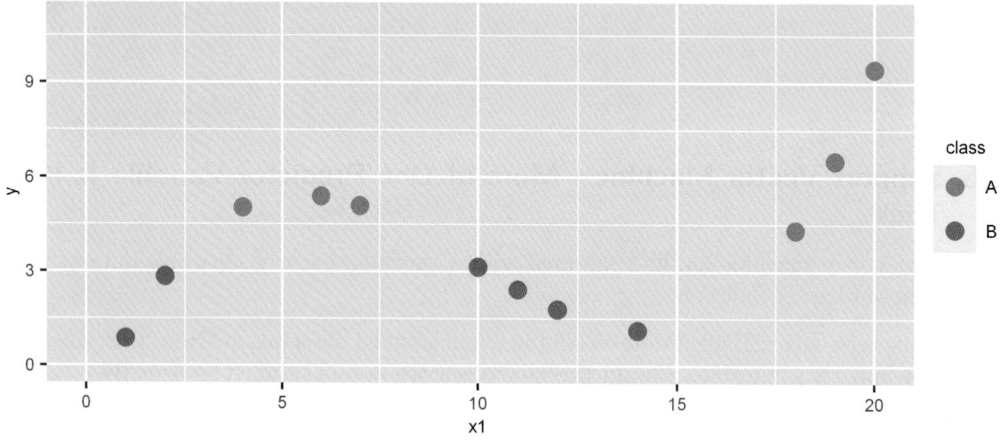

6.2.6.2 Find Support Vectors and Boundary

Here is the boundary line that separates observations of different classes and maximizes the margin.

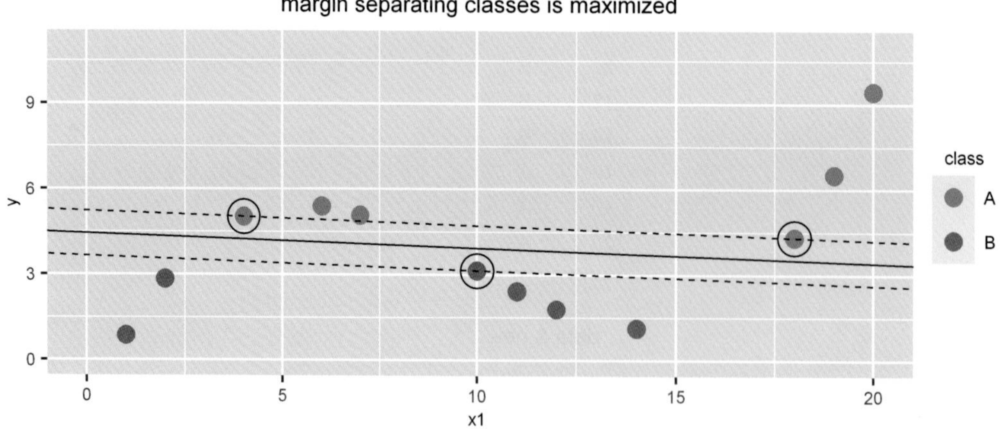

6.2.6.3 Score Observations

Score observations based on their distances from the boundary.

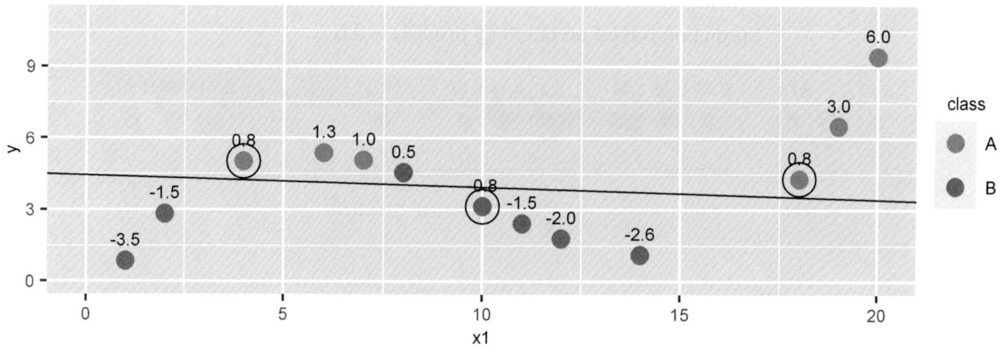

Assign probabilities to observations based on their scores.

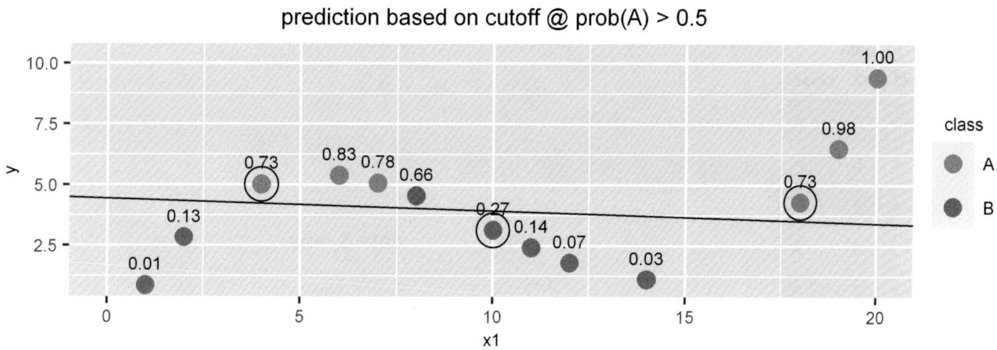

6.2.6.4 Predict

To classify the new observation, interpret its score as a probability, and make a prediction by comparing the probability with a cutoff.

Here the new observation (x_1=8) has score 0.66. Assuming cutoff 0.5, since 0.66 exceeds the cutoff, predict class A.

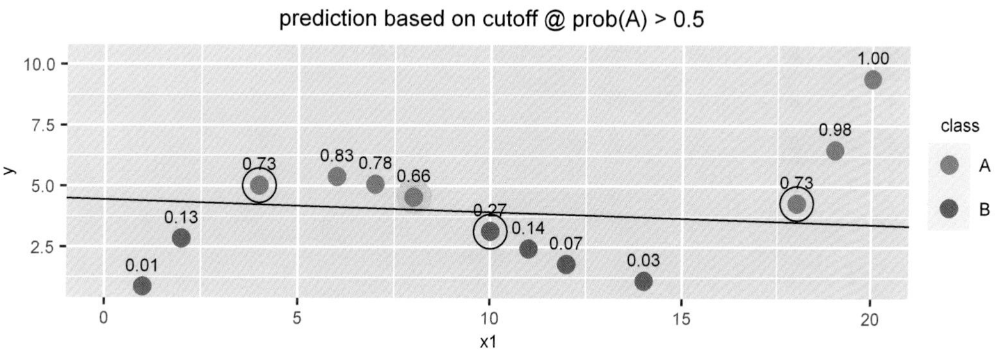

See that the support vector machine method effectively recognizes 2 groups of class A observations and 2 groups of class B observations, and constructs a classifier to place the new observation in the group to which it is closest.

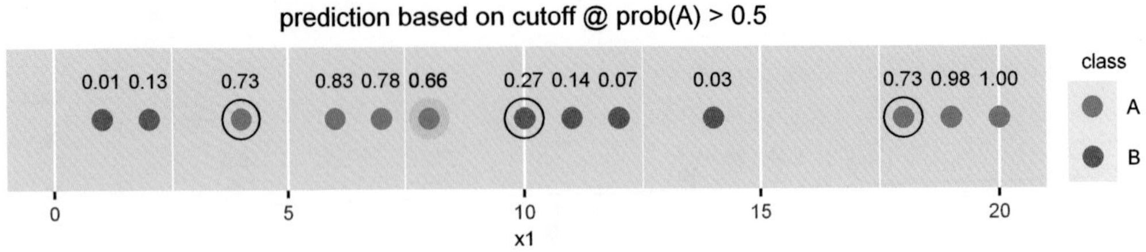

6.2.7 Support Vector Machine | Two Predictor Variables & Kernel Trick

Consider this reference classified dataset and new observation with 2 predictor variables. Note that the dataset is not linearly separable. There is no line that separates observations of different classes. Should the new observation be classified as A or B?

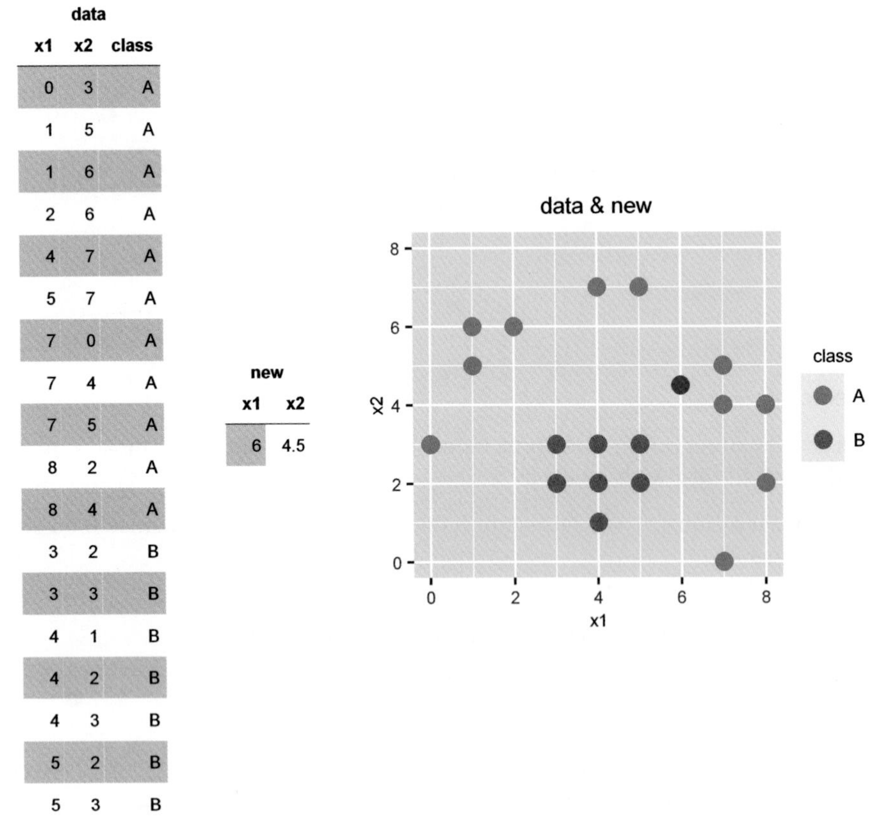

data

x1	x2	class
0	3	A
1	5	A
1	6	A
2	6	A
4	7	A
5	7	A
7	0	A
7	4	A
7	5	A
8	2	A
8	4	A
3	2	B
3	3	B
4	1	B
4	2	B
4	3	B
5	2	B
5	3	B

new

x1	x2
6	4.5

6.2.7.1 Apply Kernel

Add a synthetic variable to the dataset by applying a kernel function. You can think of this as popping the dataset into 3-dimensional space.

Here we apply the kernel function $z = (x_1 - 4)^2 + (x_2 - 2)^2$. Observations in class A map to large heights in the z- direction around the surface of a parabolic surface. Observations in class B map to small heights. Note that when viewed from this higher dimension, the dataset is linearly separable. The observations in class A can be separated from the observations in class B by the variables x_1, x_2, and z, specifically by some plane expressed in terms of x_1, x_2, and z.

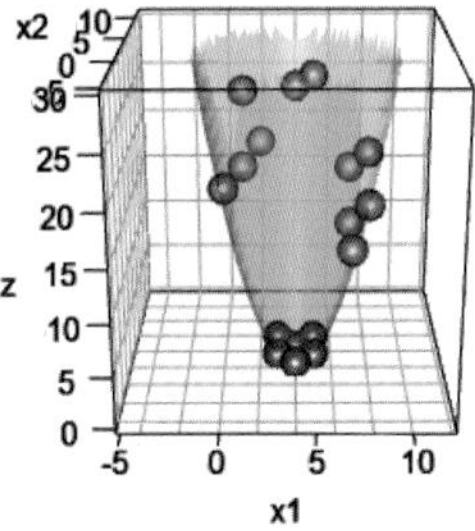

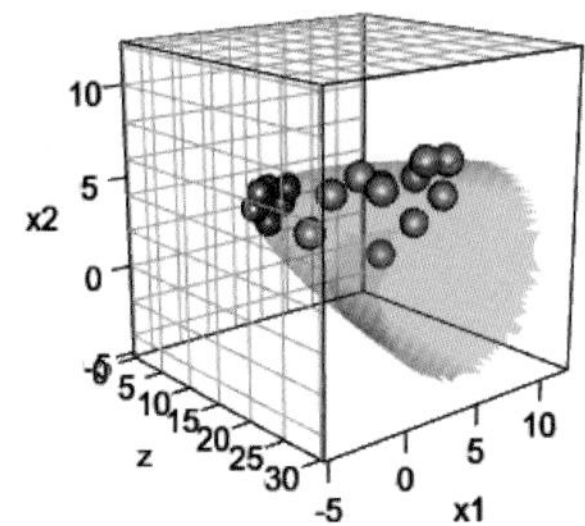

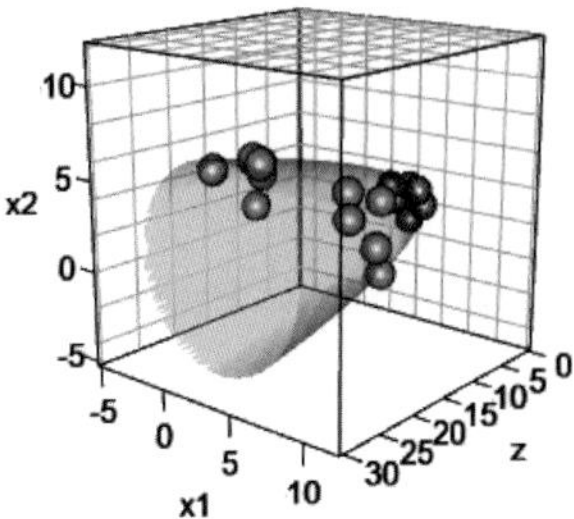

6.2.7.2 Find Support Vectors and Boundary

The support vectors are those observations at the edge of the margin separating the observations of different classes, where the margin is maximized. The boundary is the middle of the margin (a plane in 3-dimensional space).

Here is the boundary plane that separates observations of different classes and maximizes the margin. The edges of the margin are planes defined by points (x_1=0, x_2=3, z=17), (x_1=1, x_2=5, z=18), (x_1=7, x_2=4, z=13), and (x_1=4, x_2=1, z=1), which correspond to the support vectors (x_1=0, x_2=3), (x_1=1, x_2=5), (x_1=7, x_2=4), and (x_1=4, x_2=1), respectively.

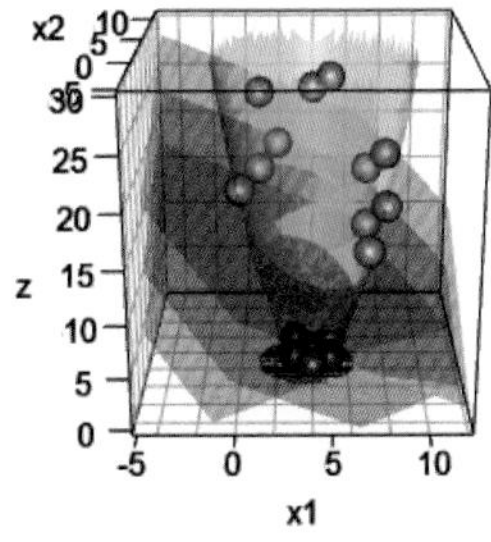

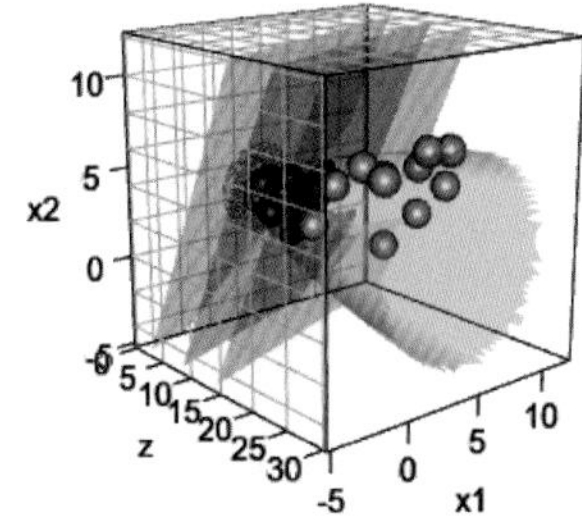

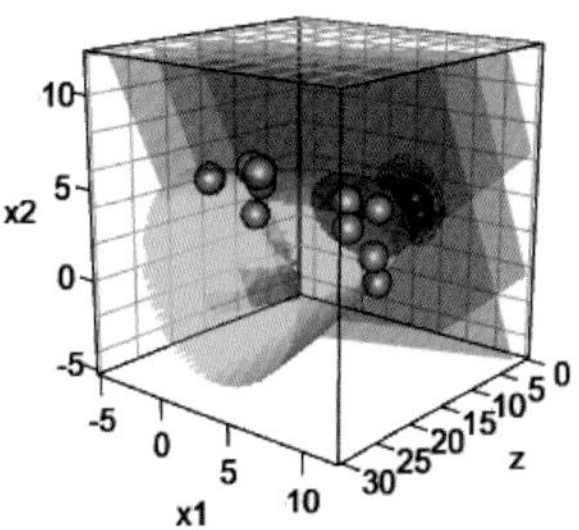

Here is a view of the dataset looking down the z-axis so that the x_1- and x_2- axes are oriented as in a 2-axis scatterplot. You can think of the dark circle surrounding the points concentrated in the center as the shadow of the boundary plane projected onto a flat surface.

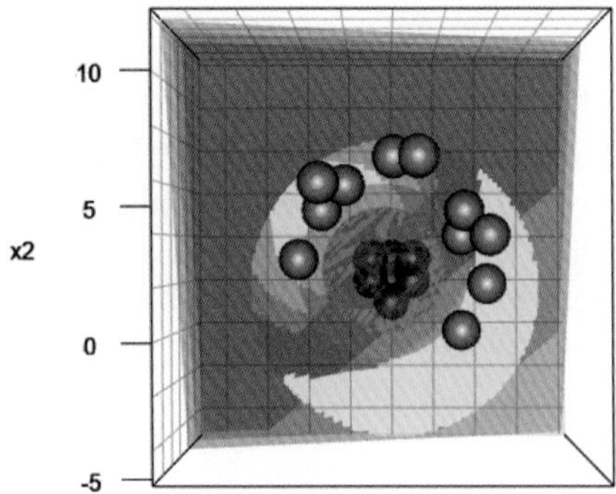

6.2.7.3 Score & Predict

To classify the new observation, calculate its score based on distance from the boundary, interpret the score as a probability, and make a prediction by comparing the probability with a cutoff.

See that the support vector machine method effectively recognizes a ring of class A observations and a bunch of class B observations, and constructs a classifier to place the new observation in the group to which it is closest.

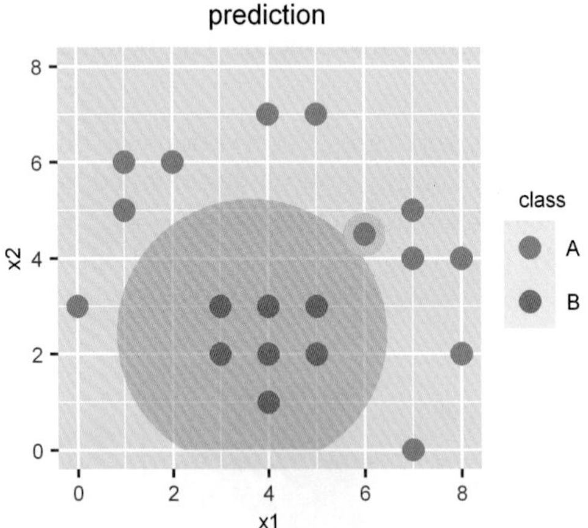

6.2.8 Support Vector Machine | Many Predictor Variables

The support vector machine method is extensible to datasets comprising many variables.

6.3 Neural Network

Construct a classifier by the neural network method.

6.3.1 Introduction

The cuttlefish has the most complex nervous system of all invertebrates. It uses it to change the color, pattern, and shape of its skin in less than a second to communicate with other cuttlefish, camouflage itself, or warn off potential predators. This involves a vast network of interconnected nerve cells sending chemical and electrical signals to each other, with signals forwarded or blocked, depending on signal strengths and cell activation thresholds.

The neural network method constructs a classifier by searching for a network configuration that best approximates a reference dataset, in a form inspired by biological neural networks.

6.3.2 About Neural Network

6.3.2.1 Overview

The **neural network method**, also called deep learning, constructs a predictive model using techniques inspired by biological neural networks. With this method, we introduce the notion of online learning, in which model construction involves iteratively updating a model-in-progress as reference data becomes available sequentially, one observation at a time. We also introduce the notion of an activation threshold, in which only some sufficiently large values are allowed to propagate through a network, while smaller values are blocked.

A **perceptron model**, the simplest type of neural network model, comprises a network of input nodes directly connected to an output node. The input nodes include 1 node for each predictor variable plus a bias node.

A **2-layer neural network model** is an extension of the perceptron model. It comprises a network of input nodes each connected to all of several hidden nodes, which in turn each connects to an output node. The input nodes include 1 node for each predictor variable plus a bias node. The hidden nodes include however many nodes are specified plus a bias node. The model is called 2-layer because we think of the input nodes as a layer, and the hidden nodes as an additional layer.

A **multilayer neural network model** is an extension of the 2-layer neural network model. It comprises a network of input nodes each connected to all of several hidden nodes, which in turn each connects to all of several more hidden nodes, and potentially more again, which ultimately each connects to an output node. The model is called multilayer because we think of the input nodes as a layer, and the hidden nodes organized into groups as additional layers.

In a neural network model, connections are **weighted** and an **activation function** is associated with the hidden and output nodes. As such, a model effectively corresponds to a potentially elaborate, non-continuous function involving weights and activations operating on values according to the arrangement of nodes in the network. Predictions are made by applying the function to new observations and interpreting the results as class probabilities. You can think of this as propagating a new observation's variable values through the input nodes into the network, combining and transforming them in various ways at each hidden and output node, eventually exiting through the output node as 1 value that indicates the probability of the observation being in 1 class or another. The job of the neural network method is to find weights for models that will result in good predictions.

The form of a neural network model is quite powerful. Indeed, ***any*** function can be approximated arbitrarily closely by a 2-layer neural network model with sufficiently many nodes. Any 2-layer neural network model can be approximated by a multilayer neural network model using fewer nodes.

6.3.2.2 Model Form

The neural network method expects you to specify an appropriate model form.

A **perceptron model** is formed of these components:

- input nodes for bias and predictor variables
- output node
- connections from input nodes to output node
- weights: 1 weight on each connection
- activation function on output node

Here is an example of a perceptron model presented as a weight matrix and as a network diagram. In the network diagram, input nodes are shown on the left in 1 vertical column, which we call the input layer. The output node is shown on the right. This model comprises 3 input nodes for bias and variables x_1 and x_2, 3 connections, 3 weights for the 3 connections, and 1 output node. The activation function on the output node is not explicitly shown.

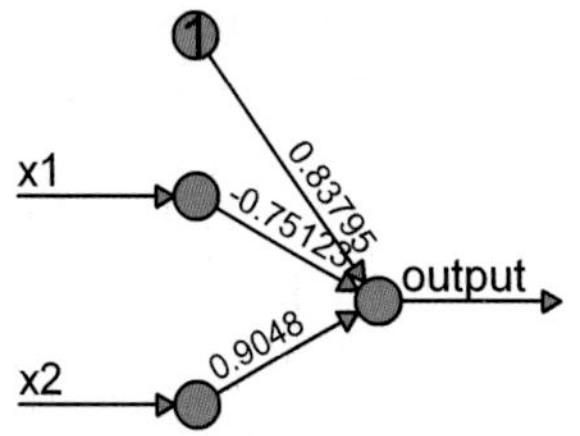

A **2-layer neural network model** is formed of these components:

- input nodes for bias and predictor variables
- hidden nodes, including a bias node
- output node
- connections from input nodes to hidden nodes, and from hidden nodes to output node
- weights: 1 weight on each connection
- activation function on hidden nodes and output node

Here is an example of a 2-layer neural network model presented as a weight matrix and as a network diagram. In the network diagram, input nodes are shown on the left in 1 vertical column, which we call the input layer. Hidden nodes are shown in the middle in 1 vertical column, which we call the **hidden layer**. The output node is shown on the right. This model comprises 3 input nodes for bias and variables x_1 and x_2, 6 connections from input nodes to hidden nodes, 3 connections from hidden nodes to output node, 9 weights for the 9 connections, and 1 output node. The activation function on the hidden nodes and output node is not explicitly shown.

weights on connections from input layer	to hidden 1	to hidden 2
from bias	0.3855	-0.6535
from x1	0.5095	0.4059
from x2	-0.3093	-2.0180

weights on connections from hidden layer	to output
from bias	0.9551
from hidden 1	0.0488
from hidden 2	0.0408

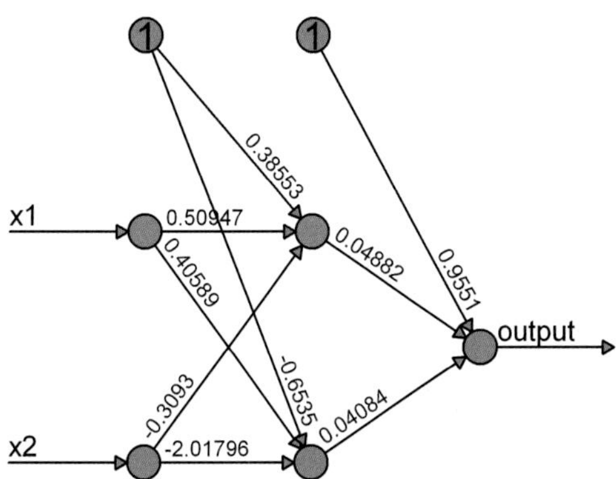

A **multilayer neural network model** is formed of these components:

- input nodes for bias and predictor variables
- hidden nodes, including bias nodes, spread across several layers
- output node
- connections from input nodes to the first layer of hidden nodes, between layers of hidden nodes, and from the last layer of hidden nodes to the output node
- weights: 1 weight on each connection
- activation function on hidden nodes and output nodes

Here is an example of a multilayer neural network model presented as a weight matrix and as a network diagram. In the network diagram, input nodes are shown on the left in 1 vertical column, which we call the input layer. Hidden nodes are shown in the middle in 2 vertical columns, which we call the hidden layers. The output node is shown on the right. This model comprises 4 input nodes for bias and variables x_1, x_2, and x_3; 12 connections from input nodes to the first layer of hidden nodes; 8 connections from the first layer of hidden nodes to the second layer of hidden nodes; 3 connections from the second layer of hidden nodes to output node; 23 weights for the 23 connections; and 1 output node. The activation function on the hidden nodes and output node is not explicitly shown.

weights on connections from input layer

	to hidden 11	to hidden 12	to hidden 13
from bias	0.4355	0.7559	-0.4342
from x1	0.5595	-1.6680	-1.0693
from x2	-0.2593	0.7801	-0.2662
from x3	-0.6035	-0.1262	1.6673

weights on connections from hidden layer 1

	to hidden 21	to hidden 22
from bias	0.2206	-0.7364
from hidden 11	0.3702	-0.1816
from hidden 12	-0.9005	1.2707
from hidden 13	0.6669	0.4487

weights on connections from hidden layer 2

	to output
from bias	0.6296
from hidden 21	1.3058
from hidden 22	-0.7943

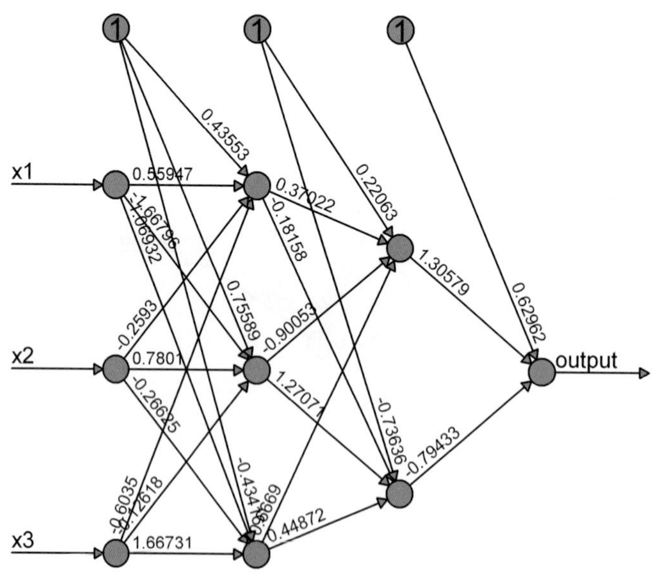

6.3.2.3 Activation Function

The neural network method expects you to specify an activation function. There are several popular choices.

The sigmoid function, also known as the logistic function, rescales any incoming value into range 0 to 1.

$$sigmoid(x) \equiv \frac{1}{1+e^{-x}}$$

The hyperbolic tangent function, also known as tanh, rescales any incoming value into range -1 to 1.

$$hyperbolic\ tangent(x) \equiv \frac{e^{2x}-1}{e^{2x}+1}$$

The softplus function is a continuous function that approximates the rectified linear unit function.

$$softplus(x) \equiv log\,(1+e^{x})$$

The rectified linear unit function, also known as ReLU, is a non-continuous function that rescales any negative value to 0, leaving positive values unchanged. Many consider this to be the preferred activation function. Theoretical and empirical studies have shown that it often leads to faster and better model construction.

$$rectified\ linear\ unit(x) \equiv \begin{Bmatrix} 0 \text{ if } x \leq 0 \\ x \text{ if } x > 0 \end{Bmatrix}$$

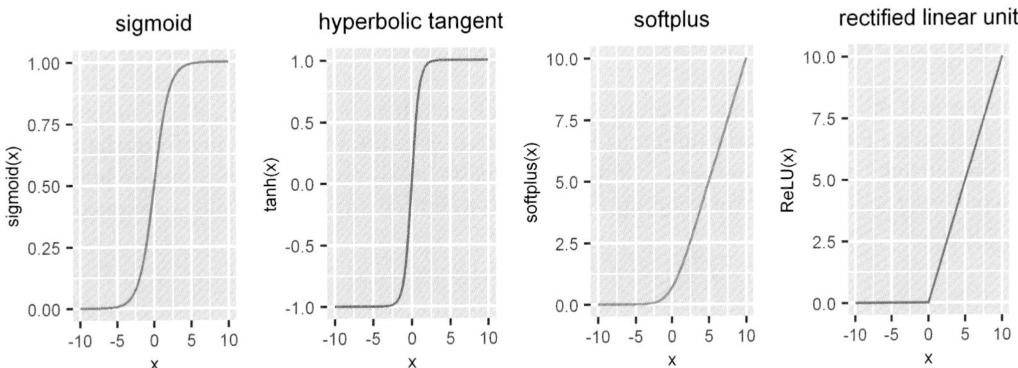

6.3.2.4 Construct Model

The neural network method tries to find weights for models that will result in good predictions.

The **perceptron method** is a variation of the neural network method to find weights for a perceptron model. It works like this:

Initialize:
Choose a cutoff
Add synthetic variable for class dummy
Choose initial weights at random
Iterate until stopping criterion is reached:
Randomize the order of observations
Iterate through all observations:
Compute output
Evaluate error based on output and class dummy
Predict class based on output and cutoff
If prediction is not correct:
Adjust weights based on error
Keep last calculated weights

If the reference dataset is linearly separable, then the perceptron method will eventually converge to specific, unchanging weights, although they might not be the best possible weights. If the reference dataset is not linearly separable, then the perceptron method will not converge to specific weights. They will continue indefinitely to change with each iteration.

The **neural network method**, more generally, works like this:

Initialize:
Choose an error function
Add a synthetic variable for class dummy
Choose initial weights at random
Iterate until stopping criterion is reached:
Randomize the order of observations
Iterate through all observations:
Compute output
Evaluate error based on output and class dummy
Adjust weights by the back-propagation algorithm
Keep last calculated weights

Output is computed like this. Compute a value for each bias node simply as 1. Compute a value for each non-bias input node simply as its associated variable value. Moving from the input side to the output side of the network, compute a value for each non-bias non-input node (hidden or output) as the activation function applied to the weighted sum of the values connected to it.

$$r_i = f\left(w_{1\to i} + (w_{j\to i} \times r_j) + (w_{k\to i} \times r_k) + \dots\right)$$

where ...

- r_i is the value for non-bias non-input node i
- f is the activation function
- $w_{1\to i}$ is the weight on the bias connection to node i
- $w_{j\to i}, w_{k\to i}, \dots$ are the weights on connections from nodes $j, k, \dots$ to node i
- $r_j, r_k, \dots$ are the values of nodes $j, k, \dots$
- nodes $j, k, \dots$ connect to node i

After computing all node values, compute output as the value of the output node.

$$output = r_o$$

where ...

- r_o is the value for the output node

In the perceptron method, weights are adjusted in proportion to their effects on the error, like this:

$$w_{1 \to output} \leftarrow w_{1 \to output} - error$$
$$w_{i \to output} \leftarrow x_i \times (w_{i \to output} - error)$$

where ...

- $w_{1 \to output}$ is the weight on the connection from the bias node to the output node
- $w_{i \to output}$ is the weight on the connection from the ith variable node to the output node
- x_i is the ith variable's value

In the neural network method, more generally, weights are adjusted by the **back-propagation algorithm**, which involves applying some calculus to the error function. In addition to the traditional back-propagation algorithm, there are several popular variations:

- traditional back-propagation (backprop)
- resilient back-propagation with weight backtracking (rprop+)
- resilient back-propagation without weight backtracking (rprop-)
- modified globally convergent with smallest absolute gradient (grprop-sag)
- modified globally convergent with smallest learning rate (grprop-slr)

6.3.2.5 Predict

To predict the class of a new observation, apply the model to the observation's variable values to compute an output. Scale the output if necessary into range 0 to 1, and interpret the output as a probability. Apply a cutoff to the probability to produce a class value.

Note that a sigmoid activation function ensures that the output will be in range 0 to 1.

6.3.3 Perceptron | Linearly Separable Data

Consider this reference classified dataset and new observation. Note that the dataset is linearly separable, since we can use a straight line to separate observations by class.

Should the new observation be classified as A or B? Let's use the perceptron method to construct a model and predict the new observation's class.

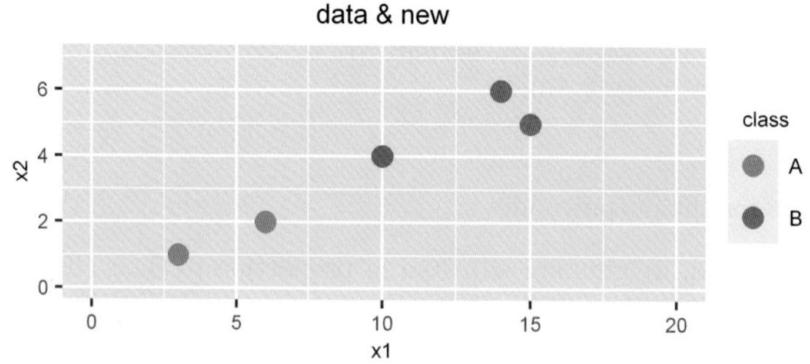

6.3.3.1 Hyper-Parameters

Set hyper-parameters to specify the model form and other method particulars.

- **activation function:** sigmoid
- **number of hidden layers:** 0
- **error function:** $output - class.bin$
- **cutoff for class A:** 0.5
- **stopping criterion:** stabilized weights

6.3.3.2 Initialize

Express the class variable *class* in dummy representation with synthetic variable *class.bin*.

Initialize weights at random.

- w_0: 0.7209 on the bias connection.
- w_1: 0.8758 on the x_1 connection.
- w_2: 0.7610 on the x_2 connection.

Here is the model-in-progress at the end of initialization.

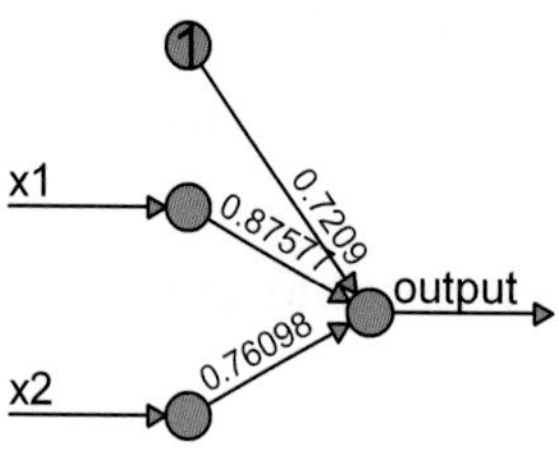

6.3.3.3 Iteration 1

Reorder observations at random. First observation goes to third position. Second observation goes to second position. Third observation goes to fourth position. Fourth observation goes to first position.

data (reordered)

	x1	x2	class
4	15	5	B
2	6	2	A
1	3	1	A
3	14	6	B

The first observation (formerly the fourth observation) is (x_1=15, x_2=5, *class*=B, *class.bin*=0). Input this observation into the model-in-progress and compute the output.

$$output = sigmoid(0.7209 + 0.8758 \times 15 + 0.7610 \times 5) = 1.0000$$

Calculate the error between the class dummy and the output.

$$error = output - class.bin = 1.0000 - 0 = 1.0000$$

Predict the observation's class, based on output and cutoff, interpreting output as a probability.

$$class.predicted = \text{A because } 1.0000 \geq 0.5$$

This prediction is wrong because the observation's predicted class is A, but its actual class is B.

status at iteration 1, step 1

	x1	x2	class	class.bin	w0	w1	w2	output	error	class.predicted
4	15	5	B	0	0.7209	0.8758	0.761	1	1	A

Because the prediction is wrong, adjust the weights. To adjust the bias connection weight, add the (negative) error. To adjust the x_1 connection weight, add 15 × the (negative) error, because the adjustment should account for the influence 15 had on producing the error in the first place. Similarly, to adjust the x_2 connection weight, add 5 × the (negative) error.

$$w_0 = 0.7209 - 1.0000 = -0.2791$$
$$w_1 = 0.8758 - (15 \times 1.0000) = -14.1242$$
$$w_2 = 0.7610 - (5 \times 1.0000) = -4.2390$$

The second observation (formerly the second observation) is (x_1=6, x_2=2, *class*=A, *class.bin*=1). Input this observation into the model-in-progress (updated with adjusted weights) and compute the output.

$$output = sigmoid(-0.2791 + -14.1242 \times 6 + -4.2390 \times 2) = 0.0000$$

Calculate the error between the class dummy and the output.

$$error = output - class.bin = 0.0000 - 1 = -1.0000$$

Predict the observation's class, based on output and cutoff, interpreting output as a probability.

$$class.predicted = \mathsf{B} \text{ because } 0.0000 < 0.5$$

status at iteration 1, step 2

	x1	x2	class	class.bin	w0	w1	w2	output	error	class.predicted
4	15	5	B	0	0.7209	0.8758	0.761	1	1	A
2	6	2	A	1	-0.2791	-14.1242	-4.239	0	-1	B

This prediction is wrong because the observation's predicted class is B, but its actual class is A. Because the prediction is wrong, adjust the weights.

$$w_0 = -0.2791 - -1.0000 = 0.7209$$
$$w_1 = -14.1242 - (6 \times -1.0000) = -8.1242$$
$$w_2 = -4.2390 - (2 \times -1.0000) = -2.2390$$

The third observation (formerly the first observation) is (x_1=3, x_2=1, *class*=A, *class.bin*=1). Input this observation into the model-in-progress (updated with adjusted weights) and compute the output.

$$output = sigmoid(0.7209 + -8.1242 \times 3 + -2.2390 \times 1) = 0.0000$$

Calculate the error between the class dummy and the output.

$$error = output - class.bin = 0.0000 - 1 = -1.0000$$

Predict the observation's class, based on output and cutoff, interpreting output as a probability.

$$class.predicted = \mathsf{B} \text{ because } 0.0000 < 0.5$$

This prediction is wrong because the observation's predicted class is B, but its actual class is A.

status at iteration 1, step 3

	x1	x2	class	class.bin	w0	w1	w2	output	error	class.predicted
4	15	5	B	0	0.7209	0.8758	0.761	1	1	A
2	6	2	A	1	-0.2791	-14.1242	-4.239	0	-1	B
1	3	1	A	1	0.7209	-8.1242	-2.239	0	-1	B

Because the prediction is wrong, adjust the weights.

$$w_0 = 0.7209 - -1.0000 = 1.7209$$
$$w_1 = -8.1242 - (3 \times -1.0000) = -5.1242$$
$$w_2 = -2.2390 - (1 \times -1.0000) = -1.2390$$

The fourth observation (formerly the third observation) is (x_1=14, x_2=6, *class*=B, *class.bin*=0). Input this observation into the model-in-progress (updated with adjusted weights) and compute the output.

$$output = sigmoid(1.7209 + -5.1242 \times 14 + -1.2390 \times 6) = 0.0000$$

Calculate the error between the class dummy and the output.

$$error = output - class.bin = 0.0000 - 0 = 0.0000$$

Predict the observation's class, based on output and cutoff, interpreting output as a probability.

$$class.predicted = \text{B because } 0.0000 < 0.5$$

This prediction is right because the observation's predicted class is B and its actual class is B, so do not adjust the weights.

status at iteration 1, step 4

	x1	x2	class	class.bin	w0	w1	w2	output	error	class.predicted
4	15	5	B	0	0.7209	0.8758	0.761	1	1	A
2	6	2	A	1	-0.2791	-14.1242	-4.239	0	-1	B
1	3	1	A	1	0.7209	-8.1242	-2.239	0	-1	B
3	14	6	B	0	1.7209	-5.1242	-1.239	0	0	B

Here is the model-in-progress at the end of iteration 1.

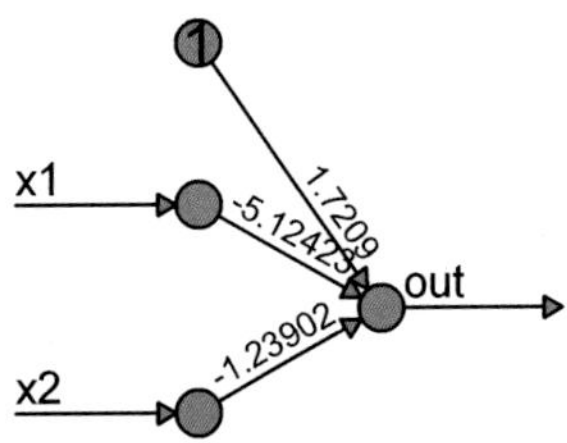

6.3.3.4 More Iterations

Continue to iterate. The weights stabilize by iteration 6, so stop there.

status at iteration 2

	x1	x2	class	class.bin	w0	w1	w2	output	error	class.predicted
2	6	2	A	1	1.721	-5.1242	-1.239	0	-1	B
3	14	6	B	0	2.721	0.8758	0.761	1	1	A
4	15	5	B	0	1.721	-13.1242	-5.239	0	0	B
1	3	1	A	1	1.721	-13.1242	-5.239	0	-1	B

status at iteration 3

	x1	x2	class	class.bin	w0	w1	w2	output	error	class.predicted
1	3	1	A	1	2.721	-10.124	-4.239	0	-1	B
3	14	6	B	0	3.721	-7.124	-3.239	0	0	B
4	15	5	B	0	3.721	-7.124	-3.239	0	0	B
2	6	2	A	1	3.721	-7.124	-3.239	0	-1	B

status at iteration 4

	x1	x2	class	class.bin	w0	w1	w2	output	error	class.predicted
3	14	6	B	0	4.721	-1.124	-1.2390	0.000	0.000	B
4	15	5	B	0	4.721	-1.124	-1.2390	0.000	0.000	B
2	6	2	A	1	4.721	-1.124	-1.2390	0.011	-0.989	B
1	3	1	A	1	5.710	4.810	0.7391	1.000	0.000	A

status at iteration 5

	x1	x2	class	class.bin	w0	w1	w2	output	error	class.predicted
3	14	6	B	0	5.71	4.81	0.7391	1.0000	1.0000	A
2	6	2	A	1	4.71	-9.19	-5.2609	0.0000	-1.0000	B
4	15	5	B	0	5.71	-3.19	-3.2609	0.0000	0.0000	B
1	3	1	A	1	5.71	-3.19	-3.2609	0.0008	-0.9992	B

status at iteration 6

	x1	x2	class	class.bin	w0	w1	w2	output	error	class.predicted
3	14	6	B	0	6.709	-0.1924	-2.262	0.0001	0.0001	B
2	6	2	A	1	6.709	-0.1924	-2.262	0.7371	-0.2629	A
4	15	5	B	0	6.709	-0.1924	-2.262	0.0006	0.0006	B
1	3	1	A	1	6.709	-0.1924	-2.262	0.9796	-0.0204	A

Here is the final model at the end of iteration 6. See that the model weights are taken from the last weights calculated in the last iteration.

weights

	to output
from bias	6.7091
from x1	-0.1924
from x2	-2.2617

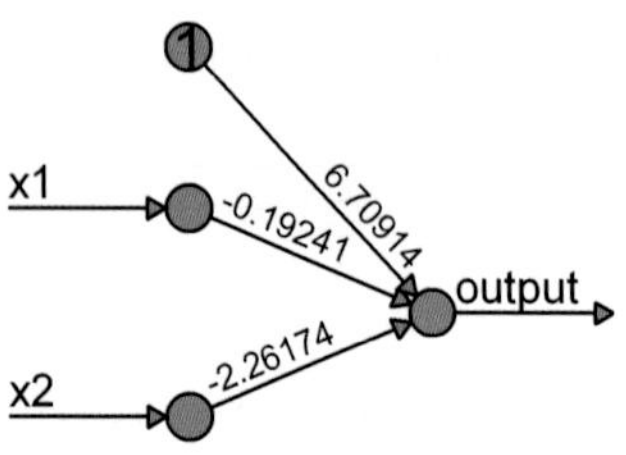

6.3.3.5 Predict

Input the new observation into the model, compute the output, and apply the cutoff to the output. We predict the new observation's class to be B.

$$output = sigmoid(6.7091 + -0.1924 \times 10 + -2.2617 \times 4) = 0.0139$$

$$class = \mathsf{B} \text{ because } 0.0139 < 0.5$$

new observation

x1	x2	output	class.predicted
10	4	0.0139	B

6.3.4 Perceptron | Non-Linearly Separable Data

Consider this reference classified dataset and new observation. Note that the dataset is not linearly separable, since there does not exist any straight line that would separate observations by class.

Should the new observation be classified as A or B? We could use the perceptron method to construct a model and predict the new observation's class. However, we should not expect such a model to predict very well because the perceptron method does not converge to stable weights when the dataset is not linearly separable.

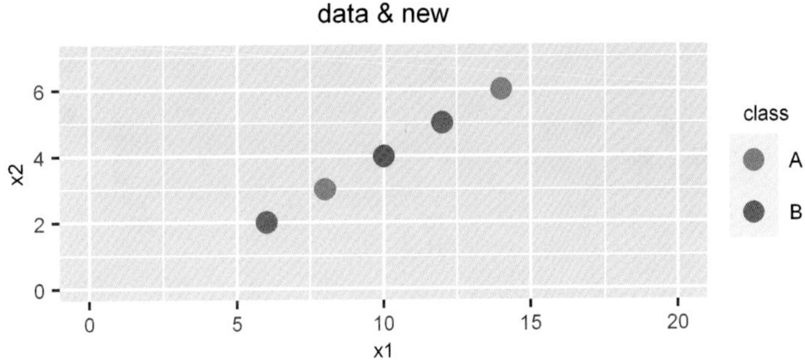

Indeed, the perceptron method run on this dataset for 100 iterations does not result in stable weights. See that weights $w_0 = -23.27$, $w_1 = -4.055$, $w_2 = 22.29$ change to $w_0 = -24.27$, $w_1 = -16.055$, $w_2 = 17.29$, and then change again to $w_0 = -23.27$, $w_1 = -8.055$, $w_2 = 20.29$. These 3 sets of weights correspond to 3 different models-in-progress, and none of them back-predicts the dataset well.

status at iteration 100

	x1	x2	class	class.bin	w0	w1	w2	output	error	class.predicted
3	14	6	A	1	-23.27	-4.055	22.29	1	0	A
4	12	5	B	0	-23.27	-4.055	22.29	1	1	A
2	8	3	A	1	-24.27	-16.055	17.29	0	-1	B
1	6	2	B	0	-23.27	-8.055	20.29	0	0	B

After 1,000 iterations, the results are no better. The weights keep changing and all of the models-in-progress make wrong back-predictions on the dataset.

status at iteration 1000

	x1	x2	class	class.bin	w0	w1	w2	output	error	class.predicted
2	8	3	A	1	-47.29	-10.671	43.00	0.0251	-0.9749	B
3	14	6	A	1	-46.32	-2.872	45.92	1.0000	0.0000	A
1	6	2	B	0	-46.32	-2.872	45.92	1.0000	1.0000	A
4	12	5	B	0	-47.32	-8.871	43.92	1.0000	1.0000	A

6.3.5 Two-Layer Neural Network

Consider this reference classified dataset and new observation. Note that the dataset is not linearly separable.

Should the new observation be classified as A or B? Let's use the neural network method to construct a 2-layer neural network model and predict the new observation's class. We can expect such a model to predict well even when the dataset is not linearly separable because the hidden layer enables an elaborate class boundary.

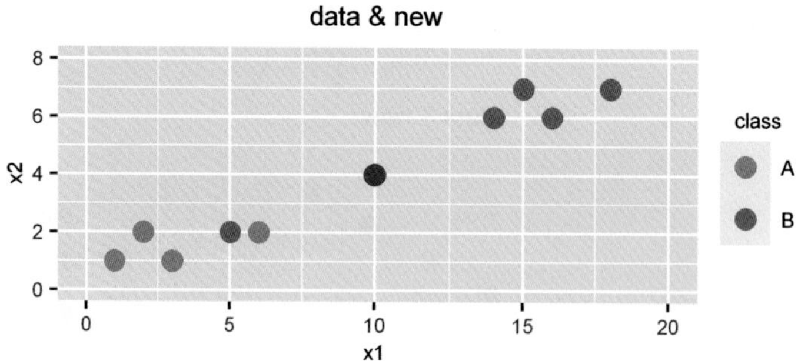

6.3.5.1 Hyper-Parameters

Set hyper-parameters to specify the model form and other method particulars.

- **activation function:** sigmoid
- **number of hidden layers:** 1
- **number of nodes in hidden layer:** 2
- **error function:** $\frac{1}{2} \times \left(output - class.bin\right)^2$
- **back-propagation algorithm:** traditional back-propagation
- **learning rate:** 0.1 (used by back-progation algorithm)
- **stopping criterion:** iterate 1,000 times

6.3.5.2 Initialize

Express the class variable *class* in dummy representation with synthetic variable *class.bin*. Initialize weights at random.

- $w_{1 \to h_1}$: 0.7209 on connection from input layer bias node to hidden node 1
- $w_{x_1 \to h_1}$: 0.8758 on connection from x_1 node to hidden node 1
- $w_{x_2 \to h_1}$: 0.7610 on connection from x_2 node to hidden node 1
- $w_{1 \to h_2}$: 0.8861 on connection from input layer bias node to hidden node 2
- $w_{x_1 \to h_2}$: 0.4565 on connection from x_1 node to hidden node 2
- $w_{x_2 \to h_2}$: 0.1664 on connection from x_2 node to hidden node 2
- $w_{1 \to output}$: 0.3251 on connection from hidden layer bias node to output node
- $w_{h_1 \to output}$: 0.5092 on connection from hidden node 1 to output node
- $w_{h_2 \to output}$: 0.7277 on connection from hidden node 2 to output node

initial weights

w.1h1	w.x1h1	w.x2h1	w.1h2	w.x1h2	w.x2h2	w.1out	w.h1out	w.h2out
0.7209	0.8758	0.761	0.8861	0.4565	0.1664	0.3251	0.5092	0.7277

Here is the model-in-progress at the end of initialization.

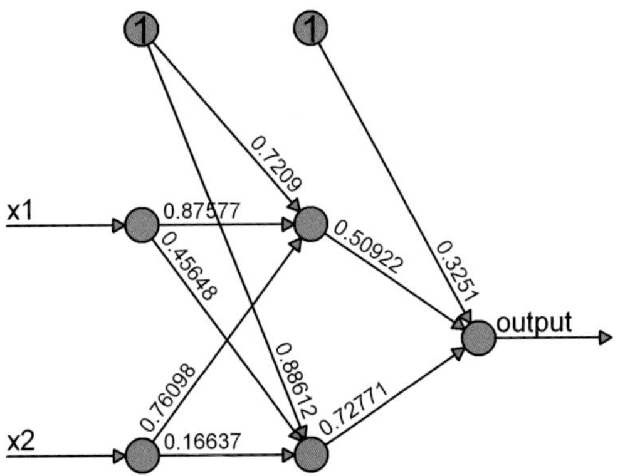

6.3.5.3 Iteration 1

Reorder observations at random.

The first observation (formerly the third observation) is (x_1=3, x_2=1, *class*=A, *class.bin*=1). Input this observation into the model-in-progress and compute the output.

$$h_1 = sigmoid(0.7209 + 0.8758 \times 3 + 0.7610 \times 1) = 0.9838$$

$$h_2 = sigmoid(0.8612 + 0.4565 \times 3 + 0.1664 \times 1) = 0.9185$$

$$output = sigmoid(0.3251 + 0.5092 \times 0.9838 + 0.7277 \times 0.9185) = 0.8167$$

Calculate the error between the class dummy and the output.

$$error = \frac{1}{2} \times \left(output - class.bin\right)^2 = \frac{1}{2} \times \left(0.8167 - 1\right)^2 = 0.0168$$

Adjust the weights by the back-propagation algorithm. The calculations involve calculus applied to the error function and the learning rate. Note that in the general neural network method, weights are adjusted at every step, unlike in the perceptron method where weights are adjusted only on steps involving incorrect predictions.

Similarly, compute outputs, calculate errors, and adjust weights for the remaining observations.

status at iteration 1

	x1	x2	class	class.bin	h1	h2	output	error	class.predicted
3	3	1	A	1	0.9838	0.9185	0.8167	0.0168	A
8	16	6	B	0	1.0000	0.9999	0.8278	0.3426	A
2	2	2	A	1	0.9819	0.8941	0.8099	0.0181	A
4	5	2	B	0	0.9987	0.9709	0.8207	0.3368	A
7	15	7	B	0	1.0000	0.9999	0.8186	0.3351	A
1	1	1	A	1	0.9136	0.8189	0.7863	0.0228	A
9	18	7	B	0	1.0000	1.0000	0.8146	0.3318	A
5	6	2	A	1	0.9994	0.9813	0.8070	0.0186	A
6	14	6	B	0	1.0000	0.9997	0.8104	0.3283	A

status at iteration 1 (weights)

	w.1h1	w.x1h1	w.x2h1	w.1h2	w.x1h2	w.x2h2	w.1out	w.h1out	w.h2out
3	0.7209	0.8758	0.7610	0.8861	0.4565	0.1664	0.3251	0.5092	0.7277
8	0.7209	0.8758	0.7610	0.8863	0.4569	0.1665	0.3278	0.5119	0.7302
2	0.7209	0.8758	0.7610	0.8863	0.4569	0.1665	0.3160	0.5001	0.7184
4	0.7210	0.8759	0.7611	0.8865	0.4573	0.1669	0.3190	0.5030	0.7210
7	0.7209	0.8759	0.7610	0.8862	0.4561	0.1664	0.3069	0.4909	0.7093
1	0.7209	0.8759	0.7610	0.8862	0.4561	0.1664	0.2947	0.4788	0.6972
9	0.7211	0.8760	0.7612	0.8866	0.4564	0.1668	0.2983	0.4821	0.7001
5	0.7211	0.8760	0.7612	0.8866	0.4564	0.1668	0.2860	0.4698	0.6878
6	0.7211	0.8760	0.7612	0.8866	0.4567	0.1669	0.2890	0.4728	0.6908

6.3.5.4 More Iterations

Continue to iterate. The stopping criterion is to iterate 1,000 times, so stop there. See that the models-in-progress correctly back-predict the class of 9 out of 10 observations in the dataset.

status iteration 1000

	x1	x2	class	class.bin	h1	h2	output	error	class.predicted
6	14	6	B	0	1.0000	0.9497	0.0851	0.0036	B
9	18	7	B	0	1.0000	0.9867	0.0722	0.0026	B
7	15	7	B	0	1.0000	0.9776	0.0751	0.0028	B
8	16	6	B	0	1.0000	0.9664	0.0788	0.0031	B
2	2	2	A	1	0.9923	0.1633	0.7959	0.0208	A
4	5	2	B	0	0.9997	0.2464	0.7266	0.2639	A
3	3	1	A	1	0.9934	0.1353	0.8135	0.0174	A
5	6	2	A	1	0.9999	0.3716	0.5882	0.0848	A
1	1	1	A	1	0.9460	0.0796	0.8490	0.0114	A

status at iteration 1000 (weights)

	w.1h1	w.x1h1	w.x2h1	w.1h2	w.x1h2	w.x2h2	w.1out	w.h1out	w.h2out
6	0.8628	1.078	0.9213	-3.229	0.1779	0.6128	1.368	0.7817	-4.764
9	0.8628	1.078	0.9213	-3.229	0.1800	0.6137	1.367	0.7811	-4.765
7	0.8628	1.078	0.9213	-3.229	0.1805	0.6139	1.367	0.7806	-4.765
8	0.8628	1.078	0.9213	-3.229	0.1813	0.6143	1.366	0.7801	-4.766
2	0.8628	1.078	0.9213	-3.229	0.1828	0.6148	1.366	0.7795	-4.766
4	0.8628	1.078	0.9214	-3.231	0.1784	0.6105	1.369	0.7828	-4.766
3	0.8628	1.078	0.9214	-3.218	0.2423	0.6361	1.355	0.7684	-4.769
5	0.8628	1.078	0.9214	-3.220	0.2376	0.6345	1.357	0.7712	-4.769
1	0.8628	1.078	0.9214	-3.231	0.1709	0.6123	1.367	0.7811	-4.765

Here is the final model at the end of iteration 1,000. See that the model weights are taken from the last weights calculated in the last iteration.

weights on connections from input layer

	to hidden 1	to hidden 2
from bias	0.8628	-3.2309
from x1	1.0784	0.1709
from x2	0.9214	0.6123

weights on connections from hidden layer

	to output
from bias	1.3674
from hidden 1	0.7811
from hidden 2	-4.7650

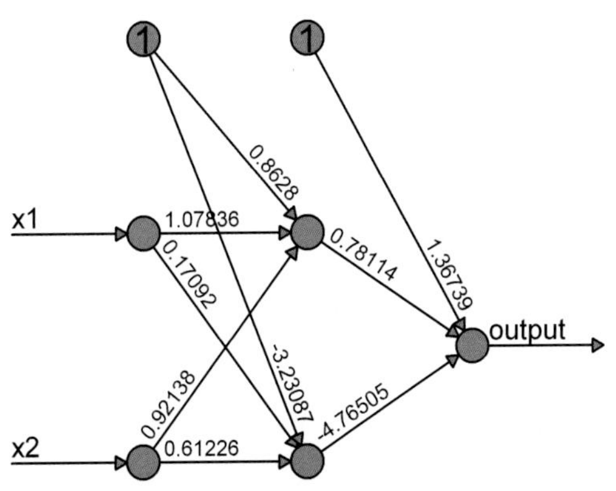

6.3.5.5 Predict

Input the new observation into the model, compute the output, and apply cutoff 0.5 to the output. We predict the new observation's class to be B.

$$h_1 = sigmoid(0.8628 + 1.0784 \times 10 + 0.9214 \times 4) = 1.0000$$

$$h_2 = sigmoid(-3.2309 + 0.1709 \times 10 + 0.6123 \times 4) = 0.7166$$

$$output = sigmoid(1.3674 + 0.7811 \times 1.0000 + -4.7650 \times 0.7166) = 0.2200$$

$$class = B \text{ because } 0.2200 < 0.5$$

new observation

x1	x2	h1	h2	output	class.predicted
10	4	1	0.7166	0.22	B

6.3.6 Multilayer Neural Network

Consider this reference classified dataset and new observation. There are 3 predictor variables and 1 class variable. Observations in class A are color-coded blue, those in class B are color-coded red. The new observation is color-coded gray.

Should the new observation be classified as A or B? Let's use the neural network method to construct a multilayer neural network model and predict the new observation's class.

data & new

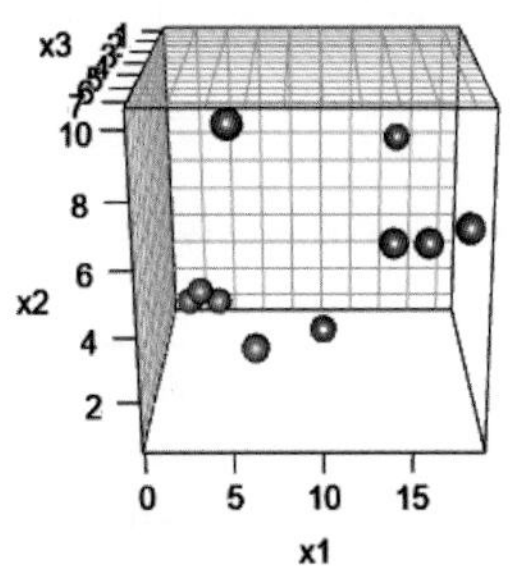

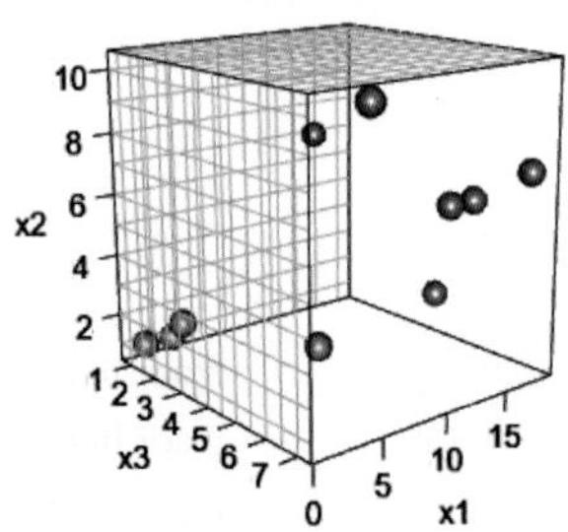

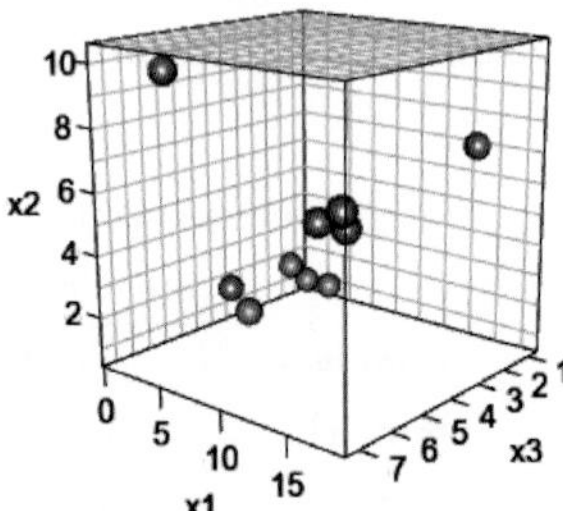

6.3.6.1 Hyper-Parameters

Set hyper-parameters to specify the model form and other method particulars.

- **activation function:** sigmoid
- **number of hidden layers:** 2
- **number of nodes in hidden layer 1:** 2
- **number of nodes in hidden layer 2:** 2
- **error function:** $(output - class.bin)^2$
- **back-propagation algorithm:** resilient back-propagation with weight backtracking (rprop+)

- **learning rate:** (not used by rprop+)
- **stopping criteria:** 100,000 iterations or weights stabilize to within 0.01, whichever comes first

6.3.6.2 Construct Model

Itialize and iterate. Here is the resulting model:

weights on connections from input layer

	to hidden 11	to hidden 12
from bias	-3.2645	3.7243
from x1	0.7640	-0.0201
from x2	-0.1844	-0.6572
from x3	-0.9640	-0.1556

weights on connections from hidden layer 1

	to_hidden 21	to hidden 22
from bias	-0.9592	1.099
from hidden 11	-3.2381	2.112
from hidden 12	3.9838	-3.580

weights on connections from hidden layer 2

	to output
from bias	-0.9034
from hidden 21	4.5853
from hidden 22	-3.5238

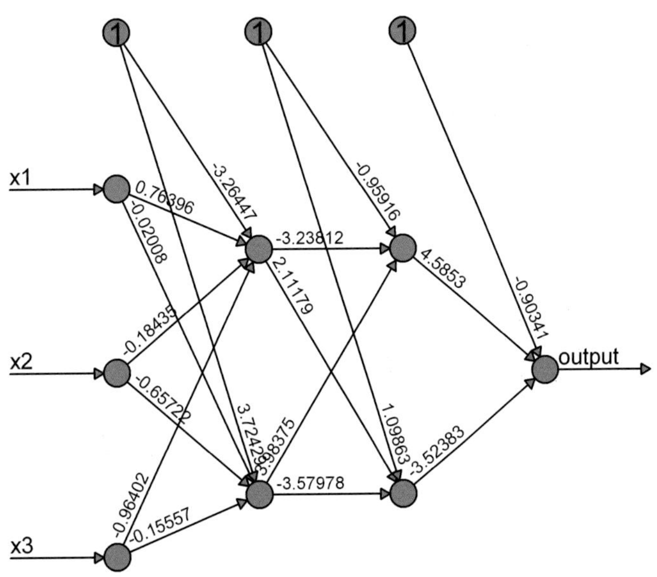

6.3.6.3 Predict

Input the new observation into the model, compute the output, and apply cutoff 0.5 to the output. We predict the new observation's class to be A.

$$h_{11} = sigmoid(-3.2645 + 0.7640 \times 10 + -0.1843 \times 4 + -0.9640 \times 7) = 0.0427$$
$$h_{12} = sigmoid(3.7243 + -0.0201 \times 10 + -0.6572 \times 4 + -0.1556 \times 7) = 0.4515$$
$$h_{21} = sigmoid(-0.9592 + -3.2381 \times 0.0427 + 3.9838 \times 0.4515) = 0.6685$$
$$h_{22} = sigmoid(1.0986 + 2.1118 \times 0.0427 + -3.5798 \times 0.4515) = 0.3947$$
$$output = sigmoid(-0.9034 + 4.5853 \times 0.6685 + -3.5238 \times 0.3947) = 0.6838$$
$$class = A \text{ because } 0.6838 \geq 0.5$$

x1	x2	x3	h11	h12	h21	h22	output	class.predicted
10	4	7	0.0427	0.4515	0.6685	0.3947	0.6838	A

6.3.7 Details of Back-Propagation Algorithm

The back-propagation algorithm adjusts the weights to account for their effect on error. It involves calculus to quantify the rate at which each weight affects the error, starting with weights on connections to the output node, and working backward through connections to nodes in hidden layers. Here we'll detail the back-propagation algorithm with these settings: 2 predictor variables, 1 hidden layer with 2 hidden nodes, sigmoid is the activation function, and $\frac{1}{2}(output - class.bin)^2$ is the error function.

At each step within an iteration, an observation is input into the model-in-progress, and error is computed based on the variable values and current weights.

$$z_{h_1} = (w_{1\to h_1} \times 1) + (w_{x_1\to h_1} \times x_1) + (w_{x_2\to h_1} \times x_2)$$
$$z_{h_2} = (w_{1\to h_2} \times 1) + (w_{x_1\to h_2} \times x_1) + (w_{x_2\to h_2} \times x_2)$$
$$z_{output} = (w_{1\to output} \times 1) + (w_{h_1\to output} \times h_1) + (w_{h_2\to output} \times h_2)$$
$$h_1 = sigmoid(z_{h_1})$$
$$h_2 = sigmoid(z_{h_2})$$
$$output = sigmoid(z_{output})$$
$$E = \frac{1}{2} \times (output - class.bin)^2$$

where ...

- x_1, x_2 are variable values
- $w_{i\to j}$ is the weight on the connection from node i to node j
- z_{h_1}, z_{h_2}, z_{output} are the weighted sums that enter hidden node 1, hidden node 2, and the output node
- h_1, h_2, $output$ are the values that exit hidden node 1, hidden node 2, and the output node
- E is the error

See how error is affected by changes to weights on connections from the hidden layer.

$$\frac{\partial E}{\partial output} = output - class.bin$$

$$\frac{\partial output}{\partial z_{output}} = output \times (1 - output)$$

$$\frac{\partial z_{output}}{\partial w_{h_1 \to output}} = h_1$$

$$\frac{\partial z_{output}}{\partial w_{h_2 \to output}} = h_2$$

$$\frac{\partial E}{\partial w_{1 \to output}} = \frac{\partial E}{\partial output} \times \frac{\partial output}{\partial z_{output}} \times 1$$

$$\frac{\partial E}{\partial w_{h_1 \to output}} = \frac{\partial E}{\partial output} \times \frac{\partial output}{\partial z_{output}} \times \frac{\partial z_{output}}{\partial w_{h_1 \to output}}$$

$$\frac{\partial E}{\partial w_{h_2 \to output}} = \frac{\partial E}{\partial output} \times \frac{\partial output}{\partial z_{output}} \times \frac{\partial z_{output}}{\partial w_{h_2 \to output}}$$

where ...

- $\frac{\partial X}{\partial Y}$ is the partial derivative of X with respect to Y (describes how a change in X is affected by a change in Y)
- Specifically, $\frac{\partial E}{\partial output}$ is from $\frac{d}{dx}\frac{1}{2}(x)^2 = x$
- Specifically, $\frac{\partial output}{\partial z_{output}}$ is from $\frac{d}{dx}sigmoid(x) = sigmoid(x) \times (1 - sigmoid(x))$

Working backward through the network, see how error is affected by changes to weights on connections from the input layer to hidden node 1.

$$\frac{\partial z_{output}}{\partial h_1} = w_{h_1 \to output}$$

$$\frac{\partial E}{\partial h_1} = \frac{\partial E}{\partial output} \times \frac{\partial output}{\partial z_{output}} \times \frac{\partial z_{output}}{\partial h_1}$$

$$\frac{\partial h_1}{\partial z_{h_1}} = h_1 \times (1 - h_1)$$

$$\frac{\partial z_{h_1}}{\partial w_{x_1 \to h_1}} = x_1$$

$$\frac{\partial z_{h_1}}{\partial w_{x_2 \to h_1}} = x_2$$

$$\frac{\partial E}{\partial w_{1 \to h_1}} = \frac{\partial E}{\partial h_1} \times \frac{\partial h_1}{\partial z_{h_1}} \times 1$$

$$\frac{\partial E}{\partial w_{x_1 \to h_1}} = \frac{\partial E}{\partial h_1} \times \frac{\partial h_1}{\partial z_{h_1}} \times \frac{\partial z h_1}{\partial w_{x_1 \to h_1}}$$

$$\frac{\partial E}{\partial w_{x_2 \to h_1}} = \frac{\partial E}{\partial h_1} \times \frac{\partial h_1}{\partial z_{h_1}} \times \frac{\partial z_{h_1}}{\partial w_{x_2 \to h_1}}$$

See also how error is affected by changes to weights on connections from the input layer to hidden node 2.

$$\frac{\partial z_{output}}{\partial h_2} = w_{h_2 \to output}$$

$$\frac{\partial E}{\partial h_2} = \frac{\partial E}{\partial output} \times \frac{\partial output}{\partial z_{output}} \times \frac{\partial z_{output}}{\partial h_2}$$

$$\frac{\partial h_2}{\partial z_{h_2}} = h_2 \times (1 - h_2)$$

$$\frac{\partial z_{h_2}}{\partial w_{x_1 \to h_2}} = x_1$$

$$\frac{\partial z_{h_2}}{\partial w_{x_2 \to h_2}} = x_2$$

$$\frac{\partial E}{\partial w_{1 \to h_2}} = \frac{\partial E}{\partial h_2} \times \frac{\partial h_2}{\partial z_{h_2}} \times 1$$

$$\frac{\partial E}{\partial w_{x_1 \to h_2}} = \frac{\partial E}{\partial h_2} \times \frac{\partial h_2}{\partial z_{h_2}} \times \frac{\partial z_{h_2}}{\partial w_{x_1 \to h_2}}$$

$$\frac{\partial E}{\partial w_{x_2 \to h_2}} = \frac{\partial E}{\partial h_2} \times \frac{\partial h_2}{\partial z_{h_2}} \times \frac{\partial z_{h_2}}{\partial w_{x_2 \to h_2}}$$

Equipped with the rates at which weights affect error, adjust each weight by its rate, amplified or attenuated by a learning rate factor.

$$w_{1 \to h_1} \leftarrow w_{1 \to h_1} - L \times \frac{\partial E}{\partial w_{1 \to h_1}}$$

$$w_{x_1 \to h_1} \leftarrow w_{x_1 \to h_1} - L \times \frac{\partial E}{\partial w_{x_1 \to h_1}}$$

$$w_{x_2 \to h_1} \leftarrow w_{x_2 \to h_1} - L \times \frac{\partial E}{\partial w_{x_2 \to h_1}}$$

$$w_{1 \to h_2} \leftarrow w_{1 \to h_2} - L \times \frac{\partial E}{\partial w_{1 \to h_2}}$$

$$w_{x_1 \to h_2} \leftarrow w_{x_1 \to h_2} - L \times \frac{\partial E}{\partial w_{x_1 \to h_2}}$$

$$w_{x_2 \to h_2} \leftarrow w_{x_2 \to h_2} - L \times \frac{\partial E}{\partial w_{x_2 \to h_2}}$$

$$w_{1 \to output} \leftarrow w_{1 \to output} - L \times \frac{\partial E}{\partial w_{1 \to output}}$$

$$w_{h_1 \to output} \leftarrow w_{h_1 \to output} - L \times \frac{\partial E}{\partial w_{h_1 \to output}}$$

$$w_{h_2 \to output} \leftarrow w_{h_2 \to output} - L \times \frac{\partial E}{\partial w_{h_2 \to output}}$$

where ...

- L is learning rate

6.4 CASE | Telecom Customer Churn

Predictive modeling with balance, naive Bayes, cross-validation, and sensitivity analysis to inform a new customer churn reduction strategy in the telecommunications industry.

6.4.1 Business Situation

A major wireless telecom operator in South Asia provides phone and internet services to about 1 million customers. Company management has become concerned about the impact of customer churn on its profit, and will implement an intervention program to reduce customer churn. The program will involve hiring and training agents to proactively call a subset of customers, inquire about the level of satisfaction with the company's service, and try to retain those that would otherwise soon switch to another operator.

- **Role:** Vice President of Customer Service
- **Decision:** Which subset of customers to intervene?
- **Approach:** Compare the effectiveness of various methods to select the subset of customers to call. Consider selection at random. Also consider selection informed by a naive Bayes classifier that predicts which customers are at risk of switching to another operator.

6.4.2 Decision Model

The decision model starts with a decision method that predicts which customers are at risk of switching operators. Customers predicted to be at risk are intervened. Customer predicted to be safe are not intervened. The business result of interest is profit.

Business parameters include the following:

- **number of customers (customers):** a value gathered from the sales organization
- **churn rate (churn_rate):** the proportion of telecom customers that would switch operators if not intervened, a value gathered from industry research

- **save rate (save_rate):** the proportion of intervened at risk customers that will not switch operators, an assumed value
- **revenue per at risk customer (safe_value):** might be different from revenue per safe customer, a value derived from the data
- **revenue per safe customer (risk_value):** might be different from revenue per at risk customer, a value derived from the data
- **cost per intervention (intervention_cost):** an assumed value

customers	churn_rate	save_rate	intervention_cost
1,000,000	0.14	0.3	300

safe_value	risk_value
derive from data	derive from data

We treat safe customers, who are not at risk, as the positive class. We treat at risk customers as the negative class. Possible results of the decision method include the following:

- correctly predicts that some customers are at risk from among those customers that are actually at risk – this proportion is the **true negative rate**
- incorrectly predicts that some customers are at risk from among those customers that are actually safe – this proportion is the **false negative rate**
- correctly predicts that some customers are safe from among the customers that are actually safe – this proportion is the **true positive rate**
- incorrectly predicts that some customers are safe from the customers that are actually at risk – this proportion is the **false positive rate**

The absolute numbers of customers in each of these groups depend on the proportions, the total number of customers, and the churn rate. The number of saved at risk customers depends on the number of intervened at risk customers and the save rate. The revenue from the saved at risk customers depends on the number of saved at risk customers and the revenue per at risk customer. The costs of intervened customers depend on the numbers of these customers and the cost per intervention. The revenue from safe customers depends on the numbers of these customers and the revenue per safe customer. Profits from each of the 3 groups depend on revenues and costs. Overall profit depends on the 3 components of profit.

Customers that are predicted safe from among customers who are actually at risk, based on the false positive rate, are not reflected in the decision model because they do not influence profit. There is no cost associated with them because they are not intervened. There is no revenue associated with them because they switch operators.

See the decision model in the influence diagram representation on the next page.

6.4.3 Data

Retrieve raw data, prepare the data, and transform the data to ready them for analysis.

6.4.3.1 Raw Data

Retrieve a reference classified dataset of historical customer behavior. Each of 2,000 observations describes a unique customer. The 13 predictor variables measure various customer characteristics. A class variable indicates whether a customer has since switched operators (Churned) or is still with the company (Active).

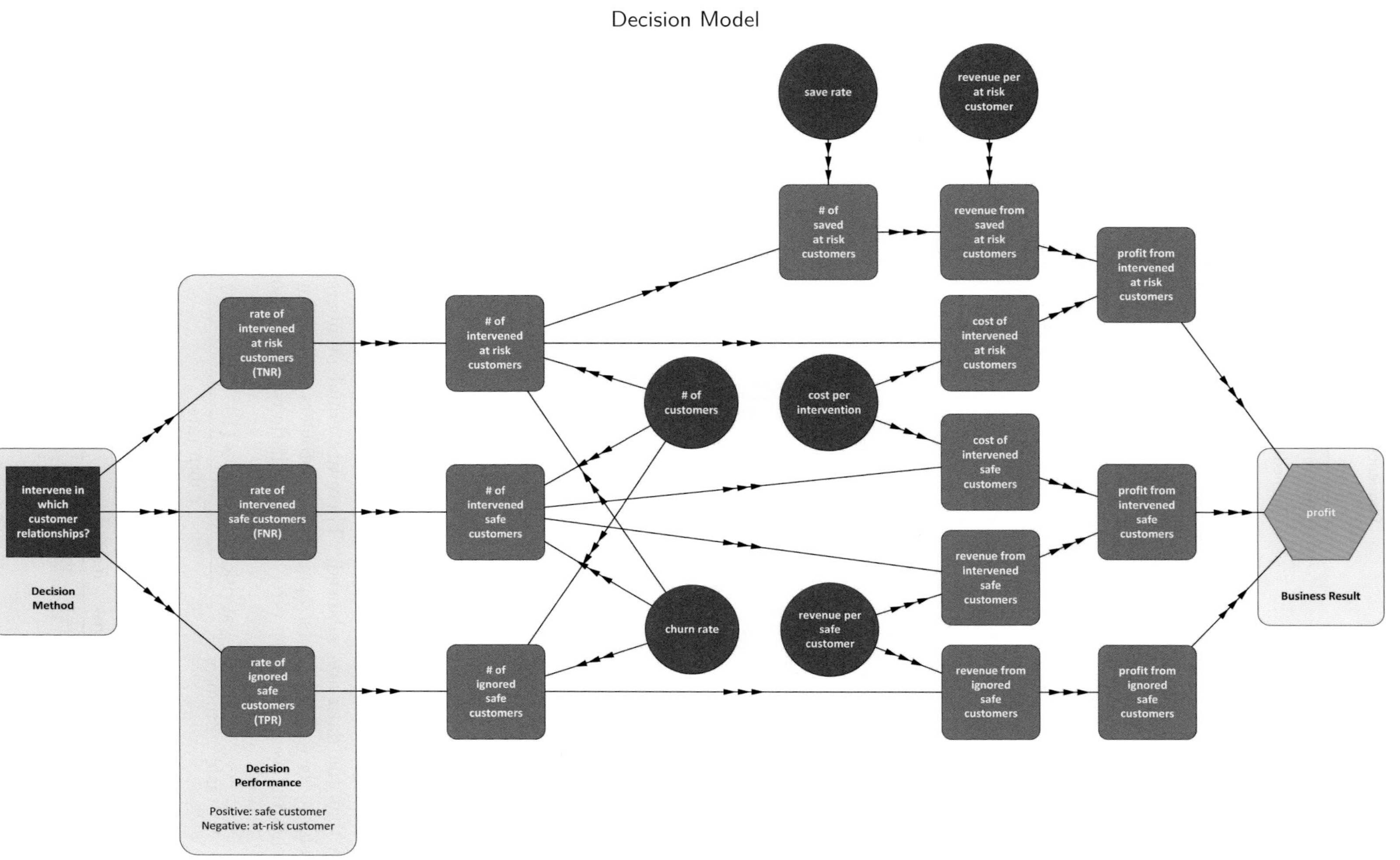

Decision Model
save rate
revenue per at risk customer
# of saved at risk customers
revenue from saved at risk customers
profit from intervened at risk customers
intervene in which customer relationships?
Decision Method
rate of intervened at risk customers (TNR)
rate of intervened safe customers (FNR)
rate of ignored safe customers (TPR)
Decision Performance
Positive: safe customer
Negative: at-risk customer
# of intervened at risk customers
# of intervened safe customers
# of ignored safe customers
# of customers
churn rate
cost per intervention
revenue per safe customer
cost of intervened at risk customers
cost of intervened safe customers
revenue from intervened safe customers
revenue from ignored safe customers
profit from intervened safe customers
profit from ignored safe customers
profit
Business Result

frequency of data.raw

Class	Freq
Active	1,000
Churned	1,000

data.raw *size 2000×14, first few observations shown, a few variables shown*

network_age	Aggregate_Total_Rev	Aggregate_SMS_Rev	Aggregate_Data_Rev	Class
1,914	1,593	23	2.5	Churned
2,073	1,404	174	27.5	Churned
3,139	86	14	5.0	Churned
139	2,315	19	52.5	Active
139	228	3	42.5	Active
143	974	22	22.5	Active

6.4.3.2 Class to Front, Rename Class Labels

For convenience, move the class variable to the front and rename class labels. Churned becomes risk, Active becomes safe.

data *size 2000×14, first few observations shown, a few variables shown*

Class	network_age	Aggregate_Total_Rev	Aggregate_SMS_Rev	Aggregate_Data_Rev
risk	1,914	1,593	23	2.5
risk	2,073	1,404	174	27.5
risk	3,139	86	14	5.0
safe	139	2,315	19	52.5
safe	139	228	3	42.5
safe	143	974	22	22.5

6.4.3.3 Unbalance

Note that the data are balanced. There are equal numbers of safe and at risk customers. Unbalance the data by bootstrapping safe customers so that the ratio of safe to at risk customers matches the assumed churn rate, a more realistic representation of reality.

$$\text{safe customers} = \frac{\text{at risk customers} \times (1 - \text{churn rate})}{\text{churn rate}} = \frac{1000 \times (1 - 0.143)}{0.143}$$

n.risk	n.safe
1,000	1,000

n.risk.target	n.safe.target
1,000	5,993

Here is the unbalanced dataset:

data *size 6993×14, first few observations shown, a few variables shown*

Class	network_age	Aggregate_Total_Rev	Aggregate_SMS_Rev	Aggregate_Data_Rev
safe	1,056	847	25.2	23.8
safe	3,704	1,045	1.8	98.8
safe	121	125	0.5	78.8
safe	256	143	0.0	3.8
safe	2,106	1,458	6.0	0.0
safe	1,493	434	35.6	91.2

Just to confirm our calculations, check that the proportion of at risk customers in the dataset is equal to the assumed churn rate.

churn_rate	churn_rate.calc
0.14	0.14

6.4.3.4 Create Five Folds

Partition the dataset into 5 folds and save for later use with cross-validation.

size(data.train[[1]])

observations	variables
5,595	14

size(data.test[[1]])

observations	variables
1,398	14

size(data.train[[2]])

observations	variables
5,594	14

size(data.test[[2]])

observations	variables
1,399	14

size(data.train[[3]])

observations	variables
5,594	14

size(data.test[[3]])

observations	variables
1,399	14

size(data.train[[4]])

observations	variables
5,595	14

size(data.test[[4]])

observations	variables
1,398	14

size(data.train[[5]])

observations	variables
5,594	14

size(data.test[[5]])

observations	variables
1,399	14

6.4.3.5 Business Parameters Derived from Data

Derive the business parameter values from the dataset as necessary. Revenue from safe customers is derived as mean of *Aggregate_Total_Rev* among safe customers. Revenue from at risk customers is derived as mean of *Aggregate_Total_Rev* among at risk customers.

customers	churn_rate	save_rate	intervention_cost
1,000,000	0.14	0.3	300

safe_value	risk_value
6,932	3,959

6.4.4 Analysis

Try 4 decision methods:

- **baseline method:** select no customers for intervention
- **random 10%:** select 10% of all customers at random for intervention
- **random 20%:** select 20% of all customers at random for intervention
- **naive Bayes:** select customers predicted by naive Bayes classifier to be at risk for intervention

6.4.4.1 Baseline

The business baseline scenario is to not implement any intervention program, and thereby select no customers for intervention. This is equivalent to a decision method that always predicts customers as safe, and so they do not merit intervention.

The in-sample accuracy of the decision method is calculated as the proportion of customers predicted safe among customers actually safe plus the proportion of customers predicted at risk among customers actually at risk. The first term accounts for all of the customers actually safe. The second term accounts for none of the customers actually at risk. So, the in-sample accuracy is the proportion of customers actually safe among all customers. Note that the cross-validation accuracy would be very close to equal to the in-sample accuracy because each fold would have very close to the same proportion of customers actually safe among all customers in the fold.

accuracy.baseline
0.86

While accuracy might be an interesting performance metric to someone, it is profit that really matters to our business.

$$\text{profit} = \text{customers} \times (1 - \text{churn rate}) \times \text{revenue per safe customer}$$

The baseline profit is 5.9 billion rupees. That's the number to beat.

profit.risk	profit.safe	profit.baseline
0	5,941,098,233	5,941,098,233

6.4.4.2 Intervene on Randomly Selected 10% of Customers

Consider the effect on profit of using a decision method that predicts that 10% of customers are at risk. Only some of the those predicted at risk will be actually at risk, so only some of the customers selected for intervention will be actually at risk. Evaluate the decision method using 5-fold cross-validation.

Classifier Construction, Probability Outputs, Predictions, & Confusion Matrix: Here is the classifier implementation of the decision method and information about its performance based on fold 1. The classifier is defined by its form and 1 parameter: intervention rate 0.1. The classifier applied to the first test observation estimates its probability of being a safe customer is 1, and so, assuming cutoff 0.5, it predicts the customer safe. Similarly for the other test observations. A confusion matrix tallies the performance across all the test observations: 1,082 predicted safe that are actually safe, 116 predicted at risk that are actually safe, 178 predicted safe that are actually at risk, and 22 predicted at risk that are actually at risk. Equivalently, 77.4% are predicted safe and actually safe, 8.3% are predicted at risk and actually safe, 12.7% are predicted safe and actually at risk, and 1.6% are predicted at risk and actually at risk.

model parameters

intervention_rate
0.1

prob
first few observations shown

safe	risk
1	0
1	0
1	0
1	0
1	0
1	0
1	0
1	0
1	0
0	1
1	0
1	0

actual vs predicted
first few observations shown

class	class.predicted
safe	safe
safe	safe
safe	safe
safe	safe
safe	safe
safe	safe
safe	safe
safe	safe
safe	safe
safe	risk
safe	safe
safe	safe

CM

	safe	risk
safe	1,082	178
risk	116	22

cm

	safe	risk
safe	0.77	0.13
risk	0.08	0.02

Confusion Matrices: Here are the confusion matrices for all 5 folds.

cm for fold 1

	safe	risk
safe	0.77	0.13
risk	0.08	0.02

cm for fold 2

	safe	risk
safe	0.78	0.13
risk	0.08	0.01

cm for fold 3

	safe	risk
safe	0.77	0.13
risk	0.08	0.01

cm for fold 4

	safe	risk
safe	0.77	0.13
risk	0.08	0.02

cm for fold 5

	safe	risk
safe	0.78	0.13
risk	0.08	0.01

Performance Metrics: From the confusion matrices, calculate the accuracy, true positive rate, false positive rate, false negative rate, and true negative rate for each fold. Calculate the cross-validation performance metrics as the means of the fold values.

fold	accuracy	tpr	fpr	fnr	tnr
1	0.79	0.90	0.89	0.10	0.11
2	0.79	0.91	0.92	0.09	0.08
3	0.78	0.90	0.93	0.10	0.07
4	0.79	0.90	0.90	0.10	0.11
5	0.79	0.91	0.90	0.10	0.10
cross-validation	0.79	0.90	0.91	0.10	0.09

Business Result: For each fold, calculate the number of customers among all 1,000,000 customers that are represented by each quadrant of the confusion matrix.

$$\text{customers predicted safe and actually safe} = \text{customers} \times (1 - \text{churn rate}) \times \text{true positive rate}$$

$$\text{customers predicted safe and actually at risk} = \text{customers} \times \text{churn rate} \times \text{false positive rate}$$

$$\text{customers predicted at risk and actually safe} = \text{customers} \times (1 - \text{churn rate}) \times \text{false negative rate}$$

$$\text{customers predicted at risk and actually at risk} = \text{customers} \times \text{churn rate} \times \text{true negative rate}$$

Then for each fold, calculate the profits from each group of customers.

$$\begin{array}{c}\text{profit from}\\ \text{customers predicted at risk}\\ \text{and actually at risk}\end{array} = \left(\begin{pmatrix}\text{customers predicted at risk and actually at risk} \times\\ \text{save rate} \times\\ \text{revenue per at risk customer}\end{pmatrix} - \begin{pmatrix}\text{customers predicted at risk and actually at risk} \times\\ \text{intervention cost}\end{pmatrix}\right)$$

$$\begin{array}{c}\text{profit from}\\ \text{customers predicted safe}\\ \text{and actually at risk}\end{array} = \begin{pmatrix}\text{customers predicted safe and actually at risk} \times\\ 0\end{pmatrix} = 0$$

$$\begin{array}{c}\text{profit from}\\ \text{customers predicted at risk}\\ \text{and actually safe}\end{array} = \left(\begin{pmatrix}\text{customers predicted at risk and actually safe} \times\\ \text{revenue per safe customer}\end{pmatrix} - \begin{pmatrix}\text{customers predicted at risk and actually safe} \times\\ \text{intervention cost}\end{pmatrix}\right)$$

$$\begin{array}{c}\text{profit for}\\ \text{customers predicted safe}\\ \text{and actually safe}\end{array} = \begin{pmatrix}\text{customers predicted safe and actually safe} \times\\ \text{revenue per safe customer}\end{pmatrix}$$

Then for each fold, calculate the overall profit as the sum of the component profits.

$$\text{profit} = \begin{pmatrix}\text{profit from customers predicted at risk and actually at risk} +\\ 0 +\\ \text{profit from customers predicted at risk and actually safe} +\\ \text{profit for customers predicted safe and actually safe}\end{pmatrix}$$

Then calculate the cross-validation profit as the average of the fold profits.

customer count

fold	safe_safe	safe_risk	risk_safe	risk_risk
1	774,018	127,270	82,982	15,730
2	776,947	131,560	80,053	11,440
3	774,088	132,990	82,912	10,010
4	772,588	127,985	84,412	15,015
5	779,806	129,415	82,972	13,585

profit

fold	safe_safe	safe_risk	risk_safe	risk_risk	total
1	5,365,830,773	0	550,372,860	13,962,874	5,930,166,508
2	5,386,135,880	0	530,946,453	10,154,818	5,927,237,151
3	5,366,316,044	0	549,908,590	8,885,465	5,925,110,099
4	5,355,917,388	0	559,857,245	13,328,198	5,929,102,831
5	5,405,955,716	0	550,306,536	12,058,846	5,968,321,098
cross-validation	NA	NA	NA	NA	5,935,987,537

6.4.4.3 Intervene on Randomly Selected 20% of Customers

Consider the effect on profit of using a decision method that predicts 20% of customers are at risk. Only some of the those predicted at risk will be actually at risk, so only some of the customers selected for intervention will be actually at risk. Evaluate the decision method using 5-fold cross-validation.

Confusion Matrices: Here are the confusion matrices for the 5 folds.

cm for fold 1

	safe	risk
safe	0.69	0.11
risk	0.17	0.03

cm for fold 2

	safe	risk
safe	0.68	0.12
risk	0.18	0.02

cm for fold 3

	safe	risk
safe	0.69	0.12
risk	0.17	0.03

cm for fold 4

	safe	risk
safe	0.69	0.11
risk	0.16	0.03

cm for fold 5

	safe	risk
safe	0.69	0.12
risk	0.16	0.03

Performance Metrics: Here are performance metrics for each fold and the cross-validation performance metrics.

fold	accuracy	tpr	fpr	fnr	tnr
1	0.72	0.80	0.76	0.20	0.24
2	0.70	0.79	0.84	0.21	0.16
3	0.71	0.80	0.83	0.20	0.17
4	0.72	0.81	0.80	0.19	0.21
5	0.72	0.81	0.81	0.20	0.19
cross-validation	0.72	0.80	0.80	0.20	0.20

Business Result: Here are the profits for each fold and the cross-validation profit.

customer count

fold	safe_safe	safe_risk	risk_safe	risk_risk
1	686,029	108,680	170,971	34,320
2	675,450	119,405	181,550	23,595
3	687,601	117,975	169,399	25,025
4	693,898	113,685	163,102	29,315
5	693,319	115,830	170,950	27,170

profit

fold	safe_safe	safe_risk	risk_safe	risk_risk	total
1	4,755,852,602	0	1,133,954,331	30,464,453	5,920,271,386
2	4,682,514,354	0	1,204,118,879	20,944,311	5,907,577,545
3	4,766,750,393	0	1,123,528,141	22,213,663	5,912,492,197
4	4,810,403,946	0	1,081,763,687	26,021,720	5,918,189,353
5	4,806,390,065	0	1,133,815,050	24,117,692	5,964,322,807
cross-validation	NA	NA	NA	NA	5,924,570,658

6.4.4.4 Intervene on Predicted At Risk Customers

Consider the effect on profit of using a naive Bayes classifier to predict which customers are at risk. Only some of the those predicted at risk will be actually at risk, so only some of the customers selected for intervention will be actually at risk. Evaluate the classifier using 5-fold cross-validation.

Fold 1 – Classifier Construction: Here is the naive Bayes classifier constructed from the training partition of fold 1. The prior probabilities are 85.7% safe customers and 14.3% at risk customers. Note that because we unbalanced the dataset to match the churn rate, the prior probability of at risk customers equals the churn rate. Had we not unbalanced the dataset, then the prior probabilities would not reflect the real-world situation and would distort any predictions.

The likelihoods for numerical variables are calculable from pairs of Gaussian functions. The likelihoods of categorical variables are calculable from pairs of relative frequency tables.

	prior
safe	0.86
risk	0.14

likelihood network_age

	mean	sd
safe	1,710	1,388
risk	1,237	1,132

likelihood Aggregate_Total_Rev

	mean	sd
safe	1,158	1,179
risk	657	1,197

likelihood Aggregate_SMS_Rev

	mean	sd
safe	28	58
risk	33	54

likelihood Aggregate_Data_Rev

	mean	sd
safe	57	139
risk	61	355

likelihood Aggregate_Data_Vol

	mean	sd
safe	3,970,847	10,716,132
risk	1,302,057	4,225,699

likelihood Aggregate_Calls

	mean	sd
safe	345	452
risk	138	233

likelihood Aggregate_ONNET_REV

	mean	sd
safe	8,783	15,674
risk	5,186	11,511

likelihood Aggregate_OFFNET_REV

	mean	sd
safe	16,498	32,588
risk	15,457	31,913

likelihood Aggregate_complaint_count

	mean	sd
safe	2.0	2.0
risk	1.7	2.5

likelihood aug_user_type

	2G	3G	Other
safe	0.20	0.6	0.19
risk	0.25	0.5	0.24

likelihood sep_user_type

	2G	3G	Other
safe	0.18	0.63	0.19
risk	0.24	0.52	0.24

likelihood aug_fav_a

	0	mobilink	ptcl	telenor	ufone	warid	zong
safe	0.04	0.14	0.17	0.15	0.22	0.13	0.15
risk	0.02	0.15	0.29	0.13	0.22	0.09	0.10

likelihood sep_fav_a

	mobilink	ptcl	telenor	ufone	warid	zong
safe	0.05	0.10	0.03	0.79	0.03	0.02
risk	0.10	0.33	0.06	0.40	0.05	0.05

Fold 1 – Probability Outputs, Predictions, & Confusion Matrix: Here are results of the classifier applied to the test partition of fold 1:

prob
first few observations shown

safe	risk
0.65	0.35
0.65	0.35
0.98	0.02
1.00	0.00
0.45	0.55
1.00	0.00
0.66	0.34
0.83	0.17
0.71	0.29
0.71	0.29
0.96	0.04
1.00	0.00

actual vs predicted
first few observations shown

class	class.predicted
safe	safe
safe	safe
safe	safe
safe	safe
safe	risk
safe	safe
safe	safe
safe	safe
safe	safe
safe	safe
safe	safe
safe	safe

CM

	safe	risk
safe	1,032	120
risk	166	80

cm

	safe	risk
safe	0.74	0.09
risk	0.12	0.06

Confusion Matrices: Here are the confusion matrices for the 5 folds:

cm for fold 1

	safe	risk
safe	0.74	0.09
risk	0.12	0.06

cm for fold 2

	safe	risk
safe	0.76	0.09
risk	0.10	0.05

cm for fold 3

	safe	risk
safe	0.76	0.08
risk	0.10	0.07

cm for fold 4

	safe	risk
safe	0.77	0.09
risk	0.08	0.05

cm for fold 5

	safe	risk
safe	0.72	0.08
risk	0.14	0.06

Performance Metrics: Here are performance metrics for each fold and the cross-validation performance metrics:

fold	accuracy	tpr	fpr	fnr	tnr
1	0.80	0.86	0.60	0.14	0.40
2	0.82	0.89	0.62	0.11	0.38
3	0.83	0.89	0.54	0.11	0.47
4	0.83	0.90	0.62	0.10	0.38
5	0.78	0.84	0.56	0.14	0.44
cross-validation	0.81	0.88	0.59	0.12	0.41

Business Result: Here are the profits for each fold and the cross-validation profit:

customer count

fold	safe_safe	safe_risk	risk_safe	risk_risk
1	738,250	85,800	118,750	57,200
2	761,937	89,375	95,063	53,625
3	761,222	76,505	95,778	66,495
4	773,303	88,660	83,697	54,340
5	720,480	79,365	118,735	63,635

profit

fold	safe_safe	safe_risk	risk_safe	risk_risk	total
1	5,117,871,378	0	787,601,856	50,774,088	5,956,247,321
2	5,282,080,005	0	630,499,328	47,600,707	5,960,180,041
3	5,277,123,313	0	635,241,520	59,024,877	5,971,389,710
4	5,360,874,081	0	555,115,053	48,235,383	5,964,224,517
5	4,994,681,978	0	787,502,369	56,486,173	5,838,670,520
cross-validation	NA	NA	NA	NA	5,938,142,422

6.4.4.5 Comparative Analysis

Let's review how the business results for the different decisions methods turned out. With business parameters set as they are, the baseline scenario would result in profit higher than either random 10% or 20%, and significantly higher than naive Bayes.

strategy	accuracy	profit	improve
baseline	0.86	5,941,098,233	0
random 10%	0.79	5,935,987,537	-5,110,696
random 20%	0.72	5,924,570,658	-16,527,576
naive Bayes	0.81	5,938,142,422	-2,955,812

customers	churn_rate	save_rate	intervention_cost	safe_value	risk_value
1,000,000	0.14	0.3	300	6,932	3,959

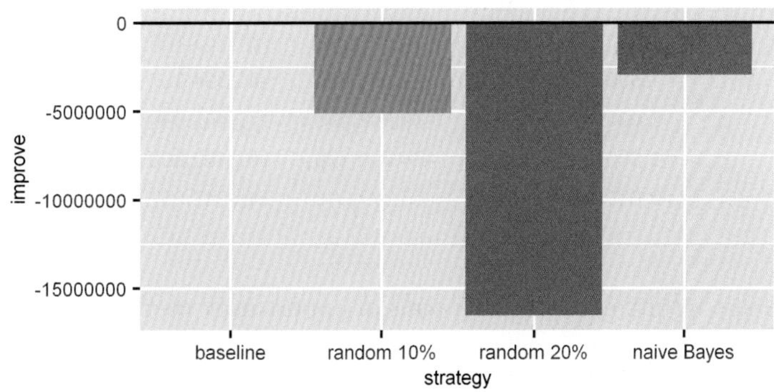

6.4.5 Sensitivity Analysis

Does the relatively poor business result coming from the random selection approach or the naive Bayes classifier approach mean that intervention is useless? Should we just skip the whole intervention program? Not at all. Sensitivity analysis on the business parameters might inspire us to action.

The Vice President of Customer Service does not have control over the number of customers, the churn rate, the revenue per safe customer, nor the revenue per at risk customer. However, she might have control over the cost per intervention and the save rate. By providing intensive training to the staff that will be conducting the interventions or by outsourcing the intervention activity to an organization known to be more effective, she might be able to change the cost per intervention and save rate. How sensitive is performance of the 4 different approaches to changes in these business parameters?

Consider this slate of alternative business parameter values. It specifies various combinations of cost per intervention and save rate values.

customers	churn_rate	intervention_cost	save_rate	safe_value	risk_value
1,000,000	0.14	250	0.15	6,932	3,959
1,000,000	0.14	250	0.25	6,932	3,959
1,000,000	0.14	250	0.40	6,932	3,959
1,000,000	0.14	500	0.15	6,932	3,959
1,000,000	0.14	500	0.25	6,932	3,959
1,000,000	0.14	500	0.40	6,932	3,959
1,000,000	0.14	1,000	0.15	6,932	3,959
1,000,000	0.14	1,000	0.25	6,932	3,959
1,000,000	0.14	1,000	0.40	6,932	3,959

Repeat our analysis assuming each combination of business parameter values. Here are the business results.

sensitivity

intervention_cost	save_rate	improve.10	improve.20	improve.nb
250	0.15	-8,132,006	-23,132,540	-29,953,604
250	0.25	-2,923,726	-12,093,250	-6,572,956
250	0.40	4,888,694	4,465,683	28,498,017
500	0.15	-32,087,556	-72,902,390	-70,319,504
500	0.25	-26,879,276	-61,863,100	-46,938,856
500	0.40	-19,066,856	-45,304,167	-11,867,883
1,000	0.15	-79,998,656	-172,442,090	-151,051,304
1,000	0.25	-74,790,376	-161,402,800	-127,670,656
1,000	0.40	-66,977,956	-144,843,867	-92,599,683

Here are the business results expressed in terms of opportunity cost of the naive Bayes classifier. The benefit of the naive Bayes classifier is the difference between the profit we can expect by using it rather than using the next best approach.

sensitivity

intervention_cost	save_rate	improve.10	improve.20	improve.nb	benefit.nb
250	0.15	-8,132,006	-23,132,540	-29,953,604	-34,842,298
250	0.25	-2,923,726	-12,093,250	-6,572,956	-11,461,650
250	0.40	4,888,694	4,465,683	28,498,017	23,609,323
500	0.15	-32,087,556	-72,902,390	-70,319,504	-75,208,198
500	0.25	-26,879,276	-61,863,100	-46,938,856	-51,827,550
500	0.40	-19,066,856	-45,304,167	-11,867,883	-16,756,577
1,000	0.15	-79,998,656	-172,442,090	-151,051,304	-155,939,998
1,000	0.25	-74,790,376	-161,402,800	-127,670,656	-132,559,350
1,000	0.40	-66,977,956	-144,843,867	-92,599,683	-97,488,377

We see that at cost 250 rupees per intervention and 40% save rate, we expect the naive Bayes classifier to result in 23.6 million rupees more profit than random intervention would, and 28.4 million rupees more profit than doing nothing would. Is it realistic to drive cost per intervention down that much and save rate up that much? For 23.6 million rupees, it might be worth trying.

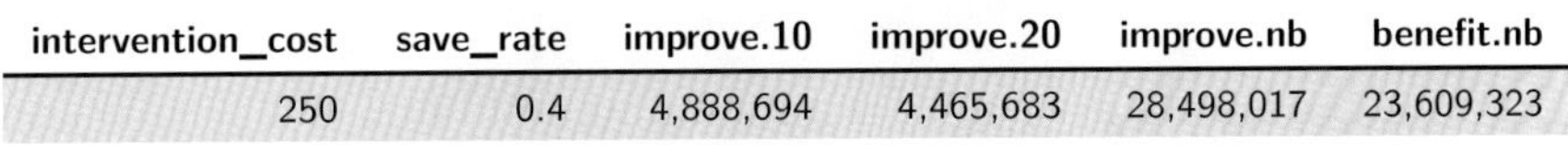

intervention_cost	save_rate	improve.10	improve.20	improve.nb	benefit.nb
250	0.4	4,888,694	4,465,683	28,498,017	23,609,323

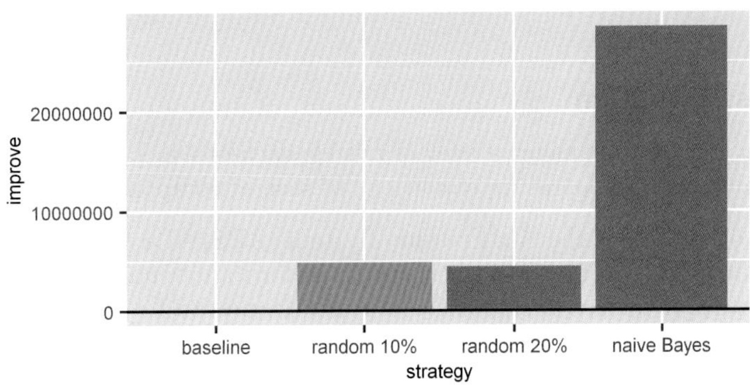

6.5 CASE | Truck Fleet Maintenance

Predictive modeling (IIoT industrial internet of things) with balance, principal component analysis, support vector machine, classifier cutoff tuning, and custom test data to inform a new adaptive truck fleet maintenance schedule in the logistics industry.

6.5.1 Business Situation

A transportation company manages a fleet of trucks, each of which is equipped with hundreds of sensors that measure the operating conditions of several components while out on the road.

One component of interest is the Air Pressure System (APS). If a truck's APS is suspected to soon fail, then the truck can be proactively called in for maintenance service at relatively low but non-zero cost. Conversely, if a truck's APS is assumed to be working properly but does fail, then the truck must be repaired in the field at relatively high cost. There are 170 sensors that measure the APS. The sensor measurements do not indicate explicitly whether or not a truck's APS is about to fail, but there might exist patterns predictive of APS health detectable in the sensor data taken from many trucks. Company management is interested in leveraging these patterns, if indeed they exist and are detectable, to improve its APS maintenance service scheduling process.

This application is an example of predictive maintenance and the industrial internet of things (IIOT).

- **Role:** Vice President of Fleet Operations
- **Decision:** Which trucks to call in for APS maintenance service?
- **Approach:** Construct a support vector machine classifier to predict imminent APS failures, using ***1*** set of hyper-parameter settings, ***1*** data representation, and ***several*** cutoffs. Determine the cutoff that results in the lowest combined maintenance service and field repair cost. Then apply the classifier with the best cutoff to new sensor measurements to schedule truck maintenance service.

6.5.2 Decision Model

The decision model starts with a decision method that predicts which trucks are about to experience an APS failure. Trucks predicted to fail are proactively called in for maintenance service. Trucks predicted as healthy are not. The business result of interest is cost.

Business parameters include the following:

- **number of good trucks (pop.ok):** a value gathered from fleet operations that reflects the proportion of good trucks, not about to fail, from among all trucks as seen in historical data
- **number of bad trucks (pop.failure):** a value gathered from fleet operations that reflects the proportion of bad trucks, about to fail, from among all trucks as seen in historical data
- **cost per maintenance service (cost.maint):** cost to service 1 truck regardless of its health, a value gathered from fleet operations
- **cost per field repair (cost.repair):** cost to repair 1 truck that has failed in the field without being called in, a value gathered from fleet operations

pop	pop.ok	pop.failure	cost.maint	cost.repair
60,000	59,000	1,000	100	5,000

We treat good trucks as the positive class. We treat bad trucks as the negative class. Possible results of the decision method include the following:

- incorrectly predict that some trucks are bad from among those that are actually good – this proportion is the **false negative rate**
- correctly predict that some trucks are bad from among those that are actually bad – this proportion is the **true negative rate**
- incorrectly predict that some trucks are good from among those that are actually bad – this is the **false positive rate**

The absolute numbers of trucks in each of these groups depend on the proportions, the number of good trucks, and the number of bad trucks. The number of trucks called in for maintenance depends on the number of good trucks predicted as bad and the number of bad trucks predicted as bad. The cost of calling in trucks for maintenance service depends on how many trucks are called in and the cost per maintenance service. The cost of repairing failed trucks depends on how many trucks failed in the field without being called in and the cost per field repair. Overall cost depends on the cost of maintenance services and the cost of field repairs.

Trucks that are predicted good from among trucks actually good, based on the true positive rate, are not reflected in the model because they do not influence cost. There is no cost for maintenance service because they are not called in, and there is no cost for field repair because they do not fail.

See the decision model in the influence diagram representation on the next page.

6.5.3 Data

Retrieve raw data, prepare the data, and transform the data to ready it for analysis.

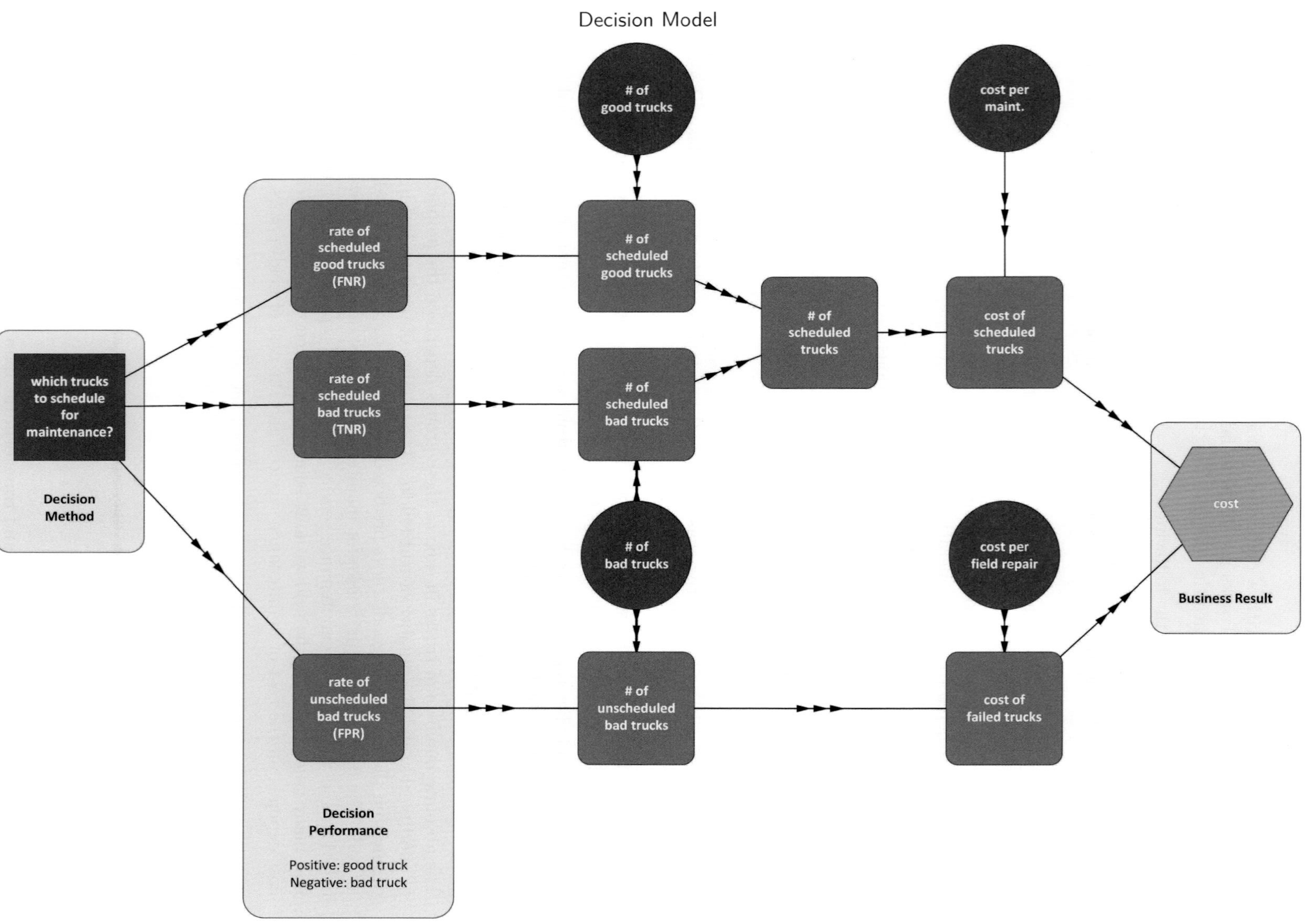
Decision Model
which trucks to schedule for maintenance?
Decision Method
rate of scheduled good trucks (FNR)
rate of scheduled bad trucks (TNR)
rate of unscheduled bad trucks (FPR)
Decision Performance
Positive: good truck
Negative: bad truck
# of good trucks
# of scheduled good trucks
# of scheduled bad trucks
# of bad trucks
# of unscheduled bad trucks
# of scheduled trucks
cost per maint.
cost of scheduled trucks
cost per field repair
cost of failed trucks
cost
Business Result

6.5.3.1 Raw Data

Retrieve a reference classified dataset of APS sensor measurements. Each of 5,000 observations describes the sensor measurements for a unique truck. The 170 predictor variables represent the 170 types of sensors. A class variable indicates whether a truck's APS has failed (pos) or not (neg).

data.raw *frequency table*

class	count	rel_freq
neg	4,916	0.9832
pos	84	0.0168

data.raw *size 5000×171, first few observations shown, first few variables shown*

class	aa_000	ab_000	ac_000	ad_000	ae_000	af_000	ag_000	ag_001	ag_002
neg	76,698	NA	2,130,706,438	280	0	0	0	0	0
neg	33,058	NA	0	NA	0	0	0	0	0
neg	41,040	NA	228	100	0	0	0	0	0
neg	12	0	70	66	0	10	0	0	0
neg	60,874	NA	1,368	458	0	0	0	0	0
neg	38,312	NA	2,130,706,432	218	0	0	0	0	0

6.5.3.2 Rename Class Labels

For convenience, rename class labels: neg becomes ok, pos becomes failure. Note that the neg value in the raw data, which is ok in the prepared data, is what we are treating as the positive class. The pos value in the raw data, which is failure in the prepared data, is what we are treating as the negative class.

data *frequency table*

class	count	rel_freq
ok	4,916	0.9832
failure	84	0.0168

data *size 5000×171, first few observations shown, first few variables shown*

class	aa_000	ab_000	ac_000	ad_000	ae_000	af_000	ag_000	ag_001	ag_002
ok	76,698	NA	2,130,706,438	280	0	0	0	0	0
ok	33,058	NA	0	NA	0	0	0	0	0
ok	41,040	NA	228	100	0	0	0	0	0
ok	12	0	70	66	0	10	0	0	0
ok	60,874	NA	1,368	458	0	0	0	0	0
ok	38,312	NA	2,130,706,432	218	0	0	0	0	0

6.5.3.3 Impute

Impute missing values with column means.

data *frequency table*

class	count	rel_freq
ok	4,916	0.9832
failure	84	0.0168

data *size 5000×171, first few observations shown, first few variables shown*

class	aa_000	ab_000	ac_000	ad_000	ae_000	af_000	ag_000	ag_001	ag_002
ok	76,698	0.5748	2,130,706,438	280.0	0	0	0	0	0
ok	33,058	0.5748	0	457.8	0	0	0	0	0
ok	41,040	0.5748	228	100.0	0	0	0	0	0
ok	12	0.0000	70	66.0	0	10	0	0	0
ok	60,874	0.5748	1,368	458.0	0	0	0	0	0
ok	38,312	0.5748	2,130,706,432	218.0	0	0	0	0	0

6.5.3.4 Filter Out Variables with Zero Variance

Remove the 1 variable (*cd*_000) that reports the same value (1209600) for all observations.

data *frequency table*

class	count	rel_freq
ok	4,916	0.9832
failure	84	0.0168

data *size 5000×170, first few observations shown, first few variables shown*

class	aa_000	ab_000	ac_000	ad_000	ae_000	af_000	ag_000	ag_001	ag_002
ok	76,698	0.5748	2,130,706,438	280.0	0	0	0	0	0
ok	33,058	0.5748	0	457.8	0	0	0	0	0
ok	41,040	0.5748	228	100.0	0	0	0	0	0
ok	12	0.0000	70	66.0	0	10	0	0	0
ok	60,874	0.5748	1,368	458.0	0	0	0	0	0
ok	38,312	0.5748	2,130,706,432	218.0	0	0	0	0	0

6.5.3.5 Principal Component Analysis

Represent the dataset in principal component form. Normalize the 170 predictor variables, use them to compute a 170×170 weight matrix, and apply the weight matrix to the predictor variables to compute 170 principal components. Retain the class variable, but replace the predictor variables with the principal components. Note that the transformed dataset still represents exactly the same 5,000 observations, though they are now expressed in terms of different predictor variables.

data *frequency table*

class	count	rel_freq
ok	4,916	0.9832
failure	84	0.0168

data *size 5000×170, first few observations shown, first few variables shown*

class	PC1	PC2	PC3	PC4	PC5	PC6	PC7	PC8	PC9
ok	-2.5017	1.1176	1.4608	0.5326	0.2873	1.0801	0.3099	-0.2265	-0.2329
ok	0.6138	0.5724	0.0115	-0.1415	0.2250	-0.0418	0.1949	0.1323	0.2997
ok	1.3116	0.1052	0.3073	-0.5898	-0.4384	-0.0493	0.0190	0.1201	0.1329
ok	3.3915	-0.1218	-0.3839	-0.3123	-0.4634	-0.5616	-0.7415	0.6139	0.0650
ok	-0.3294	-0.0117	0.7323	0.1948	0.4180	0.4738	0.2108	-0.2363	-0.6655
ok	0.9384	0.2706	0.6489	-0.3553	0.0555	0.2155	-0.2495	0.0202	0.1595

Most of the total variance in the dataset is now concentrated in the first few variables, as must be.

scree *first few observations shown*

axis	standard_deviation	variance	cum_variance	proportion	cum_proportion
PC1	7.039	49.546	49.55	0.2932	0.2932
PC2	3.012	9.073	58.62	0.0537	0.3469
PC3	2.676	7.159	65.78	0.0424	0.3892
PC4	2.415	5.833	71.61	0.0345	0.4237
PC5	2.337	5.460	77.07	0.0323	0.4560
PC6	2.051	4.208	81.28	0.0249	0.4809

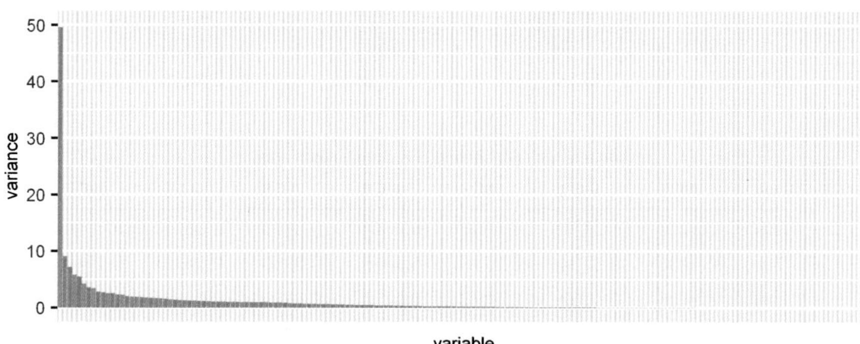

Identify the variables that comprise just over 50% of the total variance.

scree50

axis	standard_deviation	variance	cum_variance	proportion	cum_proportion
PC1	7.039	49.546	49.55	0.2932	0.2932
PC2	3.012	9.073	58.62	0.0537	0.3469
PC3	2.676	7.159	65.78	0.0424	0.3892
PC4	2.415	5.833	71.61	0.0345	0.4237
PC5	2.337	5.460	77.07	0.0323	0.4560
PC6	2.051	4.208	81.28	0.0249	0.4809
PC7	1.898	3.603	84.88	0.0213	0.5023

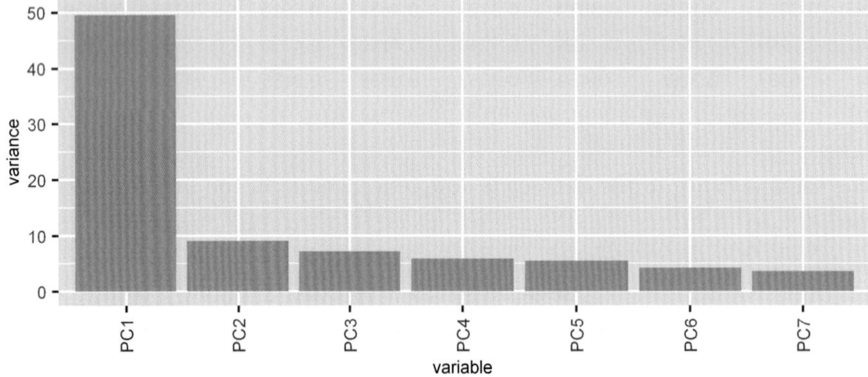

Filter in the 7 variables that comprise just over 50% of the total variance. This reduces the number of variables while likely keeping enough information to distinguish observations of different classes.

data *frequency table*

class	count	rel_freq
ok	4,916	0.9832
failure	84	0.0168

data *size 5000×8, first few observations shown*

class	PC1	PC2	PC3	PC4	PC5	PC6	PC7
ok	-2.5017	1.1176	1.4608	0.5326	0.2873	1.0801	0.3099
ok	0.6138	0.5724	0.0115	-0.1415	0.2250	-0.0418	0.1949
ok	1.3116	0.1052	0.3073	-0.5898	-0.4384	-0.0493	0.0190
ok	3.3915	-0.1218	-0.3839	-0.3123	-0.4634	-0.5616	-0.7415
ok	-0.3294	-0.0117	0.7323	0.1948	0.4180	0.4738	0.2108
ok	0.9384	0.2706	0.6489	-0.3553	0.0555	0.2155	-0.2495

6.5.3.6 Balance

Balance the dataset by bootstrapping. Some 84 failure observations are resampled with replacement to yield 4,916 failure observations, equal to the number of ok observations, for a transformed dataset of 9,832 observations. We will use the support vector machine method in our analysis, which tends to produce better performing classifiers when built using balanced data.

data *frequency table*

class	count	rel_freq
ok	4,916	0.5
failure	4,916	0.5

data *size 9832×8, first few observations shown*

class	PC1	PC2	PC3	PC4	PC5	PC6	PC7
ok	-2.5017	1.1176	1.4608	0.5326	0.2873	1.0801	0.3099
ok	0.6138	0.5724	0.0115	-0.1415	0.2250	-0.0418	0.1949
ok	1.3116	0.1052	0.3073	-0.5898	-0.4384	-0.0493	0.0190
ok	3.3915	-0.1218	-0.3839	-0.3123	-0.4634	-0.5616	-0.7415
ok	-0.3294	-0.0117	0.7323	0.1948	0.4180	0.4738	0.2108
ok	0.9384	0.2706	0.6489	-0.3553	0.0555	0.2155	-0.2495

6.5.4 Analysis I

Try decision methods as informed by a support vector machine classifier and various cutoffs.

6.5.4.1 Baseline

The business baseline scenario is the better of 2 approaches:

- **Baseline I:** Do not call in any trucks and thereby avoid any maintenance service cost. This is equivalent to a decision method that always predicts that trucks will not fail. The in-sample accuracy of the decision method is calculated as the proportion of trucks predicted not to fail among trucks that actually will not fail plus the proportion of trucks predicted to fail among trucks that actually will fail. The first term accounts for all of the trucks that actually will not fail. The second term accounts for none of the trucks that actually will fail. So, the in-sample accuracy is the proportion of trucks that actually will not fail among all trucks.
- **Baseline II:** Call in all trucks and thereby avoid any field repair cost. This is equivalent to a decision method that always predicts that trucks will fail. The in-sample accuracy of the decision method is calculated as the proportion of trucks predicted not to fail among trucks that actually will not fail plus the proportion of trucks predicted to fail among trucks that actually will fail. The first term accounts for none of the trucks that actually will not fail. The second term accounts for all of the trucks that actually will fail. So, the in-sample accuracy is the proportion of trucks that actually will fail among all trucks.

While accuracy might be an interesting performance metric to some, it is cost that really matters to our business.

$$\text{cost if call in none} = \text{trucks that will fail} \times \text{cost per field repair}$$

$$\text{cost if call in all} = \text{all trucks} \times \text{cost per maintenance service}$$

Of these 2 approaches, we can expect calling in none to result in the lower cost of $5 million.

baseline (call in none)	
accuracy	cost
0.9833	5,000,000

baseline (call in all)	
accuracy	cost
0.0167	6,000,000

The baseline cost is $5 million. That's the number to beat.

6.5.4.2 Call In Trucks Predicted to Fail

Consider the effect on cost of using a support vector machine classifier to predict which trucks will fail. Only some of the those predicted to fail would actually have failed, so only some of the trucks called in would actually have failed. Evaluate the in-sample performance of the classifier.

Classifier Construction Here is the support vector machine classifier constructed from the dataset. Hyper-parameters were set to radial basis kernel, gamma 0.1, and cost 0.1. Recall that a radial basis is effectively a Gaussian function with standard deviation the inverse of gamma. Parameters include 1,725 observations serving as support vectors to define the class separation boundary.

model parameters			
kernel	cost	gamma	support_vectors
radial	0.1	0.1	1,725

Probability Outputs Here are results of the classifier applied to the dataset. The classifier estimates for each observation the probability that it is in 1 class or the other. The classifier estimates that the first observation has probability 95.43% of being in class *ok* and probability 4.57% of being in class *failure*. We can interpret this as a 95.43% probability that the first truck will not fail and 4.57% probability that it will fail, according to the classifier. Similarly for the other observations.

prob *first few observations shown*

ok	failure
0.9543	0.0457
0.9536	0.0464
0.9527	0.0473
0.9539	0.0461
0.9470	0.0530
0.9570	0.0430

Confusion Matrices & Performance Metrics with Cutoff Tuning Here are the confusion matrices, performance metrics, and business results under 3 different assumptions for cutoff. Note that the confusion matrices differ due to different cutoffs, though they are all based on the same set of probability outputs. Predictions on the dataset made with cutoff 0.25 result in the highest true positive rate. Predictions made with cutoff 0.90 result in the highest true negative rate. Predictions made with cutoff 0.50 result in the highest accuracy.

cutoff		cm: ok	cm: failure	tnr	fnr	fpr	tpr	accuracy
0.9	ok	0.4548	0.0121	0.9758	0.0903	0.0242	0.9097	0.9427
	failure	0.0452	0.4879					

cutoff		cm: ok	cm: failure	tnr	fnr	fpr	tpr	accuracy
0.5	ok	0.4798	0.0294	0.9412	0.0405	0.0588	0.9595	0.9504
	failure	0.0202	0.4706					

cutoff		cm: ok	cm: failure	tnr	fnr	fpr	tpr	accuracy
0.25	ok	0.4853	0.0411	0.9178	0.0295	0.0822	0.9705	0.9442
	failure	0.0147	0.4589					

Business Results with Cutoff Tuning Which of performance metrics matter to us? What ultimately matters to us is not any specific performance metric, but rather the business result, which is cost calculated from a combination of the performance metrics.

Calculate the cost associated with each group of trucks and sum to the total cost.

$$\begin{aligned}
\text{trucks for necessary maintenance} &= \text{true negative rate} \times \text{trucks actually failing} \\
\text{trucks for unnecessary maintenance} &= \text{false negative rate} \times \text{trucks actually not failing} \\
\text{trucks for field repair} &= \text{false positive rate} \times \text{trucks actually failing} \\
\text{other trucks} &= \text{true positive rate} \times \text{trucks actually not failing}
\end{aligned}$$

$$\text{cost} = \begin{pmatrix} (\text{cost per maintenance service} \times \text{trucks for necessary maintenance}) + \\ (\text{cost per maintenance service} \times \text{trucks for unnecessary maintenance}) + \\ (\text{cost per field repair} \times \text{trucks for field repair}) + \\ (0 \times \text{other trucks}) \end{pmatrix}$$

Here are the business results that we can expect from the classifier when used with the different cutoffs. Note that the numbers of trucks in each group differ due to the different cutoffs.

cutoff	failure_failure	failure_ok	ok_failure	cost.maint	cost.repair	cost
	business result					
0.9	976	5,329	24	100	5,000	750,500

cutoff	failure_failure	failure_ok	ok_failure	cost.maint	cost.repair	cost
	business result					
0.5	941	2,388	59	100	5,000	627,900

cutoff	failure_failure	failure_ok	ok_failure	cost.maint	cost.repair	cost
	business result					
0.25	918	1,740	82	100	5,000	675,800

6.5.4.3 Comparative Analysis

Among the three cutoffs, we can expect the classifier used with cutoff 0.5 to result in the lowest cost of $627,900. That is an improvement of $4,372,100 over the baseline cost.

cutoff	accuracy	cost	improve
check none	0.9833	5,000,000	0
check all	0.0167	6,000,000	-1,000,000
SVM cutoff 0.90	0.9427	750,500	4,249,500
SVM cutoff 0.50	0.9504	627,900	4,372,100
SVM cutoff 0.25	0.9442	675,800	4,324,200

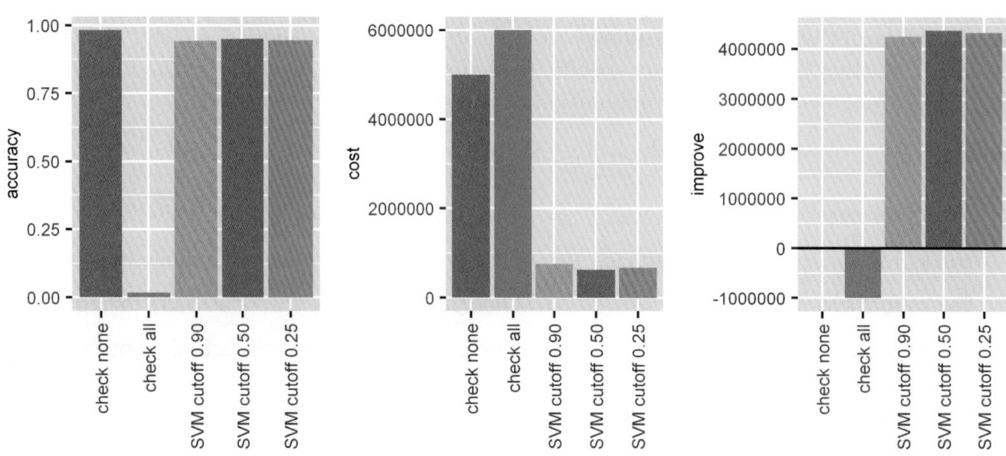

6.5.5 Custom Data for Test

Company management receives a report that a decision method has been developed that can reduce the cost of APS maintenance service from $5,000,000 down to $627,900. Under a philosophy of "trust but verify", it provides the development team with a new dataset of sensor measurements for further testing.

Prepare and transform the new dataset representation to match the original dataset representation

6.5.5.1 Raw Custom Data for Test

Retrieve a new reference classified dataset of APS sensor measurements. Each of 16,000 observations describes the sensor measurements for a unique truck. The 170 predictor variables represent the 170 types of sensors. A class variable indicates whether a truck's APS has failed (pos) or not (neg).

new.raw *frequency table*

class	count	rel_freq
neg	15,625	0.9766
pos	375	0.0234

new.raw *size 16000×171, first few observations shown, first few variables shown*

class	aa_000	ab_000	ac_000	ad_000	ae_000	af_000	ag_000	ag_001	ag_002
neg	60	0	20	12	0	0	0	0	0
neg	82	0	68	40	0	0	0	0	0
neg	66,002	2	212	112	0	0	0	0	0
neg	59,816	NA	1,010	936	0	0	0	0	0
neg	1,814	NA	156	140	0	0	0	0	0
neg	174	NA	26	24	0	0	NA	NA	NA

6.5.5.2 Rename Class Labels

To match the original dataset representation used to construct the classifier, rename class labels in the new dataset. Then neg becomes ok, pos becomes failure.

new *frequency table*

class	count	rel_freq
ok	15,625	0.9766
failure	375	0.0234

new *size 16000×171, first few observations shown, first few variables shown*

class	aa_000	ab_000	ac_000	ad_000	ae_000	af_000	ag_000	ag_001	ag_002
ok	60	0	20	12	0	0	0	0	0
ok	82	0	68	40	0	0	0	0	0
ok	66,002	2	212	112	0	0	0	0	0
ok	59,816	NA	1,010	936	0	0	0	0	0
ok	1,814	NA	156	140	0	0	0	0	0
ok	174	NA	26	24	0	0	NA	NA	NA

6.5.5.3 Impute

To match the original dataset representation, impute missing values in the **new** dataset with column means ***previously calculated from the original dataset***. Variable *ab*_000 in dataset **new** is imputed with 0.5748, which is the mean of variable *ab*_000 in dataset **data**, not the mean of variable *ab*_000 in dataset **new**. Similarly for the other variables of dataset **new**.

new *frequency table*

class	count	rel_freq
ok	15,625	0.9766
failure	375	0.0234

new *size 16000×171, first few observations shown, first few variables shown*

class	aa_000	ab_000	ac_000	ad_000	ae_000	af_000	ag_000	ag_001	ag_002
ok	60	0.0000	20	12	0	0	0.0	0.0	0
ok	82	0.0000	68	40	0	0	0.0	0.0	0
ok	66,002	2.0000	212	112	0	0	0.0	0.0	0
ok	59,816	0.5748	1,010	936	0	0	0.0	0.0	0
ok	1,814	0.5748	156	140	0	0	0.0	0.0	0
ok	174	0.5748	26	24	0	0	834.1	864.6	9,264

6.5.5.4 Filter Out Appropriate Variables

To match the original dataset representation, remove the 1 variable (cd_000) from the **new** dataset, which was ***removed from the original dataset***.

new *frequency table*

class	count	rel_freq
ok	15,625	0.9766
failure	375	0.0234

new *size 16000×170, first few observations shown, first few variables shown*

class	aa_000	ab_000	ac_000	ad_000	ae_000	af_000	ag_000	ag_001	ag_002
ok	60	0.0000	20	12	0	0	0.0	0.0	0
ok	82	0.0000	68	40	0	0	0.0	0.0	0
ok	66,002	2.0000	212	112	0	0	0.0	0.0	0
ok	59,816	0.5748	1,010	936	0	0	0.0	0.0	0
ok	1,814	0.5748	156	140	0	0	0.0	0.0	0
ok	174	0.5748	26	24	0	0	834.1	864.6	9,264

6.5.5.5 Transform to Principal Component Representation

To match the original dataset representation, represent the new dataset in principal component form according to the weight matrix ***previously calculated from the original dataset***.

new *frequency table*

class	count	rel_freq
ok	15,625	0.9766
failure	375	0.0234

new *size 16000×170, first few observations shown, first few variables shown*

class	PC1	PC2	PC3	PC4	PC5	PC6	PC7	PC8	PC9
ok	3.2847	0.0412	-0.3845	-0.3832	-0.4725	-0.6388	-0.2462	0.0346	0.3127
ok	3.3712	0.0455	-0.4232	-0.4875	-0.5128	-0.6329	-0.3279	0.0426	0.5645
ok	-1.1853	-2.1037	0.3212	1.9469	0.0514	0.4003	-1.0912	2.5433	-0.9446
ok	-0.2146	0.5111	0.8113	0.1709	-0.4885	0.4591	0.5373	-0.1037	-0.3191
ok	3.3281	0.0107	-0.3976	-0.4504	-0.4926	-0.5653	-0.2734	0.0182	0.5043
ok	1.8403	0.5320	-0.7788	-0.9272	-1.0183	0.0115	-0.6696	0.3504	0.3952

Keep the variable *class*, and the variables PC_1, PC_2, PC_3, PC_4, PC_5, PC_6, PC_7, which comprised just over 50% of total variance ***in the original dataset***.

new *frequency table*

class	count	rel_freq
ok	15,625	0.9766
failure	375	0.0234

new *size 16000×8, first few observations shown*

class	PC1	PC2	PC3	PC4	PC5	PC6	PC7
ok	3.2847	0.0412	-0.3845	-0.3832	-0.4725	-0.6388	-0.2462
ok	3.3712	0.0455	-0.4232	-0.4875	-0.5128	-0.6329	-0.3279
ok	-1.1853	-2.1037	0.3212	1.9469	0.0514	0.4003	-1.0912
ok	-0.2146	0.5111	0.8113	0.1709	-0.4885	0.4591	0.5373
ok	3.3281	0.0107	-0.3976	-0.4504	-0.4926	-0.5653	-0.2734
ok	1.8403	0.5320	-0.7788	-0.9272	-1.0183	0.0115	-0.6696

6.5.5.6 Balance

There is no need to balance the new dataset because it would not affect the form of input expected by the classifier, nor will it be used to construct a new classifier.

6.5.5.7 Business Parameters Derived from Data

The new dataset reflects a new fleet of healthy and failing trucks. So, change business parameter values accordingly. There are now 16,000 trucks, 15,625 of which will not fail and 375 of which will fail.

pop	pop.ok	pop.failure
16,000	15,625	375

6.5.6 Analysis II

Test the decision method as informed by the support vector machine classifier applied to new data.

6.5.6.1 Baseline

The business baseline scenario is again the better of two approaches:

- **Baseline I:** Do not call in any trucks and thereby avoid any maintenance service cost.
- **Baseline II:** Call in all trucks and thereby avoid any field repair cost.

Of these two approaches, we can expect calling in all to result in the lower cost of $1.6 million.

baseline (call in none)	
accuracy	cost
0.9766	1,875,000

baseline (call in all)	
accuracy	cost
0.0234	1,600,000

6.5.6.2 Probability Output, Confusion Matrix, Performance Metrics, & Business Result

Here are the results of the classifier with best cutoff 0.5 applied to the new dataset. Cost is $234,300. That's an improvement of $1,365,700 over the baseline cost.

prob *first few observations shown*

ok	failure
0.9562	0.0438
0.9561	0.0439
0.8569	0.1431
0.9582	0.0418
0.9567	0.0433
0.9532	0.0468

cutoff
0.5

cm

	ok	failure
ok	0.9393	0.0018
failure	0.0372	0.0217

performance metrics

tnr	fnr	fpr	tpr	accuracy
0.9253	0.0381	0.0747	0.9619	0.961

cutoff
0.5

business result

failure_failure	failure_ok	ok_failure	cost.maint	cost.repair	cost
347	596	28	100	5,000	234,300

7 | Classification III

Learning Objectives

Terms

Know the terms:

- Binary classifier
- Multinomial classifier
- One vs. rest (OVR)
- One vs. one (OVO)
- Round robin tournament

Effects of Assumptions

Know the effects of assumptions:

- Effects of one vs. rest approach and one vs. one approach on a model and its predictions

Use the Methods

Know how to use the methods:

- Compute a multinomial k-nearest neighbors model and use it to compute predictions.
- Compute a multinomial decision tree model and use it to compute predictions.
- Compute a multinomial naive Bayes model and use it to compute predictions.
- Compute a multinomial neural network model and use it to compute predictions.
- Compute a one vs. rest based model and use it to compute predictions.
- Compute a one vs. one based model and use it to compute predictions.

7.1 Multinomial Classification

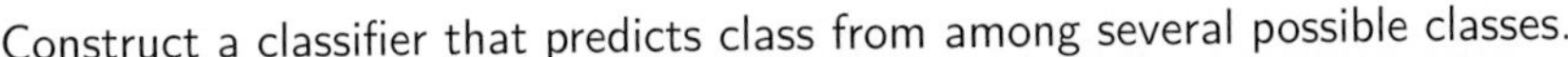
Construct a classifier that predicts class from among several possible classes.

7.1.1 Introduction

The company culture at the sports equipment manufacturer, unsurprisingly, is that most employees regularly participate in outside-of-work sports activities.

On evenings after work, many of the employees participate in swimming and diving events. In each swimming event, several contestants race against each other, and the 1 with the fastest time wins. In each diving event, several contestants each perform several dives, which are scored, and the 1 with the highest total score wins.

On Wednesday afternoons, 3 employees spend their lunch break at the nearby gym playing a friendly game of cutthroat racquetball. It keeps them fit, reduces stress, and helps them bond as a team, making them more productive when they're back at work. Each player repeatedly takes a turn playing against the 2 others, racking up his own points until his turn is over. After several turns, the player with the most points wins.

On some weekends, a few other employees grab their foils, epees, and sabers, and travel to the fencing tournaments that are frequently held throughout the region. Fencers compete in round robin style, where each fencer fights every other fencer 1 at a time, and the tournament winner is the fencer who wins the most bouts.

There are several approaches to multinomial classification. You can think of 1 approach as a swimming or diving event, where each unique class value is like a contestant trying to achieve the fastest time or highest score. You can think of another approach as a game of cutthroat racquetball, where each unique class value is like a player competing against the other players. You can think of yet another approach as a fencing tournament, where each pair of unique class values is like 2 fencers fighting each other amidst many other fencers fighting against each other.

7.1.2 About Multinomial Classification

A **binary classifier** predicts class from among 2 unique class values. A **multinomial classifier** predicts class from among more than 2 unique class values. Some classifier construction methods naturally produce multinomial classifiers, or can be easily adjusted to do so.

The k-nearest neighbors method can construct binary classifiers that calculate class probabilities based on the relative frequencies of 2 class values found among similar observations. To construct multinomial classifiers, calculate class probabilities based on the relative frequencies of more than 2 class values found among similar observations.

The decision tree method can construct binary classifiers that calculate class probabilities based on the relative frequencies of 2 class values found among the subset of observations comprising a leaf node. To construct multinomial classifiers, calculate class probabilities based on the relative frequencies of more that 2 class values found among the subset of of observations comprising a leaf node.

The naive Bayes method can construct binary classifiers that calculate prior probabilities and likelihoods for 2 class values. To construct multinomial classifiers, calculate prior probabilities and likelihoods for more than 2 class values.

The neural network method can construct binary classifiers that calculate class probability based on the output of 1 output node. To construct multinomial classifiers, specify the model form to include output nodes for all possible class values, rather than just 1 output node. Then calculate class probabilities based on outputs of all output nodes.

Any binary classifier construction method can be effectively converted to a multinomial classifier construction method by casting the multinomial version as an ensemble of binary classifiers trained on appropriate surrogate datasets. Two popular approaches include the **one vs. rest** approach and the **one vs. one** approach. The one vs. rest approach is also known as OVR. The one vs. one approach is also known as OVO.

The one vs. rest approach applied to a binary classifier construction method works like this:

```
To construct:
    For each unique class value ...
        Construct a surrogate dataset, as follows:
            Base on the reference dataset
            For each observation not assigned to the current unique class value ...
                Re-assign the observation to special class "other"
    For each surrogate dataset ...
        Construct a component binary classifier (model), as follows:
            Use the binary classifier construction method
            Base on the surrogate dataset

To predict:
    For each new observation ...
        For each component binary classifier (model) ...
            Calculate class probabilities
        Discard the class probabilities for special class "other"
        Gather the remaining class probabilities as scores
        Calculate class probabilities as relative scores
        Classify according to the highest class probability
```

Note that for n unique class values, n surrogate datasets and component models will be constructed.

$$\text{number of surrogate datasets} = \text{number of component models} = n$$

where ...

- n is number of unique class values

A variation on the one vs. rest approach is to predict based on class probabilities and several cutoffs.

The one vs. one approach applied to a binary classifier construction method works like this:

> *To construct:*
> *For each pair of unique class values ...*
> *Construct a surrogate dataset, as follows:*
> *Base on the reference dataset*
> *Remove all observations not assigned to either unique class value in the current pair*
> *For each surrogate dataset ...*
> *Construct a component binary classifier (model), as follows:*
> *Use the binary classifier construction method*
> *Base on the surrogate dataset*
>
> *To predict:*
> *For each new observation ...*
> *For each component binary classifier (model) ...*
> *Calculate class probabilities*
> *Classify according to class probabilities in a round robin tournament*

Note that for n unique class values, n choose 2 surrogate datasets and models will be constructed.

$$\text{number of surrogate datasets} = \text{number of component models} = {}_nC_2 = \frac{n!}{2!(n-2)!}$$

where ...

- n is number of unique class values

7.1.3 Multinomial k-Nearest Neighbors

Consider this classified 3-class reference dataset and unclassified new observation. Should the new observation be classified as A or B or C? Let's use multinomial k-nearest neighbors to predict the new observation's class.

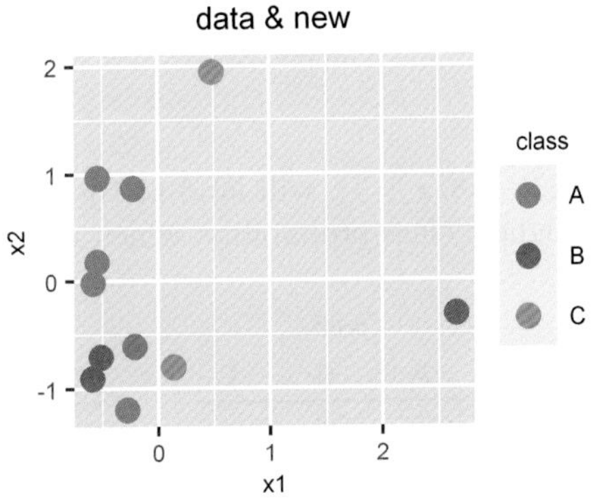

Set hyper-parameters k to 4, dissimilarity measured by Euclidean distance. See that the new observation, $(x_1 = -0.2114, x_2 = -0.6094)$, is most similar to 1 observation of class A, 2 observations of class B, and 1 observation of class C. Classify the new observation according to the highest class probability, which is class probability 0.50 for B.

new		prob			class.predicted
x1	x2	A	B	C	
-0.2114	-0.6094	0.25	0.5	0.25	B

7.1.4 Multinomial Decision Tree

Consider this classified 3-class reference dataset and unclassified new observation. Should the new observation be classified as A or B or C? Let's use multinomial decision tree to predict the new observation's class.

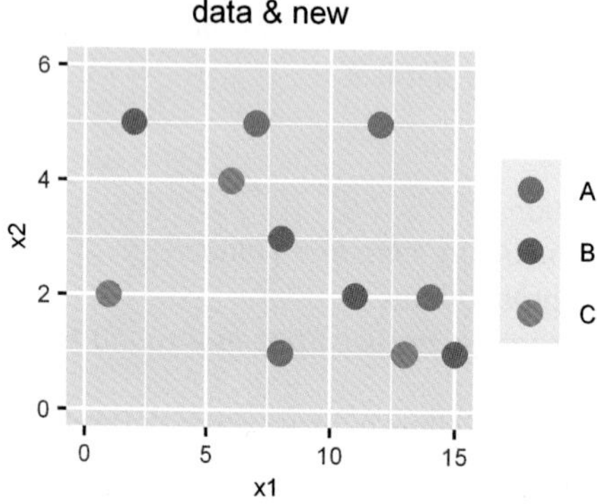

Here is a decision tree model based on the reference dataset. See that the leaf nodes show class probabilities for all 3 unique class values.

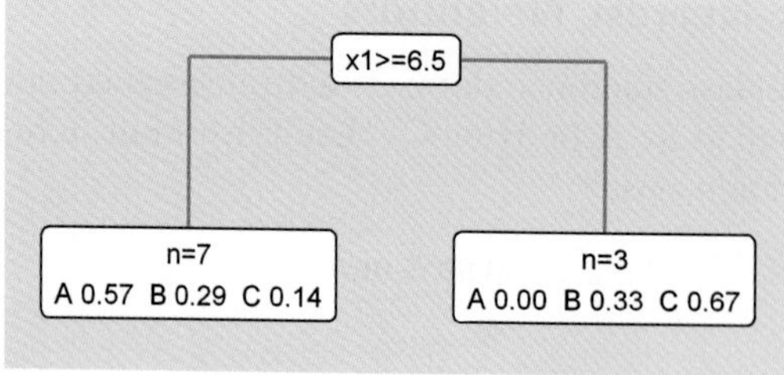

See that the new observation, $(x_1 = 8, x_2 = 3)$, will land at the left leaf node. Classify the new observation according to the highest class probability, which is class probability 0.57 for A.

new		prob			class.predicted
x1	x2	A	B	C	
8	3	0.57	0.29	0.14	A

7.1.5 Multinomial Naive Bayes

Consider this classified 3-class reference dataset and unclassified new observation. Should the new observation be classified as A or B or C? Let's use multinomial naive Bayes to predict the new observation's class.

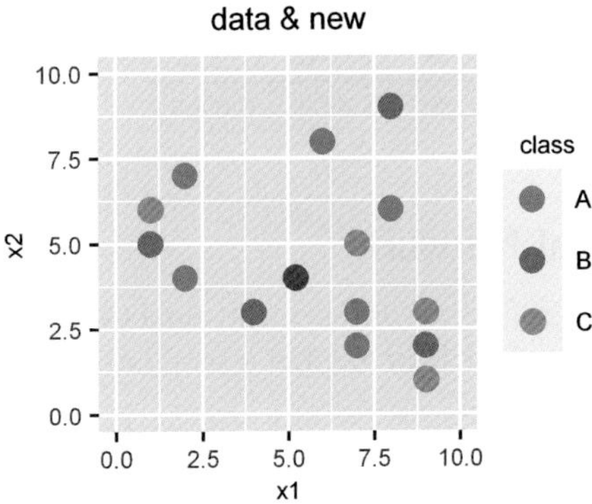

Here is a naive Bayes model based on the reference dataset. See that parameters include prior probabilities and likelihoods for all 3 unique class values.

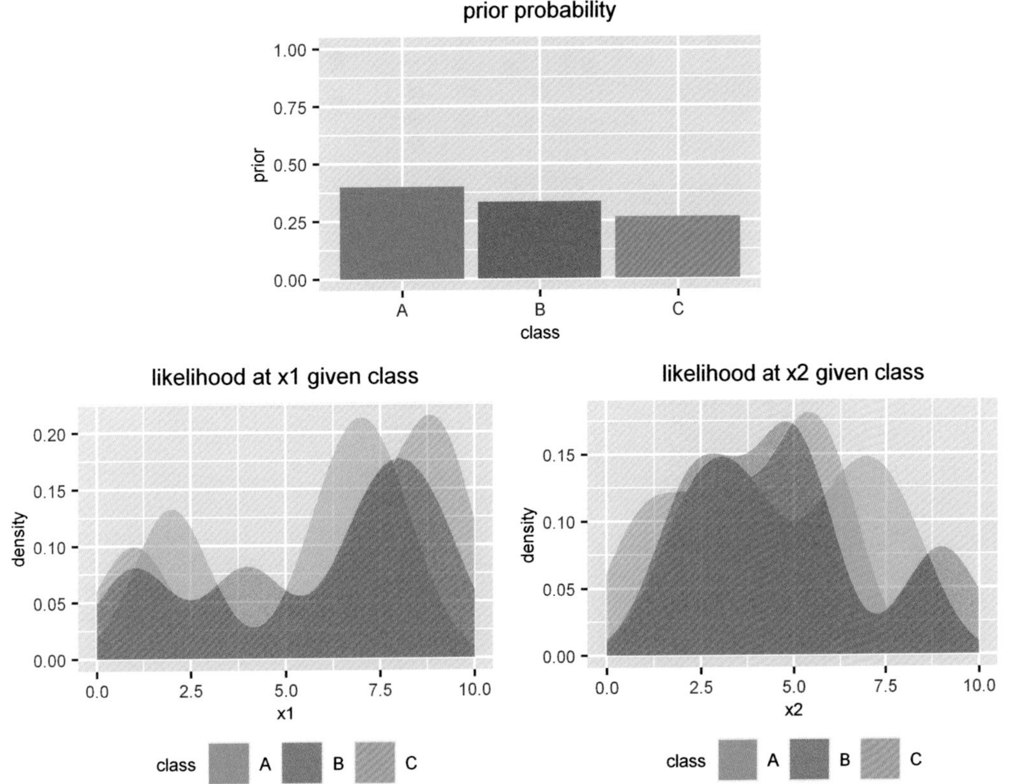

See that the new observation, $(x_1{=}5.2, x_2{=}4)$, enables relative posterior calculations for all 3 unique class values, which we interpret as class probabilities. Classify the new observation according to the highest class probability, which is class probability 0.5136 for A.

x1	x2	class	prior	likelihood.x1	likelihood.x2	posterior	rel_posterior
5.2	4	A	0.4000	0.0769	0.1257	0.0039	0.5136
5.2	4	B	0.3333	0.0564	0.1562	0.0029	0.3903
5.2	4	C	0.2667	0.0200	0.1358	0.0007	0.0961

new	
x1	x2
5.2	4

prob		
A	B	C
0.5136	0.3903	0.0961

class.predicted
A

7.1.6 Multinomial Neural Network

Consider this classified 3-class reference dataset and unclassified new observation. Should the new observation be classified as A or B or C? Let's use multinomial neural network to predict the new observation's class.

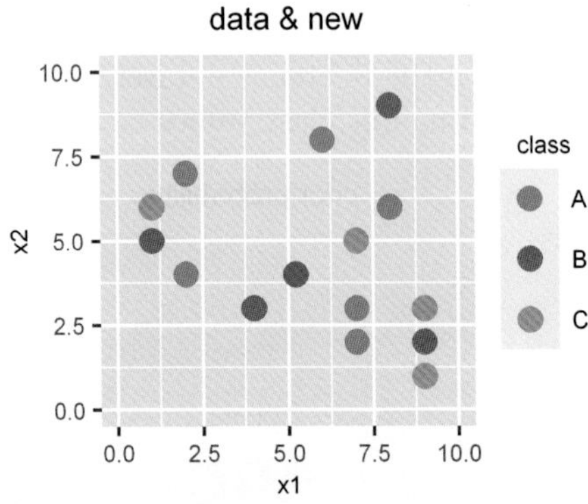

Convert the *class* variable to a set of dummy variables, but ***do not*** discard any of the dummy variables.

data		
x1	x2	class
1	5	B
1	6	C
4	3	B
2	4	A
2	7	A
6	8	A
7	2	A
7	3	A
7	5	B
7	5	C
8	6	A
8	9	B
9	1	C
9	2	B
9	3	C

data.nn				
x1	x2	class_A	class_B	class_C
1	5	0	1	0
1	6	0	0	1
4	3	0	1	0
2	4	1	0	0
2	7	1	0	0
6	8	1	0	0
7	2	1	0	0
7	3	1	0	0
7	5	0	1	0
7	5	0	0	1
8	6	1	0	0
8	9	0	1	0
9	1	0	0	1
9	2	0	1	0
9	3	0	0	1

Specify the model form to include separate output nodes for all dummy variables, which correspond to the unique class values. Here is a neural network model based on the reference dataset:

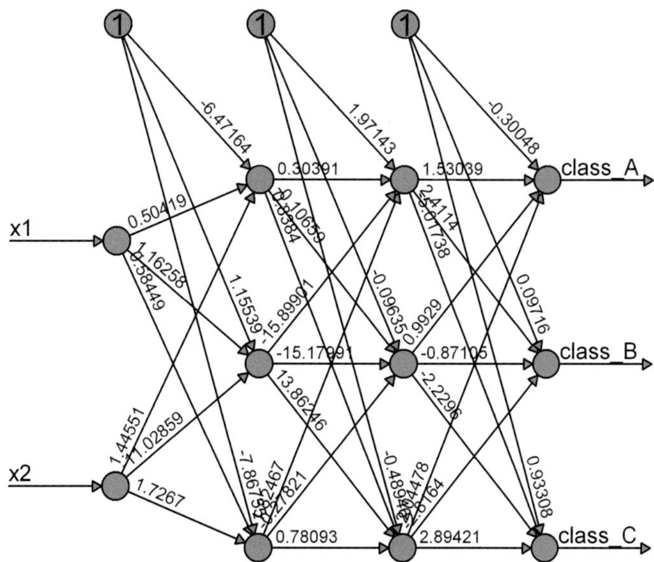

See that the new observation, (x_1=5.2, x_2=4), enables output calculations for all 3 unique class values. Each output is constrained by an activation function to be in range 0 to 1, with the collection potentially summing to 3. Calculate class probabilities as the relative outputs. Output 0.4046 for A corresponds to class probability $0.4046 \div (0.4046 + 0.3311 + 0.2461) = 0.4121$. Similarly for outputs for B and C. Classify the new observation according to the highest class probability, which is class probability 0.4121 for A.

x1	x2	output_A	output_B	output_C
5.2	4	0.4046	0.3311	0.2461

new		prob			
x1	x2	A	B	C	class.predicted
5.2	4	0.4121	0.3373	0.2507	A

7.1.7 One vs. Rest

Consider this classified 3-class reference dataset and unclassified new observation. Should the new observation be classified as A or B or C? Let's use the one vs. rest approach with logistic regression for binary classification to predict the new observation's class.

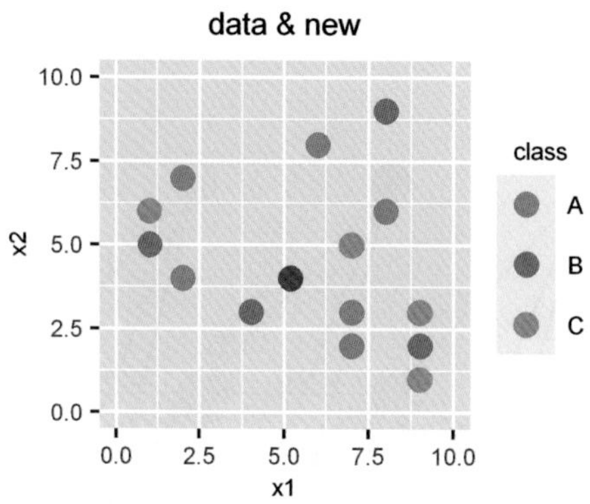

7.1.7.1 Surrogate Datasets

For each unique class value, construct a surrogate dataset:

- **Surrogate dataset for A:** Based on the reference dataset, observations not assigned to class A get re-assigned to special class other.
- **Surrogate dataset for B:** Based on the reference dataset, observations not assigned to class B get re-assigned to special class other.
- **Surrogate dataset for C:** Based on the reference dataset, observations not assigned to class C get re-assigned to special class other.

data *size 15×3*

x1	x2	class
1	5	B
1	6	C
4	3	B
2	4	A
2	7	A
6	8	A
7	2	A
7	3	A
7	5	B
7	5	C
8	6	A
8	9	B
9	1	C
9	2	B
9	3	C

data.Ao *size 15×3*

x1	x2	class
1	5	other
1	6	other
4	3	other
2	4	A
2	7	A
6	8	A
7	2	A
7	3	A
7	5	other
7	5	other
8	6	A
8	9	other
9	1	other
9	2	other
9	3	other

data.Bo *size 15×3*

x1	x2	class
1	5	B
1	6	other
4	3	B
2	4	other
2	7	other
6	8	other
7	2	other
7	3	other
7	5	B
7	5	other
8	6	other
8	9	B
9	1	other
9	2	B
9	3	other

data.Co *size 15×3*

x1	x2	class
1	5	other
1	6	C
4	3	other
2	4	other
2	7	other
6	8	other
7	2	other
7	3	other
7	5	other
7	5	C
8	6	other
8	9	other
9	1	C
9	2	other
9	3	C

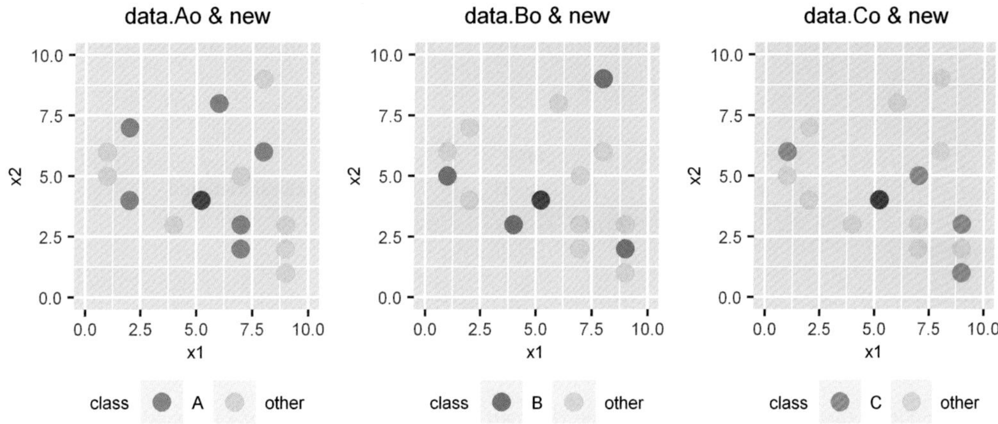

7.1.7.2 Component Models

For each surrogate dataset, construct a component model using logistic regression for binary classification. The first model will predict class A or other, the second model will predict class B or other, and the third model will predict class C or other.

model Ao

	coefficient
(Intercept)	0.5117
x1	0.0708
x2	-0.1095

model Bo

	coefficient
(Intercept)	1.0732
x1	-0.0141
x2	-0.0642

model Co

	coefficient
(Intercept)	0.4702
x1	-0.0657
x2	0.2166

7.1.7.3 Predict

Apply each component model to the new observation, (x_1=5.2, x_2=4). The first component model calculates class probability 0.3912 for A. The second component model calculates class probability 0.3223 for B. The third component model calculates class probability 0.2699 for C.

new

x1	x2
5.2	4

prob.Ao

A	other
0.3912	0.6088

prob.Bo

B	other
0.3223	0.6777

prob.Co

C	other
0.2699	0.7301

Discard the class probabilities for special class other and gather the remaining class probabilities as scores:

x1	x2	score_A	score_B	score_C
5.2	4	0.3912	0.3223	0.2699

Calculate class probabilities as the relative scores. Score 0.3912 for A corresponds to class probability $0.3912 \div (0.3912 + 0.3223 + 0.2699) = 0.3978$. Similarly for scores for B and C. Classify the new observation according to the highest class probability, which is class probability 0.3978 for A.

new		prob			
x1	x2	A	B	C	class.predicted
5.2	4	0.3978	0.3277	0.2744	A

7.1.8 One vs. One

Consider this classified 3-class reference dataset and unclassified new observation. Should the new observation be classified as A or B or C? Let's use the one vs. one approach with logistic regression for binary classification to predict the new observation's class.

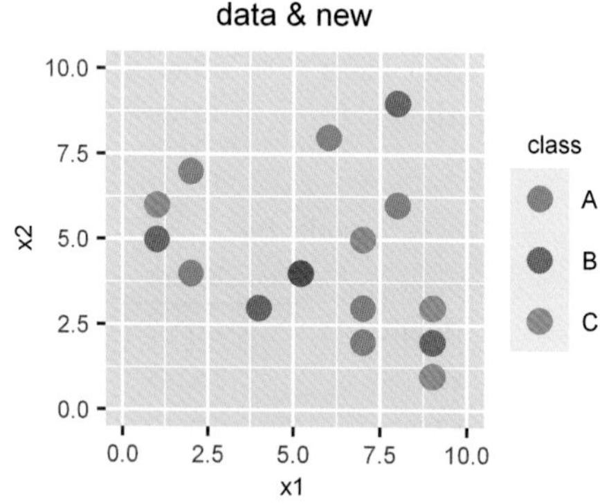

7.1.8.1 Surrogate Datasets

For each pair of unique class values, construct a surrogate dataset:

- **Surrogate dataset for A vs. B:** Based on the reference dataset, observations not assigned to class A or B get removed.
- **Surrogate dataset for A vs. C:** Based on the reference dataset, observations not assigned to class A or C get removed.
- **Surrogate dataset for B vs. C:** Based on the reference dataset, observations not assigned to class B or C get removed.

data *size 15×3*

x1	x2	class
1	5	B
1	6	C
4	3	B
2	4	A
2	7	A
6	8	A
7	2	A
7	3	A
7	5	B
7	5	C
8	6	A
8	9	B
9	1	C
9	2	B
9	3	C

data.AB *size 11×3*

x1	x2	class
1	5	B
4	3	B
2	4	A
2	7	A
6	8	A
7	2	A
7	3	A
7	5	B
8	6	A
8	9	B
9	2	B

data.AC *size 10×3*

x1	x2	class
1	6	C
2	4	A
2	7	A
6	8	A
7	2	A
7	3	A
7	5	C
8	6	A
9	1	C
9	3	C

data.BC *size 9×3*

x1	x2	class
1	5	B
1	6	C
4	3	B
7	5	B
7	5	C
8	9	B
9	1	C
9	2	B
9	3	C

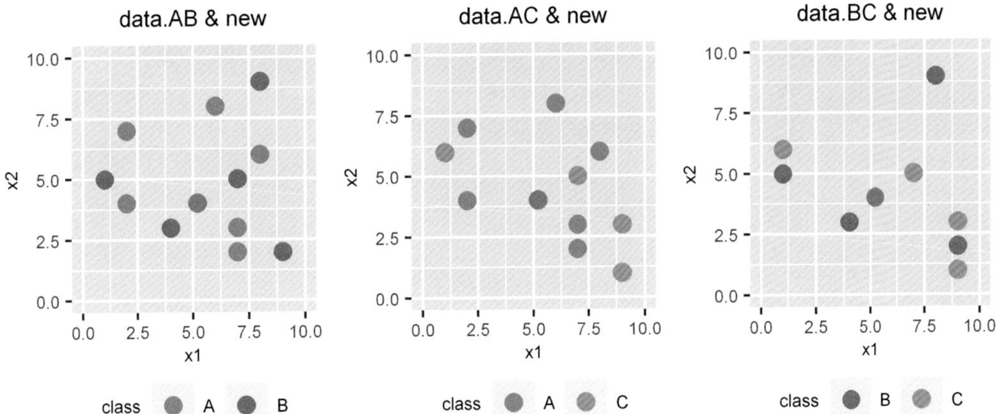

7.1.8.2 Component Models

For each surrogate dataset, construct a component model using logistic regression for binary classification. The first model will predict class A or B, the second model will predict class A or C, and the third model will predict class B or C.

model AB

	coefficient
(Intercept)	-0.3729
x1	0.0639
x2	-0.0337

model AC

	coefficient
(Intercept)	0.3307
x1	0.0567
x2	-0.2449

model BC

	coefficient
(Intercept)	0.4919
x1	0.0262
x2	-0.2055

7.1.8.3 Predict

Apply each component model to the new observation, (x_1=5.2, x_2=4). The first component model calculates class probability 0.5438 for A and 0.4562 for B. The second component model calculates class probability 0.5876 for A and 0.4124 for C. The third component model calculates class probability 0.5482 for B and 0.4518 for C.

new		prob.AB		prob.AC		prob.BC	
x1	x2	A	B	A	C	B	C
5.2	4	0.5438	0.4562	0.5876	0.4124	0.5482	0.4518

Classify the new observation according to class probabilities in a **round robin tournament** as follows. In the first round, class probability for A is higher than class probability for B, so A wins the round. In the second round, class probability for A is higher than class probability for C, so A wins that round, too. In the third round, class probability for B is higher than class probability for C, so B wins that round. Overall, A wins twice, B wins once, C never wins. A wins most often, so classify the new observation as A.

round robin tournament

model	prob.A	prob.B	prob.C	winner
AB	0.5438	0.4562	NA	A
AC	0.5876	NA	0.4124	A
BC	NA	0.5482	0.4518	B

class.predicted
A

7.2 CASE | Facial Recognition

Predictive modeling with principal component analysis and multinomial support vector machine to recognize people in photographs in the gaming industry.

7.2.1 Business Situation

A casino is ever-enhancing the gambling experience of its VIP (very important person) guests. Though it values all of its guests, treating its VIP guests with special, personalized service has proven to be especially profitable, as VIP guests who are treated well tend to spend more than the cost of service. Casino management is now experimenting with facial recognition technology to assist in recognizing its VIP customers as they enter and peruse the casino, so that staff can be alerted to their presence.

Simultaneously, the casino is also trying to exclude blacklisted guests whom it doesn't want at all. Some of these unwelcome guests have ties to organized crime, some are outright cheaters, and some are self-declared gambling addicts who could actually sue the casino if it allowed them to play. So, casino management is now experimenting with facial recognition technology to assist in distinguishing blacklisted guests, too.

Several facial recognition technology vendors are pitching their products to the casino.

- **Role:** Vice President of Technology
- **Decision:** Which guests to treat as VIPs? Which guests to treat as blacklisted?
- **Approach:** Build a multinomial model to recognize VIP guests and blacklisted guests. Use publicly available reference images to serve as proxies for images of actual guests. Treat the model as a proof-of-concept or baseline to compare other decision methods against.

7.2.2 Decision Model

The decision model includes a decision method that predicts the identities of guests from their photographs. Prediction accuracy, the number of guests, the proportion of VIP guests and blacklisted guests, what they could spend, and what they could cost the casino, all contribute to profit.

7.2.3 Data

Retrieve reference and test images, and ready them for model construction and evaluation.

7.2.3.1 Reference Data

Retrieve the reference images. There are 174 files in JPEG format, representing 6 different individuals.

files *174 files, first few files shown*

filename
Andre_Agassi_0001.jpg
Andre_Agassi_0002.jpg
Andre_Agassi_0003.jpg
Andre_Agassi_0004.jpg
Andre_Agassi_0005.jpg
Andre_Agassi_0006.jpg
Andre_Agassi_0007.jpg
Andre_Agassi_0008.jpg

who

class	count	rel_freq
Andre	33	0.1897
Arnold	39	0.2241
JK	3	0.0172
Kofi	29	0.1667
Serena	49	0.2816
Winona	21	0.1207

174 images, a few images shown

Represent the reference images as a reference dataset as follows. Convert the images from color to grayscale using some utility software, so that each image is represented as a 250 × 250 grid of pixel intensities. Then create a table, 1 observation per image, and variables to indicate the identity of the person in the image, its associated filename, and its 62,500 pixel intensities. The first variable, the identity of the person, is the class.

data.train *size 174×62502, first few observations shown, first few variables shown*

class	filename	V1	V2	V3	V4	V5	V6	V7
Andre	Andre_Agassi_0001.jpg	0.3658	0.3736	0.3775	0.3733	0.3698	0.3664	0.3700
Andre	Andre_Agassi_0002.jpg	0.0000	0.0000	0.0000	0.0000	0.0000	0.0000	0.0000
Andre	Andre_Agassi_0003.jpg	0.0000	0.0000	0.0000	0.0000	0.0000	0.0000	0.0000
Andre	Andre_Agassi_0004.jpg	0.0073	0.0073	0.0073	0.0073	0.0073	0.0073	0.0073
Andre	Andre_Agassi_0005.jpg	0.0306	0.0306	0.0306	0.0306	0.0306	0.0306	0.0306
Andre	Andre_Agassi_0006.jpg	0.0047	0.0035	0.0012	0.0023	0.0055	0.0064	0.0064

Transform the pixel intensity variables into principal component representation, using the weight matrix derived from the reference dataset. This concentrates variance in the first few principal component variables, making them appropriate for use later in model construction. Keep only the first 150 principal component variables.

data.train *size 174×152, first few observations shown, first few variables shown*

class	filename	PC1	PC2	PC3	PC4	PC5	PC6	PC7
Andre	Andre_Agassi_0001.jpg	-255.7	-73.17	-97.00	34.24	-106.932	20.631	-21.32
Andre	Andre_Agassi_0002.jpg	51.3	-60.36	-126.63	-47.49	40.097	25.441	16.80
Andre	Andre_Agassi_0003.jpg	134.4	-92.27	-62.64	11.05	74.575	-30.324	-36.92
Andre	Andre_Agassi_0004.jpg	181.2	-89.30	-120.93	46.26	1.258	-25.075	-12.79
Andre	Andre_Agassi_0005.jpg	174.5	-41.30	-98.56	87.39	-19.699	-5.517	-22.38
Andre	Andre_Agassi_0006.jpg	85.5	60.74	48.30	22.95	-55.178	74.336	-14.73

7.2.3.2 Test Data

Looking toward eventually evaluating a model, retrieve some test images of the same 6 individuals. There are 18 files in JPEG format.

files *18 files, first few files shown*

filename
Andre_Agassi_0009.jpg
Andre_Agassi_0013.jpg
Andre_Agassi_0021.jpg
Arnold_Schwarzenegger_0009.jpg
Arnold_Schwarzenegger_0013.jpg
Arnold_Schwarzenegger_0021.jpg
JK_Rowling_0001.jpg
JK_Rowling_0002.jpg
JK_Rowling_0006.jpg

files *18 files, last few files shown*

filename
Kofi_Annan_0009.jpg
Kofi_Annan_0013.jpg
Kofi_Annan_0021.jpg
Serena_Williams_0009.jpg
Serena_Williams_0013.jpg
Serena_Williams_0021.jpg
Winona_Ryder_0009.jpg
Winona_Ryder_0013.jpg
Winona_Ryder_0021.jpg

who

class	count	rel_freq
Andre	3	0.1667
Arnold	3	0.1667
JK	3	0.1667
Kofi	3	0.1667
Serena	3	0.1667
Winona	3	0.1667

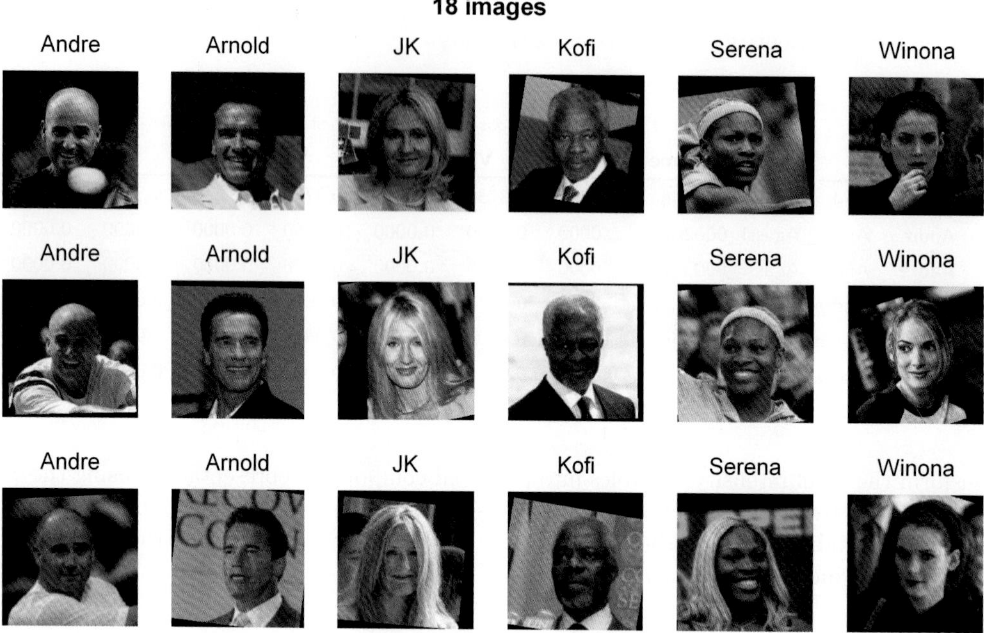

Represent the test images as a ***test*** dataset in the same way that we did earlier with reference images.

data.test *size 18×62502, first few variables shown*

class	filename	V1	V2	V3	V4	V5
Andre	Andre_Agassi_0009.jpg	0.0000	0.0000	0.0000	0.0000	0.0000
Andre	Andre_Agassi_0013.jpg	0.0023	0.0023	0.0023	0.0000	0.0000
Andre	Andre_Agassi_0021.jpg	0.0000	0.0000	0.0000	0.0000	0.0000
Arnold	Arnold_Schwarzenegger_0009.jpg	0.1345	0.1345	0.1345	0.1384	0.1384
Arnold	Arnold_Schwarzenegger_0013.jpg	0.0000	0.0000	0.0000	0.0000	0.0000
Arnold	Arnold_Schwarzenegger_0021.jpg	0.0035	0.0035	0.0012	0.0020	0.0029
JK	JK_Rowling_0001.jpg	0.0078	0.0078	0.0000	0.0000	0.3569
JK	JK_Rowling_0002.jpg	0.0287	0.0035	0.0035	0.0035	0.0012
JK	JK_Rowling_0006.jpg	0.0023	0.0023	0.0000	0.0000	0.0012
Kofi	Kofi_Annan_0009.jpg	0.0000	0.0000	0.0000	0.0000	0.0000
Kofi	Kofi_Annan_0013.jpg	0.0012	0.0012	0.0012	0.0012	0.0012
Kofi	Kofi_Annan_0021.jpg	0.0023	0.0023	0.0000	0.0000	0.0012
Serena	Serena_Williams_0009.jpg	0.0000	0.0000	0.0000	0.0000	0.0000
Serena	Serena_Williams_0013.jpg	0.0009	0.0009	0.0009	0.0009	0.0009
Serena	Serena_Williams_0021.jpg	0.0000	0.0000	0.0000	0.0000	0.0000
Winona	Winona_Ryder_0009.jpg	0.0009	0.0224	0.0035	0.0164	0.0071
Winona	Winona_Ryder_0013.jpg	0.0000	0.0000	0.0000	0.0000	0.0000
Winona	Winona_Ryder_0021.jpg	0.0071	0.0047	0.0035	0.0000	0.0032

Transform the pixel intensity variables into principal component representation, using the weight matrix derived earlier from the ***reference*** dataset. Keep only the first 150 principal component variables.

data.test *size 18×152, first few variables shown*

class	filename	PC1	PC2	PC3	PC4	PC5
Andre	Andre_Agassi_0009.jpg	132.2170	-8.796	-7.326	-36.8898	-86.427
Andre	Andre_Agassi_0013.jpg	67.4400	-57.230	-105.603	-38.9278	46.530
Andre	Andre_Agassi_0021.jpg	21.8772	-30.645	-137.253	-1.3813	21.363
Arnold	Arnold_Schwarzenegger_0009.jpg	82.5095	-112.227	-109.925	38.7622	33.789
Arnold	Arnold_Schwarzenegger_0013.jpg	-57.9217	-51.951	82.596	20.0136	25.439
Arnold	Arnold_Schwarzenegger_0021.jpg	-169.3758	-95.843	2.629	10.5005	53.361
JK	JK_Rowling_0001.jpg	-9.2428	-14.702	-38.537	26.0987	-18.842
JK	JK_Rowling_0002.jpg	-16.9734	-198.026	27.453	-11.7335	-119.157
JK	JK_Rowling_0006.jpg	0.5139	-27.584	-19.003	-114.2797	-92.285
Kofi	Kofi_Annan_0009.jpg	37.3297	44.383	109.264	-54.3699	-10.073
Kofi	Kofi_Annan_0013.jpg	-358.3924	108.843	72.070	-22.5202	43.167
Kofi	Kofi_Annan_0021.jpg	-121.5274	33.265	-64.035	-68.5268	16.568
Serena	Serena_Williams_0009.jpg	-30.7484	8.345	-17.491	-105.8964	-4.117
Serena	Serena_Williams_0013.jpg	-118.6683	-13.515	-52.728	-0.4926	-46.871
Serena	Serena_Williams_0021.jpg	-13.8593	28.145	-44.143	-78.0227	-4.344
Winona	Winona_Ryder_0009.jpg	36.7665	-33.976	86.434	59.9663	35.136
Winona	Winona_Ryder_0013.jpg	69.4040	-115.042	68.635	9.4326	-44.270
Winona	Winona_Ryder_0021.jpg	27.8783	13.667	133.870	68.9672	-104.525

7.2.4 Construct Models

Construct several multinomial models to predict *class* given the 150 principal component variables. Choose the support vector machine method, converted to multinomial form by one vs. one. For all of the models, set hyper-parameters to polynomial kernel. For each of the models, set hyper-parameters to a combination of degree 1, 2, 3, or 4; cost 0.1, 1, or 100; normalize or don't normalize.

model parameters

classes	kernel	cost	normalize	sv_count
Andre Arnold JK Kofi Serena Winona	polynomial: degree ?	?	?	?

degree
1
2
3
4

cost
0.1
1.0
100.0

normalize
FALSE
TRUE

Here is how the models perform, measured by in-sample accuracy:

		tune			
method	kernel	degree	cost	normalize	accuracy
svm	polynomial	1	0.1	FALSE	0.6667
svm	polynomial	1	0.1	TRUE	0.6667
svm	polynomial	1	1.0	FALSE	0.6667
svm	polynomial	1	1.0	TRUE	0.6667
svm	polynomial	1	100.0	FALSE	0.6667
svm	polynomial	1	100.0	TRUE	0.6667
svm	polynomial	2	0.1	FALSE	0.5556
svm	polynomial	2	0.1	TRUE	0.3333
svm	polynomial	2	1.0	FALSE	0.5556
svm	polynomial	2	1.0	TRUE	0.3333
svm	polynomial	2	100.0	FALSE	0.5556
svm	polynomial	2	100.0	TRUE	0.3333
svm	polynomial	3	0.1	FALSE	0.5556
svm	polynomial	3	0.1	TRUE	0.1667
svm	polynomial	3	1.0	FALSE	0.5556
svm	polynomial	3	1.0	TRUE	0.1667
svm	polynomial	3	100.0	FALSE	0.5556
svm	polynomial	3	100.0	TRUE	0.1667
svm	polynomial	4	0.1	FALSE	0.3333
svm	polynomial	4	0.1	TRUE	0.1667
svm	polynomial	4	1.0	FALSE	0.3333
svm	polynomial	4	1.0	TRUE	0.1667
svm	polynomial	4	100.0	FALSE	0.3333
svm	polynomial	4	100.0	TRUE	0.1667

7.2.5 Evaluate Best Model

The model specified by parameters degree 1, cost 0.1, not normalized, ties for the best performing, based on in-sample accuracy 0.6667. It happens to use 156 of the 174 reference observations as support vectors.

model parameters				
classes	kernel	cost	normalize	sv_count
Andre Arnold JK Kofi Serena Winona	polynomial: degree 1	0.1	FALSE	156

Evaluate the best performing model by applying it to the test dataset. The model always correctly recognizes 2 individuals. It correctly recognizes 3 other individuals in 2 out of 3 cases. It always confuses the 1 remaining individual.

data.test *size 18×153, first few variables shown*

class	class.predicted	filename	PC1	PC2	PC3	PC4
Andre	Andre	Andre_Agassi_0009.jpg	132.2170	-8.796	-7.326	-36.8898
Andre	Andre	Andre_Agassi_0013.jpg	67.4400	-57.230	-105.603	-38.9278
Andre	Serena	Andre_Agassi_0021.jpg	21.8772	-30.645	-137.253	-1.3813
Arnold	Arnold	Arnold_Schwarzenegger_0009.jpg	82.5095	-112.227	-109.925	38.7622
Arnold	Arnold	Arnold_Schwarzenegger_0013.jpg	-57.9217	-51.951	82.596	20.0136
Arnold	Arnold	Arnold_Schwarzenegger_0021.jpg	-169.3758	-95.843	2.629	10.5005
JK	Arnold	JK_Rowling_0001.jpg	-9.2428	-14.702	-38.537	26.0987
JK	Arnold	JK_Rowling_0002.jpg	-16.9734	-198.026	27.453	-11.7335
JK	Andre	JK_Rowling_0006.jpg	0.5139	-27.584	-19.003	-114.2797
Kofi	Kofi	Kofi_Annan_0009.jpg	37.3297	44.383	109.264	-54.3699
Kofi	Kofi	Kofi_Annan_0013.jpg	-358.3924	108.843	72.070	-22.5202
Kofi	Serena	Kofi_Annan_0021.jpg	-121.5274	33.265	-64.035	-68.5268
Serena	Serena	Serena_Williams_0009.jpg	-30.7484	8.345	-17.491	-105.8964
Serena	Serena	Serena_Williams_0013.jpg	-118.6683	-13.515	-52.728	-0.4926
Serena	Serena	Serena_Williams_0021.jpg	-13.8593	28.145	-44.143	-78.0227
Winona	Arnold	Winona_Ryder_0009.jpg	36.7665	-33.976	86.434	59.9663
Winona	Winona	Winona_Ryder_0013.jpg	69.4040	-115.042	68.635	9.4326
Winona	Winona	Winona_Ryder_0021.jpg	27.8783	13.667	133.870	68.9672

The best performing model's out-of-sample accuracy is 0.6667. Note that this much better than chance performance is achieved with only 174 reference images. We should expect further in-house developed proofs-of-concept or vendors' products to do much better with richer, larger sets of reference images.

confusion matrix	Andre	Arnold	JK	Kofi	Serena	Winona
Andre	2	0	1	0	0	0
Arnold	0	3	2	0	0	1
JK	0	0	0	0	0	0
Kofi	0	0	0	2	0	0
Serena	1	0	0	1	3	0
Winona	0	0	0	0	0	2

accuracy
0.6667

7.3 CASE | Credit Card Fraud

Comparison of predictive modeling methods to inform a credit card fraud reduction strategy in the financial services industry.

7.3.1 Business Situation

A financial services company processes credit card transactions, most of which are legitimate, but a few of which are fraudulent. Ideally, the company will alert card holders only in the event of any fraudulent transactions, confirm the fraud, and stop them in time to keep them from completing. However, distinguishing legitimate transactions from fraudulent transactions is proving to be a challenge. The company is responsible for making good to the card holder on any fraudulent transactions that it doesn't catch.

- **Role:** Vice President of Fraud Mitigation
- **Decision:** Intervene in which credit card transactions?
- **Approach:** Build predictive models to detect fraudulent transactions, using 7 different analytical methods.

7.3.2 Decision Model

The decision model starts with a decision method that predicts which transactions are fraudulent.

Agents proactively intervene in transactions predicted to be fraudulent. There are agent costs associated with interventions. When the transactions turn out to be legitimate, then there are also penalty costs to account for the effect that disturbing card holders has on customer satisfaction.

Agents reactively intervene in transactions predicted to be legitimate, in response to any disgruntled card holders who eventually call the company to report the transactions as fraudulent. In these cases, the company incurs agent costs, penalty costs, and charges, which are the transaction amounts that the company must make good on because it's too late to stop the transactions from completing. As a simplifying assumption, we treat all fraudulent transaction amounts as equal to the average fraudulent transaction amount.

Agents ignore legitimate transactions predicted to be legitimate. so there are no costs associated with these transactions.

Business parameters include the following:

- **transactions**: the total number of transactions being considered (might be larger than the total number of transactions seen in historical data)
- **fraud rate:** the proportion of fraudulent transactions from among all transactions seen in historical data
- **agent:** the cost of an agent per transaction
- **penalty:** the cost per transaction that accounts for the effect on customer satisfaction
- **charge:** the average fraudulent transaction amount

transactions	fraud_rate	agent	penalty	charge
1,000,000	determined from data	10	10	determined from data

See the decision model in influence diagram representation on the next page.

We treat fraudulent transactions as the positive class. We treat legitimate transactions as the negative class. Possible results of the decision method include the following:

- correctly predict that some transactions are fraudulent from among those that are actually fraudulent – this proportion is the ***true positive rate*** (**TPR**).
- incorrectly predict that some transactions are fraudulent from among those that are actually legitimate – this proportion is the ***false positive rate*** (**FPR**).
- incorrectly predict that some transactions are legitimate from among those that are actually fraudulent – this proportion is the ***false negative rate*** (**FNR**).

The absolute numbers of transactions in each of these groups depend on the proportions, the total number of transactions, and the fraud rate. The costs associated with each of these groups depend on their absolute numbers, agent cost per transaction, penalty cost per transaction, and charge per transaction. Total cost is the sum of the group costs.

$$\begin{aligned}
\text{cost of intervened actually fraudulent transactions} &= \text{tpr} \times \text{fraud rate} \times \text{transactions} \times \text{agent cost} \\
\text{cost of intervened actually legitimate transactions} &= \text{fpr} \times (1 - \text{fraud rate}) \times \text{transactions} \times (\text{agent cost} + \text{penalty cost}) \\
\text{cost of ignored actually fraudulent transactions} &= \text{fnr} \times \text{fraud rate} \times \text{transactions} \times (\text{agent cost} + \text{penalty cost} + \text{charge})
\end{aligned}$$

$$\text{cost} = \begin{pmatrix} \text{cost of intervened actually fraudulent transactions} + \\ \text{cost of intervened actually legitimate transactions} + \\ \text{cost of ignored actually fraudulent transactions} \end{pmatrix}$$

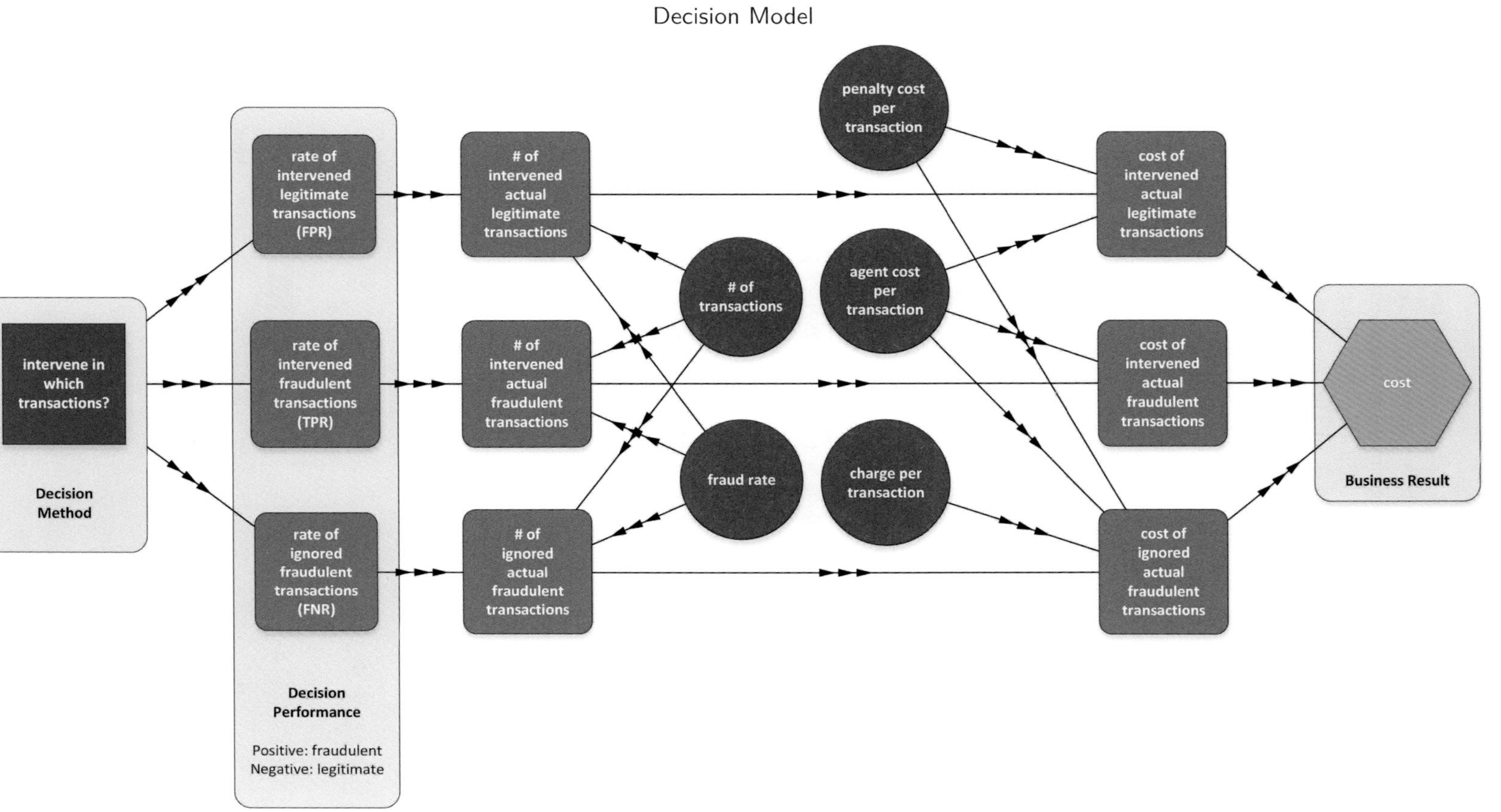

Decision Model
intervene in which transactions?
Decision Method
rate of intervened legitimate transactions (FPR)
rate of intervened fraudulent transactions (TPR)
rate of ignored fraudulent transactions (FNR)
Decision Performance
Positive: fraudulent
Negative: legitimate
# of intervened actual legitimate transactions
# of intervened actual fraudulent transactions
# of ignored actual fraudulent transactions
# of transactions
fraud rate
penalty cost per transaction
agent cost per transaction
charge per transaction
cost of intervened actual legitimate transactions
cost of intervened actual fraudulent transactions
cost of ignored actual fraudulent transactions
cost
Business Result

7.3.3 Data

Retrieve a reference classified dataset of transaction records. Each of 28,482 observations describes a unique transaction that occurred during a 2-day period. The *class* variable indicates whether a transaction is known to be legitimate or fraudulent. There is 0.18% of the transactions that are fraudulent. The *Time* variable indicates the time that a transaction occurred, measured as the number of seconds since the start of the period. The *Amount* variable indicates the transaction amount, measured in euros. Another 28 variables indicate various other features of a transaction, all transformed to principal component representation. Note that information that was contained in the pre-transformed variables is still available in the principal component variables, except for anything that could reveal the specific 28 features. This opens the dataset to analysis, while hiding the specific 28 features from nefarious actors that would otherwise exploit such knowledge to devise ways to evade detection of their own fraudulent transactions.

data *frequency table*

class	count	rel_freq
fraud	50	0.0018
legit	28,432	0.9982

data *size 28482×31, first few observations shown, first few variables shown*

class	Time	Amount	PC1	PC2	PC3	PC4	PC5	PC6	PC7	PC8
legit	12	12.99	1.1032	-0.0403	1.2673	1.2891	-0.7360	0.2881	-0.5861	0.1894
legit	14	46.80	-5.4013	-5.4501	1.1863	1.7362	3.0491	-1.7634	-1.5597	0.1608
legit	33	9.10	-0.9357	0.1704	2.7463	-1.0780	-0.3056	0.0116	-0.2962	0.4028
legit	34	21.34	1.1383	0.0570	0.6494	0.8731	-0.4685	-0.4102	-0.0139	-0.0724
legit	44	45.71	0.9271	-0.3237	0.3876	0.5445	0.2468	1.6504	-0.4276	0.6154
legit	52	6.67	1.1474	0.0590	0.2636	1.2110	-0.0441	0.3011	-0.1330	0.2279

Here is the reference dataset visualized as a scatterplot, *PC1* vs. *PC2*, color-coded by *class*. Other variables are not shown here.

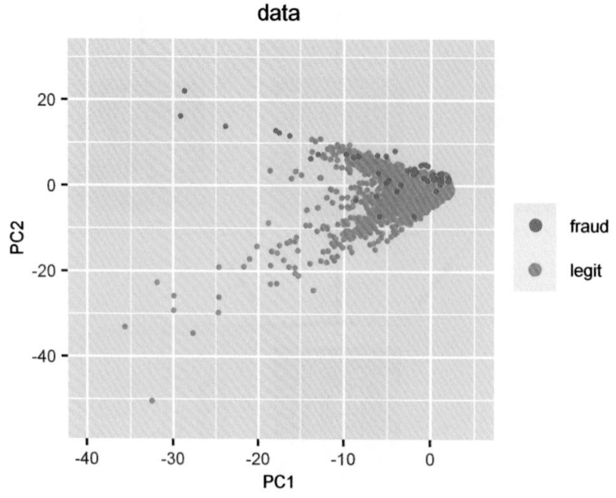

Determine the outstanding business parameters from the reference dataset. The fraud rate is 0.0018. On average, the transaction amount among fraudulent transactions is $163.60 per transaction.

transactions	fraud_rate	agent	penalty	charge
1,000,000	0.0018	10	10	163.6

Partition the reference dataset for training and testing. Choose 75% for training, 25% for testing.

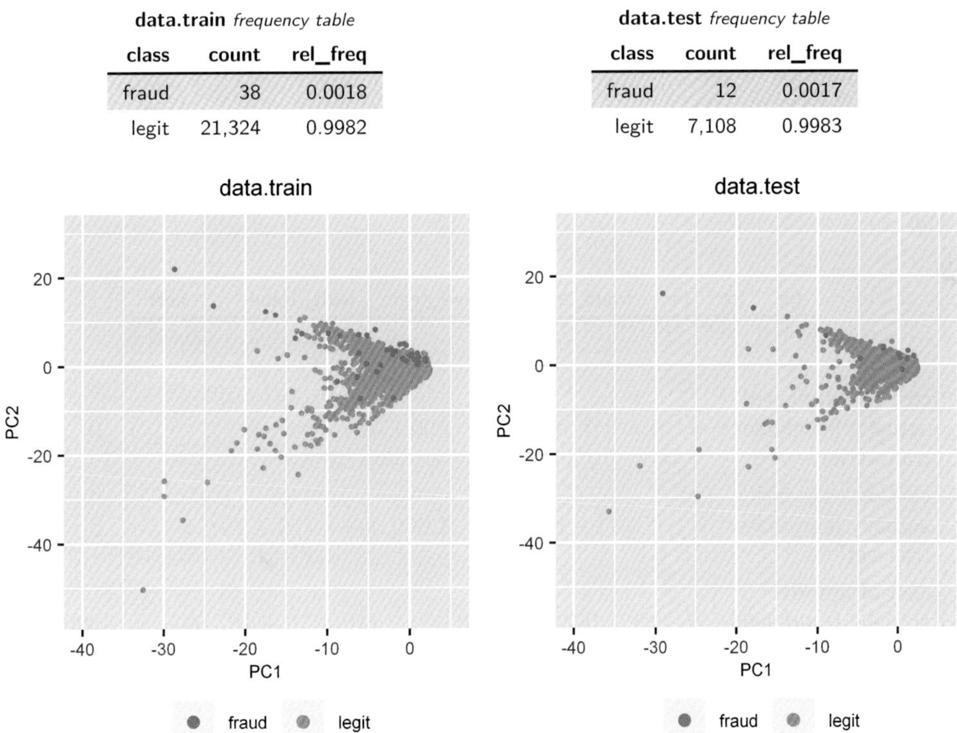

data.train *frequency table*

class	count	rel_freq
fraud	38	0.0018
legit	21,324	0.9982

data.test *frequency table*

class	count	rel_freq
fraud	12	0.0017
legit	7,108	0.9983

7.3.4 Baseline

The business baseline scenario is to use a decision method that assumes that all transactions are legitimate. This is effectively like using a model that always predicts legitimate, given any variables. Here is a scatterplot of potential transactions, each color-coded by what the model would predict about it.

When applied to the test dataset, the model correctly predicts most of the transactions to be legitimate because most of them are actually legitimate. None of the actually legitimate transactions is predicted incorrectly; the false positive rate is 0. However, the model incorrectly predicts all actually fraudulent transactions to be legitimate; the false negative rate is 1, but therefore the true positive rate is 0. Here are scatterplots of the test dataset viewed through filters that separate out the correctly predicted transactions from the incorrectly predicted ones:

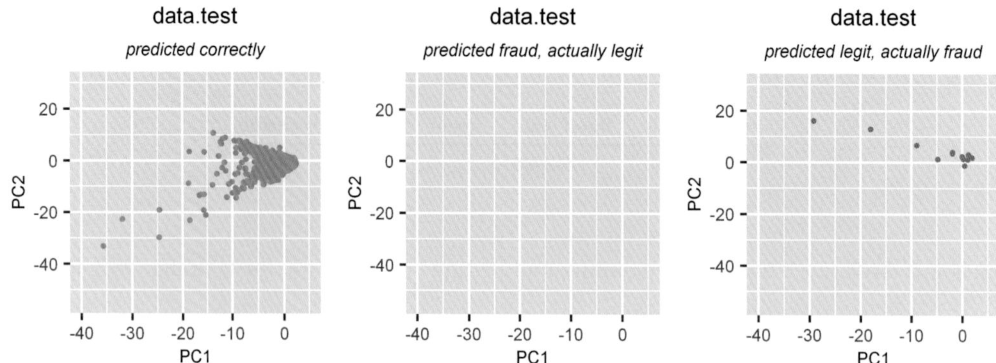

Correct predictions of actually legitimate transactions do not incur any cost. There are no incorrect predictions of actually legitimate transactions, so no costs are incurred there either. However, all actually fraudulent transactions do incur agent costs, penalty costs, and charges.

Calculate total cost based on the true negative rate, the false negative rate, the false positive rate, and the business parameters. Total cost is \$330,492. Can other decision methods beat that number?

tpr	fpr	fnr	fraud_fraud	fraud_legit	legit_fraud	cost
0	0	1	0	0	330,492	330,492

$$\text{cost of intervened actually fraudulent transactions} = 0 \times 0.0018 \times 1{,}000{,}000 \times 10 = 0$$

$$\text{cost of intervened actually legitimate transactions} = 0 \times (1 - 0.0018) \times 1{,}000{,}000 \times (10 + 10) = 0$$

$$\text{cost of ignored actually fraudulent transactions} = 1 \times 0.0018 \times 1{,}000{,}000 \times (10 + 10 + 163.60) = 330{,}492$$

$$\text{cost} = 0 + 0 + 330{,}492 = 330{,}492$$

7.3.5 Predict Fraud by k-Nearest Neighbors

Try using a k-nearest neighbors model as the decision method. Construct the model to predict *class* given *PC1*, *PC2*. Set hyper-parameters to normalize the dataset, k=2. Set cutoff to 0.5.

Here is a scatterplot of potential transactions, each color-coded by what the model would predict about it. Note the interesting shape of the boundary between predicted-legitimate and predicted-fraudulent transactions.

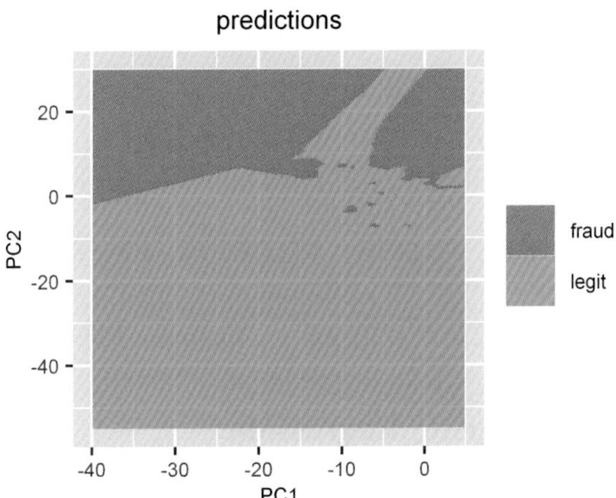

When applied to the test dataset, the model predicts with true positive rate 0.6667, false positive rate 0.0015, and false negative rate 0.3333. Here are scatterplots of the test dataset viewed through filters that separate out the correctly predicted transactions from the incorrectly predicted:

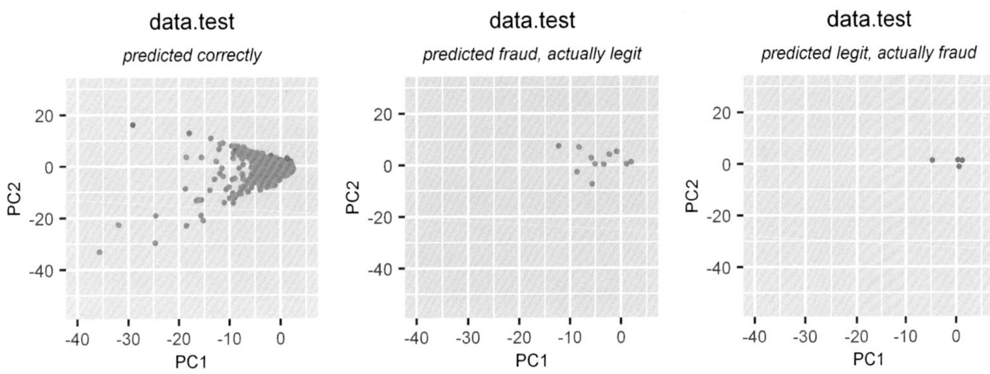

Some actually fraudulent transactions are predicted correctly and incur agent costs. The remaining actually fraudulent transactions are predicted incorrectly and incur agent costs, penalty costs, and charges. The actually legitimate transactions that are predicted incorrectly incur agent costs and penalty costs.

Calculate total cost based on the true positive rate, the false positive rate, the false negative rate, and the business parameters. Total cost is \$153,059.

tpr	fpr	fnr	fraud_fraud	fraud_legit	legit_fraud	cost
0.6667	0.0015	0.3333	12,000	30,895	110,164	153,059

$$\begin{aligned}
\text{cost of intervened actually fraudulent transactions} &= 0.6667 \times 0.0018 \times 1{,}000{,}000 \times 10 &= 12{,}000 \\
\text{cost of intervened actually legitimate transactions} &= 0.0015 \times (1 - 0.0018) \times 1{,}000{,}000 \times (10 + 10) &= 30{,}895 \\
\text{cost of ignored actually fraudulent transactions} &= 0.3333 \times 0.0018 \times 1{,}000{,}000 \times (10 + 10 + 163.60) &= 110{,}164
\end{aligned}$$

$$\text{cost} = 12{,}000 + 30{,}895 + 110{,}164 = 153{,}059$$

7.3.6 Predict Fraud by Logistic Regression

Try using a logistic regression model as the decision method. Construct the model to predict *class* given *PC1*, *PC2*. Set cutoff to 0.5.

Here is a scatterplot of potential transactions, each color-coded by what the model would predict about it. Note the simple boundary between predicted-legitimate and predicted-fraudulent transactions.

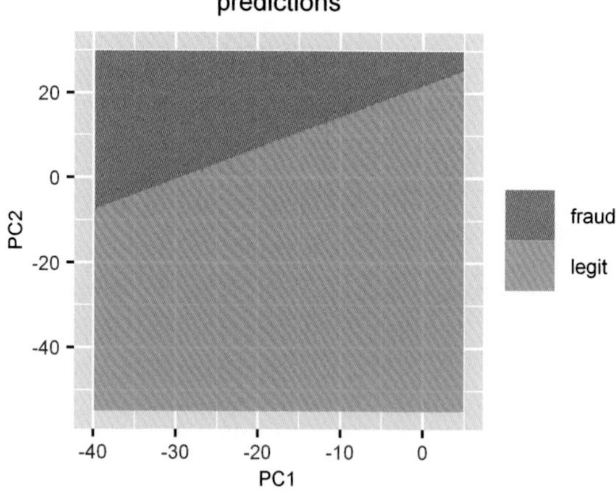

When applied to the test dataset, the model predicts with true positive rate 0.1667, false positive rate 0, and false negative rate 0.8333. Here are scatterplots of the test dataset viewed through filters that separate out the correctly predicted transactions from the incorrectly predicted:

Calculate total cost based on the true positive rate, the false positive rate, the false negative rate, and the business parameters. Total cost is \$278,410.

tpr	fpr	fnr	fraud_fraud	fraud_legit	legit_fraud	cost
0.1667	0	0.8333	3,000	0	275,410	278,410

$$\text{cost of intervened actually fraudulent transactions} = 0.1667 \times 0.0018 \times 1{,}000{,}000 \times 10 = 3{,}000$$

$$\text{cost of intervened actually legitimate transactions} = 0 \times (1 - 0.0018) \times 1{,}000{,}000 \times (10 + 10) = 0$$

$$\text{cost of ignored actually fraudulent transactions} = 0.8333 \times 0.0018 \times 1{,}000{,}000 \times (10 + 10 + 163.60) = 275{,}410$$

$$\text{cost} = 3{,}000 + 0 + 275{,}410 = 278{,}410$$

7.3.7 Predict Fraud by Decision Tree

Try using a decision tree model as the decision method. Construct the model to predict *class* given *PC1*, *PC2*. Set hyper-parameters to minimum number of splits 3, maximum depth 7. Set cutoff to 0.5.

Here is a scatterplot of potential transactions, each color-coded by what the model would predict about it. Note that the interesting shape of the boundary between predicted-legitimate and predicted-fraudulent transactions reflects how the decision tree method successively splits the 2-variable space by 1 variable value at a time.

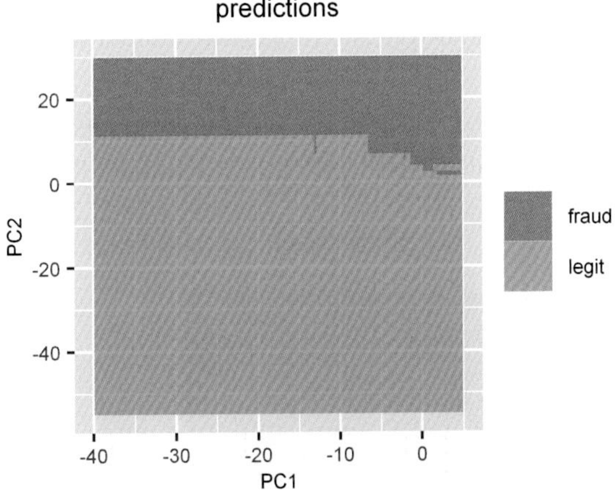

When applied to the test dataset, the model predicts with true positive rate 0.25, false positive rate 0.0003, and false negative rate 0.75. Here are scatterplots of the test dataset viewed through filters that separate out the correctly predicted transactions from the incorrectly predicted:

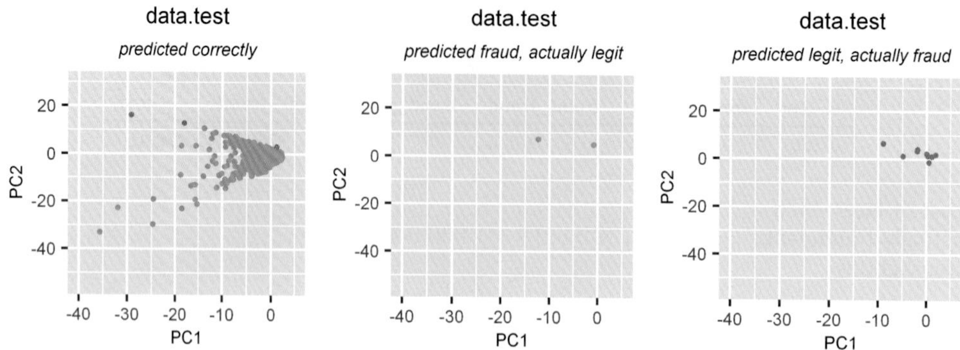

Calculate total cost based on the true positive rate, the false positive rate, the false negative rate, and the business parameters. Total cost is $257,986.

tpr	fpr	fnr	fraud_fraud	fraud_legit	legit_fraud	cost
0.25	0.0003	0.75	4,500	5,617	247,869	257,986

cost of intervened actually fraudulent transactions $= 0.25 \times 0.0018 \times 1{,}000{,}000 \times 10 = 4{,}500$

cost of intervened actually legitimate transactions $= 0.0003 \times (1 - 0.0018) \times 1{,}000{,}000 \times (10 + 10) = 5{,}617$

cost of ignored actually fraudulent transactions $= 0.75 \times 0.0018 \times 1{,}000{,}000 \times (10 + 10 + 163.60) = 247{,}869$

$$\text{cost} = 4{,}500 + 5{,}617 + 247{,}869 = 257{,}986$$

7.3.8 Predict Fraud by Naive Bayes

Try using a naive Bayes model as the decision method. Construct the model to predict *class* given *PC1*, *PC2*. Set cutoff to 0.5.

Here is a scatterplot of potential transactions, each color-coded by what the model would predict about it. Note the interesting shape of the boundary between predicted-legitimate and predicted-fraudulent transactions.

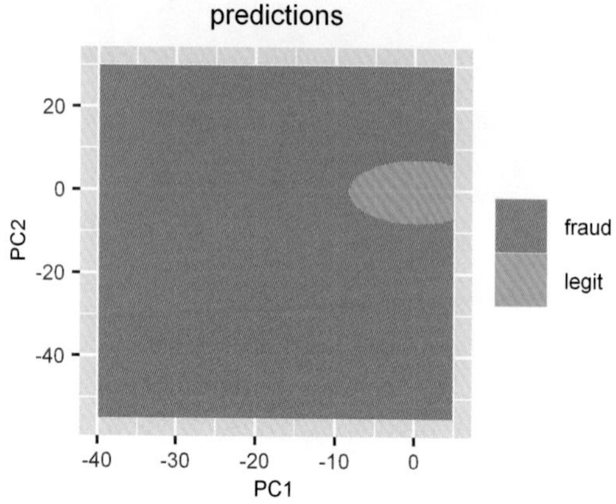

When applied to the test dataset, the model predicts with true positive rate 0.25, false positive rate 0.0148, and false negative rate 0.75. Here are scatterplots of the test dataset viewed through filters that separate out the correctly predicted transactions from the incorrectly predicted:

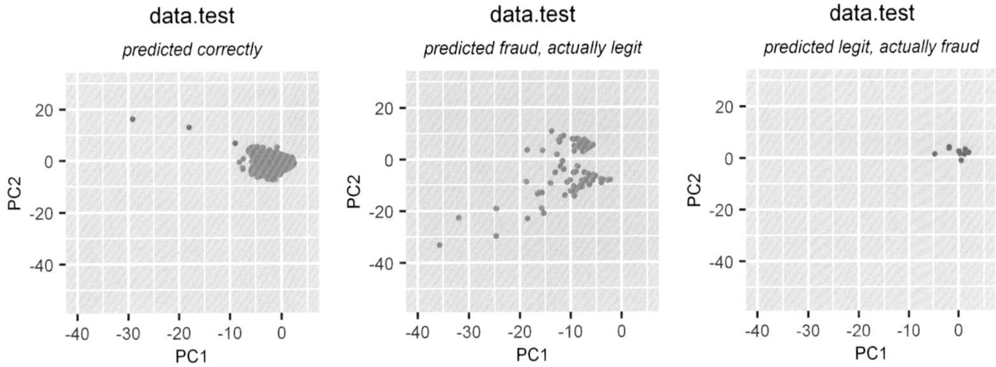

Calculate total cost based on the true positive rate, the false positive rate, the false negative rate, and the business parameters. Total cost is \$547,279.

tpr	fpr	fnr	fraud_fraud	fraud_legit	legit_fraud	cost
0.25	0.0148	0.75	4,500	294,910	247,869	547,279

$$\begin{aligned}
\text{cost of intervened actually fraudulent transactions} &= 0.25 \times 0.0018 \times 1{,}000{,}000 \times 10 &&= 4{,}500 \\
\text{cost of intervened actually legitimate transactions} &= 0.0148 \times (1 - 0.0018) \times 1{,}000{,}000 \times (10 + 10) &&= 294{,}910 \\
\text{cost of ignored actually fraudulent transactions} &= 0.75 \times 0.0018 \times 1{,}000{,}000 \times (10 + 10 + 163.60) &&= 247{,}869
\end{aligned}$$

$$\text{cost} = 4{,}500 + 294{,}910 + 247{,}869 = 547{,}279$$

7.3.9 Predict Fraud by Support Vector Machine

Try using a support vector machine model as the decision method. Construct the model to predict *class* given *PC1*, *PC2*. Set hyper-parameters to normalize the dataset, polynomial kernel of degree 4, cost 0.1. Set cutoff to 0.5.

Here is a scatterplot of potential transactions, each color-coded by what the model would predict about it. Note the interesting shape of the boundary between predicted-legitimate and predicted-fraudulent transactions.

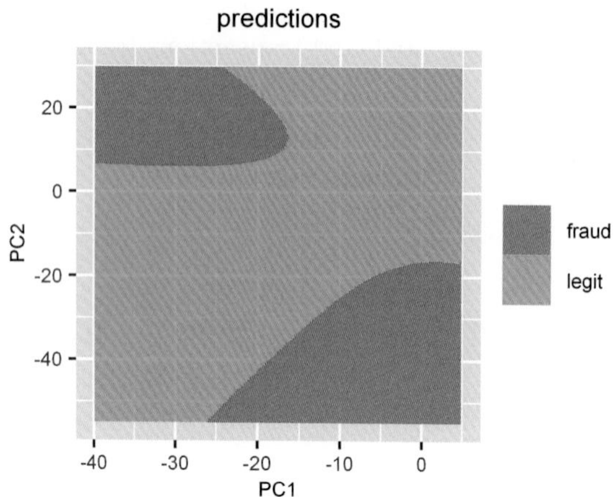

When applied to the test dataset, the model predicts with true positive rate 0.1667, false positive rate 0, and false negative rate 0.8333. Here are scatterplots of the test dataset viewed through filters that separate out the correctly predicted transactions from the incorrectly predicted:

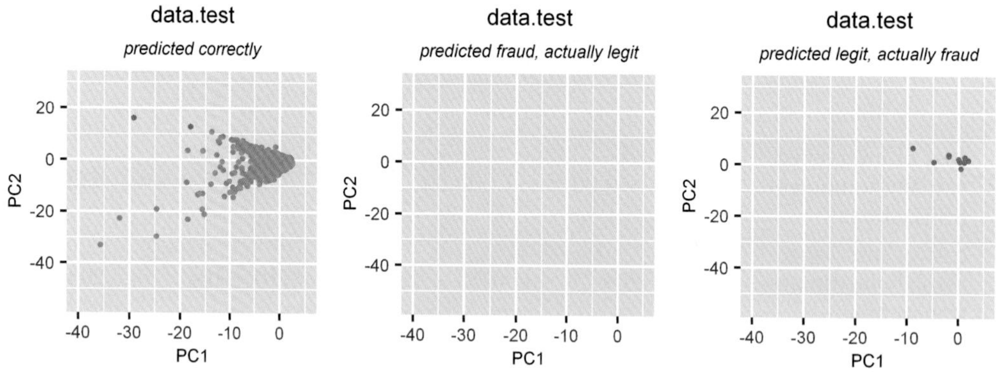

Calculate total cost based on the true positive rate, the false positive rate, the false negative rate, and the business parameters. Total cost is \$278,410.

tpr	fpr	fnr	fraud_fraud	fraud_legit	legit_fraud	cost
0.1667	0	0.8333	3,000	0	275,410	278,410

cost of intervened actually fraudulent transactions $= 0.1667 \times 0.0018 \times 1{,}000{,}000 \times 10 = 3{,}000$

cost of intervened actually legitimate transactions $= 0 \times (1 - 0.0018) \times 1{,}000{,}000 \times (10 + 10) = 0$

cost of ignored actually fraudulent transactions $= 0.8333 \times 0.0018 \times 1{,}000{,}000 \times (10 + 10 + 163.60) = 275{,}410$

$$\text{cost} = 3{,}000 + 0 + 275{,}410 = 278{,}410$$

7.3.10 Predict Fraud by Neural Network

Try using a neural network model as the decision method. Construct the model to predict *class* given *PC1*, *PC2*. Set hyper-parameters to 1 hidden layer with 2 nodes, sigmoid activation function. Set cutoff to 0.5.

Here is a scatterplot of potential transactions, each color-coded by what the model would predict about it. Note the interesting shape of the boundary between predicted-legitimate and predicted-fraudulent transactions.

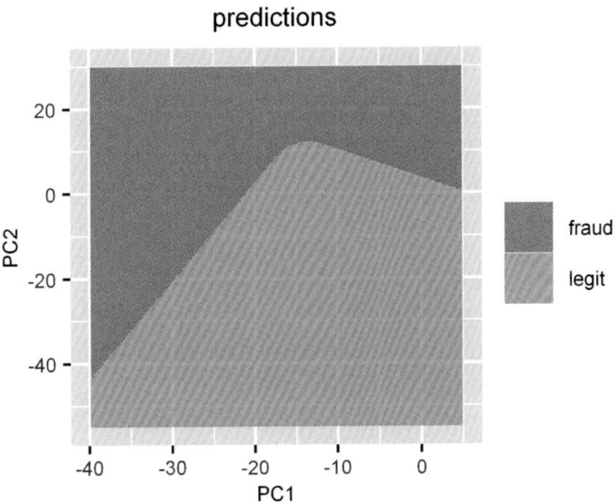

When applied to the test dataset, the model predicts with true positive rate 0.25, false positive rate 0.0004, and false negative rate 0.75. Here are scatterplots of the test dataset viewed through filters that separate out the correctly predicted transactions from the incorrectly predicted.

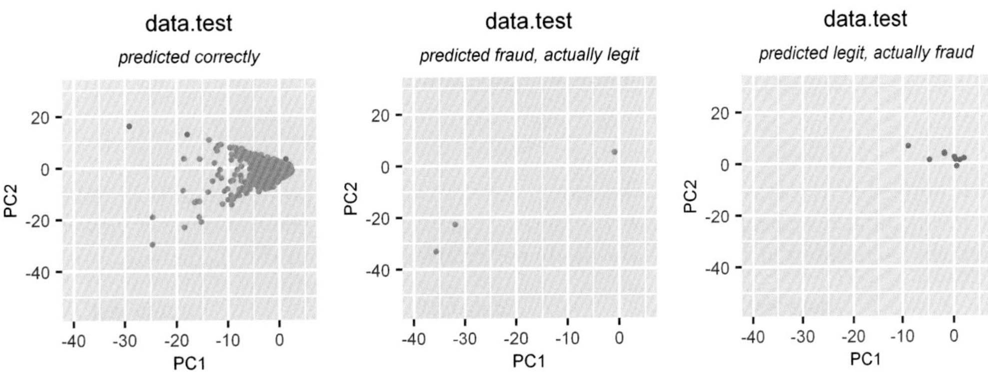

Calculate total cost based on the true positive rate, the false positive rate, the false negative rate, and the business parameters. Total cost is \$260,795.

tpr	fpr	fnr	fraud_fraud	fraud_legit	legit_fraud	cost
0.25	0.0004	0.75	4,500	8,426	247,869	260,795

cost of intervened actually fraudulent transactions	=	$0.25 \times 0.0018 \times 1{,}000{,}000 \times 10$	=	4,500
cost of intervened actually legitimate transactions	=	$0.0004 \times (1 - 0.0018) \times 1{,}000{,}000 \times (10 + 10)$	=	8,426
cost of ignored actually fraudulent transactions	=	$0.75 \times 0.0018 \times 1{,}000{,}000 \times (10 + 10 + 163.60)$	=	247,869

$$\text{cost} = 4{,}500 + 8{,}426 + 247{,}869 = 260{,}795$$

7.3.11 Predict Fraud by Stacking

Try using a k-nearest neighbors stacked model as the decision method. Construct the model to predict *class* given predictions by the decision tree model, naive Bayes model, and neural network model constructed earlier. Set hyper-parameters to normalize the dataset, k=2. Set cutoff to 0.5.

Here is a scatterplot of potential transactions, each color-coded by what the model would predict about it. Note that the interesting shape of the boundary between predicted-legitimate and predicted-fraudulent transactions reflects a blend of the predictions that would be made by the constituent models.

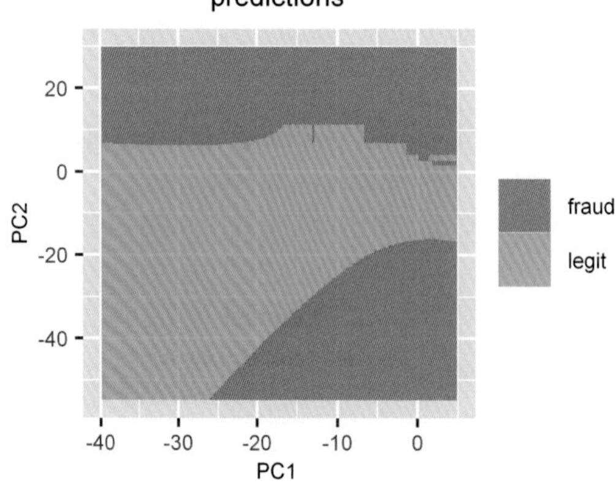

When applied to the test dataset, the model predicts with true positive rate 0.25, false positive rate 0.0003, and false negative rate 0.75. Here are scatterplots of the test dataset viewed through filters that separate out the correctly predicted transactions from the incorrectly predicted:

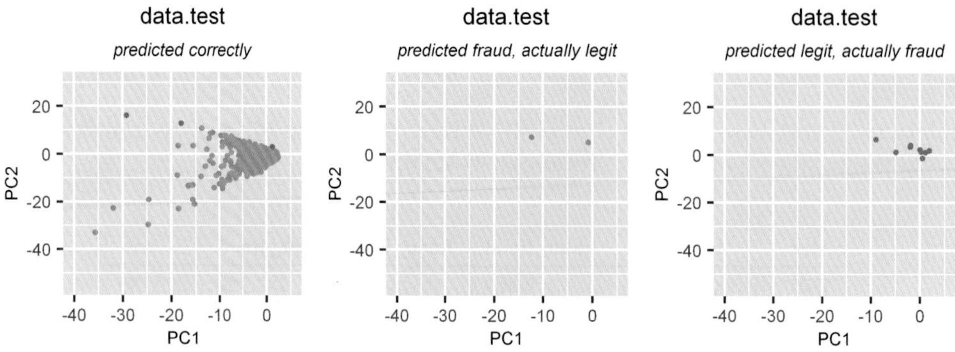

Calculate total cost based on the true positive rate, the false positive rate, the false negative rate, and the business parameters. Total cost is \$257,986.

tpr	fpr	fnr	fraud_fraud	fraud_legit	legit_fraud	cost
0.25	0.0003	0.75	4,500	5,617	247,869	257,986

$$\begin{aligned}
\text{cost of intervened actually fraudulent transactions} &= 0.25 \times 0.0018 \times 1{,}000{,}000 \times 10 &&= 4{,}500 \\
\text{cost of intervened actually legitimate transactions} &= 0.0003 \times (1 - 0.0018) \times 1{,}000{,}000 \times (10 + 10) &&= 5{,}617 \\
\text{cost of ignored actually fraudulent transactions} &= 0.75 \times 0.0018 \times 1{,}000{,}000 \times (10 + 10 + 163.60) &&= 247{,}869
\end{aligned}$$

$$\text{cost} = 4{,}500 + 5{,}617 + 247{,}869 = 257{,}986$$

7.3.12 Comparative Analysis

From our analysis, we can expect that if we don't even try to identify fraudulent transactions, then we'll incur a cost of \$330,492 per every 1,000,000 transactions. If we use a naive Bayes model to try to identify fraudulent transactions, we can expect to do even worse: \$547,279 per every 1,000,000 transactions. However, if we use any of the other models, we can expect to do better. Notably, using a k-nearest neighbors model will incur a cost of only \$153,059 per 1,000,000 transactions. That's the decision method to use.

Note that the logistic regression model and the support vector machine model, which are constructed by very different methods, make the same predictions on the test dataset. Stacking, which often improves predictive performance over its constituent models, doesn't help much in this case. The stacked model makes the same predictions on the test dataset that its constituent decision tree model does. To generalize this notion, when we consider all potential transactions, the various models make very different sets of predictions, as we can see from the variety of predicted-legitimate vs. predicted-fraudulent boundaries. However, when we focus on just the transactions that we're likely to really encounter in our business, as represented by the test dataset, then most of the models produce about the same business result. You can think of the models as neighboring tribes that each embrace a unique belief about how the world works. So long as they remain provincial, living in only a small part of the world, then they don't experience much that's inconsistent with any of their beliefs. One belief explains the world pretty much as well as any other. Only when tribes travel to new lands are their beliefs challenged by new experiences that defy their expectations.

results

method	tpr	fpr	fnr	cost
baseline	0.0000	0.0000	1.0000	330,492
knn	0.6667	0.0015	0.3333	153,059
logistic regression	0.1667	0.0000	0.8333	278,410
decision tree	0.2500	0.0003	0.7500	257,986
naive bayes	0.2500	0.0148	0.7500	547,279
svm	0.1667	0.0000	0.8333	278,410
neural network	0.2500	0.0004	0.7500	260,795
stacked	0.2500	0.0003	0.7500	257,986

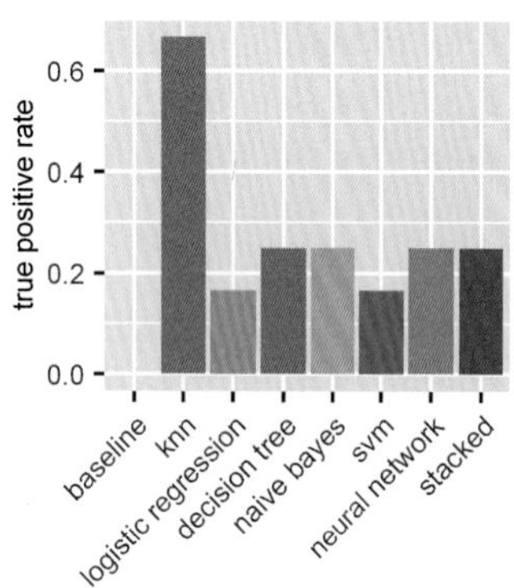

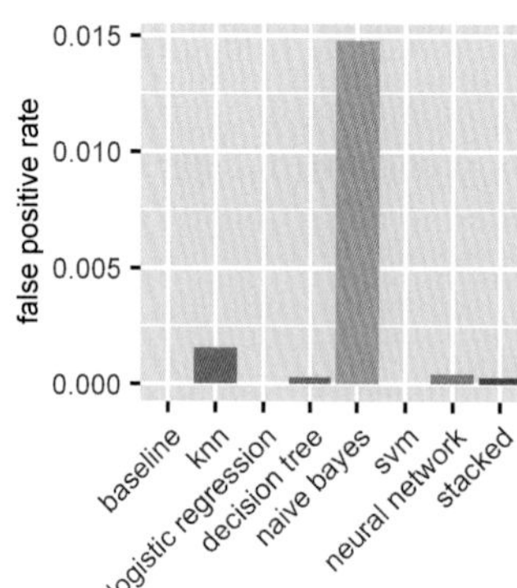

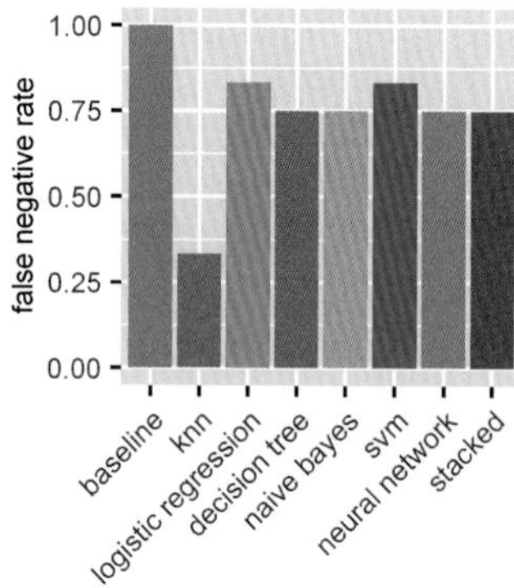

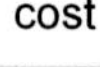

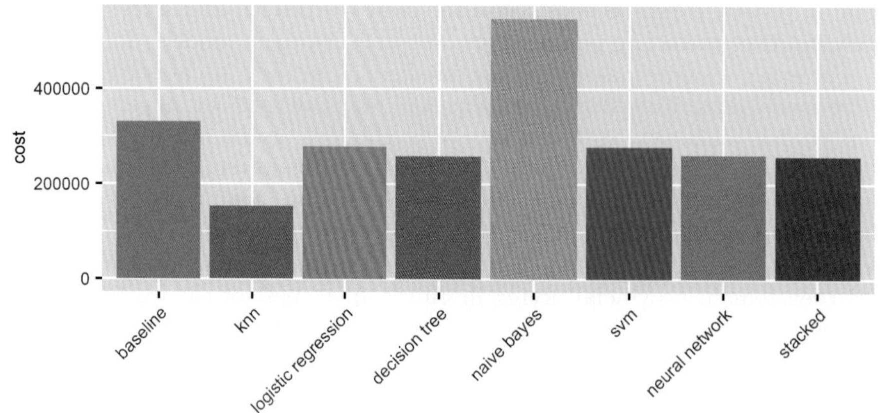

8 | Regression

Learning Objectives

Terms

Know the terms:

- Regression
- Regressor
- Construction
- Prediction
- Evaluation
- Reference known-outcome dataset
- New unknown-outcome dataset
- Predictor variable
- Outcome variable
- Hyper-parameter
- Parameter
- Error table
- Performance metric
- Mean absolute error (MAE)
- Mean square error (MSE)
- Root mean square error (RMSE)
- Mean absolute percent error (MAPE)
- Training data
- Testing data
- In-sample performance
- Out-of-sample performance
- Holdin data
- Holdout data
- Cross-validation performance
- Fold
- Linear regression method
- Linear regression model
- Simple linear regression
- Multiple linear regression
- Best-fit line
- Best-fit plane
- Best-fit hyper-plane
- Dummy-coding
- Index-coding

Effects of Assumptions

Know the effects of assumptions:

- Effect of evaluating a model's performance by in-sample vs. out-of-sample vs. cross-validation

Use the Methods

Know how to use the methods:

- Frame your thinking about regression based on the regression methodology.
- Compute the error table for a model with respect to a test dataset by in-sample evaluation.
- Compute the error table for a model with respect to a test dataset by out-of-sample evaluation.
- Compute the error table for a model with respect to a test dataset by cross-validation evaluation.
- Compute a performance metric value for a model by error table analysis.
- Compute a simple linear regression model.
- Compute a multiple linear regression model.

- Compute a multiple linear model with log outcome, log predictor, polynomial predictor, interaction predictor, and/or categorical predictor preparation.
- Compute a prediction using a linear regression model.
- Calculate a prediction using a linear regression model.
- Compute a k-nearest neighbors model (regression version) and use it to compute predictions.
- Compute a decision tree model (regression version) and use it to compute predictions.
- Compute a support vector machine model (regression version) and use it to compute predictions.
- Compute a neural network model (regression version) and use it to compute predictions.

8.1 Regression Methodology

Construct a regressor, use it to predict, and evaluate its performance.

8.1.1 Introduction

In 1900, sponge divers near the Greek island of Antikythera came upon a Roman shipwreck bestrewn with ancient statues, jewelry, and other treasure, and an odd looking, very encrusted gear mechanism. Retrieved and then studied for decades, it took until 1974 for scientists to unravel the mystery of the mechanism's purpose. It was a computer, designed and built in Egypt around 100 BCE, that could predict the positions of the sun, moon, and planets, and the timings of solar eclipses and Olympic Games events.

Regressor construction methods construct regressors that can make predictions. They do so by identifying patterns in some reference known-outcome data, where known-outcome here means a dataset that includes some ***numerical*** variable with known values that indicate the outcome of each observation. The regressors constructed by these methods then leverage the patterns to predict the outcome of each observation in some new unknown-outcome dataset.

Regressors are useful in a variety of business applications, notably any time it is advantageous to have numerical predictions about the future based on what happened in the past, which is pretty much all the time. For example, you may want to predict how long a project will take based on how long projects took in the past, or predict when a machine part will fail based on what caused machine parts to fail in the past, or predict how much customers will pay for a new product based on what kind of customers paid a premium for products in the past, or predict how much revenue will be lost due to fraudulent credit card transactions based on circumstances around fraudulent credit card transactions in the past. Regressors are also useful for making predictions about the past, present, or future based on the past, present, or future, in general. For example, you may want to predict a city's present demand for electric power from a utility based on past solar and wind power installations, present demand in other cities, and projected future economic conditions.

Let's consider more carefully how we might predict when a machine part will fail. Repairing a part that won't fail soon is an unnecessary expense, repairing a part just before it fails is a modest expense, and repairing an already failed part is a large expense. Operating conditions of parts throughout our factory are continuously monitored by copious sensors, which once per hour report their pressure and temperature measurements to a central computer via wireless internet connection. Technicians report information about failed parts whenever they make repairs, which is sent to the same central computer and aligned with the pressure and temperature data. The combined data are transformed to a representation in which each observation corresponds to a part, the pressures and temperatures of the part over a year, the pressures and temperatures of other parts over a year, and the date on which the part last had to be repaired. A regressor construction method is applied to the data weekly, which finds patterns that identify when parts are likely to fail, and constructs a regressor to predict that. The regressor is applied to new data as the data are updated over the week, predicts when parts are likely to fail, and generates notifications to technicians to preemptively investigate and repair parts likely to fail soon but before they do, avoiding significant expense.

There are several popular regressor construction methods, including linear regression and regression versions of k-nearest neighbors, decision tree, support vector machine, and neural network.

8.1.2 About Regression Methodology

The **regression** methodology and classification methodology are similar to each other, but not quite the same. To make clear what's the same and what's different, the discourse here on regression methodology parallels the discourse presented earlier on classification methodology. The same wording is used in places to describe aspects of the methodologies common to both, while different wording is used in places to draw attention to where the methodologies differ.

The regression methodology comprises three parts:

- **Construction** of a regressor, using some regressor construction method and some **reference known-outcome dataset**
- **Prediction** of outcome variable values, using the regressor applied to some new **unknown-outcome dataset**
- **Evaluation** of regressor performance, which estimates the quality of a regressor's predictions

8.1.2.1 Construction

In construction, a **regressor** construction method takes as input some reference known-outcome data and hyper-parameter settings. The job of the regressor construction method is to detect patterns in the reference known-outcome data that imply observation outcomes, and output a regressor with knowledge of those patterns built into it. The resulting regressor is defined by its form and parameter settings, both determined by the regressor construction method. Note that we have here a method constructing a method. The constructed regressor is not a set of predictions, but rather is a method to make predictions.

Hyper-parameters are provided by a regressor construction method as a way to configure its specific behavior. Each particular regressor construction method provides its own set of hyper-parameters. You can think of hyper-parameters as switches and dials to set the operating conditions of a regressor construction machine. Hyper-parameters allow for several variations of any particular regressor model construction method, effectively expanding the set of methods available for regressor construction.

Parameters, in contrast to hyper-parameters, are components of a regressor, set by a regressor construction method. You can think of parameters as switches and dials to set the operating conditions of a regressor machine.

Construction is also known as supervised learning, supervised machine learning, training, modeling, model building, model fitting, or predictive data analytics.

Here we see a reference known-outcome dataset with 5 observations and 9 variables. There are 8 variables treated as **predictor variables** and 1 numerical variable treated as the **outcome variable**. The regressor construction method is configured to specific behavior by you setting the hyper-parameters. The method outputs a regressor that will accept a new unknown-outcome dataset with 8 predictor variables as input and predict outcomes as output.

Construct a Regressor

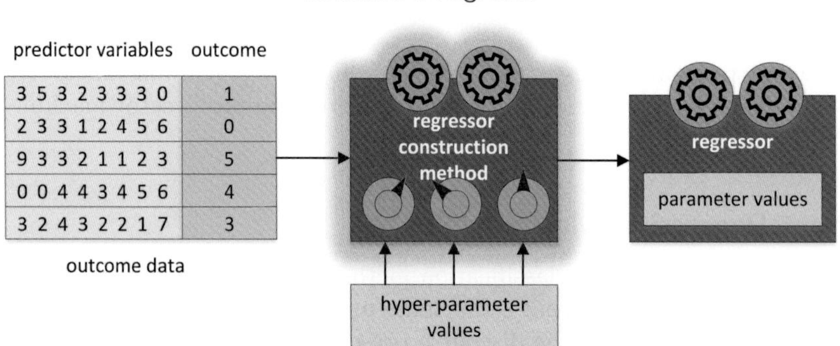

8.1.2.2 Prediction

In prediction, a regressor takes as input some new unknown-outcome dataset. The job of the regressor is then to use its built-in knowledge of patterns in a reference known-outcome dataset to predict the outcomes of observations in the new unknown-outcome dataset. Each observation in the new unknown-outcome dataset gets its own predicted outcome value. Note that we have here a method constructed by a method – the regressor is the output of a regressor construction method, and the regressor is itself a method to make predictions.

Prediction, in this context, is also known as regression.

Here we see a new unknown-outcome dataset with five observations and eight predictor variables. The regressor accepts the dataset as input and outputs predicted outcomes. The regressor predicts that the first observation's outcome should be 1.5. Similarly for the other observations.

Use a Regressor to Make Predictions

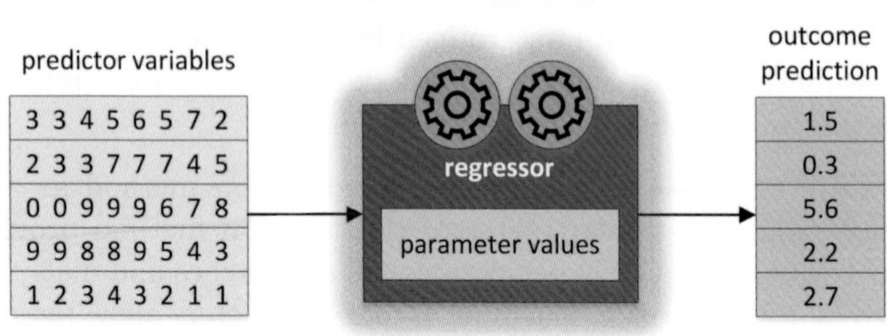

8.1.2.3 Evaluation

In evaluation, we usually estimate the quality a regressor's predictions by examining not the regressor directly, but rather by examining 1 or more other similar regressors. We'll call the regressor we're evaluating the prime regressor and call the other similar regressors the evaluation regressors. The evaluation regressors are constructed using the same regressor construction method and hyper-parameter settings as for the prime regressor, but using only subsets of the reference known-outcome dataset as inputs. Because the evaluation regressors are constructed in almost the same way as the prime regressor, we make the assumption that their performance will be similar to that of the prime regressor. We can then take estimates of the evaluation regressors' performance as an estimate of the prime regressor's performance. The reason that we usually do not examine a prime regressor directly, but rather examine evaluation regressors, is so that we can leverage reference known-outcome data in various useful ways.

Note that evaluation regressors are required only for estimating the prime regressor's performance. We can discard the evaluation regressors after the prime regressor's performance has been estimated. Their job will have been done.

Evaluation is also known as validation or testing.

Here we see a regressor being evaluated. The reference known-outcome dataset used to construct the prime regressor is provided to a process that partitions the dataset into subsets as necessary. The dataset subsets are input to a regressor construction method that constructs evaluation regressors. Performance metric values are calculated for the evaluation regressors based on how well they back-predict. A single performance metric value for the prime regressor, here RMSE 1.36, is derived from the collection of performance metric values across the evaluation regressors.

Evaluate a Regressor

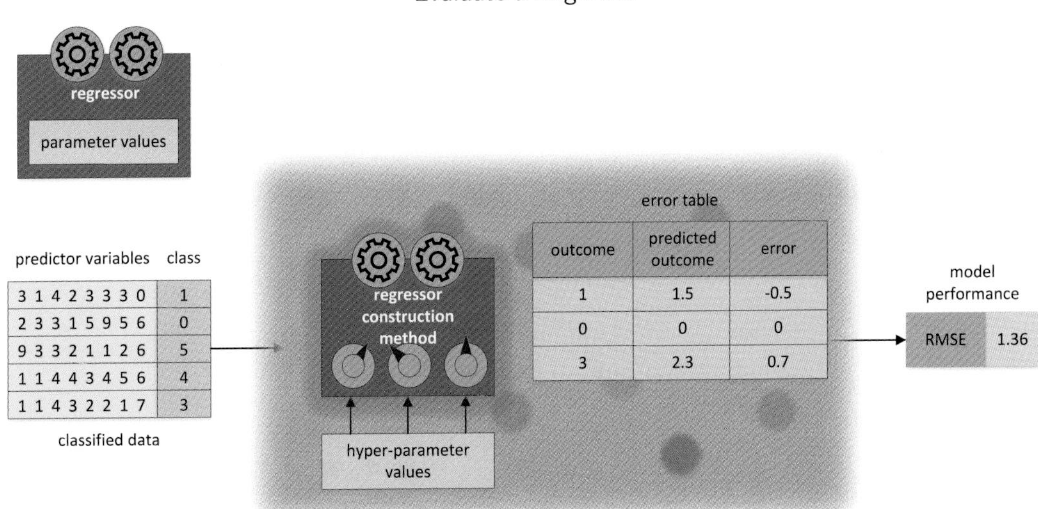

8.1.3 Construction

Construction involves applying a regressor construction method to a reference known-outcome dataset to calculate regressor parameter values.

Consider this reference known-outcome dataset. Note that the outcome variable is numerical and indicates each observation's known outcome.

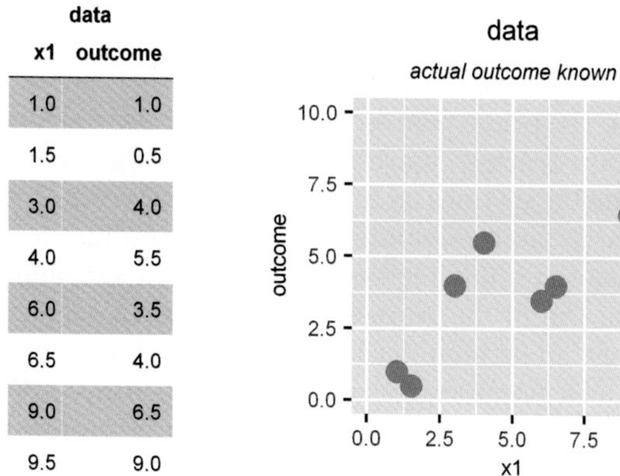

data

x1	outcome
1.0	1.0
1.5	0.5
3.0	4.0
4.0	5.5
6.0	3.5
6.5	4.0
9.0	6.5
9.5	9.0

Use a regressor construction method to construct a regressor. Here we use the "My Special Method" method, with its hyper-parameter set to 0.0, applied to the reference known-outcome dataset. The resulting regressor has a form that is not completely transparent to us, but we do see that it is defined by parameter settings 0.45 and 0.75, and will accept new unknown-outcome datasets with 1 predictor variable x_1 as input. Note that the hyper-parameter setting is not present in the classifier, though it is reflected in how the parameter settings were determined.

model

method	vars	parameter_1	parameter_2
My Special Method	x1	0.4471	0.7512

8.1.4 Prediction

Prediction involves applying a regressor to a new unknown-outcome observation or dataset to predict outcome values.

Consider this new unknown-outcome dataset:

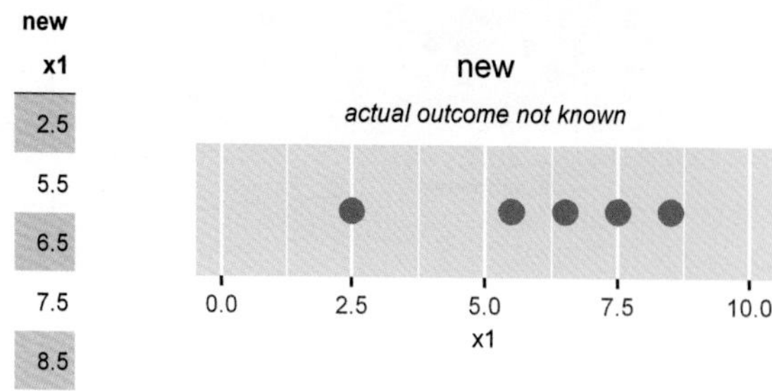

new

x1
2.5
5.5
6.5
7.5
8.5

Use the regressor applied to the new unknown-outcome dataset to predict outcomes:

	new
x1	outcome.predicted
2.5	2.325
5.5	4.579
6.5	5.330
7.5	6.081
8.5	6.832

Here is the reference known-outcome dataset compared with the new unknown-outcome dataset as the regressor would have predicted outcomes:

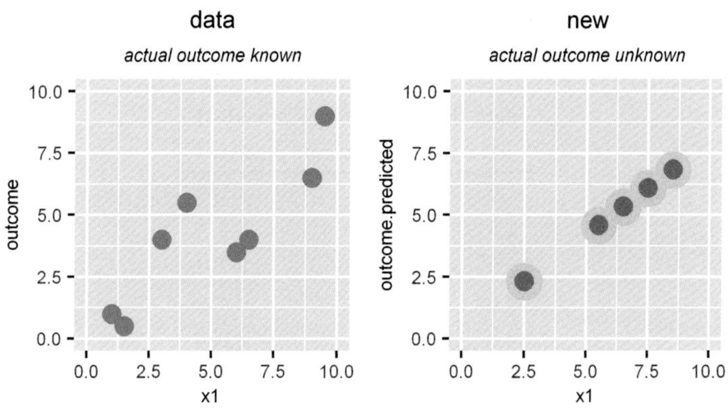

8.1.5 Evaluation

Evaluation involves back-predicting a known-outcome dataset and comparing predicted outcome values with known outcome values.

8.1.5.1 Back-Prediction

We can know how close to correct a regressor predicts only when we can compare predicted outcome values with known outcome values. Back-prediction involves using a regressor to predict outcome values of observations whose outcome values are already known, but in a way that the known outcome values are hidden from the regressor. Then the regressor's predicted outcome values can be compared with the known outcome values. Back-prediction can be applied to the reference known-outcome dataset that was used to construct the regressor, or to a subset of that dataset, or to a completely different dataset.

Here we apply back-prediction to the reference known-outcome dataset with the outcome values hidden:

data	
x1	outcome
1.0	1.0
1.5	0.5
3.0	4.0
4.0	5.5
6.0	3.5
6.5	4.0
9.0	6.5
9.5	9.0

data (known outcome is hidden)
x1
1.0
1.5
3.0
4.0
6.0
6.5
9.0
9.5

Use the regressor (previously constructed) to predict outcome values. The predicted outcome values might be different from the known outcome values.

data (known outcome is hidden)	
x1	outcome.predicted
1.0	1.198
1.5	1.574
3.0	2.701
4.0	3.452
6.0	4.954
6.5	5.330
9.0	7.208
9.5	7.583

8.1.5.2 Comparison

Compare the predicted outcome values to the known-outcome values. Mark each observation with the prediction error, which is the difference between the known outcome value and the predicted outcome value.

data	
x1	outcome
1.0	1.0
1.5	0.5
3.0	4.0
4.0	5.5
6.0	3.5
6.5	4.0
9.0	6.5
9.5	9.0

data (known outcome is hidden)		
x1	outcome.predicted	error
1.0	1.198	-0.1983
1.5	1.574	-1.0739
3.0	2.701	1.2993
4.0	3.452	2.0481
6.0	4.954	-1.4542
6.5	5.330	-1.3298
9.0	7.208	-0.7078
9.5	7.583	1.4166

Here is a visualization of the dataset showing the prediction errors for specific observations:

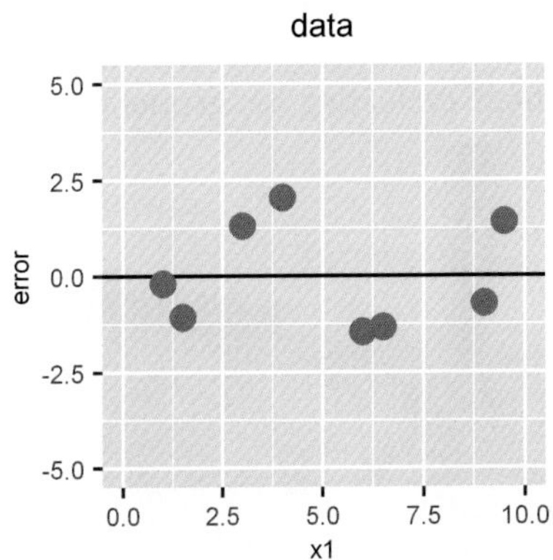

Calculate some performance metric based on the prediction errors. Here we calculate the proportion of prediction errors within 2 of the mean error. This is our estimate of the quality of our regressor's predictions.

proportion.of.prediction.errors.within.2.of.mean
0.875

8.2 Regressor Evaluation

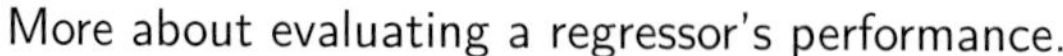
More about evaluating a regressor's performance.

8.2.1 Introduction

When a regressor construction method produces a regressor, that regressor might or might not make good predictions. If we think that it will make good predictions, then perhaps we should use it to inform our business decisions. If we think that it won't, then perhaps we should discard it as useless. We don't know in advance how good the predictions will be, but we can estimate that. Let's look further into estimating how good a classifier's predictions will be.

8.2.2 Error Table

Consider this reference known-outcome dataset. Note that the outcome variable is numerical and indicates each observation's known outcome.

data

x1	outcome
1.0	1.0
1.5	0.5
3.0	4.0
4.0	5.5
6.0	3.5
6.5	4.0
9.0	6.5
9.5	9.0

An **error table** summarizes how close to correct a regressor back-predicts outcome values, and provides a convenient way to calculate performance metrics.

Here we see an error table for a previously constructed regressor applied to back-predict the reference known-outcome dataset:

error_table

outcome	outcome.predicted	error
1.0	1.198	-0.1983
0.5	1.574	-1.0739
4.0	2.701	1.2993
5.5	3.452	2.0481
3.5	4.954	-1.4542
4.0	5.330	-1.3298
6.5	7.208	-0.7078
9.0	7.583	1.4166

Interpretation of the error table:

- The first observation's predicted outcome is 0.20 higher than its known outcome.
- The second observation's predicted outcome is 1.07 higher than its known outcome.
- The third observation's predicted outcome is 1.30 lower than its known outcome.
- Similarly for the other observations.

8.2.3 Performance Metrics

From an error table, we can calculate any of several useful regressor **performance metrics**.

Essential regressor performance metrics:

- **mean absolute error (MAE):** $mean\left(|\text{error}_1|, |\text{error}_2|, |\text{error}_3|, \dots\right)$
- **mean square error (MSE):** $mean\left(\text{error}_1{}^2, \text{error}_2{}^2, \text{error}_3{}^2, \dots\right)$
- **root mean square error (RMSE):** $\sqrt{mean\left(\text{error}_1{}^2, \text{error}_2{}^2, \text{error}_3{}^2, \dots\right)}$
- **mean absolute percent error (MAPE):**

$$100 \times mean\left(\left|\frac{\text{error}_1}{\text{known value}_1}\right|, \left|\frac{\text{error}_2}{\text{known value}_2}\right|, \left|\frac{\text{error}_3}{\text{known value}_3}\right|, \dots\right)$$

Here we see an error table and the corresponding essential performance metric values:

error_table

outcome	outcome.predicted	error
1.0	1.198	-0.1983
0.5	1.574	-1.0739
4.0	2.701	1.2993
5.5	3.452	2.0481
3.5	4.954	-1.4542
4.0	5.330	-1.3298
6.5	7.208	-0.7078
9.0	7.583	1.4166

mae	mse	rmse	mape
1.191	1.683	1.297	50.72

Considerations about performance metrics:

- MSE has the disadvantage that it is not on the same scale as the outcomes.
- RMSE has the advantage that it is on the same scale as the outcomes. It has the disadvantage that its interpretation requires knowledge of the scale of the outcomes.
- MAPE has the advantage that its interpretation does not require knowledge of the scale of the outcomes. It has the disadvantage that it can be nonsensical at small outcomes and is not defined at all at outcome 0.

8.2.4 Evaluation by In-Sample Performance

Evaluation by **in-sample performance** is 1 of 3 popular versions of evaluation. It uses all of the reference known-outcome dataset, referred to in this context as **training data**, to construct 1 evaluation regressor. It uses all of the same reference known-outcome dataset, referred to in this context as **testing data**, to predict and compare outcome values.

Here we see evaluation by in-sample performance of a regressor.

Use the "My Special Method" method applied to the 8-observation reference known-outcome dataset to construct the prime regressor.

data

x1	outcome
1.0	1.0
1.5	0.5
3.0	4.0
4.0	5.5
6.0	3.5
6.5	4.0
9.0	6.5
9.5	9.0

model.prime

method	vars	parameter_1	parameter_2
My Special Method	x1	0.4471	0.7512

Use the same "My Special Method" method applied to the reference known-outcome dataset to construct an evaluation regressor, which in this case is exactly the same as the prime regressor.

data.train

x1	outcome
1.0	1.0
1.5	0.5
3.0	4.0
4.0	5.5
6.0	3.5
6.5	4.0
9.0	6.5
9.5	9.0

model.evaluation

method	vars	parameter_1	parameter_2
My Special Method	x1	0.4471	0.7512

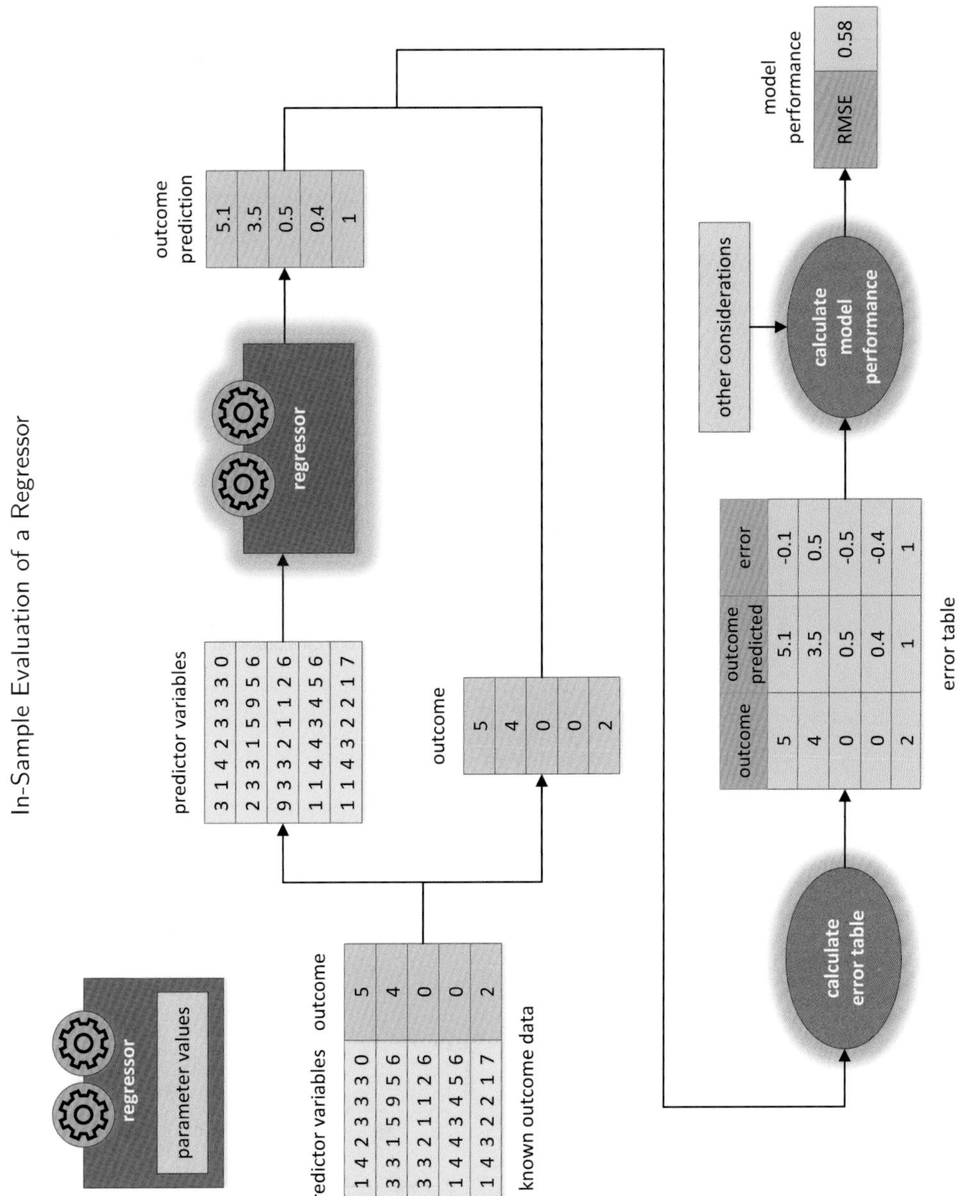
In-Sample Evaluation of a Regressor
regressor
parameter values
predictor variables
outcome
3 1 4 2 3 3 3 0
2 3 3 1 5 9 5 6
9 3 3 2 1 1 2 6
1 1 4 4 3 4 5 6
1 1 4 3 2 2 1 7
5
4
0
0
2
known outcome data
predictor variables
outcome
regressor
outcome prediction
5.1
3.5
0.5
0.4
1
calculate error table
outcome
outcome predicted
error
5 5.1 -0.1
4 3.5 0.5
0 0.5 -0.5
0 0.4 -0.4
2 1 1
error table
other considerations
calculate model performance
model performance
RMSE
0.58

Input the same reference dataset with the outcome variable hidden to the evaluation regressor to predict outcomes. Construct an error table and use it to compute a performance metric, in this example RMSE 1.30, which is an estimate of the prime regressor's performance.

data.test		data.test (known outcome is hidden)		error table			
x1	**outcome**	**x1**	**outcome.predicted**	**outcome**	**outcome.predicted**	**error**	**RMSE**
1.0	1.0	1.0	1.198	1.0	1.198	-0.1983	1.297
1.5	0.5	1.5	1.574	0.5	1.574	-1.0739	
3.0	4.0	3.0	2.701	4.0	2.701	1.2993	
4.0	5.5	4.0	3.452	5.5	3.452	2.0481	
6.0	3.5	6.0	4.954	3.5	4.954	-1.4542	
6.5	4.0	6.5	5.330	4.0	5.330	-1.3298	
9.0	6.5	9.0	7.208	6.5	7.208	-0.7078	
9.5	9.0	9.5	7.583	9.0	7.583	1.4166	

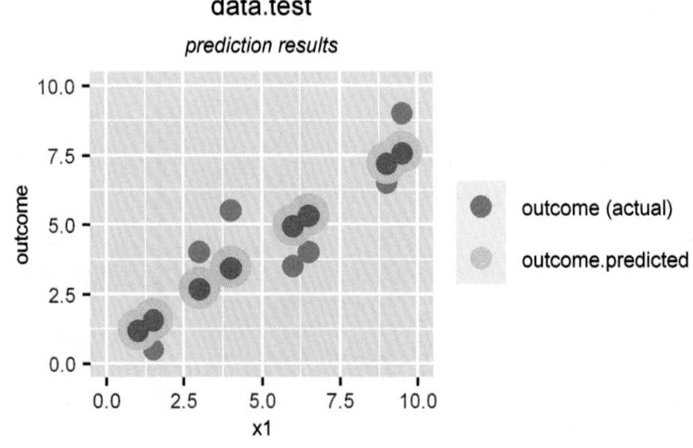

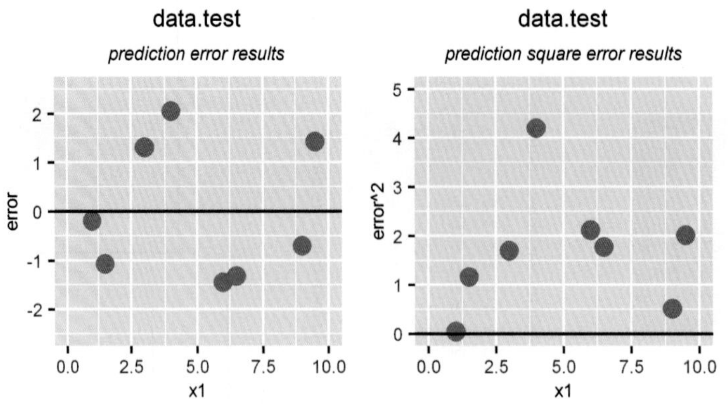

8.2.5 Evaluation by Out-of-Sample Performance

Evaluation by **out-of-sample performance** is another 1 of 3 popular versions of evaluation. It uses some of the reference known-outcome dataset, referred to in this context as **holdin data**, to construct an evaluation regressor. It uses the rest of the reference known-outcome dataset, referred to in this context as **holdout data**, to predict and compare outcome values.

Out-of-sample performance is also known as holdout performance.

Here we see evaluation by out-of-sample performance of a classifier.

Use the "My Special Method" applied to the 8-observation reference known-outcome dataset to construct the prime regressor.

data

x1	outcome
1.0	1.0
1.5	0.5
3.0	4.0
4.0	5.5
6.0	3.5
6.5	4.0
9.0	6.5
9.5	9.0

model.prime

method	vars	parameter_1	parameter_2
My Special Method	x1	0.4471	0.7512

Partition the reference known-observation dataset into a holdin part for training and a holdout part for testing. Here we choose to tag 30% of the dataset's observations, sampled at random, as holdout: observations 3 and 6. We tag the remaining 70% of the dataset as holdin: observations 1, 2, 4, 5, 7, and 8.

holdout
6
3

data.test

x1	outcome
6.5	4
3.0	4

holdin
1
2
4
5
7
8

data.train

x1	outcome
1.0	1.0
1.5	0.5
4.0	5.5
6.0	3.5
9.0	6.5
9.5	9.0

Input the 6-observation holdin dataset to the "My Special Method" method to construct an evaluation regressor, which will be different from the prime regressor.

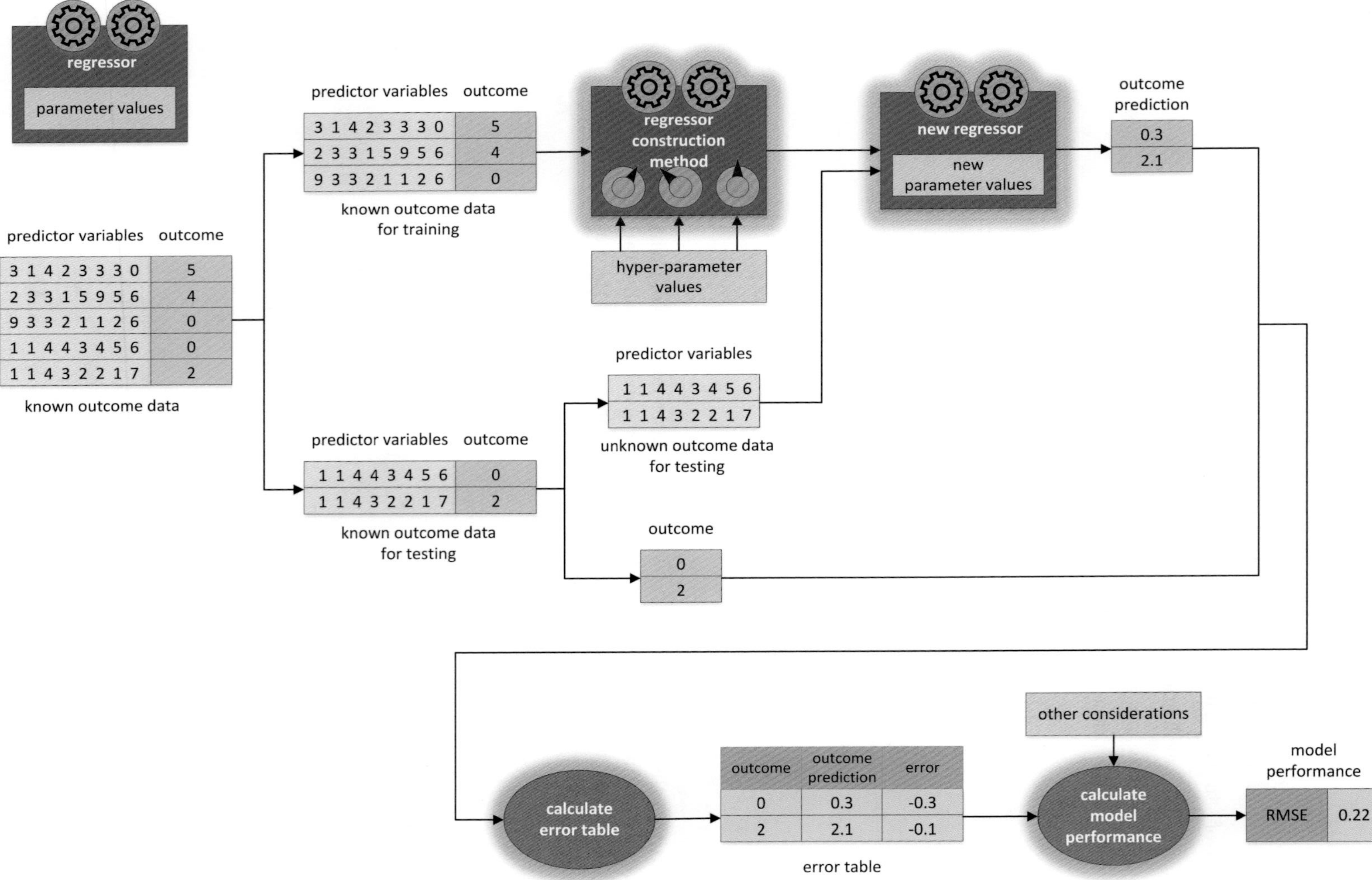
Out-of-Sample Evaluation of a Regressor
regressor
parameter values
predictor variables
outcome
3 1 4 2 3 3 3 0
5
2 3 3 1 5 9 5 6
4
9 3 3 2 1 1 2 6
0
1 1 4 4 3 4 5 6
0
1 1 4 3 2 2 1 7
2
known outcome data
known outcome data for training
known outcome data for testing
regressor construction method
hyper-parameter values
new regressor
new parameter values
unknown outcome data for testing
outcome prediction
0.3
2.1
calculate error table
outcome prediction
error
-0.3
-0.1
error table
other considerations
calculate model performance
model performance
RMSE
0.22

data.train

x1	outcome
1.0	1.0
1.5	0.5
4.0	5.5
6.0	3.5
9.0	6.5
9.5	9.0

model.evaluation

method	vars	parameter_1	parameter_2
My Special Method	x1	0.0948	0.8204

Input the 2-observation holdout dataset to the evaluation regressor to predict outcomes, and in turn compare them with the known outcomes. From there, construct an error table and use it to compute a performance metric, in this example RMSE 1.44, which is an estimate of the prime regressor's performance. At this point, we can discard the evaluation regressor.

data.test

x1	outcome
6.5	4
3.0	4

data.test (unknown outcome)

x1	outcome.predicted	error	square_error
6.5	5.427	-1.427	2.037
3.0	2.556	1.444	2.085

RMSE
1.436

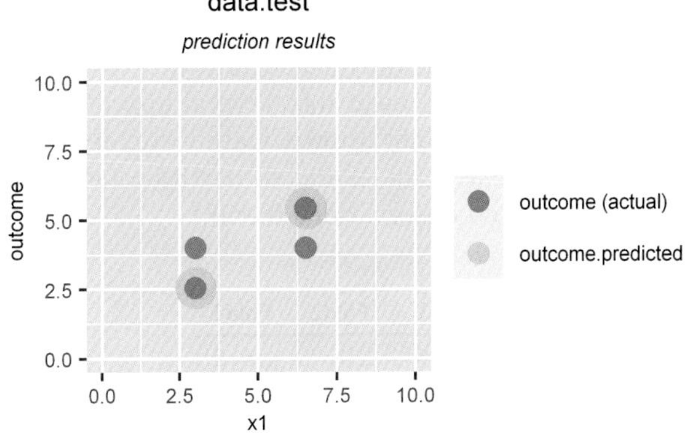

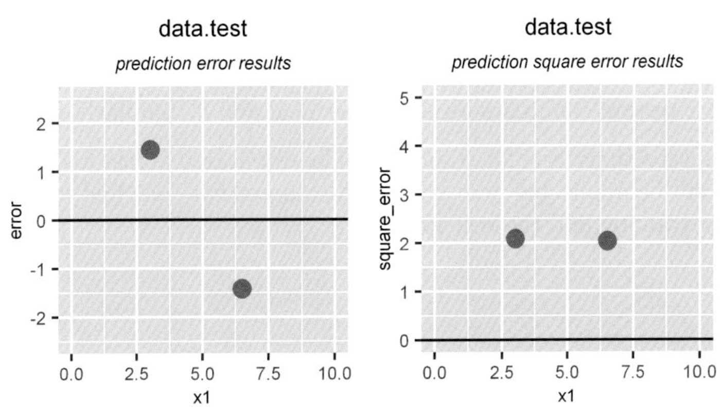

8.2.6 Evaluation by Cross-Validation Performance

Evaluation by **cross-validation performance** is yet another 1 of 3 popular versions of evaluation. It works by organizing a reference known-outcome dataset into several approximately equally sized **folds**, where each fold comprises a subset of the dataset for training and the rest of the dataset for testing. It uses all of the reference known-outcome dataset, but only 1 subset at a time, to construct several evaluation regressors. It uses all of the reference known-outcome dataset, but only 1 subset at a time, to predict and compare outcomes.

Here we see evaluation by cross-validation performance of a regressor.

Use the "My Special Method" applied to the 8-observation reference known-outcome dataset to construct the prime regressor.

data

x1	outcome
1.0	1.0
1.5	0.5
3.0	4.0
4.0	5.5
6.0	3.5
6.5	4.0
9.0	6.5
9.5	9.0

model.prime

method	vars	parameter_1	parameter_2
My Special Method	x1	0.4471	0.7512

Organize the reference known-outcome dataset into several approximately equally sized folds. Do this by first partitioning the dataset into approximately equally-sized subsets, sampling at random. Here we choose to organize as 3 folds, and so partition into 3 subsets: observations 1, 3, and 5; observations 2, 4, and 7; and observations 6 and 8.

Fold1	Fold2	Fold3
1, 3, 5	2, 4, 7	6, 8

For each fold, assign the reference known-outcome dataset subset to be its testing dataset. Then for each fold, assign the part of the reference dataset not used for testing in that fold to be its training dataset. Here the first fold comprises a 5-observation dataset for training and a 3-observation dataset for testing. The dataset for training comprises observations 2, 4, 6, 7, and 8. The dataset for testing comprises observations 1, 3, and 5. Similarly for folds 2 and 3.

Note that some observations used for training will be duplicated across folds, but no observations used for testing will be duplicated across folds. Also note that each fold uses all of the reference dataset, some for training and the rest for testing.

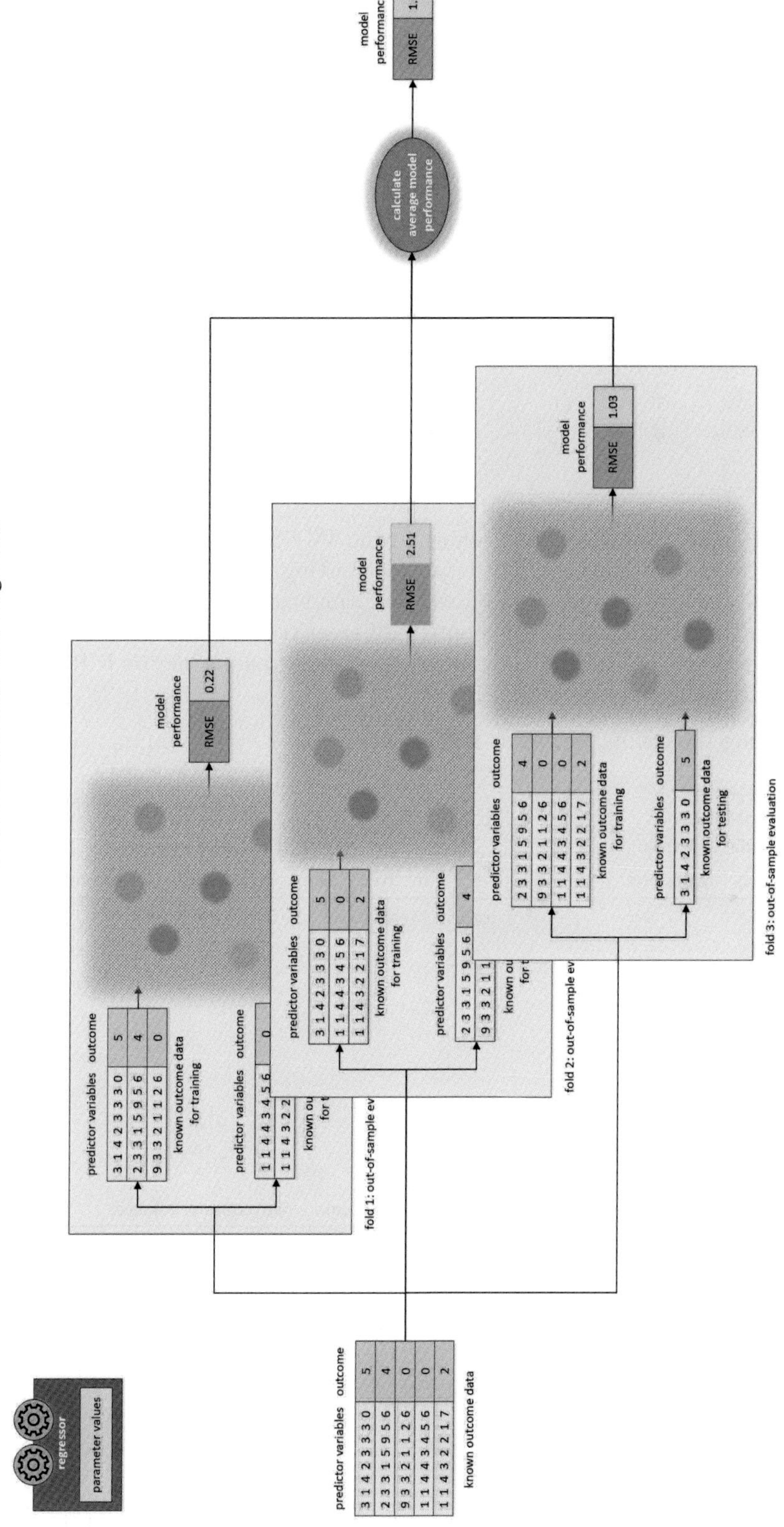
Cross-Validation Evaluation of a Regressor
regressor
parameter values
predictor variables outcome
3 1 4 2 3 3 3 0 5
2 3 3 1 5 9 5 6 4
9 3 3 2 1 1 2 6 0
1 1 4 4 3 4 5 6 0
1 1 4 3 2 2 1 7 2
known outcome data
known outcome data for training
known outcome data for testing
fold 1: out-of-sample evaluation
fold 2: out-of-sample evaluation
fold 3: out-of-sample evaluation
model performance
RMSE 0.22
RMSE 2.51
RMSE 1.03
calculate average model performance
RMSE 1.25

data_1.train

x1	outcome
1.5	0.5
4.0	5.5
6.5	4.0
9.0	6.5
9.5	9.0

data_2.train

x1	outcome
1.0	1.0
3.0	4.0
6.0	3.5
6.5	4.0
9.5	9.0

data_3.train

x1	outcome
1.0	1.0
1.5	0.5
3.0	4.0
4.0	5.5
6.0	3.5
9.0	6.5

data_1.test

x1	outcome
1	1.0
3	4.0
6	3.5

data_2.test

x1	outcome
1.5	0.5
4.0	5.5
9.0	6.5

data_3.test

x1	outcome
6.5	4
9.5	9

For each fold, input its dataset for training to the "My Special Method" method to construct an evaluation regressor, and input its dataset for testing to that regressor to predict outcomes, construct an error table, and compute a performance metric. Note that we construct 3 different evaluation regressors and compute 3 different performance metrics. Here the first fold performance metric is RMSE 1.20, the second fold performance metric is RMSE 1.41, and the third fold performance metric is RMSE 1.58.

Fold 1: Here are the results for fold 1. Note that the fold 1 evaluation regressor's performance is RMSE 1.20.

data_1.train

x1	outcome
1.5	0.5
4.0	5.5
6.5	4.0
9.0	6.5
9.5	9.0

model_1.evaluation

method	vars	parameter_1	parameter_2
My Special Method	x1	0.1346	0.814

data_1.test

x1	outcome
1	1.0
3	4.0
6	3.5

data_1.test (known outcome is hidden)

x1	outcome.predicted
1	0.9486
3	2.5766
6	5.0186

error_table_1

outcome	outcome.predicted	error
1.0	0.9486	0.0514
4.0	2.5766	1.4234
3.5	5.0186	-1.5186

RMSE_1
1.202

Fold 2: Here are the results for fold 2. Note that the fold 2 evaluation regressor's performance is RMSE 1.41.

data_2.train

x1	outcome
1.0	1.0
3.0	4.0
6.0	3.5
6.5	4.0
9.5	9.0

model_2.evaluation

method	vars	parameter_1	parameter_2
My Special Method	x1	0.2529	0.7783

data_2.test

x1	outcome
1.5	0.5
4.0	5.5
9.0	6.5

data_2.test (known outcome is hidden)

x1	outcome.predicted
1.5	1.420
4.0	3.366
9.0	7.258

error_table_2

outcome	outcome.predicted	error
0.5	1.420	-0.9203
5.5	3.366	2.1339
6.5	7.258	-0.7575

RMSE_2
1.411

Fold 3: Here are the results for fold 3. Note that the fold 3 evaluation regressor's performance is RMSE 1.58.

data_3.train

x1	outcome
1.0	1.0
1.5	0.5
3.0	4.0
4.0	5.5
6.0	3.5
9.0	6.5

model_3.evaluation

method	vars	parameter_1	parameter_2
My Special Method	x1	0.8355	0.6525

data_3.test

x1	outcome
6.5	4
9.5	9

data_3.test (known outcome is hidden)

x1	outcome.predicted
6.5	5.077
9.5	7.035

error_table_3

outcome	outcome.predicted	error
4	5.077	-1.077
9	7.035	1.965

RMSE_3
1.585

Here is a comparison of the prediction results across the 3 folds:

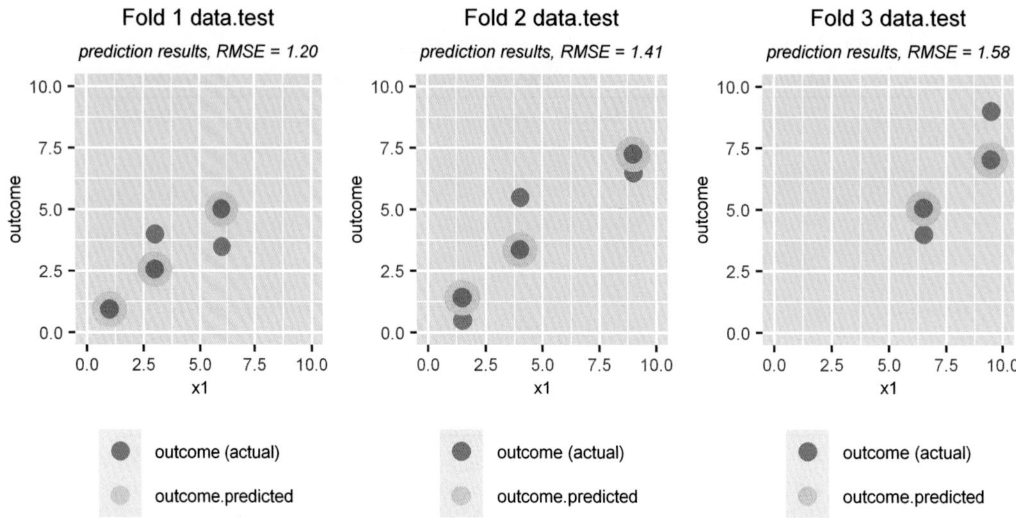

Compute the average of the 3 performance metrics, in this example RMSE 1.40, which is an estimate of the prime regressor's performance. At this point, we can discard all 3 of the evaluation regressors.

fold	RMSE
1	1.202
2	1.411
3	1.585

RMSE.cv
1.399

8.3 Linear Regression

Construct a regressor by the linear regression method.

8.3.1 Introduction

Spring is in the air, the flowers in are bloom, and the bees are hard at work collecting pollen. Much research has gone into uncovering how they find their way back to the hive. They don't all follow precisely the same path, but they roughly do. At times, the path is nearly a straight line. At other times, it takes on other familiar shapes. You can think of the linear regression method as searching for the path that the bees will take. When you discover the path, you can predict where the bees will be.

8.3.2 About Linear Regression

Linear regression is a method to construct a regressor. Various versions of linear regression all use optimization techniques to find the best-fit line, plane, or hyper-plane through a set of reference observations.

Simple linear regression constructs a predictive model that takes ***1*** numerical predictor as input and produces ***1*** numerical outcome as output. The form of the model is an equation for a ***line***, or more specifically, the intercept and coefficient that define a line.

The method relies on having some optimization technique to search for the unique **best-fit line**, where we specify best-fit as the one that minimizes the sum of squared errors between the reference observations and the line. For any set of observations, there are many lines that minimize the sum of errors, there are many lines that minimize the sum of absolute errors, but there is exactly 1 line that minimizes the sum of squared errors.

Note that error is not necessarily the shortest distance from an observation to a line, but rather the distance along a vertical path.

Consider these examples of lines passing through a set of 4 observations. In both example 1 and example 2, the errors between observations and the line sum to 0. In example 1, the squared errors sum to 9. In example 2, the squared errors sum to 10.44. It turns out that there is no line that does better than sum of squared errors 9, so the example 1 line is the best-fit line.

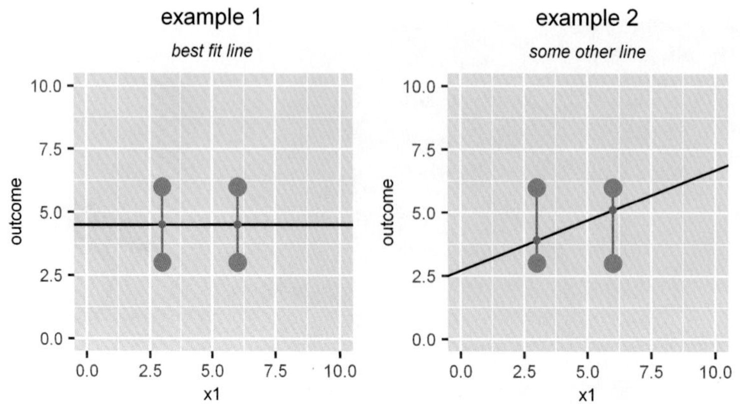

data

x1	outcome
3	6
3	3
6	6
6	3

example 1 errors

error	abs_error	squared_error
1.5	1.5	2.25
-1.5	1.5	2.25
1.5	1.5	2.25
-1.5	1.5	2.25

example 2 errors

error	abs_error	squared_error
2.1	2.1	4.41
-0.9	0.9	0.81
0.9	0.9	0.81
-2.1	2.1	4.41

example 1 error sums

sum_error	sum_abs_error	sum_squared_error
0	6	9

example 2 error sums

sum_error	sum_abs_error	sum_squared_error
0	6	10.44

Multiple linear regression constructs a predictive model that takes ***many*** numerical predictors as input and produces ***1*** numerical outcome as output. The form of the model is an equation for a ***plane*** if 2 predictors, or an equation for a ***hyper-plane*** if 3 or more predictors, or more specifically, the intercept and the coefficients that define that plane or hyper-plane.

Similar to simple linear regression, the method relies on having an optimization technique to search for the unique **best-fit plane** or **best-fit hyper-plane**, where we specify best-fit as the one that minimizes the sum of squared errors between the reference observations and the plane or hyper-plane. Note that a hyper-plane and errors between observations and a hyper-plane might be difficult (and not useful) to visualize, but they are straightforward to compute.

Consider these examples of planes passing through a set of 8 observations. In example 1, the squared errors sum to 18. In example 2, the squared errors sum to 19.41. It turns out that there is no plane that does better than sum of squared errors 18, so the example 1 plane is the best-fit plane.

example 1: best-fit plane

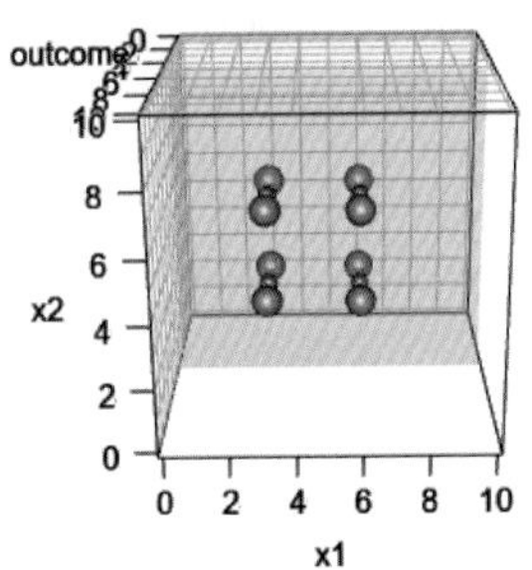

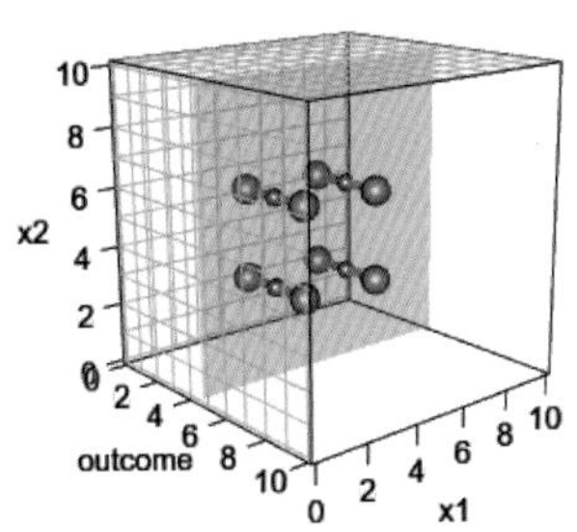

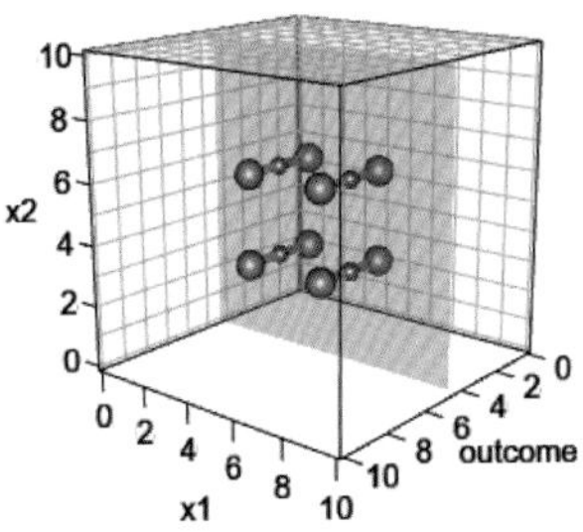

example 2: some other plane

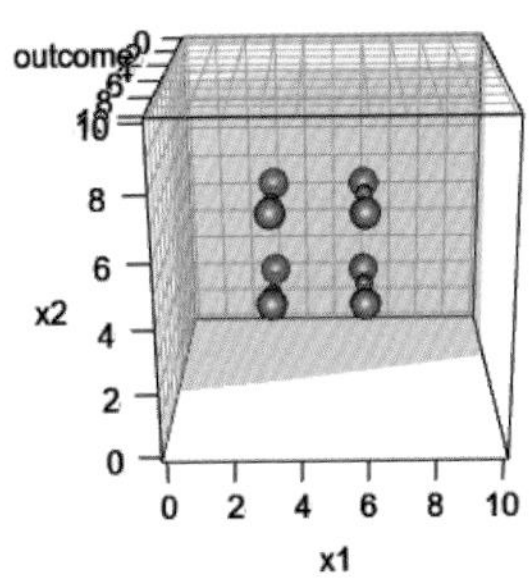

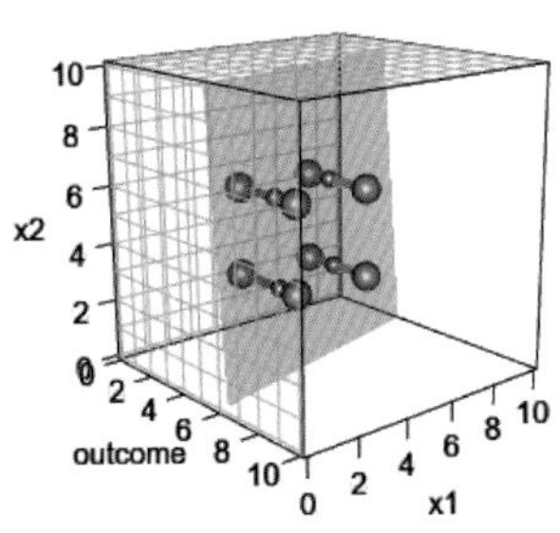

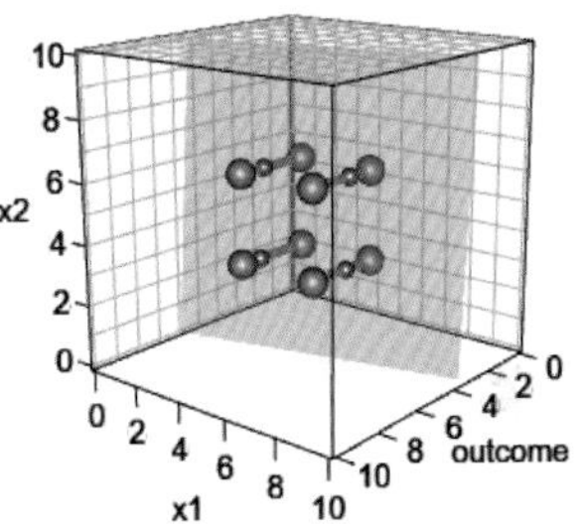

data

x1	x2	outcome
3	3	6
3	3	3
6	3	6
6	3	3
3	6	6
3	6	3
6	6	6
6	6	3

example 1 errors

error	abs_error	squared_error
1.5	1.5	2.25
-1.5	1.5	2.25
1.5	1.5	2.25
-1.5	1.5	2.25
1.5	1.5	2.25
-1.5	1.5	2.25
1.5	1.5	2.25
-1.5	1.5	2.25

example 2 errors

error	abs_error	squared_error
0.8957	0.8957	0.8023
-2.1043	2.1043	4.4279
1.6777	1.6777	2.8148
-1.3223	1.3223	1.7484
1.1090	1.1090	1.2299
-1.8910	1.8910	3.5759
1.8910	1.8910	3.5759
-1.1090	1.1090	1.2299

example 1 error sums

sum_error	sum_abs_error	sum_squared_error
0	12	18

example 2 error sums

sum_error	sum_abs_error	sum_squared_error
-0.8531	12	19.41

Note that every set of observations has its best-fit line, plane, or hyper-plane, although it's possible that the best-fit might not be very good if its sum of squared errors is large.

Linear regression has the impressive and very useful feature that the models it generates can be interpreted as ***any*** shape, not just as lines, planes, and hyper-planes, when provided with datasets that are cleverly prepared with appropriate synthetic variables. As such, linear regression can detect non-linear patterns, not just linear patterns.

8.3.3 Simple Linear Regression

Consider this reference known-outcome dataset and new unknown-outcome observation. The dataset includes 1 predictor variable and 1 outcome variable. The new observation includes 1 predictor variable. What should the new observation's outcome be? Let's use the simple linear regression method to predict the new observation's outcome.

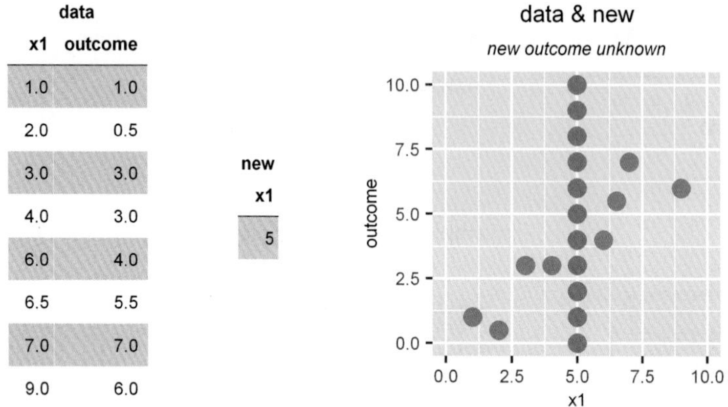

data

x1	outcome
1.0	1.0
2.0	0.5
3.0	3.0
4.0	3.0
6.0	4.0
6.5	5.5
7.0	7.0
9.0	6.0

new

x1
5

8.3.3.1 Construct Model: Best-Fit Line

Rely on some optimization technique to find the best-fit line that passes through the reference observations:

$$outcome = -0.0091 + 0.7811x_1$$

This line minimizes the sum of squared errors to be 5.681. This line is the model.

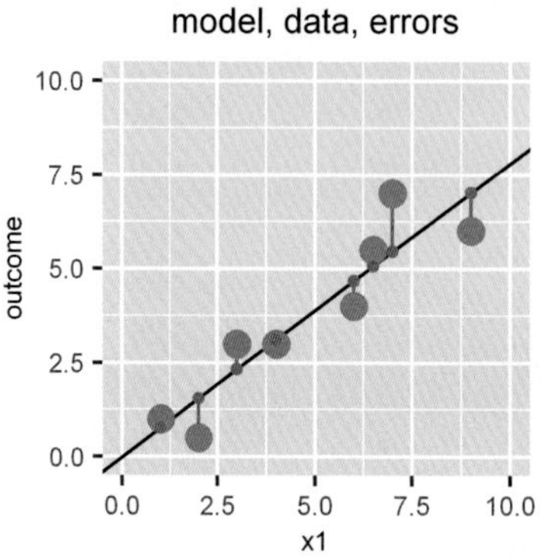

x1	outcome	outcome.predicted	error	squared_error
1.0	1.0	0.772	0.2280	0.0520
2.0	0.5	1.553	-1.0531	1.1090
3.0	3.0	2.334	0.6658	0.4433
4.0	3.0	3.115	-0.1153	0.0133
6.0	4.0	4.678	-0.6776	0.4591
6.5	5.5	5.068	0.4319	0.1865
7.0	7.0	5.459	1.5413	2.3756
9.0	6.0	7.021	-1.0209	1.0423

sum_error	sum_squared_error
0	5.681

8.3.3.2 Predict

Apply the best-fit line model to the new observation:

$$outcome = -0.0091 + 0.7811x_1 = -0.0091 + 0.7811 \times 5 = 3.897$$

The model predicts the new observation's outcome to be 3.897.

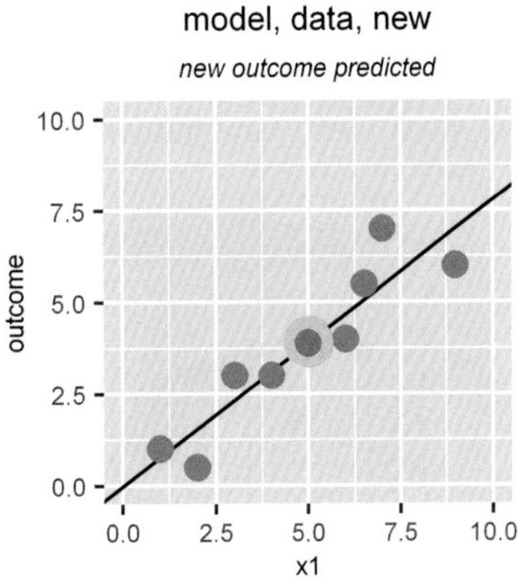

8.3.4 Multiple Linear Regression

Consider this reference known-outcome dataset and new unknown-outcome observation. The dataset includes 2 predictor variables and 1 outcome variable. The new observation includes 2 predictor variables. What should the new observation's outcome be? Let's use the multiple linear regression method to predict the new observation's outcome.

data

x1	x2	outcome
1.0	5.0	1.0
2.0	7.0	0.5
3.0	2.0	3.0
4.0	4.0	3.0
6.0	3.0	4.0
6.5	1.0	5.5
7.0	2.0	7.0
9.0	2.5	6.0

new

x1	x2
5	5

data & new: new outcome unknown

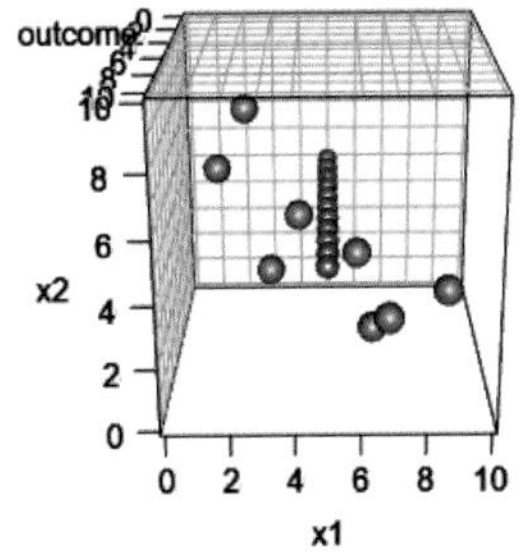

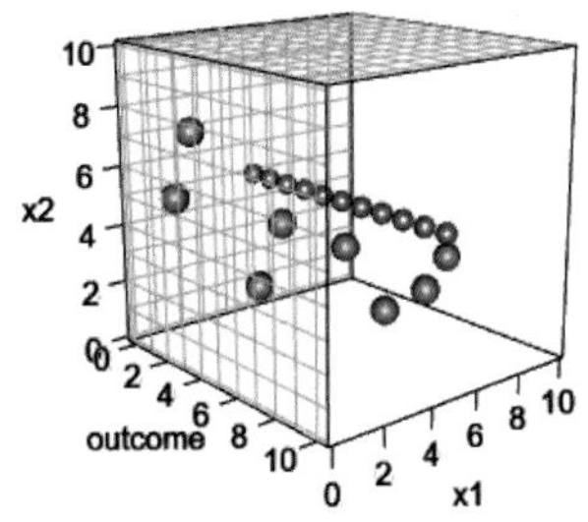

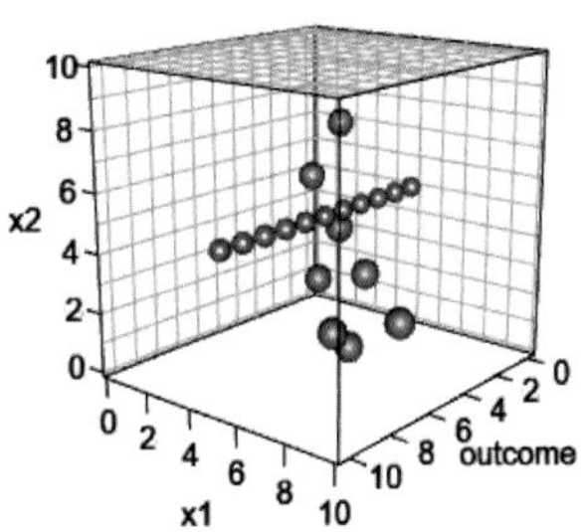

8.3.4.1 Construct Model: Best-Fit Plane

Rely on some optimization technique to find the best-fit plane that passes through the reference observations:

$$outcome = 2.5487 + 0.5622x_1 + -0.4542x_2$$

This plane minimizes the sum of squared errors. This plane is the model.

model, data, new: new outcome unknown

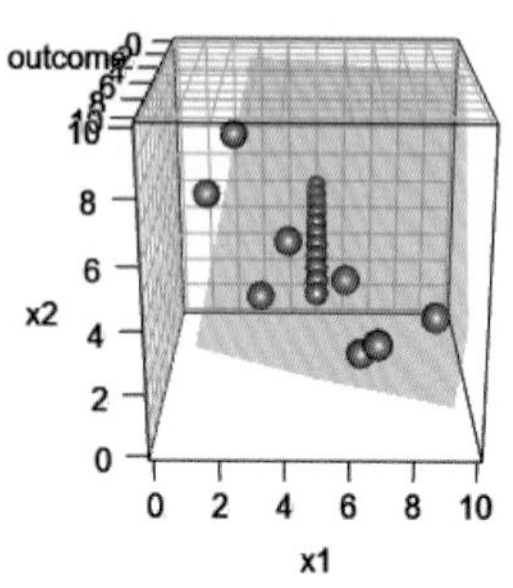

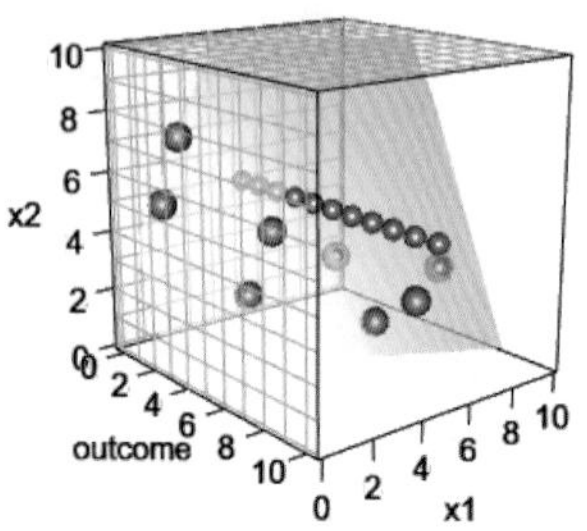

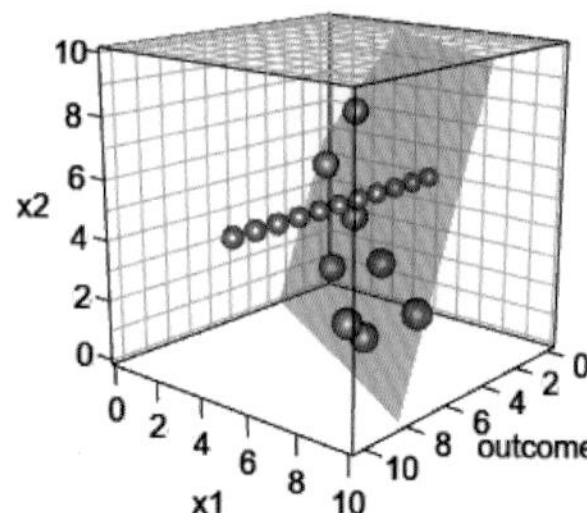

8.3.4.2 Predict

Apply the best-fit plane model to the new observation:

$$outcome = 2.5487 + 0.5622x_1 + -0.4542x_2 = 2.5487 + 0.5622 \times 5 + -0.4542 \times 5 = 3.089$$

The model predicts the new observation's outcome to be 3.089.

model, data, new: new outcome predicted

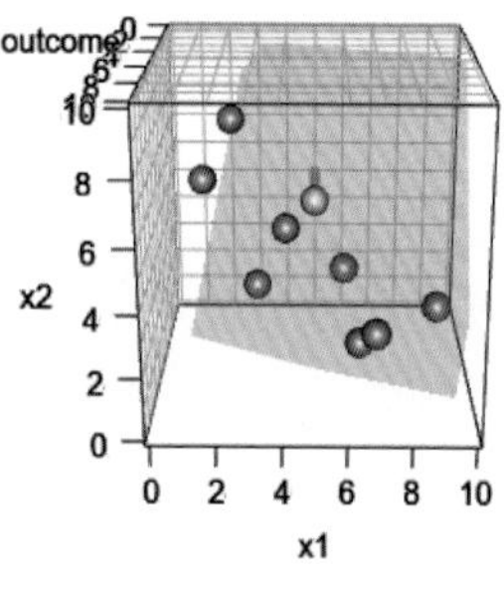

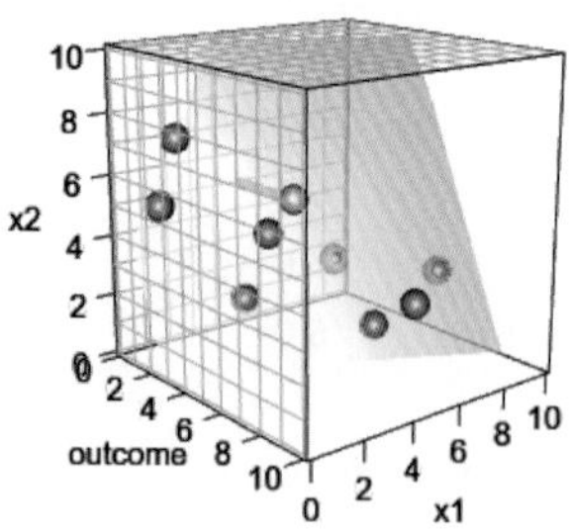

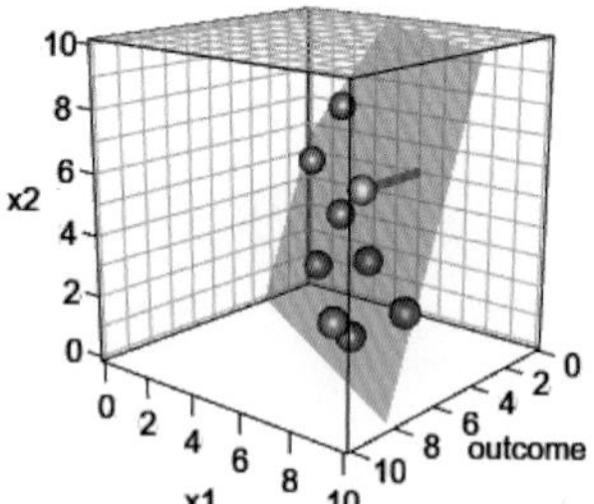

Here is the new observation's predicted outcome visualized in scatterplots in terms of only 1 predictor variable at a time. Note that the new observation's predicted outcome does not necessarily fall on some best-fit line that passes through the reference observations. There is no best-fit line to fall on. Rather, the new observation falls on the best-fit plane, which is not visible in these scatterplots.

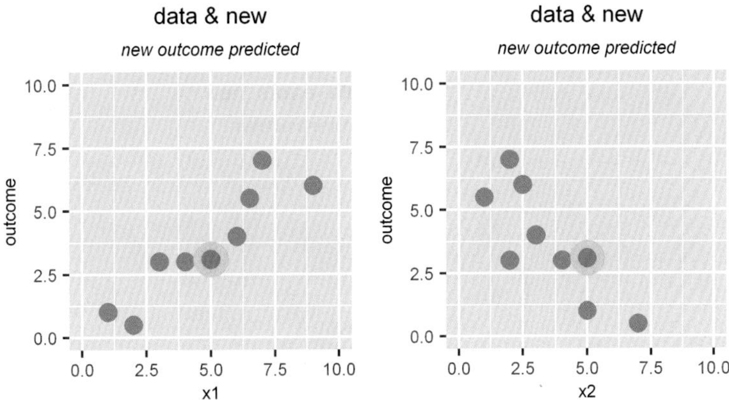

8.3.5 Linear Regression with Log Outcome Preparation

Consider this reference known-outcome dataset and new unknown-outcome observation. The dataset includes 1 predictor variable and 1 outcome variable. The new observation includes 1 predictor variable. We could construct a model by finding the best-fit line through the reference observations, but perhaps that would not feel satisfying. At low x_1 values, outcomes are high. At about (x_1=4), outcomes drop precipitously. As x_1 increases from there, outcomes continue to decrease only slightly, gradually leveling off. That doesn't seem like a linear pattern suited to a best-fit line. Rather, perhaps some kind of logarithmic pattern would feel more appropriate.

What should the new observation's outcome be? Let's use the simple linear regression method applied to the dataset prepared with a log of outcome synthetic variable to predict the new observation's outcome.

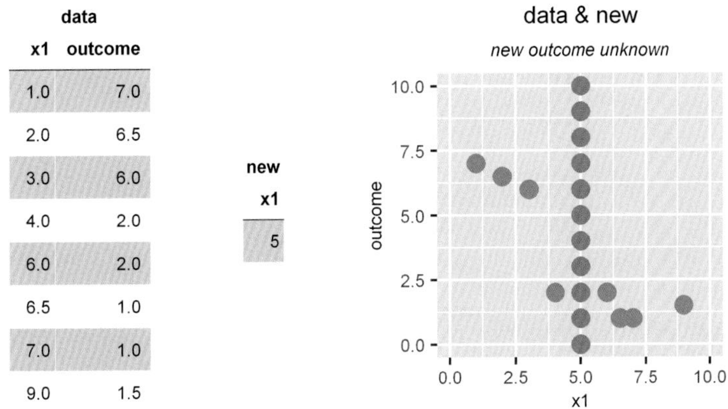

data

x1	outcome
1.0	7.0
2.0	6.5
3.0	6.0
4.0	2.0
6.0	2.0
6.5	1.0
7.0	1.0
9.0	1.5

new

x1
5

8.3.5.1 Construct Model & Predict without Preparation

For comparison purposes, let's first use the simple linear regression method to construct a best-fit line model and apply it to the new observation:

$$outcome = 7.4578 + -0.8484x_1 = 7.4578 + -0.8484 \times 5 = 3.216$$

The model predicts the new observation's outcome to be 3.216, which perhaps feels too high since it doesn't fit well into the reference observations' logarithmic pattern.

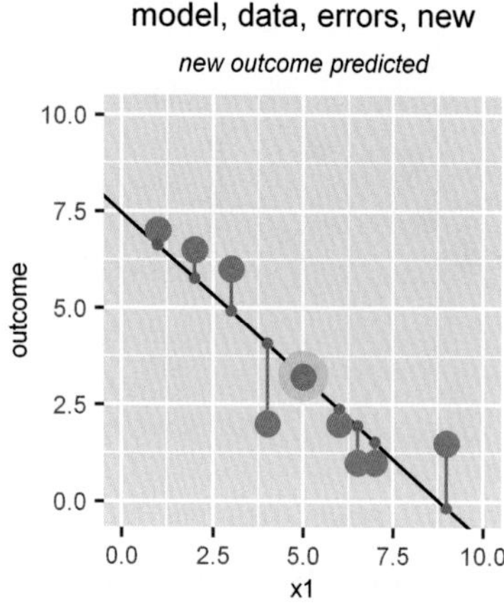

8.3.5.2 Construct Model & Predict with Preparation

Construct another model, this one accounting for the logarithmic pattern. Add a synthetic variable named *logoutcome* to the dataset, specified as the log of the *outcome* variable. Note that, as always, adding a synthetic variable does not gather, discard, or replace any data, but rather just changes the representation of the data.

data (prepared)

x1	log_outcome	outcome
1.0	1.9459	7.0
2.0	1.8718	6.5
3.0	1.7918	6.0
4.0	0.6931	2.0
6.0	0.6931	2.0
6.5	0.0000	1.0
7.0	0.0000	1.0
9.0	0.4055	1.5

new

x1
5

Rely on some optimization technique to find the best-fit line that passes through the reference observations, considering only the *logoutcome* and x_1 variables, and apply it to the new observation:

$$logoutcome = 2.1947 + -0.2638x_1 = 2.1947 + -0.2638 \times 5 = 0.8757$$

The model predicts the new observation's *logoutcome* to be 0.8757.

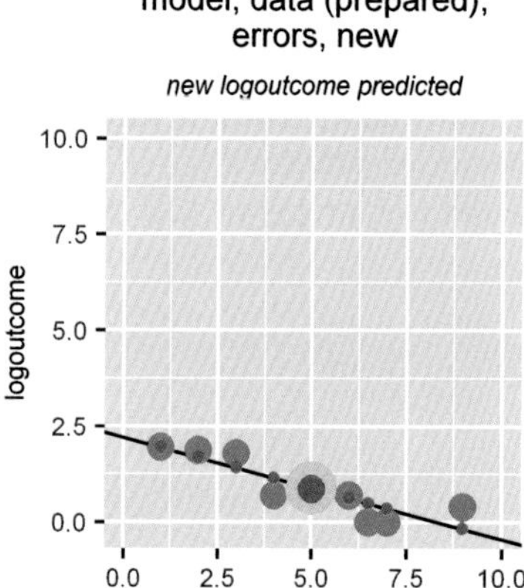

We now have the new observation's predicted *logoutcome*, but ultimately we are interested in predicting the new observation's *outcome*. The simple linear regression method treated *logoutput* as a variable. It has no awareness of the variable being a synthetic variable. It has no awareness of the variable being computed as the log of anything. However, we can interpret *logoutput* as $log(outcome)$ because we know how it was specified. So, unwind the prediction by exponentiating it:

$$outcome = e^{logoutcome} = e^{0.8757} = e^{log(outcome)} = e^{log(5)} = 2.401$$

The model, when interpreted appropriately, predicts the new observation's outcome to be 2.401.

Here is the new observation's predicted outcome visualized in a scatterplot in terms of the *outcome* variable, rather than the *logoutcome* variable. Note that the best-fit line for *logoutcome* appears as a logarithmic shape when viewed from this perspective. Perhaps predicting the outcome to be 2.401 rather than 3.216 feels more satisfying since the new observation would better fit into the reference observations' logarithmic pattern.

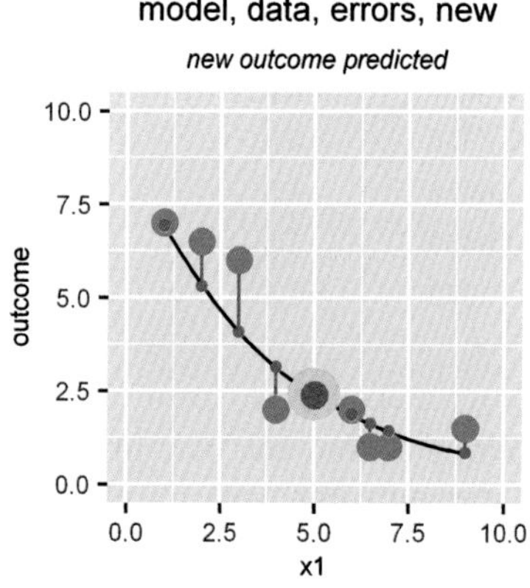

8.3.6 Linear Regression with Log Predictor Preparation

Consider again this reference known-outcome dataset and new unknown-outcome observation. We can account for the logarithmic pattern with a synthetic predictor variable, rather than with a synthetic outcome variable. That might lead to a model that predicts even more satisfying outcomes, depending on the specific characteristics of the data. Let's use the simple linear regression method applied to the dataset prepared with a log of x_1 synthetic variable to predict the new observation's outcome.

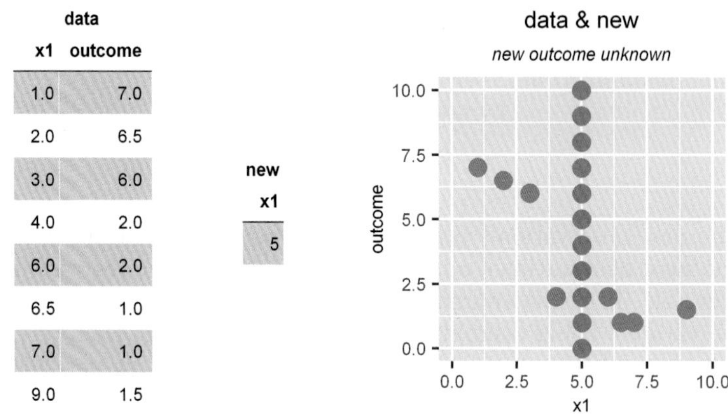

data

x1	outcome
1.0	7.0
2.0	6.5
3.0	6.0
4.0	2.0
6.0	2.0
6.5	1.0
7.0	1.0
9.0	1.5

new

x1
5

8.3.6.1 Construct Model & Predict with Preparation

Add a synthetic variable named $logx_1$ to the dataset and to the new observation, specified as the log of the x_1 variable:

data (prepared)

x1	log_x1	outcome
1.0	0.0000	7.0
2.0	0.6931	6.5
3.0	1.0986	6.0
4.0	1.3863	2.0
6.0	1.7918	2.0
6.5	1.8718	1.0
7.0	1.9459	1.0
9.0	2.1972	1.5

new (prepared)

x1	log_x1
5	1.609

Rely on some optimization technique to find the best-fit line that passes through the reference observations, considering only the *outcome* and $logx_1$ variables, and apply it to the new observation:

$$outcome = 7.830 + -3.245 logx_1 = 7.830 + -3.245 \times 1.609 = 2.608$$

The simple linear regression method treated $logx_1$ as a variable. It has no awareness of the variable being a synthetic variable. It has no awareness of the variable being the log of anything. However, we can interpret $logx_1$ as $\log(x_1)$ because we know how it was specified:

$$outcome = 7.830 + -3.245log(x_1) = 7.830 + -3.245 \times log(5) = 2.608$$

The model, when provided appropriate input, predicts the new observation's outcome to be 2.608. Note that to make this prediction, the model was provided $log(x_1)$ as input, not x_1 as input.

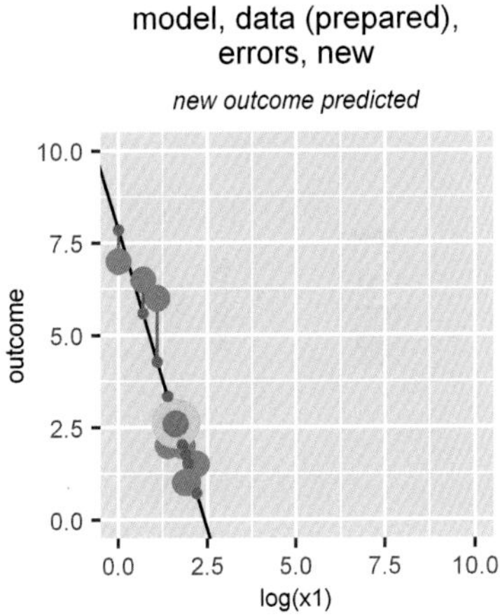

Here is the new observation's predicted outcome visualized in a scatterplot in terms of the x_1 variable, rather than the $logx_1$ variable. Note that the best-fit line for $logx_1$ appears as a logarithmic shape when viewed from this perspective. Perhaps predicting the outcome to be 2.608 rather than 3.216 or 2.401 feels more satisfying since the new observation would better fit into the reference observations' logarithmic pattern.

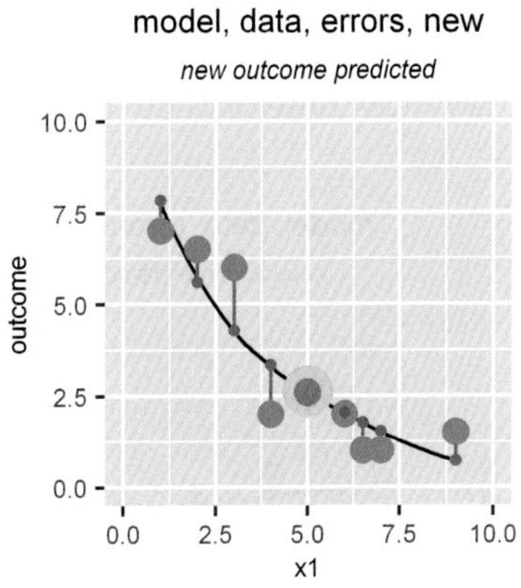

8.3.7 Linear Regression with Polynomial Predictor Preparation

Consider this reference known-outcome dataset and new unknown-outcome observation. The dataset includes 1 predictor variable and 1 outcome variable. The new observation includes 1 predictor variable. At low and high x_1 values, outcomes are high. In between, outcomes are low. That doesn't seem like a linear pattern suited to a best-fit line. Rather, perhaps some kind of parabolic pattern feels more appropriate. What should the new observation's outcome be? Let's use the multiple linear regression method applied to the dataset prepared with a squared x_1 synthetic variable to predict the new observation's outcome.

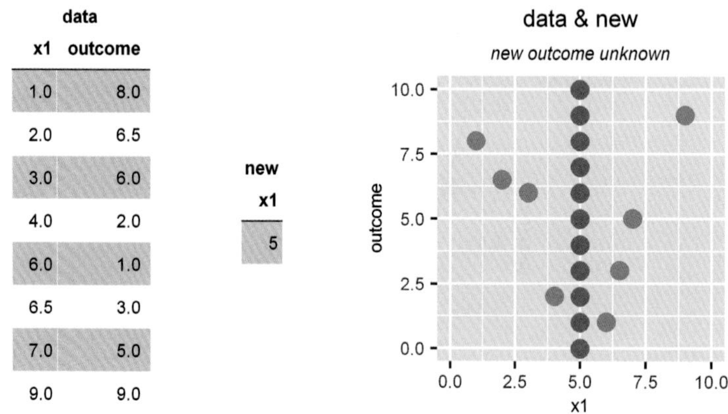

data

x1	outcome
1.0	8.0
2.0	6.5
3.0	6.0
4.0	2.0
6.0	1.0
6.5	3.0
7.0	5.0
9.0	9.0

new

x1
5

8.3.7.1 Construct Model & Predict without Preparation

For comparison purposes, let's first use the simple linear regression method to construct a best-fit line model and apply it to the new observation:

$$outcome = 5.6445 + -0.1209x_1 = 5.6445 + -0.1209 \times 5 = 5.0400$$

The model predicts the new observation's outcome to be 5.0400, which perhaps feels too high since it doesn't fit well into the reference observations' parabolic pattern.

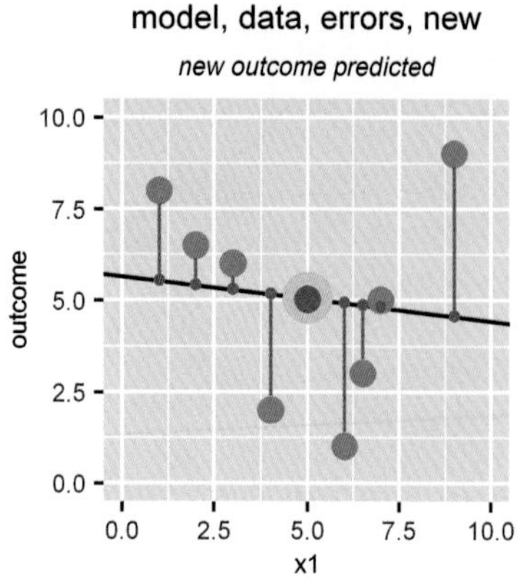

8.3.7.2 Construct Model & Predict with Preparation

Construct another model, this one accounting for the parabolic pattern. Add a synthetic variable named $x_1 square$ to the dataset and new observation, specified as the square of the x_1 variable.

data (prepared)

x1	x1.square	outcome
1.0	1.00	8.0
2.0	4.00	6.5
3.0	9.00	6.0
4.0	16.00	2.0
6.0	36.00	1.0
6.5	42.25	3.0
7.0	49.00	5.0
9.0	81.00	9.0

new (prepared)

x1	x1.square
5	25

Rely on some optimization technique to find the best-fit line that passes through the reference observations, considering all the *outcome*, x_1, and $x_1 square$ variables, and apply it to the new observation:

$$outcome = 12.6973 + -4.1381 x_1 + 0.4123 x_1 square = 12.6973 + -4.1381 \times 5 + 0.4123 \times 25 = 2.3150$$

The multiple linear regression method treated $x_1 square$ as a variable. However, we can interpret $x_1 square$ as ${x_1}^2$ because we know how it was specified:

$$outcome = 12.6973 + -4.1381 x_1 + 0.4123 {x_1}^2 = 12.6973 + -4.1381 \times 5 + 0.4123 \times 5^2 = 2.3150$$

The model, when provided appropriate inputs, predicts the new observation's outcome to be 2.3150. Note that to make this prediction, the model was provided x_1 and $x_1 square$ as inputs, not just x_1 alone or $x_1 square$ alone as input.

model, data (prepared), new: new outcome predicted

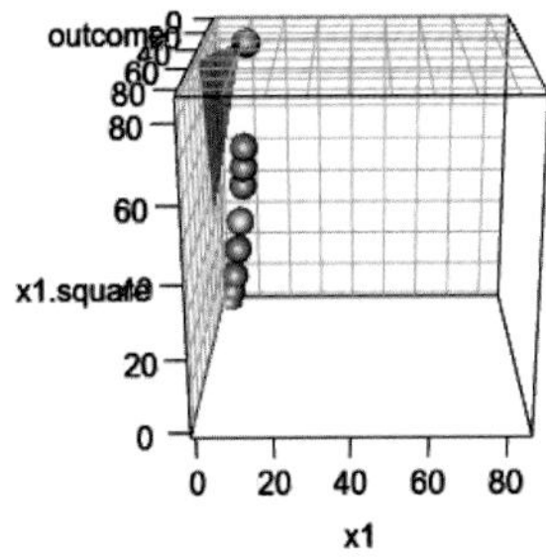

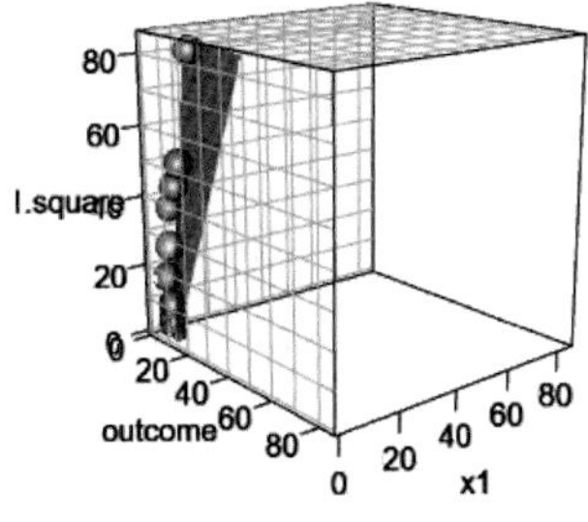

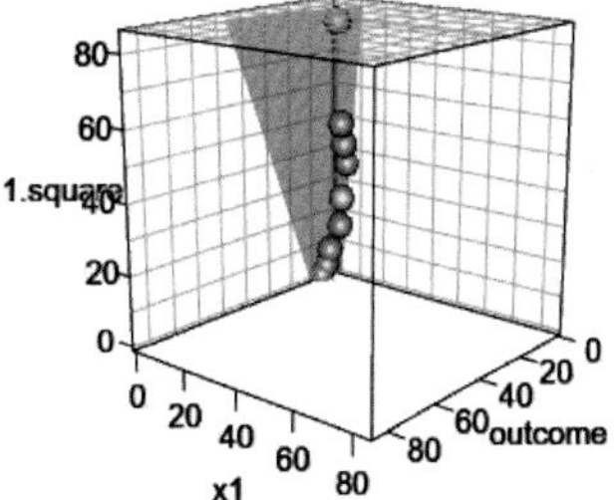

Here is the new observation's predicted outcome visualized in a scatterplot in terms of the x_1 variable. Note that the best-fit plane appears as a parabolic shape when viewed from this perspective. Perhaps predicting outcome to be 2.3150 rather than 5.0400 feels more satisfying since the new observation would better fit into the reference observations' parabolic pattern.

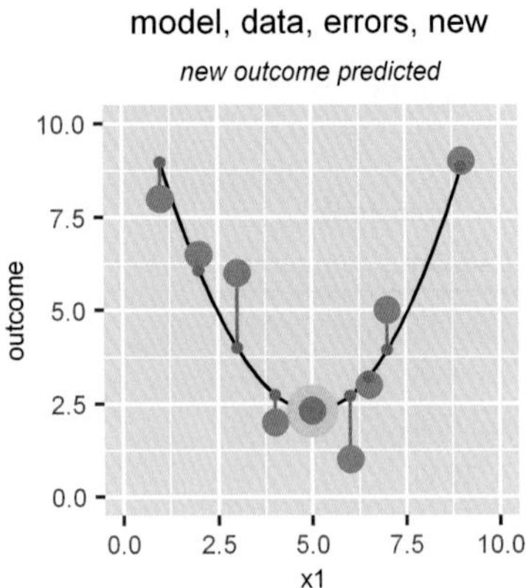

8.3.8 Linear Regression with Interaction Predictor Preparation

Consider this reference known-outcome dataset and new unknown-outcome observation. The dataset includes 2 predictor variables and 1 outcome variable. The new observation includes 2 predictor variables. It's possible that the predictor variables are highly interactive, in the sense that the value of 1 variable could strongly influence the value of the other variable. To account for this possibility, let's use the multiple linear regression method applied to the dataset prepared with an interaction synthetic variable to predict the new observation's outcome.

data

x1	x2	outcome
1.0	5.0	1.0
2.0	7.0	0.5
3.0	2.0	3.0
4.0	4.0	3.0
6.0	3.0	4.0
6.5	1.0	5.5
7.0	2.0	7.0
9.0	2.5	6.0

new

x1	x2
5	5

data & new: new outcome unknown

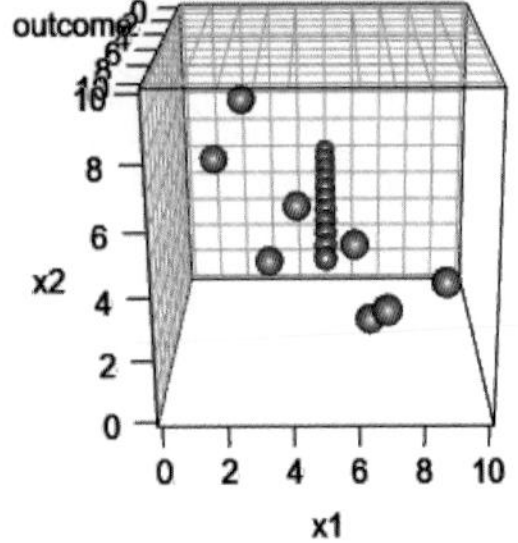

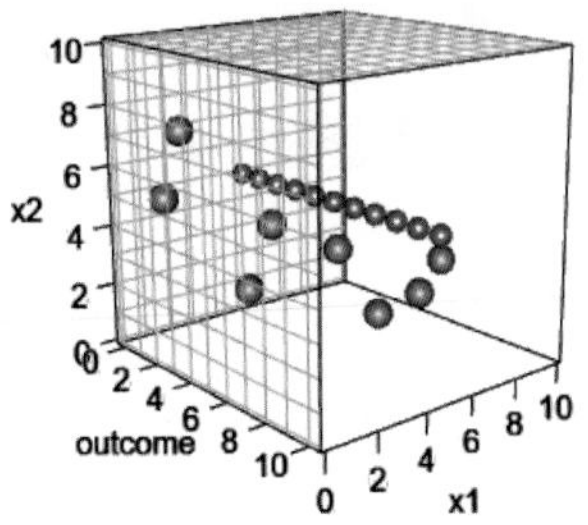

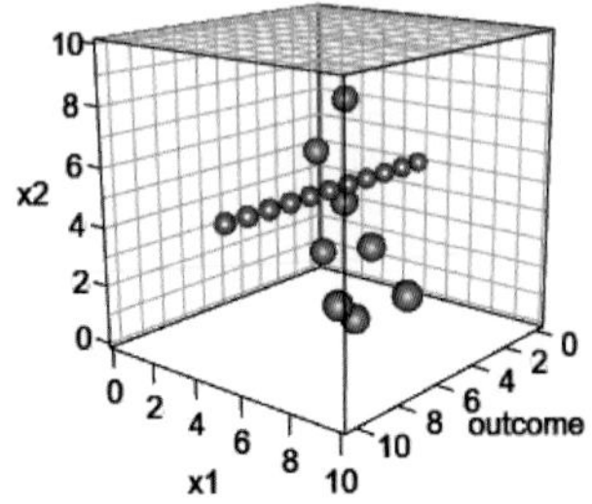

8.3.8.1 Construct Model & Predict without Preparation

For comparison purposes, let's first use the multiple linear regression method to construct a best-fit plane model and apply it to the new observation:

$$outcome = 2.5487 + 0.5622x_1 + -4.4542x_2 = 2.5487 + 0.5622 \times 5 + -4.4542 \times 5 = 3.0890$$

The model predicts the new observation's outcome to be 3.0890, which perhaps feels like it fits the observations' pattern pretty well.

model, data, new: new outcome predicted

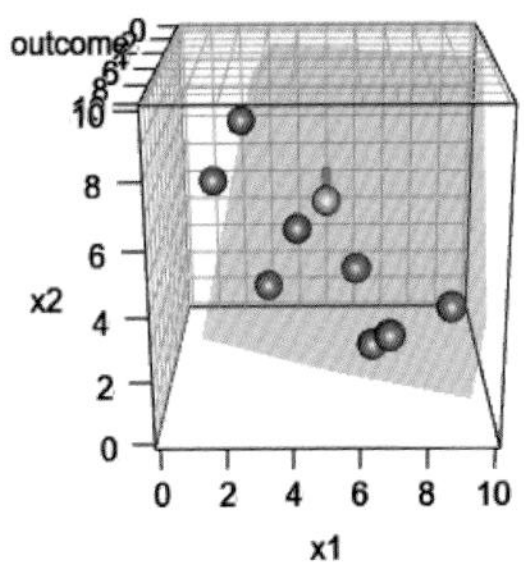

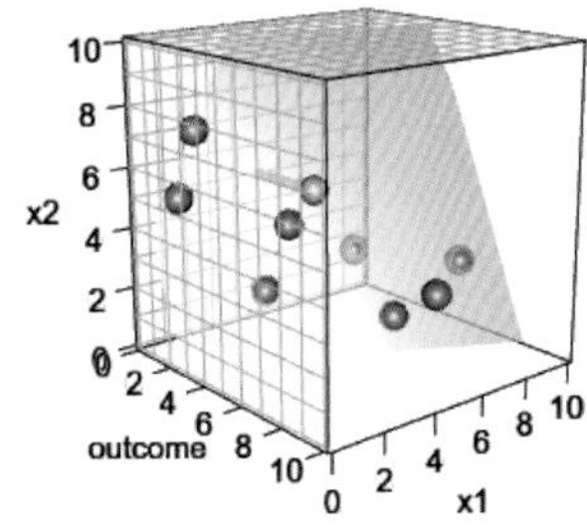

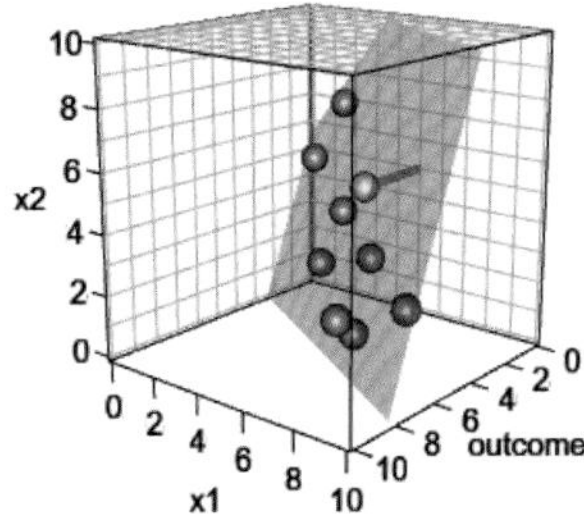

8.3.8.2 Construct Model & Predict with Preparation

Construct another model, this one accounting for possible interaction between predictor variables. Add a synthetic variable named x_1x_2 to the dataset and new observation, specified as the product of the x_1 and x_2 variables. This interaction variable varies along both predictor variables. When either of the predictor variables go high or low, so goes the interaction variable. In this way, the predictor variables cannot vary freely without their influence on each other being reflected in the data.

data (prepared)

x1	x2	x1x2	outcome
1.0	5.0	5.0	1.0
2.0	7.0	14.0	0.5
3.0	2.0	6.0	3.0
4.0	4.0	16.0	3.0
6.0	3.0	18.0	4.0
6.5	1.0	6.5	5.5
7.0	2.0	14.0	7.0
9.0	2.5	22.5	6.0

new (prepared)

x1	x2	x1x2
5	5	25

Rely on some optimization technique to find the best-fit hyper-plane that passes through the reference observations, considering all the *outcome*, x_1, x_2, and x_1x_2 variables, and apply it to the new observation:

$$\begin{aligned} outcome &= 1.8770 + 0.7399x_1 + -0.2688x_2 + -0.0625x_1x_2 \\ &= 1.8770 + 0.7399 \times 5 + -0.2688 \times 5 + -0.0625 \times 25 \\ &= 2.6690 \end{aligned}$$

The multiple linear regression method treated x_1x_2 as a variable. However, we can interpret x_1x_2 as $x_1 \times x_2$ because we know how it was specified:

$$\begin{aligned} outcome &= 1.8770 + 0.7399x_1 + -0.2688x_2 + -0.0625x_1x_2 \\ &= 1.8770 + 0.7399 \times 5 + -0.2688 \times 5 + -0.0625 \times (5 \times 5) \\ &= 2.6690 \end{aligned}$$

The model, when provided appropriate inputs, predicts the new observation's outcome to be 2.6690. Note that to make this prediction, the model was provided x_1, x_2, and x_1x_2 as inputs, not just x_1 and x_2 as inputs.

Here is the new observation's predicted outcome visualized in a scatterplot in terms of only 2 predictor variables. Note that the new observation's predicted outcome does not necessarily fall on some best-fit plane that passes through the reference observations. There is no best-fit plane to fall on. Rather, the new observation falls on the best-fit hyper-plane, which is not visible in this scatterplot. Perhaps predicting the outcome to be 2.6690 rather than 3.0890 feels more satisfying since the new observation reflects interaction between predictor variables.

data, new: new outcome predicted

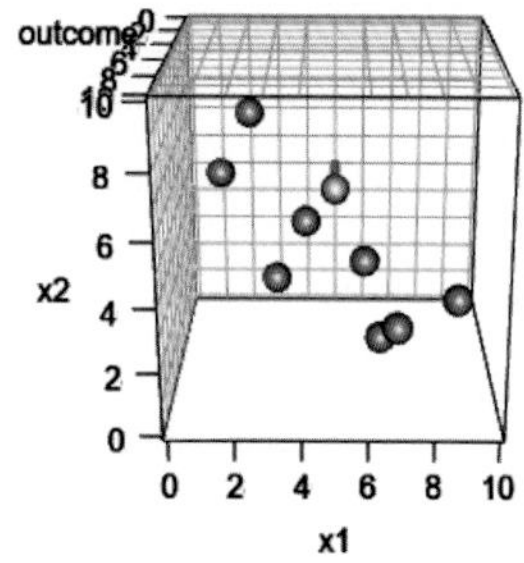

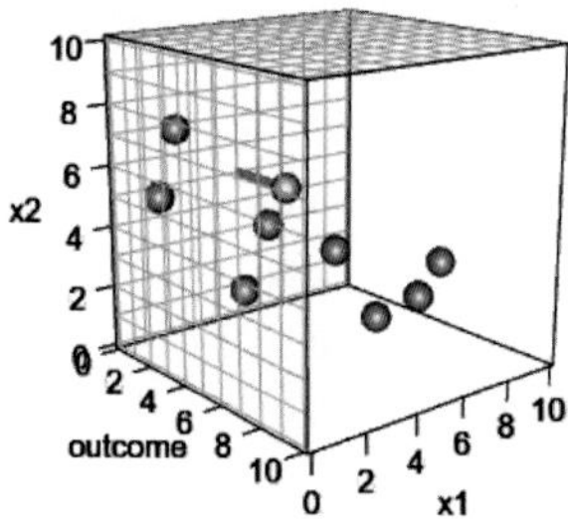

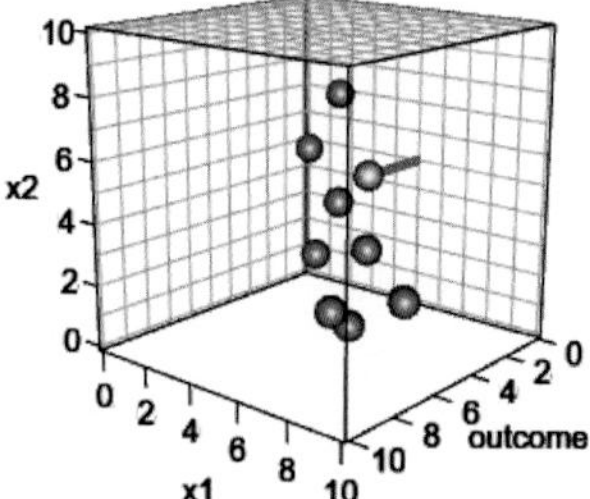

8.3.9 Linear Regression with Categorical Predictor Variables

Consider this reference known-outcome dataset and new unknown-outcome observation. The dataset includes 1 numerical predictor variable, 1 categorical predictor variable, and 1 outcome variable. The new observation includes 1 numerical predictor variable and 1 categorical predictor variable. The linear regression method requires all numerical predictor variables, but any categorical variables can be represented as numerical variables using **dummy-coding** or **index-coding**, so linear regression is still applicable. Let's use the multiple linear regression method applied to the dataset prepared with index or dummy synthetic variables to predict the new observation's outcome. We'll see that it's typically better to use dummy-coding rather than index-coding.

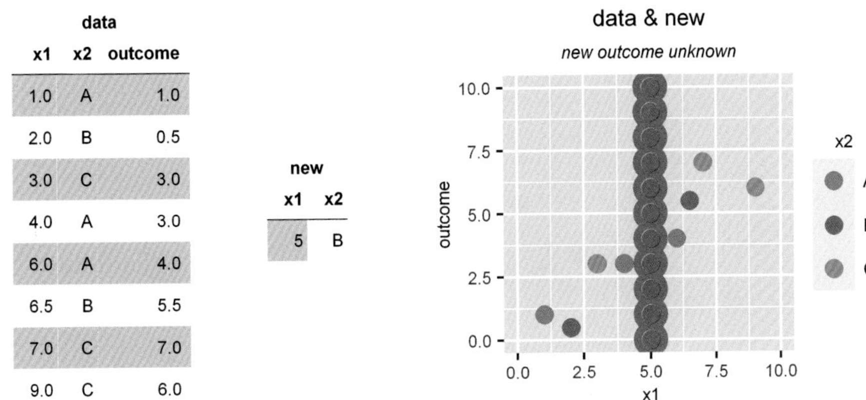

data

x1	x2	outcome
1.0	A	1.0
2.0	B	0.5
3.0	C	3.0
4.0	A	3.0
6.0	A	4.0
6.5	B	5.5
7.0	C	7.0
9.0	C	6.0

new

x1	x2
5	B

8.3.9.1 Construct Model & Predict with Dummy-Coding Preparation

To prepare with dummy-coding, add synthetic variables to the dataset and new observation to represent the categorical variable x_2 as numerical variables named x_{2B} and x_{2C}. Recall that dummy representation involves replacing the orignal categorical variable with a set of new variables, 1 for each value except the first 1 in the categorical variable's domain.

data (prepared dummy-coding)

x1	x2_B	x2_C	outcome
1.0	0	0	1.0
2.0	1	0	0.5
3.0	0	1	3.0
4.0	0	0	3.0
6.0	0	0	4.0
6.5	1	0	5.5
7.0	0	1	7.0
9.0	0	1	6.0

new (prepared dummy-coding)

x1	x2_B	x2_C
5	1	0

Rely on some optimization technique to find the best-fit hyper-plane that passes through the reference observations:

$$\begin{aligned} outcome &= 0.0503 + 0.7136x_1 + -0.0829x_{2B} + 0.7638x_{2C} \\ &= 0.0503 + 0.7136 \times 5 + -0.0829 \times 1 + 0.7638 \times 0 \\ &= 3.535 \end{aligned}$$

The model, when provided appropriate inputs, predicts the new observation's outcome to be 3.535. Note that to make this prediction, the model was provided x_1, x_{2B}, and x_{2C} as inputs, and did not leave out x_{2C} as an input.

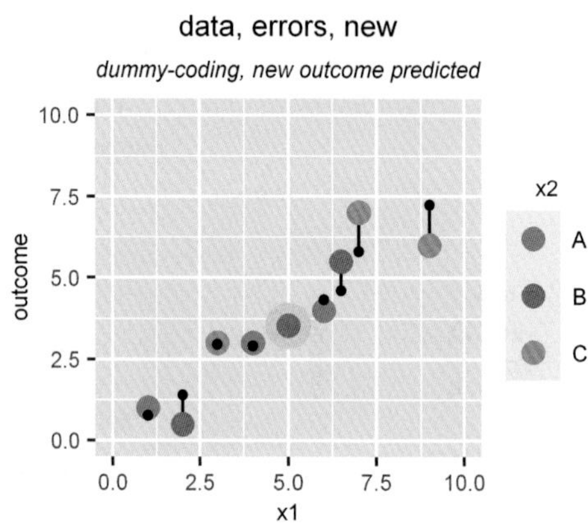

8.3.9.2 Construct Model & Predict with Index-Coding Preparation

To prepare with index-coding, as an alternative to preparing with dummy-coding, add a synthetic variable to the dataset and new observation to represent the categorical variable x_2 as a numerical variable named x_{2i}. Recall that index-coding involves replacing the original categorical variable with a new variable that maps values from the categorical variable's domain to numbers.

data (prepared index-coding)

x1	x2.i	outcome
1.0	1	1.0
2.0	2	0.5
3.0	3	3.0
4.0	1	3.0
6.0	1	4.0
6.5	2	5.5
7.0	3	7.0
9.0	3	6.0

new (prepared index-coding)

x1	x2.i
5	2

Rely on some optimization technique to find the best-fit plane that passes through the reference observations:

$$outcome = -0.4744 + 0.7259x_1 + 0.3654x_{2i} = -0.4744 + 0.7259x_1 + 0.3654x_{2i} = 3.886$$

The model, when provided appropriate inputs, predicts the new observation's outcome to be 3.886. Note that to make this prediction, the model was provided x_1 and x_{2i} as inputs.

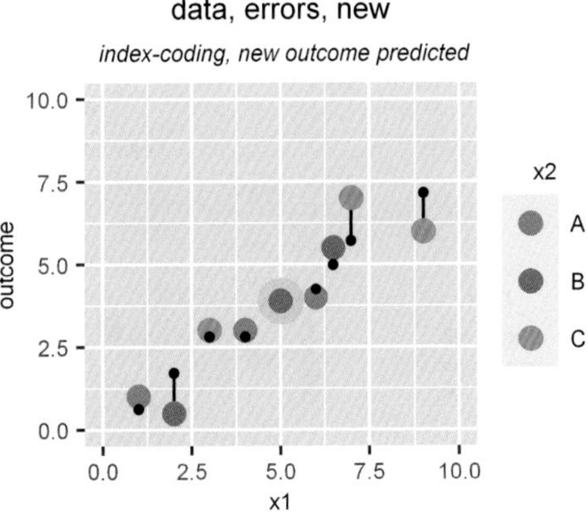

8.3.9.3 Dummy-Coding vs. Index-Coding

The 2 models, 1 constructed from dummy-coding preparation and the other from index-coding preparation, make different predictions. The dummy-coding version back-predicts the reference observations slightly better, as measured by RMSE, and so perhaps it predicts new observation outcomes slightly better, too. This is a typical result and why it's typically preferable to use dummy-coding rather than index-coding.

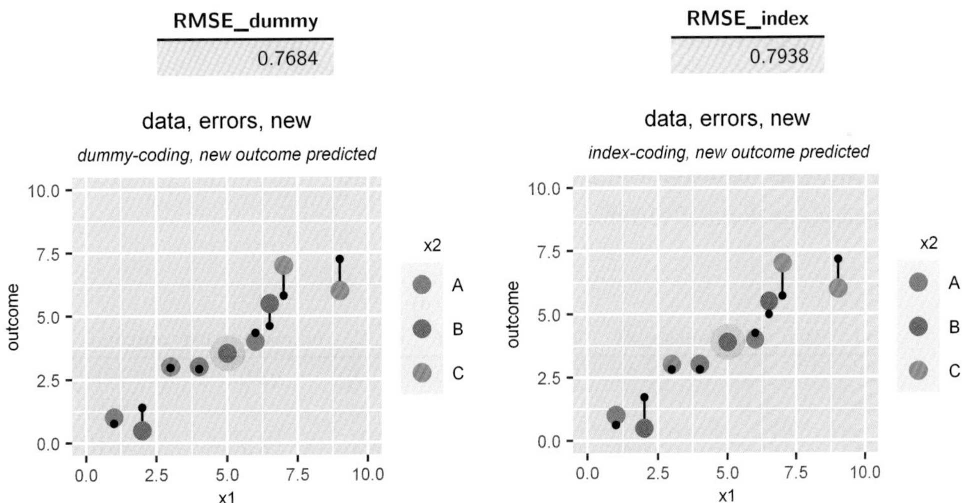

8.3.10 Complex Linear Regression

Consider this reference known-outcome dataset and new unknown-outcome observation. There could be a logarithmic pattern in there. There could be a parabolic pattern in there. There could be a higher polynomial pattern in there. There is a mix of numerical and categorical predictor variables.

Linear regression can produce models that account for any combination of patterns and variable types that we see or even just suspect. Let's use the multiple linear regression method applied to the dataset prepared with a variety of synthetic variables accounting for combination of patterns to predict the new observation's outcome.

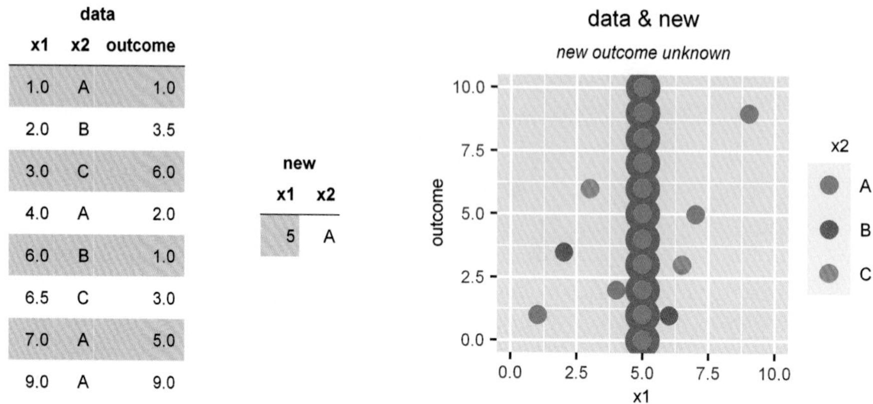

data

x1	x2	outcome
1.0	A	1.0
2.0	B	3.5
3.0	C	6.0
4.0	A	2.0
6.0	B	1.0
6.5	C	3.0
7.0	A	5.0
9.0	A	9.0

new

x1	x2
5	A

8.3.10.1 Construct Model & Predict with Preparation

Prepare the dataset and new observation by adding a variety of synthetic variables.

Add a synthetic variable to the dataset:

- Specify *logoutcome* as the log of the *outcome* variable.

Add synthetic variables to the dataset and new observation:

- Specify $cubex_1$ as the cube of the x_1 variable.
- Specify $squarex_1$ as the square of the x_1 variable.
- Specify $logx_1$ as the log of the x_1 variable.
- Represent x_2 as dummy variables x_{2B} and x_{2C}.

data (prepared)

x1	cube_x1	square_x1	log_x1	x2_B	x2_C	outcome	log_outcome
1.0	1.0	1.00	0.0000	0	0	1.0	0.0000
2.0	8.0	4.00	0.6931	1	0	3.5	1.2528
3.0	27.0	9.00	1.0986	0	1	6.0	1.7918
4.0	64.0	16.00	1.3863	0	0	2.0	0.6931
6.0	216.0	36.00	1.7918	1	0	1.0	0.0000
6.5	274.6	42.25	1.8718	0	1	3.0	1.0986
7.0	343.0	49.00	1.9459	0	0	5.0	1.6094
9.0	729.0	81.00	2.1972	0	0	9.0	2.1972

new (prepared)

x1	cube_x1	square_x1	log_x1	x2_B	x2_C
5	125	25	1.609	0	0

Rely on some optimization technique to find the best-fit hyper-plane that passes through the reference observations, without considering the *outcome* variable. Interpret the synthetic predictor variables based on how they were specified. Unwind $log(outcome)$ by exponentiating it. Apply the model to the new observation.

$$
\begin{aligned}
log(outcome) &= 15.31 + -0.083x_1{}^3 + 1.94x_1{}^2 + -17.18x_1 + \\
&\quad 20.57log(x_1) + -0.97x_{2B} + 0.069x_{2C}
\end{aligned}
$$

$$
\begin{aligned}
outcome &= e^{\left(15.31 \;+\; -0.083x_1{}^3 \;+\; 1.94x_1{}^2 \;+\; -17.18x_1 \;+\; 20.57log(x_1) \;+\; -0.97x_{2B} \;+\; 0.069x_{2C}\right)} \\
&= e^{\left(15.31 \;+\; -0.083\times5^3 \;+\; 1.94\times5^2 \;+\; -17.18\times5 \;+\; 20.57\times log(5) \;+\; -0.97\times0 \;+\; 0.069\times0\right)} \\
&= 1.778
\end{aligned}
$$

The model, when interpreted appropriately and provided appropriate inputs, predicts the new observation's outcome to be 1.778.

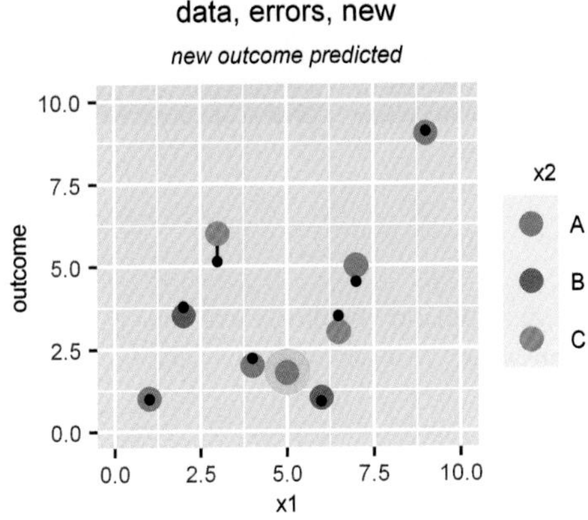

8.4 Regression Versions

Construct a regressor by the regression version of a model construction method.

8.4.1 Introduction

Regression versions of model construction methods are based on classifier construction methods, but adjusted to construct regressors.

8.4.2 Data

Consider this reference known-outcome dataset and new unknown-outcome observation. There are 2 predictor variables x_1 and x_2, and an outcome variable *outcome*. The new observation is $(x_1{=}5.5, x_2{=}7.5)$. What should we predict for the new observation's outcome? Let's use the regressor versions of k-nearest neighbors, decision tree, support vector machine, and neural network methods to construct regressors and make predictions.

data

x1	x2	outcome
2	3	1
5	6	2
3	9	3
9	7	4
3	4	5
2	8	6
1	3	7
4	8	8
6	9	9
2	0	4
9	9	3

new

x1	x2
5.5	7.5

data & new: outcome vs. x1. vs x2

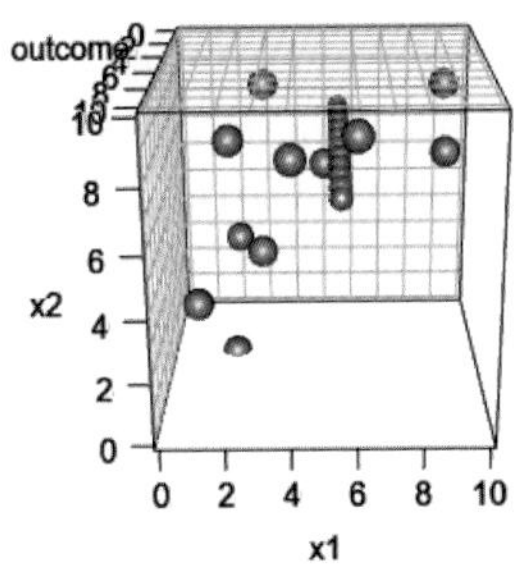

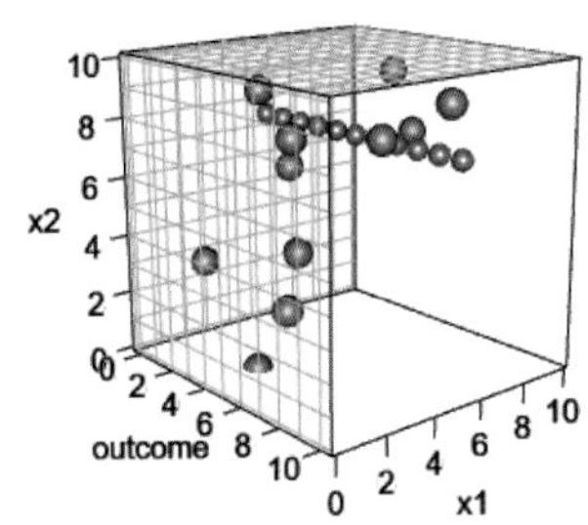

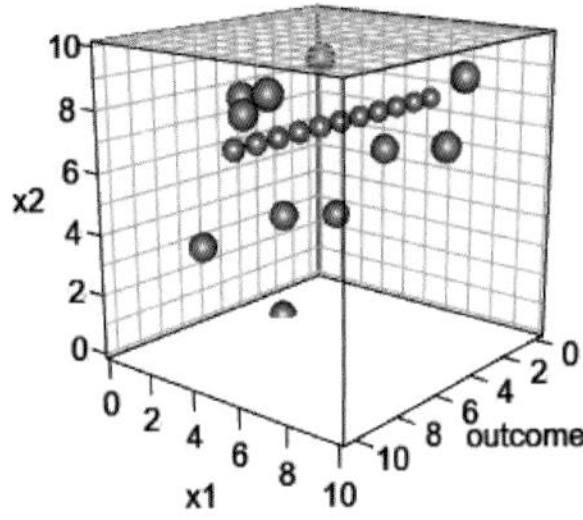

8.4.3 Regression by k-Nearest Neighbors

In its classification version, k-nearest neighbors predictions are made by finding the reference observations most similar to a new observation, noting the class values of those observations, and interpreting the relative proportion of positive class values to be the probability that the new observation's class is positive.

In its regression version, k-nearest neighbors predictions are made by finding the reference observations most similar to a new observation, noting the outcomes of those observations, and interpreting the mean of the those outcomes to be the new observation's outcome.

Here the 3 nearest neighbor observations to the new observation $(x_1{=}5.5, x_2{=}7.5)$ are $(x_1{=}5, x_2{=}6)$, $(x_1{=}4, x_2{=}8)$, and $(x_1{=}6, x_2{=}9)$. Their outcomes are 2, 8, and 9, with mean 6.333. So, predict the new observation's outcome to be 6.333.

model		new		
method	k	x1	x2	outcome.predicted
k-nearest neighbors	3	5.5	7.5	6.333

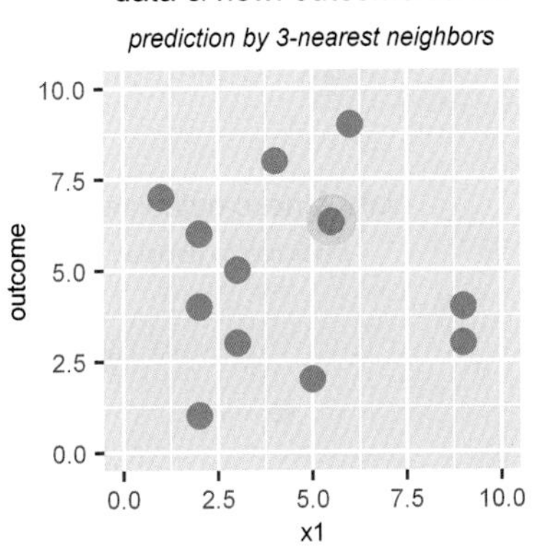

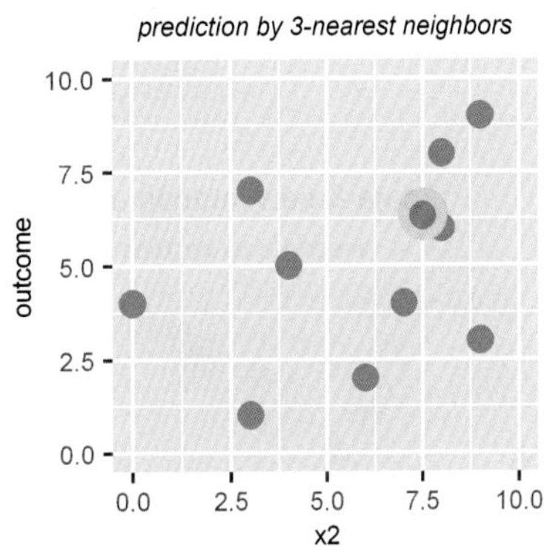

8.4.4 Regression by Decision Tree

In its classification version, the decision tree method constructs a model in the form of a tree with leaf nodes corresponding to subsets of the reference dataset. Each leaf node indicates the relative proportion of positive class values in its subset. Predictions are made by navigating the tree, directed by a new observation, and interpreting the proportion indicated by the leaf node at the end of the path to be the probability that the new observation's class is positive.

In its regression version, the decision tree method constructs a model in the form of a tree with leaf nodes corresponding to subsets of the reference dataset. Each leaf node indicates the mean of the outcome values in its subset. Predictions are made by navigating the tree, directed by a new observation, and interpreting the mean outcome indicated by the leaf node at the end of the path to be the new observation's outcome.

Here the new observation leads to the right of split node $x_2<7.5$, to the right of split node $x_1 \geq 7.5$, and to the right of split node $x_1<3.5$, arriving at the leaf node corresponding to the subset of the reference dataset comprising observations ($x_1=4, x_2=8$) and ($x_1=6, x_2=9$). Their outcomes are 8 and 9, with mean 8.50. So, predict the new observation's outcome to be 8.50.

model (decision tree)

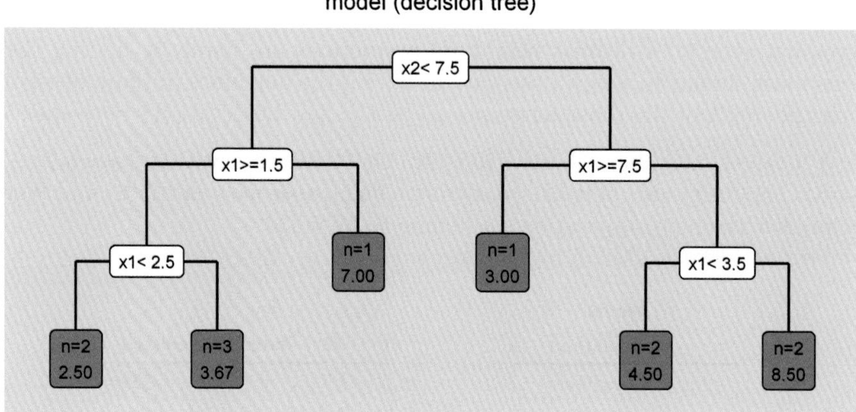

new

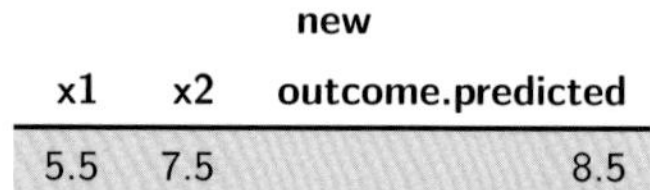

x1	x2	outcome.predicted
5.5	7.5	8.5

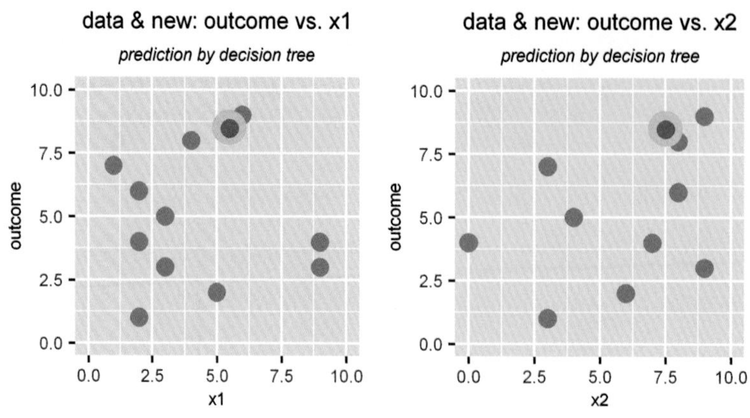

8.4.5 Regression by Support Vector Machine

In its classification version, the support vector machine method constructs a boundary through the reference dataset. Predictions are made by interpreting the proximity of a new observation to the boundary to be the probability that the new observation's class is positive.

In its regression version, the support vector machine method constructs a boundary through the reference dataset. Predictions are made by interpreting the distance of a new observation to the boundary to be the new observation's outcome.

Regression by support vector machine is also known as support vector regression or SVR.

Here predict the new observation's outcome to be 5.786.

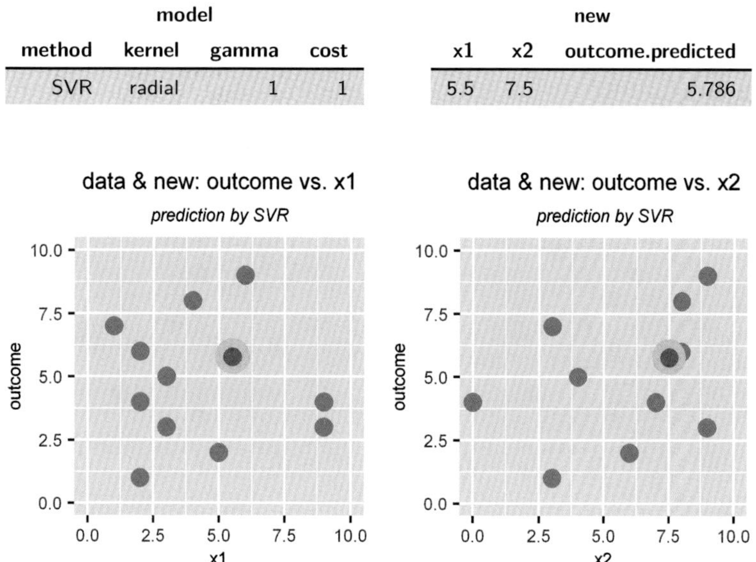

model			
method	kernel	gamma	cost
SVR	radial	1	1

new		
x1	x2	outcome.predicted
5.5	7.5	5.786

8.4.6 Regression by Neural Network

In its classification version, an activation function is applied to the output node to constrain the result to the range 0 to 1.

In its regression version, no activation function is applied to the output node, so the result is not so constrained. All hidden nodes still have activation functions applied to them. Back-propagation is still used to adjust the model weights by considering the errors between the output node values and actual reference values. Predictions are made by interpreting the output as the new observation's outcome.

Here the new observation leads to output 4.667. So, predict the new observation's outcome to be 4.667.

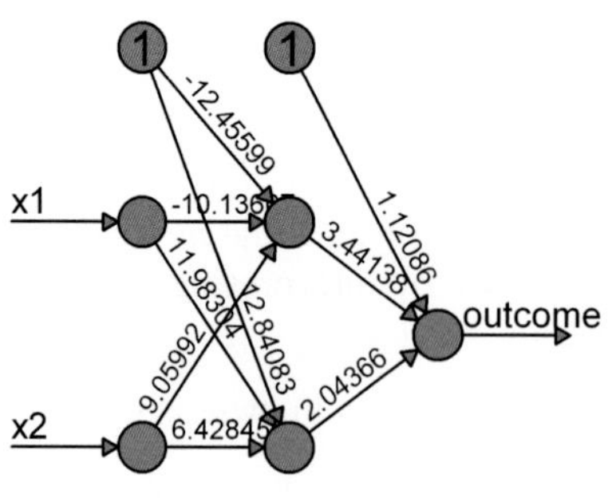

new

x1	x2	outcome.predicted
5.5	7.5	4.667

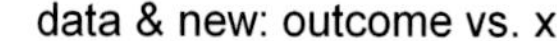

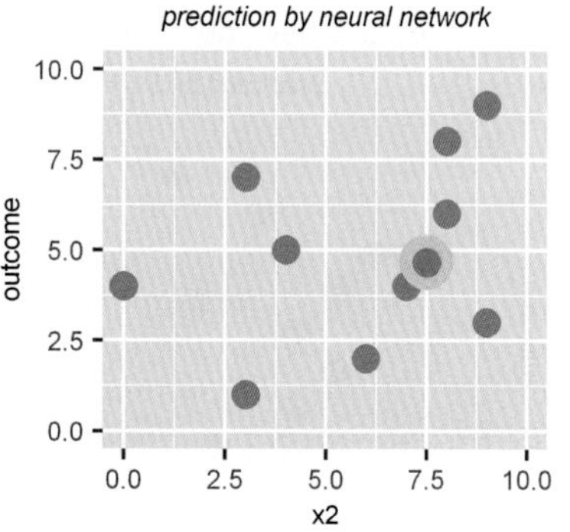

8.5 CASE | Call Center Scheduling

Predictive modeling with linear regression to inform a partnership agreement between a large retail pet supply client and a business process outsourcing provider.

8.5.1 Business Situation

A business process outsourcing company (the call center) is negotiating with a pet supplies company (the client) to provide customer service to the client's customers next year. The contract calls for the client to pay the call center per call handled, based on a reasonable rate and assuming the client's call volume will be about the same as it was last year. Also, the call center will be charged a penalty for any unanswered calls beyond a certain threshold per day. The call center will decide the appropriate daily agent staffing levels, but the schedule must be committed to in advance. Note that the call center's profit will depend on a trade-off between saving agent staffing costs and incurring customer dissatisfaction penalties. The call center must also consider the client's cost savings from outsourcing and the customers' satisfaction level, or risk losing the client altogether.

- **Role:** Vice President of Call Center Operations at a business process outsourcing company.
- **Decision:** Schedule for call center agents?
- **Approach:** Assume some fixed staffing levels and propose schedules for the required number of call center agents accordingly. Also build several linear regression regressors to predict daily call volumes and propose schedules for the required number of call center agents accordingly. Estimate and compare call center profit, client cost savings, and customer satisfaction resulting from the various proposed schedules.

8.5.2 Decision Models

There are two decision models relevant here, one that describes how a decision method influences the call center's business result, and another one that describes how a decision method influences the client's business result.

8.5.2.1 Call Center Perspective

The call center decision model starts with a decision method that predicts the number of calls that will arrive on each day over some time period, so that an appropriate number of call center agents can be scheduled for each day over that time period. The business result of interest is profit measured as the revenue from answering calls minus the costs of agents and penalties.

Business parameters include the following:

- **number of calls (call_count):** assumed to be the same as last year, a value derived from the data
- **call handle rate:** maximum number of calls that can be handled by an agent per day, a value gathered from call center operations
- **agent pay rate:** cost per scheduled agent per day, a value gathered from call center operations
- **answered call pay rate:** a value negotiated between call center and client
- **unanswered call penalty rate:** a value negotiated between call center and client
- **threshold:** penalty applied on days when number of unanswered calls exceeds this count, a value negotiated between call center and client

business parameters

name	value
agent_pay_rate	100
call_handle_rate	30
answered_call_pay_rate	7
unanswered_call_penalty_rate	25
threshold	10
call_count	to be derived from data

Possible results of the decision method include the following:

- days where the predicted number of calls is too high from among all days – this is the ***over-prediction rate***.
- average amount by which predicted number of calls is too high on days where predicted number of calls is too high – this is the ***mean over-prediction error***.
- days where the predicted number of calls is too low from among all days – this is the ***under-prediction rate***.
- average amount by which predicted number of calls is too low on days where predicted number of calls is too low – this is the ***mean under-prediction error***.

The number of predicted calls can be inferred from over-prediction and under-prediction rates and mean errors. The number of answered calls depends on the over-prediction rate, under-prediction rate, and mean under-prediction error because calls get answered on both over-predicted days and under-predicted days. The number of answered calls does not depend on mean over-prediction error, because on days when there are enough agents to answer all calls it is irrelevant how many extra agents are available. The number of unanswered calls depends only on under-prediction rate and mean under-prediction error because calls go unanswered only on under-predicted days.

Agents are scheduled to cover predicted calls, so agent cost depends on the number of predicted calls, agent pay rate, and call handle rate. Revenue comes from answering calls at a pay rate. Penalty costs come from leaving calls unanswered at a penalty rate, but subject to exceeding a threshold. Profit is revenue less agent and penalty costs.

8.5.2.2 Client Perspective

The client decision model starts with the same decision method that predicts the number of calls that will arrive on each day of some time period, and assumes that the call center schedules the appropriate number of call center agents accordingly. The 2 business results of interest are cost savings measured as the budget for call center operations less the cost of call center operations, and customer satisfaction measured as the probability of getting a call answered.

Business parameters include the following:

- **budget:** budget for call center operations, a value gathered from company general management
- **number of calls (call_count):** assumed to be the same as last year, a value derived from the data
- **answered call pay rate:** a value negotiated between call center and client
- **unanswered call penalty rate:** a value negotiated between call center and client
- **threshold:** penalty applied on days when number of unanswered calls exceeds this count, a value negotiated between call center and client

business parameters

name	value
budget	1,000,000
answered_call_pay_rate	7
unanswered_call_penalty_rate	25
threshold	10
call_count	to be derived from data

Possible results of the decision method include the following:

- days where the predicted number of calls is too high from among all days – this is the ***over-prediction rate***.
- days where the predicted number of calls is too low from among all days – this is the ***under-prediction rate***.
- average amount by which predicted number of calls is too low on days where predicted number of calls is too low – this is the ***mean under-prediction error***.

Mean over-prediction error and number of predicted calls are not considered because they are irrelevant from the client perspective. Any extra agents available due to predicting too high do not affect client costs because the client pays for calls answered, not for agents scheduled. Similarly, extra agents do not affect customer satisfaction because customers care about calls answered, not about agents scheduled.

The number of answered calls depends on the over-prediction rate, under-prediction rate, and mean under-prediction error because calls get answered on both over-predicted days and

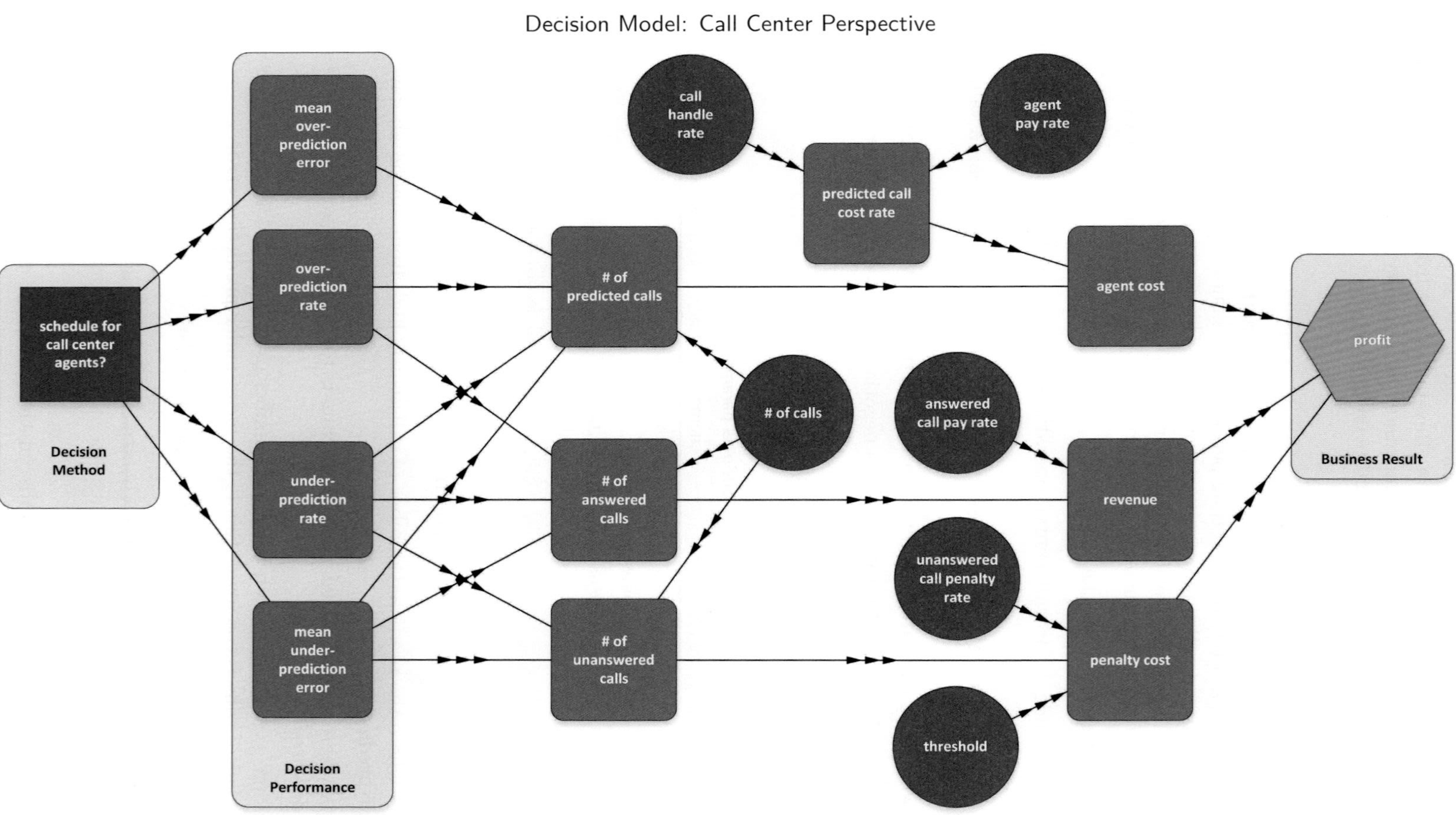
Decision Model: Call Center Perspective
schedule for call center agents?
Decision Method
mean over-prediction error
over-prediction rate
under-prediction rate
mean under-prediction error
Decision Performance
# of predicted calls
# of answered calls
# of unanswered calls
call handle rate
predicted call cost rate
agent pay rate
# of calls
answered call pay rate
unanswered call penalty rate
threshold
agent cost
revenue
penalty cost
profit
Business Result

under-predicted days. The number of unanswered calls depends only on under-prediction rate and mean under-prediction error because calls go unanswered only on under-predicted days.

Call cost comes from answering calls at a pay rate. Penalty credit comes from leaving calls unanswered at a penalty rate, but subject to exceeding a threshold. Cost savings is budget less call costs adjusted by penalty credit. Customer satisfaction, the probability of getting a call answered, is the number of answered calls from among all calls.

8.5.3 Data

Retrieve a reference known-outcome dataset of daily call volumes over a 2-year time period. Each of 711 observations describes a unique day. Predictor variables capture calendar features information about store promotions that could potentially affect call volume. An outcome variable indicates the call volume.

all_variables
Date, Day, WOM, Month, Year, Holidays, Promotions, Actual..Call.Volume

Prepare the dataset for analysis. For convenience, rename and change the case of some of the variables, and set the holiday variable's blank entries to be "none". To simplify upcoming data visualizations, convert the date variable from categorical to a special date type.

data *size 711×8, first few observations shown, first few variables shown*

date	day	wom	month	year
2014-01-01	Wednesday	1	Jan	2,014
2014-01-02	Thursday	1	Jan	2,014
2014-01-03	Friday	1	Jan	2,014
2014-01-04	Saturday	1	Jan	2,014
2014-01-05	Sunday	1	Jan	2,014

data *size 711×8, first few observations shown, last few variables shown*

holidays	promotions	volume
New Year's Day	25% Off,FS on $49	373
Next Day of the-New Year's Day	No Email Drop	497
none	No Email Drop	467
none	No Email Drop	430
none	25% Off,FS on $49	523

8.5.4 Model A: Staffing Level Is Set to Fixed High

Consider a simplistic, aggressive approach to staffing call center agents. Just schedule a fixed high number of agents, say enough to answer 500 calls per day. Note that this is like always predicting call volume to be 500 calls per day.

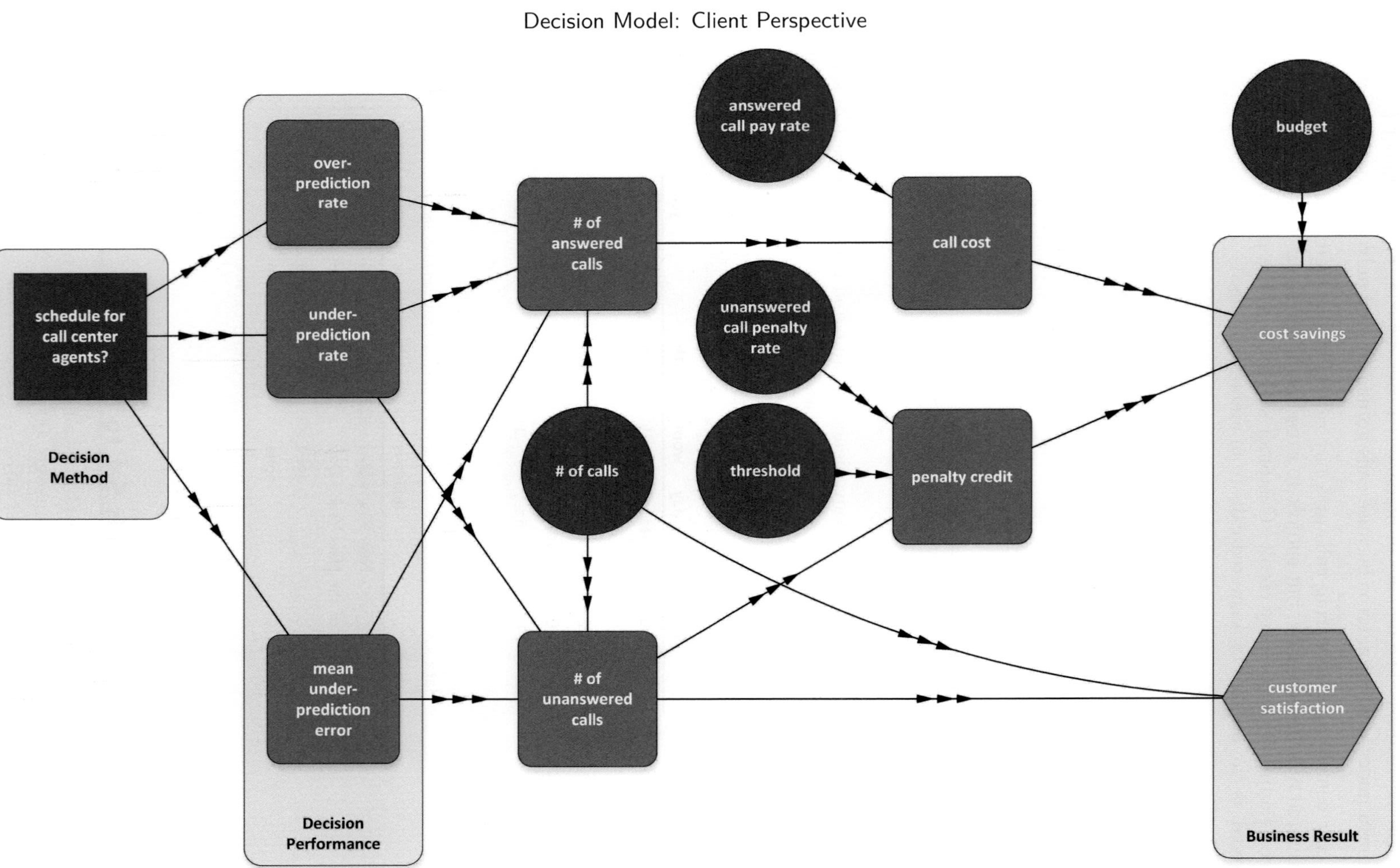
Decision Model: Client Perspective
schedule for call center agents?
Decision Method
over-prediction rate
under-prediction rate
mean under-prediction error
Decision Performance
# of answered calls
# of calls
# of unanswered calls
answered call pay rate
unanswered call penalty rate
threshold
call cost
penalty credit
budget
cost savings
customer satisfaction
Business Result

8.5.4.1 Partition Dataset

We don't really need a training dataset because it wouldn't be necessary for building a model that always predicts 500 calls per day. Let's hold out the second year as the testing dataset. We need only the date and volume variables: date for the upcoming data visualization, volume to compare against the upcoming predicted volume.

data.test *size 346×2, first few observations shown*

date	volume
2015-01-01	300
2015-01-02	419
2015-01-03	340
2015-01-04	404

8.5.4.2 Construct Model

Trivially construct a model that always predicts 500 calls per day.

model

volume.predicted
500

8.5.4.3 Evaluate Model

Here are the actual call volumes and predicted call volumes across the testing time period. The number of agents scheduled corresponds to the number of calls predicted. We see that on most days, there are plenty of agents available to answer calls.

data.test *first few observations shown*

date	volume	volume.predicted
2015-01-01	300	500
2015-01-02	419	500
2015-01-03	340	500
2015-01-04	404	500

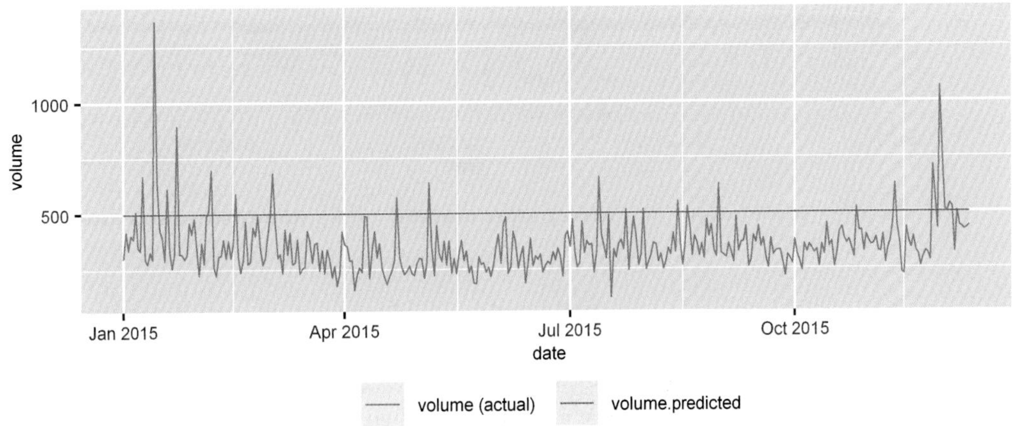

On some days, predicting call volumes too high results in over-staffing and excess calls, which are calls that could have be answered but never arrived. On other days, predicting call volumes too low results in under-staffing and missed calls, which are calls that arrived but were not answered.

Here is a closer look at how predicted call volumes affect the number of excess calls and number of missed calls:

Predicted call volumes too high:

$$\begin{aligned}\text{volume excess} &= \text{volume predicted} - \text{volume actual}\\ \text{volume missed} &= 0\end{aligned}$$

Predicted call volume too low:

$$\begin{aligned}\text{volume missed} &= \text{volume actual} - \text{volume predicted}\\ \text{volume excess} &= 0\end{aligned}$$

Treat a day as overstaffed when the number of excess calls is 0 or more. Treat a day as understaffed when number of missed calls exceeds the threshold.

data.test *first few observations shown*

date	volume	volume.predicted	volume.excess	overstaffed	volume.missed	understaffed
2015-01-01	300	500	200	TRUE	0	FALSE
2015-01-02	419	500	81	TRUE	0	FALSE
2015-01-03	340	500	160	TRUE	0	FALSE
2015-01-04	404	500	96	TRUE	0	FALSE

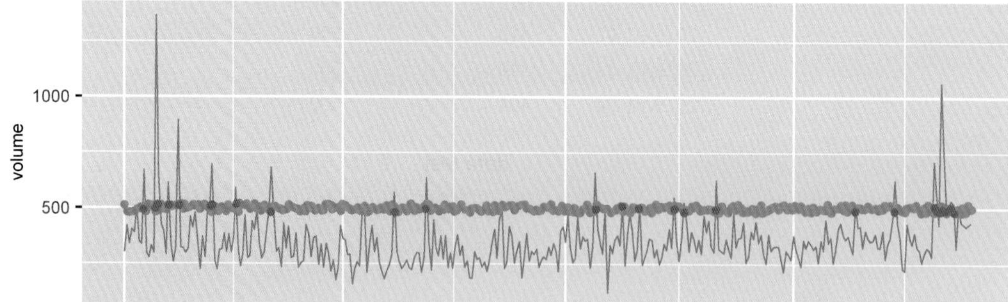

8.5.4.4 Business Results

Calculate business results from the call center perspective and from the client perspective per the decision model, business parameters, and model evaluation.

Call center perspective:

$$\text{revenue} = \text{answered call pay rate} \times \left(\begin{array}{l}\text{actual number of calls while overstaffed} + \\ \text{predicted number of calls while understaffed}\end{array}\right)$$

$$\text{agent cost} = \left(\frac{\text{agent pay rate}}{\text{call handle rate}}\right) \times \text{number of calls predicted}$$

$$\text{penalty cost} = \left(\begin{array}{l}\text{unanswered call penalty rate} \times \\ \text{number of calls missed while understaffed}\end{array}\right)$$

$$\text{cost} = \text{agent cost} + \text{penalty cost}$$

$$\text{profit} = \text{revenue} - \text{cost}$$

model	revenue	agent_cost	penalty_cost	cost	profit
Fixed High	947,807	576,667	102,125	678,792	269,015

Client perspective:

$$\text{call cost} = \text{answered call pay rate} \times \left(\begin{array}{l}\text{actual number of calls while overstaffed} + \\ \text{predicted number of calls while understaffed}\end{array}\right)$$

$$\text{penalty credit} = \left(\begin{array}{l}\text{unanswered call penalty rate} \times \\ \text{number of calls missed while understaffed}\end{array}\right)$$

$$\text{cost} = \text{call cost} - \text{penalty credit}$$

$$\text{savings} = \text{budget} - \text{cost}$$

$$\text{customer satisfaction} = 1 - \left(\frac{\text{number of calls missed}}{\text{number of calls}}\right)$$

model	call_cost	penalty_credit	cost	savings	csat
Fixed High	947,807	102,125	845,682	154,318	0.9665

Under the fixed high scheduling approach, we can expect the call center to make a modest profit of \$269,015 per year. The client will pay a high cost of \$845,682 per year, but in return will reach a high 96.65% customer satisfaction score.

8.5.5 Model B: Staffing Level Is Set to Fixed Low

Next consider a simplistic, lax approach. Schedule a fixed low number of agents, say enough to answer 350 calls per day. Note that this is like always predicting call volume to be 350 calls per day.

8.5.5.1 Partition Dataset

As before, hold out the second year as the testing dataset and keep just the date and volume variables.

data.test *size 346×2, first few observations shown*

date	volume
2015-01-01	300
2015-01-02	419
2015-01-03	340
2015-01-04	404

8.5.5.2 Construct Model

Trivially construct a model that always predicts 350 calls per day.

model

volume.predicted
350

8.5.5.3 Evaluate Model

Here are the actual call volumes and predicted call volumes across the testing time period. The number of agents scheduled corresponds to the number of calls predicted. We see that on most days, there are not enough agents available to answer calls.

data.test *first few observations shown*

date	volume	volume.predicted	volume.excess	overstaffed	volume.missed	understaffed
2015-01-01	300	350	50	TRUE	0	FALSE
2015-01-02	419	350	0	TRUE	69	TRUE
2015-01-03	340	350	10	TRUE	0	FALSE
2015-01-04	404	350	0	TRUE	54	TRUE

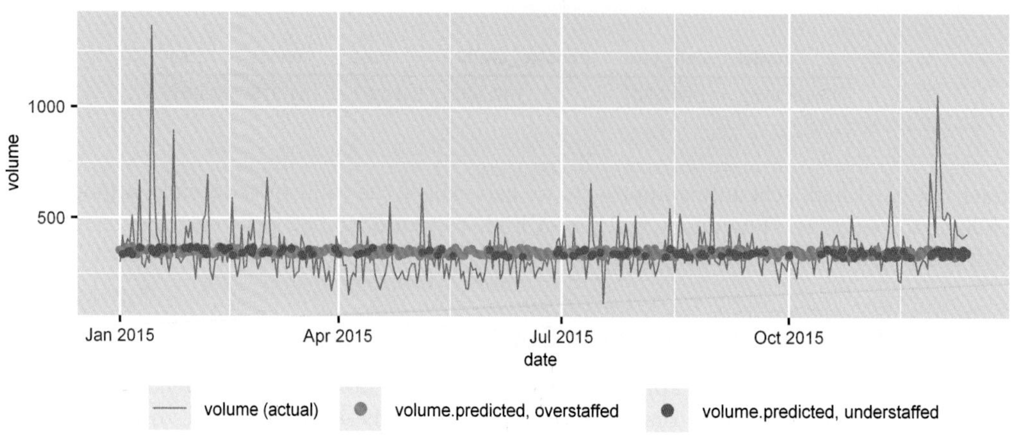

8.5.5.4 Business Result

Here are the business results from the call center perspective and from the client perspective.

call center persepctive

model	revenue	agent_cost	penalty_cost	cost	profit
Fixed Low	1,175,307	403,667	366,100	769,767	405,540

client perspective

model	call_cost	penalty_credit	cost	savings	csat
Fixed Low	1,175,307	366,100	809,207	190,793	0.8797

Under the fixed low scheduling approach, we can expect the call center to make a hefty profit of \$405,540 per year. The client will pay a low cost of \$809,207 per year, but suffer a low 87.97% customer satisfaction score.

These business results expose a problem at the root of the call center–client relationship. The call center is incentivized to provide poor customer service because that way it would make a larger profit. The client is incentivized to drive down the call center's profit because that way its customers would be more satisfied. However, if the call center provides customer service that's too bad, it will soon find itself without a client and no profit at all. Likewise, if the client drives down the call center's profit too much, it will soon find itself without a call center center and no customer service at all.

8.5.6 Model C: Staffing Level Is Set by Linear Regression

A compromise is in order, where the call center makes a reasonable profit and the client's customer get a reasonable level of customer service. That would require a better model, one that doesn't cause too much over-staffing or too much under-staffing. Consider a linear regression model as a candidate.

8.5.6.1 Further Prepare Data

The linear regression method only works with numerical predictor variables. Convert the *day*, *month*, *holidays*, and *promotion* categorical variables to dummy variables.

data *size 711×167, first few observations shown, first few variables shown*

date	wom	year	volume	day_Monday	day_Saturday	day_Sunday	day_Thursday
2014-01-01	1	2,014	373	0	0	0	0
2014-01-02	1	2,014	497	0	0	0	1
2014-01-03	1	2,014	467	0	0	0	0
2014-01-04	1	2,014	430	0	1	0	0

data *size 711×167, first few observations shown, a few variables shown*

month_Aug	month_Dec	month_Feb	month_Jan	month_Jul	month_Jun	month_Mar
0	0	0	1	0	0	0
0	0	0	1	0	0	0
0	0	0	1	0	0	0
0	0	0	1	0	0	0

data *size 711×167, first few observations shown, a few variables shown*

holidays_Labor Day	holidays_Martin Luther King Jr. Day	holidays_Memorial Day
0	0	0
0	0	0
0	0	0
0	0	0

data *size 711×167, first few observations shown, a few variables shown*

promotions_20% Off on Halloween, FS on $49	promotions_20% Off on Supplies,FS on $49
0	0
0	0
0	0
0	0

8.5.6.2 Partition Dataset

Use the first year as the training dataset and hold out the second year as the testing dataset.

size of data.train

observations	variables
365	167

size of data.test

observations	variables
346	167

8.5.6.3 Construct Model

Use linear regression to construct a model to predict call volume given the other predictor variables, excluding *date*. Here are a few of the resulting model's parameters. Note that the *year* variable was effectively not used because there is no variation in *year* values in the training dataset. They're all value 2014. Also note that each dummy variable gets a coefficient, effectively acting as a way to adjust volume predicted up or down based on new observations occurring on specific days, months, holidays, or during specific promotions.

model parameters
first few coefficients shown

	coefficient
(Intercept)	529.429
wom	-6.781
year	NA
day_Monday	75.887
day_Saturday	-38.587
day_Sunday	-45.567
day_Thursday	-31.884
day_Tuesday	61.416
day_Wednesday	29.158
month_Aug	-72.427

8.5.6.4 Evaluate Model

Here are the actual call volumes and predicted call volumes across the testing time period. The number of agents scheduled corresponds to the number of calls predicted. We see that there is a mix of overstaffed and understaffed days.

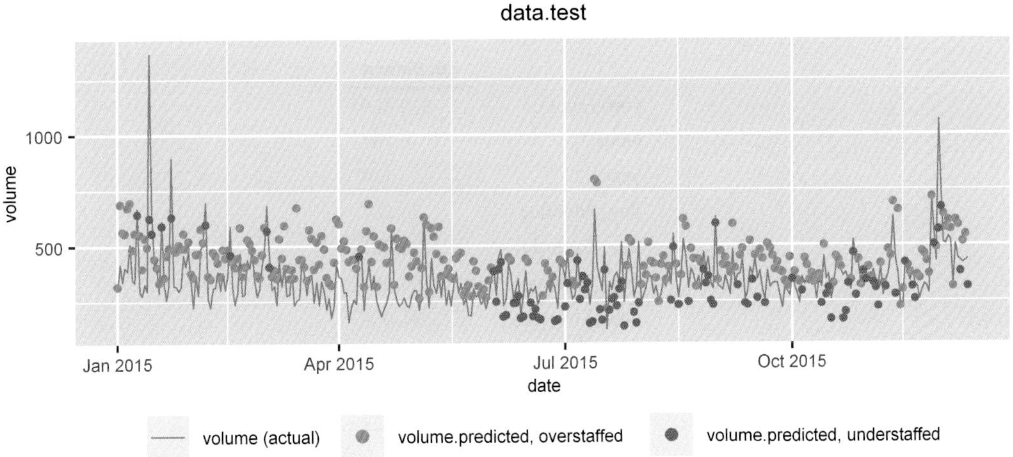

8.5.6.5 Business Result

Here are the business results from the call center perspective and from the client perspective.

call center perspective

model	revenue	agent_cost	penalty_cost	cost	profit
LinReg	1,060,117	471,982	208,692	680,674	379,443

client perspective

model	call_cost	penalty_credit	cost	savings	csat
LinReg	1,060,117	208,692	851,425	148,575	0.9313

Under the scheduling by linear regression model approach, we can expect the call center to make a reasonable profit of \$379,443 per year. The client will pay a reasonable cost of \$851,425 per year, and achieve a reasonable 93.13% customer satisfaction score.

These business results show that better prediction leads to a better business relationship. It is in the interest of both parties to collaborate and invest in developing better prediction capability.

8.5.7 Model D: Staffing Level Is Set by Linear Regression with Buffer

Perhaps the compromise between call center profit and client customer satisfaction suits both parties. More likely, they will continue to negotiate terms, trying to gain at least some small advantage, though stopping short of risking their good relationship. For example, the client might suggest adding a small buffer to the volume predicted. This could potentially increase customer satisfaction significantly without decreasing call center profit much. If so, that might be worth doing.

8.5.7.1 Construct Model

Adjust the linear regression model by adding 50 to the intercept parameter. This adjusted model will predict 50 calls more than the original linear regression model would, given the same predictor variable values as inputs.

model parameters
first few coefficients shown

	coefficient
(Intercept)	579.429
wom	-6.781
year	NA
day_Monday	75.887
day_Saturday	-38.587
day_Sunday	-45.567
day_Thursday	-31.884
day_Tuesday	61.416
day_Wednesday	29.158
month_Aug	-72.427

8.5.7.2 Evaluate Model

Here are the actual call volumes and predicted call volumes across the testing time period. The number of agents scheduled corresponds to the number of calls predicted. We see that there is a mix of overstaffed and understaffed days, but more overstaffed days.

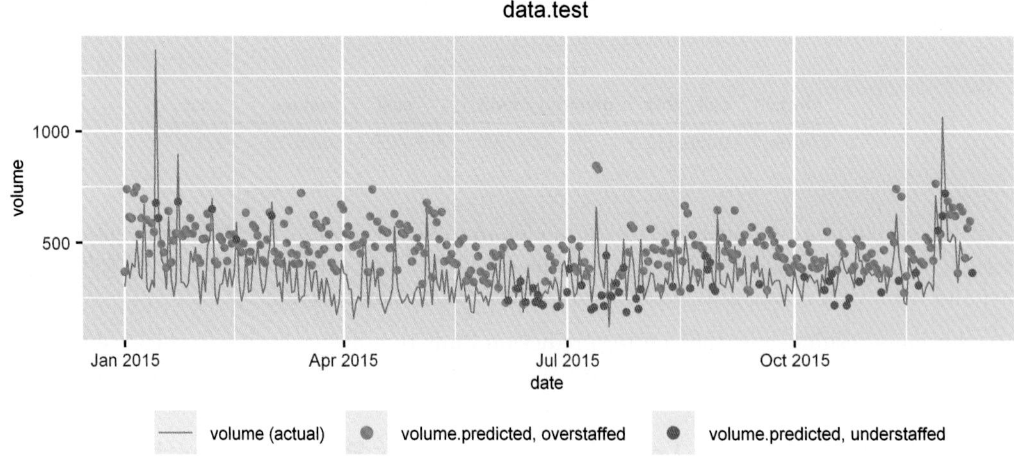

8.5.7.3 Business Result

Here are the business results from the call center perspective and from the client perspective.

call center perspective

model	revenue	agent_cost	penalty_cost	cost	profit
LinReg Buffer	991,559	529,649	107,967	637,616	353,944

client perspective

model	call_cost	penalty_credit	cost	savings	csat
LinReg Buffer	991,559	107,967	883,592	116,408	0.9643

Under the scheduling by linear regression model plus buffer approach, we can expect the call center to make a reasonable profit of \$353,944 per year. The client will pay a reasonable cost of \$883{,}592 per year, and rise to a 96.43% customer satisfaction score.

Adding a buffer to the predictions drops the call center's profit by \$379,443 – \$353,944 = \$25,499 per year, and increases the client's customer satisfaction score by 96.43% – 93.13% = 3.3%. Is it worth \$25,499 per year to please the client? Is it worth a 3.3% increase in customer satisfaction to displease the call center? Perhaps so.

8.5.8 Model E: Staffing Level Is Set by Piece-Wise Linear Regression

Perhaps you noticed that the linear regression model tends to over-predict in the first half of the year, and tends to more evenly over-predict and under-predict in the second half of the year. This leads us to suspect that something about the first half differs from the second half. If so, it might not be appropriate to use just 1 model to make predictions about 2 different environments.

8.5.8.1 Further Prepare Data

Add a synthetic variable *half* to the dataset to distinguish observations in the first half of the year from those in the second. Specify *half* as 1 or 2, depending on whether a particular month dummy variable is 1 or 0.

data *first few observations shown, first few variables shown*

half	date	wom	year	volume	day_Monday	day_Saturday	day_Sunday
1	2014-01-01	1	2,014	373	0	0	0
1	2014-01-02	1	2,014	497	0	0	0
1	2014-01-03	1	2,014	467	0	0	0
1	2014-01-04	1	2,014	430	0	1	0

8.5.8.2 Partition Data

Partition the each of the training and testing datasets further into parts based on the *half* variable. This yields training and testing datasets for the first half of a year, and different training and testing datasets for the second half of a year.

size of data.train.1st_half

observations	variables
181	168

size of data.train.2nd_half

observations	variables
184	168

size of data.test.1st_half

observations	variables
181	168

size of data.test.2nd_half

observations	variables
165	168

8.5.8.3 Construct Models

Use linear regression to construct 2 models to predict call volume given the other predictor variables, excluding *date*. The first model, constructed based on the first-half training dataset, will be for predicting call volumes in the first half of a year. The second model, constructed based on the second-half training dataset, will be for predicting call volumes in the second half of the year.

Here are few of the models' parameters. The models are quite unlike the model based on a whole year training dataset, and are quite unlike each other. Also note that the first model effectively does not use the *month_Aug* variable (and does not use other second-half month variables) because there is no variation in *month_Aug* values in the training dataset. They're all value 0. Similarly in the second model for first-half month variables.

model.1st_half parameters
first few coefficients shown

	coefficient
(Intercept)	535.88
wom	-11.22
year	NA
day_Monday	73.28
day_Saturday	-46.94
day_Sunday	-25.41
day_Thursday	-55.34
day_Tuesday	91.06
day_Wednesday	35.35
month_Aug	NA

model.2nd_half parameters
first few coefficients shown

	coefficient
(Intercept)	362.6360
wom	0.7428
year	NA
day_Monday	68.6023
day_Saturday	-36.5842
day_Sunday	-75.7766
day_Thursday	-26.0436
day_Tuesday	1.6211
day_Wednesday	11.0452
month_Aug	0.4317

8.5.8.4 Evaluate Models

Apply each of the 2 models to its appropriate testing dataset. For each model, here are the actual call volumes and predicted call volumes across the testing time periods. The number of agents scheduled corresponds to the number of calls predicted.

data.test.1st_half
first few observations shown, a few variables shown

half	date	volume	volume.predicted
1	2015-01-01	300	278.6
1	2015-01-02	419	725.5
1	2015-01-03	340	565.7
1	2015-01-04	404	587.2

data.test.2nd_half
first few observations shown, a few variables shown

half	date	volume	volume.predicted
2	2015-07-01	349	226.1
2	2015-07-02	471	323.8
2	2015-07-03	327	458.0
2	2015-07-04	257	245.3

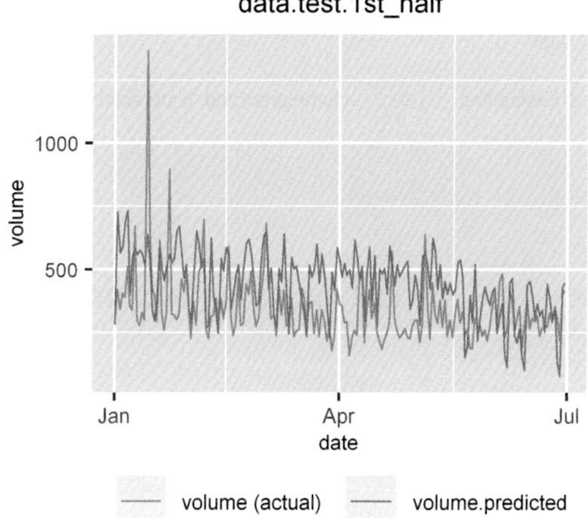

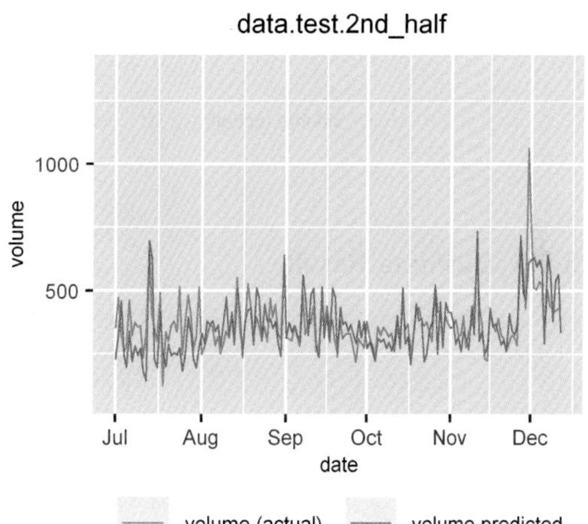

Concatenate the 2 evaluations to visualize altogether in 1 lineplot. Note that the lineplot shows predictions from 2 different models.

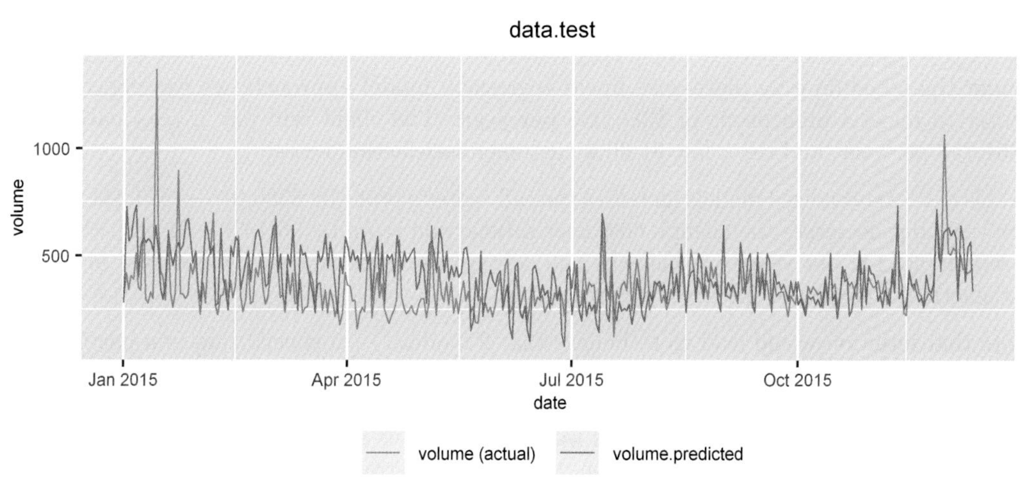

We see that in the first half of the year, there is a more even mix of over-prediction and under-prediction than with the whole year model, though still tending to over-predict. In the second half of the year, the mix is much more even.

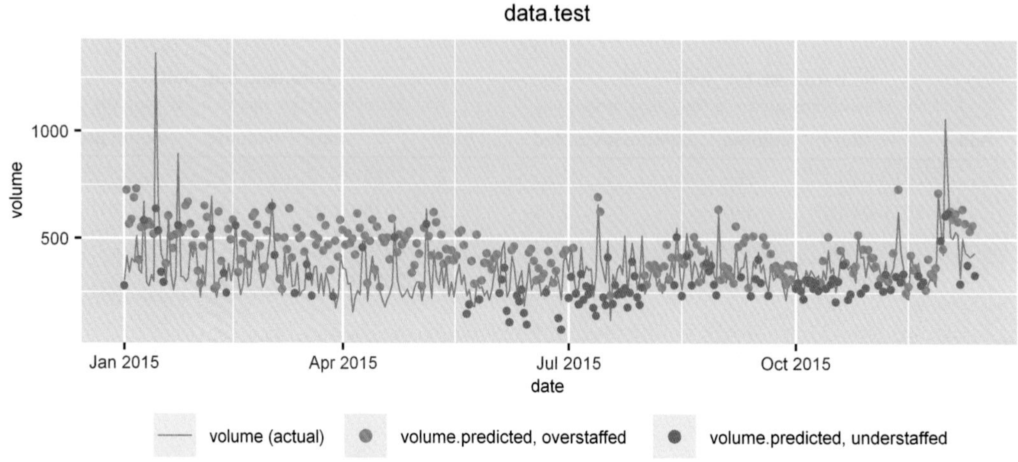

8.5.8.5 Business Result

Here are the business results from the call center perspective and from the client perspective.

call center perspective

model	revenue	agent_cost	penalty_cost	cost	profit
LinReg Piece-Wise	1,104,974	465,671	253,216	718,887	386,086

client perspective

model	call_cost	penalty_credit	cost	savings	csat
LinReg Piece-Wise	1,104,974	253,216	851,758	148,242	0.9166

Under the scheduling by piece-wise linear regression model approach, we can expect the call center to make a high profit of \$386,086 per year. The client will pay a reasonable cost of \$851,758 per year, and see a low 91.66% customer satisfaction score.

In this case, 2 specialized models increases the call center's profit by $\$386{,}086 - \$353{,}944 = \$32{,}142$ per year, but decreases the client's customer satisfaction score by $96.43\% - 91.66\% = 4.77\%$. Is it worth \$32,142 per year to please the call center? Is it worth a 4.77% decrease in customer satisfaction to displease the client? Perhaps not.

Note that intuition would lead us to believe that 2 models, each specializing in a particular part of the year, would predict better that 1 general model would. And in some cases that would be true. However, as always, business results are more important than performance metrics. In this case, we can expect that using 2 models would only lead us away from an amicable compromise between profit and customer satisfaction, and toward a strained business relationship.

8.5.9 Comparative Analysis

Let's summarize our analysis. From the call center's financial perspective, fixed high and piece-wise linear regression approaches to prediction are best, regardless of the client's concerns.

call center business results

model	revenue	agent_cost	penalty_cost	cost	profit
Fixed High	947,807	576,667	102,125	678,792	269,015
Fixed Low	1,175,307	403,667	366,100	769,767	405,540
LinReg	1,060,117	471,982	208,692	680,674	379,443
LinReg Buffer	991,559	529,649	107,967	637,616	353,944
LinReg Piece-Wise	1,104,974	465,671	253,216	718,887	386,086

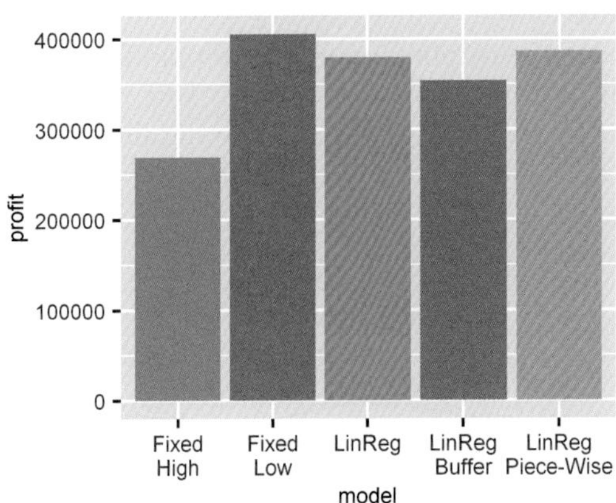

From the client's financial perspective, fixed low is best, and fixed high, linear regression, and piece-wise linear regression roughly tie for second best. From the client's customer satisfaction perspective, fixed high and linear regression plus buffer are best.

client business results

model	call_cost	penalty_credit	cost	savings	csat
Fixed High	947,807	102,125	845,682	154,318	0.9665
Fixed Low	1,175,307	366,100	809,207	190,793	0.8797
LinReg	1,060,117	208,692	851,425	148,575	0.9313
LinReg Buffer	991,559	107,967	883,592	116,408	0.9643
LinReg Piece-Wise	1,104,974	253,216	851,758	148,242	0.9166

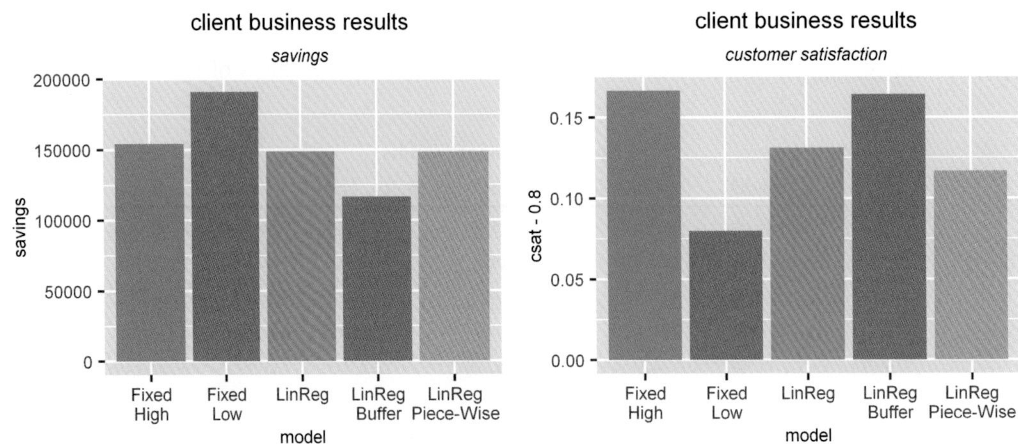

Various decisions about which scheduling approach to take will lead to various business results. This analysis doesn't tell us which decision is best. But it does tell us what the the likely business results would be, so that parties with conflicting incentives can negotiate with a clear understanding toward an amicable compromise. There's always a trade-off, and there's always a trade.

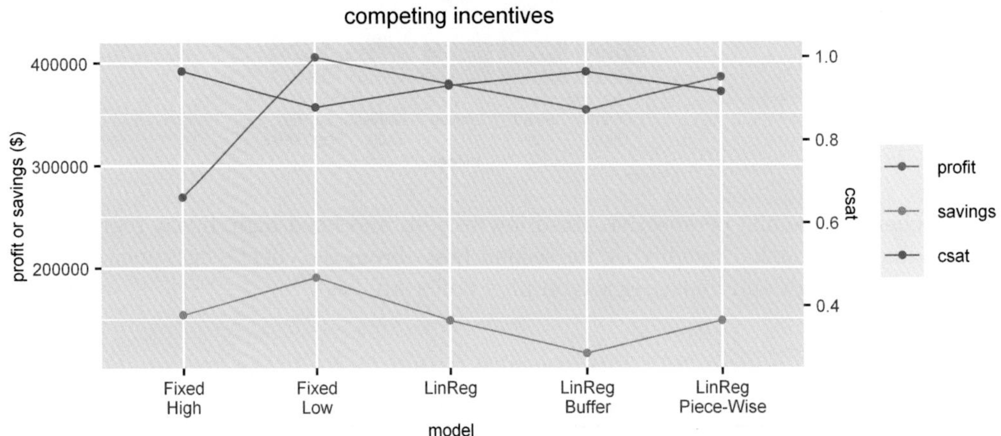

9 | Ensemble Assembly

Learning Objectives

Terms

Know the terms:

- Ensemble assembly
- Ensemble model
- Component model
- Bagging method
  (or bootstrap aggregating method)
- Bagged model
- Bootstrap sample
- Boosting method
- Boosted model
- Stacking method
- Stacked model

Effects of Assumptions

Know the effects of assumptions:

- Effect of probability within the bagging method
- Effect of probability within the boosting method
- Effect of choice of component model construction methods within stacking method

Use the Methods

Know how to use the methods:

- Compute a bagged model and use it to compute predictions.
- Compute a boosted model and use it to compute predictions.
- Compute a stacked model and use it to compute predictions.

9.1 Bagging

Combine predictive model construction methods by the bagging method, as with a committee of general experts.

9.1.1 Introduction

Could a European swallow fly a coconut from the African continent to the British Isles? You can think of bagging as convening a committee of ***general*** experts to answer some questions, perhaps questions involving aerodynamics (the study of flying), carpology (the study of seeds and fruits like coconuts), and ornithology (the study of birds like swallows).

Each expert is well versed in all 3 fields, but each has learned about them from both a set of books read by all the experts and a set of books read only by the single expert. One of the experts, Annie, concludes that our swallow could not perform such a feat. The second expert, Jacob, concludes that our swallow could indeed do it. Annie and Jacob are both experts, but they can make different conclusions about the same question because their reasonings are not based on same books. The third expert, Rongsen, also concludes that our swallow is incapable of flying so far carrying a coconut, this time reasoning based on yet a third set of books.

The committee needs to commit to just 1 answer, so the experts vote. The committee answers no because the 2-to-1 majority voted no.

Another example: consider a software application running on your computer to detect ransomware attacks, an increasingly important business application. The application incorporates a model built using the decision tree method and a portion of a log file as the reference dataset, which includes log entries made during normal computer operation and some entries made in the presence of ransomware. The model can quickly conclude whether or not patterns in new log files indicate ransomware, but not with perfect accuracy. The application incorporates several other models, too, each built using the same decision tree method but with a different portion of the log file as the reference dataset. Each model makes its own conclusion about the presence of ransomware when presented with new log files. The application sounds an alarm when the majority of the models concludes that a ransomware attack has occurred.

9.1.2 About Bagging

Ensemble assembly is about combining several predictive models to build a new predictive model, one that synergizes the strengths of the **component models**.

The **bagging method** is a specific ensemble assembly method that combines predictive models built using a single model construction method and a single set of hyper-parameter values, but using different bootstrap samples of a single reference dataset. The resulting **bagged model** makes predictions based on the most popular of the component models' predictions. The bagging method is also known as the **bootstrap aggregating method**.

Bagging works like this: Get several bootstrap samples of a reference dataset. For each sample, build a model using a single model construction method and a single set of hyper-parameter values. Treat these models as components of a new model that makes predictions based on the most popular of the component models' predictions.

9.1.3 Bagging

Consider this reference dataset and new observation. The scatterplot shows the observations jittered to expose those with identical x_1, x_2 values.

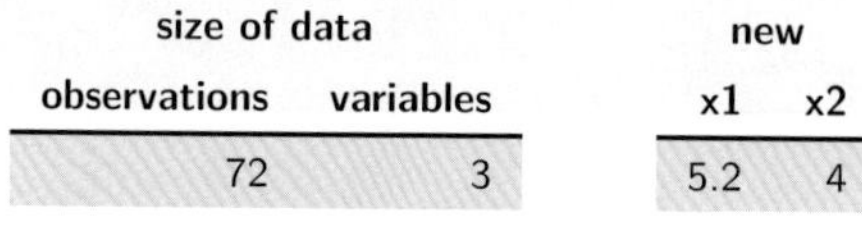

size of data		new	
observations	variables	x1	x2
72	3	5.2	4

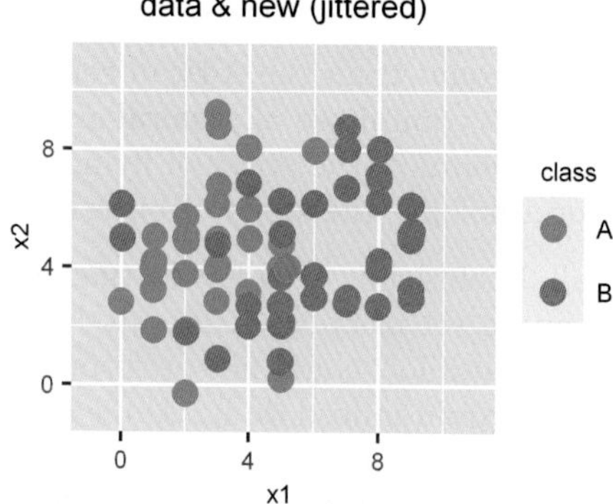

9.1.3.1 Bootstrap Samples

A **bootstrap sample** from a dataset is a set of randomly selected observations from that dataset, with replacement allowed. The number of observations in the bootstrap sample should be the same as the number of observations in the dataset from which it is taken. Usually, many of the observations in the bootstrap sample are duplicates of each other.

Here we take 3 different bootstrap samples from the dataset:

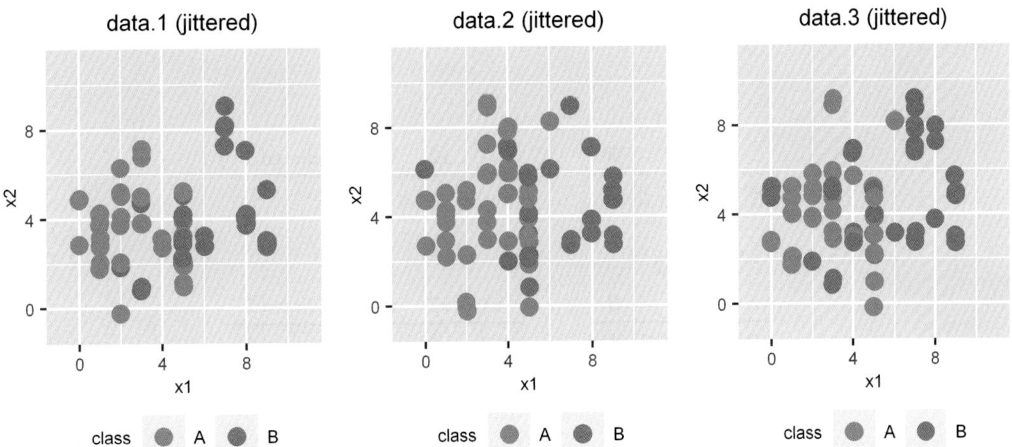

9.1.3.2 Component Models Based on Bootstrap Samples

We can build several models, using the same method and hyper-parameter values, but based on the different bootstrap samples of the reference dataset.

Here we build 3 such models:

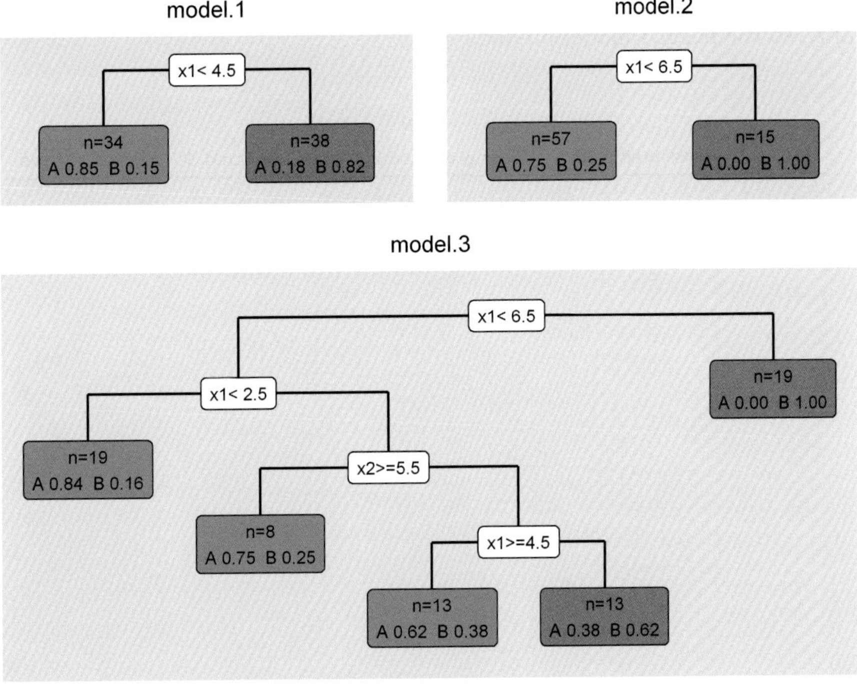

9.1.3.3 Predictions

We use the 3 models to make 3 different predictions of the new observation's class:

prob.1

A	B
0.1842	0.8158

new

x1	x2	class.predicted.1
5.2	4	B

prob.2

A	B
0.7544	0.2456

new

x1	x2	class.predicted.2
5.2	4	A

prob.3

A	B
0.6154	0.3846

new

x1	x2	class.predicted.3
5.2	4	A

9.1.3.4 Vote

We compare the predictions of the models and vote for the most popular prediction. Model 1 predicts that the new observation's class is B, and models 2 and 3 predict A. The vote is 2 to 1 in favor of A, so the bagged model predicts A.

new

x1	x2	class.predicted.1	class.predicted.2	class.predicted.3	class.predicted
5.2	4	B	A	A	A

9.2 Boosting

Combine predictive model construction methods by the boosting method, as with a committee of general and specialized experts.

9.2.1 Introduction

Could a European swallow fly a coconut from the African continent to the British Isles? You can think of boosting as convening a committee of ***specialized*** experts to answer some questions, perhaps questions involving aerodynamics (the study of flying), carpology (the study of seeds and fruits like coconuts), and ornithology (the study of birds like swallows).

One expert expert, Kijahre, is well versed in all 3 fields. To join the committee, Kijahre must first take an exam to certify his levels of expertise. He does pretty well, especially on questions involving aerodynamics, but misses a few questions on carpology and ornithology.

A second expert, Laura, has had access to the same books used by Kijahre, but Laura studied less about aerodynamics and more about carpology and ornithology. So Laura is more specialized. It may be good to have Laura join the committee since she may be more likely to correctly answer the kinds of questions that Kijahre would more likely get wrong. Laura takes an exam covering mostly carpology and ornithology. She does pretty well, especially on questions involving carpology, but misses a few questions on ornithology.

A third expert, Waiyam, studied ornithology extensively, but studied just a little about aerodynamics and carpology. Waiyam is the most specialized. It may be good to have Waiyam join the committee to help with Laura's weaker expertise in ornithology.

Now, the 3 experts committee proceed to make conclusions about our swallow. Kijahre says no, Laura says yes, Waiyam says no. The committee needs to commit to just 1 answer, so the experts vote. The committee answers no because the 2-to-1 majority voted no. Note that the question involved all 3 fields, so the question could not have been delegated to just a few specialized experts. Rather, all the experts make their own conclusions, which are then reconciled by voting.

Another example: consider a firm that places data analyst contractors at its clients' companies. The firm uses a software application to predict how likely a candidate is to be successful at a job given the candidate's qualification report and a job description. The application incorporates 3 models, each built using the naive Bayes method. One model was built using a database of historical placement information, and it is very accurate at predicting success for candidates without programming skills. A second model was built using just the portion of the database that mostly includes placement information about candidates with programming skills, and it is very accurate at predicting success for candidates without R programming skills. A third model was built using just the portion of the database that mostly includes placement information about candidates with R programming skills. The application predicts that a candidate will be successful when the majority of the models predict success.

9.2.2 About Boosting

Ensemble assembly is about combining several predictive models to build a new predictive model, one that synergizes the strengths of the **component models**.

The **boosting method** is a specific ensemble assembly method that combines predictive models built using a single model construction method and a single set of hyper-parameter values, but using different ***weighted*** bootstrap samples of a single reference dataset so that they emphasize observations predicted incorrectly by other models. The resulting **boosted model** makes predictions based on the most popular of the component models' predictions.

Boosting works like this: Build a model, make predictions about the reference data, and note the prediction errors. Then build another model, using the same model construction method and hyper-parameter values, but based on a bootstrap sample of the reference data weighted to emphasize the observations associated with the prediction errors. Continue in this way to build more models. Treat these models as the components of a new model that makes predictions based on the most popular of the component models' predictions.

9.2.3 Boosting

Consider this dataset and new unclassified observation. The scatterplot shows the observations jittered to expose those with identical x_1, x_2 values.

size of data	
observations	**variables**
72	3

new	
x1	**x2**
5.2	4

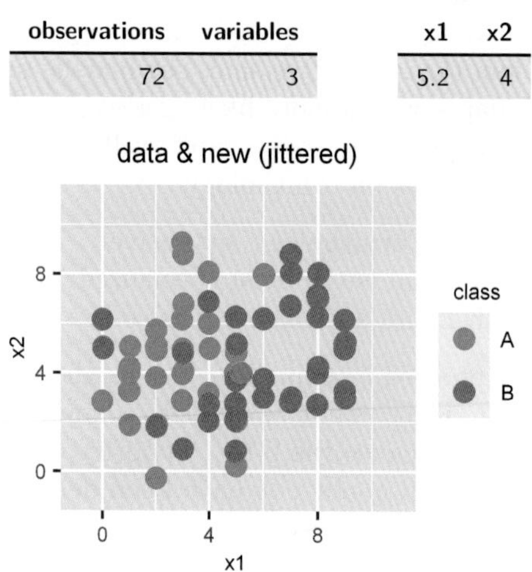

9.2.3.1 Component Models Based on Boosting

First we build several component models that will ultimately be combined as an ensemble model.

Model 1: Build model 1 based on the original dataset. Here we use the decision tree method to build the model.

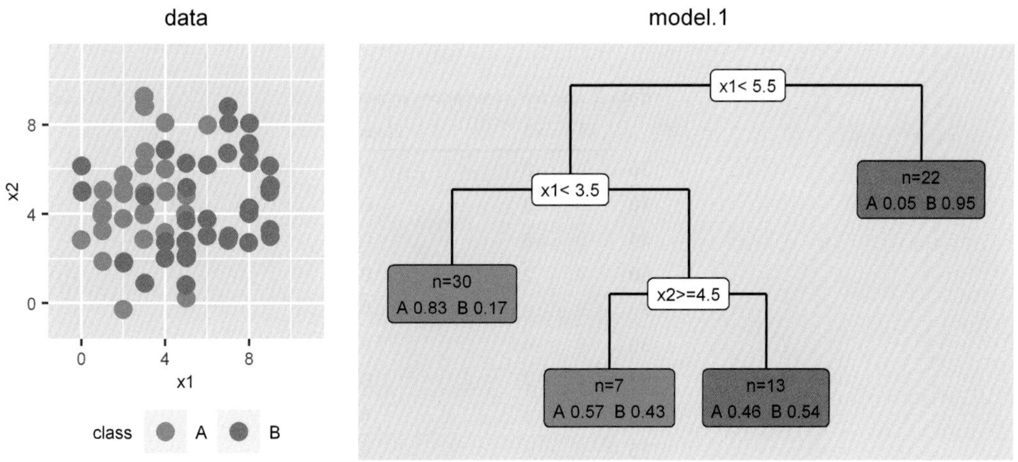

Model 2: Assess model 1's ability to predict the original dataset's observation classes.

data *first few observations shown*

x1	x2	class	class.predicted.1	hit.1
1	3	A	A	TRUE
2	2	A	A	TRUE
3	6	A	A	TRUE
4	5	A	A	TRUE
3	4	A	A	TRUE
2	5	A	A	TRUE
5	3	A	B	FALSE
4	8	A	A	TRUE
3	9	A	A	TRUE
2	0	A	A	TRUE

data *a few "hit" observations*

x1	x2	class	class.predicted.1	hit.1
1	3	A	A	TRUE
2	2	A	A	TRUE
3	6	A	A	TRUE
4	5	A	A	TRUE
3	4	A	A	TRUE
2	5	A	A	TRUE
4	8	A	A	TRUE
3	9	A	A	TRUE
2	0	A	A	TRUE
3	9	A	A	TRUE

data *a few "miss" observations*

x1	x2	class	class.predicted.1	hit.1
5	3	A	B	FALSE
5	0	A	B	FALSE
5	2	A	B	FALSE
5	1	A	B	FALSE
4	3	A	B	FALSE
5	4	A	B	FALSE
6	8	A	B	FALSE
3	1	B	A	FALSE
2	2	B	A	FALSE
3	5	B	A	FALSE

Resample the original dataset; choose observations predicted incorrectly by model 1 with high probability. This becomes dataset 2.

Here we choose the incorrectly predicted observations with 10 times greater chance than the correctly predicted observations. Note that observation (x_1=5, x_2=3, $class$=A) (which appears seventh in the original dataset) was predicted incorrectly by model 1 and so it is not surprising that it appears in dataset 2.

data.2 *first few observations shown*

	x1	x2	class
36	6	8	A
48	9	3	B
24	0	5	A
50	4	2	B
7	5	3	A
35	5	4	A
53	4	7	B
28	5	1	A
15	3	5	A
71	9	5	B

Build model 2 based on dataset 2. We expect this model to better predict the classes of those observations that model 1 predicted incorrectly.

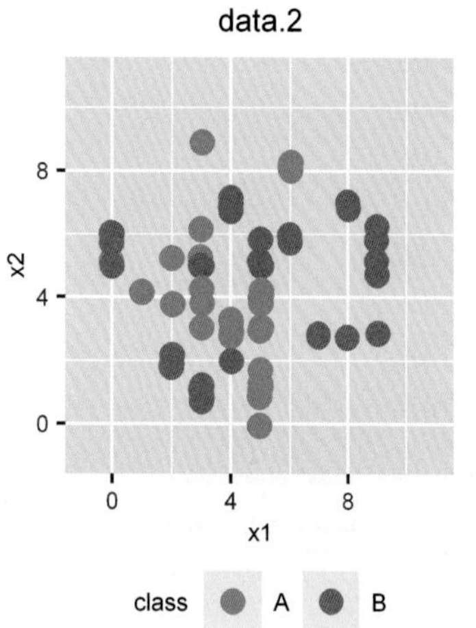

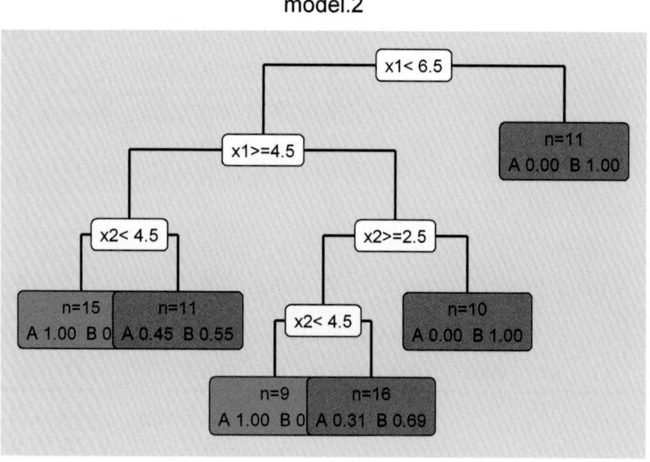

Model 3: Assess model 2's ability to predict dataset 2's observation classes.

data.2 *first few observations shown*

	x1	x2	class	class.predicted.2	hit.2
36	6	8	A	B	FALSE
48	9	3	B	B	TRUE
24	0	5	A	B	FALSE
50	4	2	B	B	TRUE
7	5	3	A	A	TRUE
35	5	4	A	A	TRUE
53	4	7	B	B	TRUE
28	5	1	A	A	TRUE
15	3	5	A	B	FALSE
71	9	5	B	B	TRUE

data.2 *a few "hit" observations*

x1	x2	class	class.predicted.2	hit.2
9	3	B	B	TRUE
4	2	B	B	TRUE
5	3	A	A	TRUE
5	4	A	A	TRUE
4	7	B	B	TRUE
5	1	A	A	TRUE
9	5	B	B	TRUE
4	3	A	A	TRUE
5	4	A	A	TRUE
2	4	A	A	TRUE

data.2 *a few "miss" observations*

x1	x2	class	class.predicted.2	hit.2
6	8	A	B	FALSE
0	5	A	B	FALSE
3	5	A	B	FALSE
6	8	A	B	FALSE
6	8	A	B	FALSE
6	8	A	B	FALSE
3	9	A	B	FALSE
2	5	A	B	FALSE
3	6	A	B	FALSE
6	8	A	B	FALSE

Resample dataset 2; choose observations predicted incorrectly by model 2 with high probability. This becomes dataset 3.

Here we choose the incorrectly predicted observations with 10 times greater chance than the correctly predicted observations.

data.3 *first few observations shown*

	x1	x2	class
52	5	6	B
53.3	4	7	B
28.3	5	1	A
56	6	6	B
36.1	6	8	A
3	3	6	A
36.2	6	8	A
15	3	5	A
38	2	2	B
50	4	2	B

Build model 3 based on dataset 3. We expect this model to better predict the classes of those observations that model 2 predicted incorrectly.

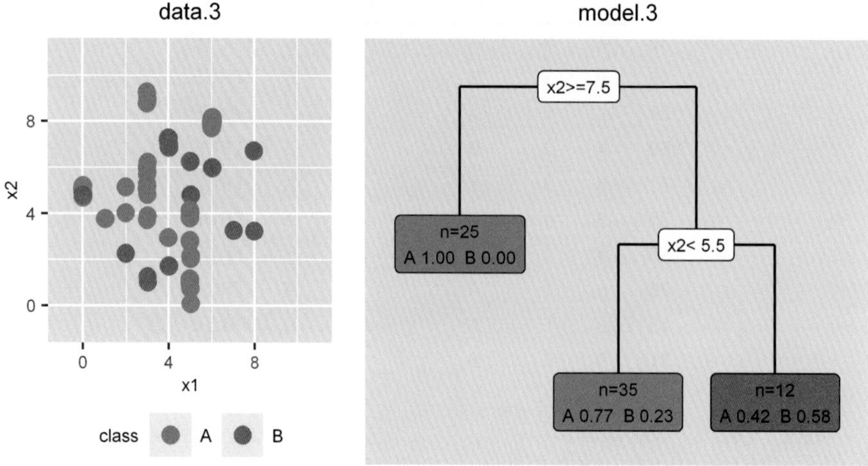

9.2.3.2 Predictions

We use the 3 models to make 3 different predictions of the new observation's class.

prob.1	
A	B
0.4615	0.5385

new		
x1	x2	class.predicted.1
5.2	4	B

prob.2	
A	B
1	0

new		
x1	x2	class.predicted.2
5.2	4	A

prob.3	
A	B
0.7714	0.2286

new		
x1	x2	class.predicted.3
5.2	4	A

9.2.3.3 Vote

We compare the predictions of the models and vote for the most popular prediction. Model 1 predicts that the new observation's class is B, and models 2 and 3 predict A. The vote is 2 to 1 in favor of A, so the boosted model predicts A.

new					
x1	x2	class.predicted.1	class.predicted.2	class.predicted.3	class.predicted
5.2	4	B	A	A	A

9.3 Stacking

Combine predictive model construction methods by the stacking method, as with an expert on a committee of experts.

9.3.1 Introduction

Could a European swallow fly a coconut from the African continent to the British Isles? You can think of stacking as hiring an expert on a committee of experts to answer some questions, perhaps questions involving aerodynamics (the study of flying), carpology (the study of seeds and fruits like coconuts), and ornithology (the study of birds, such as swallows).

The committee here comprises 3 experts. Ina studied all 3 fields by reading books. Soumik also studied all 3 fields, but by attending classes. Atticus studied all 3 fields by watching video tutorials. The 3 experts developed their expertise by studying the same material, but they used different methods to do so. Accordingly, we can expect that they will not always make the same conclusions about some questions.

Ye Joon is not an expert in any of the 3 fields, but he has been studying the committee itself. He has noticed a pattern in the committee's answers. When Ina and Soumik agree on a conclusion, they are usually wrong.

Now the 3 experts on the committee proceed to make conclusions about our swallow. Ina says yes, Soumik says yes, Atticus says no. The committee experts are free to reconcile their different conclusions however they want to, but we are free to ignore them. Rather, we look to Ye Joon for an answer. Ina and Soumik agree on yes, Ye Joon knows that when they agree they are usually wrong, so Ye Joon answers no. We take Ye Joon's no as the final answer. Note that even though a 2-to-1 majority favored a specific answer, we ultimately chose to take a different answer.

Another example: consider a hedge fund firm that predicts stock prices. Several other firms predict stock prices, too, but they do so based on looking at company financials and other factors. Our firm predicts stock prices by accounting for the other firms' predictions and their records for getting their predictions right.

9.3.2 About Stacking

Ensemble assembly is about combining several predictive models to build a new predictive model, one that synergizes the strengths of the **component models**.

Stacking is a specific ensemble assembly method that combines predictive models built using different model construction methods, but using a single reference dataset. Final predictions are made by a **stacked model**, built using the other models' predictions as its new reference dataset. Effectively, the component models transform the original reference dataset representation to a stacked form to be used by the stacked model.

Stacking works like this: Build several models and make predictions. Then build a new model based on the predictions that the other models would make about the original data.

9.3.3 Stacking

Consider this reference dataset and new unclassified observation. The scatterplot shows the observations jittered to expose those with identical x_1, x_2 values.

size of data	
observations	variables
72	3

new	
x1	x2
5.2	4

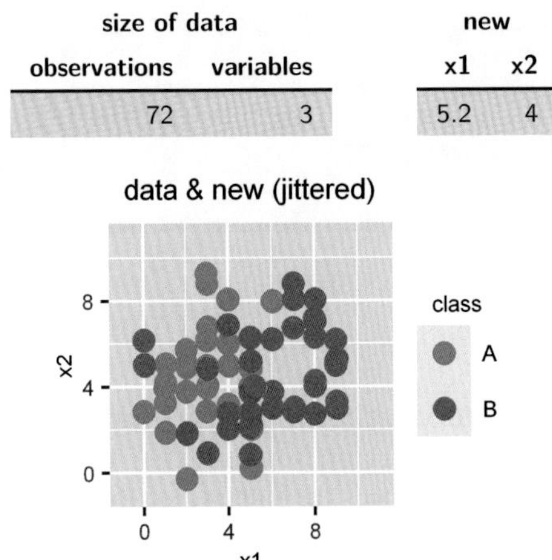

9.3.3.1 Component Models Based on Original Data

Build several models, using different methods and/or different hyper-parameter values, but based on the same reference dataset.

Model 1: Here we build a decision tree model (with maximum depth 1):

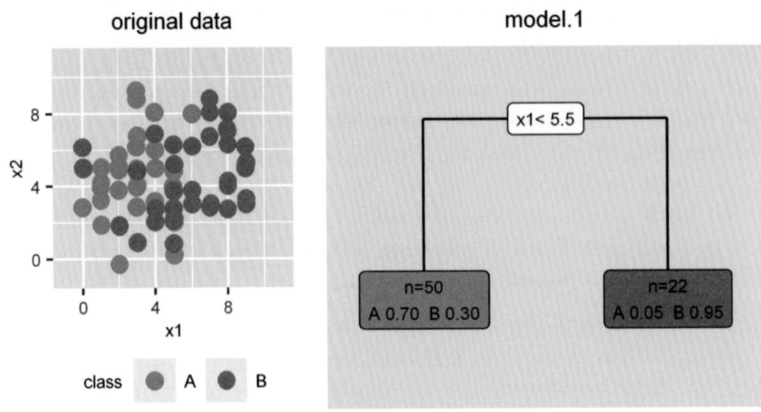

Model 2: Here we build a naive Bayes model:

	prior
A	0.5
B	0.5

	likelihood x1	
	mean	sd
A	2.722	1.614
B	6.056	2.461

	likelihood x2	
	mean	sd
A	4.333	2.178
B	4.528	2.077

Model 3: Here we build a support vector machine model:

model parameters

classes	kernel	cost	normalize	sv_count
A B	polynomial: degree 3, gamma 0.5, coef 0	0.1	TRUE	56

9.3.3.2 Transformed Data

The component models make these predictions about the original dataset's observation classes:

data *first few observations shown*

x1	x2	class	class.predicted.1	class.predicted.2	class.predicted.3
1	3	A	A	A	A
2	2	A	A	A	A
3	6	A	A	A	A
4	5	A	A	A	A
3	4	A	A	A	A
2	5	A	A	A	A
5	3	A	A	B	A
4	8	A	A	A	A
3	9	A	A	A	A
2	0	A	A	A	A

So, the transformed data look like this, based on the models' predictions about the original data's classes:

data (transformed) *first few observations shown*

class.predicted.1	class.predicted.2	class.predicted.3	class
A	A	A	A
A	A	A	A
A	A	A	A
A	A	A	A
A	A	A	A
A	A	A	A
A	B	A	A
A	A	A	A
A	A	A	A
A	A	A	A

9.3.3.3 Stacked Model Based on Component Model Predictions

Build a model using the transformed data.

Stacked Model: Here we build a logistic regression model:

model parameters

	coefficients
(Intercept)	-1.288
class.predicted.1B	18.848
class.predicted.2B	1.624
class.predicted.3B	-16.294

9.3.3.4 Prediction

Express the new observation in terms of how its class is predicted by the component models.

The new observation $(x_1{=}5.2, x_2{=}4)$ can be expressed as (*class.predicted.1*=A, *class.predicted.2*=B, *class.predicted.3*=A) because model 1 predicts the class of $(x_1{=}5.2, x_2{=}4)$ to be A, model 2 predicts it to be B, and model 3 predicts it to be A.

prob.1

A	B
0.7	0.3

new

x1	x2	class.predicted.1
5.2	4	A

prob.2

A	B
0.3268	0.6732

new

x1	x2	class.predicted.2
5.2	4	B

prob.3

A	B
0.5699	0.4301

new

x1	x2	class.predicted.3
5.2	4	A

new (transformed)

class.predicted.1	class.predicted.2	class.predicted.3
A	B	A

Use the stacked model to predict the class of a new observation.

Here the stacked model predicts the class of the transformed new observation (*class.predicted.1*=A, *class.predicted.2*=B, *class.predicted.3*=A) to be B, which means it predicts the class of new observation $(x_1{=}5.2, x_2{=}4)$ to be B.

Note that the stacked model predicts this new observation's class to be B, even though 2 of the 3 component models would predict it to be A.

prob.stack

A	B
0.4167	0.5833

new (transformed)

class.predicted.1	class.predicted.2	class.predicted.3	class.predicted
A	B	A	B

new

x1	x2	class.predicted
5.2	4	B

10 | Cluster Analysis

Learning Objectives

Terms

Know the terms:

- Cluster analysis
- Cluster model
- Construction
- Evaluation
- Hyper-parameter
- Euclidean distance
- Linkage
- Centroid
- Centroid linkage
- Gower centroid linkage
- Median linkage
- Single linkage
- Complete linkage
- Average linkage
- McQuitty linkage
- Inter-observation distance
- Inter-cluster distance
- Mean intra-cluster dispersion
- Mean mean intra-cluster dispersion
- Mean inter-cluster dispersion
- Dispersion ratio
- Akaike Information Criterion (or AIC)
- Bayesian Information Criterion (or BIC)
- Mallow's Cp
- Distance matrix
- k-means method
- k-means model
- Hierarchical agglomeration method (or agglomerative hierarchical clustering or AHC)
- Hierarchical agglomeration model
- Dendrogram
- Cutline
- Gaussian mixture method (or GMM method, or GMM-EM method)
- Gaussian mixture model (or GMM)
- Gaussian function
- Bi-variate Gaussian function

Effects of Assumptions

Know the effects of assumptions:

- Effect of the choice of cluster analysis method on a cluster model
- Effect of the number of variables within a cluster analysis method
- Effect of the specification for observation dissimilarity on cluster model evaluation
- Effect of the inter-cluster linkage on cluster model evaluation
- Effect of normalizing a dataset prior to applying the k-means method
- Effect of centroid initialization within the k-means method
- Effect of normalizing a dataset prior to applying the hierarchical agglomeration method
- Effect of a cutline within the hierarchical agglomeration method
- Effect of Gaussian function parameter initialization within the Gaussian mixture method

Use the Methods

Know how to use the methods:

- Frame your thinking about cluster analysis based on the cluster analysis methodology.
- Compute the mean mean intra-cluster dispersion of a cluster model.
- Compute the mean inter-cluster dispersion of a cluster model.
- Compute the dispersion ratio of a cluster model.
- Compute a cluster model using the k-means method.
- Calculate centroids at any step within the k-means method.
- Compute a cluster model using the hierarchical agglomeration method.
- Calculate the distance matrix at any iteration within the hierarchical agglomeration method.
- Compute a dendrogram visualization.
- Interpret a dendrogram.
- Select the number of clusters using dendrogram analysis.
- Compute a cluster model using the Gaussian mixture method.
- Calculate Gaussian function sizes, means, and standard deviations in any iteration within the Gaussian mixture method applied to a 1-variable dataset.
- Calculate partial class assignments in any iteration within the Gaussian mixture method applied to a 1-variable dataset.

10.1 Cluster Analysis Methodology

Construct a cluster model and evaluate its quality.

10.1.1 Introduction

The platypus is a remarkable animal. It's characterized by a combination of features that suggest it could belong to any of a few different animal classes. It lays eggs and has a bill like a bird does. It produces milk and has fur like a mammal does. The male platypus carries venomous spikes on its feet, not common for either birds or mammals. Which animal class best suits the platypus? More generally, how should animals be organized into clusters? How many different clusters should there be? Which combinations of features should be considered? What criteria should be used to determine whether animals are similar or dissimilar? What is the benefit of organizing animals into clusters?

Cluster analysis methods organize observations into distinct clusters in some way that distinguishes how the observations differ from each other. Some observations will constitute one cluster, other observations will constitute another cluster, and still other observations could constitute other clusters.

Cluster analysis is useful in a variety of business applications, notably market segmentation. You might want to treat all your customers as individuals. For example, you might want to advertise to each individual customer in a way that specifically targets that customer, or you might want to build a product for each individual customer that is specifically designed for that customer's needs, or provide a custom service to each individual customer. If your business is, say, a management consulting firm with only 6 clients, then you might be able to do that. However, if you have limited resources (as all businesses do) and many customers, that might not be practical. Rather, you can conduct a market segmentation exercise, assigning some customers to one class and other customers to other classes. Then treat one cluster of customers one way and other clusters in different ways. Assuming that customers in one cluster are all similar to each other and customers in other clusters are dissimilar, then making business decisions about advertising, product development, or service provision based on market segmentation is often a good approach.

Let's consider further how we might distinguish different types of customers so as to assign them to different clusters. There are certainly many features we could employ. Income level may be a reasonable feature to employ when making a business decision about product development: build an inexpensive product for customers with low income and build an expensive product for customers with high income. Age might also be a reasonable feature to employ: build a product for young customers and another product for mature customers. When we consider the combination of income level and age, though, we're led to building 4 products: 1 product for low-income young customers, 1 for low-income mature customers, 1 for high-income young customers, and 1 for high-income mature customers. When we consider combinations of even more features, we're led to building an increasing number of products, which quickly becomes impractical. Restricting ourselves to a limited number of clusters and a corresponding limited number of products could result in some similar customers being split across different clusters, like having some low-income customers in 1 cluster and other low-income customers in another cluster. But we still want the customers in any 1 cluster to be relatively similar to each other and customers in other clusters to be relatively dissimilar. We need cluster analysis to determine sensible organizations when we want to consider many features but are limited to few clusters.

Cluster analysis is also known as unsupervised machine learning.

There are several popular cluster analysis methods, including hierarchical agglomeration, k-means, and Gaussian mixture.

10.1.2 About Cluster Analysis Methodology

Cluster analysis comprises construction and evaluation. **Construction** is about constructing a **cluster model** based on some unclassified dataset. **Evaluation** is about evaluating the quality of the resulting cluster model.

Cluster model construction in some contexts is referred to as training, modeling, building a model, or fitting a model. Cluster model evaluation is some contexts is referred to as testing.

10.1.2.1 Construction

For construction, use some cluster analysis method that receives an unclassified dataset as input and generates a cluster model as output. The form of the cluster model is the dataset itself extended by one additional class variable.

Here we see an unclassified dataset with 5 observations and 8 numerical variables being input to a cluster analysis method. The specific version of the method is set by **hyper-parameters**. The method outputs a cluster model, comprising the 5 observations that are now classified into 2 classes, A and B. The first, second, and fifth observations are assigned to class A. The third and fourth observations are assigned to class B. The 2 classes A and B correspond to 2 clusters.

We won't know whether this cluster analysis method applied to this dataset generated a good cluster model until we evaluate it.

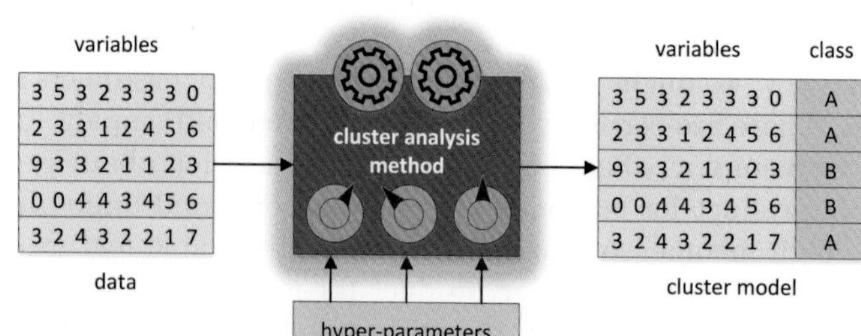

10.1.2.2 Evaluation

For evaluation, use some method that receives a cluster model as input and generates a quality metric score as output. Typically, the method will involve measures of how dissimilar observations in any 1 cluster are to each other and how dissimilar they are to observations in the other clusters.

Here we see a cluster model with 5 observations. The method outputs a quality score of 0.5 on some AIC scale.

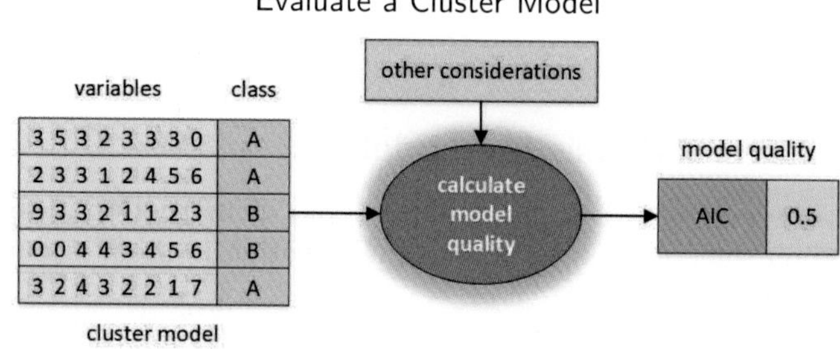

10.1.2.3 Cluster Analysis & Similarity

Often, both construction and evaluation rely on having some way to measure similarity between observations and between clusters. To determine how similar one observation is to another observation, we can measure **Euclidean distance** or other kind of distance. To determine how similar one cluster is to another cluster, it's not enough to have a specification for **inter-observation distance**. Rather, use some specification for **inter-cluster distance** that can be calculated given the specification for inter-observation distance and summary information about the observations constituting the clusters. Treat distance between clusters as a measure of their similarity.

Here are some popular specifications for distance between 2 clusters. The general version of each is referred to as a **linkage**, and specific versions are defined by which specifications of inter-observation distance are used, which could be Euclidean distance or any other kind of distance. The term ***non-coresident observations*** used in these descriptions indicates that 1 observation is in 1 cluster and the other observation is in another cluster.

- **Centroid linkage** specifies that the distance between 2 clusters is the inter-observation distance between their centroids. A cluster's **centroid** is the point at the variable means across all of its constituent observations.

- **Gower centroid linkage** specifies that the distance between 2 clusters is the Gower distance between their non-coresident observations, which is a special recursively defined, computation-efficient approximation of the distance between their centroids.
- **Median linkage** specifies that the distance between 2 clusters is the inter-observation distance between their medians.
- **Single linkage** specifies that the distance between 2 clusters is the inter-observation distance between the closest pair of non-coresident observations.
- **Complete linkage** specifies that the distance between 2 clusters is the inter-observation distance between the farthest pair of non-coresident observations.
- **Average linkage** specifies that the distance between 2 clusters is the mean of inter-observation distances between every pair of non-coresident observations.
- **McQuitty linkage** specifies that the distance between 2 clusters is the mean of inter-observation distances between every pair of non-coresident observations, not weighted by the number of observations in the clusters.

In our discourse, we usually specify inter-cluster distance to be centroid linkage with Euclidean distance.

10.1.3 Cluster Analysis Methodology

Consider this unclassified 3-variable dataset and its corresponding normalized representation. Let's construct some cluster models from this dataset.

data (not normalized)

	x1	x2	x3
a	2.0	3.5	10.0
b	2.5	9.0	9.0
c	4.0	8.5	10.5
d	6.5	11.0	2.0
e	8.0	2.5	1.5
f	9.0	1.0	1.0
g	10.0	4.0	9.5
h	10.5	7.5	11.0

data

	x1	x2	x3
a	-1.3562	-0.6628	0.7167
b	-1.2076	0.8721	0.4918
c	-0.7617	0.7326	0.8291
d	-0.0186	1.4303	-1.0820
e	0.4273	-0.9419	-1.1945
f	0.7246	-1.3605	-1.3069
g	1.0218	-0.5233	0.6043
h	1.1705	0.4535	0.9415

Here is the dataset with a synthetic class variable added. Note that class values are initially unknown.

data (with unknown class values)

	x1	x2	x3	class
a	-1.3562	-0.6628	0.7167	NA
b	-1.2076	0.8721	0.4918	NA
c	-0.7617	0.7326	0.8291	NA
d	-0.0186	1.4303	-1.0820	NA
e	0.4273	-0.9419	-1.1945	NA
f	0.7246	-1.3605	-1.3069	NA
g	1.0218	-0.5233	0.6043	NA
h	1.1705	0.4535	0.9415	NA

10.1.3.1 Construction with One Variable

We can construct cluster models from the dataset by considering just 1 variable, say x_1.

Perhaps we need only partition observations into 2 classes without any special class assignment criteria. Here is such a cluster model constructed from random class assignments.

- Cluster A comprises the 3 observations **c**, **f**, **g**.
- Cluster B comprises the 5 observations **a**, **b**, **d**, **e**, **h**.

Note that this cluster does not seem very useful.

data (with class values)

	x1	x2	x3	class
a	-1.3562	-0.6628	0.7167	B
b	-1.2076	0.8721	0.4918	B
c	-0.7617	0.7326	0.8291	A
d	-0.0186	1.4303	-1.0820	B
e	0.4273	-0.9419	-1.1945	B
f	0.7246	-1.3605	-1.3069	A
g	1.0218	-0.5233	0.6043	A
h	1.1705	0.4535	0.9415	B

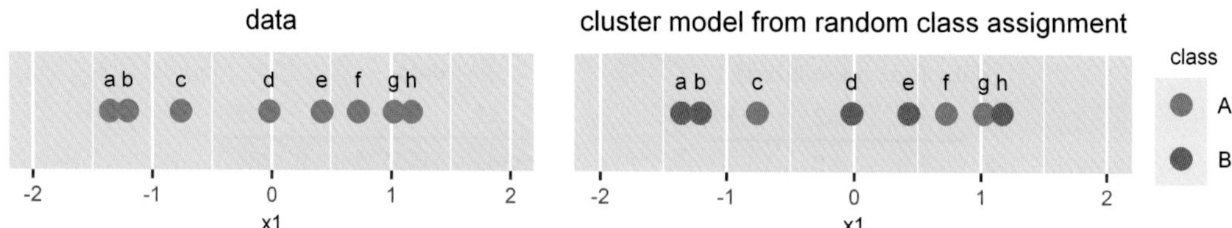

Perhaps it would be more useful for us to partition observations into 2 classes with class assignment based on proximity. Here is such a model constructed from class assignments made according to inter-observation distance specified as Euclidean distance, and considering only the x_1 variable.

- Cluster A comprises the 3 observations **a**, **b**, **c**, which are closer to each other than they are to cluster B observations.
- Cluster B comprises the 5 observations **d**, **e**, **f**, **g**, **h**, which are closer to each other than they are to cluster A observations.

data (with class values)

	x1	x2	x3	class
a	-1.3562	-0.6628	0.7167	A
b	-1.2076	0.8721	0.4918	A
c	-0.7617	0.7326	0.8291	A
d	-0.0186	1.4303	-1.0820	B
e	0.4273	-0.9419	-1.1945	B
f	0.7246	-1.3605	-1.3069	B
g	1.0218	-0.5233	0.6043	B
h	1.1705	0.4535	0.9415	B

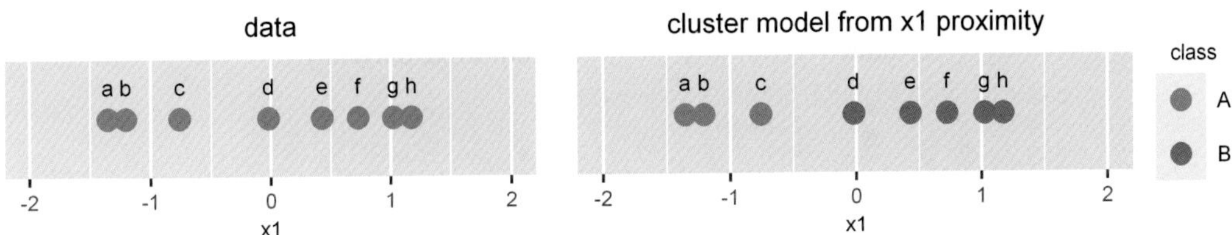

10.1.3.2 Construction with Two Variables

We can construct cluster models from the dataset by considering just 2 variables, say x_1 and x_2, taken 1 at at time.

The distribution of x_1 values suggests perhaps 2 classes assigned according to proximity. Here is such a cluster model constructed by considering only the x_1 variable.

- Cluster A comprises observations **a**, **b**, **c**.
- Cluster B comprises observations **d**, **e**, **f**, **g**, **h**.

The distribution of x_2 values also suggests perhaps 2 classes assigned according to proximity. However, the arrangement of values in the x_2 variable is different than in the x_1 variable. So, here also is another cluster model, this one constructed by considering only the x_2 variable.

- Cluster A comprises observations **a**, **e**, **f**, **g**.
- Cluster B comprises observations **b**, **c**, **d**, **h**.

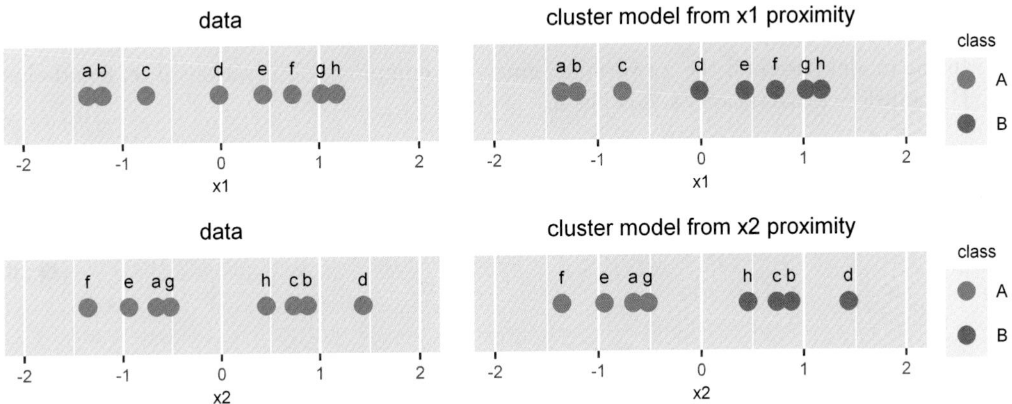

We can also construct cluster models from the dataset by considering just 2 variables, say x_1 and x_2, taken in combination. Note that proximity viewed in any one dimension looks different from proximity viewed in 2 dimensions. The distributions of x_1 and x_2 taken in combination suggest perhaps different class assignments. Here is such a cluster model with 2 classes constructed by considering the x_1 and x_2 variables taken in combination.

- Cluster A comprises observations **a**, **b**, **c**, **d**.
- Cluster B comprises observations **e**, **f**, **g**, **h**.

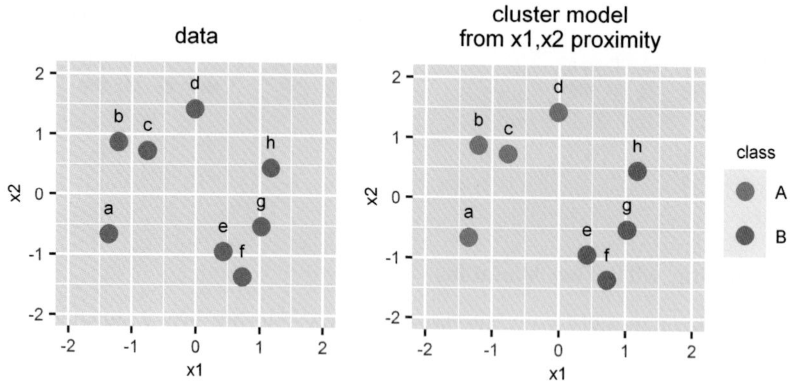

10.1.3.3 Construction with Three Variables

We can construct cluster models from the dataset by considering just 3 variables, say x_1, x_2, and x_3, taken one at a time.

The distribution of x_3 values suggests perhaps 2 classes assigned according to proximity. However, the arrangement of values in the x_3 variable is different from either the x_1 and x_2 variable. So, here are 3 different cluster models: 1 constructed by considering only the x_1 variable, another constructed by considering only the x_2 variable, and yet another constructed by considering only the x_3 variable.

- In the model based on the x_1 variable, cluster A comprises observations **a**, **b**, **c** and cluster B comprises observations **d**, **e**, **f**, **g**, **h**.
- In the model based on the x_2 variable, cluster A comprises observations **a**, **e**, **f**, **g** and cluster B comprises observations **b**, **c**, **d**, **h**.
- In the model based on the x_3 variable, cluster A comprises observations **d**, **e**, **f** and cluster B comprises observations **a**, **b**, **c**, **g**, **h**.

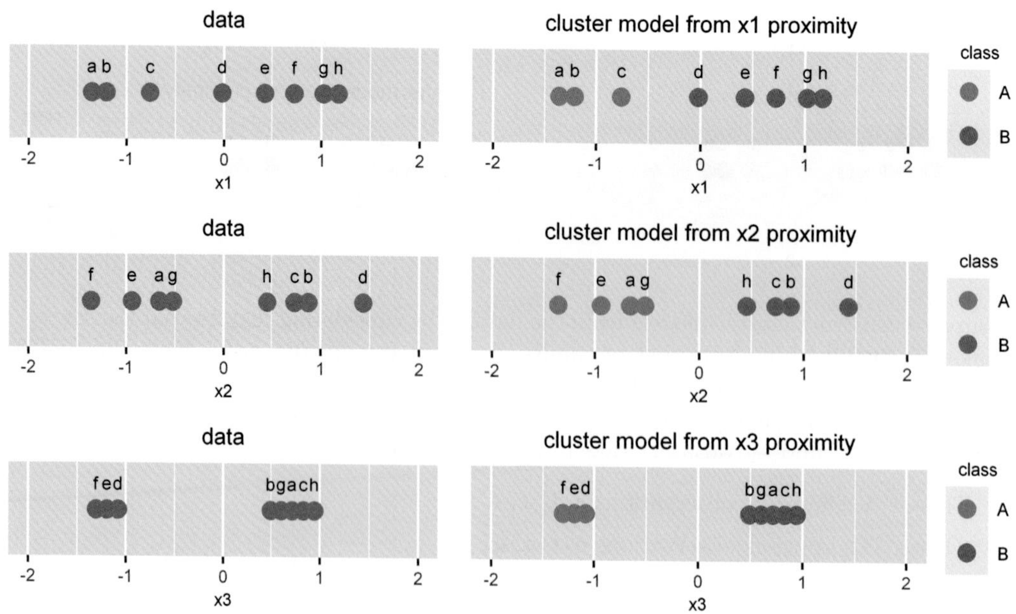

We can also construct cluster models from the dataset by considering just 2 variables taken in combination. Note that proximity viewed in any combination of 2 variables looks different from proximity viewed in another combination of 2 variables.

Here is a cluster model with 2 classes constructed by considering the x_1 and x_2 variables taken in combination.

- Cluster A comprises observations **a**, **b**, **c**, **d**.
- Cluster B comprises observations **e**, **f**, **g**, **h**.

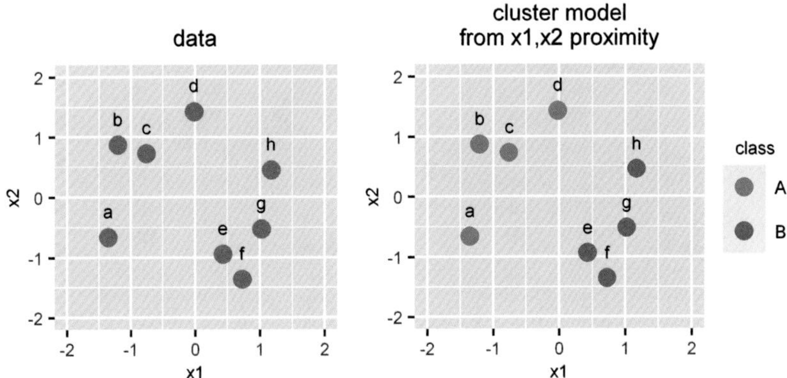

Here is a cluster model with 3 classes constructed by considering the x_1 and x_3 variables taken in combination.

- Cluster A comprises observations **a**, **b**, **c**.
- Cluster B comprises observations **d**, **e**, **f**.
- Cluster C comprises observations **g**, **h**.

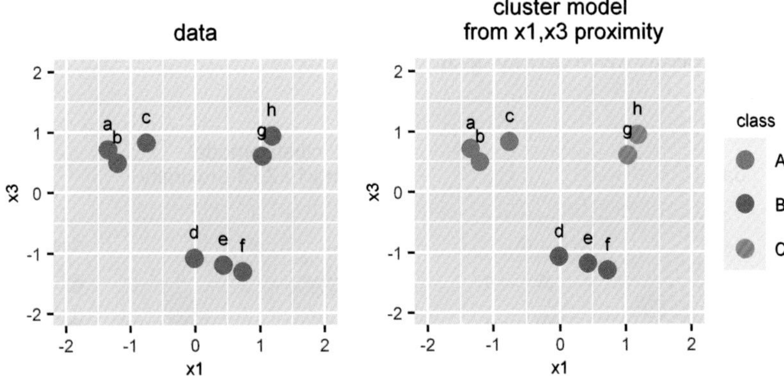

Here is a cluster model with 4 classes constructed by considering the x_2 and x_3 variables taken in combination.

- Cluster A comprises observations **e**, **f**.
- Cluster B comprises observations **a**, **g**.
- Cluster C comprises observations **b**, **c**, **h**.
- Cluster D comprises observation **d**.

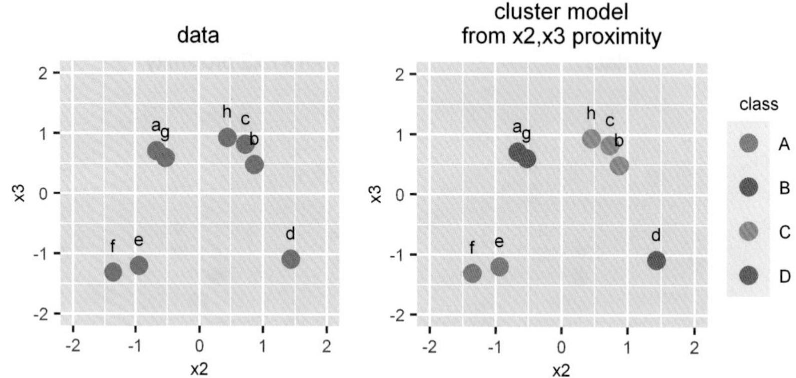

We can also construct cluster models from the dataset by considering just 3 variables, say x_1, x_2, and x_3, taken in combination, visualized as a bubbleplot. Note that proximity viewed in any 2 variables looks different from proximity viewed in 3 variables. The distributions of x_1, x_2, and x_3 taken in combination suggest perhaps different class assignments. Here is such a cluster model with 4 classes constructed by considering the x_1, x_2, and x_3 variables taken in combination.

- Cluster A comprises observations **a**, **b**, **c**.
- Cluster B comprises observation **d**.
- Cluster C comprises observations **e**, **f**.
- Cluster D comprises observations **g**, **h**.

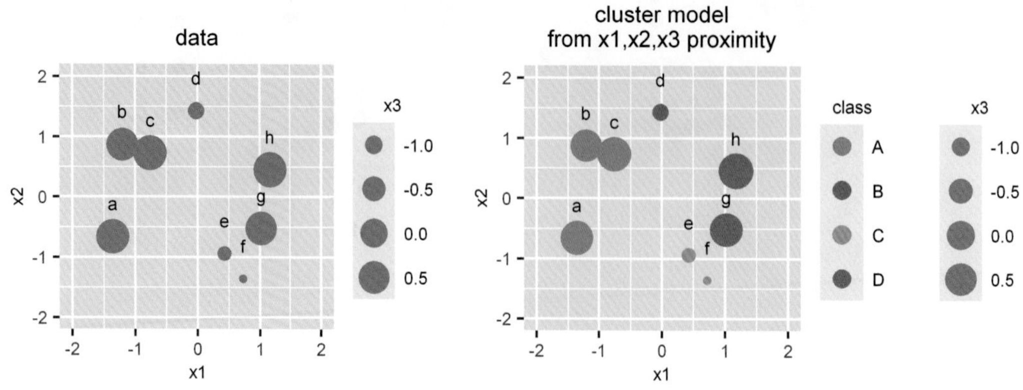

Here is the cluster model visualized as a 3-axis scatterplot projection.

cluster model from x1,x2,x3 proximity

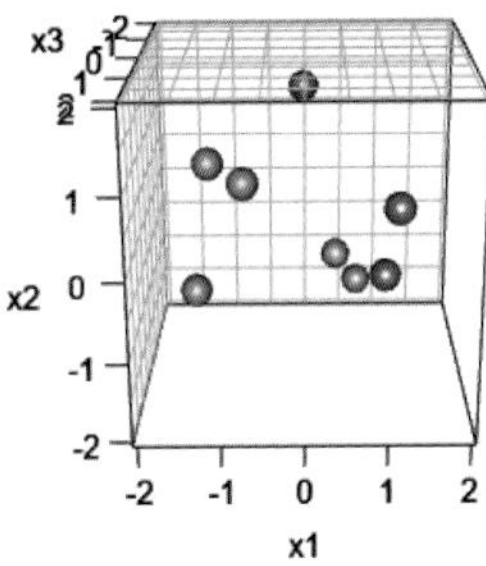

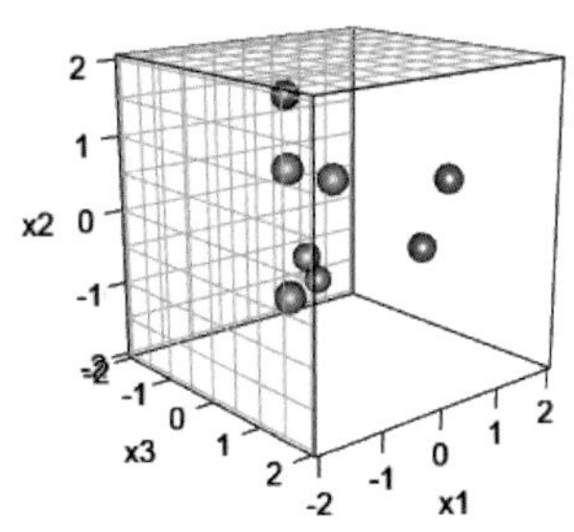

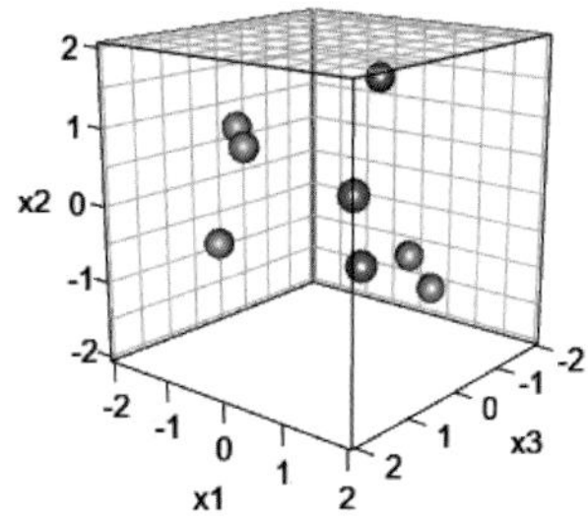

Here are 3 other cluster models visualized as 3-axis scatterplot projections. The first organizes observations into 2 clusters. The second organizes observations into 2 clusters in a different way. The third organizes observations into 4 clusters.

a 2-cluster model

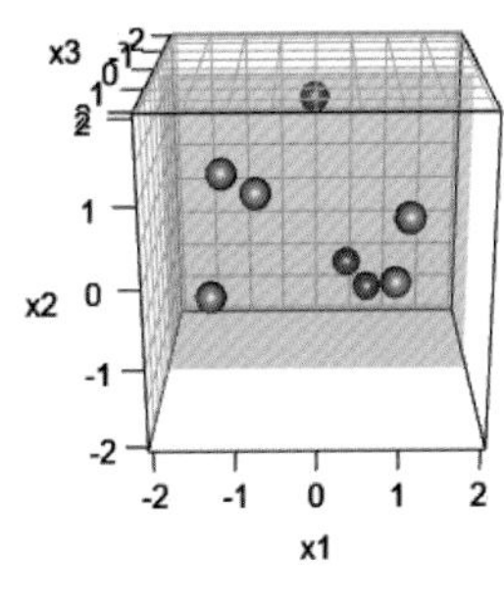

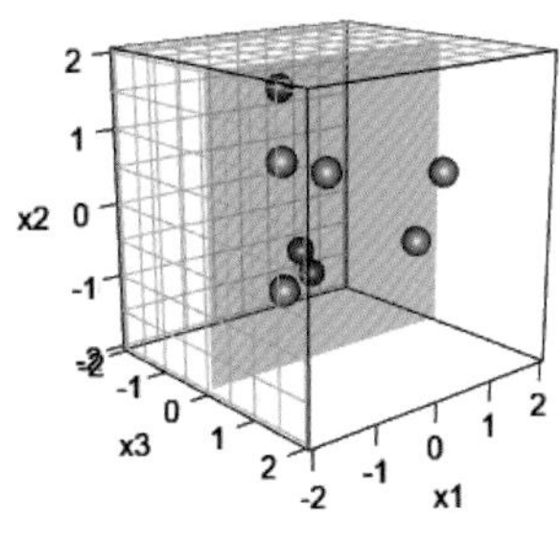

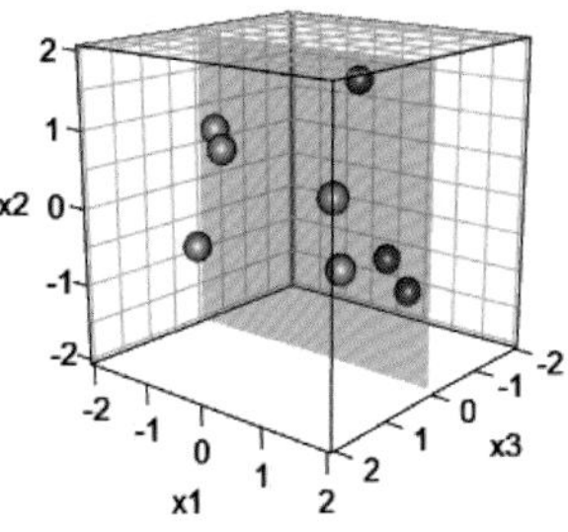

another 2-cluster model

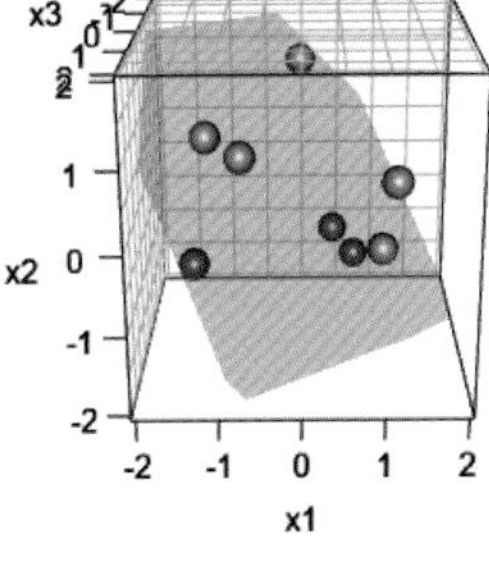

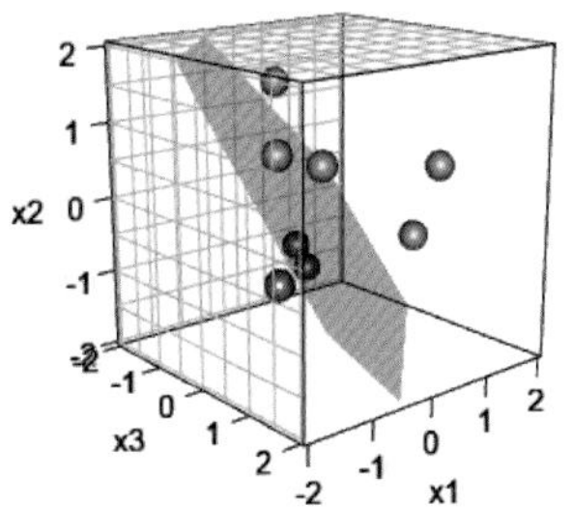

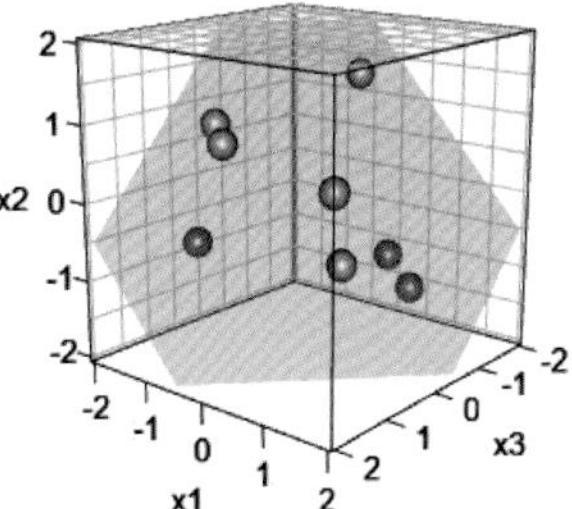

another 4-cluster model

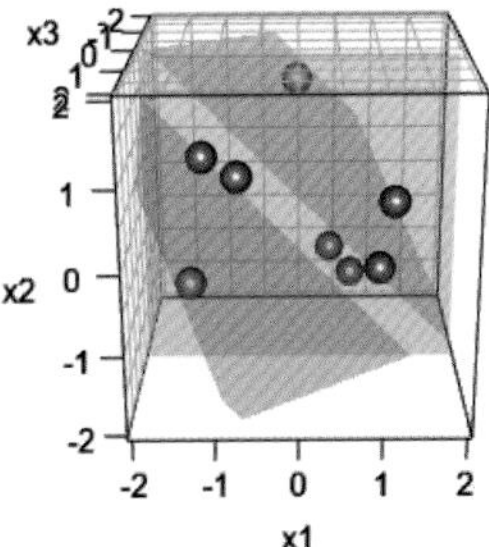

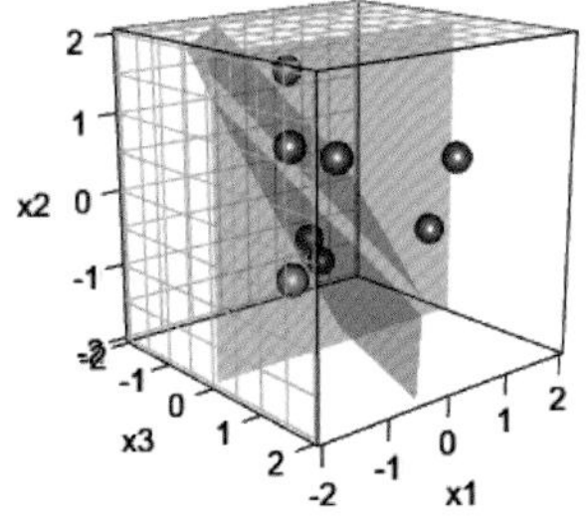

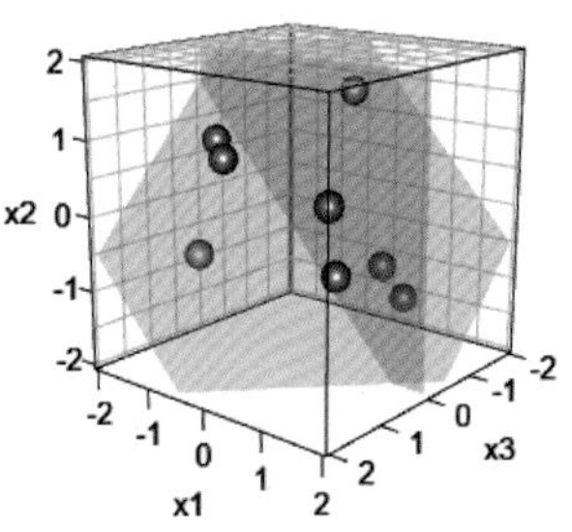

10.1.3.4 Evaluation

To get a quality score for each cluster model, apply an evaluation method appropriate for the business to each cluster model produced. Select the cluster model with the best quality score.

10.2 Cluster Model Evaluation

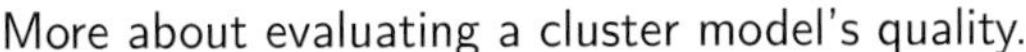

More about evaluating a cluster model's quality.

10.2.1 Introduction

When a cluster analysis method produces a cluster model, that cluster model might or might not organize observations in a way useful to your business. If you think that it is useful, then perhaps you should use it to inform your business decisions. If you think that it isn't, then perhaps you should discard it as useless. You don't know in advance how good it will turn out to be, but you can estimate that. Let's look further into estimating how good a cluster model could be.

10.2.2 About Cluster Model Evaluation

To evaluate how useful a cluster model is likely to be, use some method that receives a cluster model as input and generates a quality metric score as output. Typically, the method will involve measures of how dissimilar observations in any 1 cluster are to each other and how dissimilar they are to observations in the other clusters.

Here are some popular quality metrics for scoring cluster models:

- **Mean mean intra-cluster dispersion** is the average distance between observations within a cluster, averaged across all clusters.
- **Mean inter-cluster dispersion** is the average distance between clusters
- **Dispersion ratio** is the average distance between clusters as compared to average distance between observations within a cluster, across all clusters. This metric accounts for dissimilarity between observations both within and between clusters.
- **Akaike Information Criterion (AIC)** is the likelihood that the cluster model represents the underlying process as compared with other possible cluster models, accounting for the complexity of the models.

- **Bayesian Information Criterion (BIC)** is similar to AIC, but accounts for complexity of models differently.
- **Mallow's Cp** is a special case of AIC.

Some cluster model evaluation methods (and some cluster model construction methods) employ distance matrices to aid with various calculations. A **distance matrix** is a square matrix: columns are observation numbers, rows are observation numbers, and entries record the distance between each pair of observations.

Note that in our discourse we usually rate cluster models by dispersion ratio.

10.2.3 Cluster Model Evaluation by Dispersion Ratio

Consider this cluster model, shown as a classified 4-variable dataset, and its corresponding normalized representation. How good is this cluster model? Is it likely to be useful to our business? Let's evaluate the quality of the cluster model, rated by dispersion ratio. To calculate the dispersion ratio, we'll first calculate the component mean intra-cluster dispersion of each cluster, the mean mean intra-cluster dispersion, and the mean inter-cluster dispersion, and then combine these scores into one score. We'll specify inter-cluster distance to be centroid linkage and inter-observation distance to be Euclidean distance.

data (not normalized)

	x1	x2	x3	class
a	2.0	3.5	10.0	A
b	2.5	9.0	9.0	A
c	4.0	8.5	10.5	A
d	6.5	11.0	2.0	B
e	8.0	2.5	1.5	C
f	9.0	1.0	1.0	C
g	10.0	4.0	9.5	D
h	10.5	7.5	11.0	D

data

	x1	x2	x3	class
a	-1.3562	-0.6628	0.7167	A
b	-1.2076	0.8721	0.4918	A
c	-0.7617	0.7326	0.8291	A
d	-0.0186	1.4303	-1.0820	B
e	0.4273	-0.9419	-1.1945	C
f	0.7246	-1.3605	-1.3069	C
g	1.0218	-0.5233	0.6043	D
h	1.1705	0.4535	0.9415	D

10.2.3.1 Mean Intra-Cluster Dispersion

Mean intra-cluster dispersion is a measure of how dissimilar observations are from each other within a cluster. It is calculated as the mean of the distances between each pair of observations within a cluster.

$$\text{mean intra-cluster dispersion} = mean\begin{pmatrix} distance_{1,2},\ distance_{1,3},\ distance_{1,4},\ \ldots,\ distance_{1,n}, \\ distance_{2,3},\ distance_{2,4},\ \ldots,\ distance_{2,n}, \\ \ldots, \\ distance_{n-1,n} \end{pmatrix}$$

where ...

- $distance_{x,y}$ is the distance between observation x and observation y within a cluster
- $n-1$ is the penultimate observation and n is the last observation within a cluster

Here we calculate the mean intra-cluster dispersion for each cluster in the cluster model.

Cluster A comprises 3 observations: **a**, **b**, and **c**. This makes for 3 intra-cluster distances: the Euclidean distance 1.5584 between **a** and **b**, the Euclidean distance 1.521 between **a** and **c**, and the Euclidean distance 0.5762 between **b** and **c**, as shown in the distance matrix. The mean intra-cluster dispersion of cluster A, the mean of these 3 distances, is 1.218. Note that the mean intra-cluster dispersion can be equivalently calculated as the mean of all distance matrix entries below the diagonal.

data.A

	x1	x2	x3	class
a	-1.3562	-0.6628	0.7167	A
b	-1.2076	0.8721	0.4918	A
c	-0.7617	0.7326	0.8291	A

distance_matrix.A

	a	b	c
a	0.000	1.5584	1.5209
b	1.558	0.0000	0.5762
c	1.521	0.5762	0.0000

distance

observation_pair	distance
a_b	1.5584
a_c	1.5209
b_c	0.5762

cluster	mean_intracluster_dispersion
A	1.218

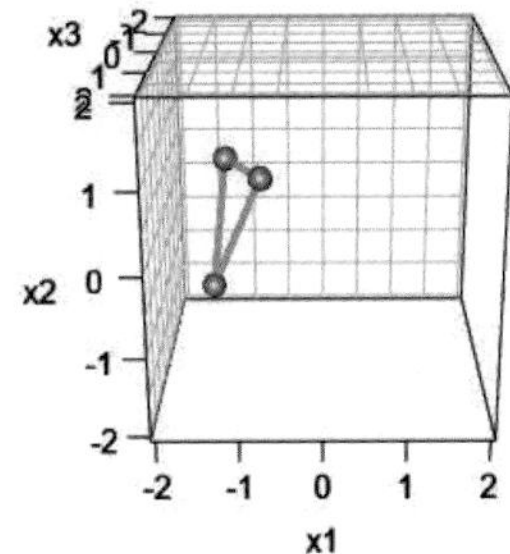

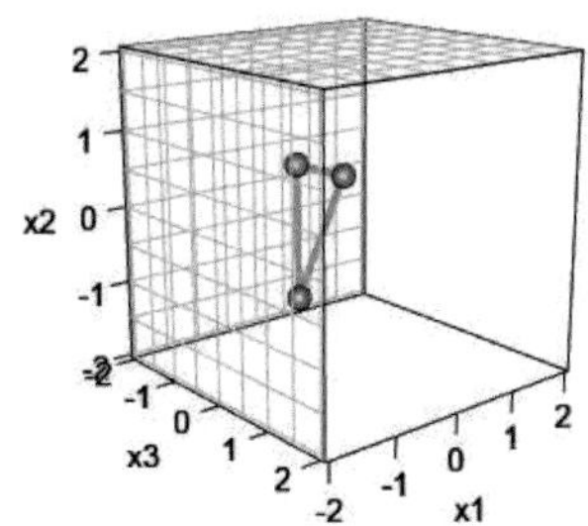

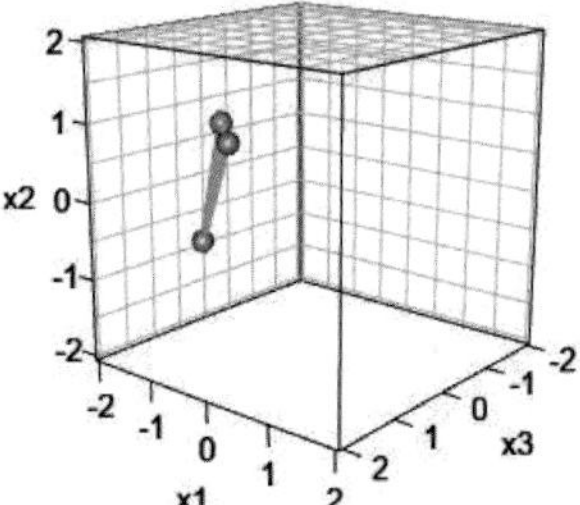

Cluster B comprises only 1 observation: **d**. This makes for no intra-cluster distances. The mean intra-cluster dispersion of cluster B, without any distances to average, is 0.

data.B

x1	x2	x3	class
-0.0186	1.43	-1.082	B

distance_matrix.B

	d
d	0

cluster	mean_intracluster_dispersion
B	0

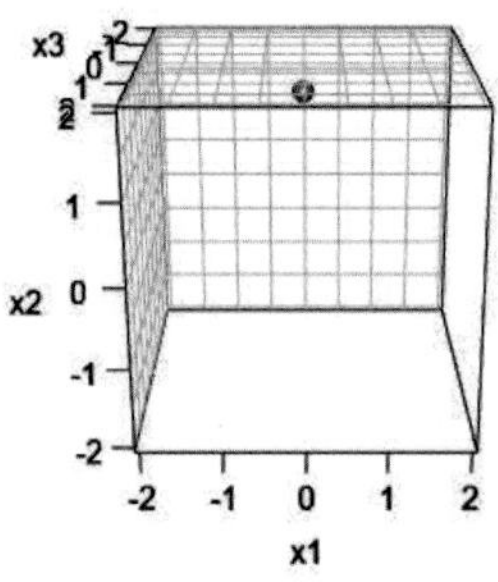
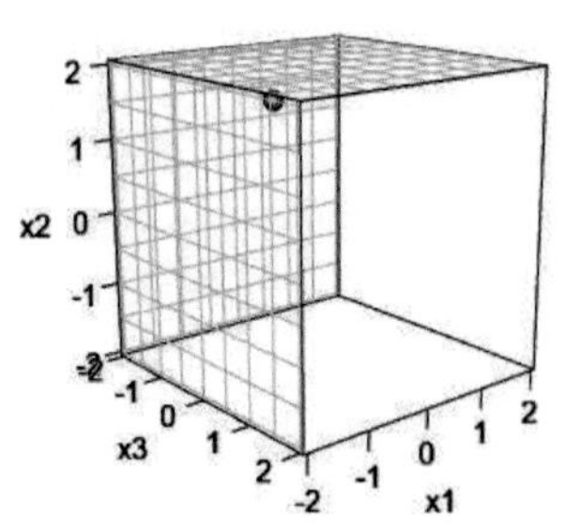
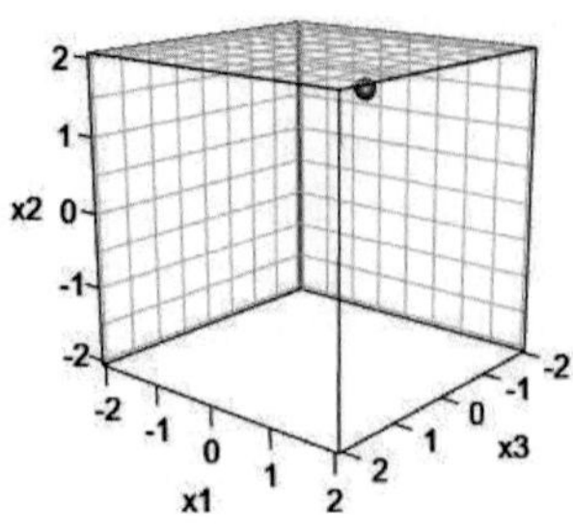

Cluster C comprises 2 observations: **e** and **f**. This makes for 1 relevant intra-cluster distance: the distance between **e** and **f**. The mean intra-cluster dispersion of cluster C, the mean of this 1 distance, is 0.5256.

data.C

x1	x2	x3	class
0.4273	-0.9419	-1.194	C
0.7246	-1.3605	-1.307	C

distance_matrix.C

	e	f
e	0.0000	0.5256
f	0.5256	0.0000

distance

observation_pair	distance
e_f	0.5256

cluster	mean_intracluster_dispersion
C	0.5256

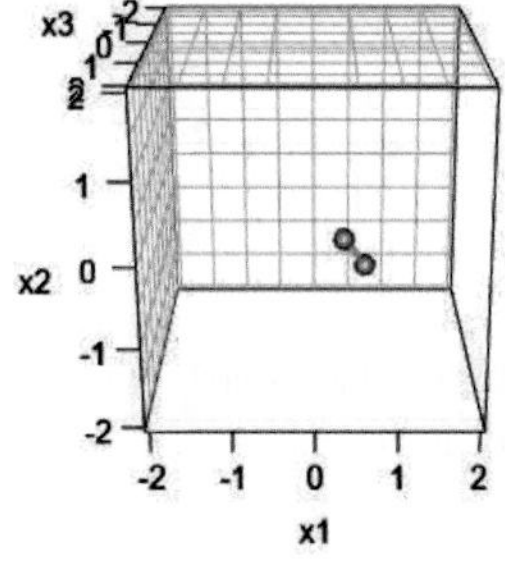
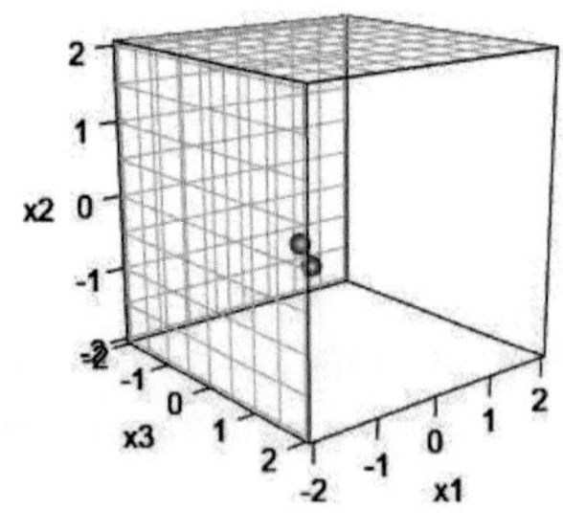
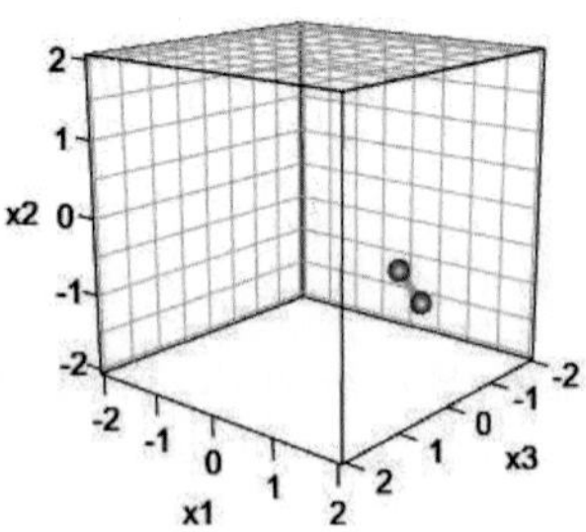

Cluster D comprises 2 observations: **g** and **h**. This makes for 1 relevant intra-cluster distance: the distance between **g** and **h**. The mean intra-cluster dispersion of cluster D, the mean of this 1 distance, is 1.044.

data.D

x1	x2	x3	class
1.022	-0.5233	0.6043	D
1.171	0.4535	0.9415	D

distance_matrix.D

	g	h
g	0.000	1.044
h	1.044	0.000

distance

observation_pair	distance
g_h	1.044

cluster	mean_intracluster_dispersion
D	1.044

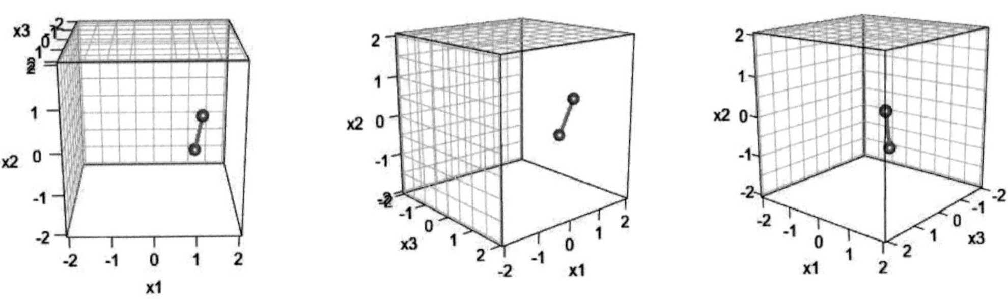

10.2.3.2 Mean Mean Intra-Cluster Dispersion

Mean mean intra-cluster dispersion is a measure of how dissimilar observations are from each other within a cluster, across all clusters. It is calculated as the mean of the mean intra-cluster dispersions of all clusters in the cluster model.

$$\begin{array}{c}\text{mean mean}\\\text{intra-cluster}\\\text{dispersion}\end{array} = mean\begin{pmatrix}\text{mean intra-cluster dispersion}_A,\\\text{mean intra-cluster dispersion}_B,\\\ldots,\\\text{mean intra-cluster dispersion}_N\end{pmatrix}$$

where ...

- mean intra-cluster dispersion$_X$ is the mean intra-cluster dispersion of cluster X
- N is the last cluster

Here we calculate the mean mean intra-cluster dispersion of the cluster model, the mean of 1.218, 0, 0.5256, and 1.0440, to be 0.697.

summary

class	mean_intracluster_dispersion
A	1.2185
B	0.0000
C	0.5256
D	1.0440

mean_mean_intracluster_dispersion
0.697

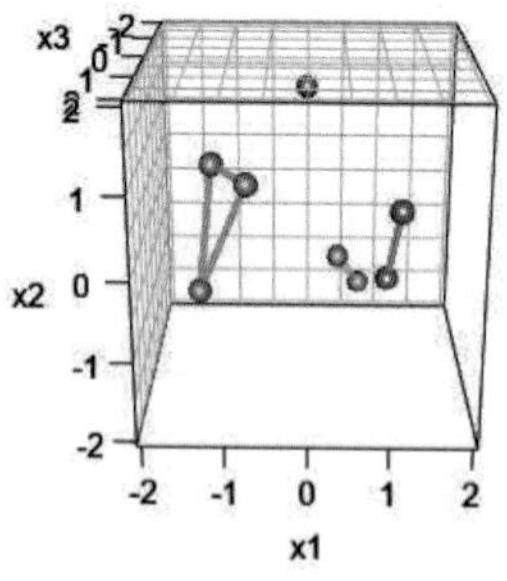
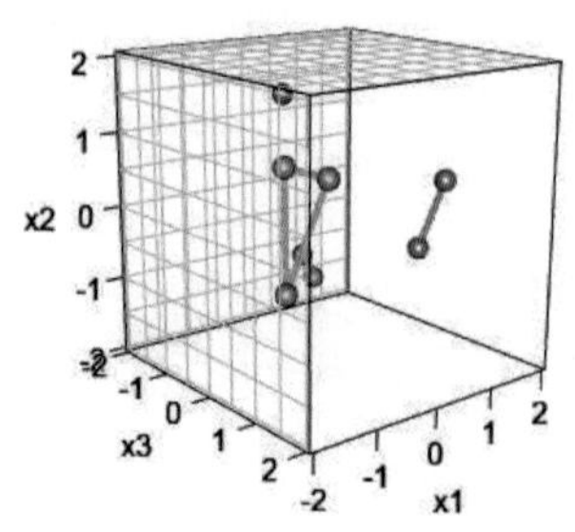
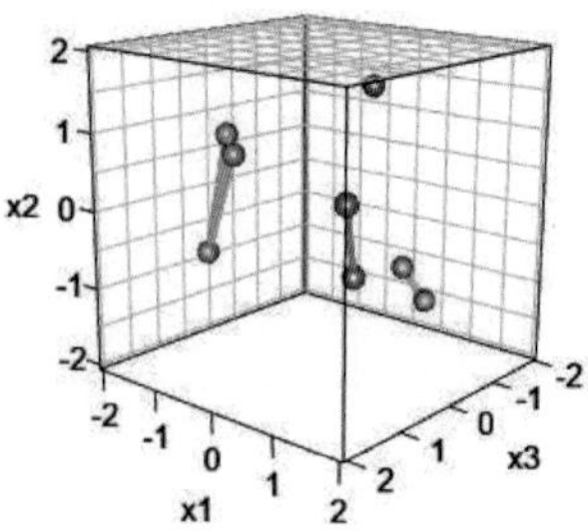

10.2.3.3 Mean Inter-Cluster Dispersion

Mean inter-cluster dispersion is a measure of how dissimilar clusters are from each other. It is calculated as the mean of the distances between each pair of clusters in the cluster model.

$$\text{mean inter-cluster dispersion} = mean\begin{pmatrix} Distance_{A,B},\ Distance_{A,C},\ Distance_{A,D},\ \ldots,\ Distance_{A,N}, \\ Distance_{B,C},\ Distance_{B,D},\ \ldots,\ Distance_{B,N}, \\ \ldots, \\ Distance_{N-1,N} \end{pmatrix}$$

where ...

- $Distance_{X,Y}$ is the distance between cluster X and cluster Y
- $N-1$ is the penultimate cluster and N is the last cluster

Here we calculate the mean inter-cluster dispersion of the cluster model. First, for each cluster, we determine its centroid derived from the means of its relevant variables.

data.A

x1	x2	x3	class
-1.3562	-0.6628	0.7167	A
-1.2076	0.8721	0.4918	A
-0.7617	0.7326	0.8291	A

centroid.A

x1	x2	x3
-1.109	0.314	0.6792

data.B

x1	x2	x3	class
-0.0186	1.43	-1.082	B

centroid.B

x1	x2	x3
-0.0186	1.43	-1.082

data.C

x1	x2	x3	class
0.4273	-0.9419	-1.194	C
0.7246	-1.3605	-1.307	C

centroid.C

x1	x2	x3
0.5759	-1.151	-1.251

data.D

x1	x2	x3	class
1.022	-0.5233	0.6043	D
1.171	0.4535	0.9415	D

centroid.D

x1	x2	x3
1.096	-0.0349	0.7729

Here are the 4 cluster centroids:

	centroid		
class	x1	x2	x3
A	-1.1085	0.3140	0.6792
B	-0.0186	1.4303	-1.0820
C	0.5759	-1.1512	-1.2507
D	1.0961	-0.0349	0.7729

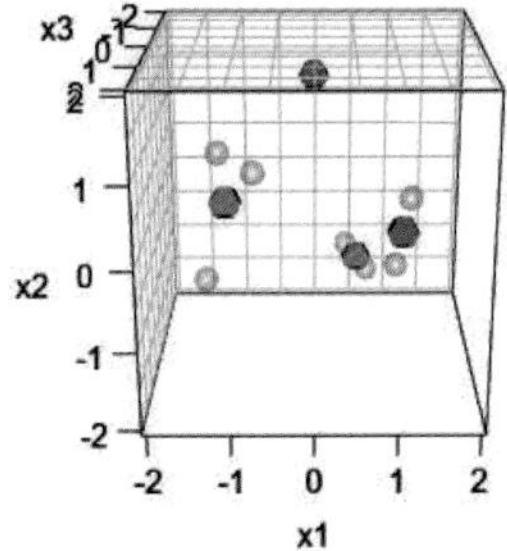

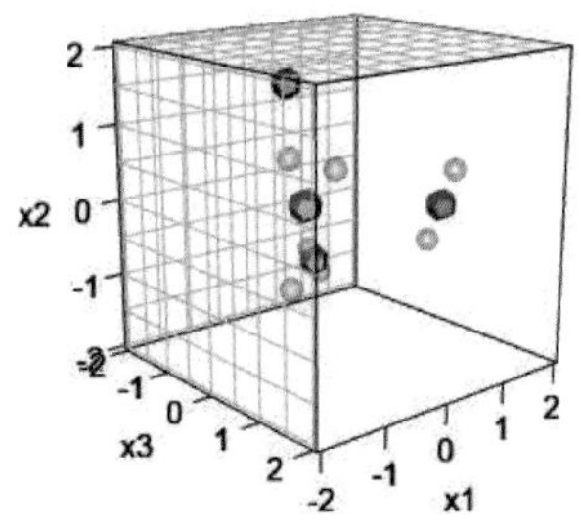

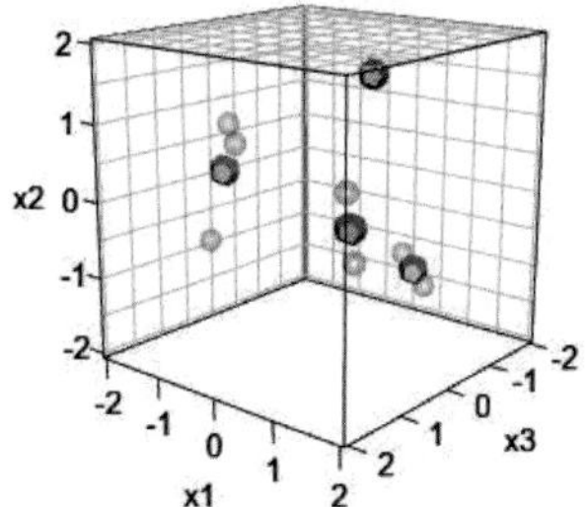

Then we determine the distances between the centroids and the mean of those distances.

distance_matrix.centroid

	A	B	C	D
A	0.000	2.353	2.951	2.234
B	2.353	0.000	2.654	2.613
C	2.951	2.654	0.000	2.369
D	2.234	2.613	2.369	0.000

distance

cluster_pair	distance
A_B	2.353
A_C	2.951
A_D	2.234
B_C	2.654
B_D	2.613
C_D	2.369

mean_intercluster_dispersion
2.529

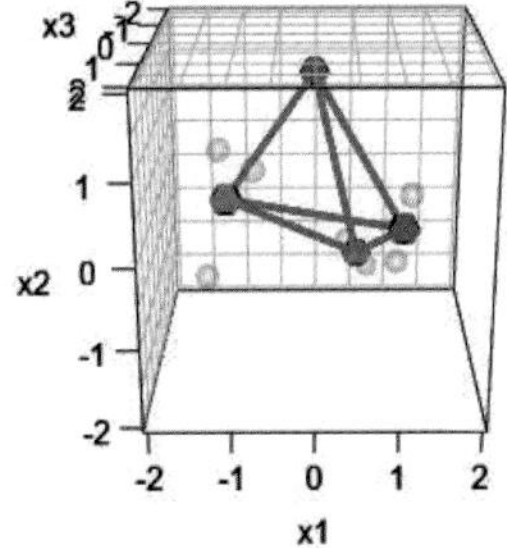

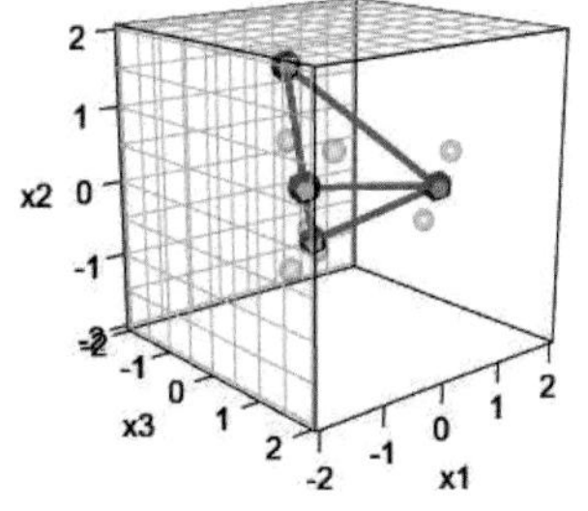

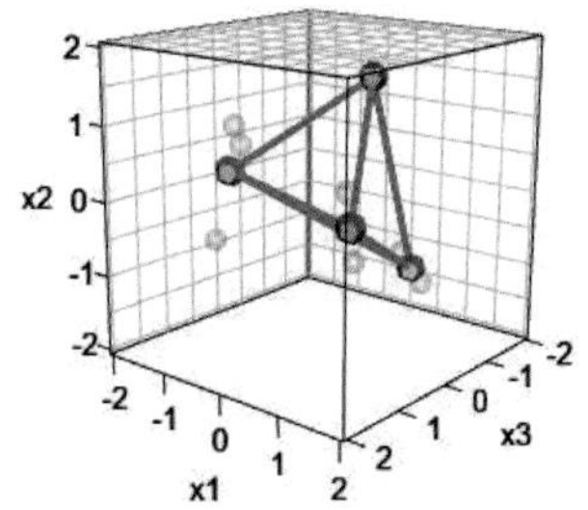

10.2.3.4 Dispersion Ratio

Dispersion ratio is a measure of both how dissimilar observations are from each other within a cluster and how dissimilar clusters are from each other. It is calculated as the inter-cluster dispersion divided by the mean mean intra-cluster dispersion.

$$\text{dispersion ratio} = \frac{\text{mean inter-cluster dispersion}}{\text{mean mean intra-cluster dispersion}}$$

Here we calculate the dispersion ratio of the cluster model:

mean_mean_intracluster_dispersion	mean_intercluster_dispersion	dispersion_ratio
0.697	2.529	3.628

A large dispersion ratio implies that observations constituting a cluster tend to be more similar to each other than they are to observations in other clusters. Conversely, a small dispersion ratio implies that observations constituting a cluster are not any more similar to each other than they are to observations in other clusters. In many business applications, the goal is to construct cluster models with large dispersion ratios.

We've quantified the quality of our cluster model as dispersion ratio 3.628. We can go on to compare this score to those of other cluster models to select the one likely to be most useful to our business.

10.3 k-Means

Construct a cluster model by the k-means method.

10.3.1 Introduction

As planets form in an emerging solar system, absorbing more and more dust, each planet's mass, its gravitational center, and its pull on dust still out there changes over time. Eventually, dust that started nearest 1 planet might move closer to another. You can think of the k-means method as dust moving around in space, affected by planets' evolving influence.

You can also think of the k-means method as a way to form clubs. Imagine establishing a club about the wind energy industry and a club about the solar energy industry. People in the community join the clubs in which they are more interested. However, many of the people interested in green energy in general are split across two different clubs. Further, many people not interested in green energy at all are stuck in clubs with people who are. So sometime later, a few people in the wind club who don't like green energy but do really like international trade see that there are many people in the solar club who really like international trade, so they move over to join that club. Doing this increases the concentration of people in the wind club interested in green energy. So in turn, the wind club looks more attractive to people in the solar club who are really interested in green energy, and they move over to join the wind club. This goes on for a while with the clubs becoming more or less attractive to various people moving between them. Eventually, what was the wind club has effectively become a green energy club and what was the solar energy club has become an international trade club. In this way, people organize themselves into satisfying groups.

10.3.2 About k-Means

The **k-means method** organizes observations into distinct clusters. With this method, we rely on the notions of distance as a measure of dissimilarity, and of a centroid, which is the datapoint at the variable means of a set of observations.

The k-means method works like this:

> *Initialize: Choose initial centroids at random*
> *Iterate:*
>   *Assign observations to classes based on distances to centroids*
>   *Re-position centroids based on class assignments*
> *Commit: Keep the latest class assignments*

First, establish classes to name the clusters, and randomly choose several centroids, 1 associated with each class.

Second, iterate over the following 2 steps. For each observation, calculate its distance to each centroid, and assign it to the class associated with the closest centroid. Then for each centroid, re-calculate its position to be the centroid of the observations assigned to its associated class. The re-calculated centroid's first variable value becomes the mean of its nearby observations' first variable values. Similarly for the other variables. In this way, the centroids move around, attracting and severing class assignments, while the observations retain their positions. Following several iterations, each observation tends to stay assigned to 1 class.

Third, for each observation, keep the latest class assignment. The observations, now finally assigned to classes, indicate which observations belong in which clusters. The observations and their class assignments constitute a **k-means model**.

Because the k-means method incorporates distance calculations, normalizing the observations in advance typically leads to more useful results.

The k-means method can appear in any of several variations as specified by hyper-parameters, including number of clusters, how distance between observations is measured, and how distance between clusters is measured (linkage). Also, the k-means method incorporates randomness. Specifically, the method gets initialized by centroids chosen at random. As such, the specific k-means model produced depends on which method variation gets used and how it gets initialized.

10.3.3 k-Means

Consider this unclassified 2-variable dataset. The observation numbers, 1 through 6, are shown. The observations could be organized into clusters in a variety of ways. Perhaps put observations with low versus high x_1 values in their own clusters. Or perhaps organize by x_2 values. Or perhaps organize by some function of both variables. Or perhaps put every other observation in 1 cluster and put the rest in another cluster. Would this expose any useful insights about their similarity and dissimilarity?

How should the observations be organized? Let's use the k-means method to organize the observations into 2 clusters.

data

	x1	x2
1	2	1
2	2	4
3	3	4
4	5	4
5	10	4
6	12	4

10.3.3.1 Hyper-parameters

Set hyper-parameters to specify which version of the method to use.

- **Number of clusters:** 2
- **Specification of inter-observation distance:** Euclidean distance
- **Specification of inter-cluster distance:** centroid linkage

10.3.3.2 Initialize

Randomly position the cluster centroids.

Here we see the centroid of cluster A at (x_1=1, x_2=3) and the centroid of cluster B at (x_1=4, x_2=4).

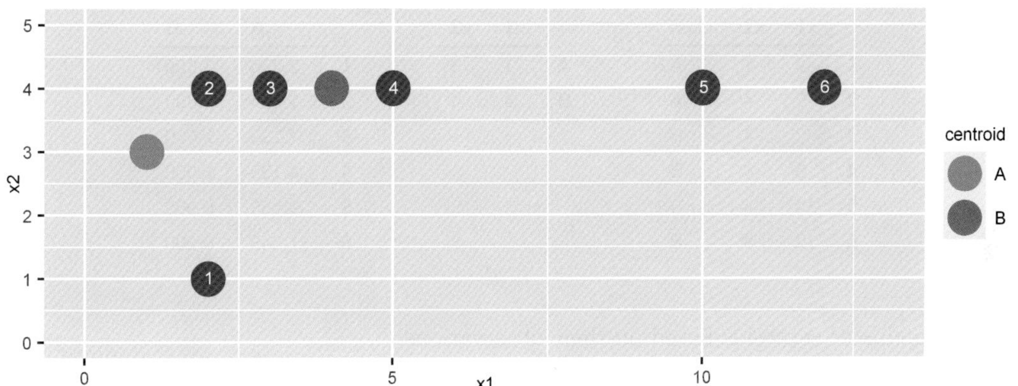

data

	x1	x2
1	2	1
2	2	4
3	3	4
4	5	4
5	10	4
6	12	4

centroid

	x1	x2
A	1	3
B	4	4

10.3.3.3 Iterate

Iterate, re-positioning the cluster centroids at each step. You can interrupt the method at the step that provides you with a satisfactory cluster model, or you can let it go until it converges on a stable cluster model.

Iteration 1: Calculate distances from the observations to the centroids. Tentatively assign each observation to the cluster associated with its nearest centroid.

Here we see that observations 1 and 2 are closer to centroid A than they are to centroid B, so those observations are tentatively assigned to cluster A. Similarly, observations 3, 4, 5, and 6 are tentatively assigned to cluster B.

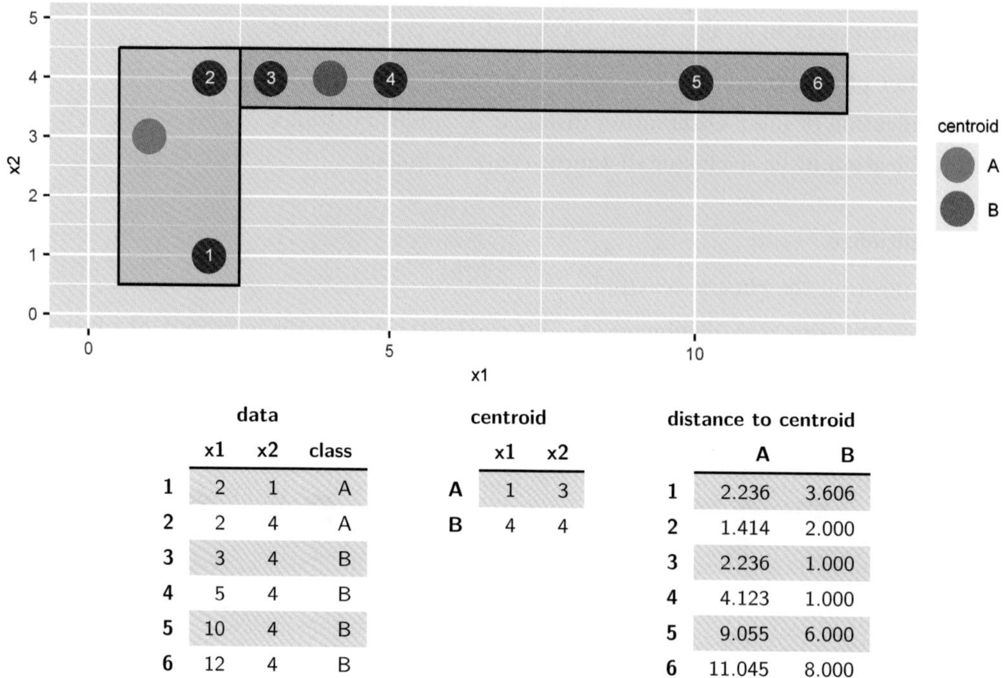

data

	x1	x2	class
1	2	1	A
2	2	4	A
3	3	4	B
4	5	4	B
5	10	4	B
6	12	4	B

centroid

	x1	x2
A	1	3
B	4	4

distance to centroid

	A	B
1	2.236	3.606
2	1.414	2.000
3	2.236	1.000
4	4.123	1.000
5	9.055	6.000
6	11.045	8.000

Re-position cluster centroids based on their observations.

Here we see centroid A re-positioned at (x_1=2.0, x_2=2.5) based on observations 1 and 2. Similarly, centroid B is re-positioned at (x_1=7.5, x_2=4.0) based on observations 3, 4, 5, and 6.

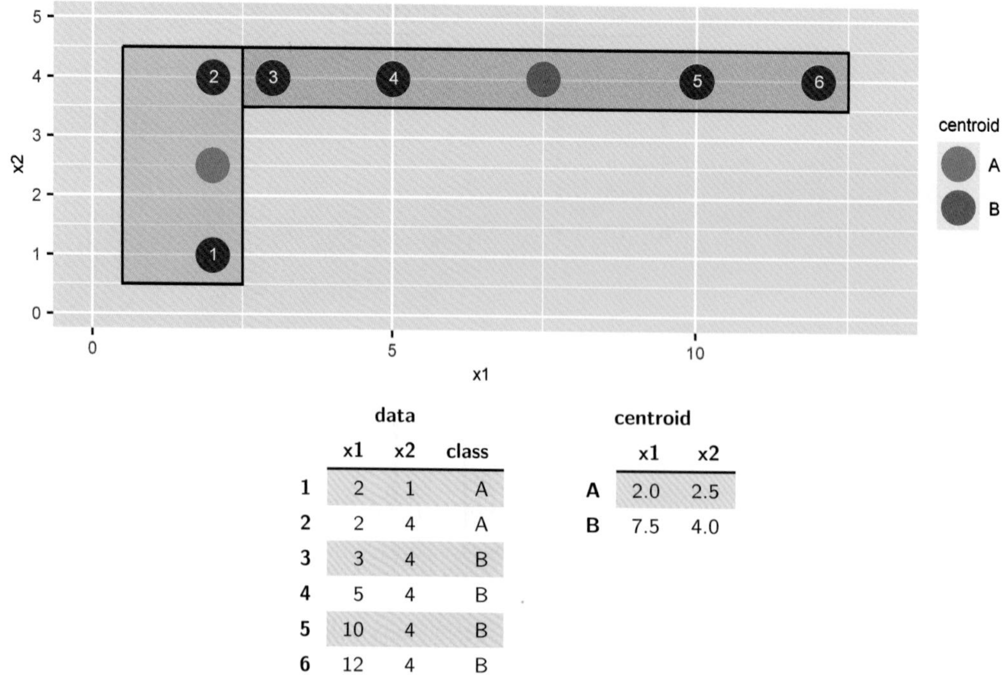

data

	x1	x2	class
1	2	1	A
2	2	4	A
3	3	4	B
4	5	4	B
5	10	4	B
6	12	4	B

centroid

	x1	x2
A	2.0	2.5
B	7.5	4.0

Iteration 2: Calculate distances from the observations to the centroids. Tentatively assign each observation to the cluster associated with its nearest centroid. Note that the observations do not change position, but some may change class.

Here we see that observations 1, 2, and 3 are closer to centroid A than they are to centroid B, so those observations are tentatively assigned to cluster A. Similarly, observations 4, 5, and 6 are tentatively assigned to cluster B.

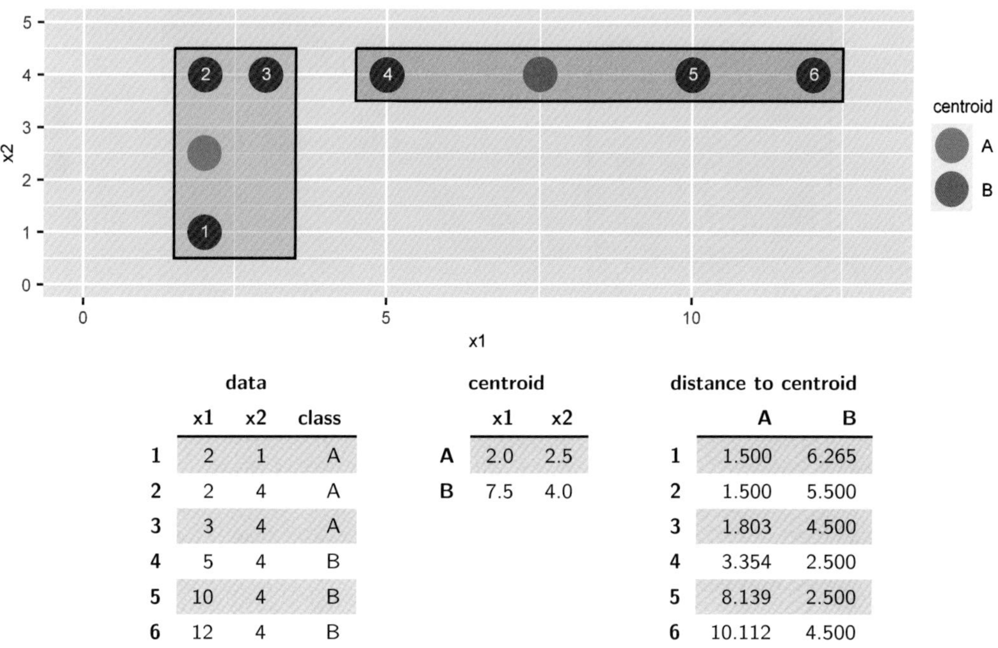

data

	x1	x2	class
1	2	1	A
2	2	4	A
3	3	4	A
4	5	4	B
5	10	4	B
6	12	4	B

centroid

	x1	x2
A	2.0	2.5
B	7.5	4.0

distance to centroid

	A	B
1	1.500	6.265
2	1.500	5.500
3	1.803	4.500
4	3.354	2.500
5	8.139	2.500
6	10.112	4.500

Re-position cluster centroids based on their observations.

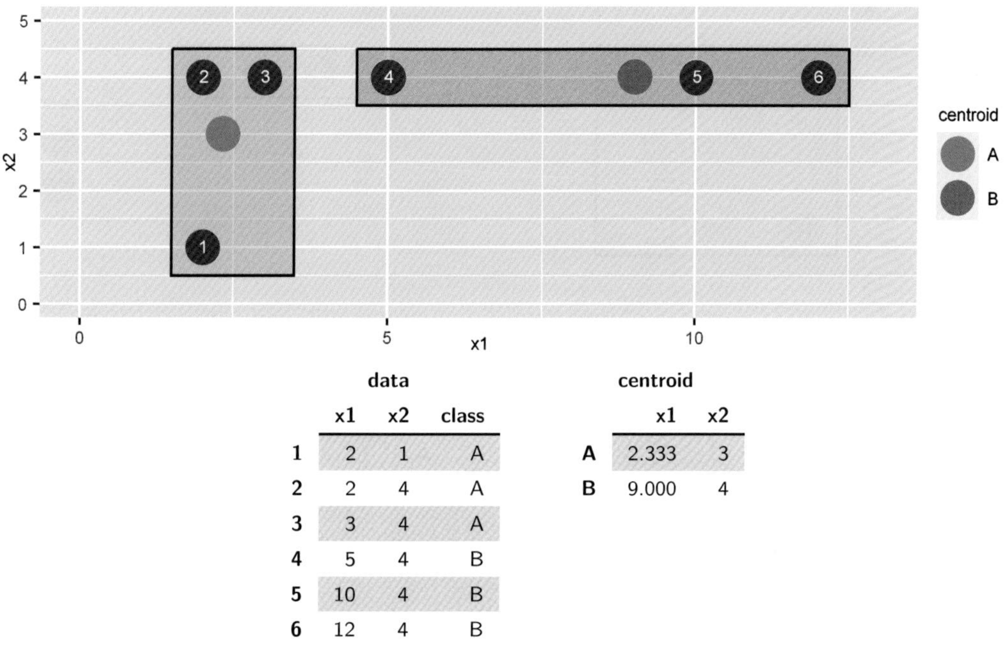

data

	x1	x2	class
1	2	1	A
2	2	4	A
3	3	4	A
4	5	4	B
5	10	4	B
6	12	4	B

centroid

	x1	x2
A	2.333	3
B	9.000	4

Iteration 3: Calculate distances from the observations to the centroids. Tentatively assign each observation to the cluster associated with its nearest centroid.

Here we see that observations 1, 2, 3, and 4 are closer to centroid A than they are to centroid B, so those observations are tentatively assigned to cluster A. Similarly, observations 5 and 6 tentatively are assigned to cluster B.

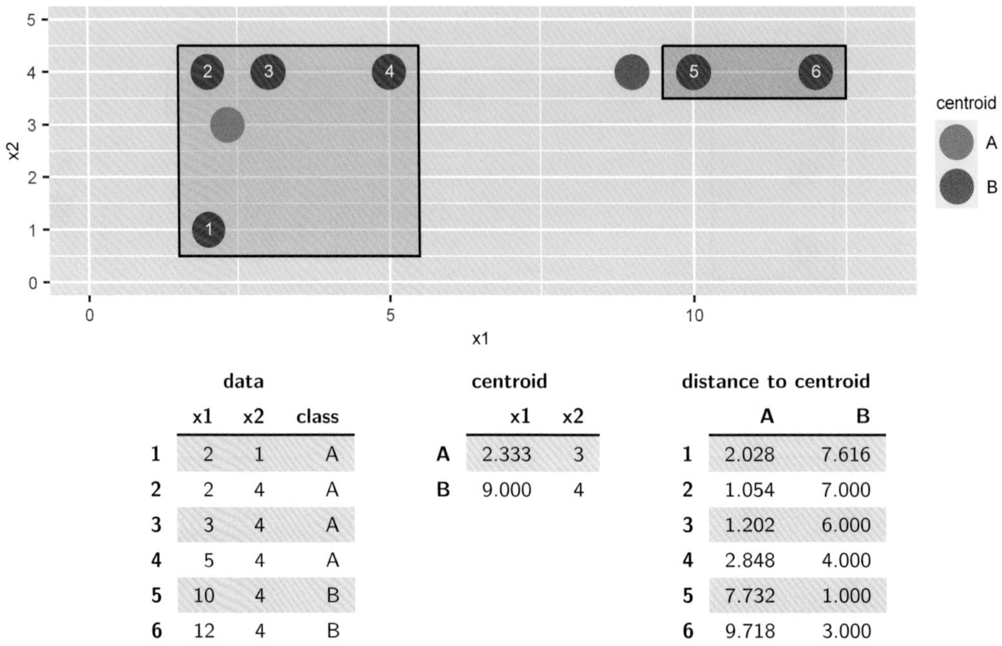

data

	x1	x2	class
1	2	1	A
2	2	4	A
3	3	4	A
4	5	4	A
5	10	4	B
6	12	4	B

centroid

	x1	x2
A	2.333	3
B	9.000	4

distance to centroid

	A	B
1	2.028	7.616
2	1.054	7.000
3	1.202	6.000
4	2.848	4.000
5	7.732	1.000
6	9.718	3.000

Re-position cluster centroids based on their observations.

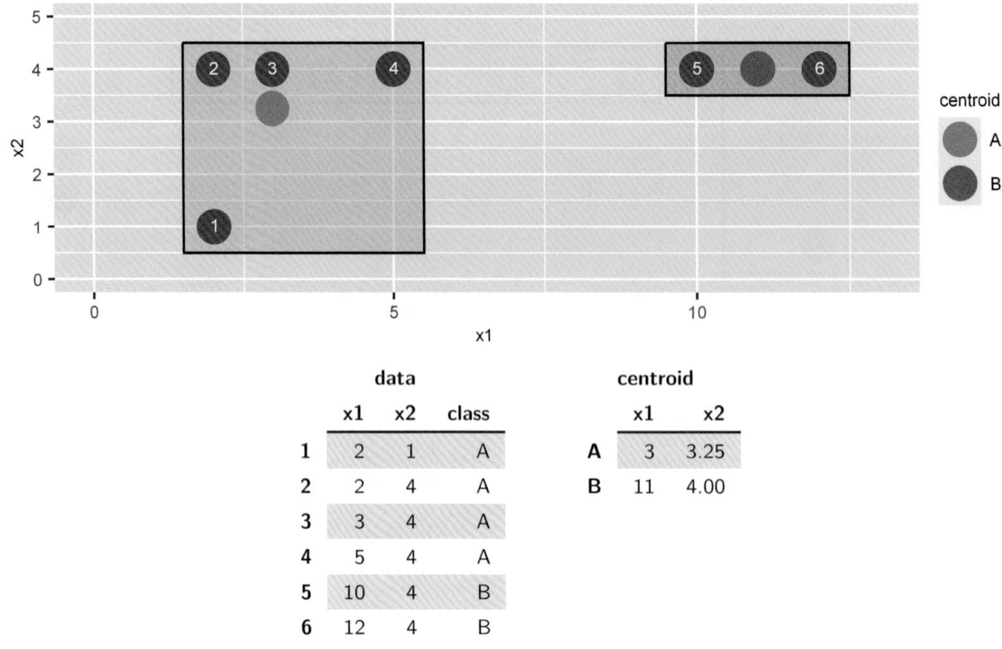

data

	x1	x2	class
1	2	1	A
2	2	4	A
3	3	4	A
4	5	4	A
5	10	4	B
6	12	4	B

centroid

	x1	x2
A	3	3.25
B	11	4.00

Iteration 4: Calculate distances from the observations to the centroids. Tentatively assign each observation to the cluster associated with its nearest centroid. At this step, there is no change in cluster assignments, so centroids would not change in any subsequent steps.

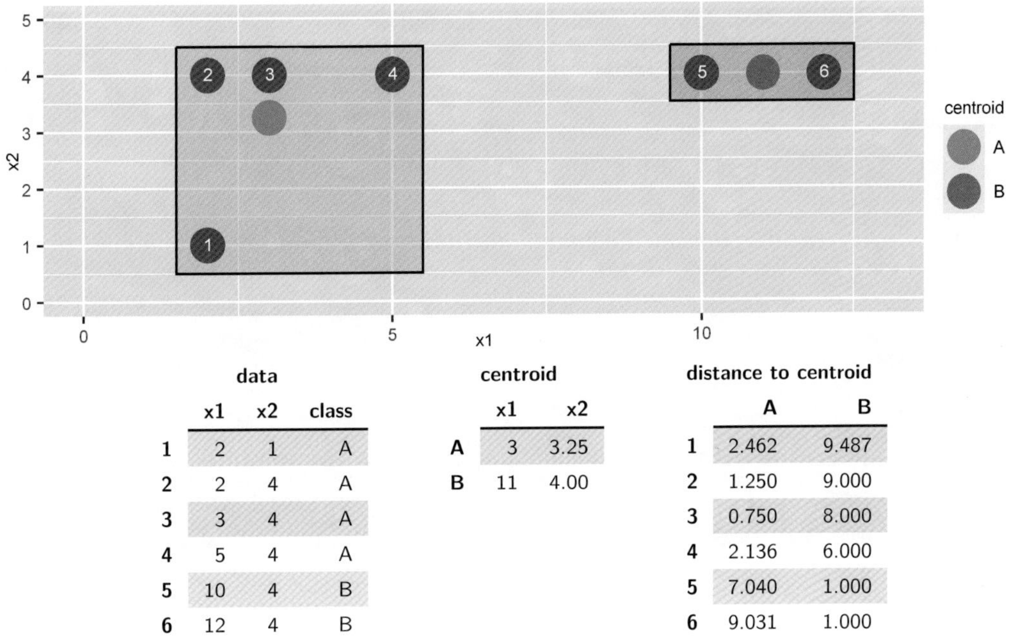

data

	x1	x2	class
1	2	1	A
2	2	4	A
3	3	4	A
4	5	4	A
5	10	4	B
6	12	4	B

centroid

	x1	x2
A	3	3.25
B	11	4.00

distance to centroid

	A	B
1	2.462	9.487
2	1.250	9.000
3	0.750	8.000
4	2.136	6.000
5	7.040	1.000
6	9.031	1.000

10.3.3.4 Commit Cluster Assignments

We have converged on a stable cluster model and commit cluster assignments accordingly.

Here we see the resulting cluster model:

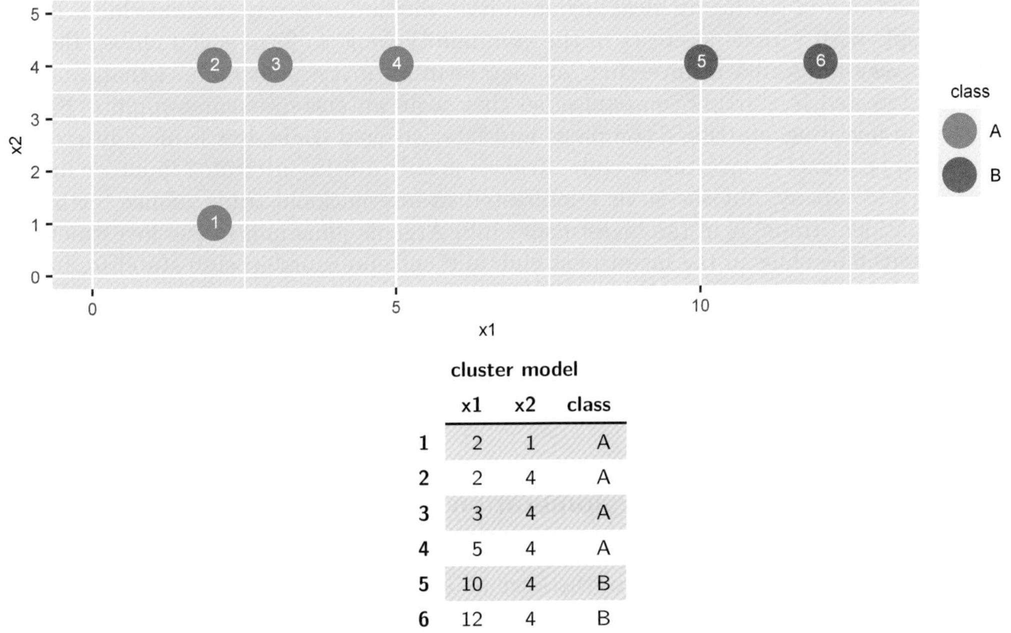

cluster model

	x1	x2	class
1	2	1	A
2	2	4	A
3	3	4	A
4	5	4	A
5	10	4	B
6	12	4	B

10.4 Hierarchical Agglomeration

Construct a cluster model by the hierarchical agglomeration method.

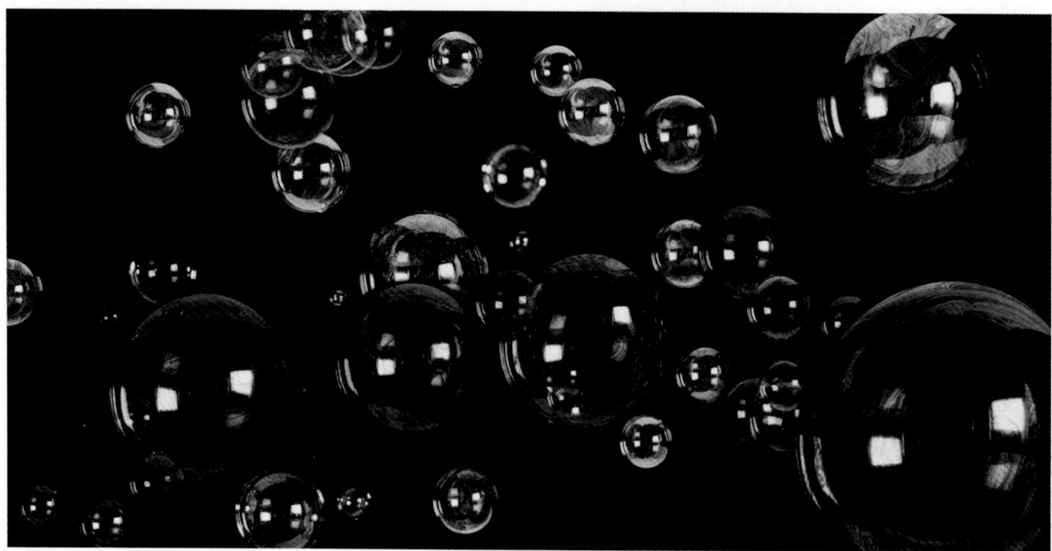

10.4.1 Introduction

As soap bubbles float around in the air, a few touch each other and combine into larger soap bubbles. Sometime later, those soap bubbles touch yet others to combine further. Eventually, the number of soap bubbles decreases while the sizes of the combined soap bubbles increases. We're left with just a few large soap bubbles. You can think of the hierarchical agglomeration method as combining soap bubbles.

You can also think of the hierarchical agglomeration method as a way to form clubs. Imagine several people with various interests in the community want to form social clubs. Ilene and Ishaan are very interested in investing, so they form an investment club. Ethan and Ebru are very interested in starting companies, so they form an entrepreneurship club. Saahil is interested in investing, starting a company, and international trade, but is most interested in investing, so he joins the investment club. Argenis is only a little interested in either investing or starting a company, but she is very interested in international trade. Since Saahil, who likes international trade, is in the investment club, Argenis joins him in the investment club. Eventually, memberships in the investment club and entrepreneurship club stabilize, but each club would like a larger membership, so they merge with each other to form a business club. People in the business club don't all have really similar interests like they did back when they were in the investment club and entrepreneurship club, but still somewhat similar, at least as compared with how similar they'd be to people in other clubs. In this way, people organize themselves into satisfying groups.

10.4.2 About Hierarchical Agglomeration

The **hierarchical agglomeration method** organizes observations into distinct clusters. With this method, we rely on the notion of distance as a way to characterize dissimilarity, and a **dendrogram** as way to represent iteration history.

The hierarchical agglomeration method works like this:

> *Initialize:*
> *Treat each observation as a cluster*
> *Calculate distance matrix and minimum distance*
> *Iterate:*
> *Agglomerate pair of clusters closest to each other*
> *Re-calculate distance matrix and minimum distance*
> *Keep track of iteration history*
> *Dendrogram Analysis:*
> *Represent iteration history as dendrogram*
> *Clip dendrogram based on dendrogram analysis*
> *Commit: Assign classes based on dendrogram clips*

First, establish a record to track the creation and replacement of clusters. The record comprises entries for all clusters, initially treating each observation as its own cluster of size 1. The record starts out looking exactly like the dataset, but will subsequently evolve as we iterate. Calculate the distance matrix of distances between all pairs of clusters, using your choice of how to measure distance between clusters. From the matrix, determine the minimum distance between pairs of clusters.

Second, iterate over the following 2 steps. Agglomerate the 2 closest clusters by putting them both into a new cluster. Update the record by replacing the entries for those 2 closest clusters with an entry for the new cluster. The new entry must include enough information about the new cluster to allow for the calculation of its distance to all other clusters. Then re-calculate the distance matrix based on the updated record. Note that in each iteration the number of entries decreases by 1 because 2 clusters get replaced by 1 cluster. Keep track of which clusters get agglomerated in each iteration, typically in an agglomeration dendrogram. Following several iterations, the record reduces to an entry for just 1 cluster. In this way, the method accumulates a set of cluster models, 1 of size equal to the number of observations, 1 of size 1, and others of every size in between.

Third, represent the iteration history as a dendrogram, which exposes the relationships among intra-cluster distances and inter-cluster distances at each iteration. Slide a **cutline** vertically along the dendrogram to determine the best trade-off between intra-cluster distances and inter-cluster distances. Clip the dendrogram at the best cutline.

Fourth, assign each observation to the class indicated by the dendrogram and best cutline. The observations and their class assignments constitute a cluster model.

Because the hierarchical agglomeration method incorporates distance calculations, normalizing the observations in advance typically leads to more useful results.

The hierarchical agglomeration method can appear in any of several variations as specified by hyper-parameters, including how distance between observations is measured and how distance between clusters is measured. Note that the number of clusters is typically not explicitly specified, but rather will be determined from the dendrogram analysis. The hierarchical agglomeration method does not incorporate randomness. As such, the specific cluster model produced depends on which method variation gets used, but not on initialization.

The hierarchical agglomeration method is also known as **agglomerative hierarchical clustering** or **AHC**.

10.4.3 Hierarchical Agglomeration

Consider this unclassified 2-variable dataset. The observation numbers, 1 through 6, are shown. The observations could be organized into clusters in a variety of ways. Perhaps put observations with low versus high x_1 values in their own clusters. Or perhaps organize by x_2 values. Or perhaps organize by some function of both variables. Or perhaps put every other observation in one cluster and put the rest in another cluster. Would this expose any useful insights about their similarity and dissimilarity?

How should the observations be organized? Let's use the hierarchical agglomeration method to organize the observations into 2 clusters.

data

	x1	x2
1	2	1
2	2	4
3	3	4
4	5	4
5	10	4
6	12	4

10.4.3.1 Hyper-parameters

Set hyper-parameters to specify which version of the method to use.

- **Specification of inter-observation distance:** Euclidean distance
- **Specification of inter-cluster distance:** centroid linkage

10.4.3.2 Initialize

Establish a record of clusters, treating each observation as a cluster. Calculate the distance matrix of distances between each pair of clusters, using Euclidean distance and centroid linkage as the way to measure distance between clusters. From that, determine the minimum distance between pairs of clusters, which here is distance 1.0 between cluster 2 and cluster 3.

Were we to interrupt the method at initialization, we would have a 6-cluster model.

record

	x1	x2
1	2	1
2	2	4
3	3	4
4	5	4
5	10	4
6	12	4

distance matrix

	1	2	3	4	5	6
1	0.0000	3.0000	3.1623	4.2426	8.5440	10.4403
2	3.0000	0.0000	1.0000	3.0000	8.0000	10.0000
3	3.1623	1.0000	0.0000	2.0000	7.0000	9.0000
4	4.2426	3.0000	2.0000	0.0000	5.0000	7.0000
5	8.5440	8.0000	7.0000	5.0000	0.0000	2.0000
6	10.4403	10.0000	9.0000	7.0000	2.0000	0.0000

min distance
1.0000

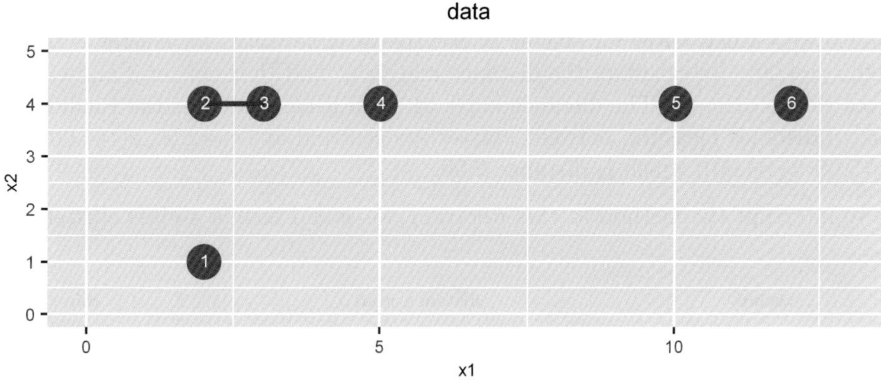

10.4.3.3 Iterate

Iterate, agglomerating 2 clusters at each iteration until there is just 1 cluster left.

Iteration 1: We see that cluster 2 and cluster 3 are the closest to each other at distance 1.0, so agglomerate them. They don't get re-positioned, but they do get put into a new cluster, which we'll call cluster A. Then update the record of clusters, replacing entries for cluster 2 and cluster 3 with a new entry for cluster A. Set the variable values to reflect cluster A's position according to our choice of linkage, which here is the cluster's centroid at (x_1=2.50, x_2=4.00). Then re-calculate the distance matrix and identify the new minimum distance, which here is distance 2.00 between cluster 5 and cluster 6.

Were we to interrupt the method at this iteration, we would have a 5-cluster model.

	record	
	x1	x2
1	2.0	1
4	5.0	4
5	10.0	4
6	12.0	4
A	2.5	4

	distance matrix				
	1	4	5	6	A
1	0.0000	4.2426	8.5440	10.4403	3.0414
4	4.2426	0.0000	5.0000	7.0000	2.5000
5	8.5440	5.0000	0.0000	2.0000	7.5000
6	10.4403	7.0000	2.0000	0.0000	9.5000
A	3.0414	2.5000	7.5000	9.5000	0.0000

min
distance
2.0000

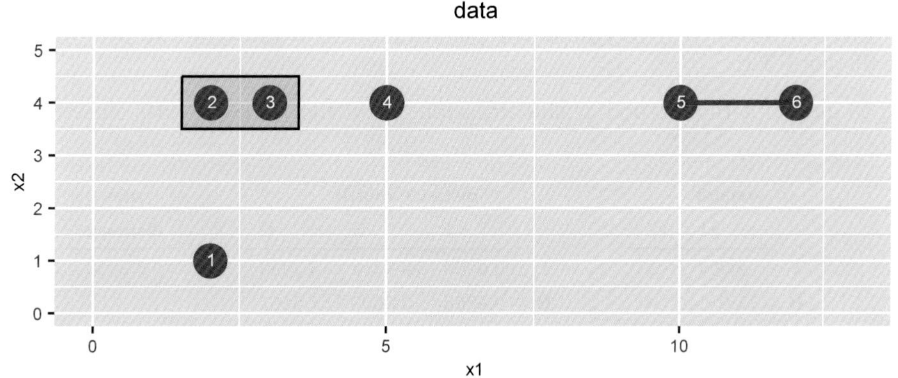

Iteration 2: Agglomerate the re-assessed closest clusters, cluster 5 and cluster 6, and put them into a new cluster, which we'll call cluster B. Update the record by replacing entries for cluster 5 and cluster 6 with a new entry for cluster B. Set the variable values for cluster B to its centroid (x_1=11.00, x_2=4.00). Re-calculate the distance matrix to find that cluster 4 and cluster A have become the closest clusters. The distance between them is calculated as the Euclidean distance, our choice of distance measure, between cluster A's centroid at (x_1=2.50, x_2=4.00) and cluster 4 at (x_1=5.00, x_2=4.00), which is distance 2.50.

Were we to interrupt the method at this iteration, we would have a 4-class cluster model.

record	x1	x2
1	2.0	1
4	5.0	4
A	2.5	4
B	11.0	4

distance matrix	1	4	A	B
1	0.0000	4.2426	3.0414	9.4868
4	4.2426	0.0000	2.5000	6.0000
A	3.0414	2.5000	0.0000	8.5000
B	9.4868	6.0000	8.5000	0.0000

min distance
2.5000

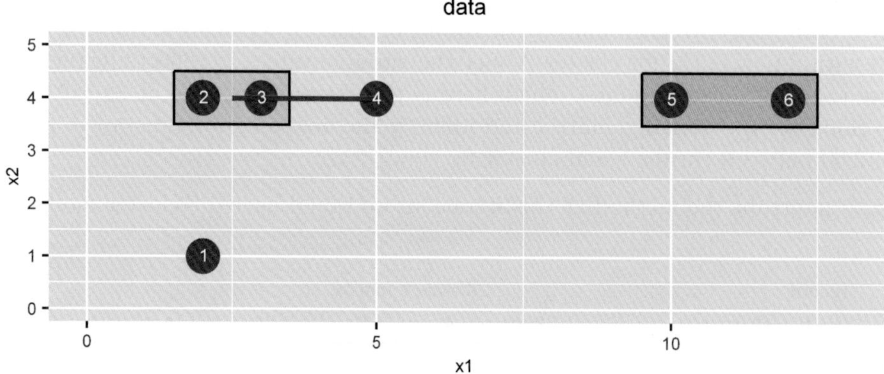

Iteration 3: Agglomerate the re-assessed closest clusters, cluster A and cluster 4, and put them into a new cluster, which we'll call cluster C. Update the record by replacing entries for cluster A and cluster 4 with a new entry for cluster C. Set the variable values for cluster C to its centroid (x_1=3.33, x_2=4.00). Note that cluster C's centroid is calculated as the variable means of the observations 2, 3, and 4 residing in it. Re-calculate the distance matrix to find that cluster 1 and cluster C have become the closest clusters. The distance is calculated as the Euclidean distance between cluster C's centroid at (x_1=3.33, x_2=4.00) and cluster 1 at (x_1=2.00, x_2=1.00), which is distance 3.28.

Were we to interrupt the method at this iteration, we would have a 3-class cluster model.

record	x1	x2
1	2.000	1
B	11.000	4
C	3.333	4

distance matrix	1	B	C
1	0.0000	9.4868	3.2830
B	9.4868	0.0000	7.6667
C	3.2830	7.6667	0.0000

min distance
3.2830

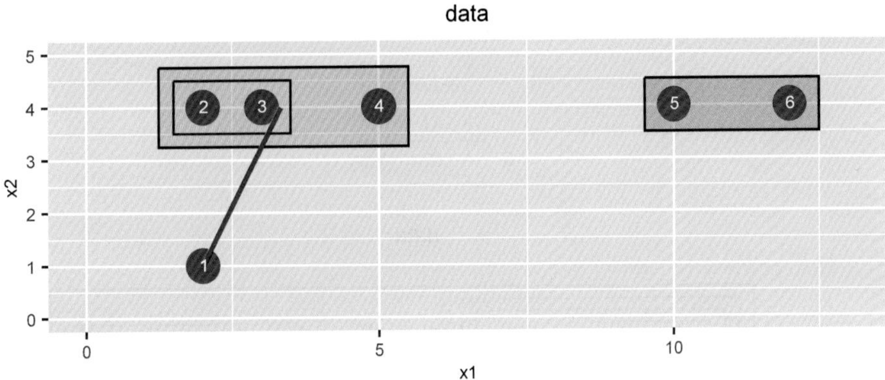

Iteration 4: Agglomerate the re-assessed closest clusters, cluster C and cluster 1, and put them into a new cluster, which we'll call cluster D. Update the record by replacing entries for cluster C and cluster 1 with a new entry for cluster D. Set the variable values for cluster D to its centroid (x_1=3.00, x_2=3.25). Note that cluster D's centroid is calculated as the variable means of the observations 1, 2, 3, and 4 residing in it. Re-calculate the distance matrix to find that cluster B and cluster D have become the closest clusters. Actually, they are the the only pair left. The distance is calculated as the Euclidean distance between cluster B's centroid at (x_1=11.00, x_2=4.00) and cluster D's centroid at (x_1=3.00, x_2=3.25), which is distance 8.04.

Were we to interrupt the method at this step, we would have a 2-class cluster model.

record

	x1	x2
B	11	4.00
D	3	3.25

distance matrix

	B	D
B	0.0000	8.0351
D	8.0351	0.0000

min distance
8.0351

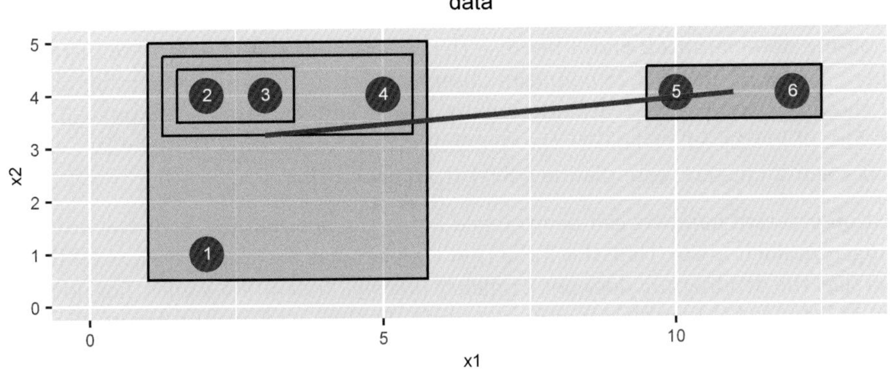

Iteration 5: By iteration 5, we are left with only 1 pair, which gets put into a new cluster we'll call cluster E.

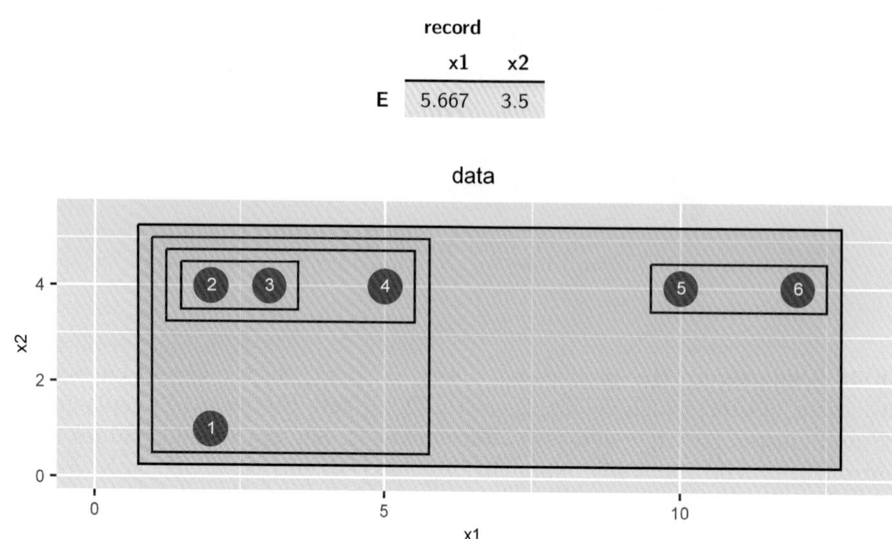

10.4.3.4 Dendrogram Analysis

Having tracked the iteration history, now represent it as a dendrogram. The horizontal axis indicates observation number, and the vertical axis indicates distance. Observations and clusters of observations are connected by forks of various heights, indicating their inter-cluster distances.

We see that observations 2 and 3 are connected by a fork of height 1.00. That shows that observations 2 and 3, treated as clusters 2 and 3, were agglomerated into a single cluster in some iteration because they were distance 1.00 from each other. Observations 5 and 6 are connected by a fork of height 2.00. They were agglomerated into a single cluster because they were distance 2.00 from each other. Observation 4 is connected by a fork of height 2.50 to the fork connecting observations 2 and 3. This shows that observation 4 was agglomerated with the cluster housing observations 2 and 3 because the observation and cluster were distance 2.5 from each other. A fork of height 3.28 connects observation 1 to the fork connecting observations 2, 3, and 4 showing that the observation and cluster were agglomerated at distance 3.28 from each other. A fork of height 8.04 connects the remaining clusters showing that the last agglomeration happened when 2 clusters were distance 8.04 from each other.

Note that observation numbers can be arranged along the horizontal axis in any order. Here they are arranged in such a way that the forks don't cross, just to simplify the overall appearance. Note also that the dendrogram does not explicitly convey observation values, nor does it explicitly convey how distance between clusters was measured. Rather, it shows the results after observation values and a way of measuring distance were provided to the hierarchical agglomeration method. For this specific dendrogram, we can infer the order in which agglomerations occurred based on fork heights. Agglomerations associated with shorter heights must have occurred before those associated with longer heights.

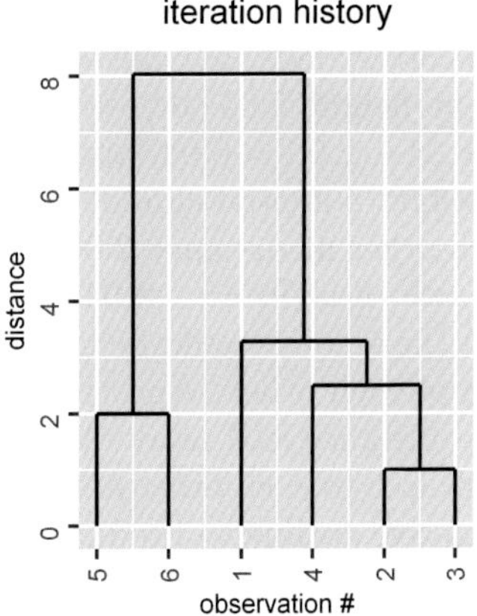

Next try cutting the dendrogram with cutlines at various heights. The clipped lower portions of the dendrogram correspond to sets of clusters as they appeared in various iterations.

Here we try cutlines at heights 5.66, 2.89, and 2.25. A cutline at height 5.66 clips the dendrogram in 2 places, leaving 1 cluster housing observations 5 and 6, and another cluster housing observations 1, 2, 3, and 4. Sliding the cutline down to height 2.89, we clip the dendrogram in 3 places to get 3 clusters. Sliding down to height 2.25, we clip in 4 places to get 4 clusters.

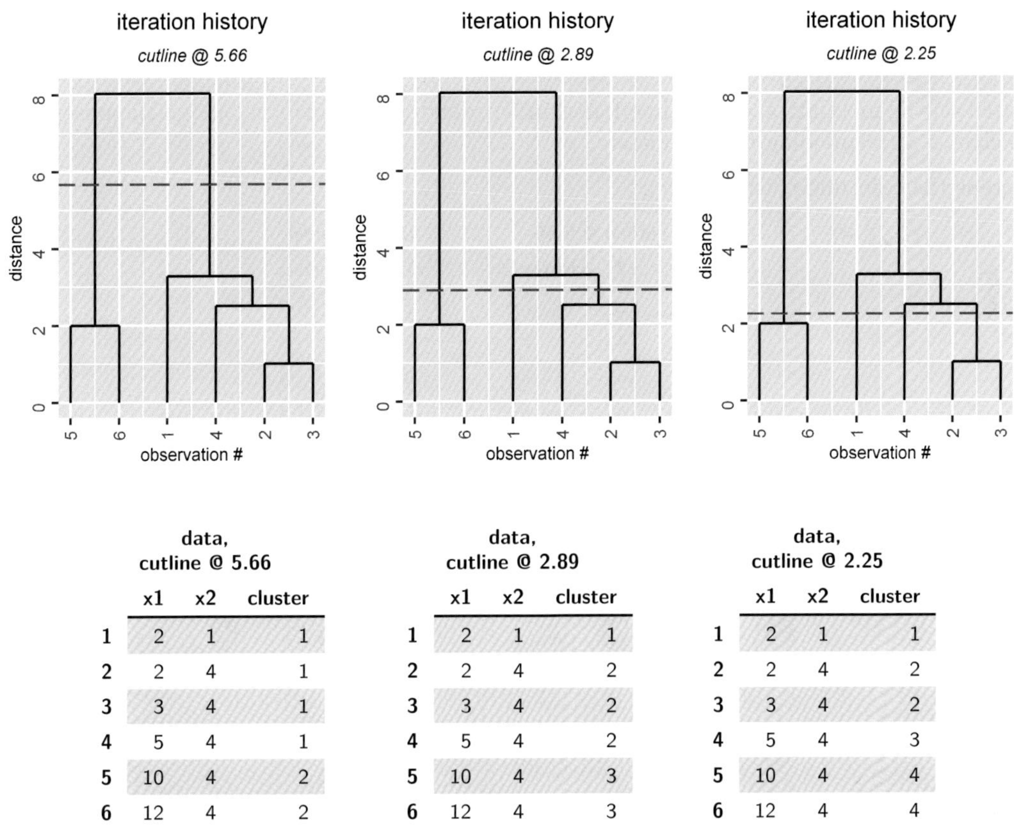

data, cutline @ 5.66

	x1	x2	cluster
1	2	1	1
2	2	4	1
3	3	4	1
4	5	4	1
5	10	4	2
6	12	4	2

data, cutline @ 2.89

	x1	x2	cluster
1	2	1	1
2	2	4	2
3	3	4	2
4	5	4	2
5	10	4	3
6	12	4	3

data, cutline @ 2.25

	x1	x2	cluster
1	2	1	1
2	2	4	2
3	3	4	2
4	5	4	3
5	10	4	4
6	12	4	4

Any cutline would result in a set of clusters that could serve as our cluster model. However, in practice, some cutlines produce more useful cluster models than others do. A cutline that clips relatively long fork segments corresponds to a cluster model in which clusters are relatively far from each other. A cutline at height 5.66, or any height between 3.28 and 8.4, would clip one fork segment of length $8.04 - 2.00 = 6.04$, and clip a second fork segment of length $8.04 - 3.28 = 4.76$. Looking at the first potential clip, observations 5 and 6 in the first would-be cluster are relatively close to each other at distance 2.00, but this first cluster is relatively far from the second would-be cluster, which is distance 8.04 away. Looking at the second potential clip, observations 1, 2, 3, and 4 in the second would-be cluster are relatively close to each other. They are all within distance 3.28 of each other. And this second cluster is relatively far from the first would-be cluster, which is distance 8.04 away. As we've seen before, it's often better to keep observations within a cluster close to each other and the clusters themselves far from each other. So, this seems like an attractive cutline to produce a useful cluster model.

Compare that to a cutline at height 2.89, or any height between 2.50 and 3.28. Such a cutline would clip 3 fork segments, one of length $8.04 - 2.00 = 6.04$, one of length $3.28 - 0 = 3.28$, and one of length $3.28 - 2.5 = 0.78$. The first and second would-be clusters look all right. But observations 2, 3, and 4 in the third would-be cluster are already distance 2.5 from each other. They are only distance 0.78 farther away from observation 1 in the second would-be cluster than they are from each other. In other words, the second would-be cluster and the third would-be cluster seem relatively similar to each other. And if that's the case, it might not be useful to organize observations into these 2 separate clusters that way. Better to avoid this cutline.

Similarly, we can see that other cutlines are not as attractive as the cutlines that clip just 2 fork segments.

10.4.3.5 Commit

Based on the most attractive cutline found in our dendrogram analysis, assign the observations to classes corresponding to the clusters.

Here is the resulting cluster model:

data, cutline @ 5.66

	x1	x2	cluster
1	2	1	1
2	2	4	1
3	3	4	1
4	5	4	1
5	10	4	2
6	12	4	2

cluster model

x1	x2	class
2	1	A
2	4	A
3	4	A
5	4	A
10	4	B
12	4	B

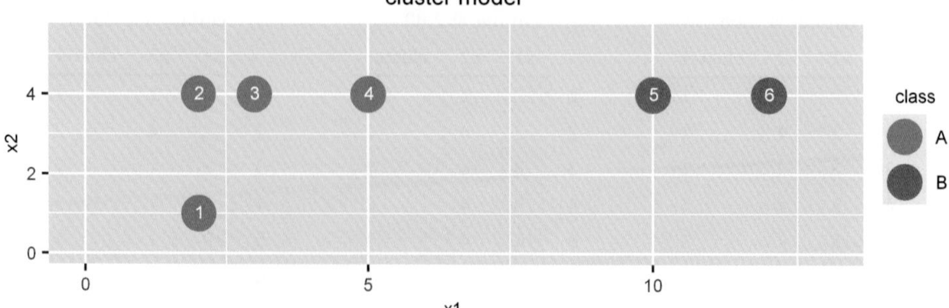

10.4.4 More Dendrogram Analysis

Consider this unclassified 2-variable dataset and iteration history showing the results of hierarchical agglomeration applied to the dataset.

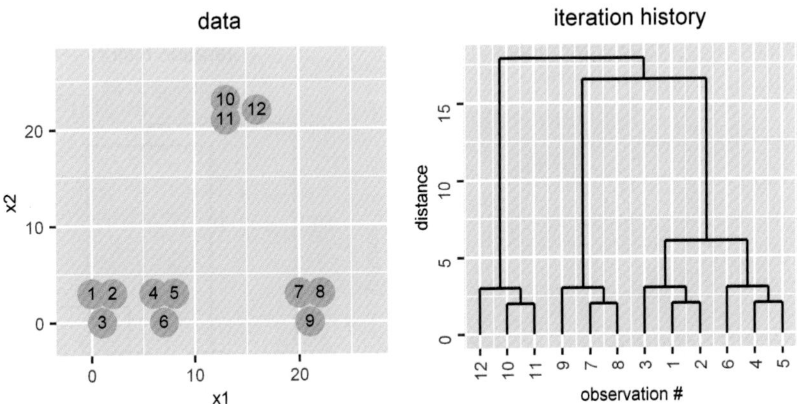

Any cutline between 3 and 6 would produce a 4-cluster model.

The forks of height 3 reflect that each of the 4 clusters house observations up to distance 3 apart from each other. The fork of height 6 reflects what would happen were cluster 1,2,3 to be agglomerated with cluster 4,5,6. The taller fork of height 6 is only length $6 - 3 = 3$ taller than the shorter fork of height 3. That difference is relatively small when compared with the shorter fork height. Interpret this like so: the observations in cluster 1,2,3 are relatively similar to the observations in cluster 4,5,6.

The 4-cluster model seems somewhat satisfying because intra-cluster distances are small, although at least 1 inter-cluster distance is also small.

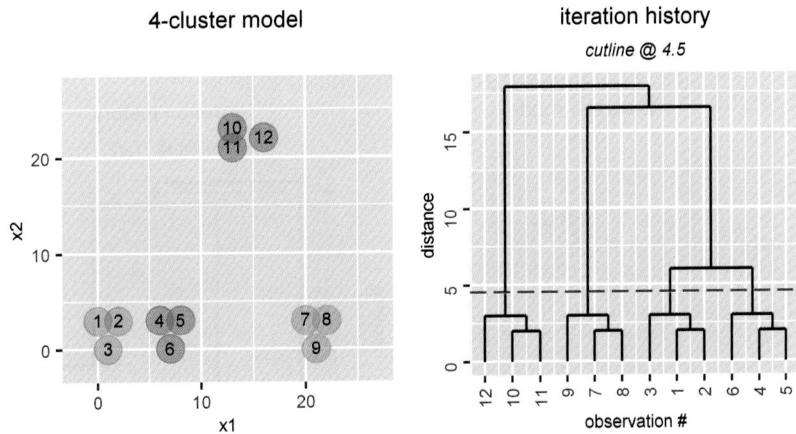

Any cutline between 6 and 16.5 would produce a 3-cluster model.

The fork of height 6 reflects that 1 cluster houses observations that are up to distance 6 apart from each other. The fork of height 16.5 reflects what would happen were cluster 1,2,3,4,5,6 to be agglomerated with cluster 7,8,9. The taller fork of height 16.5 is length $16.5 - 6 = 10.5$ taller than the shorter fork of height 6. That difference is relatively large when compared with the shorter fork height. Interpret this like so: the observations in cluster 1,2,3,4,5,6 are relatively dissimilar to the observations in cluster 7,8,9.

The 3-cluster model seems very satisfying because intra-cluster distances are small and inter-cluster distances are large.

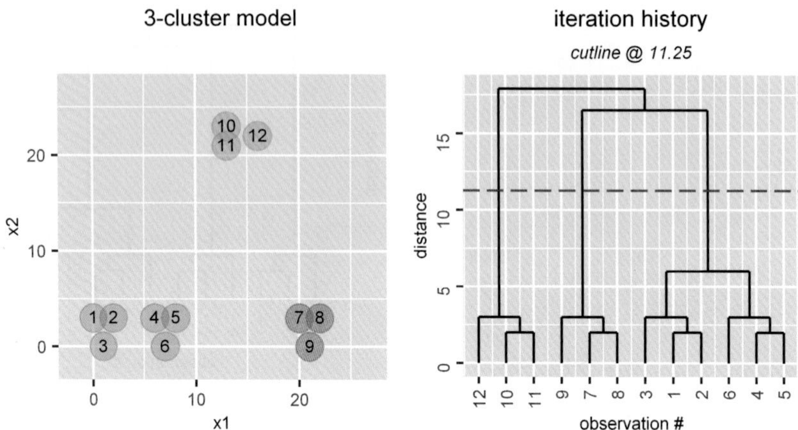

Any cutline between 16.5 and 17.9 would produce a 2-cluster model.

The fork of height 16.5 reflects that 1 cluster houses observations that are up to distance 16.5 apart from each other. The fork of height 17.90 reflects what would happen were cluster 1,2,3,4,5,6,7,8,9 to be agglomerated with cluster 10,11,12. The taller fork of height 17.9 is only length $17.9 - 16.5 = 1.4$ taller than the shorter fork of height 16.5. That difference is relatively small when compared with the shorter fork height. Interpret this like so: the observations in cluster 1,2,3,4,5,6,7,8,9 are already dissimilar to each other, making the observations in cluster 10,11,12 not much more distinctive.

The 2-cluster model seems not satisfying because intra-cluster distances are large and inter-cluster distances are not much larger than intra-cluster distances.

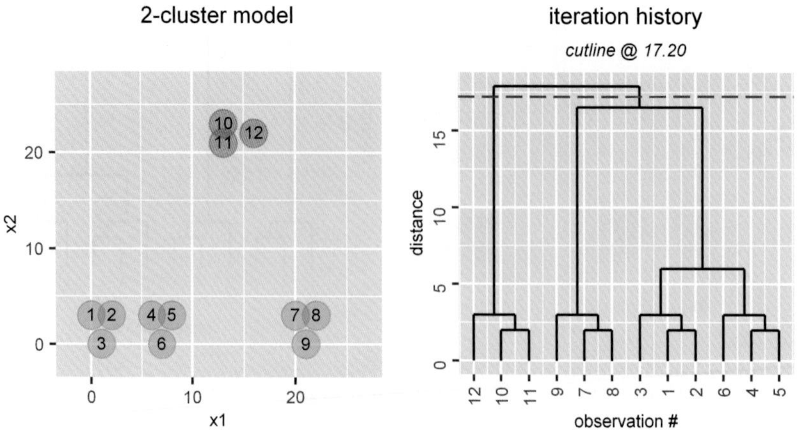

From our dendrogram analysis, we select the 3-cluster model as likely the most useful way to organize the observations.

10.5 Gaussian Mixture

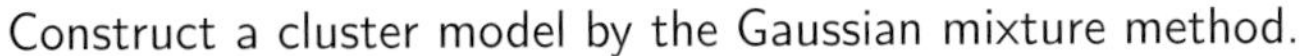
Construct a cluster model by the Gaussian mixture method.

10.5.1 Introduction

As a relentless wind blows over a desert landscape, dunes of loose sand pile up, transforming mounds to mountains, or conversely disperse, transforming mountains to mounds. They seem animated as peaks roam about. Each animal living among the dunes adapts to the continuously changing environment, at times most affected by 1 dune, at other times more so by others. You can think of the Gaussian mixture method as organizing animals according to the shifting sand dunes that most affect them.

You can also think of the Gaussian mixture method as a way to form clubs. Imagine establishing a club about green energy and a club about international trade with China. Each person in the community joins both clubs. Citlalli is very interested in wind energy and somewhat interested in international trade with China, so she spends 4 days per week at the energy club and only 1 day per week at the trade club. Ming is somewhat interested in solar energy and very interested in international trade with India. Neither really fits his interests well, but the trade club fits better than the energy club does, so he spends 1 day per week at the energy club and 4 days per week at the trade club. Other people similarly participate in 1 club more than the other based on their own interests. After a while, the energy club leadership notices that most of its engagement comes from people very interested in wind energy, so it re-positions the club as a wind energy club. The trade club leadership notices that most of its engagement comes from people interested in international trade with countries ranging from India to China to Japan, so it re-positions the club as an international trade with Asia club. In this the way, people organize themselves into satisfying groups.

10.5.2 About Gaussian Mixture

The Gaussian mixture method organizes observations into distinct clusters. With this method, we introduce the notion of ***partial*** class assignment, in which an observation can be assigned to all possible classes, but with each class for that observation being associated with a particular weight.

10.5.2.1 Overview

The **Gaussian mixture method** works like this:

> *Initialize: Choose initial Gaussian functions at random*
> *Iterate:*
>   *Expectation Step: Calculate weights based on Gaussian functions*
>   *Maximization Step: Shift the Gaussian functions based on weights*
> *Commit: Assign classes based on latest weights*

First, establish classes to name the clusters, and randomly choose several **Gaussian functions**, 1 associated with each class. Note that a specific Gaussian function of 1 variable is specified by 3 parameters: size (or area under the curve), mean (or center), and standard deviation (or flatness). A specific Gaussian function of more than 1 variable would be similarly specified, but with more parameters.

Second, iterate over the following 2 steps. For each observation, partially assign it to all classes, using the Gaussian functions evaluated at those observations' values to guide how to weight the classes. Because the Gaussian functions were chosen at random, the partial class assignment weights will initially look somewhat random, too. We call this partial class assignment the ***expectation*** step, because the Gaussian functions tell us what we should expect the weights to be. Then for each Gaussian function, change its parameter values, re-calculating based on all the observations' weights. Re-calculated size becomes relative weight, using the proportion of weights for 1 class with respect to the weights for all classes. Re-calculated mean becomes the weighted average of all the observations' values. Re-calculated standard deviation becomes the weighted standard deviation of all the observations' values. In this way, the Gaussian functions shift their areas under the curves, centers, and flatness. We call this re-calculation of Gaussian parameter values the ***maximization*** step, because the changed Gaussian functions better reflect which observations belong in which clusters. Following several iterations, each observation's weights tend to concentrate in just 1 class.

Third, for each observation, assign (not partially assign) it to the class based on its most heavily weighted, partially assigned class. The observations, now fully assigned to classes, indicate which observations belong in which clusters. The observations and their class assignments constitute a cluster model, specifically a **Gaussian mixture model**.

Because the Gaussian mixture method does not incorporate distance calculations, normalizing the observations in advance does not necessarily lead to more useful results.

The Gaussian mixture method can appear in any of several variations as specified by hyper-parameters, including number of clusters. Also, the Gaussian mixture method incorporates randomness. Specifically, the method gets initialized by Gaussian functions chosen at random. As such, the specific cluster model produced depends on which method variation gets used and how it gets initialized.

The Gaussian mixture method is also known as the **GMM method**, or **GMM-EM method**. A Gaussian mixture model is also known as a **GMM**.

10.5.2.2 Detailed Description

Elaborating on the overview, here is a detailed description of the Gaussian mixture method to produce a ***1-variable*** cluster model.

Initialize: Choose the number of clusters and establish classes to name the clusters. With classes A, B, ..., Z we would be implying that we want to organize observations into some clusters A, B, ..., Z. Specify 1 Gaussian function for class A, 1 Gaussian function for class B, ..., and 1 Gaussian function for class Z. Any random values for the parameters size, mean, and standard deviation will do, subject to the constraints that the sizes and standard deviations are positive, and that the sizes sum to 1.

For class A: Gaussian function parameters are ... $s_A = rand_+ \quad \mu_A = rand \quad \sigma_A = rand_+$

For class B: Gaussian function parameters are ... $s_B = rand_+ \quad \mu_B = rand \quad \sigma_B = rand_+$

$\vdots \qquad \vdots \qquad \vdots \qquad \vdots$

For class Z: Gaussian function parameters are ... $s_Z = rand_+ \quad \mu_Z = rand \quad \sigma_Z = rand_+$

all constrained by ...

$$s_A + s_B + \cdots + s_Z = 1$$

where ...

- $s_A, s_B, \ldots, s_Z$ are the sizes of the Gaussian functions for classes A, B, ..., Z
- $\mu_A, \mu_B, \ldots, \mu_Z$ are the means of the Gaussian functions for classes A, B, ..., Z
- $\sigma_A, \sigma_B, \ldots, \sigma_Z$ are the standard deviations of the Gaussian functions for classes A, B, ..., Z
- $rand$ is some random number
- $rand_+$ is some random positive number

Iterate: Adjust the observations' weights and shift the Gaussian functions by iterating through expectation-maximization.

Iterate | Expectation Step: Calculate weights based on the Gaussian functions like this: For each class, for each observation, evaluate the Gaussian function associated with the class at that observation's value, and divide by the sum of all Gaussian functions evaluated at that observation's value. In this way, each observation gets a weight for class A, a weight for class B, ..., and a weight for class Z. Note that an observation has weights for ***all*** classes, effectively being partially assigned to all classes. Further note that an observation's weights sum to 1.

$$\text{For class A:} \quad w_{Ai} = \frac{g_A(x_i)}{g_A(x_i) + g_B(x_i) + \ldots + g_Z(x_i)}$$

$$\text{For class B:} \quad w_{Bi} = \frac{g_B(x_i)}{g_A(x_i) + g_B(x_i) + \ldots + g_Z(x_i)}$$

$$\vdots \qquad \vdots$$

$$\text{For class Z:} \quad w_{Zi} = \frac{g_Z(x_i)}{g_A(x_i) + g_Z(x_i) + \ldots + g_Z(x_i)}$$

where . . .

- x_i is the ith observation's value
- $g_A, g_B, \ldots, g_Z$ are the Gaussian functions for classes A, B, . . . , Z
- $w_{Ai}, w_{Bi}, \ldots, w_{Zi}$ are the weights applied to the ith observation for classes A, B, . . . , Z

Iterate | Maximization Step: Change each Gaussian function to better reflect those observations that are more heavily weighted to its associated class. Do so by re-calculating each Gaussian function's size, mean, and standard deviation based on ***all*** observations' values, but weight some observations' values more heavily than others. Note that the sizes still sum to 1.

For class A:

$$s_A = \frac{\sum_{i=1}^{n} w_{Ai}}{\sum_{i=1}^{n} w_{Ai} + \sum_{i=1}^{n} w_{Bi} + \cdots + \sum_{i=1}^{n} w_{Zi}} \quad \mu_A = \frac{\sum_{i=1}^{n} w_{Ai} x_i}{\sum_{i=1}^{n} w_{Ai}} \quad \sigma_A = \sqrt{\frac{\sum_{i=1}^{n} w_{Ai}(x_i - \mu_A)^2}{\sum_{i=1}^{n} w_{Ai}}}$$

For class B:

$$s_B = \frac{\sum_{i=1}^{n} w_{Bi}}{\sum_{i=1}^{n} w_{Ai} + \sum_{i=1}^{n} w_{Bi} + \cdots + \sum_{i=1}^{n} w_{Zi}} \quad \mu_B = \frac{\sum_{i=1}^{n} w_{Bi} x_i}{\sum_{i=1}^{n} w_{Bi}} \quad \sigma_B = \sqrt{\frac{\sum_{i=1}^{n} w_{Bi}(x_i - \mu_B)^2}{\sum_{i=1}^{n} w_{Bi}}}$$

$$\vdots \qquad \vdots \qquad \vdots$$

For class Z:

$$s_Z = \frac{\sum_{i=1}^{n} w_{Zi}}{\sum_{i=1}^{n} w_{Ai} + \sum_{i=1}^{n} w_{Bi} + \cdots + \sum_{i=1}^{n} w_{Zi}} \quad \mu_Z = \frac{\sum_{i=1}^{n} w_{Zi} x_i}{\sum_{i=1}^{n} w_{Zi}} \quad \sigma_Z = \sqrt{\frac{\sum_{i=1}^{n} w_{Zi}(x_i - \mu_Z)^2}{\sum_{i=1}^{n} w_{Zi}}}$$

where ...

- n is the number of observations
- x_i is the ith observation's value
- $w_{Ai}, w_{Bi}, \ldots, w_{Zi}$ are the weights applied to the ith observation for classes A, B, ..., Z
- $s_A, s_B, \ldots, s_Z$ are the sizes of the new Gaussian functions for classes A, B, ..., Z
- $\mu_A, \mu_B, \ldots, \mu_Z$ are the means of the new Gaussian functions for classes A, B, ..., Z
- $\sigma_A, \sigma_B, \ldots, \sigma_Z$ are the standard deviations of the new Gaussian functions for classes A, B, ..., Z

Commit: Following many iterations, ultimately assign each observation to the class that corresponds to its heaviest weight. These class assignments indicate which observations belong in which clusters. The observations and their class assignments constitute a cluster model.

$$c_i = q \text{ such that } w_{qi} = max(w_{Ai}, w_{Bi}, \ldots, w_{Zi})$$

where ...

- q is a class
- w_{qi} is the final weight applied to the ith observation for class q
- $w_{Ai}, w_{Bi}, \ldots, w_{Zi}$ are the final weights applied to the ith observation for classes A, B, ..., Z
- c_i is the ith observation's class at commitment

10.5.3 Gaussian Mixture | One Variable, Two Classes

Consider this unclassified 1-variable dataset. The observations could be organized into clusters in a variety of ways. Perhaps put left-side observations in 1 cluster and put right-side observations in another cluster. This would expose their similarity and dissimilarity based on their proximity to each other. Or perhaps put the very left and very right observations in 1 cluster and put the rest in another cluster. This would expose their similarity and dissimilarity based on their proximity to their center or average. Or perhaps put every other observation in 1 cluster and put the rest in another cluster. Would this expose any useful insights about their similarity and dissimilarity?

How should the observations be organized? Let's use the Gaussian mixture method to organize the observations into 2 clusters.

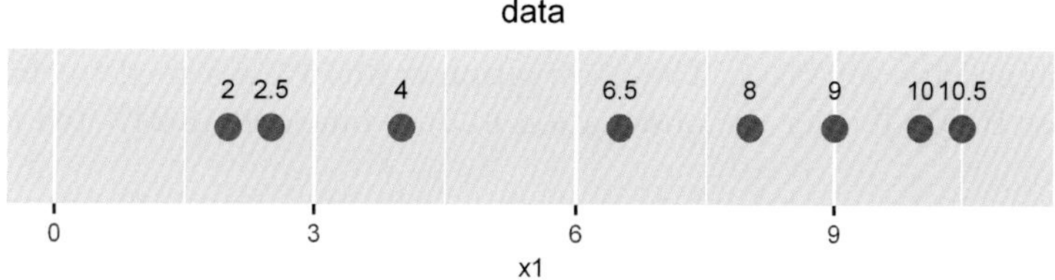

10.5.3.1 Hyper-parameters

Set hyper-parameters to specify which version of the method to use.

- **Number of clusters:** 2

10.5.3.2 Initialize

Establish 2 classes, A and B, to name the clusters. Specify 2 Gaussian functions, 1 for class A and 1 for class B. For the Gaussian function associated with class A, randomly set size to 0.5, randomly set mean to 9, and randomly set standard deviation to 1. For the Gaussian function associated with class B, set size to 0.5 because the sizes should sum to 1, randomly set mean to 10, and randomly set standard deviation to 1.

It's useful to visualize the Gaussian functions overlaid onto the observations.

Gaussian parameters at initialization

class	size	mean	sd
A	0.5	9	1
B	0.5	10	1

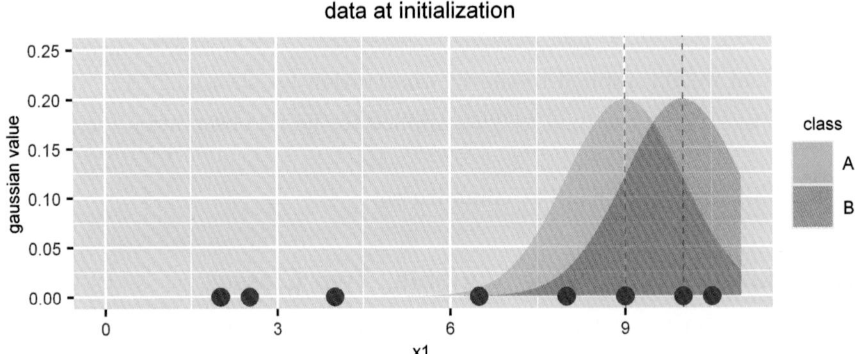

10.5.3.3 Iterate

Iterate through expectation-maximization to adjust the observations' weights and shift the Gaussian functions.

In the first iteration, consider the observation (x_1=8). We see that the Gaussian function associated with class A evaluates to a score of 0.1210 at (x_1=8). The Gaussian function associated with class B evaluates to a score of 0.0270 at (x_1=8). From a comparison of these 2 scores to their sum, we calculate 2 weights for the observation, 1 for class A and 1 for class B. The weight for class A is $0.1210 \div (0.1210 + 0.0270) = 0.8176$. The weight for class B is $0.0270 \div (0.1210 + 0.0270) = 0.1824$. These weights are measures of how much the observation is partially assigned to each class. The observation is 81.76% assigned to class A and 18.24% assigned to class B. We'll color the observation 81.76% blue and 18.24% red to reflect that.

Gaussian parameters at iteration 1, at start of iteration

class	size	mean	sd
A	0.5	9	1
B	0.5	10	1

one observation at iteration 1, after expectation step

x1	g.A	g.B	weight.A	weight.B
8	0.121	0.027	0.8176	0.1824

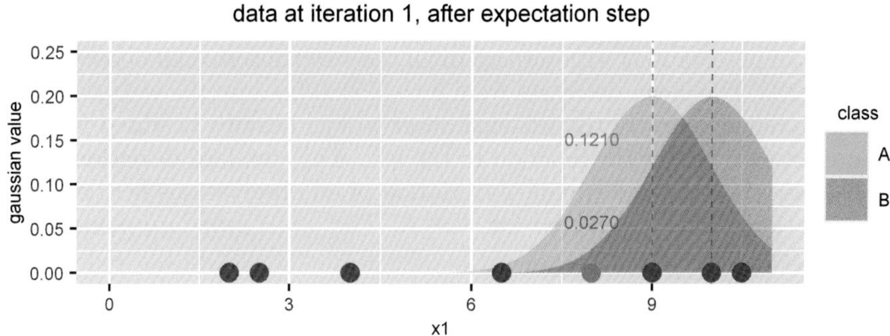

Now consider all the observations. Each observation gets 2 scores, 1 from each Gaussian function, and from these scores each observation gets 2 weights. At observation (x_1=2), both Gaussian functions evaluate to scores near 0, and yet the Gaussian function associated with class A evaluates to a score 1,665 times larger than the Gaussian function associated with class B does. For this observation, we calculate the weights to be 0.9994 for class A and 0.0006 for class B. We'll color the observation mostly blue to reflect that it's over 99% partially assigned to class A, though it's still just slightly partially assigned to class B, too. At observation (x_1=10.5), the Gaussian function associated with class A evaluates to a score of 0.0648; the Gaussian function associated with class B evaluates to a score of 0.1760. That makes the weights $0.0648 \div (0.0648 + 0.1760) = 0.2689$ for class A and $0.1760 \div (0.0648 + 0.1760) = 0.7311$ for class B. We'll color the observation a bit more red than blue to reflect that it's 26.89% partially assigned to class A and 73.11% partially assigned to class B. Similarly for the other observations.

Gaussian parameters at iteration 1, at start of iteration

class	size	mean	sd
A	0.5	9	1
B	0.5	10	1

data at iteration 1, after expectation step

x1	g.A	g.B	weight.A	weight.B
2.0	0.0000	0.0000	0.9994	0.0006
2.5	0.0000	0.0000	0.9991	0.0009
4.0	0.0000	0.0000	0.9959	0.0041
6.5	0.0088	0.0004	0.9526	0.0474
8.0	0.1210	0.0270	0.8176	0.1824
9.0	0.1995	0.1210	0.6225	0.3775
10.0	0.1210	0.1995	0.3775	0.6225
10.5	0.0648	0.1760	0.2689	0.7311

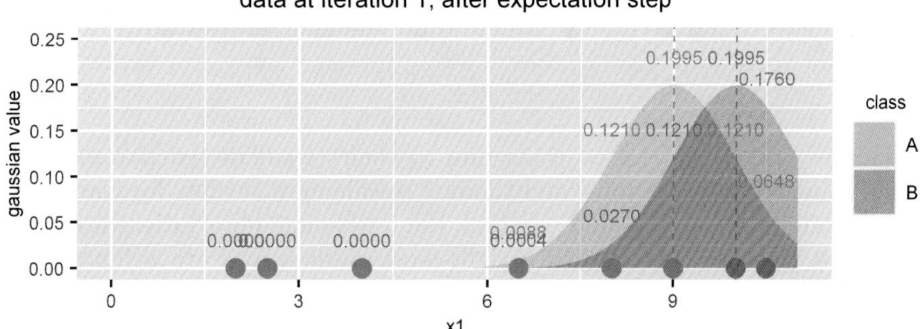

With weights now calculated, we use them to re-calculate the Gaussian parameter values.

The Gaussian function associated with class A increases in size because the proportion of weights for class A across all observations with respect to all the weights across all observations increases from 50% to 75.42%. The mean decreases from 9 to 5.5380 because the weighted average of all observations here reflects mostly the left-side observations heavily weighted for class A. The smaller mean effectively moves the function to the left. The standard deviation increases from 1 to 2.9222 because the weighted standard deviation of all observations here reflects the wide spread of observations heavily weighted for class A. The larger standard deviation effectively flattens the function.

The Gaussian function associated with class B decreases in size, reflecting a decrease in the weights for class B from 50% to 24.58%. The mean decreases from 10 to 9.7060, which is not as much as the other function's mean decreases. This is because the weighted average of all observations here reflects many left-side observations, but they are weighted only lightly for class B. The weighted average also reflects the right-side observations, weighted heavily for class B, but there are only a few of them. The slightly smaller mean effectively moves the function slightly to the left. The standard deviation decreases only very slightly from 1 to 0.9917 because the weighted standard deviation here reflects mostly the narrow spread of the few observations heavily weighted for class B. The very slightly smaller standard deviation effectively very slightly pinches the function.

You can think of re-calculating these Gaussian parameter values like this: the observations heavily weighted for class A tug on the Gaussian function for class A, stretching it out and siphoning some size from the other Gaussian function.

Gaussian parameters at iteration 1, after maximization step

class	size	mean	sd
A	0.7542	5.538	2.9222
B	0.2458	9.706	0.9917

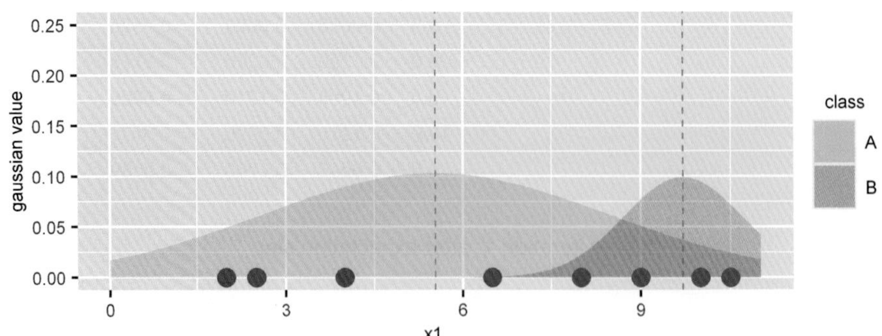

With the Gaussian functions shifted according to their re-calculated parameter values, we evaluate them at all the observations, and thereby re-calculate weights for class A and class B for all the observations. By this second iteration, the 5 left-most observations are weighted more heavily for class A than for class B. The 3 right-most observations are weighted more heavily for class B. Note that observation (x_1=8) is weighted 76.22% for class A and still favors class A over class B, but not as much as it did in the first iteration when it was weighted 81.76% for class A. Note also that observation (x_1=9) went from weight 62.25% for class A to weight

60.06% for class B. This observation flipped from being mostly partially assigned to class A to mostly partially assigned to class B.

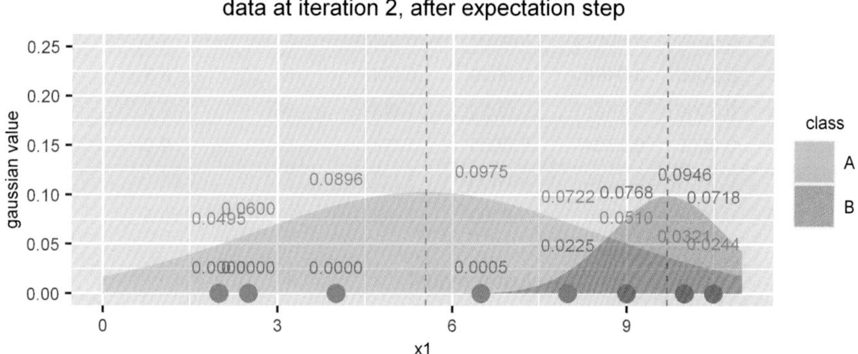

As we continue to iterate through expectation-maximization, the 2 Gaussian functions continue to shift around and the 8 observations' partial class assignments continue to evolve. By iteration 100, the Gaussian functions have largely separated from each other, reflecting a large distance between their means relative to their standard deviations. The Gaussian function associated with class A has shrunk in size to 37.37%, while the Gaussian function associated with class B has grown in size to 62.63%.

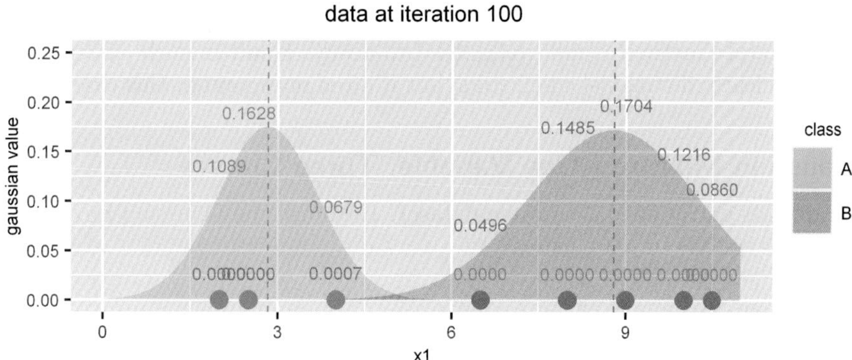

10.5.3.4 Commit

We eventually arrive at Gaussian functions that produce extreme partial class assignments. Three observations are each more than 98% partially assigned to class A. Five observations are each more than 99% partially assigned to class B.

Since each observation's partial class assignment overwhelmingly favors 1 class over the other, we disregard the small influence of its unfavored class. We commit each observation entirely to the class it favors, effectively converting partial class assignments to full class assignments. The observations along with their full class assignments constitute a cluster model.

data at commitment with class assignments

x1	g.A	g.B	weight.A	weight.B	class
2.0	0.1089	0.0000	1.0000	0.0000	A
2.5	0.1628	0.0000	0.9999	0.0001	A
4.0	0.0679	0.0007	0.9892	0.0108	A
6.5	0.0000	0.0496	0.0003	0.9997	B
8.0	0.0000	0.1485	0.0000	1.0000	B
9.0	0.0000	0.1704	0.0000	1.0000	B
10.0	0.0000	0.1216	0.0000	1.0000	B
10.5	0.0000	0.0860	0.0000	1.0000	B

cluster model

x1	class
2.0	A
2.5	A
4.0	A
6.5	B
8.0	B
9.0	B
10.0	B
10.5	B

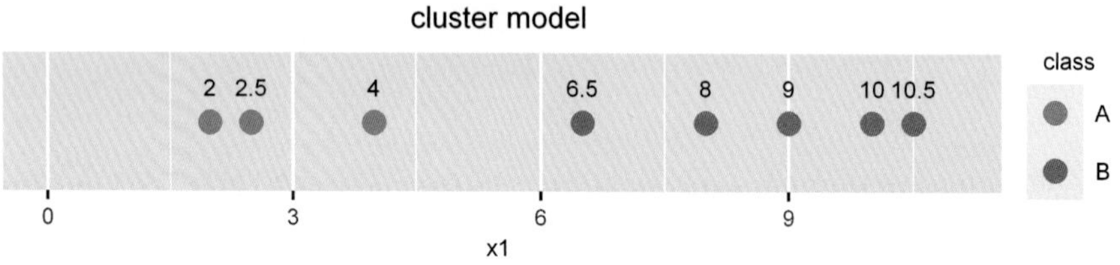

The Gaussian mixture method, initialized with 2 specific Gaussian functions, effectively detected a pattern in the dataset that it used to organize the observations. The 3 left-most observations are relatively close to each other, the 5 right-most observations are relatively close to each other, and these 2 sets of observations are relatively far from each other. So, the method put the 3 left-most observations into 1 cluster and put the 5 right-most observations into another cluster.

The Gaussian mixture method is not guaranteed to always result in such extreme partial class assignments and clearly distinguished clusters, but it often does, and in this case it certainly did.

10.5.4 Gaussian Mixture | One Variable, Three Classes

Consider again this unclassified 1-variable dataset. Let's use the Gaussian mixture method to organize the observations into 3 clusters.

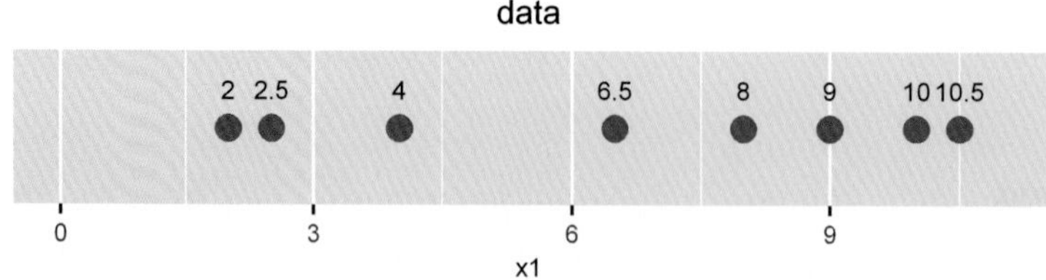

10.5.4.1 Hyper-parameters

Set hyper-parameters to specify which version of the method to use.

- **Number of clusters:** 3

10.5.4.2 Initialize

Establish 3 classes, A, B, and C, to name the clusters. Specify 3 Gaussian functions, 1 for class A, 1 for class B, and 1 for class C. For the Gaussian function associated with class A, randomly set size to 0.33, randomly set mean to 9, and randomly set standard deviation to 1. For the Gaussian function associated with class B, randomly set size to 0.33, randomly set mean to 10, and randomly set standard deviation to 1. For the Gaussian function associated with class C, set size to 0.33 because the sizes should sum to 1, randomly set mean to 8, and randomly set standard deviation to 1.

Gaussian parameters at initialization

class	size	mean	sd
A	0.33	9	1
B	0.33	10	1
C	0.33	8	1

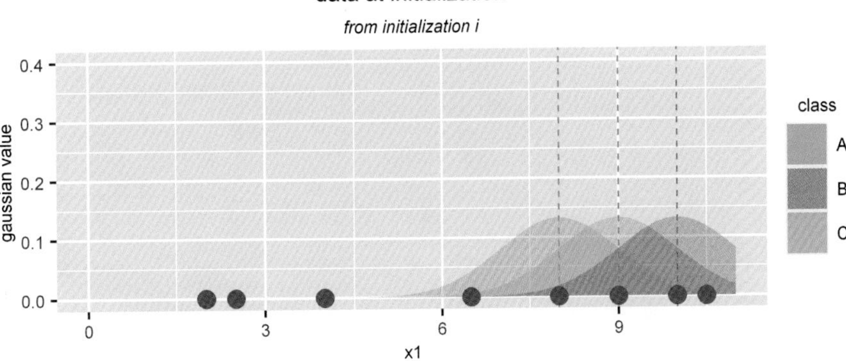

10.5.4.3 Iterate

Iterate through expectation-maximization to adjust the observations' weights and shift the Gaussian functions.

In the first iteration, 1 observation is weighted most heavily for class A because, even though all Gaussian functions evaluate to high scores for this observation, the Gaussian function associated with class A evaluates to the highest score. Two of the observations are most heavily weighted for class B, as determined by evaluating the Gaussian functions at these observations. Most of the observations are heavily weighted for class C because, even though all the Gaussian functions evaluate to low scores at these observations, the Gaussian function associated with class C evaluates to much higher scores than the other 2 Gaussian functions do. The weights are measures of how much each observation is partially assigned to each of the 3 classes. We'll color the observations mixtures of blue, red, and green to reflect their partial class assignments.

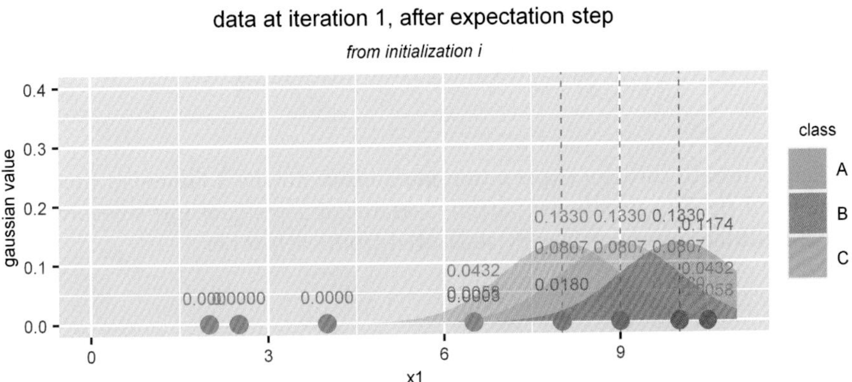

With weights now calculated, we use them to re-calculate the Gaussian parameter values.

The Gaussian function associated with class A retains its mean value because the observations with values on either side of it contribute equally to the weighted average. The function flattens to better span the observations modestly weighted for class A.

The Gaussian function associated with class B moves right and pinches, affected mostly by the 2 right-most observations heavily weighted for class B.

The Gaussian function associated with class C increases in size, moves left, and flattens, affected mostly by the many left-side observations spread out and heavily weighted for class C. The Gaussian functions associated with classes A and B shrink in size correspondingly.

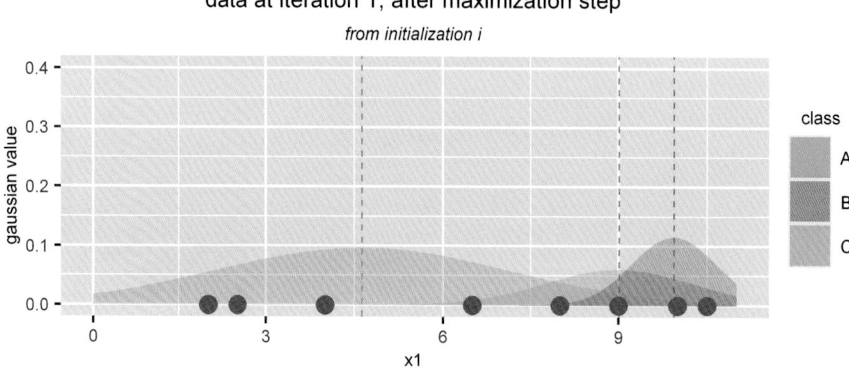

With the Gaussian functions shifted according to their re-calculated parameter values, we evaluate them at all the observations, and thereby re-calculate weights for class A, class B, and class C for all the observations.

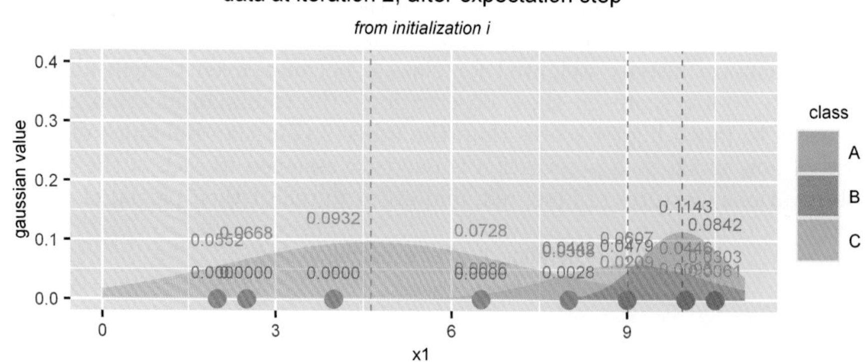

As we continue to iterate through expectation-maximization, the 3 Gaussian functions continue to shift around and the 8 observations' partial class assignments continue to evolve. By iteration 100, the Gaussian functions have largely separated from each other.

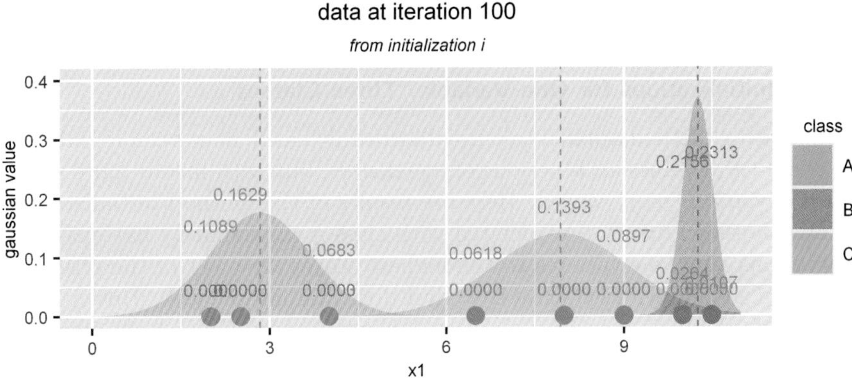

10.5.4.4 Commit

We eventually arrive at Gaussian functions that produce extreme partial class assignments. Three observations are each almost 100% partially assigned to class A. Two observations are each more than 89% partially assigned to class B. Three observations are each more than 99% partially assigned to class C.

Since each observation's partial class assignment overwhelmingly favors 1 class over the others, we commit to full class assignments by disregarding the small influence of unfavored classes and produce a cluster model.

data at commitment with class assignments

x1	g.A	g.B	g.C	weight.A	weight.B	weight.C	class
2.0	0.000	0.000	0.109	0.000	0.000	1.000	C
2.5	0.000	0.000	0.163	0.000	0.000	1.000	C
4.0	0.000	0.000	0.068	0.005	0.000	0.995	C
6.5	0.062	0.000	0.000	1.000	0.000	0.000	A
8.0	0.139	0.000	0.000	1.000	0.000	0.000	A
9.0	0.090	0.000	0.000	1.000	0.000	0.000	A
10.0	0.026	0.216	0.000	0.109	0.891	0.000	B
10.5	0.011	0.231	0.000	0.044	0.956	0.000	B

cluster model

x1	class
2.0	C
2.5	C
4.0	C
6.5	A
8.0	A
9.0	A
10.0	B
10.5	B

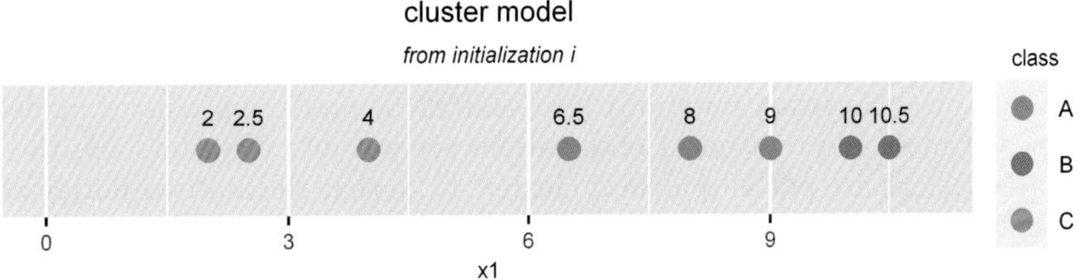

The Gaussian mixture method, initialized with 3 specific Gaussian functions, effectively detected a pattern in the dataset that it used to organize the observations. The 3 left-most observations are relatively close to each other, the 3 mid-space observations are relatively close to each other, the 2 right-most observations are relatively close to each other, and these 3 sets of observations are relatively far from each other. So, the method distributed the observations among 3 clusters accordingly.

10.5.4.5 Other Initializations for One Variable, Three Classes

The Gaussian mixture method applied to our dataset could easily have been initialized differently. Perhaps we could try 3 Gaussian functions of equal sizes, but with means more spread out and with standard deviations more varied. Here are results of the method initialized that way. In iteration 1, the Gaussian function associated with class A immediately flattens to better span all the observations, and so evaluates to the highest scores for most of the observations. The Gaussian function associated with class B at first doesn't compete well. However, by iteration 200 the Gaussian function associated with class A has moved back and been pinched to close to its initial shape. The method initialized this way produces the same cluster model as with the earlier initialization, albeit with different arbitrarily chosen cluster names.

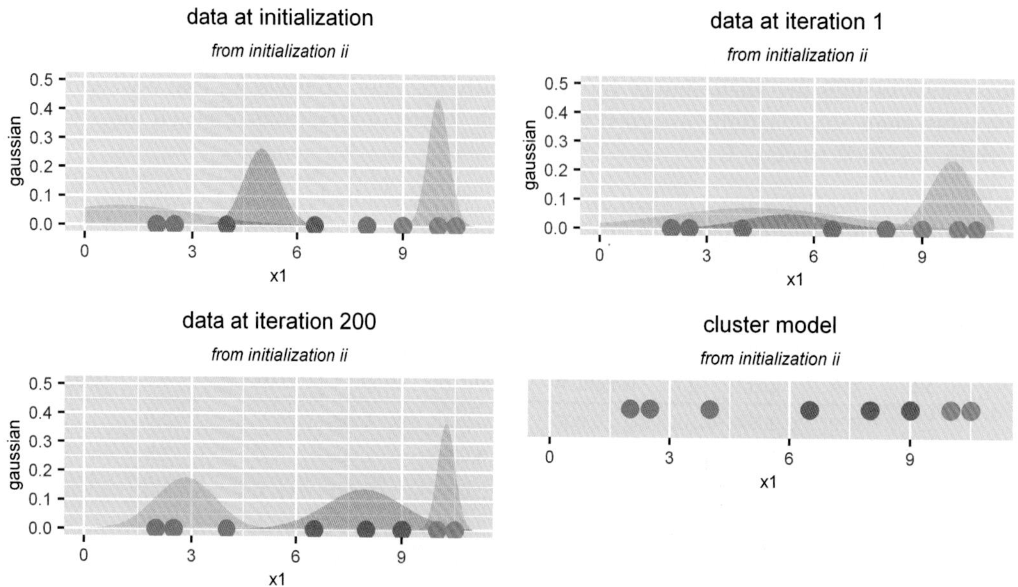

Let's try initializing with yet different Gaussian functions, this time with unequal sizes but equal standard deviations. In iteration 1, the Gaussian function associated with class A is pinched to better span only the 2 left-most observations because the right-side observations have little effect on it. You can think of this as the 2 left-most observations getting an early start toward their assignment to class A.

By iteration 200, the Gaussian functions have shifted to produce a cluster model in which the outer few left-most and right-most observations are put into 2 clusters and the remaining mid-space observations are put into a third cluster. Note that the method initialized this way produces a different cluster model than it did with the earlier initializations.

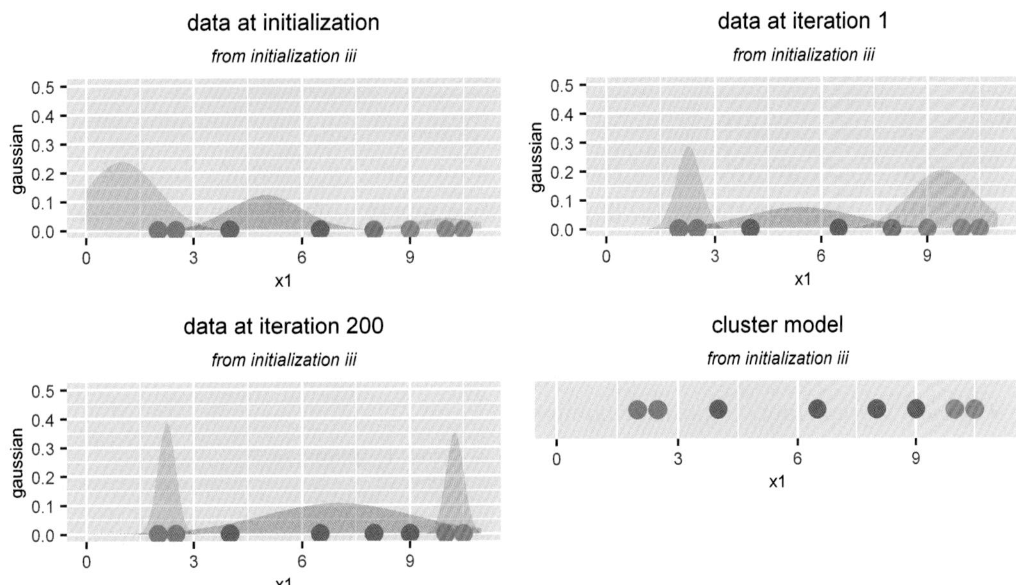

10.5.5 More about Gaussian Mixture

Here is a detailed description of the Gaussian mixture method to produce a ***2-variable*** cluster model. It works similarly to the 1-variable version, except that each Gaussian function is ***bi-variate*** in the sense that it takes 2 variables as input rather than 1, and is specified by 6 parameters rather than 3.

Initialize: Choose the number of clusters and establish classes to name the clusters. With classes A, B, ..., Z we would be implying that we want to organize observations into some clusters A, B, ..., Z. Specify 1 bi-variate Gaussian function for class A, 1 bi-variate Gaussian function for class B, ..., and 1 bi-variate Gaussian function for class Z. Note that a specific Gaussian function is specified by 6 parameters: size (or volume under the curve in 3-dimensional space), a pair of means (or center in 2-dimensional space), a pair of standard deviations (or flatness in 2-dimensional space), and correlation between the variables (or rotation in 2-dimensional space). Any random values for the parameters will do, subject to the constraints that the sizes and standard deviations are positive, the correlations are in range -1 to 1, and that the sizes sum to 1.

For class A: Gaussian function parameters are ...

$$s_A = rand_+ \quad \mu_A = (rand, rand) \quad \sigma_A = (rand_+, rand_+) \quad cor_A = rand_{-1,1}$$

For class B: Gaussian function parameters are ...

$$s_B = rand_+ \quad \mu_B = (rand, rand) \quad \sigma_B = (rand_+, rand_+) \quad cor_B = rand_{-1,1}$$

$$\vdots \qquad \vdots \qquad \vdots \qquad \vdots$$

For class Z: Gaussian function parameters are ...

$$s_Z = rand_+ \quad \mu_Z = (rand, rand) \quad \sigma_Z = (rand_+, rand_+) \quad cor_Z = rand_{-1,1}$$

$$\text{all constrained by ...}$$
$$s_A + s_B + \cdots + s_Z = 1$$

where ...

- s_A, s_B, ..., s_Z are the sizes of the Gaussian functions for classes A, B, ..., Z
- μ_A, μ_B, ..., μ_Z are the means of the Gaussian functions for classes A, B, ..., Z
- σ_A, σ_B, ..., σ_Z are the standard deviations of the Gaussian functions for classes A, B, ..., Z
- cor_A, cor_B, ..., cor_Z are the correlations between the 2 variables for classes A, B, ..., Z
- $rand$ is some random number
- $rand_+$ is some random positive number
- $rand_{-1,1}$ is some random number between -1 and 1, inclusive

Iterate: Shift the Gaussian functions and adjust the observations' weights by iterating through expectation-maximization.

Iterate | Expectation Step: Calculate weights based on the Gaussian functions.

$$\text{For class A:} \quad w_{Ai} = \frac{g_A(x_{1i}, x_{2i})}{g_A(x_{1i}, x_{2i}) + g_B(x_{1i}, x_{2i}) + \ldots + g_Z(x_{1i}, x_{2i})}$$

$$\text{For class B:} \quad w_{Bi} = \frac{g_B(x_{1i}, x_{2i})}{g_A(x_{1i}, x_{2i}) + g_B(x_{1i}, x_{2i}) + \ldots + g_Z(x_{1i}, x_{2i})}$$

$$\vdots \qquad \vdots$$

$$\text{For class Z:} \quad w_{Zi} = \frac{g_Z(x_{1i}, x_{2i})}{g_A(x_{1i}, x_{2i}) + g_B(x_{1i}, x_{2i}) + \ldots + g_Z(x_{1i}, x_{2i})}$$

where ...

- x_{1i} is the ith observation's x_1 value
- x_{2i} is the ith observation's x_2 value
- g_A, g_B, ..., g_Z are the Gaussian functions for classes A, B, ..., Z
- w_{Ai}, w_{Bi}, ..., w_{Zi} are the weights applied to the ith observation for classes A, B, ..., Z

Iterate | Maximization Step: Change each Gaussian function to better reflect those observations that are more heavily weighted to its associated class. Re-calculated size becomes relative weight, using the proportion of weights for 1 class with respect to the weights for all classes. Re-calculated means become the weighted averages of all the observations' x_1 and x_2 values. For convenience, the standard deviations and correlation can be expressed together as a covariance matrix. The re-calculated covariance matrix becomes the weighted covariance matrix of all the observations' x_1 and x_2 values, from which standard deviations and correlation can be extracted.

For class A:

$$s_A = \frac{\sum_{i=1}^{n} w_{Ai}}{\sum_{i=1}^{n} w_{Ai} + \sum_{i=1}^{n} w_{Bi} + \cdots + \sum_{i=1}^{n} w_{Zi}} \qquad \mu_{1A} = \frac{\sum_{i=1}^{n} w_{Ai}x_{1i}}{\sum_{i=1}^{n} w_{Ai}} \qquad \mu_{2A} = \frac{\sum_{i=1}^{n} w_{Ai}x_{2i}}{\sum_{i=1}^{n} w_{Ai}}$$

$$K_{x_1x_2A} = \textit{weighted covariance matrix}(x_1, x_2, w_A)$$

For class B:

$$s_B = \frac{\sum_{i=1}^{n} w_{Bi}}{\sum_{i=1}^{n} w_{Ai} + \sum_{i=1}^{n} w_{Bi} + \cdots + \sum_{i=1}^{n} w_{Zi}} \qquad \mu_{1B} = \frac{\sum_{i=1}^{n} w_{Bi}x_{1i}}{\sum_{i=1}^{n} w_{Bi}} \qquad \mu_{2B} = \frac{\sum_{i=1}^{n} w_{Bi}x_{2i}}{\sum_{i=1}^{n} w_{Bi}}$$

$$K_{x_1x_2B} = \textit{weighted covariance matrix}(x_1, x_2, w_B)$$

$$\vdots \qquad \vdots \qquad \vdots \qquad \vdots$$

For class Z:

$$s_Z = \frac{\sum_{i=1}^{n} w_{Zi}}{\sum_{i=1}^{n} w_{Ai} + \sum_{i=1}^{n} w_{Bi} + \cdots + \sum_{i=1}^{n} w_{Zi}} \qquad \mu_{1Z} = \frac{\sum_{i=1}^{n} w_{Zi}x_{1i}}{\sum_{i=1}^{n} w_{Zi}} \qquad \mu_{2Z} = \frac{\sum_{i=1}^{n} w_{Zi}x_{2i}}{\sum_{i=1}^{n} w_{Zi}}$$

$$K_{x_1x_2Z} = \textit{weighted covariance matrix}(x_1, x_2, w_Z)$$

where ...

- n is the number of observations
- x_{1i} is the ith observation's x_1 value
- x_{2i} is the ith observation's x_2 value
- w_{Ai}, w_{Bi}, ..., w_{Zi} are the weights applied to the ith observation for classes A, B, ..., Z
- x_1 is all the observations' x_1 values
- x_2 is all the observations' x_2 values
- w_A, w_B, ..., w_Z are the weights applied to all the observations for classes A, B, ..., Z
- s_A, s_B, ..., s_Z are the sizes of the new Gaussian functions for classes A, B, ..., Z
- μ_{1A}, μ_{1B}, ..., μ_{1Z} are the first means of the new Gaussian functions for classes A, B, ..., Z
- μ_{2A}, μ_{2B}, ..., μ_{2Z} are the second means of the new Gaussian functions for classes A, B, ..., Z
- $K_{x_1x_2A}$, $K_{x_1x_2B}$, ..., $K_{x_1x_2Z}$ are the covariance matrices representing to the standard deviations and correlations of the new Gaussian functions for classes A, B, ..., Z

Commit: Following many iterations, ultimately assign each observation to the class that corresponds to its heaviest weight. These class assignments indicate which observations belong in which clusters. The observations and their class assignments constitute a cluster model.

$$c_i = q \text{ such that } w_{qi} = max(w_{Ai}, w_{Bi}, \ldots, w_{Zi})$$

where ...

- q is a class
- w_{qi} is the final weight applied to the ith observation for class q
- w_{Ai}, w_{Bi}, ..., w_{Zi} are the final weights applied to the ith observation for classes A, B, ..., Z
- c_i is the ith observation's class at commitment

10.5.6 Gaussian Mixture | Two Variables, Two Classes

Consider this unclassified 2-variable dataset. The observations could be organized into clusters in a variety of ways. How should the observations be organized? Let's use the Gaussian mixture method to organize the observations into 2 clusters.

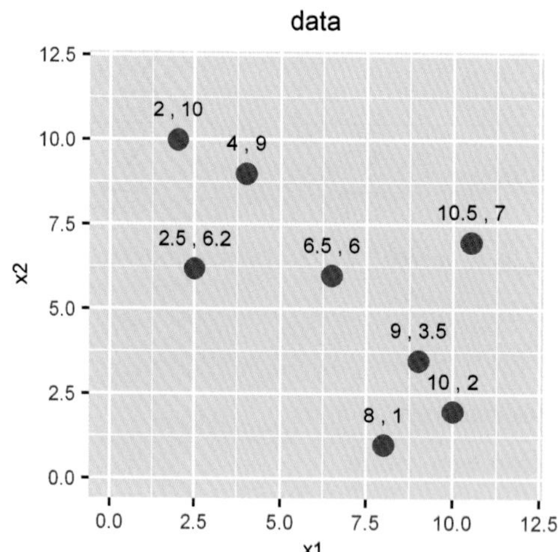

10.5.6.1 Hyper-parameters

Set hyper-parameters to specify which version of the method to use.

- **Number of clusters:** 2

10.5.6.2 Initialize

Establish 2 classes, A and B to name the clusters. Specify 2 bi-variate Gaussian functions, 1 for class A and 1 for class B.

For the Gaussian function associated with class A, randomly set size to 0.5. Randomly set means to 5 and 2, which makes the function's center (x_1=5, x_2=2). Randomly set standard deviation to 2 and 1, which makes the function flatten along the x_1-axis more than along the x_2-axis. Randomly set correlation to 0, which indicates no rotation.

For the Gaussian function associated with class B, set size to 0.5 because the sizes should sum to 1. Randomly set means to 8 and 2, which puts the function's center at $(x_1{=}8, x_2{=}2)$, which is right of the other function's center. Randomly set standard deviations to 2 and 1, and randomly set correlation to 0.

It's useful to visualize the Gaussian functions as clouds overlaid onto the observations. We'll color the cloud for the Gaussian function associated with class A blue and the cloud for the Gaussian function associated with class B red. The intensity of cloud color at any point corresponds to the Gaussian function score as evaluated at that point.

Gaussian parameters at initialization

class	size	mean.x1	mean.x2	sd.x1	sd.x2	cor
A	0.5	5	2	2	1	0
B	0.5	8	2	2	1	0

10.5.6.3 Iterate

Iterate through expectation-maximization to adjust the observations' weights and shift the Gaussian functions.

In the first iteration, left-side observations are heavily weighted for class A, affected mostly by the Gaussian function with low x_1 mean. The right-side observations are heavily weighted for class B, affected mostly by the Gaussian function with high x_1 mean. One observation is weighted exactly equally for class A and class B, as it sits midway between the Gaussian functions' x_1 means. We'll color the observations mixtures of blue and red to reflect their partial class assignments.

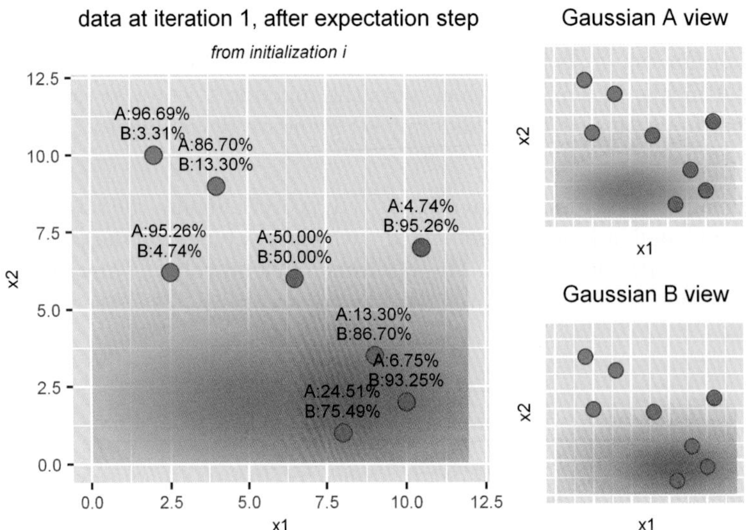

With weights now calculated, we use them to re-calculate the Gaussian parameter values. See that the upper-left observations, and to a lesser extent the lower-right observations, tug on the Gaussian function associated with class A, stretching it mainly along a downward-sloping diagonal. The function has effectively rotated. The upper-left observations also tug on the Gaussian function associated with class B, but not as much as the observation (x_1=10.5, x_2=7) does, so that the function rotates slightly but gets stretched mainly along the x_2-axis. Note that the rotations are reflected in the now non-zero correlations.

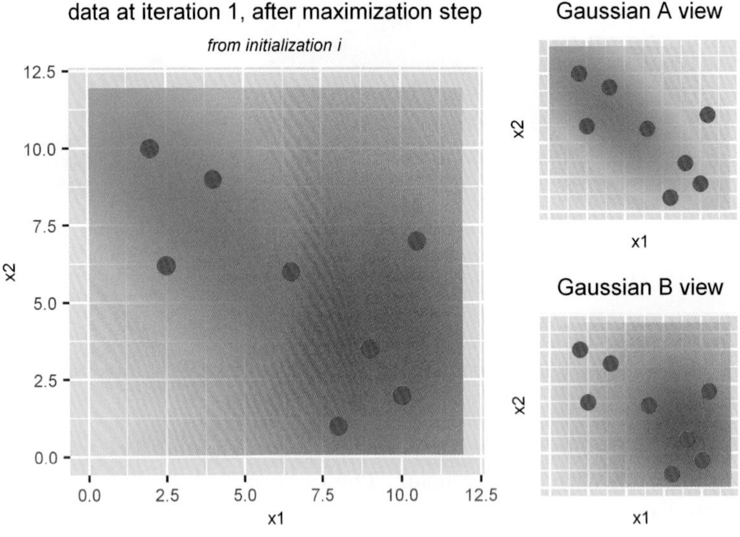

With the Gaussian functions shifted according to their re-calculated parameter values, we evaluate them at all the observations, and thereby re-calculate weights for class A and class B for all the observations.

By iteration 20, both Gaussian functions have narrowed. Around the lower-right observations, both functions evaluate to high scores, but the Gaussian function associated with class B evaluates to higher scores.

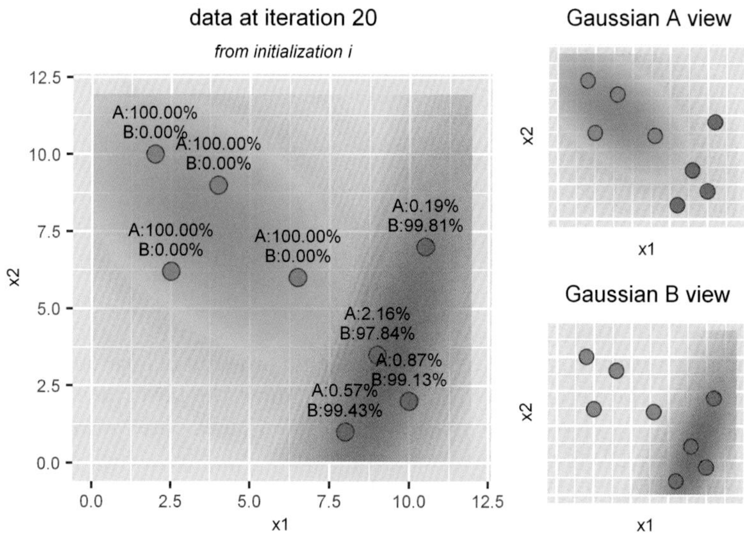

10.5.6.4 Commit

We eventually arrive at Gaussian functions that produce extreme partial class assignments. Four observations are each almost 100% partially assigned to class A. Four observations are each more than 97% partially assigned to class B.

Here is the resulting cluster model:

data at commitment with class assignments

x1	x2	g.A	g.B	weight.A	weight.B	class
2.0	10.0	0.0119	0.0000	1.0000	0.0000	A
2.5	6.2	0.0076	0.0000	1.0000	0.0000	A
4.0	9.0	0.0163	0.0000	1.0000	0.0000	A
6.5	6.0	0.0097	0.0000	1.0000	0.0000	A
8.0	1.0	0.0001	0.0185	0.0057	0.9943	B
9.0	3.5	0.0008	0.0342	0.0216	0.9784	B
10.0	2.0	0.0001	0.0130	0.0087	0.9913	B
10.5	7.0	0.0000	0.0155	0.0019	0.9981	B

cluster model

x1	x2	class
2.0	10.0	A
2.5	6.2	A
4.0	9.0	A
6.5	6.0	A
8.0	1.0	B
9.0	3.5	B
10.0	2.0	B
10.5	7.0	B

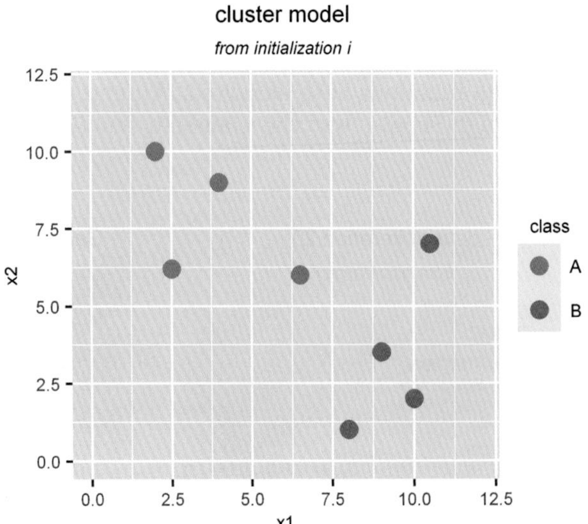

The Gaussian mixture method, initialized with 2 specific bi-variate Gaussian functions, effectively detected a pattern in the dataset that it used to organize the observations. The 4 upper-left observations are relatively close to each other, the 4 lower-right observations are relatively close to each other, and these 2 sets of observations are relatively far from each other. So, the method puts the observations into 2 clusters accordingly.

10.5.6.5 Other Initializations for Two Variables, Two Classes

Here
ways.

At initialization ii, the method detects that some observations lie along a diagonal, while others lie below the diagonal.

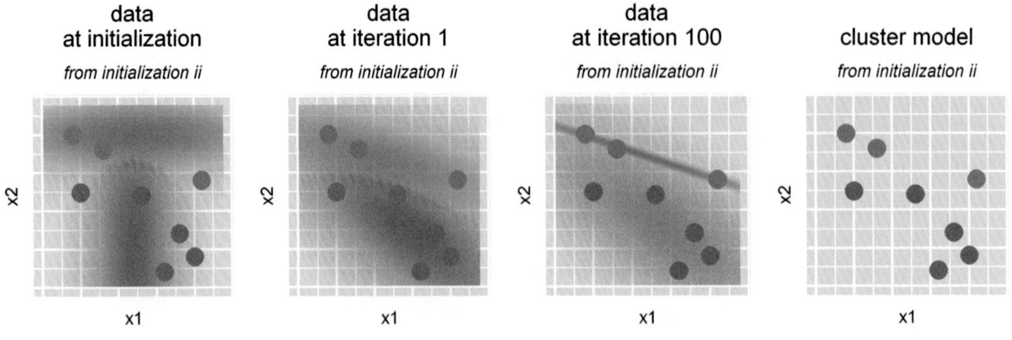

At initialization iii, the method detects that some observations lie along a downward-sloping diagonal, while others lie along an upward-sloping diagonal. Note that observations are not organized strictly by their proximity to others in their respective clusters.

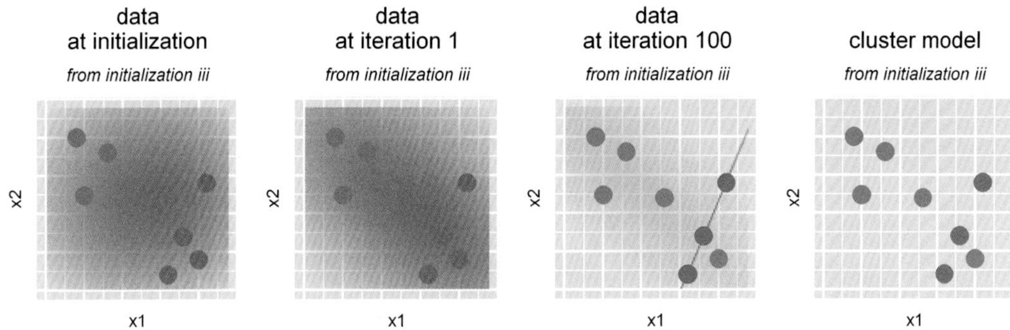

At initialization iv, the method detects that some observations lie along a downward-sloping diagonal, while others do not. Note that at commitment, the Gaussian associated with class B is centered on the observations on the diagonal. However, it's very spread out, while the Gaussian associated with class A is concentrated along the diagonal. So, the Gaussian function associated with class A evaluates to higher scores at observations on the diagonal, putting these observations in their own cluster. You can think of the class B observations as belonging to the "everything else that doesn't follow a nice pattern" cluster.

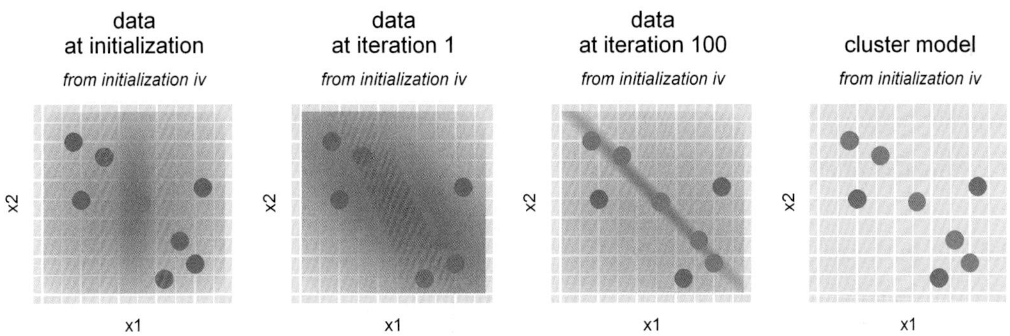

At initialization v, the method also detects that some observations lie along a downward-sloping diagonal, while others do not. However, it's more strict about what constitutes the diagonal.

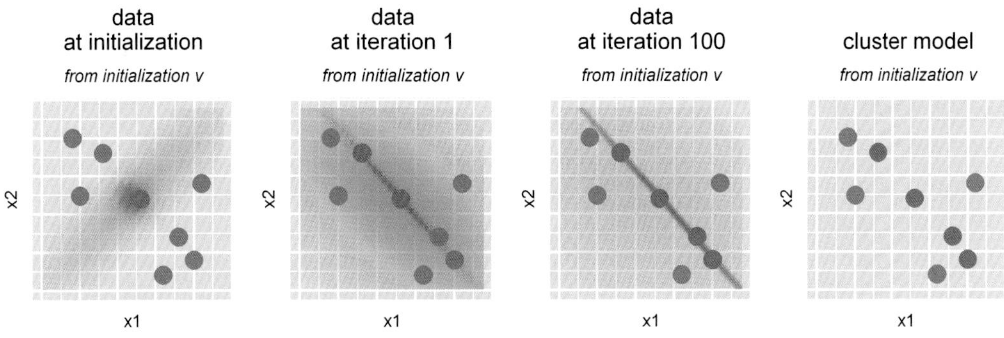

10.5.7 Gaussian Mixture | Two Variables, Three Classes

Consider again this unclassified 2-variable dataset. Let's use the Gaussian mixture method to organize the observations into 3 clusters.

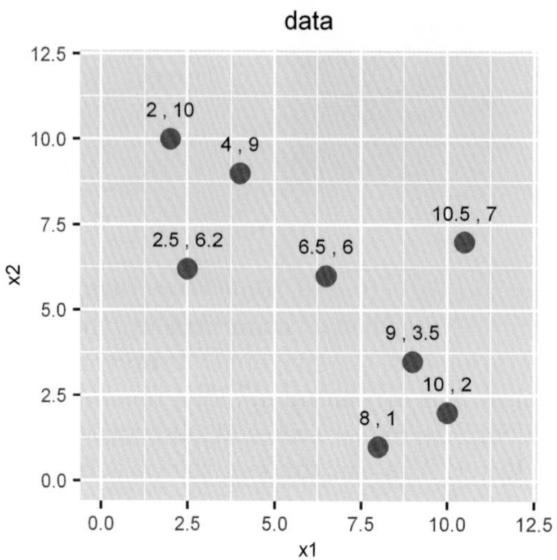

10.5.7.1 Hyper-parameters

Set hyper-parameters to specify which version of the method to use.

- **Number of clusters:** 3

10.5.7.2 Initialize

Establish 3 classes A, B, and C to name the clusters. Specify 3 bi-variate Gaussian functions, 1 for class A, 1 for class B, and 1 for class C. For the Gaussian function associated with class A, randomly set size to 0.33, randomly set means to 4 and 6, randomly set standard deviations to 1.5 and 1.5, and randomly set correlation to 0. For the Gaussian function associated with class B, randomly set size to 0.33, randomly set means to 6 and 6, randomly set standard deviations to 1.5 and 1.5, and randomly set correlation to 0. For the Gaussian function associated with class C, set size to 0.33 because the sizes should sum to 1, randomly set means to 8 and 6, randomly set standard deviation to 1, and randomly set correlation to 0.

Gaussian parameters at initialization

class	size	mean.x1	mean.x2	sd.x1	sd.x2	cor
A	0.33	4	6	1.5	1.5	0
B	0.33	6	6	1.5	1.5	0
C	0.33	8	6	1.5	1.5	0

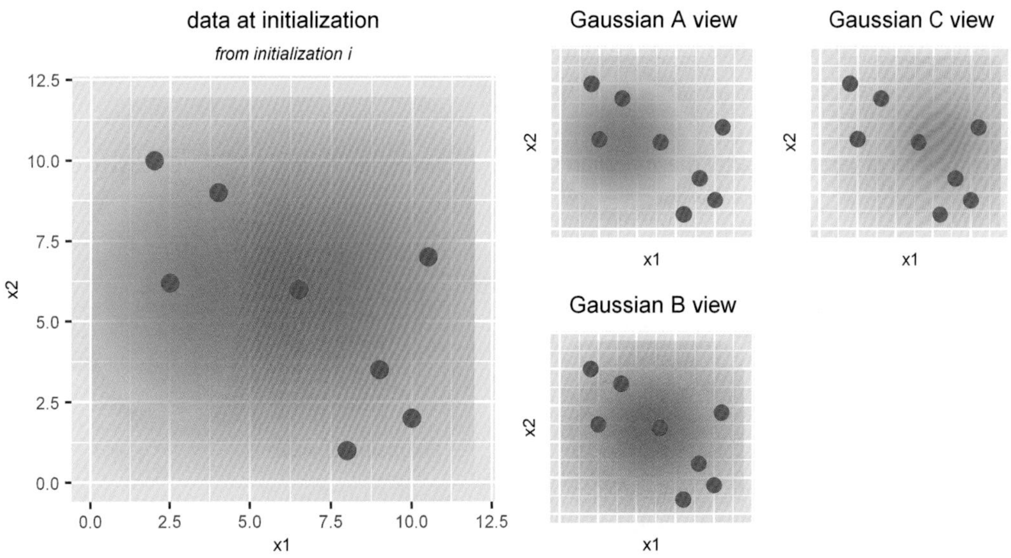

10.5.7.3 Iterate

Iterate through expectation-maximization to adjust the observations' weights and shift the Gaussian functions.

In the first iteration, we use the Gaussian functions to calculate weights for all classes for all observations.

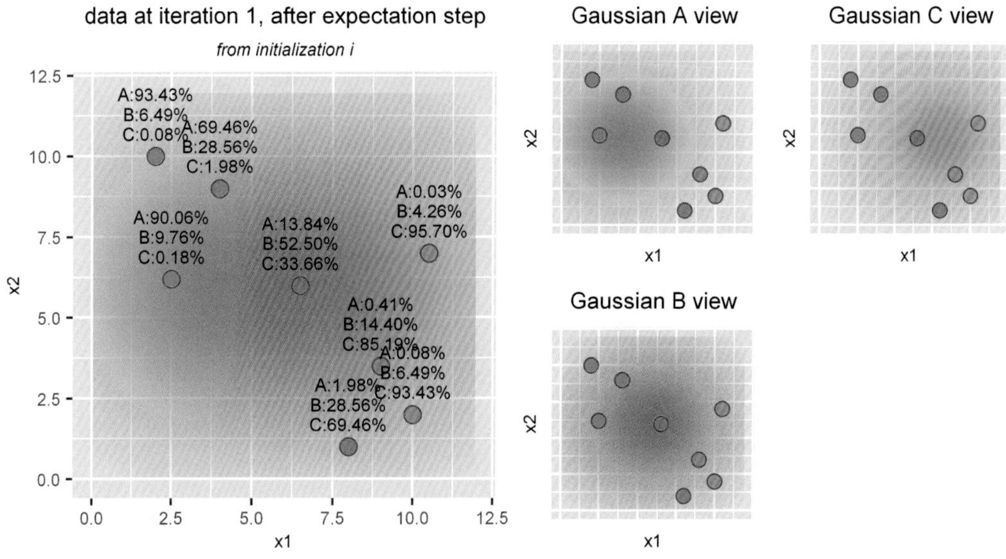

Then we use the calculated weights to re-calculate the Gaussian parameter values. See that the Gaussian function associated with class A moves upward left, affected mostly by the upper-left observations, but also rotates slightly toward the lower-right observations that are lightly weighted for class A. The Gaussian function associated with class B rotates dramatically, affected roughly equally by the upper-left observations and the lower-right observations. The Gaussian function associated with class C rotates slightly toward the right-side observations that are heavily weighted for class C. Note that the now non-zero negative and positive correlations reflect the rotations.

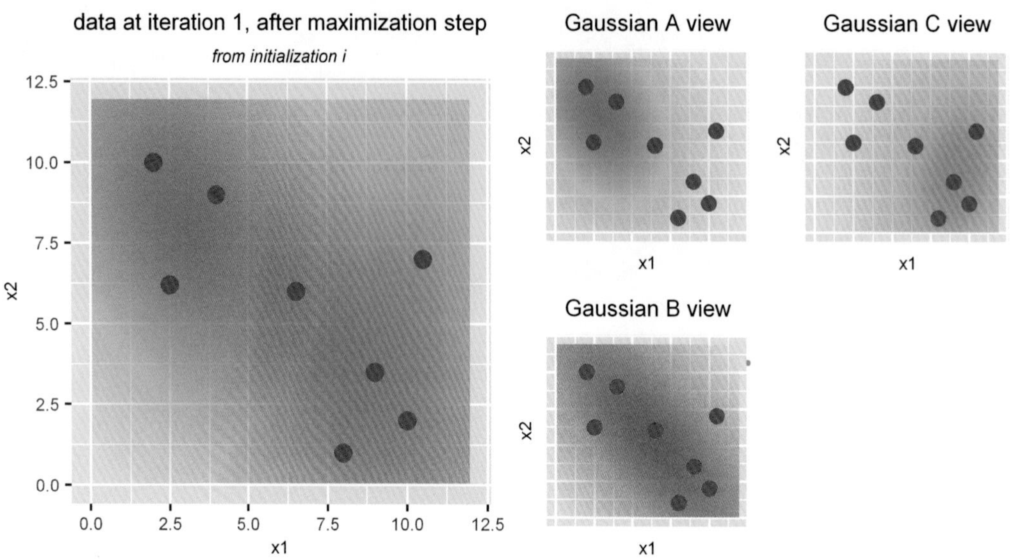

By iteration 7, the Gaussian functions are ready for us to commit class assignments.

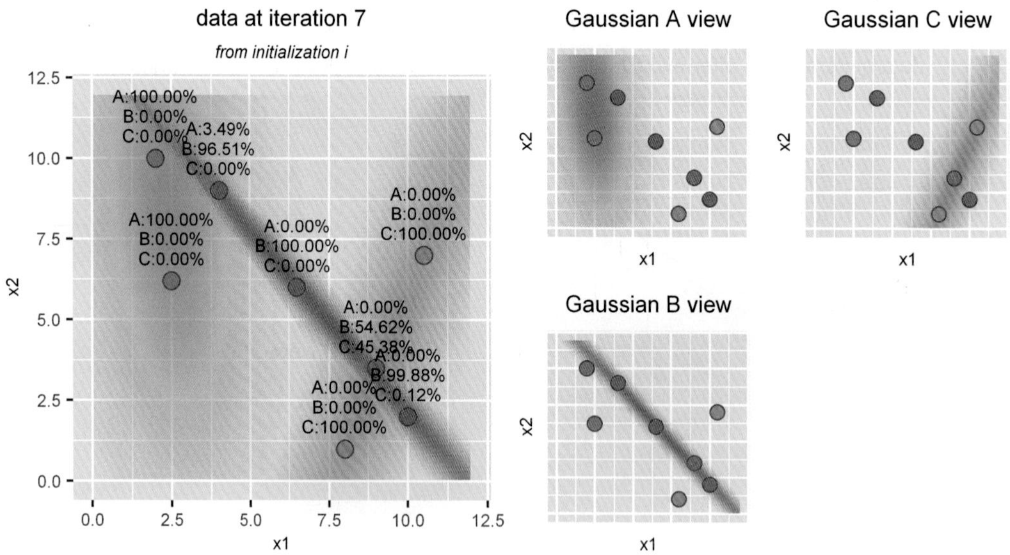

10.5.7.4 Commit

We eventually arrive at Gaussian functions that produce extreme partial class assignments. Two observations are each almost 100% partially assigned to class A. Three observations are each almost 100% partially assigned to class B. Three observations are each more than 90% partially assigned to class C.

Here is the resulting cluster model:

data at commitment with class assignments

x1	x2	g.A	g.B	g.C	weight.A	weight.B	weight.C	class
2.0	10.0	0.02	0.00	0.00	1.00	0.00	0.00	A
2.5	6.2	0.02	0.00	0.00	1.00	0.00	0.00	A
4.0	9.0	0.00	0.05	0.00	0.03	0.97	0.00	B
6.5	6.0	0.00	0.10	0.00	0.00	1.00	0.00	B
8.0	1.0	0.00	0.00	0.02	0.00	0.00	1.00	C
9.0	3.5	0.00	0.04	0.04	0.00	0.55	0.45	B
10.0	2.0	0.00	0.05	0.00	0.00	1.00	0.00	B
10.5	7.0	0.00	0.00	0.02	0.00	0.00	1.00	C

cluster model

x1	x2	class
2.0	10.0	A
2.5	6.2	A
4.0	9.0	B
6.5	6.0	B
8.0	1.0	C
9.0	3.5	B
10.0	2.0	B
10.5	7.0	C

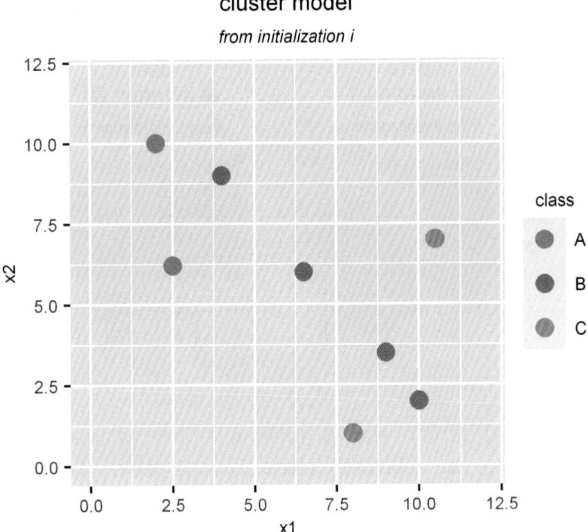

The Gaussian mixture method, initialized with 3 specific bi-variate Gaussian functions, effectively detected a pattern in the dataset that it used to organize the observations. Two observations lie on the left side, the others lie on the right side. Among those on the right side, some lie along a downward-sloping diagonal, while others lie along an upward-sloping diagonal. So, the method puts the observations into 3 clusters accordingly.

10.5.7.5 Other Initializations for Two Variables, Three Classes

Here
ways.

At initialization ii, the method detects that some observations lie along a diagonal, while others lie below the diagonal. Note that the cluster for class A observations is empty because the extreme partial class assignments at the last iteration do not include any large partial class assignments for class A. So, the result is effectively a 2-cluster model. Note also that the cluster model is the same as one produced by the method initialized with 2 Gaussian functions.

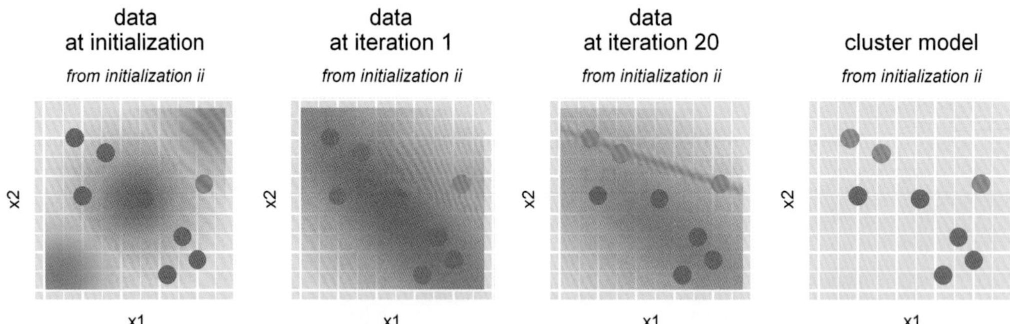

At initialization iii, the method detects that the upper-left observations are relatively close to each other, the 4 lower-right observations are relatively close to each other, and these 2 sets of observations are relatively far from each other. The cluster for class C observations is empty, so the result is effectively a 2-cluster model. Note also that the cluster model is the same as one produced by the method initialized with 2 Gaussian functions.

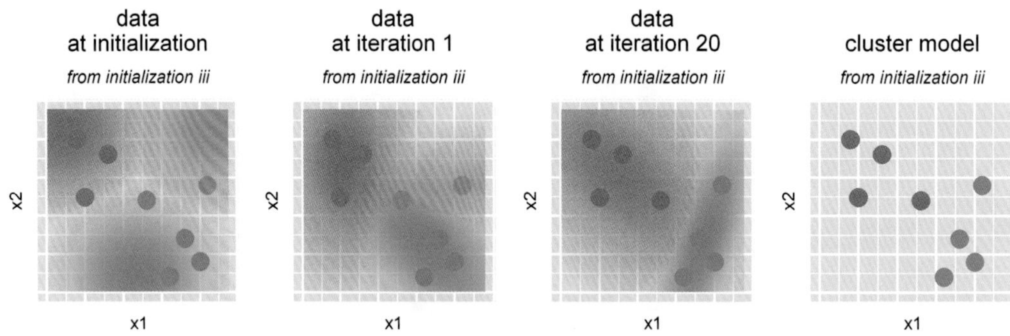

At initialization iv, the method detects that 3 upper-left observations are relatively close to each other, 2 mid-space observations are relatively close to each other, 3 lower-right observations are relatively close to each other, and these 3 sets of observations are relatively far from each other.

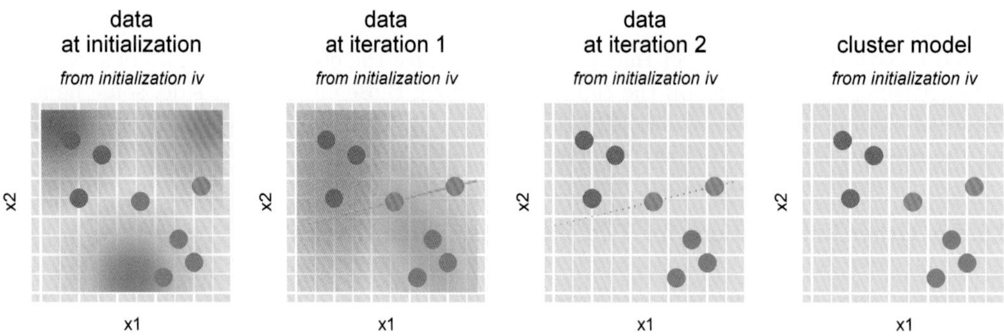

At initialization v, the method detects that some observations lie along a downward-sloping diagonal, while others do not. The cluster for class B observations is empty, so the result is effectively a 2-cluster model. Note also that the cluster model is the same as one produced by the method initialized with 2 Gaussian functions.

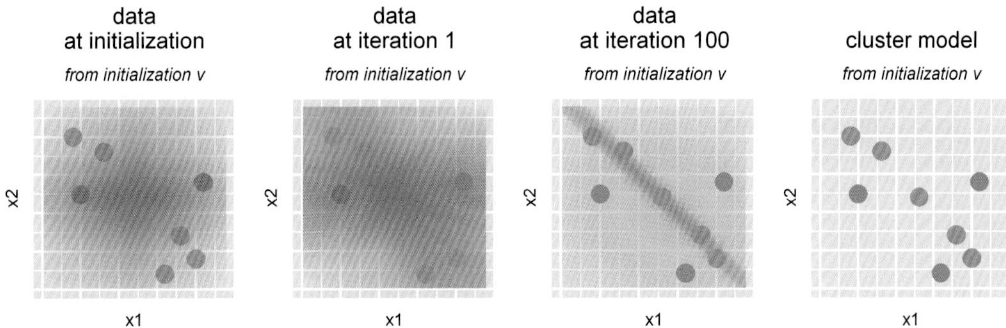

10.5.8 Gaussian Mixture | Many Variables, Many Classes

The Gaussian mixture method can be extended to work on many-variable datasets and produce many-cluster models.

To extend to many-variable datasets, extend the Gaussian functions to a form that accepts many variables as input. Each function will then be specified by a size, means for all variables, and a covariance matrix that incorporates standard deviations for all variables and correlations between all pairs of variables.

To extend to many clusters, increase the number of Gaussian functions and classes to suit the desired number of clusters.

Consider this unclassified 3-variable dataset:

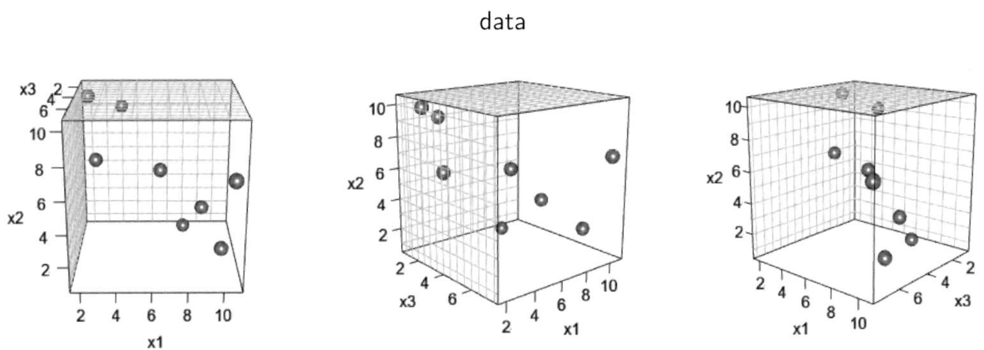

Here are cluster models produced by the Gaussian mixture method initialized with 3, 4, and 5 Gaussian functions:

3-cluster model

x1	x2	x3	class
2.0	10.0	2.0	1
2.5	6.2	3.0	1
4.0	9.0	1.0	1
6.5	6.0	4.0	2
8.0	1.0	2.0	2
9.0	3.5	4.0	2
10.0	2.0	6.0	2
10.5	7.0	7.3	3

4-cluster model

x1	x2	x3	class
2.0	10.0	2.0	1
2.5	6.2	3.0	1
4.0	9.0	1.0	1
6.5	6.0	4.0	2
8.0	1.0	2.0	3
9.0	3.5	4.0	2
10.0	2.0	6.0	2
10.5	7.0	7.3	4

5-cluster model

x1	x2	x3	class
2.0	10.0	2.0	1
2.5	6.2	3.0	2
4.0	9.0	1.0	1
6.5	6.0	4.0	3
8.0	1.0	2.0	4
9.0	3.5	4.0	3
10.0	2.0	6.0	3
10.5	7.0	7.3	5

3-cluster model

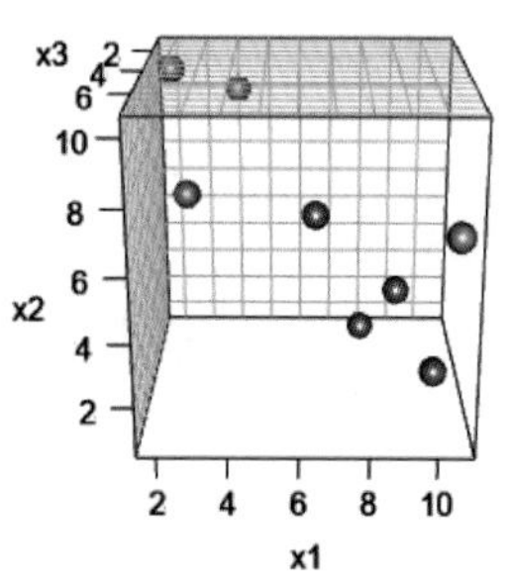

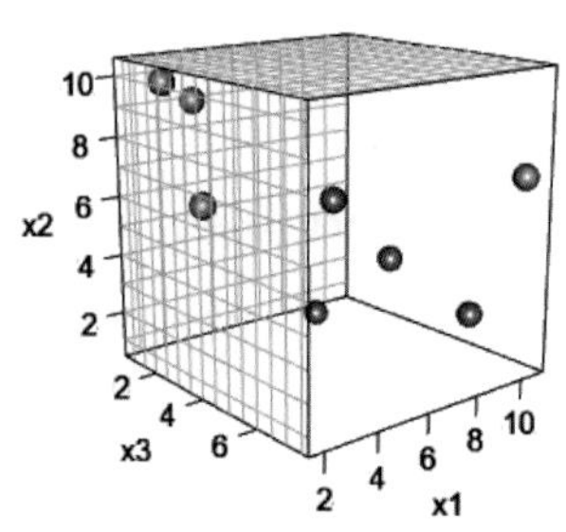

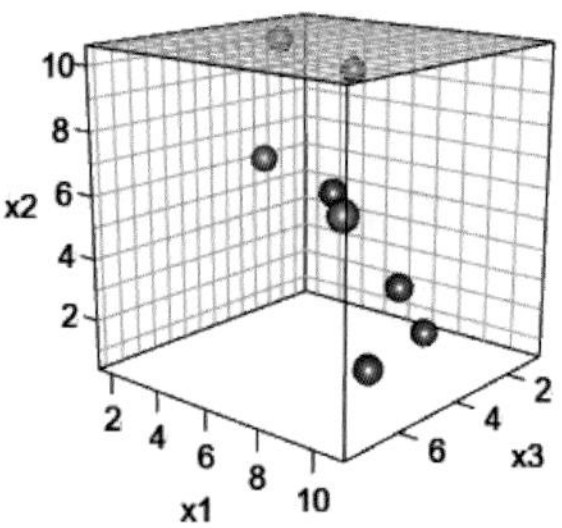

4-cluster model

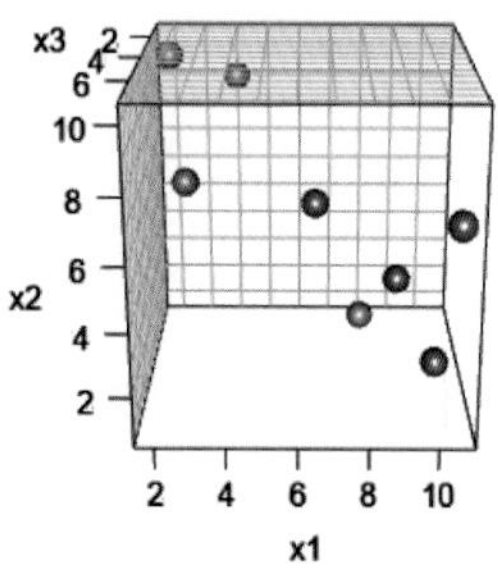

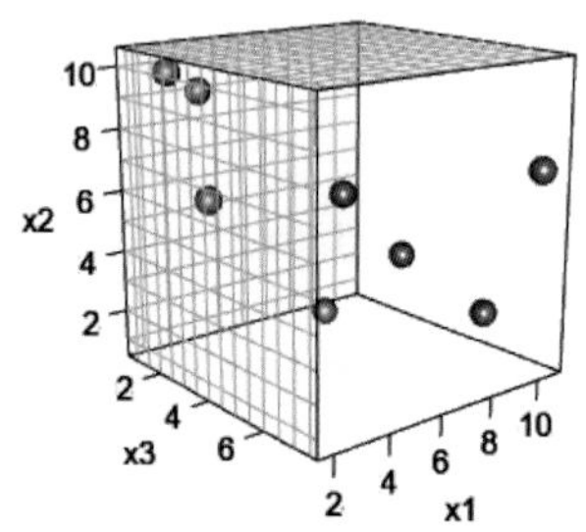

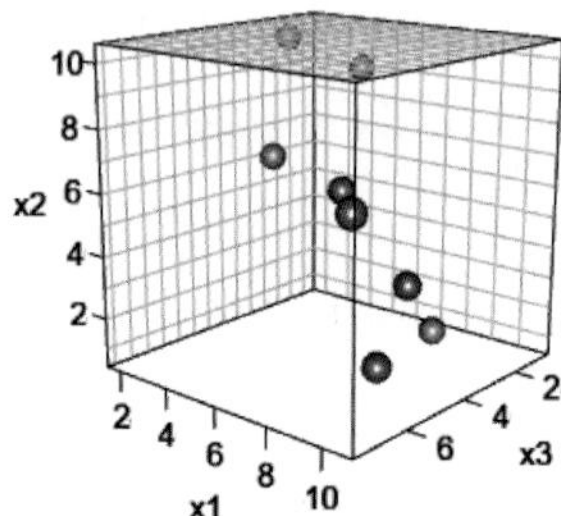

5-cluster model

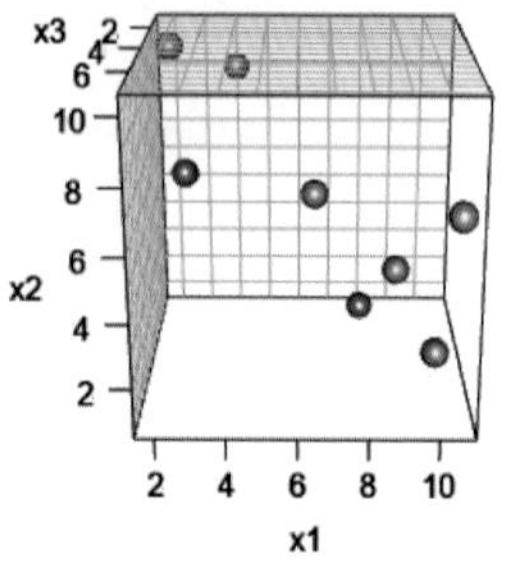

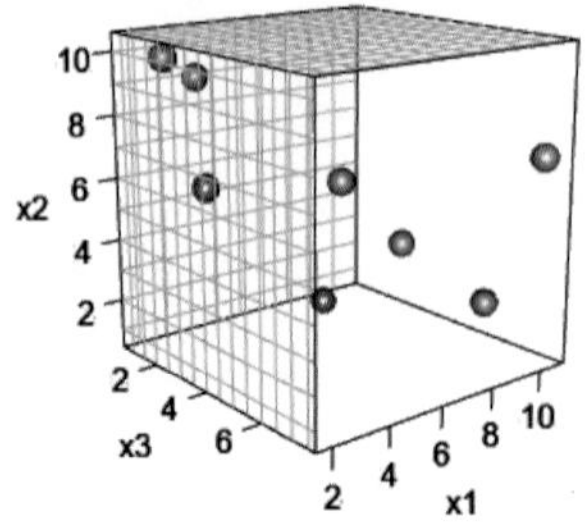

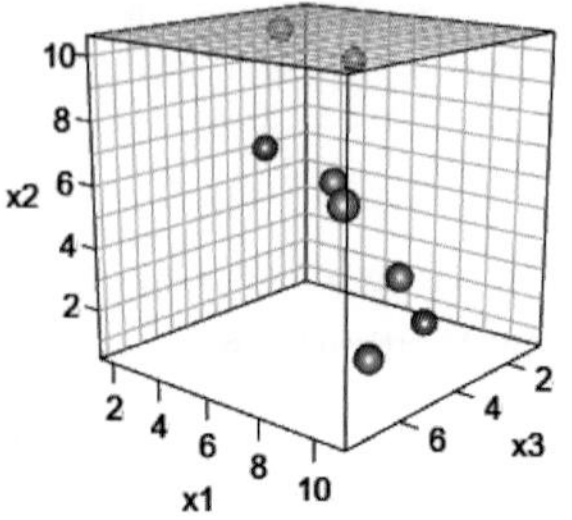

10.6 CASE | Fortune 500 Diversity

Cluster analysis to expose race and gender diversity in Fortune 500 companies.

10.6.1 Business Situation

The year is 2017. A company's investors and customers are inquiring about its workforce diversity, concerned that it could be at a competitive disadvantage if it's less diverse than industry norms. Company management wants to know how its workforce compares with those of other companies, and thereby inform a decision about initiating a program to encourage further workforce diversification.

- **Role:** Vice President of Human Resources
- **Decision:** Initiate a program to further diversify workforce?
- **Approach:** Use the Gaussian mixture method applied to publicly available workforce diversity data to organize some Fortune 500 companies into clusters based on similarities in their workforce diversity. Then identify the characteristics of companies that distinguish them from each other. Compare the company's workforce diversity with industry norms exposed by the analysis.

10.6.2 Data

Retrieve an unclassified dataset about Fortune 500 company workforce diversity. Each of 500 observations summarizes a survey response from a unique company about its workforce. Eight variables identify the company and reporting period, and a further 204 variables break down employee counts by gender, race, and position categories.

all_variables

f500.2017.rank, name, data.avail, data.url, diversity.pg.url, data.year, PAYROLL_START, PAYROLL_END, HISPM1, HISPM1_2, HISPM2, HISPM3, HISPM4, HISPM5, HISPM6, HISPM7, HISPM8, HISPM9, HISPM10, HISPM11, HISPF1, HISPF1_2, HISPF2, HISPF3, HISPF4, HISPF5, HISPF6, HISPF7, HISPF8, HISPF9, HISPF10, HISPF11, WHM1, WHM1_2, WHM2, WHM3, WHM4, WHM5, WHM6, WHM7, WHM8, WHM9, WHM10, WHM11, BLKM1, BLKM1_2, BLKM2, BLKM3, BLKM4, BLKM5, BLKM6, BLKM7, BLKM8, BLKM9, BLKM10, BLKM11, NHOPIM1, NHOPIM1_2, NHOPIM2, NHOPIM3, NHOPIM4, NHOPIM5, NHOPIM6, NHOPIM7, NHOPIM8, NHOPIM9, NHOPIM10, NHOPIM11, ASIANM1, ASIANM1_2, ASIANM2, ASIANM3, ASIANM4, ASIANM5, ASIANM6, ASIANM7, ASIANM8, ASIANM9, ASIANM10, ASIANM11, AIANM1, AIANM1_2, AIANM2, AIANM3, AIANM4, AIANM5, AIANM6, AIANM7, AIANM8, AIANM9, AIANM10, AIANM11, TOMRM1, TOMRM1_2, TOMRM2, TOMRM3, TOMRM4, TOMRM5, TOMRM6, TOMRM7, TOMRM8, TOMRM9, TOMRM10, TOMRM11, WHF1, WHF1_2, WHF2, WHF3, WHF4, WHF5, WHF6, WHF7, WHF8, WHF9, WHF10, WHF11, BLKF1, BLKF1_2, BLKF2, BLKF3, BLKF4, BLKF5, BLKF6, BLKF7, BLKF8, BLKF9, BLKF10, BLKF11, NHOPIF1, NHOPIF1_2, NHOPIF2, NHOPIF3, NHOPIF4, NHOPIF5, NHOPIF6, NHOPIF7, NHOPIF8, NHOPIF9, NHOPIF10, NHOPIF11, ASIANF1, ASIANF1_2, ASIANF2, ASIANF3, ASIANF4, ASIANF5, ASIANF6, ASIANF7, ASIANF8, ASIANF9, ASIANF10, ASIANF11, AIANF1, AIANF1_2, AIANF2, AIANF3, AIANF4, AIANF5, AIANF6, AIANF7, AIANF8, AIANF9, AIANF10, AIANF11, TOMRF1, TOMRF1_2, TOMRF2, TOMRF3, TOMRF4, TOMRF5, TOMRF6, TOMRF7, TOMRF8, TOMRF9, TOMRF10, TOMRF11, FT1, FT1_2, FT2, FT3, FT4, FT5, FT6, FT7, FT8, FT9, FT10, FT11, MT1, MT1_2, MT2, MT3, MT4, MT5, MT6, MT7, MT8, MT9, MT10, MT11, TOTAL1, TOTAL1_2, TOTAL2, TOTAL3, TOTAL4, TOTAL5, TOTAL6, TOTAL7, TOTAL8, TOTAL9, TOTAL10, TOTAL11

data.raw *size 500×212, first few observations shown, a few variables shown*

f500.2017.rank	name	data.year	HISPM1	HISPM1_2	HISPM2	HISPM3
1	Wal-Mart Stores	2,015	NA	NA	NA	NA
2	Berkshire Hathaway	NA	NA	NA	NA	NA
3	Apple	2,016	2	411	799	1,709
4	Exxon Mobil	NA	NA	NA	NA	NA
5	McKesson	NA	NA	NA	NA	NA
6	UnitedHealth Group	NA	NA	NA	NA	NA

Only 14 of 500 companies responded to surveys with complete information. For our analysis, remove the companies with incomplete information.

data *size 14×212, a few variables shown*

f500.2017.rank	name	data.year	HISPM1	HISPM1_2	HISPM2	HISPM3
3	Apple	2,016	2	411	799	1,709
12	Amazon.com	2,016	1	489	790	117
16	Costco Wholesale	2,016	4	1,401	149	292
27	Alphabet	2,016	0	340	1,107	29
28	Microsoft	2,016	6	323	1,937	0
47	Intel	2,016	1	322	1,654	1,112
60	Cisco Systems	NA	4	180	898	1
61	HP	NA	29	303	1,906	440
98	Facebook	NA	9	22	163	5
119	Qualcomm	NA	41	106	290	58
310	eBay	NA	2	33	46	1
391	Jones Lang LaSalle	NA	4	99	241	0
443	Adobe Systems	2,015	3	44	69	0
498	Yahoo	2,015	5	22	115	3

10.6.3 Analysis I

Apply the Gaussian mixture method to the dataset, set to 2 clusters, based on the employee count variables. The resulting cluster model comprises 1 cluster including Amazon and Costco, and another cluster including the other 12 companies. Amazon and Costco appear similar to each other and different from the rest when considering all aspects of diversity.

data *a few variables shown*

class	f500.2017.rank	name	data.year	HISPM1	HISPM1_2	HISPM2	HISPM3
1	3	Apple	2,016	2	411	799	1,709
2	12	Amazon.com	2,016	1	489	790	117
2	16	Costco Wholesale	2,016	4	1,401	149	292
1	27	Alphabet	2,016	0	340	1,107	29
1	28	Microsoft	2,016	6	323	1,937	0
1	47	Intel	2,016	1	322	1,654	1,112
1	60	Cisco Systems	NA	4	180	898	1
1	61	HP	NA	29	303	1,906	440
1	98	Facebook	NA	9	22	163	5
1	119	Qualcomm	NA	41	106	290	58
1	310	eBay	NA	2	33	46	1
1	391	Jones Lang LaSalle	NA	4	99	241	0
1	443	Adobe Systems	2,015	3	44	69	0
1	498	Yahoo	2,015	5	22	115	3

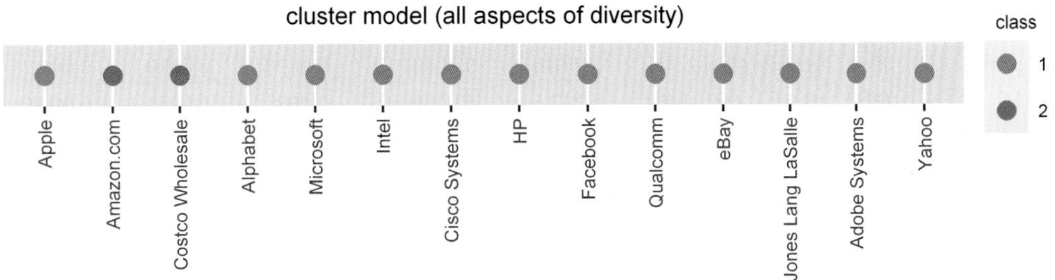

Perhaps the situation is different when considering only gender diversity. So, apply the Gaussian mixture method to the dataset, set to 2 clusters, based on the gender-related employee count variables. The result is that Amazon and Costco still appear different from the rest.

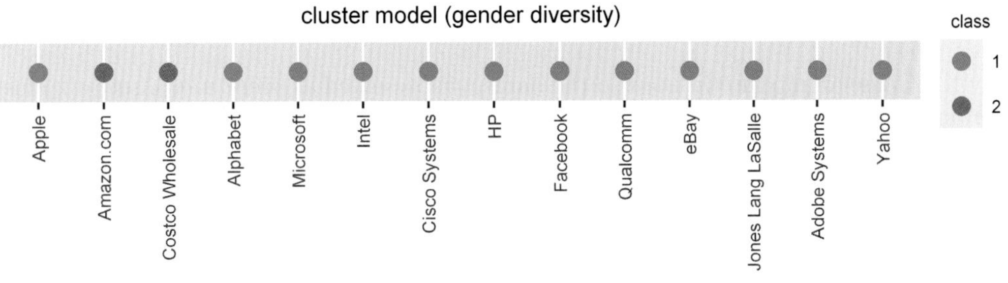

Perhaps the situation is different when considering only race diversity. So, apply the Gaussian mixture method to the dataset, set to 2 clusters, based on the race-related employee count variables. The result is that Amazon and Costco still appear different from the rest.

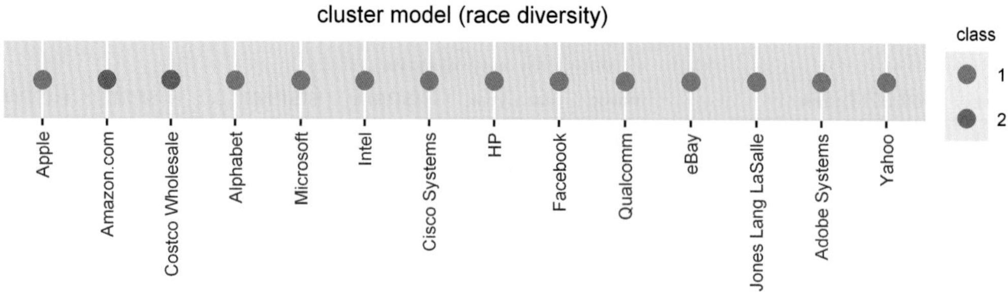

Amazon and Costco both have large workforces relative to some of the other companies' workforces. Perhaps the cluster models are reflecting that. To assess workforce diversity without regard to size of the company, represent the variable values as proportions of all company employees rather than as absolute employee counts. Take care to account for the current and previous years, since some employee count variables are meant to go with the current year and some with the previous year.

data (as proportion of all employees) *a few variables shown*

f500.2017.rank	name	data.year	HISPM1	HISPM1_2	HISPM2	HISPM3
3	Apple	2,016	0.0000	0.0053	0.0104	0.0221
12	Amazon.com	2,016	0.0000	0.0028	0.0045	0.0007
16	Costco Wholesale	2,016	0.0000	0.0098	0.0010	0.0021
27	Alphabet	2,016	0.0000	0.0083	0.0269	0.0007
28	Microsoft	2,016	0.0001	0.0063	0.0377	0.0000
47	Intel	2,016	0.0000	0.0059	0.0306	0.0205
60	Cisco Systems	NA	0.0001	0.0048	0.0239	0.0000
61	HP	NA	0.0004	0.0042	0.0264	0.0061
98	Facebook	NA	0.0011	0.0026	0.0193	0.0006
119	Qualcomm	NA	0.0023	0.0059	0.0161	0.0032
310	eBay	NA	0.0003	0.0050	0.0070	0.0002
391	Jones Lang LaSalle	NA	0.0002	0.0045	0.0109	0.0000
443	Adobe Systems	2,015	0.0005	0.0067	0.0105	0.0000
498	Yahoo	2,015	0.0007	0.0030	0.0156	0.0004

Apply the Gaussian mixture method to the dataset represented as proportions, set to 2 clusters, based on the employee proportion variables. The result is that Amazon and Costco still appear different from the rest.

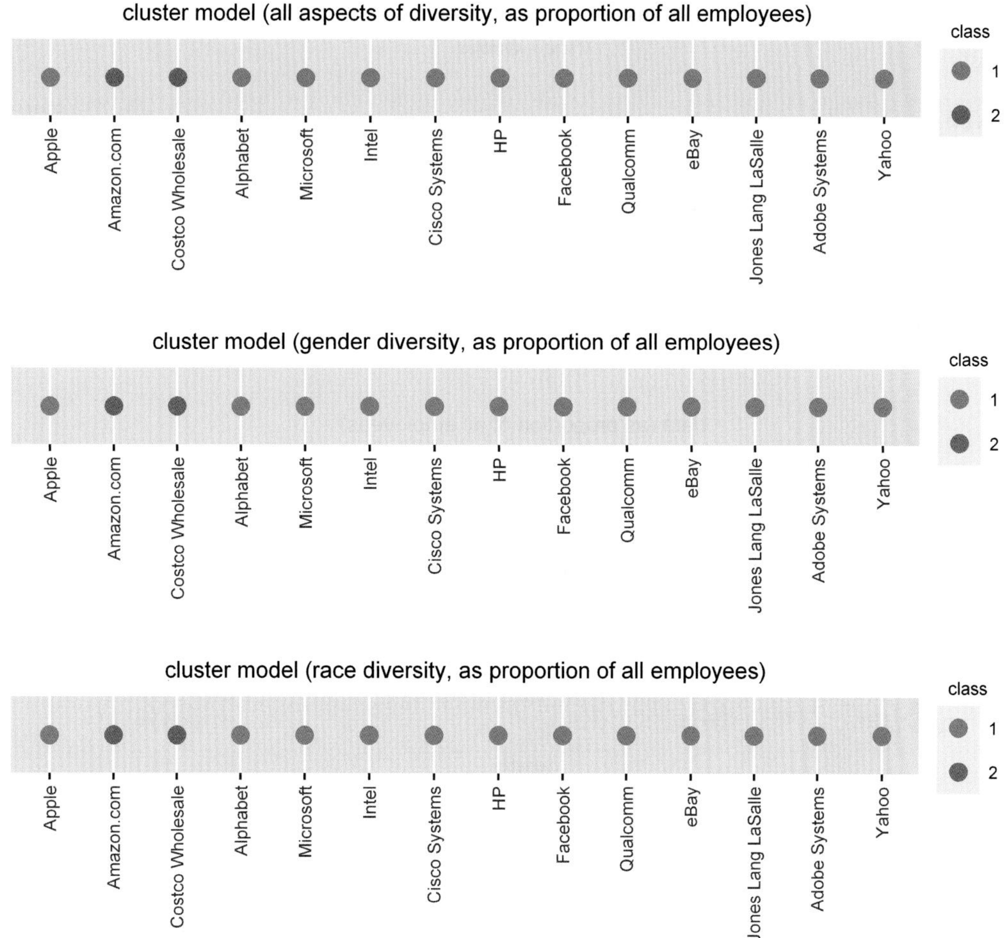

Without a cluster analysis, it wouldn't be obvious which companies are alike and which are different. With a cluster analysis, it becomes obvious that Amazon and Costco are alike, so we can focus on investigating what distinguishes just these 2 companies.

Here is the dataset cross-tabulated and visualized as a scatterplot with variable names along the horizontal axis and employee proportions along the vertical axis. For clarity, employees proportions belonging to the same company are shown connected by line segments. Points and line segments are color-coded by class so that it's easy to see which variables make Amazon and Costco so different from the others: higher values for HISPM10, HISPM11, HISPF10, HISPF11, BLKM8, BLKM10, BLKM11, WHF10, WHF11, FT10, FT11, and lower values for WHM10, WHM11, ASIANM2, ASIANM10, ASIANM11, ASIANF2, ASIANF10, ASIANF11, MT2, MT10, MT11.

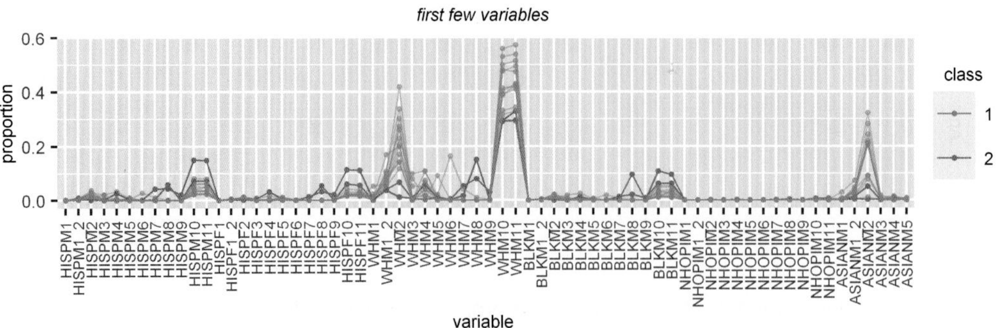

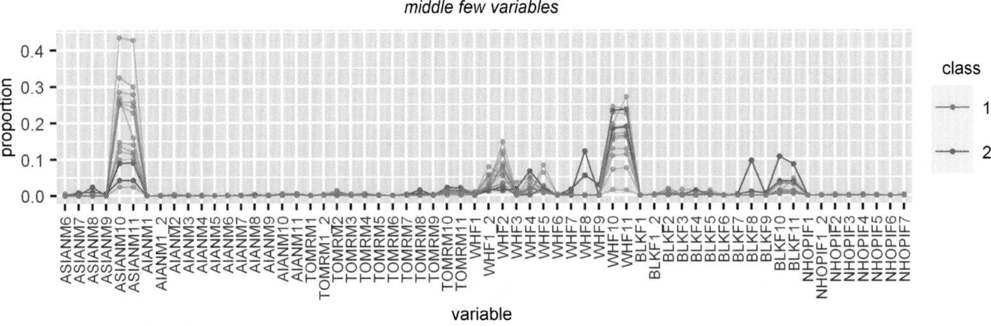

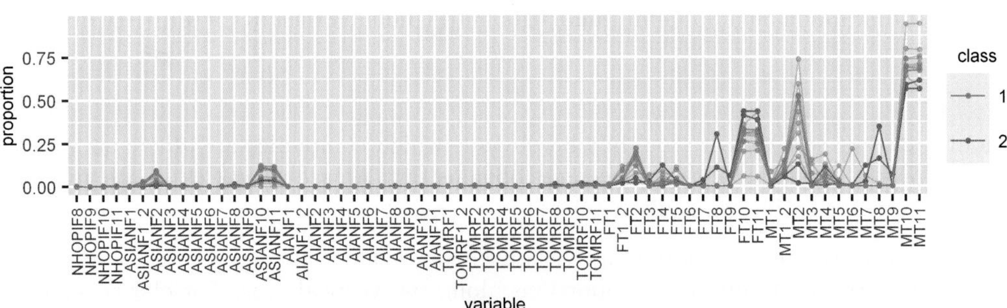

According to this analysis, Amazon and Costco distinguish themselves from other companies by employing unusually high proportions of Hispanic men and women, black men, white women, and women overall in both the current and previous year. They employ unusually low proportions of white men, Asian men and women, and men overall in both the current and previous year.

As the Vice President of Human Resources thinks through these results, he concludes that perhaps Amazon and Costco should serve as a high standard for workforce diversity to guide his company. However, further analysis is calling.

10.6.4 Analysis II

Apply the Gaussian mixture method to the dataset, set to 2 clusters, based on the management-related employee proportion variables.

These are the management-related employee proportion variables:

middle_management_variables

HISPM1_2, HISPF1_2, WHM1_2, BLKM1_2, NHOPIM1_2, ASIANM1_2, AIANM1_2, TOMRM1_2, WHF1_2, BLKF1_2, NHOPIF1_2, ASIANF1_2, AIANF1_2, TOMRF1_2, FT1_2, MT1_2

executive_management_variables

HISPM1, HISPF1, WHM1, BLKM1, NHOPIM1, ASIANM1, AIANM1, TOMRM1, WHF1, BLKF1, NHOPIF1, ASIANF1, AIANF1, TOMRF1, FT1, MT1

The dataset must be transformed again, this time in 2 ways. First, for each company, filter in just the middle management-related employee count variables and divide each by the total middle management employee count to express as proportions of middle management. Second, do similarly for executive management.

The resulting cluster model based on only the middle management-related employee proportion variables makes Costco its own cluster.

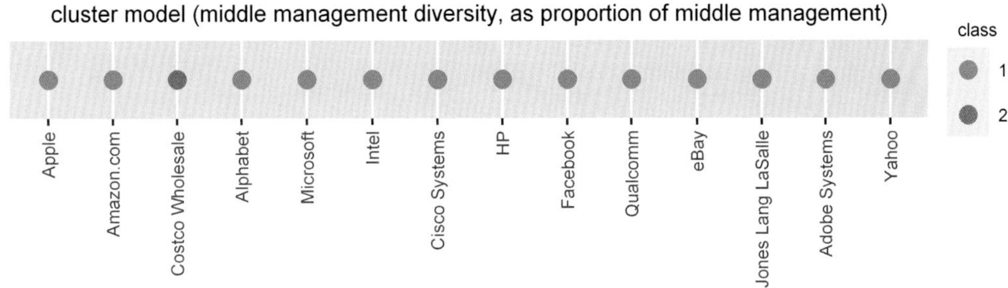

The resulting cluster model based on only the executive management-related employee proportion variables also makes Costco its own cluster.

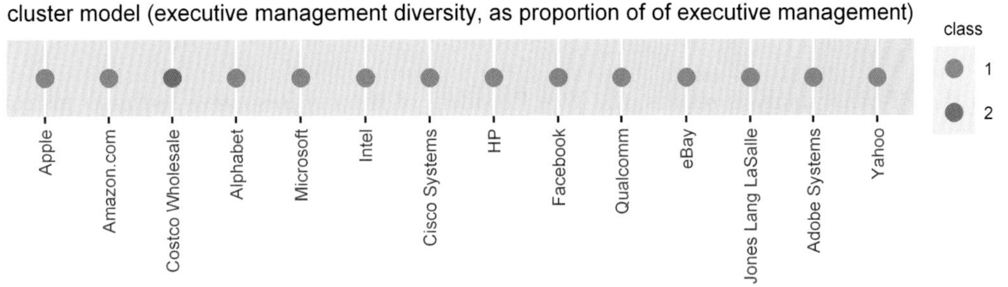

Both cluster models expose Costco management diversity as very different from the other companies' management diversity. Through the lens of middle management, Costco has higher values for HSPM1_2, HSPF1_2, BLKM1_2, BLKF1_2, and lower values for ASIANM1_2, ASIANF1_2. Through the lens of executive management, Costco has higher values for HSPM1, WHM1, MT1, and lower values for ASIANM1, WHF1, ASIANF1, FT1.

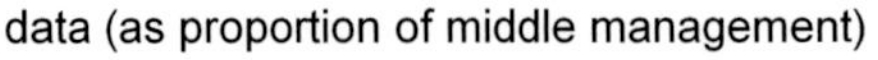

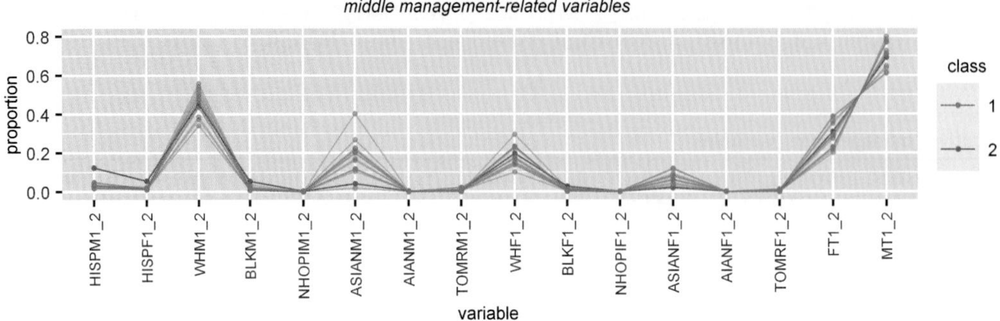

data (as proportion of executive management)

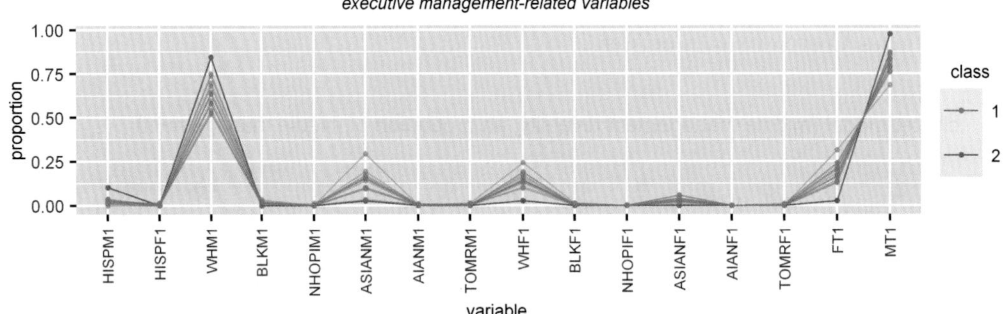

According to this further analysis, Costco distinguishes itself from other companies in two ways. Costco's middle management is made up of unusually high proportions of Hispanic and black men and women, and unusually low proportions of Asian men and women. Women overall make up middle management not especially more or less than at other companies. Costco's executive management is a different story. Its executive management is made up of unusually high proportions of Hispanic and white men, and unusually low proportions of black and Asian men and women, and an unusually low proportion of women overall. What at first might have appeared very diverse turns out to be relatively homogeneous when viewed through another lens.

With these further analysis results, the Vice President of Human Resources re-thinks his earlier conclusions. Perhaps the company needs several workforce diversity standards to account for several different categories of employees. Perhaps it needs programs to encourage further workforce diversity for some categories and not so much for others.

Note: By 2021, Costco Wholesale had reported that women accounted for 36.4% of management.

10.7 CASE | Music Market Segmentation

Cluster analysis with principal component analysis and sensitivity analysis to segment a market for new bands in the music industry.

10.7.1 Business Situation

A record label company is planning to develop new bands to serve its evolving market, based on survey responses it has compiled on music tastes of potential customers.

- Many market segments would require many bands. Each band would be developed to narrowly, strongly appeal to a group of homogeneous potential customers with similar tastes. This would positively affect profit due to relatively high demand within a group. However, this would also negatively affect profit due to small group sizes and high development costs spread across many bands.
- Few market segments would require only a few bands. Each band would be developed to broadly, lightly appeal to a group of heterogeneous potential customers with a variety of tastes. This would positively affect profit due to large group sizes and low development costs spread over only a few bands. However, this would also negatively affect profit due to relatively low demand within a group.

The record label company must balance the trade-off between the number of market segments, the appeal of the bands, and the cost of development.

- **Role:** Head of Artists & Repertoire at a record label company.
- **Decision:** How to segment the market to best serve consumers with new band products? How many and what kind of bands to develop?
- **Approach:** Apply Gaussian mixture to music taste survey data to segment the market in various ways and compare relative business value of various band development strategies.

10.7.2 Decision Model

The decision model starts with a decision method that constructs a cluster model, where each cluster corresponds to a market segment. A new band will be developed for each market segment. The business result of interest is profit.

Business parameters include the following:

- **market size:** the total number of potential customers
- **calibration:** a calibration factor involved in a formula to estimate the share of a segment that will buy products, based on similarity of tastes within a segment
- **price:** unit price of product
- **cost.fixed:** fixed cost to develop a new band
- **cost.variable:** variable cost of product, which may include marketing, production, delivery, and other costs associated with each unit

business parameters

market_size	calibration	price	cost.fixed	cost.variable
10,000,000	3	1.49	1,000,000	0.05

We treat the intra-cluster dispersion of each cluster as a measure of the dissimilarity in tastes among potential customers in the corresponding market segment. The potential market share associated with each segment is proportional to the size of the corresponding cluster. The market share associated with each segment then depends on the potential market share, adjusted by its calibrated reciprocal intra-cluster dispersion – the higher the intra-cluster dispersion, the lower the market share, because we assume that groups of heterogeneous potential customers will have lower demand for products. Volume of products depends on the market size and market share. Revenue depends on volume and price. Total fixed cost depends on fixed cost per new band and number of new bands, which is the number of segments. Total variable cost depends on variable cost and volume. Total cost depends on total fixed cost and total variable cost. Profit depends on revenue and total cost.

Note that fixed cost is variable in terms of number of segments, but not variable in terms of volume.

10.7.3 Data

Retrieve a reference unclassified dataset of music taste survey responses. Each of 8,124 observations describes the responses for a unique respondent. One variable, named V_1, we'll set aside for now. The other 22 variables, named V_2 through V_{23}, correspond to 22 questions on the survey, each of the form: "Which of the following songs do you like most?" Values indicate the checkbox numbers that the respondent marked. See, for example, that respondent 1 marked checkbox 2 for the first question, marked checkbox 9 for the second question, marked checkbox 10 for the third question, and so on. Note that checkbox numbering starts at 0.

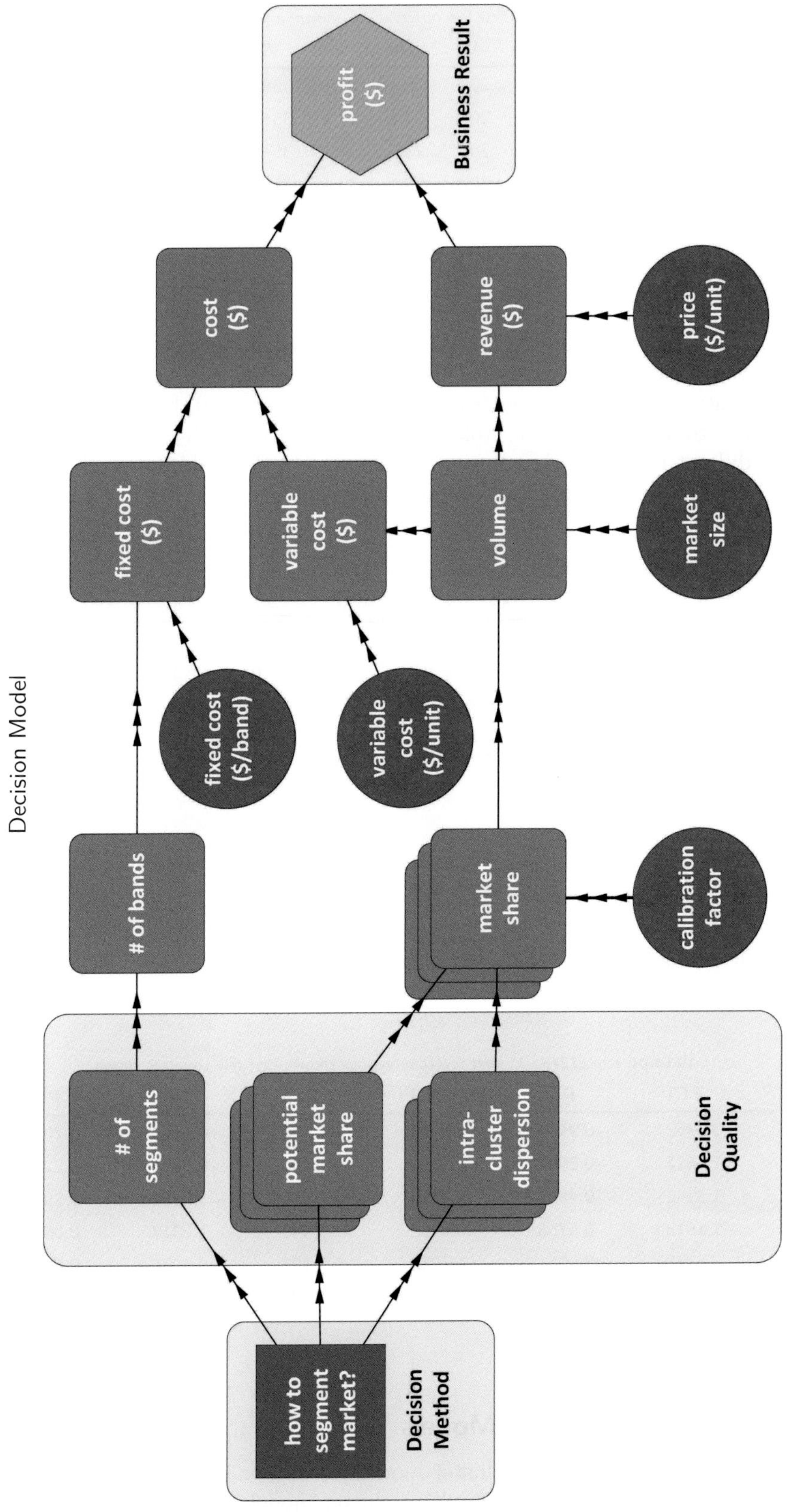
Decision Model
how to segment market?
Decision Method
# of segments
potential market share
intra-cluster dispersion
Decision Quality
# of bands
market share
calibration factor
fixed cost ($/band)
variable cost ($/unit)
fixed cost ($)
variable cost ($)
volume
market size
cost ($)
revenue ($)
price ($/unit)
profit ($)
Business Result

data *size 8124×23, first few observations shown, a few variables shown*

V2	V3	V4	V5	V6	V7	V8	V9	V10
2:1	9:1	10:1	20:1	29:1	33:1	35:1	39:1	40:1
2:1	9:1	19:1	20:1	22:1	33:1	35:1	38:1	40:1
0:1	9:1	18:1	20:1	23:1	33:1	35:1	38:1	41:1
2:1	8:1	18:1	20:1	29:1	33:1	35:1	39:1	41:1
2:1	9:1	13:1	21:1	28:1	33:1	36:1	38:1	40:1
2:1	8:1	19:1	20:1	22:1	33:1	35:1	38:1	41:1

Prepare the dataset by converting it to dummy representation. In the raw dataset, each variable is effectively categorical, with each checkbox number acting as a categorical value. In the dummy representation, all 8,124 observations have been retained, but original variables have been replaced with 126 dummy variables named X_1 through X_{126}. See, for example, that respondent 1 did not mark checkbox 0 (now represented by X_1), did not mark checkbox 1 (now represented by X_2), did mark checkbox 3 (now represented by X_3), and so on.

data *size 8124×126, first few observations shown, first few variables shown*

X1	X2	X3	X4	X5	X6	X7	X8	X9	X10
0	0	1	0	0	0	0	0	0	1
0	0	1	0	0	0	0	0	0	1
1	0	0	0	0	0	0	0	0	1
0	0	1	0	0	0	0	0	1	0
0	0	1	0	0	0	0	0	0	1
0	0	1	0	0	0	0	0	1	0

For later data visualization, convert the dummy representation to principal component representation, and set the resulting transformed dataset aside for now. In principal component representation, all 8,124 observations have been retained, but the 126 dummy variables have been replaced with 126 principal component variables.

data.pc *size 8124×126, first few observations shown, first few variables shown*

PC1	PC2	PC3	PC4	PC5	PC6
0.9962	-0.9469	0.8025	-1.267	-0.9847	0.2021
1.4417	-0.1642	1.0682	-1.490	-0.5736	0.2284
1.5241	-0.4087	0.8532	-1.686	-0.2150	-0.2984
1.1518	-0.6758	0.6298	-1.440	-1.2317	0.0416
0.6175	-0.9961	1.7259	1.428	-0.1936	0.5725
1.5003	0.0236	0.7028	-1.588	-0.6194	0.0557

10.7.4 Market Segmentation Models

Use Gaussian mixture to construct cluster models, based on data in dummy representation. Try 2, 3, and 4 clusters. Here are the resulting cluster models. The data visualizations show a point for each respondent, color-coded by assigned segment. Note that these data visualizations expose the relative sizes of the segments, but not much else.

2-segment model

segment	size
1	4,964
2	3,160

3-segment model

segment	size
1	801
2	3,745
3	3,578

4-segment model

segment	size
1	800
2	3,868
3	1,728
4	1,728

2-segment model
list representation
segment
1 2

3-segment model
list representation
segment
1 2 3

4-segment model
list representation
segment
1 2 3 4

To get deeper insight into the patterns in the data detected by the Gaussian mixture method, visualize the dataset as a scatterplot of the first and second principal component variables, color-coded by segment. From this perspective, we see that the 2-segment model effectively proposes establishing segments for potential customers with tastes similar to those of low vs. high PC_1 respondents. The 3-segment model effectively proposes establishing a segment for potential customers with tastes similar to those of near-zero PC_1 respondents, a second segment for potential customers with tastes similar to those of moderately low and moderately high PC_1 respondents, and a third a segment for potential customers with tastes similar to those of very low and very high PC_1 respondents. Similarly for the 4-segment model.

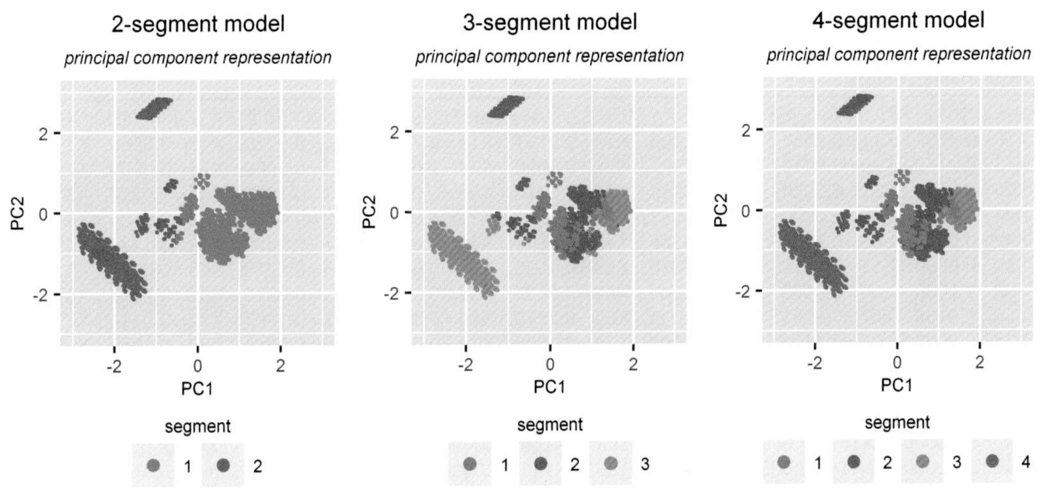

10.7.5 Evaluation

Evaluate the quality of the proposed segmentations by the usual dispersion-related quality metrics.

Here are the metrics for the 2-segment model. Note that these metrics are calculated based on distances between points in 126-dimensional space, since there are 126 variables in the cluster model, not including the class variable. See, for example, the cluster centroids required to calculate mean inter-cluster dispersion are each a point expressed as 126 values.

2-segment model, segment metrics

segment	size	intracluster_dispersion
1	4,964	4.400
2	3,160	4.141

2-segment model, model metrics

metric	value
mean_intercluster_dispersion	2.7038
mean_intracluster_dispersion	4.2705
dispersion_ratio	0.6331

2-segment model, centroid of segment 1

all_variable_values
X1=0.0890, X2=0.0004, X3=0.4817, X4=0.3789, X5=0.0435, X6=0.0064, X7=0.3300, X8=0.0008, X9=0.3284, X10=0.3409, X11=0.2764, X12=0.0338, X13=0.0024, X14=0.2401, X15=0.0016, X16=0.0290, X17=0.0016, X18=0.1257, X19=0.2087, X20=0.0806, X21=0.6801, X22=0.3199, X23=0.0806, X24=0.0806, X25=0.0387, X26=0.0000, X27=0.0580, X28=0.0000, X29=0.6906, X30=0.0516, X31=0.0000, X32=0.0387, X33=0.0000, X34=0.9613, X35=0.0000, X36=0.7454, X37=0.2546, X38=0.0000, X39=0.8622, X40=0.1378, X41=0.0822, X42=0.2111, X43=0.0000, X44=0.0592, X45=0.0645, X46=0.0048, X47=0.0129, X48=0.2125, X49=0.0981, X50=0.0193, X51=0.2224, X52=0.0129, X53=0.4198, X54=0.5802, X55=0.4915, X56=0.1031, X57=0.0000, X58=0.2256, X59=0.0000, X60=0.0387, X61=0.1410, X62=0.1064, X63=0.0032, X64=0.0290, X65=0.8614, X66=0.1120, X67=0.0419, X68=0.0290, X69=0.8171, X70=0.0032, X71=0.0000, X72=0.0000, X73=0.1160, X74=0.0387, X75=0.1160, X76=0.0193, X77=0.7067, X78=0.0000, X79=0.0048, X80=0.0000, X81=0.0000, X82=0.1160, X83=0.0387, X84=0.1160, X85=0.0193, X86=0.7051, X87=0.0000, X88=1.0000, X89=0.0000, X90=0.0193, X91=0.0193, X92=0.9613, X93=0.0000, X94=0.0000, X95=0.8791, X96=0.1209, X97=0.0000, X98=0.1950, X99=0.0056, X100=0.0000, X101=0.0000, X102=0.7994, X103=0.0000, X104=0.0000, X105=0.3771, X106=0.3965, X107=0.0097, X108=0.0637, X109=0.0145, X110=0.0097, X111=0.0097, X112=0.1096, X113=0.0097, X114=0.0774, X115=0.0596, X116=0.0806, X117=0.2514, X118=0.3167, X119=0.2143, X120=0.3457, X121=0.0419, X122=0.0588, X123=0.0274, X124=0.0741, X125=0.0387, X126=0.4134

2-segment model, centroid of segment 2

all_variable_values
X1=0.0032, X2=0.0006, X3=0.4003, X4=0.4022, X5=0.1937, X6=0.0000, X7=0.2158, X8=0.0000, X9=0.5108, X10=0.2734, X11=0.2886, X12=0.0000, X13=0.0101, X14=0.2051, X15=0.0025, X16=0.0000, X17=0.0025, X18=0.2772, X19=0.0013, X20=0.2127, X21=0.0000, X22=1.0000, X23=0.0000, X24=0.0000, X25=0.0000, X26=0.1823, X27=0.5924, X28=0.0114, X29=0.0316, X30=0.0000, X31=0.1823, X32=0.0057, X33=0.0000, X34=0.9943, X35=0.0000, X36=0.9848, X37=0.0152, X38=0.0000, X39=0.4215, X40=0.5785, X41=0.0000, X42=0.0000, X43=0.5468, X44=0.1386, X45=0.1367, X46=0.0000, X47=0.0000, X48=0.1383, X49=0.0016, X50=0.0000, X51=0.0310, X52=0.0070, X53=0.4532, X54=0.5468, X55=0.4228, X56=0.0139, X57=0.0000, X58=0.0000, X59=0.0000, X60=0.0000, X61=0.5633, X62=0.0076, X63=0.0025, X64=0.7051, X65=0.2848, X66=0.0139, X67=0.0241, X68=0.6835, X69=0.2785, X70=0.1367, X71=0.1367, X72=0.0114, X73=0.0000, X74=0.0000, X75=0.4101, X76=0.0000, X77=0.3025, X78=0.0025, X79=0.1544, X80=0.1367, X81=0.0114, X82=0.0000, X83=0.0000, X84=0.4101, X85=0.0000, X86=0.2797, X87=0.0076, X88=1.0000, X89=0.0000, X90=0.0000, X91=0.0000, X92=0.9975, X93=0.0025, X94=0.0114, X95=0.9886, X96=0.0000, X97=0.0000, X98=0.5722, X99=0.0063, X100=0.4101, X101=0.0114, X102=0.0000, X103=0.0000, X104=0.0000, X105=0.0000, X106=0.0000, X107=0.0000, X108=0.4165, X109=0.0000, X110=0.0000, X111=0.0000, X112=0.5835, X113=0.0000, X114=0.0000, X115=0.0139, X116=0.0000, X117=0.0000, X118=0.7810, X119=0.2051, X120=0.1367, X121=0.1975, X122=0.0000, X123=0.3190, X124=0.0000, X125=0.0000, X126=0.3468

Here are the metrics for the 3-segment model:

3-segment model, segment metrics

segment	size	intracluster_dispersion
1	801	4.203
2	3,745	4.576
3	3,578	4.080

3-segment model, model metrics

metric	value
mean_intercluster_dispersion	2.4412
mean_intracluster_dispersion	4.2864
dispersion_ratio	0.5695

Here are the metrics for the 4-segment model:

4-segment model, segment metrics

segment	size	intracluster_dispersion
1	800	4.202
2	3,868	4.595
3	1,728	3.048
4	1,728	3.126

4-segment model, model metrics

metric	value
mean_intercluster_dispersion	3.1524
mean_intracluster_dispersion	3.7425
dispersion_ratio	0.8423

Compare the quality of the 3 proposed segmentations, as measured by dispersion ratio. The 4-segment model looks better than 2-segment and 3-segment models. In the 4-segment model, the dissimilarity between segments is more pronounced: mean inter-cluster dispersion 3.1524 vs. 2.7038 or 2.4412. In the 4-segment model, the dissimilarity among members of a segment is on average less pronounced: mean intra-cluster dispersion 3.7425 vs. 4.2705 or 4.2864. The 4-segment model boasts the highest dispersion ratio due to having both the highest mean inter-cluster dispersion and lowest intra-cluster dispersion.

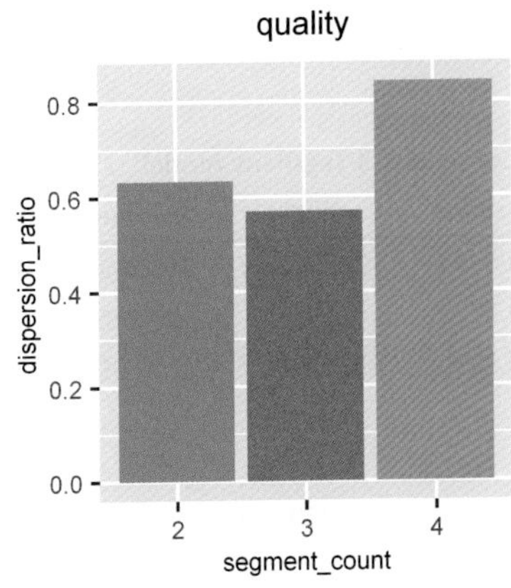

10.7.6 Business Results

Which among the quality metrics matters to us? What ultimately matters to us is not any specific quality metric, but rather the business result, which is profit calculated from the intra-cluster dispersions. So, calculate and compare the business results that you can expect from each segmentation model.

For each model, calculate the profit from each segment, then sum to the total profit:

For each segment ...

$$\begin{aligned}
\text{potential market share} &= \frac{\text{cluster size}}{\text{dataset size}} \\
\text{market share} &= min\left(1, \frac{1}{\text{intra-cluster dispersion}} \times \text{calibration}\right) \\
\text{volume} &= \text{market size} \times \text{market share} \\
\text{revenue} &= \text{volume} \times \text{price} \\
\text{cost} &= \text{fixed cost} + (\text{variable cost} \times \text{volume}) \\
\text{profit} &= \text{revenue} - \text{cost}
\end{aligned}$$

Here are the business results for the 2-segment, 3-segment, and 4-segment models. Even though the highest quality, 4-segment model would suggest that we partition the market into 4 segments, we can rather expect the best business results – profit of $8,057,034 – if we partition the market into 2 segments and develop only 2 new bands.

business result, 2-segment model

segment	pot_share	intra	share	volume	revenue	cost	profit	total_profit
1	0.611	4.400	0.4166	4,165,947	6,207,261	1,208,297	4,998,963	8,057,034
2	0.389	4.141	0.2818	2,818,105	4,198,976	1,140,905	3,058,071	

business result, 3-segment model

segment	pot_share	intra	share	volume	revenue	cost	profit	total_profit
1	0.0986	4.203	0.0704	703,746	1,048,581	1,035,187	13,394	7,028,616
2	0.4610	4.576	0.3022	3,021,977	4,502,746	1,151,099	3,351,647	
3	0.4404	4.080	0.3239	3,238,594	4,825,505	1,161,930	3,663,575	

business result, 4-segment model

segment	pot_share	intra	share	volume	revenue	cost	profit	total_profit
1	0.0985	4.202	0.0703	703,097	1,047,615	1,035,155	12,460	7,443,486
2	0.4761	4.595	0.3109	3,108,791	4,632,099	1,155,440	3,476,660	
3	0.2127	3.048	0.2093	2,093,395	3,119,158	1,104,670	2,014,489	
4	0.2127	3.126	0.2042	2,041,582	3,041,957	1,102,079	1,939,878	

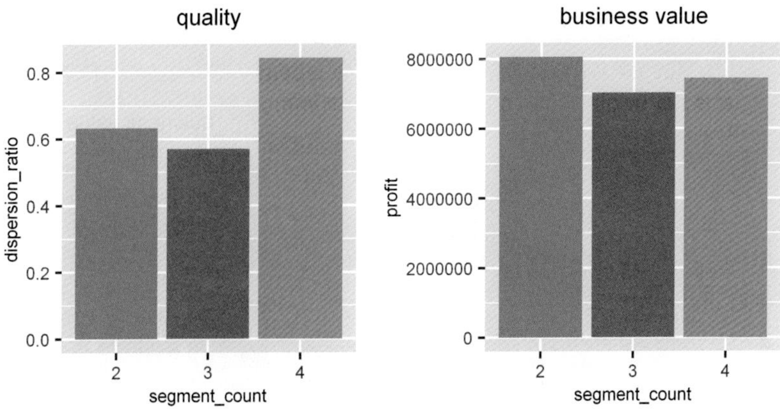

10.7.7 Sensitivity Analysis

It's worth doing some sensitivity analysis to get a feel for how much our assumptions, reflected in the business parameters, could affect the business results.

Would we try a different strategy if we could develop new bands at a lower fixed cost? Developing 4 new bands would result in the highest profit if we could get fixed cost down from $1,000,000 per band to $500,000 per band.

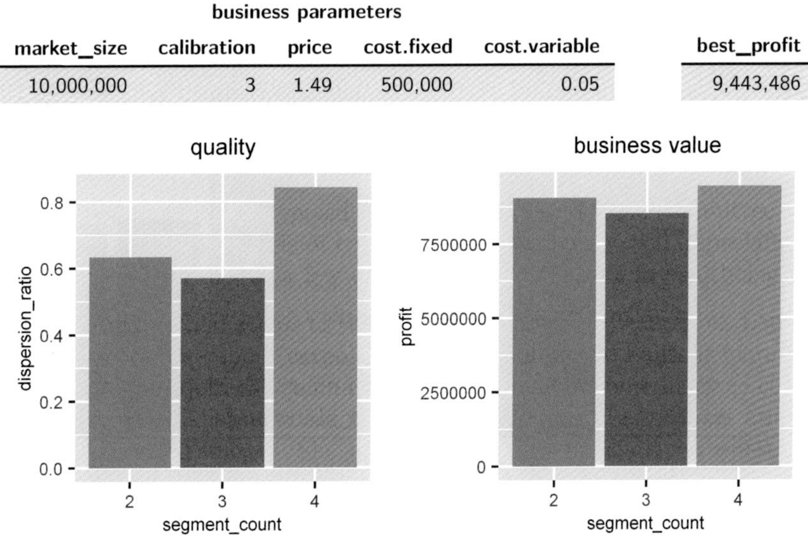

business parameters						best_profit
market_size	calibration	price	cost.fixed	cost.variable		best_profit
10,000,000	3	1.49	500,000	0.05		9,443,486

Would we try a different strategy if we could sell product at a higher price? Developing 4 bands would result in highest profit if we could charge $2.49 per unit instead of $1.49 per unit.

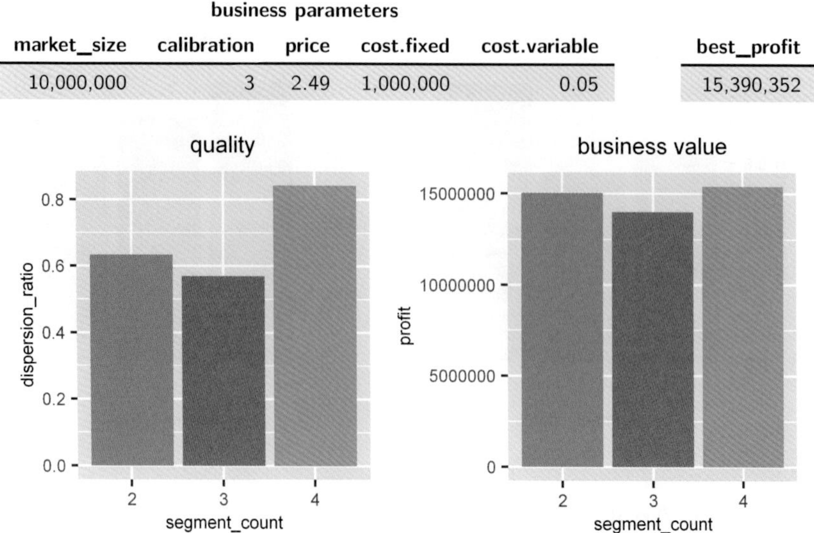

business parameters						best_profit
market_size	calibration	price	cost.fixed	cost.variable		best_profit
10,000,000	3	2.49	1,000,000	0.05		15,390,352

How sure are we about the formula to estimate market share? Would we try a different strategy if only small changes in the formula could produce a wide variety of business results? Developing 2 bands would still result in highest profit if we assumed calibration factor 2 instead of 3, though that highest profit would be lower.

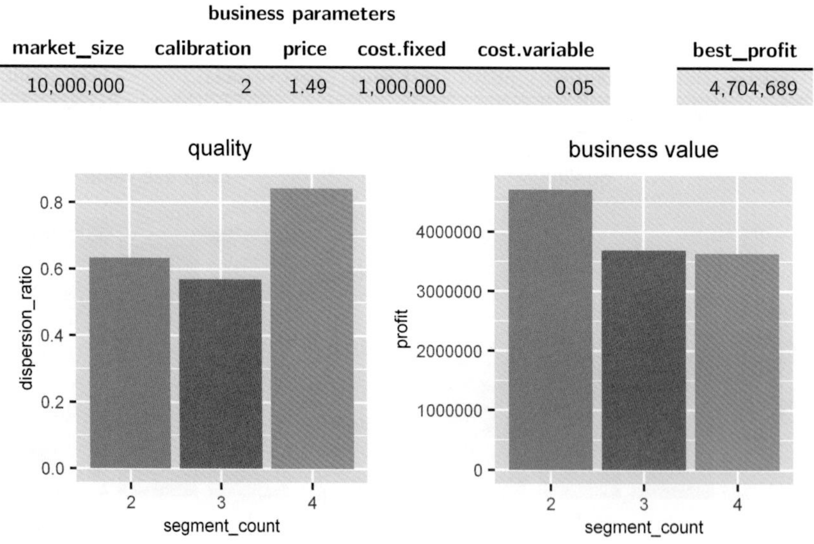

business parameters						best_profit
market_size	calibration	price	cost.fixed	cost.variable		best_profit
10,000,000	2	1.49	1,000,000	0.05		4,704,689

10.7.8 Reveal

The reference dataset used here to demonstrate market segmentation by cluster analysis is actually based on the classic mushroom dataset, which describes 22 features of 8,124 observed mushrooms. Here are the 22 variables, their meanings, and their possible values.

var	meaning
X7	cap-surface=fibrous
X8	cap-surface=grooves
X9	cap-surface=scaly
X10	cap-surface=smooth

var	meaning
X62	stalk-surface-above-ring=fibrous
X63	stalk-surface-above-ring=scaly
X64	stalk-surface-above-ring=silky
X65	stalk-surface-above-ring=smooth

var	meaning
X90	veil-color=brown
X91	veil-color=orange
X92	veil-color=white
X93	veil-color=yellow

var	meaning
X21	bruises?=bruises
X22	bruises?=no

var	meaning
X39	gill-size=broad
X40	gill-size=narrow

var	meaning
X53	stalk-shape=enlarging
X54	stalk-shape=tapering

var	meaning
X36	gill-spacing=close
X37	gill-spacing=crowded
X38	gill-spacing=distant

var	meaning
X88	veil-type=partial
X89	veil-type=universal

var	meaning
X94	ring-number=none
X95	ring-number=one
X96	ring-number=two

var	meaning
X32	gill-attachment=attached
X33	gill-attachment=descending
X34	gill-attachment=free
X35	gill-attachment=notched

var	meaning
X66	stalk-surface-below-ring=fibrous
X67	stalk-surface-below-ring=scaly
X68	stalk-surface-below-ring=silky
X69	stalk-surface-below-ring=smooth

var	meaning
X1	cap-shape=bell
X2	cap-shape=conical
X3	cap-shape=convex
X4	cap-shape=flat
X5	cap-shape=knobbed
X6	cap-shape=sunken

var	meaning
X55	stalk-root=bulbous
X56	stalk-root=club
X57	stalk-root=cup
X58	stalk-root=equal
X59	stalk-root=rhizomorphs
X60	stalk-root=rooted
X61	stalk-root=missing

var	meaning
X114	population=abundant
X115	population=clustered
X116	population=numerous
X117	population=scattered
X118	population=several
X119	population=solitary

var	meaning
X70	stalk-color-above-ring=brown
X71	stalk-color-above-ring=buff
X72	stalk-color-above-ring=cinnamon
X73	stalk-color-above-ring=gray
X74	stalk-color-above-ring=orange
X75	stalk-color-above-ring=pink
X76	stalk-color-above-ring=red
X77	stalk-color-above-ring=white
X78	stalk-color-above-ring=yellow

var	meaning
X79	stalk-color-below-ring=brown
X80	stalk-color-below-ring=buff
X81	stalk-color-below-ring=cinnamon
X82	stalk-color-below-ring=gray
X83	stalk-color-below-ring=orange
X84	stalk-color-below-ring=pink
X85	stalk-color-below-ring=red
X86	stalk-color-below-ring=white
X87	stalk-color-below-ring=yellow

var	meaning
X11	cap-color=brown
X12	cap-color=buff
X13	cap-color=cinnamon
X14	cap-color=gray
X15	cap-color=green
X16	cap-color=pink
X17	cap-color=purple
X18	cap-color=red
X19	cap-color=white
X20	cap-color=yellow

var	meaning
X23	odor=almond
X24	odor=anise
X25	odor=creosote
X26	odor=fishy
X27	odor=foul
X28	odor=musty
X29	odor=none
X30	odor=pungent
X31	odor=spicy

var	meaning
X105	spore-print-color=black
X106	spore-print-color=brown
X107	spore-print-color=buff
X108	spore-print-color=chocolate
X109	spore-print-color=green
X110	spore-print-color=orange
X111	spore-print-color=purple
X112	spore-print-color=white
X113	spore-print-color=yellow

var	meaning
X41	gill-color=black
X42	gill-color=brown
X43	gill-color=buff
X44	gill-color=chocolate
X45	gill-color=gray
X46	gill-color=green
X47	gill-color=orange
X48	gill-color=pink
X49	gill-color=purple
X50	gill-color=red
X51	gill-color=white
X52	gill-color=yellow

var	meaning
X97	ring-type=cobwebby
X98	ring-type=evanescent
X99	ring-type=flaring
X100	ring-type=large
X101	ring-type=none
X102	ring-type=pendant
X103	ring-type=sheathing
X104	ring-type=zone

var	meaning
X120	habitat=grasses
X121	habitat=leaves
X122	habitat=meadows
X123	habitat=paths
X124	habitat=urban
X125	habitat=waste
X126	habitat=woods

The classic mushroom dataset also includes a class variable. That's the V_1 variable that we set aside when we first retrieved the dataset. The class variable indicates whether an observed mushroom is edible (0) or poison (1). Here is the dataset visualized as a scatterplot of the first and second principal component variables, color-coded by edible/poison class. We see that mushrooms with lower PC_1 values are mostly poison, and mushrooms with higher PC_1 values are mostly edible, except for several mushrooms with PC_1 values around 1 and PC_2 values around 0 or -1.

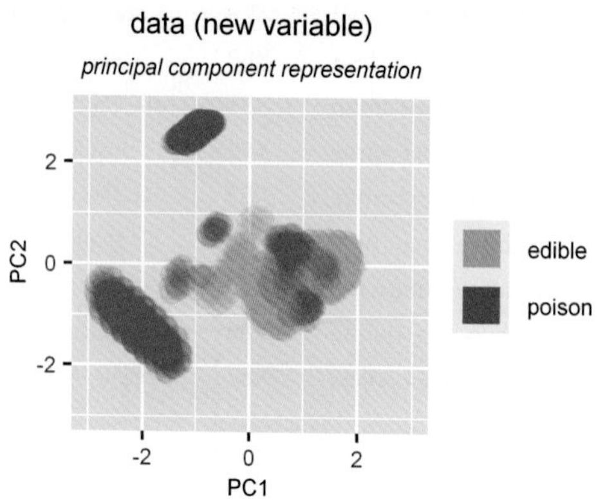

How well did our segmentation models, when viewed as mushroom cluster models, detect the poison mushrooms? Here are the models visualized as scatterplots of the dataset's first and second principal component variables, color-coded by cluster, overlaid on clouds color-coded by edible/poison class. The 4-cluster model did pretty well at detecting the poison mushrooms. All mushrooms in cluster 3 and 90% of mushrooms in cluster 1 are edible. All mushrooms in cluster 4 are poison. Mushrooms in cluster 2 are those for which it's just too hard tell.

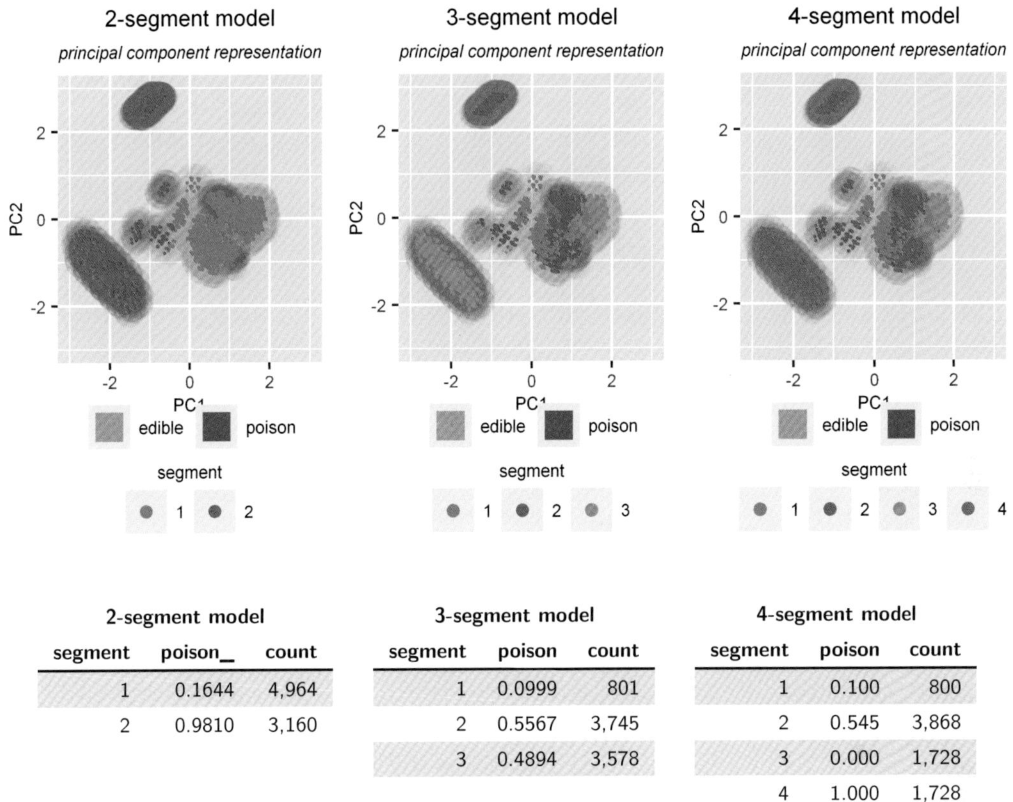

2-segment model

segment	poison_	count
1	0.1644	4,964
2	0.9810	3,160

3-segment model

segment	poison	count
1	0.0999	801
2	0.5567	3,745
3	0.4894	3,578

4-segment model

segment	poison	count
1	0.100	800
2	0.545	3,868
3	0.000	1,728
4	1.000	1,728

Note that the same one cluster analysis here produced useful results under 2 completely different interpretations of what the reference dataset even represents: music taste survey responses, mushroom features.

11 | Special Data Types

Learning Objectives

Terms

Know the terms:

- Text mining
- Text processing
- Natural language processing (NLP)
- Corpus
- Document
- Simplified text
- Document-term matrix (DTM)
- Stopwords
- Stemming
- Token
- Tokenization
- Bag of words
- Bi-gram
- n-gram
- Sparse variable
- Pruning
- Time series
- Timestep
- Forecast
- Viewpoint
- Horizon
- Lookback
- Lookahead
- Direct approach
- Recursive approach
- Time series cross-validation
- Network
- Nodes
- Links
- Network diagram
- Adjacency matrix
- Link list
- Shortest path length
- Indegree
- Outdegree
- Betweenness centrality
- Average path length
- Closeness centrality
- Eccentricity
- Eigenvector centrality
- Random walk method
- PageRank
- PageRank with dampening
- PageRank method
- Collaborative filtering method
- Bipartite graph (or bigraph)
- Inter-observation correlation
- Simple collaborative filtering
- Collaborative filtering with weighting
- Collaborative filtering with calibrated weighting
- Collaborative filtering with calibrated weighting, item-based

Effects of Assumptions

Know the effects of assumptions:

- Effect of simplifying text on a model and its predictions
- Effect of the n-gram degree on a model and its predictions
- Effect of removing sparse variables on a model and its predictions
- Effect of forecasting by direct approach vs. recursive approach
- Effect of dampening within the PageRank method

Use the Methods

Know how to use the methods:

- Transform a corpus to simplified text representation.
- Transform a corpus to document-term matrix representation.
- Prune a document-term matrix by sparse variable analysis.
- Transform a new document to ready it for prediction.
- Compute a model based on text data.
- Compute a prediction using a model based on text data.
- Prepare time series data for analytical modeling.
- Compute models based on prepared time series data.
- Prepare a new observation for forecasting.
- Forecast a horizon using the direct approach.
- Forecast a horizon using the recursive approach.
- Evaluate a model based on the direct approach by in-sample, out-of-sample, and cross-validation performance.
- Evaluate a model based on the recursive approach by in-sample, out-of-sample, and cross-validation performance.
- Compute a variety of network statistics applied to a network.
- Compute the PageRank values of nodes in a network, without dampening.
- Compute the PageRank values of nodes in a network, with dampening.
- Calculate the revised PageRank value of a node at any iteration within the PageRank method.
- Compute a recommendation by collaborative filtering, simple version.
- Compute a recommendation by collaborative filtering, weighted version.
- Compute a recommendation by collaborative filtering, adjusted weighted version.

11.1 Text Data

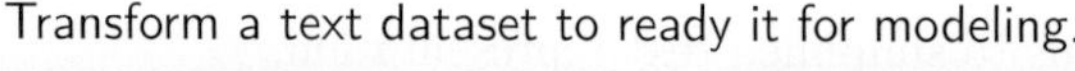
Transform a text dataset to ready it for modeling.

11.1.1 Introduction

Polonius: "What do you read, my lord?"
Hamlet: "Words. words, words."

Modeling relies on the presence of patterns in reference datasets, and some of those patterns might occur in text. For example, customer service operations at an application service provider might need to know if customer comments on social media indicate satisfaction or dissatisfaction with the company's products. There could be many thousands of comments across many channels, so getting people to read all of them would be slow and costly. Operations would be glad of a predictive model that automatically discerns sentiment expressed in the comments.

11.1.2 About Text Data

Analysis with text data is about applying analysis methods to text documents represented as a multivariate dataset, rich with information about document features. Analysis with text data is also known as **text mining**, **text processing**, **natural language processing** (when the text is a natural language), and **NLP**.

A **corpus** is a collection of text **documents**. Each document can be a book, an article, a page, a paragraph, a sentence, or any unit of text.

In analysis with text, a corpus is often represented as **simplified text**, and further as a **document-term matrix**, also known as a **DTM**.

Text in simplified text representation is text that has been transformed by any of several operations, rendering it easier to find relationships among the text elements. Some information is lost in the transformation of the corpus from its original representation, but that can be acceptable if it facilitates effective modeling. Popular operations include these:

- **Encoding:** Replace any unusual characters with similar standard Latin letters.
- **Case:** Replace any upper case letters with corresponding lower case letters.
- **Numbers:** Remove any numbers.
- **Punctuation:** Remove any punctuation.
- **Special Characters:** Remove any special characters.
- **Stopwords:** Remove any inconsequential words, like "a", "the", "we", "in", and so on. These are known as **stopwords**.
- **Stemming:** Reduce all words to their roots, or close approximations, by stripping common suffixes like "-ing", "-ion", "-ness", "-s", "-e", and so on. This is known as **stemming**.
- **Whitespace:** Remove any whitespace like spaces, new lines, etc.

Text in document-term matrix representation is text that has been transformed into a table, in which each observation corresponds to a document, each variable corresponds to some feature of the document called a **token**, and each value indicates the number of times the token appears in the document. Each token corresponds to a text element, like a word, or a set of text elements that appear next to each other. A token corresponding to 1 text element is a 1-gram, a token corresponding to a pair of text elements is a 2-gram, and, in general, a token corresponding to n text elements is an **n-gram**. **Tokenization** is the process of identifying the tokens. Some information is lost in the transformation of the corpus from its original representation, but that can be acceptable if it facilitates effective modeling. Popular versions of document-term matrix include these:

- **Bag of Words:** The set of tokens (variables) is all unique words (1-grams) appearing anywhere in the corpus.
- **2-Gram:** The set of tokens (variables) is all unique pairs of words appearing next to each other (2-grams) anywhere in the corpus.
- **1,2-Gram:** The set of tokens (variables) is all unique words (1-grams) plus all unique pairs of words appearing next to each other (2-grams) anywhere in the corpus.
- *and many others ...*

A corpus in document-term matrix representation can include many **sparse variables**, which contain mostly 0 values, and are oftentimes not very useful for modeling. **Pruning** removes sparse variables from the document-term matrix, resulting in a smaller and more useful representation.

Models can be constructed using any of a variety of model construction methods applied to a reference corpus in document-term matrix representation.

To predict the class or outcome of new documents, first transform the new documents to document-term matrix representation as expected by the model making the predictions. This involves simplifying and tokenizing the new documents in the same way that the reference corpus was. Further, reconcile variables in the new document-term matrix by removing any variables that don't appear in the reference corpus, and adding any variables that are missing. Set the values of the added variables to 0 to indicate no appearance of the corresponding tokens in the new documents.

11.1.3 Data

Consider this reference classified corpus and new unclassified document. The corpus is represented as a dataset comprising 10 observations and 2 variables. Each observation corresponds to a document, which in this case is a sentence. The class variable indicates the source of the text, A or B. The text variable indicates the text itself.

data

class	text
A	Good decisions come from experience. Experience comes from making bad decisions.
A	There are lies, there are damn lies, and then there are statistics.
A	A person with a new idea is a crank until the idea succeeds.
A	When everyone is looking for gold, it's a good time to be in the pick and shovel business.
A	The secret of success is making your vocation your vacation.
B	No person will make a great business who wants to do it all himself or get all the credit.
B	There is no way of making a business successful that can vie with the policy of promoting those who render exceptional service.
B	No man can become rich without himself enriching others.
B	The secret of success lies not in doing your own work but in recognizing the best person to do it.
B	Surplus wealth is a sacred trust which its possessor is bound to administer in his lifetime for the good of the community.

new

text
My axiom is, to succeed in business: avoid my example.

Does the new document come from source A or B? Let's transform the corpus to a representation appropriate for modeling, construct a model, and predict the source of the new document.

11.1.4 Transform

Transform the reference corpus first to simplified text representation and then to document-term matrix representation.

11.1.4.1 Simplified Text Representation

Simplify the text in these 8 ways:

- Replace any unusual characters with similar standard Latin letters.
- Replace any upper-case letters with corresponding lower case letters.
- Remove any numbers.
- Remove any punctuation.
- Remove any special characters.
- Remove any stopwords.
- Stem all words.
- Remove any whitespace.

Here is the resulting corpus in simplified text representation:

data

class	text
A	good decis come experi experi come make bad decis
A	lie damn lie statist
A	person new idea crank idea succeed
A	everyon look gold good time pick shovel busi
A	secret success make vocat vacat
B	person will make great busi want get credit
B	way make busi success can vie polici promot render except servic
B	man can becom rich without enrich other
B	secret success lie work recogn best person
B	surplus wealth sacr trust possessor bound administ lifetim good communiti

11.1.4.2 Document-Term Matrix Representation

Transform the simplified text to document-term matrix representation.

Bag of Words Start by transforming the simplified text to a bag of words, which is the simplest version of document-term matrix. Each observation still corresponds to 1 of the 10 unique documents. Each variable corresponds to a 1-gram token: 1 of the 56 unique words appearing anywhere in the corpus. Values indicate the number of times the token appears in the document. See that the token "administ" appears once in document 10; the token "busi" appears once in document 4, once in document 6, and once in document 7; the token "come" appears twice in document 1; and similarly for the other tokens.

dtm *size 10×56, first few variables shown*

administ	bad	becom	best	bound	busi	can	come	communiti	crank	credit	damn
0	1	0	0	0	0	0	2	0	0	0	0
0	0	0	0	0	0	0	0	0	0	0	1
0	0	0	0	0	0	0	0	0	1	0	0
0	0	0	0	0	1	0	0	0	0	0	0
0	0	0	0	0	0	0	0	0	0	0	0
0	0	0	0	0	1	0	0	0	0	1	0
0	0	0	0	0	1	1	0	0	0	0	0
0	0	1	0	0	0	1	0	0	0	0	0
0	0	0	1	0	0	0	0	0	0	0	0
1	0	0	0	1	0	0	0	1	0	0	0

1,2-Grams To further describe the text, enhance the document-term matrix by adding variables for 2-gram tokens, which are pairs of words that appear next to each other anywhere in the text. That results in 120 variables: 56 corresponding to 1-gram tokens plus 64 corresponding to 2-gram tokens. See that the token "administ_lifetim" appears once in document 10, as reflected by the words "administ" and "lifetim" appearing next to each other there. Similarly for the other tokens. We could potentially describe the text in even more detail by adding even more variables to indicate other relationships between words, but we'll stop here.

dtm *size 10×120, first few variables shown*

administ	administ_lifetim	bad	bad_decis	becom	becom_rich	best	best_person	bound
0	0	1	1	0	0	0	0	0
0	0	0	0	0	0	0	0	0
0	0	0	0	0	0	0	0	0
0	0	0	0	0	0	0	0	0
0	0	0	0	0	0	0	0	0
0	0	0	0	0	0	0	0	0
0	0	0	0	0	0	0	0	0
0	0	0	0	1	1	0	0	0
0	0	0	0	0	0	1	1	0
1	1	0	0	0	0	0	0	1

Pruning Every variable contains at least 1 non-zero value. However, most of the variables don't contain much more than that, and so are not very useful for distinguishing documents. For example, see that the token "administ" appears in only 1 out of 10 documents. So, while the *administ* variable does say something about how 1 document is different from the others, it does not say anything about how the other 90% of documents differ from each other.

Remove the sparse variables, since they are not very useful. Here we choose to remove variables which contain more than 85% 0 values. That leaves 9 variables: 8 corresponding to 1-gram tokens plus 1 corresponding to a 2-gram token.

dtm *size 10×9*

busi	can	good	lie	make	person	secret	secret_success	success
0	0	1	0	1	0	0	0	0
0	0	0	2	0	0	0	0	0
0	0	0	0	0	1	0	0	0
1	0	1	0	0	0	0	0	0
0	0	0	0	1	0	1	1	1
1	0	0	0	1	1	0	0	0
1	1	0	0	1	0	0	0	1
0	1	0	0	0	0	0	0	0
0	0	0	1	0	1	1	1	1
0	0	1	0	0	0	0	0	0

Replace the text variable with the matrix variables. The reference corpus has now been transformed to a representation appropriate for modeling.

data *size 10×10*

class	busi	can	good	lie	make	person	secret	secret_success	success
A	0	0	1	0	1	0	0	0	0
A	0	0	0	2	0	0	0	0	0
A	0	0	0	0	0	1	0	0	0
A	1	0	1	0	0	0	0	0	0
A	0	0	0	0	1	0	1	1	1
B	1	0	0	0	1	1	0	0	0
B	1	1	0	0	1	0	0	0	1
B	0	1	0	0	0	0	0	0	0
B	0	0	0	1	0	1	1	1	1
B	0	0	1	0	0	0	0	0	0

11.1.5 Model

Build a predictive model based on the reference corpus. Here we choose to build the model using the decision tree method:

model

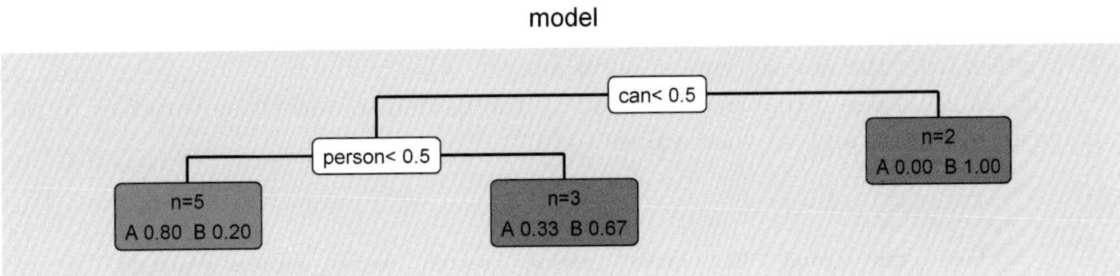

Evaluate the model by applying it to the reference corpus. In-sample accuracy is 80%. False positive rate and false negative rate are both 20%.

data *size 10×11*

class	class.predicted	busi	can	good	lie	make	person	secret	secret_success	success
A	A	0	0	1	0	1	0	0	0	0
A	A	0	0	0	2	0	0	0	0	0
A	B	0	0	0	0	0	1	0	0	0
A	A	1	0	1	0	0	0	0	0	0
A	A	0	0	0	0	1	0	1	1	1
B	B	1	0	0	0	1	1	0	0	0
B	B	1	1	0	0	1	0	0	0	1
B	B	0	1	0	0	0	0	0	0	0
B	B	0	0	0	1	0	1	1	1	1
B	A	0	0	1	0	0	0	0	0	0

11.1.6 Predict

Simplify the text of the new document, using the same simplifications that were applied to the text of the reference corpus.

new

text
axiom succeed busi avoid exampl

Transform the simplified text to document-term matrix representation, using the same 1,2-gram tokenization that was applied to the simplified text of the reference corpus. Do not remove sparse variables – with just 1 document, there aren't any sparse variables, but you wouldn't remove any even if there were. That results in 9 variables: 5 corresponding to 1-gram tokens plus 4 corresponding to 2-gram tokens. Note that these variables are not the same as those in the reference document-term matrix.

dtm *size 1×9*

avoid	avoid_exampl	axiom	axiom_succeed	busi	busi_avoid	exampl	succeed	succeed_busi
1	1	1	1	1	1	1	1	1

Reconcile variables in the new document-term matrix with the variables expected by the model, which are *busi, can, good, lie, make, person, secret, secret success, success*. In the new document-term matrix, *busi* is the only variable expected by the model, so remove the other variables from the new document-term matrix. Also in the new document-term matrix, some variables are missing that are expected by the model, so add those variables to the new document-term matrix and set their values to 0.

dtm *size 1×9*

busi	can	good	lie	make	person	secret	secret_success	success
1	0	0	0	0	0	0	0	0

Replace the text variable with the matrix variables. The new document has now been transformed to a representation appropriate for prediction by the model.

new *size 1×9*

busi	can	good	lie	make	person	secret	secret_success	success
1	0	0	0	0	0	0	0	0

Predict the class of the new document, using the model applied to the new document-term matrix. The model predicts that the document comes from source A.

new

class.predicted	busi	can	good	lie	make	person	secret	secret_success	success
A	1	0	0	0	0	0	0	0	0

Here is the prediction shown alongside of the new document in its original, non-transformed representation:

new

class.predicted	text
A	My axiom is, to succeed in business: avoid my example.

11.2 Time Series Data

Transform a time series dataset to ready it for modeling.

11.2.1 Introduction

Plato: "Time is the moving image of reality."
Albert Einstein: "The only reason for time is so that everything doesn't happen at once."
Doctor Who: "People assume that time is a strict progression of cause to effect, but actually, from a non-linear, non-subjective viewpoint, it's more like a big ball of wibbly-wobbly, timey-wimey stuff."

Analytical modeling relies on the presence of patterns in reference datasets, and some of those patterns might occur over time. For example, planners at a power plant might need to forecast customer demand for electricity a few days from now. They need to know in advance because electricity generation doesn't happen instantly at the push of a button, but rather it ramps up over time, so it must be anticipated. It doesn't shut off instantly either, but rather ramps down over time. If the planners underestimate demand, then there won't be enough by the time customers are ready for it. If the planners overestimate, it'll be costly. The planners know that there are several factors affecting demand: temperature, day of the week, time of the year, energy efficiency programs, and more. But here it is key that the planners can get an even better idea of what demand will be just by looking back at what recent demand has been.

Analysis with time series data is about applying analysis methods to time series data represented as an unordered, multivariate dataset, rich with information about temporal relationships.

11.2.2 About Time Series Data

A **time series** dataset is a dataset in which the order of observations is meaningful. Each observation is about something measured at a particular **timestep**. The order of observations reflects a chronological sequence of evenly spaced timesteps.

A **forecast** is a special kind of prediction, where the predictor variables provide information about the past, and the class or outcome variable is about something that could happen in the future. A forecast must therefore be made with respect to a **viewpoint**, which is a particular timestep separating the past from the future. A viewpoint prevents information from the future being used to forecast the future. A **horizon** is the set of timesteps in the future being forecasted.

Many otherwise useful analytical modeling methods don't work with time series data because they don't recognize the order of observations in a dataset as meaningful. However, any times series dataset can be prepared by adding synthetic variables in such a way so that these methods do work with it. A **lookback** is a synthetic variable calculated as the class or outcome variable offset forward by some number of timesteps. For any observation then, this effectively incorporates information into the observation about classes or outcomes that occurred previously, exposing patterns over time without the need to preserve the order of observations. Similarly, a **lookahead** is a synthetic variable calculated as the class or outcome variable offset backward by some number of timesteps. This effectively incorporates information into an observation about classes or outcomes that will occur later.

$$b_{1i} = x_{i-1} \quad b_{2i} = x_{i-2} \quad b_{3i} = x_{i-3} \quad \ldots$$
$$a_{1i} = x_{i+1} \quad a_{2i} = x_{i+2} \quad a_{3i} = x_{i+3} \quad \ldots$$

where ...

- x_{i-1}, x_{i-2}, x_{i-3}, ... are the classes or outcomes at timesteps $i-1$, $i-2$, $i-3$, ...
- b_{1i}, b_{2i}, b_{3i}, ... are the lookbacks at timestep i
- a_{1i}, a_{2i}, a_{3i}, ... are the lookaheads at timestep i

For example, see here how observations in a portion of a time series dataset get prepared with 3 lookbacks and 3 lookaheads.

time series dataset	prepared dataset						
outcome	outcome	back.1	back.2	back.3	ahead.1	ahead.2	ahead.3
10	10	0	-10	-20	20	30	40
20	20	10	0	-10	30	40	50
30	30	20	10	0	40	50	60
40	40	30	20	10	50	60	70

There are 2 popular approaches to model construction and forecasting with prepared time series data. In the **direct approach**, construct several models, each to predict a lookahead corresponding to a different timestep in the horizon. In the **recursive approach**, construct 1 model to predict the outcome at the viewpoint, and then iteratively advance the viewpoint and predict again until all timesteps in the horizon have been predicted, substituting earlier predictions for any unavailable lookbacks along the way.

Here is how the ***direct approach*** works:

$$\hat{x}_{v+i} \quad = \quad model_i(b_{1v}, b_{2v}, \ldots), \; {\scriptstyle v+i \in H}$$

where ...

- v is the viewpoint (a timestamp)
- H is the horizon (a set of timestamps occurring later than the viewpoint)
- $\hat{x}_{v+i}$ is the predicted class or outcome at timestep $v{+}i$
- $model_i$ is the model to predict lookahead i
- b_{1v}, b_{2v}, ... are the lookbacks at viewpoint v

Here is how the ***recursive approach*** works:

$$\begin{aligned}
\hat{x}_v &= model_0(b_{1v}, b_{2v}, b_{3v}, \ldots) \\
\hat{x}_{v+1} &= model_0(x_v, b_{1v}, b_{2v}, \ldots) \\
\hat{x}_{v+2} &= model_0(x_{v+1}, x_v, b_{1v}, \ldots) \\
&\vdots \\
\hat{x}_{v+i} &= model_0(x_{v+i-1}, x_{v+i-2}, x_{v+i-3}, \ldots),\ {\scriptstyle v+i \in H}
\end{aligned}$$

where ...

- v is the viewpoint (a timestamp)
- H is the horizon (a set of timestamps occurring later than the viewpoint)
- $\hat{x}_{v+i}$ is the predicted class or outcome at timestep $v{+}i$
- $model_0$ is the model to predict class or outcome
- b_{1v}, b_{2v}, ... are the lookbacks at viewpoint v

Both the direct and recursive approaches are subject to in-sample, out-of-sample, and cross-validation evaluation, with the caveat that the timesteps known to a training partition must occur earlier than any timesteps known to its corresponding testing partition.

For out-of-sample evaluation, choose a timestep to serve as the train/test boundary, then assign all observations with information about timesteps occurring earlier than the boundary to the training partition, and assign all observations with information about timestamps occurring at or later than the boundary to the testing partition. The observations at timesteps near the boundary will typically include lookaheads with information about timesteps at or later than the boundary, or lookbacks with information about timesteps earlier than the boundary, so exclude these observations from both the training and testing partitions.

time series dataset (1000 observations, 25% holdout)

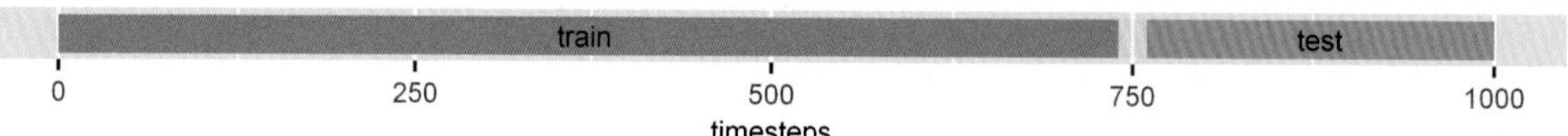

For cross-validation evaluation, choose a number of folds n. Separate the dataset into $n{+}1$ parts, approximately equal-sized, preserving the order of observations. Treat the observations in parts

2, 3, 4, ..., $n+1$ as the test partitions for folds 1, 2, 3, ..., n. Treat the observations at the corresponding earlier timesteps as the training partitions for folds 1, 2, 3, ..., n.

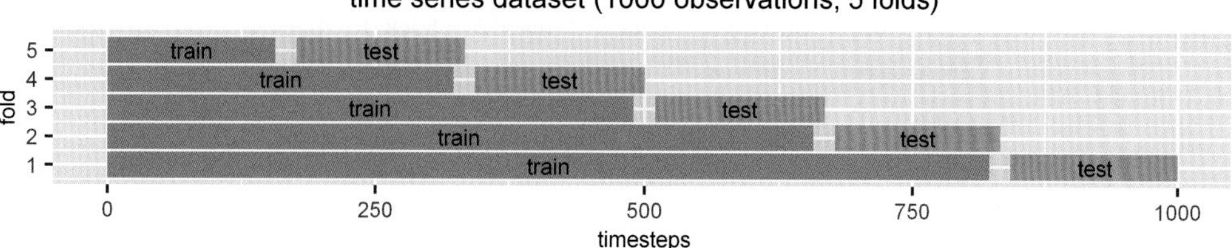

11.2.3 Data

Consider this reference time series dataset of outcomes spanning just over a year. What outcome can you expect next? Let's forecast the outcomes over a 3-day horizon starting 1 day ahead of a viewpoint at January 29, 2014.

data *size 396×2, first few observations shown*

day	outcome
2013-01-01	58,714
2013-01-02	59,472
2013-01-03	56,288
2013-01-04	56,493
2013-01-05	57,718
2013-01-06	61,021

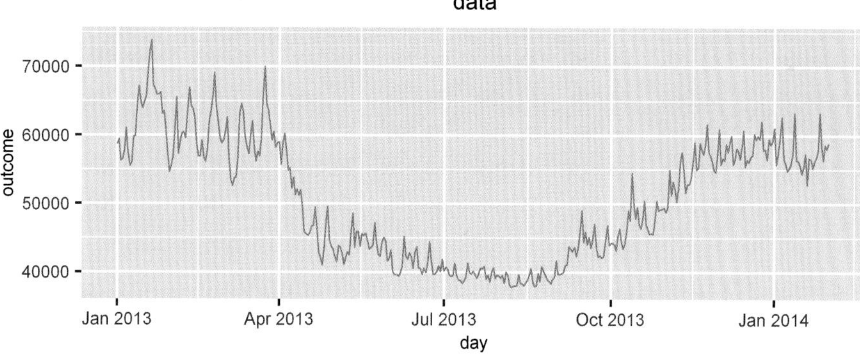

11.2.4 Prepare Data

Convert the time series dataset to cross-sectional representation, given some lookbacks and lookaheads. Here we choose lookbacks and lookaheads to forecast a 3-day horizon starting 1 day ahead of a viewpoint, based on what happened the previous 4 days:

- lookbacks: 1, 2, 3, 4
- lookaheads: 1, 2, 3

For each lookback, add a synthetic variable derived from the outcome variable shifted forward by the appropriate number of days.

data *size 396×6, first few observations shown*

day	outcome	back.1	back.2	back.3	back.4
2013-01-01	58,714	NA	NA	NA	NA
2013-01-02	59,472	58,714	NA	NA	NA
2013-01-03	56,288	59,472	58,714	NA	NA
2013-01-04	56,493	56,288	59,472	58,714	NA
2013-01-05	57,718	56,493	56,288	59,472	58,714
2013-01-06	61,021	57,718	56,493	56,288	59,472

For each lookahead, add a synthetic variable derived from the outcome variable shifted backward by the appropriate number of days.

data *size 396×9, first few observations shown*

day	outcome	back.1	back.2	back.3	back.4	ahead.1	ahead.2	ahead.3
2013-01-01	58,714	NA	NA	NA	NA	59,472	56,288	56,493
2013-01-02	59,472	58,714	NA	NA	NA	56,288	56,493	57,718
2013-01-03	56,288	59,472	58,714	NA	NA	56,493	57,718	61,021
2013-01-04	56,493	56,288	59,472	58,714	NA	57,718	61,021	57,471
2013-01-05	57,718	56,493	56,288	59,472	58,714	61,021	57,471	55,542
2013-01-06	61,021	57,718	56,493	56,288	59,472	57,471	55,542	56,025

data *size 396×9, last few observations shown*

day	outcome	back.1	back.2	back.3	back.4	ahead.1	ahead.2	ahead.3
2014-01-26	63,299	57,701	56,789	56,251	55,231	58,416	56,355	58,649
2014-01-27	58,416	63,299	57,701	56,789	56,251	56,355	58,649	58,043
2014-01-28	56,355	58,416	63,299	57,701	56,789	58,649	58,043	58,932
2014-01-29	58,649	56,355	58,416	63,299	57,701	58,043	58,932	NA
2014-01-30	58,043	58,649	56,355	58,416	63,299	58,932	NA	NA
2014-01-31	58,932	58,043	58,649	56,355	58,416	NA	NA	NA

Discard the first 4 observations and last 3 observations of the resulting dataset because those observations are missing data. The dataset doesn't tell us what happened 1 to 4 days back from the first day of data, nor does it say what happens 1 to 3 days ahead of the last day of data.

data *size 386×9, first few observations shown*

day	outcome	back.1	back.2	back.3	back.4	ahead.1	ahead.2	ahead.3
2013-01-08	55,542	57,471	61,021	57,718	56,493	56,025	59,837	59,900
2013-01-09	56,025	55,542	57,471	61,021	57,718	59,837	59,900	64,332
2013-01-10	59,837	56,025	55,542	57,471	61,021	59,900	64,332	67,181
2013-01-11	59,900	59,837	56,025	55,542	57,471	64,332	67,181	65,087
2013-01-12	64,332	59,900	59,837	56,025	55,542	67,181	65,087	63,969
2013-01-13	67,181	64,332	59,900	59,837	56,025	65,087	63,969	64,919

data *size 386×9, last few observations shown*

day	outcome	back.1	back.2	back.3	back.4	ahead.1	ahead.2	ahead.3
2014-01-23	56,251	55,231	56,494	56,709	52,766	56,789	57,701	63,299
2014-01-24	56,789	56,251	55,231	56,494	56,709	57,701	63,299	58,416
2014-01-25	57,701	56,789	56,251	55,231	56,494	63,299	58,416	56,355
2014-01-26	63,299	57,701	56,789	56,251	55,231	58,416	56,355	58,649
2014-01-27	58,416	63,299	57,701	56,789	56,251	56,355	58,649	58,043
2014-01-28	56,355	58,416	63,299	57,701	56,789	58,649	58,043	58,932

11.2.5 Construct Models

Build 4 models, 1 for outcome and 1 each for the 3 lookaheads, all trained on the reference dataset. Here we choose the linear regression method to build all 4 models:

- ***model.0*** will predict the outcome given a viewpoint and its lookbacks.
  That's effectively forecasting the outcome at the viewpoint given outcomes at 1, 2, 3, and 4 timesteps prior to the viewpoint.
- ***model.1*** will predict the first lookahead given a viewpoint and its lookbacks.
  That's effectively forecasting the outcome at 1 timestep ahead of the viewpoint given outcomes at 1, 2, 3, and 4 timesteps prior to the viewpoint.
- ***model.2*** will predict the second lookahead given a viewpoint and its lookbacks.
  That's effectively forecasting the outcome at 2 timesteps ahead of the viewpoint given outcomes at 1, 2, 3, and 4 timesteps prior to the viewpoint.
- ***model.3*** will predict the third lookahead given a viewpoint and its lookbacks.
  That's effectively forecasting the outcome at 3 timesteps ahead of the viewpoint given outcomes at 1, 2, 3, and 4 timesteps prior to the viewpoint.

model.0

	coefficients
(Intercept)	1,177.8042
back.1	0.8697
back.2	-0.0491
back.3	0.0635
back.4	0.0925

model.1

	coefficients
(Intercept)	2,003.1225
back.1	0.6887
back.2	0.0355
back.3	0.0328
back.4	0.2033

model.2

	coefficients
(Intercept)	2,350.1753
back.1	0.5864
back.2	0.0225
back.3	-0.0555
back.4	0.4002

model.3

	coefficients
(Intercept)	2,588.6769
back.1	0.4715
back.2	-0.0497
back.3	0.1196
back.4	0.4074

11.2.6 Forecast

Set the viewpoint to January 29, 2014. Set the horizon to 3 days starting 1 day ahead of the viewpoint. Also provide an outcome history covering the 4 days prior to the viewpoint because the models require those 4 lookbacks.

history

day	outcome
2014-01-25	57,701
2014-01-26	63,299
2014-01-27	58,416
2014-01-28	56,355

viewpoint

day
2014-01-29

horizon

day
2014-01-30
2014-01-31
2014-02-01

11.2.6.1 Direct Approach

To forecast by the direct approach, prepare a viewpoint observation and apply ***model.1***, ***model.2***, and ***model.3***.

Here is the prepared viewpoint observation. It includes the predictor variables required by the models, which are the 4 lookback variables. The values come from the outcome history: *back*.1 is 56,355, which is the outcome at January 28, 1 timestep prior to the viewpoint January 29; *back*.2 is 58,416, which is the outcome at 2 timesteps prior to the viewpoint; *back*.3 is 63,299, which is 3 timesteps back; *back*.4 is 57,701.

viewpoint

day	back.1	back.2	back.3	back.4
2014-01-29	56,355	58,416	63,299	57,701

Here are the models' predictions given the viewpoint observation. ***model.1*** predicts *ahead*.1 to be 56,698, which corresponds to outcome at January 30. ***model.2*** predicts *ahead*.2 to be 56,290, which corresponds to outcome at January 31. ***model.3*** predicts *ahead*.3 to be 57,337, which corresponds to outcome at February 1. Together they comprise a forecast of the horizon.

horizon

day	outcome.predicted
2014-01-30	56,698
2014-01-31	56,290
2014-02-01	57,337

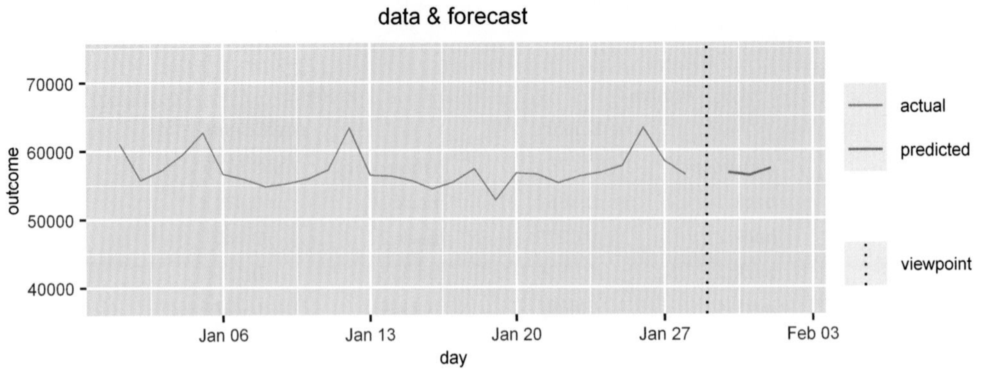

11.2.6.2 Recursive Approach

To forecast by the recursive approach, prepare a viewpoint observation and apply only the model that predicts outcome, several times in succession.

Here is the first prepared viewpoint observation and model prediction. Call this observation **viewpoint.0**. ***model.0*** predicts outcome to be 56,677 at January 29, given **viewpoint.0**.

viewpoint.0

day	back.1	back.2	back.3	back.4
2014-01-29	56,355	58,416	63,299	57,701

prediction.0
56,677

Now that we have a prediction of the outcome at January 29, we can move the viewpoint to January 30 and predict outcome there.

Prepare a new viewpoint at January 30. Call this observation **viewpoint.1**. The values come from the previous prediction and **viewpoint.0**:

- *back*.1 of **viewpoint.1** is 56,677, which is the predicted outcome at January 29, 1 timestep prior to January 30
- *back*.2 of **viewpoint.1** is 56,355, which is *back*.1 of **viewpoint.0**, the outcome at 2 timesteps prior to January 30
- *back*.3 of **viewpoint.1** is 58,416, which is 3 timesteps back
- *back*.4 of **viewpoint.1** is 63,299

model.0 predicts outcome to be 57,266 at January 30, given **viewpoint.1**.

viewpoint.1

day	back.1	back.2	back.3	back.4
2014-01-30	56,677	56,355	58,416	63,299

prediction.1
57,266

Prepare a new viewpoint at January 31. Call this observation **viewpoint.2**. The values come from the previous prediction and **viewpoint.1**:

- *back*.1 of **viewpoint.2** is 57,266, which is the predicted outcome at January 30, 1 timestep prior to January 31
- *back*.2 of **viewpoint.2** is 56,677, which is *back*.1 of **viewpoint.1**, the outcome at 2 timesteps prior to January 31
- *back*.3 of **viewpoint.2** is 56,355, which is 3 timesteps back
- *back*.4 of **viewpoint.2** is 58,416

model.0 predicts outcome to be 57,180 at January 31, given **viewpoint.2**.

viewpoint.2

day	back.1	back.2	back.3	back.4
2014-01-31	57,266	56,677	56,355	58,416

prediction.2
57,180

Prepare a new viewpoint at February 1. Call this observation **viewpoint.3**. The values come from the previous prediction and **viewpoint.2**:

- *back*.1 of **viewpoint.3** is 57,180, which is the predicted outcome at January 31, 1 timestep prior to February 1
- *back*.2 of **viewpoint.3** is 56,266, which is *back*.1 of **viewpoint.2**, the outcome at 2 timesteps prior to February 1
- *back*.3 of **viewpoint.3** is 56,677, which is 3 timesteps back
- *back*.4 of **viewpoint.3** is 56,355

model.0 predicts outcome to be 56,907 at February 1, given **viewpoint.3**.

viewpoint.3

day	back.1	back.2	back.3	back.4
2014-02-01	57,180	57,266	56,677	56,355

prediction.3
56,907

Here are the model predictions given the several viewpoint observations. Together they comprise a forecast of the horizon.

horizon

day	outcome.predicted
2014-01-30	57,266
2014-01-31	57,180
2014-02-01	56,907

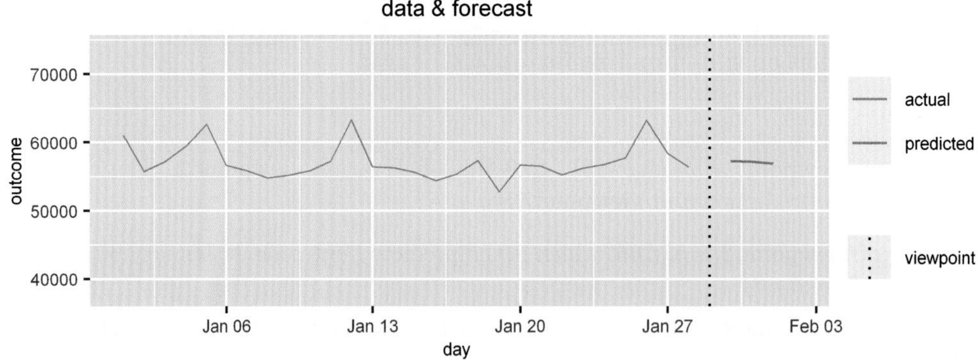

11.2.7 Evaluate by In-Sample Performance

Evaluate the in-sample performance of both the direct approach and recursive approach to predicting 3 timesteps ahead.

11.2.7.1 Direct Approach

To evaluate the direct approach's ability to predict 3 timesteps ahead of a viewpoint, treat all observations of the reference dataset as viewpoints to be tested. Apply ***model.3*** to the viewpoints and compare the actual *ahead*.3 values to the predicted *ahead*.3 values. In-sample RMSE of ***model.3*** to predict 3 timesteps ahead using the direct approach is 3,274.

model.3

	coefficients
(Intercept)	2,588.6769
back.1	0.4715
back.2	-0.0497
back.3	0.1196
back.4	0.4074

data *first few observations shown, a few variables shown*

day	ahead.3	ahead.3.predicted	error
2013-01-08	59,900	56,575	3,325
2013-01-09	64,332	56,736	7,596
2013-01-10	67,181	57,980	9,201
2013-01-11	65,087	58,077	7,010
2013-01-12	63,969	57,189	6,780
2013-01-13	64,919	59,928	4,990

RMSE
3,274

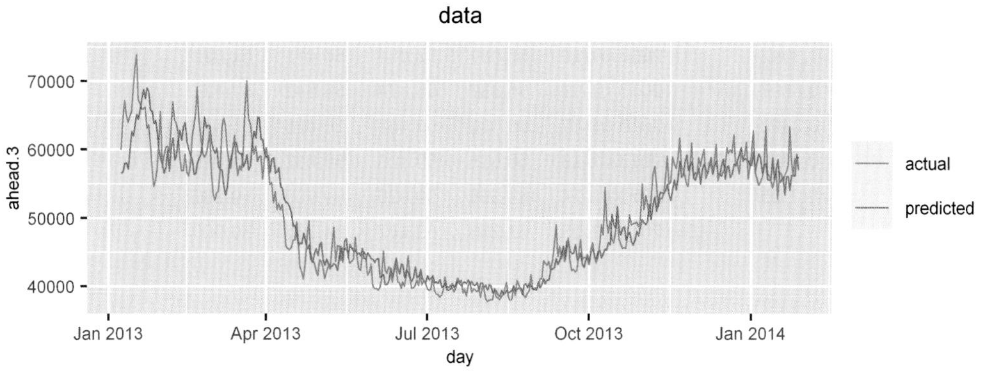

11.2.7.2 Recursive Approach

To evaluate the recursive approach's ability to predict 3 timesteps ahead of a viewpoint, treat all observations of the reference dataset as viewpoints. Apply ***model.0*** to the viewpoints, then revise the dataset according to the predictions and apply ***model.0*** again, several times in succession.

Here are the model predictions given viewpoints taken from the reference dataset:

model.0

	coefficients
(Intercept)	1,177.8042
back.1	0.8697
back.2	-0.0491
back.3	0.0635
back.4	0.0925

data *first few observations shown, a few variables shown*

day	back.1	back.2	back.3	back.4	outcome.predicted
2013-01-08	57,471	61,021	57,718	56,493	57,054
2013-01-09	55,542	57,471	61,021	57,718	55,874
2013-01-10	56,025	55,542	57,471	61,021	56,468
2013-01-11	59,837	56,025	55,542	57,471	59,309
2013-01-12	59,900	59,837	56,025	55,542	59,029
2013-01-13	64,332	59,900	59,837	56,025	63,167

Revise the dataset like this: advance day values; replace *back*.2, *back*.3, and *back*.4 with *back*.1, *back*.2, and *back*.3; replace *back*.1 with the just-predicted outcomes. This effectively creates a new set of viewpoints, each with 1 of its lookbacks predicted by ***model.0***. Apply ***model.0*** to the revised dataset.

model.0

	coefficients
(Intercept)	1,177.8042
back.1	0.8697
back.2	-0.0491
back.3	0.0635
back.4	0.0925

data.1 *first few observations shown, a few variables shown*

day	back.1	back.2	back.3	back.4	outcome.predicted
2013-01-09	57,054	57,471	61,021	57,718	57,189
2013-01-10	55,874	55,542	57,471	61,021	56,337
2013-01-11	56,468	56,025	55,542	57,471	56,380
2013-01-12	59,309	59,837	56,025	55,542	58,515
2013-01-13	59,029	59,900	59,837	56,025	58,555
2013-01-14	63,167	64,332	59,900	59,837	62,293

Revise the dataset again. This effectively creates a new set of viewpoints, each with 2 of its lookbacks predicted by ***model.0***. Apply ***model.0*** to the revised dataset.

model.0

	coefficients
(Intercept)	1,177.8042
back.1	0.8697
back.2	-0.0491
back.3	0.0635
back.4	0.0925

data.2 *first few observations shown, a few variables shown*

day	back.1	back.2	back.3	back.4	outcome.predicted
2013-01-10	57,189	57,054	57,471	61,021	57,406
2013-01-11	56,337	55,874	55,542	57,471	56,273
2013-01-12	56,380	56,468	56,025	55,542	56,133
2013-01-13	58,515	59,309	59,837	56,025	58,138
2013-01-14	58,555	59,029	59,900	59,837	58,542
2013-01-15	62,293	63,167	64,332	59,900	61,877

Revise the dataset again. This effectively creates a new set of viewpoints, each with 3 of its lookbacks predicted by ***model.0***. Apply ***model.0*** to the revised dataset. Note that these new outcome predictions are effectively *ahead*.3 predictions from a viewpoint 3 timesteps back.

model.0

	coefficients
(Intercept)	1,177.8042
back.1	0.8697
back.2	-0.0491
back.3	0.0635
back.4	0.0925

data.3 *first few observations shown, a few variables shown*

day	back.1	back.2	back.3	back.4	outcome.predicted
2013-01-11	57,406	57,189	57,054	57,471	57,234
2013-01-12	56,273	56,337	55,874	55,542	56,037
2013-01-13	56,133	56,380	56,468	56,025	55,995
2013-01-14	58,138	58,515	59,309	59,837	58,167
2013-01-15	58,542	58,555	59,029	59,900	58,505
2013-01-16	61,877	62,293	63,167	64,332	61,894

Return to the original reference dataset and compare the actual *ahead*.3 values with the predicted *ahead*.3 values. In-sample RMSE of ***model.0*** to predict 3 timesteps ahead using the recursive approach is 3,449.

data *first few observations shown, a few variables shown*

day	ahead.3	ahead.3.predicted	error
2013-01-08	59,900	57,234	2,666
2013-01-09	64,332	56,037	8,295
2013-01-10	67,181	55,995	11,186
2013-01-11	65,087	58,167	6,920
2013-01-12	63,969	58,505	5,464
2013-01-13	64,919	61,894	3,024

RMSE
3,449

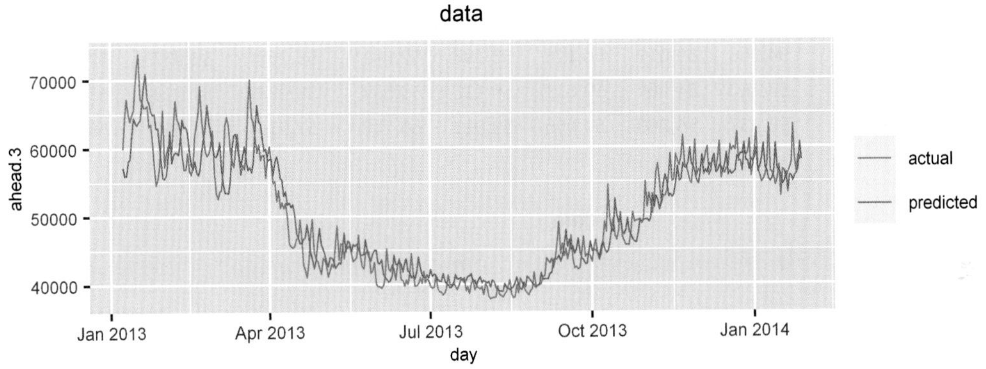

data

11.2.8 Evaluate by Time Series Out-of-Sample Performance

Evaluate the out-of-sample performance of both the direct approach and recursive approach to predicting 3 timesteps ahead.

Here we choose to hold out 20% of the reference dataset for testing, and hold in the remaining 80% for training. Because it's time series data, do not choose observations at random, but rather set the train/test boundary to November 11, 2013, which is the 80% of the way through the reference dataset. The training partition then includes the observations with any information involving timesteps prior to that date. Note that the training partition's latest day is November 7, 2013, because that observation includes information about the outcome at November 10, 2013, in its *ahead*.3 variable. The test partition includes the observations with any information involving timesteps at or after November 11, 2013. The test partition's earliest day is November 15, 2013, because that observation includes information about the outcome at November 11, 2013, in its *back*.4 variable.

data.train *first few observations shown*

day	outcome	back.1	back.2	back.3	back.4	ahead.1	ahead.2	ahead.3
2013-01-08	55,542	57,471	61,021	57,718	56,493	56,025	59,837	59,900
2013-01-09	56,025	55,542	57,471	61,021	57,718	59,837	59,900	64,332
2013-01-10	59,837	56,025	55,542	57,471	61,021	59,900	64,332	67,181
2013-01-11	59,900	59,837	56,025	55,542	57,471	64,332	67,181	65,087
2013-01-12	64,332	59,900	59,837	56,025	55,542	67,181	65,087	63,969
2013-01-13	67,181	64,332	59,900	59,837	56,025	65,087	63,969	64,919

data.test *first few observations shown*

day	outcome	back.1	back.2	back.3	back.4	ahead.1	ahead.2	ahead.3
2013-11-15	53,597	52,841	52,879	51,674	54,831	56,118	59,011	54,966
2013-11-16	56,118	53,597	52,841	52,879	51,674	59,011	54,966	55,260
2013-11-17	59,011	56,118	53,597	52,841	52,879	54,966	55,260	58,937
2013-11-18	54,966	59,011	56,118	53,597	52,841	55,260	58,937	57,915
2013-11-19	55,260	54,966	59,011	56,118	53,597	58,937	57,915	57,257
2013-11-20	58,937	55,260	54,966	59,011	56,118	57,915	57,257	58,624

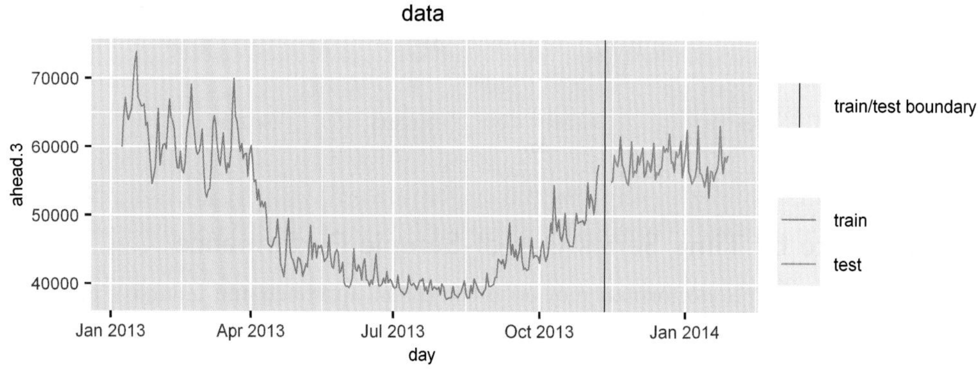

11.2.8.1 Direct Approach

To evaluate the direct approach's ability to predict 3 timesteps ahead, construct a model to predict 3 days ahead based on the training partition. Call this ***model.3.train***. Treat all observations of the test partition as viewpoints to be tested. Apply ***model.3.train*** to the viewpoints and compare the actual *ahead*.3 values to the predicted *ahead*.3 values. Out-of-sample RMSE of ***model.3*** to predict 3 timesteps ahead using the direct approach is 2,617.

model.3

	coefficients
(Intercept)	2,588.6769
back.1	0.4715
back.2	-0.0497
back.3	0.1196
back.4	0.4074

model.3.train

	coefficients
(Intercept)	3,007.1293
back.1	0.5298
back.2	-0.0929
back.3	0.0765
back.4	0.4232

RMSE
2,617

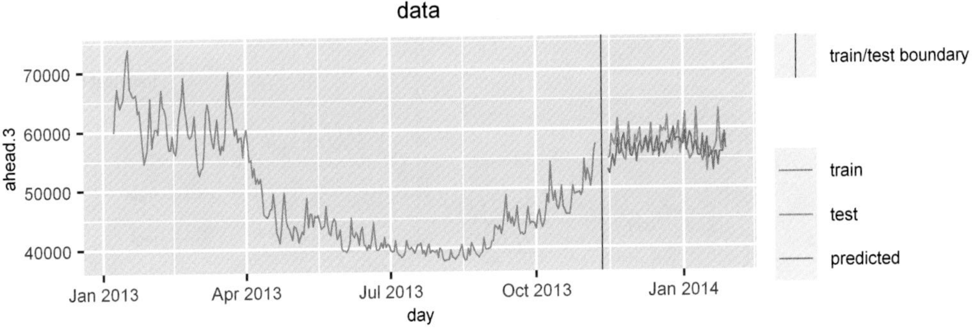

11.2.8.2 Recursive Approach

To evaluate the recursive approach's ability to predict 3 timesteps ahead, construct a model to predict outcome based on the training partition. Call this ***model.0.train***. Treat all observations of the test partition as viewpoints to be tested. Apply ***model.0.train*** to the viewpoints, then revise the dataset according to the predictions and apply ***model.0*** again, several times in succession. Compare the actual *ahead*.3 values to the predicted *ahead*.3 values. Out-of-sample RMSE of ***model.0*** to predict 3 timesteps ahead using the recursive approach is 2,870.

model.0

	coefficients
(Intercept)	1,177.8042
back.1	0.8697
back.2	-0.0491
back.3	0.0635
back.4	0.0925

model.0.train

	coefficients
(Intercept)	1,173.4612
back.1	0.9587
back.2	-0.1034
back.3	0.0481
back.4	0.0719

RMSE
2,870

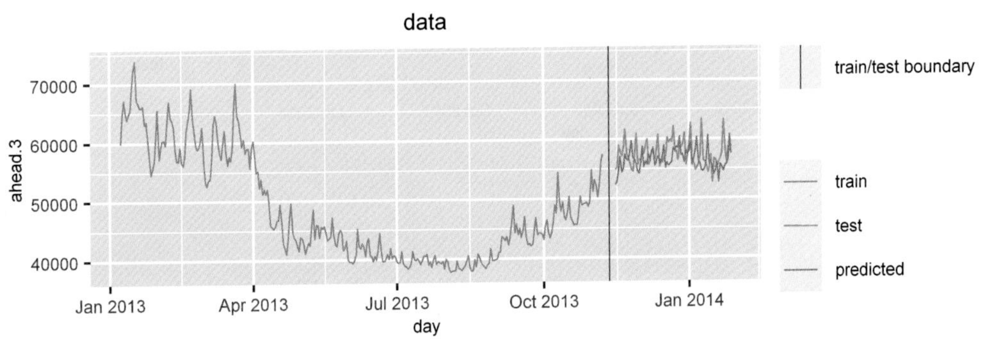

11.2.9 Evaluate by Time Series Cross-Validation Performance

Evaluate the cross-validation performance of both the direct approach and recursive approach to predicting 3 timesteps ahead.

Here we choose 3 folds. Because it's time series data, do not choose observations at random, but rather set the folds like this: fold 1 is 75% for training and 25% for testing; fold 2 is 50% for training and 25% for testing; fold 3 is 25% for training and 25% for testing.

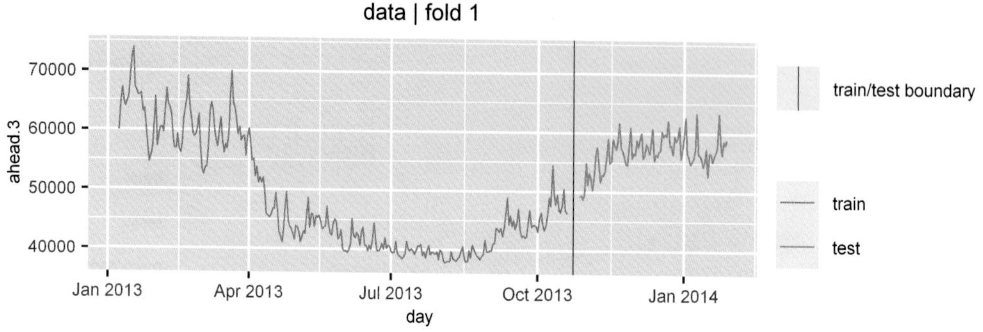

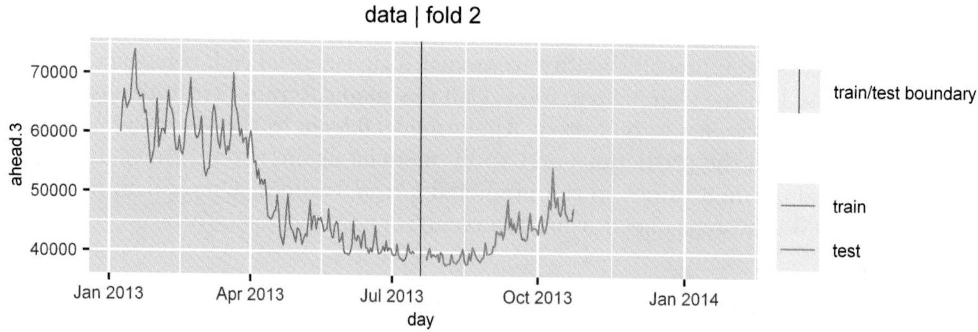

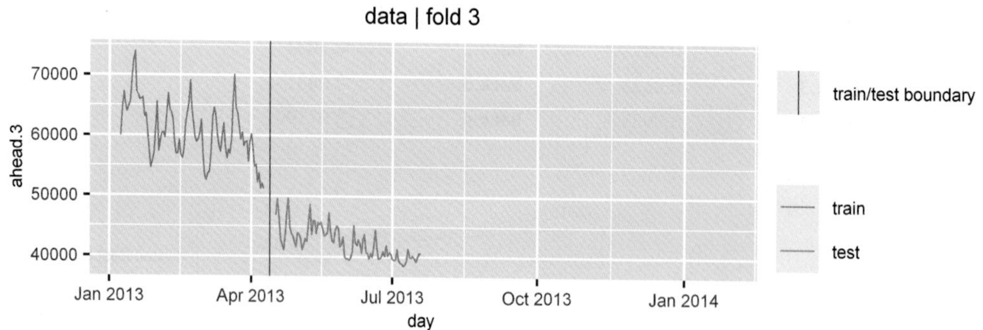

11.2.9.1 Direct Approach

To evaluate the direct approach's ability to predict 3 timesteps ahead, for each fold, construct a model to predict 3 days ahead based on the training partition. Treat all observations in the corresponding test partition as viewpoints to be tested. Apply the model to the viewpoints and compare the actual *ahead.3* values with the predicted *ahead.3* values. Estimate performance to be mean performance across the 3 folds.

RMSE for fold 1 is 2,760.

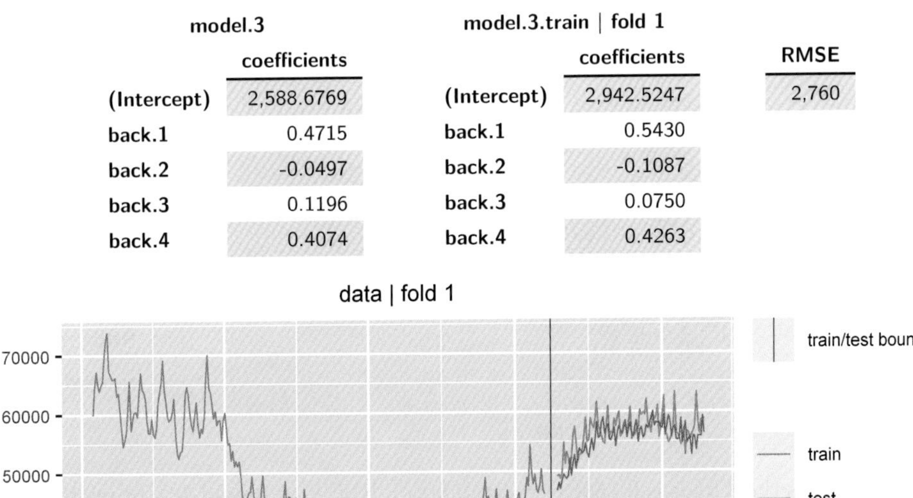

model.3

	coefficients
(Intercept)	2,588.6769
back.1	0.4715
back.2	-0.0497
back.3	0.1196
back.4	0.4074

model.3.train | fold 1

	coefficients
(Intercept)	2,942.5247
back.1	0.5430
back.2	-0.1087
back.3	0.0750
back.4	0.4263

RMSE
2,760

RMSE for fold 2 is 2,029.

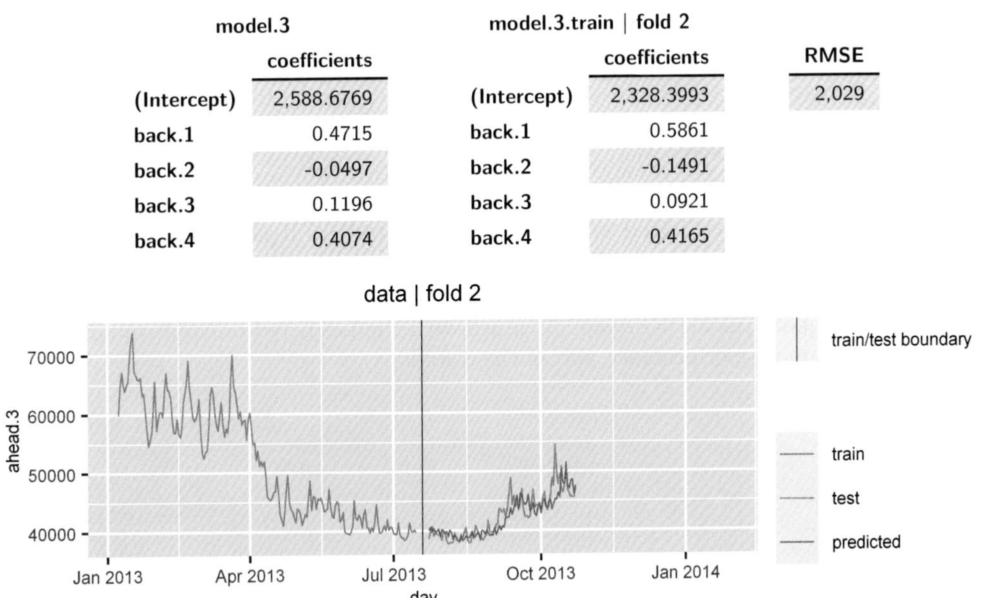

model.3

	coefficients
(Intercept)	2,588.6769
back.1	0.4715
back.2	-0.0497
back.3	0.1196
back.4	0.4074

model.3.train | fold 2

	coefficients
(Intercept)	2,328.3993
back.1	0.5861
back.2	-0.1491
back.3	0.0921
back.4	0.4165

RMSE
2,029

RMSE for fold 3 is 13,679.

model.3

	coefficients
(Intercept)	2,588.6769
back.1	0.4715
back.2	-0.0497
back.3	0.1196
back.4	0.4074

model.3.train | fold 3

	coefficients
(Intercept)	44,555.7417
back.1	0.3956
back.2	-0.3001
back.3	0.1125
back.4	0.0558

RMSE
13,679

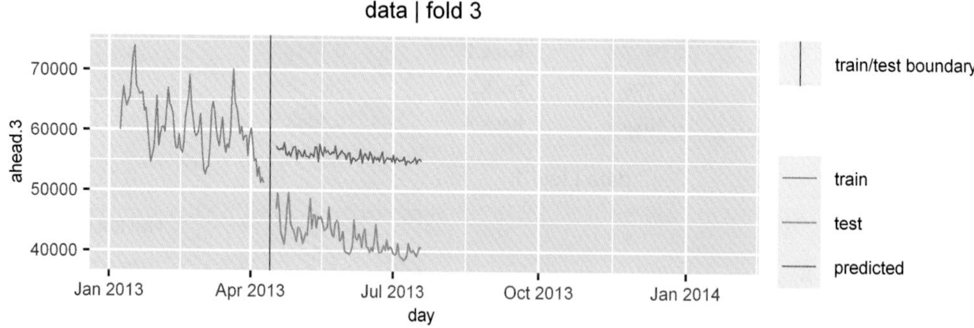

Mean RMSE across the 3 folds is 6,156. Cross-validation RMSE of ***model.3*** to predict 3 timesteps ahead using the direct approach is 6,156.

	RMSE
1	2,760
2	2,029
3	13,679

RMSE.cv
6,156

11.2.9.2 Recursive Approach

To evaluate the recursive approach's ability to predict 3 timesteps ahead, for each fold, construct a model to predict outcome based on the training partition. Treat all observations in the corresponding test partition as viewpoints to be tested. Apply the model to the viewpoints, then revise the test partition according to the predictions and apply the model again, several times in succession. Compare the actual *ahead*.3 values with the predicted *ahead*.3 values. Estimate performance to be mean performance across the 3 folds.

RMSE for fold 1 is 2,992.

model.0	coefficients
(Intercept)	1,177.8042
back.1	0.8697
back.2	-0.0491
back.3	0.0635
back.4	0.0925

model.0.train | fold 1	coefficients
(Intercept)	1,112.6341
back.1	0.9790
back.2	-0.1271
back.3	0.0540
back.4	0.0703

RMSE
2,992

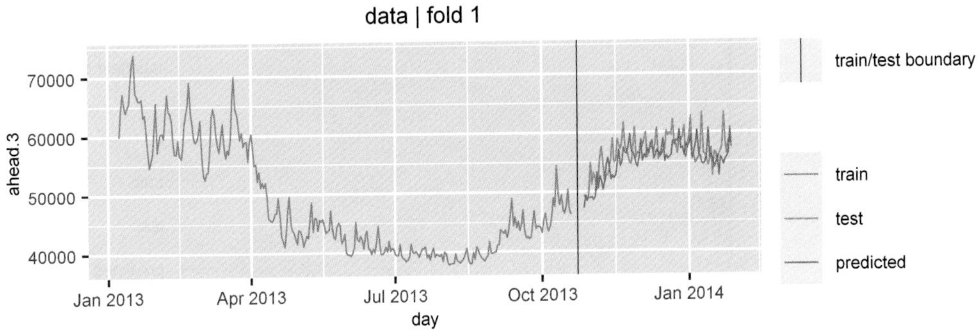

RMSE for fold 2 is 2,188.

model.0	coefficients
(Intercept)	1,177.8042
back.1	0.8697
back.2	-0.0491
back.3	0.0635
back.4	0.0925

model.0.train | fold 2	coefficients
(Intercept)	2,328.3993
back.1	0.5861
back.2	-0.1491
back.3	0.0921
back.4	0.4165

RMSE
2,188

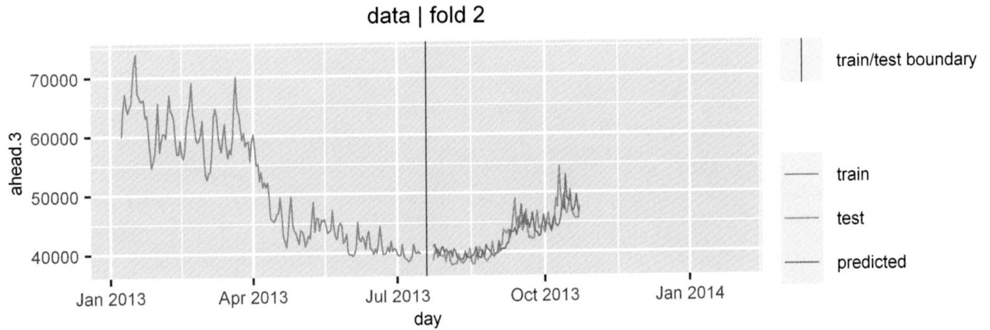

RMSE for fold 3 is 16,725.

model.0

	coefficients
(Intercept)	1,177.8042
back.1	0.8697
back.2	-0.0491
back.3	0.0635
back.4	0.0925

model.0.train | fold 3

	coefficients
(Intercept)	44,555.7417
back.1	0.3956
back.2	-0.3001
back.3	0.1125
back.4	0.0558

RMSE
16,725

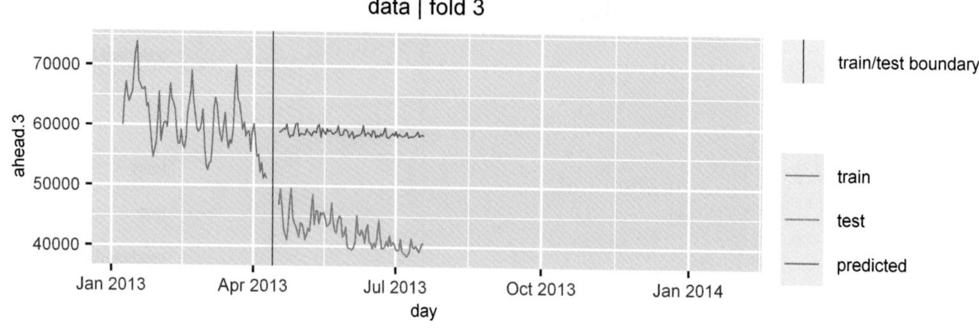

Mean RMSE across the 3 folds is 7,302. Cross-validation RMSE of ***model.0*** to predict 3 timesteps ahead using the direct approach is 7,302.

	RMSE
1	2,992
2	2,188
3	16,725

RMSE.cv
7,302

11.3 Network Data

Summarize a network with just a few numbers.

11.3.1 Introduction

The city manager is looking for ways to reduce the time that drivers wait at traffic lights. He analyzes the network of traffic lights. The airport operations manager is looking for ways to improve average on-time performance. She analyzes the network of airports. The logistics manager is scheduling deliveries to shorten the time that ships are in transit. He analyzes the network of ports. The social media blogger is looking to increase subscriptions. She analyzes the network of current subscribers connected to other users. The utility manager is forecasting demand for water to ensure that there will be sufficient supply. He analyzes the network of pipes connecting water reservoirs to customer homes. The cybersecurity expert is investigating a slowdown in system performance. She analyzes the network of servers, routers, and switches across the enterprise. The telecommunications engineer is investigating a surge in dropped cell phone calls. He analyzes the network of cellular towers.

Descriptive statistics for network data are about characterizing networks to facilitate analysis.

11.3.2 About Network Data

A **network** is something that can be described by a set of **nodes**, some of which are connected to each other by **links**. A network is also called a graph. Nodes are also called vertices or actors. Links are also called connectors or edges.

A **network diagram** can be a useful way to visualize a network. Nodes are shown as circles and links are shown as line segments tipped with arrowheads connecting the appropriate circles.

Network data can be represented in any of several ways, depending on which is most useful to a particular analysis. An **adjacency matrix** represents network data as a table, where rows correspond to nodes from which links might originate, columns correspond to nodes to which links might destinate, and values 0 or 1 indicate whether there actually is a link between nodes. A **link list** represents network data as a list of pairs of nodes, where each pair indicates a link.

Several useful descriptive statistics have been defined especially for analysis involving network data.

11.3.2.1 Node-Level Statistics

Here are some network statistics useful for characterizing nodes.

Shortest Path Length between a pair of nodes is the smallest number of links that connect a pair of nodes.

Indegree of a node is the number of links to a node. Calculate as the sum of a column of the adjacency matrix.

Outdegree of a node is the number of links from a node. Calculate as the sum of a row of the adjacency matrix.

Betweenness Centrality of a node is the ratio of the number of shortest paths between 2 nodes that include this node to the number of shortest paths between the 2 nodes. This statistic measures the tendency of a node to reside on shortest paths. You can think of a node with high betweenness centrality as a power broker that can block dissemination of information.

$$betweenness(v) = \sum_{i,j} \frac{g_{ivj}}{g_{ij}}$$

where ...

- v is a node
- i,j is an arbitrary pair of nodes; $i \neq j$, $i \neq v$, $j \neq v$
- g_{ivj} is the number of shortest paths from i through v to j
- g_{ij} is the number of shortest paths from i to j

Average Path Length of a node is the mean of the lengths of shortest paths between this node and any other node.

$$average\ path\ length(v) = \underset{j}{mean}(s_{vj})$$

where ...

- v is a node
- j is an arbitrary node; $j \neq v$
- s_{vj} is the length of the shortest path from v to j

Closeness Centrality of a node is the inverse of the sum of the lengths of shortest paths. You can think of a node with high closeness centrality as a broadcaster that can enable dissemination of information.

$$closeness(v) = \frac{1}{\sum_{j} s_{vj}}$$

where ...

- v is a node
- j is an arbitrary node; $j \neq v$
- s_{vj} is the length of the shortest path from v to j

Eccentricity of a node is the length of the shortest path to the farthest other node. You can think of a node with high eccentricity as an outcast that has little communication with most other nodes.

$$eccentricity(v) = \underset{j}{max}(s_{vj})$$

where ...

- v is a node
- j is an arbitrary node; $j \neq v$
- s_{vj} is the length of the shortest path from v to j

Eigenvector Centrality of a node is a value from the first eigenvector of the adjacency matrix. This statistic measures the degree to which a node is linked to by other nodes, taking into account the eigenvector centrality of those other nodes. Note that this statistic is recursively defined, so you'll need to rely on some algorithm to calculate it. You can think of a node with high eigenvector centrality as an influencer that communicates with other nodes that have high eigenvector centrality. The **PageRank** statistic is a variant of eigenvector centrality.

11.3.2.2 Network-Level Statistics

Here are some network statistics useful for characterizing whole networks.

Size of a network is the number of links.

Order of a network is the number of nodes.

Diameter of a network is the number of nodes on the longest shortest path.

$$diameter(N) = \underset{i,j}{max}(s_{ij}) + 1$$

where ...

- N is a network
- i,j is an arbitrary pair of nodes; $i \neq j$
- s_{ij} is the length of the shortest path from i to j

Average Path Length of a network is the mean of the lengths of the shortest paths.

$$average\ path\ length(N) = \underset{i,j}{mean}(s_{ij})$$

where ...

- N is a network
- i,j is an arbitrary pair of nodes; $i \neq j$
- s_{ij} is the length of the shortest path from i to j

Density of a network is the ratio of the size to the potential size if all pairs of nodes were linked. Calculate the potential size as the order permute 2.

$$density(N) = \frac{z}{{}_nP_2} = \frac{z}{\left(\dfrac{n!}{(n-2)!}\right)}$$

where ...

- N is a network
- z is the network size
- n is the network order

11.3.3 Data

Consider this network visualized as a network diagram, and represented as an adjacency matrix and a link list. See that node A is linked to node B. In the network diagram, the circle labeled A is connected by a line segment tipped with an arrowhead to the circle labeled B. In the adjacency matrix, the value 1 at first row A and second column B indicates that there is a link from node A to node B. In the link list, the first element labeled A→B indicates that there is a link from node A to node B.

Similarly, node B links to node A, going in the reverse direction.

However, while node C links to node B, node B does not link to node C. In the network diagram, the circle labeled C and the circle labeled B are connected by a line segment with arrowhead pointing only toward B. In the adjacency matrix, the value 1 at third row C and second column B indicates that there is a link from node C to node B. The value 0 at second row B and third column C indicates that there is no link from node B to node C. In the link list, there is an element labeled C→B, but no element labeled B→C.

data (shown as network diagram)

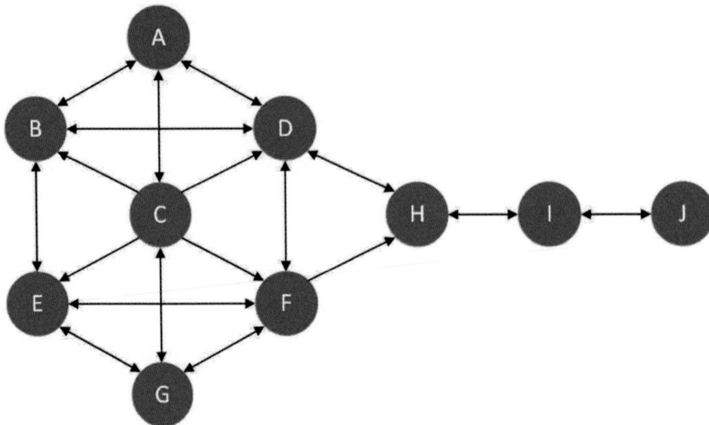

data *shown as adjacency matrix*

	A	B	C	D	E	F	G	H	I	J
A	0	1	1	1	0	0	0	0	0	0
B	1	0	0	1	1	0	0	0	0	0
C	1	1	0	1	1	1	1	0	0	0
D	1	1	0	0	0	1	0	1	0	0
E	0	1	0	0	0	1	1	0	0	0
F	0	0	0	1	1	0	1	1	0	0
G	0	0	1	0	1	1	0	0	0	0
H	0	0	0	1	0	0	0	0	1	0
I	0	0	0	0	0	0	0	1	0	1
J	0	0	0	0	0	0	0	0	1	0

data *shown as link list*

link
A→B, A→C, A→D, B→A, B→D, B→E, C→A, C→B, C→D, C→E, C→F, C→G, D→A, D→B, D→F, D→H, E→B, E→F, E→G, F→D, F→E, F→G, F→H, G→C, G→E, G→F, H→D, H→I, I→H, I→J, J→I

Let's use descriptive statistics to characterize the nodes in the network, and to characterize the whole network.

11.3.4 Node-Level Statistics

Here we characterize each pair of nodes in the network, shown as a shortest path length matrix. The shortest paths from node A to nodes B, C, D, E, F, G, H, I, J are lengths 1, 1, 1, 2, 2, 2, 2, 3, 4. Similarly for shortest paths between other pairs of nodes.

shortest path length

	A	B	C	D	E	F	G	H	I	J
A	0	1	1	1	2	2	2	2	3	4
B	1	0	2	1	1	2	2	2	3	4
C	1	1	0	1	1	1	1	2	3	4
D	1	1	2	0	2	1	2	1	2	3
E	2	1	2	2	0	1	1	2	3	4
F	2	2	2	1	1	0	1	1	2	3
G	2	2	1	2	1	1	0	2	3	4
H	2	2	3	1	3	2	3	0	1	2
I	3	3	4	2	4	3	4	1	0	1
J	4	4	5	3	5	4	5	2	1	0

Here we characterize each node in the network:

	node-level statistics						
	indegree	outdegree	betweenness	average_path_length	closeness	eccentricity	eigencentrality
A	3	3	5.0	2.000	0.0556	4	0.6682
B	4	3	4.0	1.889	0.0556	4	0.8520
C	2	6	4.0	1.667	0.0667	4	0.3801
D	5	4	28.0	1.556	0.0667	3	1.0000
E	4	3	2.5	1.889	0.0556	4	0.7980
F	4	4	14.5	1.556	0.0667	3	0.8321
G	3	3	2.0	2.000	0.0556	4	0.6018
H	3	2	28.0	1.667	0.0526	3	0.6083
I	2	2	16.0	2.333	0.0400	4	0.2000
J	1	1	0.0	3.222	0.0303	5	0.0599

Node A has indegree 3 because there are 3 links from other nodes to it:

- 1 link from B to A
- 1 link from C to A
- 1 link from D to A

Node A has outdegree 3 because there are 3 links from it to other nodes:

- 1 link from A to B
- 1 link from A to C
- 1 link from A to D

Node A has betweenness centrality 5 because there are 5 pairs of nodes that each includes node A in its 1 shortest path:

- The 1 shortest path from B to C is B $\rightarrow$ A $\rightarrow$ C
- The 1 shortest path from D to C is D $\rightarrow$ A $\rightarrow$ C
- The 1 shortest path from H to C is H $\rightarrow$ D $\rightarrow$ A $\rightarrow$ C
- The 1 shortest path from I to C is I $\rightarrow$ H $\rightarrow$ D $\rightarrow$ A $\rightarrow$ C
- The 1 shortest path from J to C is J $\rightarrow$ I $\rightarrow$ H $\rightarrow$ D $\rightarrow$ A $\rightarrow$ C

Node E has betweenness centrality 2.5 because there is 1 pair of nodes that includes node E in its 1 shortest path, and 3 pairs of nodes that each includes node E in 1 of its 2 shortest paths:

- The 1 shortest path from B to G is B $\rightarrow$ E $\rightarrow$ G
- 1 of 2 shortest paths from B to F is B $\rightarrow$ E $\rightarrow$ F
- 1 of 2 shortest paths from F to B is F $\rightarrow$ E $\rightarrow$ B
- 1 of 2 shortest paths from G to B is G $\rightarrow$ E $\rightarrow$ B

Node A has average path length 2, calculated as $mean(1, 1, 1, 2, 2, 2, 2, 3, 4) = 2$.

Node A has closeness centrality 0.0556, calculated as $1 \div (1+1+1+2+2+2+2+2+3+4) = 0.0556$.

Node A has eccentricity 4 because the longest shortest path from node A is length 4:

- The shortest path from A to J is A $\rightarrow$ D $\rightarrow$ H $\rightarrow$ I $\rightarrow$ J

Node A has eigenvector centrality 0.6682, calculated by a search algorithm that finds the first eigenvector of the adjacency matrix.

Similarly for node-level statistics of other nodes.

11.3.5 Network-Level Statistics

Here we summarize the whole network:

network-level statistics

size	order	diameter	average_path_length	density
31	10	5	2.156	0.3444

The network size is 31 because there are 31 directed links.

The network order is 10 because there are 10 nodes: A, B, C, D, E, F, G, H, I, J.

The network diameter is 5 because the longest shortest paths are length 4, each traversing 5 nodes:

- The shortest path from B to J is B $\rightarrow$ D $\rightarrow$ H $\rightarrow$ I $\rightarrow$ J
- The shortest path from E to J is E $\rightarrow$ F $\rightarrow$ H $\rightarrow$ I $\rightarrow$ J

The network average path length is 2.156, calculated as the mean of every pair of nodes' shortest path length.

The network density is 0.3444, calculated as $31 \div {}_{10}P_2 = 31 \div \frac{10!}{(10-2)!} = 0.3444$.

11.4 PageRank for Network Data

Find the most important nodes in a network.

11.4.1 Introduction

In the 1990s, an enterprising young entrepreneur has an idea for a new business. She searches the internet for information about the market using the popular search engines of the time. The searches quickly return links to many relevant websites. Too many websites. There are thousands to comb through, and they are not presented to her in any particularly useful order. The entrepreneur would, of course, prefer that the most important websites be prioritized and presented to her first.

You can think of PageRank as a way to assess websites' importance, and thereby assist in prioritizing search engine results. Indeed, that's what it was developed for. It was so good at it that soon after its development a whole new company was created around it – a company called Google.

11.4.2 About PageRank

The **random walk method** calculates the probability of encountering a certain node while randomly following links in a network. A node encountered with high probability can be considered important in the sense that it is frequently visited. Effectively, such a probability is a measure of a node's importance as reflected by the importance of other nodes that link to it.

The random walk method works like this:

Initialize:
    Choose a current node at random
    Keep track of the current node encountered
Iterate:
    Choose a link emitting from the current node at random

> *Follow the link to select a new current node*
> *Keep track of the (new) current node encountered*
> *Summarize: Calculate probabilities of encounter*

PageRank is a node-level descriptive statistic for network data, and approximates the probability of encountering a node while randomly following links in a network. It captures the notion of a user searching for something online by following website hyper-links. **PageRank with dampening** is a variation of PageRank. Where PageRank measures the probability of encountering a node while following links, PageRank with dampening measures the probability of encountering a node while usually following links, but occasionally jumping to a distant node at random. It captures the notion of a user searching for something online by following website hyper-links until losing patience and jumping to some random website.

The **PageRank method** works like this:

> *Initialize:*
> *For each node ...*
> *Randomly choose a PageRank*
> *Iterate:*
> *For each node ...*
> *Revise PageRank to be weighted sum of PageRanks contributed by all nodes that link to it*

At initialization, PageRank values across all nodes should sum to 1. At iteration, the weight that goes with a certain node's contribution is based on how many links emit from that node.

Here is how to revise PageRank:

$$pagerank_i \leftarrow \sum_{j \in C(i)} \frac{pagerank_j}{L(j)}$$

where ...

- $pagerank_i$ is the PageRank of the ith node
- $pagerank_j$ is the PageRank of the jth node
- $C(i)$ is the set of nodes that link to the ith node
- $L(j)$ is the outdegree of the jth node

Here is how to revise PageRank with dampening:

$$pagerank_i \leftarrow d \times \left(\sum_{j \in C(i)} \frac{pagerank_j}{L(j)} \right) + \frac{1-d}{N}$$

where ...

- $pagerank_i$ is the PageRank of the ith node
- $pagerank_j$ is the PageRank of the jth node
- d is a dampening factor $(0 \leq d \leq 1)$

- $C(i)$ is the set of nodes that link to the ith node
- $L(j)$ is the outdegree of the jth node
- N is the number of nodes (i.e., the network order)

11.4.3 Data

Consider this network. Node A links to both node B and node C. Node B links only to node D. Node C links to both node D and node E. Node D also links to node E, which links back to node A. How important is each of the nodes?

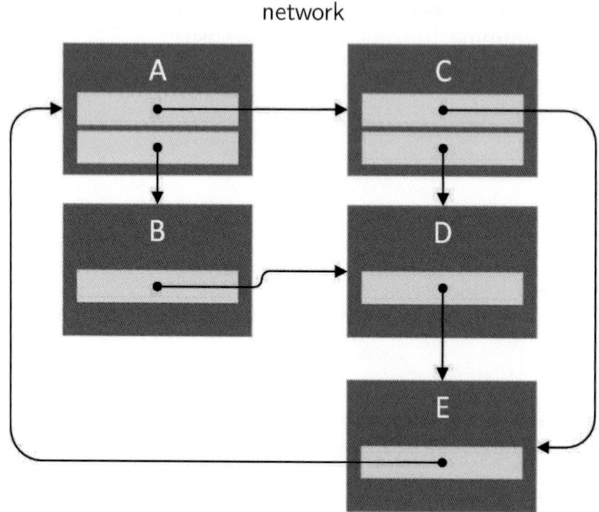

You can think of this network as 5 websites with various hyper-links to each other. If these websites were returned by a search algorithm as being relevant to a user's query, in what order should they be presented to the user? Which website is likely to be the most important and should therefore be presented first? Let's use the random walk method and PageRank method to calculate their importance and so prioritize them.

11.4.4 Random Walk

Take a random walk of 20 steps through the network. We randomly choose to start with node C, which has links to both node D and node E. Keep track of encountering node C once so far. Next, randomly choose to follow the link node E and keep track of encountering node E once so far. E has a link only to node A, so follow it to node A. Continue to iterate until reaching node D at step 20.

a_random_walk_of_20_steps

```
C > E > A > B > D > E > A > C > E > A > B > D > E > A > B > D > E > A > C > D
```

Looking over the 20 steps, node A was encountered at $5 \div 20 = 25\%$ of the steps, nodes B and C were each encountered at $3 \div 20 = 15\%$ of the steps, node D at $4 \div 20 = 20\%$ of the steps, and node E at $5 \div 20 = 25\%$ of the steps.

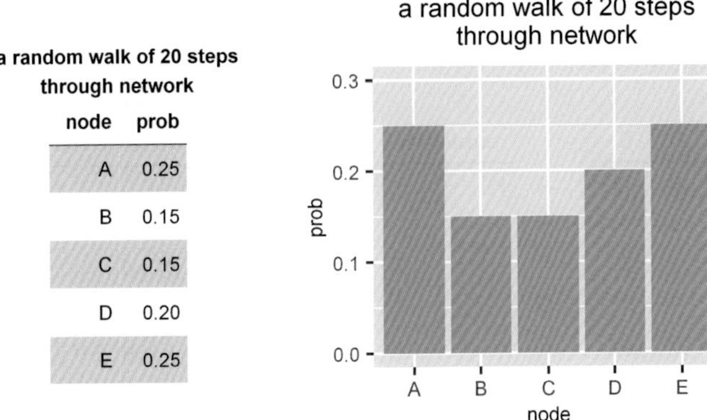
a random walk of 20 steps through network

node	prob
A	0.25
B	0.15
C	0.15
D	0.20
E	0.25

To get a better estimate of the probabilities of encounter, take a random walk of 1,000,000 steps. That refines the probabilities to node A 26.67%, node B 13.33%, node C 13%, node D 19.99%, and node E 26.67%.

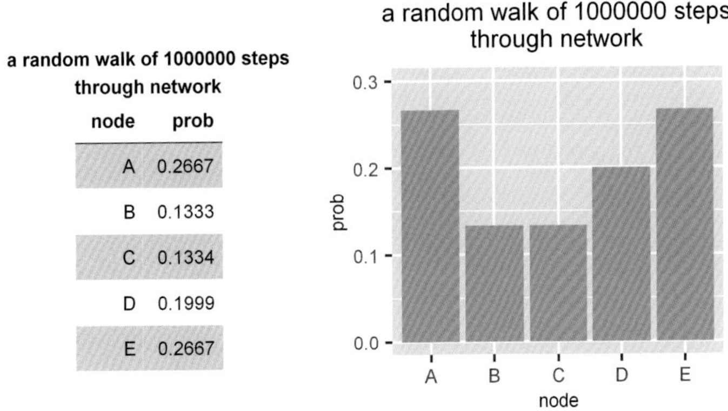
a random walk of 1000000 steps through network

node	prob
A	0.2667
B	0.1333
C	0.1334
D	0.1999
E	0.2667

11.4.5 PageRank

Calculate the PageRank of each node in the network.

11.4.5.1 Initialize

Initialize by representing the network as an adjacency matrix. Construct an outdegree vector populated with the outdegree of each node, which is conveniently calculated as the row sums of the adjacency matrix.

Construct a weight matrix to indicate the proportion of influence each node has on the nodes it links to. The weight matrix organizes relationships between nodes in the same way that the adjacency matrix does, with number of columns and number of rows both equal to number of nodes. Populate each row of the weight matrix with corresponding values from the adjacency matrix, but divided by the appropriate outdegree. For example, the weight matrix value of 0.5 for row A, column B is calculated as the adjacency matrix value of 1 for row A, column B, divided by outdegree 2 for row A. We can interpret the 0.5 value like this: half of node A's importance contributes to node B's importance because half of node A's links point to node B.

Construct a PageRank vector, populated with randomly chosen PageRank values of 0.2 for each node. Note that the PageRank values sum to $0.2 \times 5 = 1$.

data

	A	B	C	D	E
A	0	1	1	0	0
B	0	0	0	1	0
C	0	0	0	1	1
D	0	0	0	0	1
E	1	0	0	0	0

	outdegree
A	2
B	1
C	2
D	1
E	1

weight

	A	B	C	D	E
A	0	0.5	0.5	0.0	0.0
B	0	0.0	0.0	1.0	0.0
C	0	0.0	0.0	0.5	0.5
D	0	0.0	0.0	0.0	1.0
E	1	0.0	0.0	0.0	0.0

	pagerank
A	0.2
B	0.2
C	0.2
D	0.2
E	0.2

11.4.5.2 Iterate

Iteratively revise each node's PageRank value to the weighted sum of PageRank values of nodes that link to it, which is conveniently calculated as the sum product of the weight matrix column for the node and the PageRank vector.

$$\text{revised } PageRank(x) = \begin{pmatrix} weight_{A,x} \times PageRank(A) & + \\ weight_{B,x} \times PageRank(B) & + \\ weight_{C,x} \times PageRank(C) & + \\ weight_{D,x} \times PageRank(D) & + \\ weight_{E,x} \times PageRank(E) & \end{pmatrix}$$

At iteration 1 ...

$$\begin{aligned}
\text{revised } PageRank(A) &= (0 \times 0.2) + (0 \times 0.2) + (0 \times 0.2) + (0 \times 0.2) + (1 \times 0.2) &= 0.2 \\
\text{revised } PageRank(B) &= (0.5 \times 0.2) + (0 \times 0.2) + (0 \times 0.2) + (0 \times 0.2) + (0 \times 0.2) &= 0.1 \\
\text{revised } PageRank(C) &= (0.5 \times 0.2) + (0 \times 0.2) + (0 \times 0.2) + (0 \times 0.2) + (0 \times 0.2) &= 0.1 \\
\text{revised } PageRank(D) &= (0 \times 0.2) + (1 \times 0.2) + (0.5 \times 0.2) + (0 \times 0.2) + (0 \times 0.2) &= 0.3 \\
\text{revised } PageRank(E) &= (0 \times 0.2) + (0 \times 0.2) + (0.5 \times 0.2) + (1 \times 0.2) + (0 \times 0.2) &= 0.3
\end{aligned}$$

weight

	A	B	C	D	E
A	0	0.5	0.5	0.0	0.0
B	0	0.0	0.0	1.0	0.0
C	0	0.0	0.0	0.5	0.5
D	0	0.0	0.0	0.0	1.0
E	1	0.0	0.0	0.0	0.0

	pagerank.old
A	0.2
B	0.2
C	0.2
D	0.2
E	0.2

	pagerank.new
A	0.2
B	0.1
C	0.1
D	0.3
E	0.3

At iteration 2 ...

$$\begin{aligned}
\text{revised } PageRank(A) &= (0 \times 0.2) + (0 \times 0.1) + (0 \times 0.1) + (0 \times 0.3) + (1 \times 0.3) &= 0.3 \\
\text{revised } PageRank(B) &= (0.5 \times 0.2) + (0 \times 0.1) + (0 \times 0.1) + (0 \times 0.3) + (0 \times 0.3) &= 0.1 \\
\text{revised } PageRank(C) &= (0.5 \times 0.2) + (0 \times 0.1) + (0 \times 0.1) + (0 \times 0.3) + (0 \times 0.3) &= 0.1 \\
\text{revised } PageRank(D) &= (0 \times 0.2) + (1 \times 0.1) + (0.5 \times 0.1) + (0 \times 0.3) + (0 \times 0.3) &= 0.15 \\
\text{revised } PageRank(E) &= (0 \times 0.2) + (0 \times 0.1) + (0.5 \times 0.1) + (1 \times 0.3) + (0 \times 0.3) &= 0.35
\end{aligned}$$

weight	A	B	C	D	E
A	0	0.5	0.5	0.0	0.0
B	0	0.0	0.0	1.0	0.0
C	0	0.0	0.0	0.5	0.5
D	0	0.0	0.0	0.0	1.0
E	1	0.0	0.0	0.0	0.0

	pagerank.old
A	0.2
B	0.1
C	0.1
D	0.3
E	0.3

	pagerank.new
A	0.30
B	0.10
C	0.10
D	0.15
E	0.35

At 100 iterations, the PageRank values have essentially stabilized. Note that the PageRank values closely approximate the probabilities of encounter calculated by the random walk method.

weight	A	B	C	D	E
A	0	0.5	0.5	0.0	0.0
B	0	0.0	0.0	1.0	0.0
C	0	0.0	0.0	0.5	0.5
D	0	0.0	0.0	0.0	1.0
E	1	0.0	0.0	0.0	0.0

	pagerank.old
A	0.2666
B	0.1334
C	0.1334
D	0.2000
E	0.2665

	pagerank.new
A	0.2665
B	0.1333
C	0.1333
D	0.2001
E	0.2667

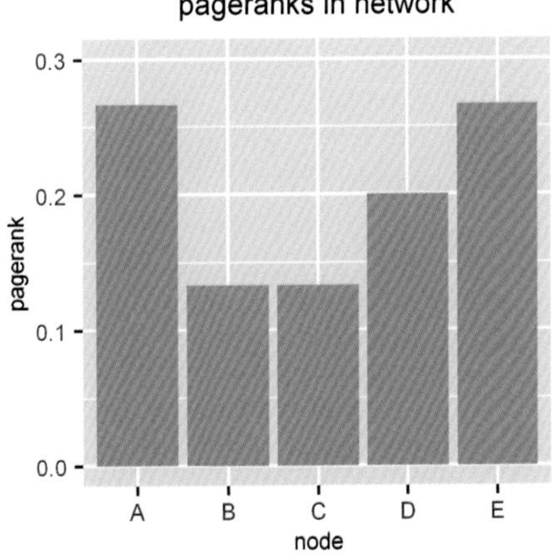

11.4.6 PageRank with Dampening

Calculate the PageRank, adjusted with dampening, of each node in the network.

11.4.6.1 Initialize

Initialize by constructing an outdegree vector, weight matrix, and PageRank vector of values chosen at random, as before.

data

	A	B	C	D	E
A	0	1	1	0	0
B	0	0	0	1	0
C	0	0	0	1	1
D	0	0	0	0	1
E	1	0	0	0	0

	outdegree
A	2
B	1
C	2
D	1
E	1

weight

	A	B	C	D	E
A	0	0.5	0.5	0.0	0.0
B	0	0.0	0.0	1.0	0.0
C	0	0.0	0.0	0.5	0.5
D	0	0.0	0.0	0.0	1.0
E	1	0.0	0.0	0.0	0.0

	pagerank
A	0.2
B	0.2
C	0.2
D	0.2
E	0.2

11.4.6.2 Iterate

Set the dampening factor to 0.85. Iteratively revise each node's PageRank value to the weighted sum of PageRank values of nodes that link to it, adjusted by the dampening factor.

$$\begin{matrix}\text{revised}\\ \mathit{PageRank}(x)\end{matrix} = \left(\mathit{damp} \times \begin{pmatrix} \mathit{weight}_{A,x} \times \mathit{PageRank}(A) & + \\ \mathit{weight}_{B,x} \times \mathit{PageRank}(B) & + \\ \mathit{weight}_{C,x} \times \mathit{PageRank}(C) & + \\ \mathit{weight}_{D,x} \times \mathit{PageRank}(D) & + \\ \mathit{weight}_{E,x} \times \mathit{PageRank}(E) & \end{pmatrix} \right) + \left(\frac{1 - \mathit{damp}}{\text{number of nodes}} \right)$$

At iteration 1 ...

$$\text{revised } PageRank(A) = \left(0.85 \times \left((0 \times 0.2) + (0 \times 0.2) + (0 \times 0.2) + (0 \times 0.2) + (1 \times 0.2)\right)\right) + \left(\frac{1 - 0.85}{5}\right) = 0.2$$

$$\text{revised } PageRank(B) = \left(0.85 \times \left((0.5 \times 0.2) + (0 \times 0.2) + (0 \times 0.2) + (0 \times 0.2) + (0 \times 0.2)\right)\right) + \left(\frac{1 - 0.85}{5}\right) = 0.115$$

$$\text{revised } PageRank(C) = \left(0.85 \times \left((0.5 \times 0.2) + (0 \times 0.2) + (0 \times 0.2) + (0 \times 0.2) + (0 \times 0.2)\right)\right) + \left(\frac{1 - 0.85}{5}\right) = 0.115$$

$$\text{revised } PageRank(D) = \left(0.85 \times \left((0 \times 0.2) + (1 \times 0.2) + (0.5 \times 0.2) + (0 \times 0.2) + (0 \times 0.2)\right)\right) + \left(\frac{1 - 0.85}{5}\right) = 0.285$$

$$\text{revised } PageRank(E) = \left(0.85 \times \left((0 \times 0.2) + (0 \times 0.2) + (0.5 \times 0.2) + (1 \times 0.2) + (0 \times 0.2)\right)\right) + \left(\frac{1 - 0.85}{5}\right) = 0.285$$

damp
0.85

weight	A	B	C	D	E
A	0	0.5	0.5	0.0	0.0
B	0	0.0	0.0	1.0	0.0
C	0	0.0	0.0	0.5	0.5
D	0	0.0	0.0	0.0	1.0
E	1	0.0	0.0	0.0	0.0

	pagerank.old
A	0.2
B	0.2
C	0.2
D	0.2
E	0.2

	pagerank.new
A	0.200
B	0.115
C	0.115
D	0.285
E	0.285

At iteration 2 …

$$\text{revised } \textit{PageRank}(A) = \left(0.85 \times \left(\begin{array}{ll}(0 \times 0.2) & + \\ (0 \times 0.115) & + \\ (0 \times 0.115) & + \\ (0 \times 0.285) & + \\ (1 \times 0.285) & \end{array}\right)\right) + \left(\frac{1-0.85}{5}\right) = 0.2723$$

$$\text{revised } \textit{PageRank}(B) = \left(0.85 \times \left(\begin{array}{ll}(0.5 \times 0.2) & + \\ (0 \times 0.115) & + \\ (0 \times 0.115) & + \\ (0 \times 0.285) & + \\ (0 \times 0.285) & \end{array}\right)\right) + \left(\frac{1-0.85}{5}\right) = 0.115$$

$$\text{revised } \textit{PageRank}(C) = \left(0.85 \times \left(\begin{array}{ll}(0.5 \times 0.2) & + \\ (0 \times 0.115) & + \\ (0 \times 0.115) & + \\ (0 \times 0.285) & + \\ (0 \times 0.285) & \end{array}\right)\right) + \left(\frac{1-0.85}{5}\right) = 0.115$$

$$\text{revised } \textit{PageRank}(D) = \left(0.85 \times \left(\begin{array}{ll}(0 \times 0.2) & + \\ (1 \times 0.115) & + \\ (0.5 \times 0.115) & + \\ (0 \times 0.285) & + \\ (0 \times 0.285) & \end{array}\right)\right) + \left(\frac{1-0.85}{5}\right) = 0.1766$$

$$\text{revised } \textit{PageRank}(E) = \left(0.85 \times \left(\begin{array}{ll}(0 \times 0.2) & + \\ (0 \times 0.115) & + \\ (0.5 \times 0.115) & + \\ (1 \times 0.285) & + \\ (0 \times 0.285) & \end{array}\right)\right) + \left(\frac{1-0.85}{5}\right) = 0.3211$$

damp
0.85

weight	A	B	C	D	E
A	0	0.5	0.5	0.0	0.0
B	0	0.0	0.0	1.0	0.0
C	0	0.0	0.0	0.5	0.5
D	0	0.0	0.0	0.0	1.0
E	1	0.0	0.0	0.0	0.0

	pagerank.old
A	0.200
B	0.115
C	0.115
D	0.285
E	0.285

	pagerank.new
A	0.2723
B	0.1150
C	0.1150
D	0.1766
E	0.3211

Here are the PageRank values calculated with dampening factor 0.85 at 100 iterations:

damp
0.85

	weight				
	A	B	C	D	E
A	0	0.5	0.5	0.0	0.0
B	0	0.0	0.0	1.0	0.0
C	0	0.0	0.0	0.5	0.5
D	0	0.0	0.0	0.0	1.0
E	1	0.0	0.0	0.0	0.0

	pagerank.old
A	0.2542
B	0.1380
C	0.1380
D	0.2060
E	0.2638

	pagerank.new
A	0.2542
B	0.1380
C	0.1380
D	0.2060
E	0.2638

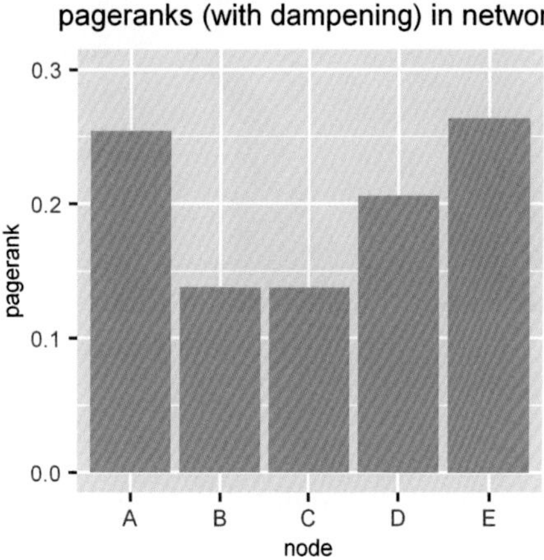

11.5 Collaborative Filtering for Network Data

Recommend an item to someone based on what others like.

11.5.1 Introduction

Zhengxin has just finished reading a very enjoyable book on data science. She goes online to visit her favorite bookseller website and rates the book as 5 out of 5 to indicate how much she enjoyed it, adding to a long list of ratings she's given to the many other books she's purchased. She then proceeds to ask for a recommendation for what she might enjoy reading next. Perhaps she'd like something rated highly by other readers with tastes similar to hers. Or perhaps she'd like something that other readers find similar to another book that she rated highly?

11.5.2 About Collaborative Filtering

Collaborative filtering is about making recommender systems.

The **collaborative filtering method** predicts how various users would rate various items, based either on what similar users would do or on how similar items were rated. With this method, we introduce the notion of a bipartite graph as a special kind of network, and inter-observation correlation as a way of defining similarity.

A **bipartite graph** is a network in which several nodes, which you can call user nodes, each link to any number of other nodes, which you can call item nodes. The links are uni-directional from user nodes to item nodes, but not from item nodes to user nodes. User nodes don't link to other user nodes, and item nodes don't link to other item nodes.

Inter-observation correlation is a descriptive statistic on 2 observations. Each observation is treated as a vector, and the correlation function is applied as usual, skipping over any pairs with missing values.

Simple collaborative filtering predicts that a user will rate items the same way that its most similar user does. Similarity between users is defined as their inter-observation correlation if non-negative, otherwise 0.

$$\hat{r}_{u,i} = r_{x,i}$$

where ...

- $\hat{r}_{u,i}$ is the predicted user u's rating of item i
- x is the index of the user most similar to user u
- $r_{x,i}$ is user x's rating of item i

Collaborative filtering with weighting predicts that a user will rate items the same way that all other users do, but weighs more similar users more heavily.

$$\hat{r}_{u,i} = \frac{\sum\limits_{x \in N_u} w_{x,u} r_{x,i}}{\sum\limits_{x \in N_u} w_{x,u}}$$

where ...

- $\hat{r}_{u,i}$ is the predicted user u's rating of item i
- N_u are the indices of the users other than user u
- $w_{x,u}$ is the measure of how similar user x is to user u
- $r_{x,i}$ is user x's rating of item i

Collaborative filtering with calibrated weighting accounts for differences in standards between users. It corrects for users that tend to rate highly and users that tend to rate lowly by comparing deviations from their mean ratings rather than comparing ratings directly. Two parameters can be adjusted to tune performance: threshold sets the number of similar users to consider, and alpha factor sets the magnitude of the similar users' influence.

$$\hat{r}_{u,i} = \bar{r}_u + \alpha \left(\frac{\sum\limits_{x \in N_u^t} w_{x,u} (r_{x,i} - \bar{r}_x)}{\sum\limits_{x \in N_u^t} w_{x,u}} \right)$$

where ...

- $\hat{r}_{u,i}$ is the prediction for user u's rating of item i
- $\bar{r}_u$ is the average of user u's ratings for all rated items
- $\bar{r}_x$ is the average of user x's ratings for all rated items
- t (threshold) is the number of similar users to consider
- α (alpha factor) is the magnitude of similar users' influence
- N_u^t are the indices of the t users most similar to user u
- $w_{x,u}$ is the measure of how similar user x is to user u
- $r_{x,i}$ is user x's rating of item i

Collaborative filtering with calibrated weighting, item-based is a variation of the method. It predicts that a user will rate items based on the way that it rates other similar items, where similarity between items is based on how other users rate items. Essentially, this variation swaps users and items.

$$\hat{r}_{i,u} = \bar{r}_i + \alpha \left(\frac{\sum_{x \in N_i^t} w_{x,i}(r_{x,u} - \bar{r}_x)}{\sum_{x \in N_i^t} w_{x,i}} \right)$$

where ...

- $\hat{r}_{i,u}$ is the predicted item i's rating by user u
- $\bar{r}_i$ is the average of item i's ratings by all rating users
- $\bar{r}_x$ is the average of item x's ratings by all rating users
- t (threshold) is the number of similar items to consider
- α (alpha factor) is the magnitude of similar items' influence
- N_i^t are the indices of the t items most similar to item i
- $w_{x,i}$ is the measure of how similar item x is to item i
- $r_{x,u}$ is item x's rating by user u

11.5.3 Data

Consider this network data shown as a bipartite network diagram representing how users rate items. Links are uni-directional from users to items, and are notated with ratings. User A has experience with items 1, 2, 3, 5, and 6, but no experience with item 4. He rates items 2 and 3 as 5 on a scale of 1 to 5, items 1 and 5 as 4, and item 6 as only 1. Similarly, user B rates items 1, 3, 4, 5, and 6. User C rates only items 2, 3, 5, and 6. User D rates only items 1, 4, 5, and 6.

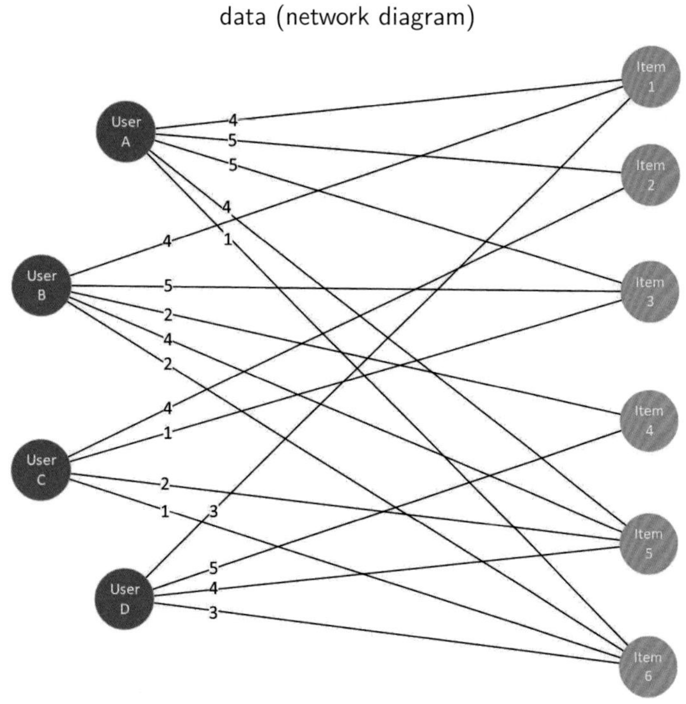

Here is the network shown as an adjacency matrix. Note that only the upper-right quadrant contains any non-zero values, so we can work with an abridged adjacency matrix without loss of information.

data (adjacency matrix)

	user_a	user_b	user_c	user_d	item_1	item_2	item_3	item_4	item_5	item_6
user_a	0	0	0	0	1	1	1	0	1	1
user_b	0	0	0	0	1	0	1	1	1	1
user_c	0	0	0	0	0	1	1	0	1	1
user_d	0	0	0	0	1	0	0	1	1	1
item_1	0	0	0	0	0	0	0	0	0	0
item_2	0	0	0	0	0	0	0	0	0	0
item_3	0	0	0	0	0	0	0	0	0	0
item_4	0	0	0	0	0	0	0	0	0	0
item_5	0	0	0	0	0	0	0	0	0	0
item_6	0	0	0	0	0	0	0	0	0	0

data (adjacency matrix, abridged)

	item_1	item_2	item_3	item_4	item_5	item_6
user_a	1	1	1	0	1	1
user_b	1	0	1	1	1	1
user_c	0	1	1	0	1	1
user_d	1	0	0	1	1	1

To represent the ratings along with the links in the matrix, replace 1s with the appropriate ratings and remove 0s.

data

	item_1	item_2	item_3	item_4	item_5	item_6
user_a	4	5	5	NA	4	1
user_b	4	NA	5	2	4	2
user_c	NA	4	1	NA	2	1
user_d	3	NA	NA	5	4	3

Would user A like item 4? Would user B like item 2? Would user C like item 1 more than item 4? Would user D like item 2 more than item 3? Let's use collaborative filtering to predict users' preferences and make some recommendations.

11.5.4 Similarity Matrix

Construct the similarity matrix. Define similarity between observations as inter-observation correlation. Treat any observation pairs with negative correlation as having no similarity.

$$\begin{aligned}
cor(A,B) &= cor((4,5,5,-,4,1),(4,-,5,2,4,2)) &&= cor((4,5,4,1),(4,5,4,2)) &&= 0.9941\\
cor(A,C) &= cor((4,5,5,-,4,1),(-,4,1,-,2,1)) &&= cor((5,5,4,1),(4,1,2,1)) &&= 0.4981\\
cor(A,D) &= cor((4,5,5,-,4,1),(3,-,-,5,4,3)) &&= cor((4,4,1),(3,4,3)) &&= 0.5\\
cor(B,C) &= cor((4,-,5,2,4,2),(-,4,1,-,2,1)) &&= cor((5,4,2),(1,2,1)) &&= 0.189\\
cor(B,D) &= cor((4,-,5,2,4,2),(3,-,-,5,4,3)) &&= cor((4,2,4,2),(3,5,4,3)) &&= -0.3 < 0\\
cor(C,D) &= cor((-,4,1,-,2,1),(3,-,-,5,4,3)) &&= cor((2,1),(4,3)) &&= 1
\end{aligned}$$

user similarity matrix

	user_a	user_b	user_c	user_d
user_a	1.0000	0.9941	0.4981	0.5
user_b	0.9941	1.0000	0.1890	0.0
user_c	0.4981	0.1890	1.0000	1.0
user_d	0.5000	0.0000	1.0000	1.0

11.5.5 Simple Collaborative Filtering

Simple collaborative filtering predicts that a user will rate items the same way that its most similar user does.

To predict how user A would rate item 4, look to the most similar user. User B is most similar to user A, with similarity 0.9941. User B rates item 4 as 2, so predict that user A would rate item 4 as 2.

calculation for user_a rating of item_4

similar_user	rating
user_b	2

prediction

user	item_4
user_a	2

Here is a table listing all users and their most similar user's ratings for all items:

similar user's ratings

user	similar_user	item_1	item_2	item_3	item_4	item_5	item_6
user_a	user_b	4	NA	5	2	4	2
user_b	user_a	4	5	5	NA	4	1
user_c	user_d	3	NA	NA	5	4	3
user_d	user_c	NA	4	1	NA	2	1

Predict all missing ratings, taken from the table of similar users' ratings. Predict that user A would rate item 4 as 2 because that's what user B does. Predict that user B would rate item 2 as 5 because that's what user A does. Predict user C would rate item 1 as 3 because that's what user D does. Similarly, predict the other missing ratings.

data.filtered

	item_1	item_2	item_3	item_4	item_5	item_6
user_a	4	5	5	2	4	1
user_b	4	5	5	2	4	2
user_c	3	4	1	5	2	1
user_d	3	4	1	5	4	3

11.5.6 Collaborative Filtering with Weighting

Collaborative filtering with weighting predicts that a user will rate items the same way that all other users do, but weighs more similar users more heavily.

To predict how user A would rate item 4, look to all other users. User B rates item 4 as 2. User C does not rate item 4. User D rates item 4 as 5.

Weigh these ratings according to how similar the users are to user A. User B's rating gets weighed 0.9941. User D's rating gets weighed 0.5000. The relative weight for user B is then $0.9941 \div (0.9941 + 0.5000) = 0.6654$ and the relative weight for user D is $0.5000 \div (0.9941 + 0.5000) = 0.3346$. User B's rating gets weighted about twice as heavily as user D's rating. We do this because user B is about 2 times more similar to user A than user D is.

Predict that user A would rate item 4 as the weighted average of the other users' ratings of item 4, which is $(0.6654 \times 2) + (0.3346 \times 5) = 3.004$.

calculation for user_a rating of item_4

user	rating	weight	rel_weight	contribution
user_b	2	0.9941	0.6654	1.331
user_c	NA	NA	NA	NA
user_d	5	0.5000	0.3346	1.673

prediction

user	item_4
user_a	3.004

Here are the predicted ratings for all users for all items:

predicted ratings

user	item_1	item_2	item_3	item_4	item_5	item_6
user_a	3.665	4.000	3.665	3.004	3.500	2.001
user_b	4.000	4.840	4.361	NaN	3.680	1.000
user_c	3.407	5.000	5.000	4.523	4.000	2.297
user_d	4.000	4.333	2.333	NaN	2.667	1.000

Keep the known ratings, but filter in all missing ratings, taken from the table of predicted ratings.

data.filtered

	item_1	item_2	item_3	item_4	item_5	item_6
user_a	4.000	5.000	5.000	**3.004**	4	1
user_b	4.000	**4.840**	5.000	2.000	4	2
user_c	**3.407**	4.000	1.000	**4.523**	2	1
user_d	3.000	**4.333**	**2.333**	5.000	4	3

11.5.7 Collaborative Filtering with Calibrated Weighting

Collaborative filtering with calibrated weighting accounts for differences in standards between users.

Set the threshold to 2, which indicates the number of similar users to consider. Set the alpha factor to 1, which indicates the magnitude of the similar users' influence.

hyper-parameters

threshold	alpha
2	1

To predict how user A would rate item 4, look to the 2 most similar users since threshold is set to 2. User B rates item 4 as 2. User D rates item 4 as 5.

Weigh these ratings according to how similar the users are to user A. Calculate the relative weights.

Calculate the mean rating for each similar user. User B rates item 1 as 4, item 3 as 5, item 4 as 2, item 5 as 4, and item 6 as 2. User B's mean rating is then $(4 + 5 + 2 + 4 + 2) \div 5 = 3.40$. User D's mean rating is $(3 + 5 + 4 + 3) \div 4 = 3.75$. Note that B tends to rate items lower than user D does. You can think of user B as having a higher standard, or think of user D as being an easier grader.

Since the similar users rate according to different standards, express each user's rating in terms of the deviation from that user's standard. That effectively calibrates the ratings. User B's rating of 2 is a deviation of 1.40 below the mean rating of 3.40. User D's rating of 5 is 1.25 above 3.75.

User A's mean rating is $(4 + 5 + 5 + 4 + 1) \div 5 = 3.8$. The weighted average of the similar users' deviations is $(0.6654 \times -1.40) + (0.3346 \times 1.25) = -0.5132$. Predict that user A would rate item 4 to be a deviation from its mean rating, specifically $3.8 + -0.5132 = 3.287$. Or more generally, adjust the deviation by the alpha factor of 1, and predict a rating of $3.8 + (1 \times -0.5132) = 3.287$.

calculation for user_a rating of item_4

similar_user	rating	weight	rel_weight	mean_rating	deviation	contribution
user_b	2	0.9941	0.6654	3.40	-1.40	-0.9315
user_d	5	0.5000	0.3346	3.75	1.25	0.4183

prediction

user	mean_rating	alpha	deviation	item_4
user_a	3.8	1	-0.5132	3.287

Here are the predicted deviations and predicted ratings for all users for all items. Predicted ratings have been clipped to minimum 1 and maximum 5, where necessary, to remain interpretable as values on a 1 to 5 scale.

weighted average of others' deviations

	item_1	item_2	item_3	item_4	item_5	item_6
user_a	0.1482	0.000	1.6000	-0.5132	0.4829	-1.183
user_b	0.2000	1.328	0.8486	0.0000	0.1681	-2.513
user_c	-0.4342	1.200	1.2000	1.2500	0.2334	-1.432
user_d	0.2000	1.733	-0.2667	0.0000	0.0667	-1.600

predicted ratings

	item_1	item_2	item_3	item_4	item_5	item_6
user_a	3.948	3.800	5.000	3.287	4.283	2.618
user_b	3.600	4.728	4.249	3.400	3.568	1.000
user_c	1.566	3.200	3.200	3.250	2.233	1.000
user_d	3.950	5.000	3.483	3.750	3.817	2.150

Keep the known ratings, but filter in all missing ratings, taken from the table of predicted ratings.

data.filtered

	item_1	item_2	item_3	item_4	item_5	item_6
user_a	4.000	5.000	5.000	3.287	4	1
user_b	4.000	4.728	5.000	2.000	4	2
user_c	1.566	4.000	1.000	3.250	2	1
user_d	3.000	5.000	3.483	5.000	4	3

11.5.8 Collaborative Filtering with Calibrated Weighting, Item-Based

As an alternative to user-based collaborative filtering, we can instead use item-based.

Transpose the data table so that rows represent items and columns represent users.

data (transposed)

	user_a	user_b	user_c	user_d
item_1	4	4	NA	3
item_2	5	NA	4	NA
item_3	5	5	1	NA
item_4	NA	2	NA	5
item_5	4	4	2	4
item_6	1	2	1	3

Here is the item similarity matrix calculated based on the transposed data table:

item similarity matrix

	item_1	item_2	item_3	item_4	item_5	item_6
item_1	1	NA	NA	0	NA	0.0000
item_2	NA	1	1.0	NA	1.0000	NA
item_3	NA	1	1.0	NA	1.0000	0.5000
item_4	0	NA	NA	1	NA	1.0000
item_5	NA	1	1.0	NA	1.0000	0.5222
item_6	0	NA	0.5	1	0.5222	1.0000

Set threshold to 2 and alpha factor to 1.

parameters

threshold	alpha
2	1

Here are the predicted ratings for all items for all users:

predicted ratings, item-based

	user_a	user_b	user_c	user_d
item_1	3.667	3.667	3.667	3.667
item_2	5.000	5.000	2.417	5.000
item_3	4.167	4.167	2.667	4.167
item_4	2.750	3.750	2.750	4.750
item_5	4.417	4.833	1.917	3.500
item_6	2.250	1.000	1.000	2.907

Keep the known ratings, but filter in all missing ratings, taken from the table of predicted ratings.

data.filtered, item-based

	user_a	user_b	user_c	user_d
item_1	4.00	4	**3.667**	3.000
item_2	5.00	5	4.000	**5.000**
item_3	5.00	5	1.000	**4.167**
item_4	**2.75**	2	**2.750**	5.000
item_5	4.00	4	2.000	4.000
item_6	1.00	2	1.000	3.000

11.5.9 Recommendation

Based on collaborative filtering with calibrated weighting, advise user A that he can expect item 4 to be only modestly satisfying. The predicted rating of 3.287 is not too low, but not too high either. User B can expect to like item 2, with a predicted high rating of 4.728. User C can expect to be only modestly impressed with item 4 and its predicted rating of 3.25, but even less so with item 1 and its predicted rating of 1.566. Recommend item 2 more strongly than item 3 to user D because item 2's predicted rating of 5 is higher than item 3's predicted rating of 3.483.

11.6 CASE | Deceptive Hotel Reviews

Predictive modeling on text data to detect fraudulent customer surveys and inform a customer service improvement strategy in the hospitality industry.

11.6.1 Business Situation

Management at a large hotel regularly analyzes reviews from its customers about their stays. Customers are encouraged to provide ratings and text about their experiences, which they do by the thousands every month. Management considers ratings of 4 or 5 to be good, but ratings of 1, 2, or 3 to be poor. Receiving too many poor ratings is treated with alarm and can trigger a special project to address customer satisfaction issues before they get even worse. Such projects can be expensive and disruptive. They can require significant investments in process change. They can involve assigning employees to special tasks, taking them away from their normal duties. They are undertaken only if really necessary. The hotel's standard is that receiving more than 10% poor reviews in a month indicates that it's really necessary and should trigger a special project.

Complicating matters, the hotel is dealing with a recent increase in deceptive reviews. For a variety of reasons, people that have not actually stayed at the hotel are posting fabricated reviews. In a month with many poor reviews, it's hard to tell whether there are really customer satisfaction issues or merely that deceptive reviews are distorting the situation.

This month, there are an alarming number of poor reviews.

- **Role:** Vice President of Customer Service
- **Decision:** Launch a special project to address customer satisfaction issues?
- **Approach:** Build a predictive model using support vector machine applied to text data to distinguish truthful reviews from deceptive reviews. Base the decision to launch a special project on the predicted truthful reviews.

11.6.2 Data

Retrieve the monthly hotel review dataset. There are 1,185 reviews, each described by 19 variables. The *reviews.rating* variable indicates the reviewers' ratings. The *reviews.text* variable captures the reviewers' comments. Note that comments come in multiple languages, which will not obstruct our modeling method at all.

data *size 1185×3, a few observations shown*

reviews.rating	reviews.title	reviews.text
5	Outstanding Customer Service	The hotel was in a great location. The rooms were beautiful and very clean. The customer service was outstanding!!! It was nice to be greeted by name without them having to look at my credit card first!
5	Wonderful	The hotel was great. Staff went above and beyond bringing hot tea to room at 11:30 pm at no charge!
5	Sehr sch??nes Hotel	Tolles Zimmer, nettes Personal
4	A pleasant stay.	Very friendly staff; good location. Child and pet friendly. Great swimming pool. Nice, interesting decor; clean. Overall, a very good hotel.
2	Very Disappointing	Not sure why this is called a 5 star hotel. nothing 5 star about it. was very disappointed with the hotel..
1	Worst hotel I've ever visited	I stay at dozens of upscale hotels every year. This hotel is being renovated and ought to be closed until those renovations are complete. I can not exaggerate how lousy my stay was.

Here is a summary of the ratings. Note that 11.05% of the ratings are 1, 2, or 3, which constitutes more than 10% poor reviews. How many of these poor reviews are truthful and how many are deceptive?

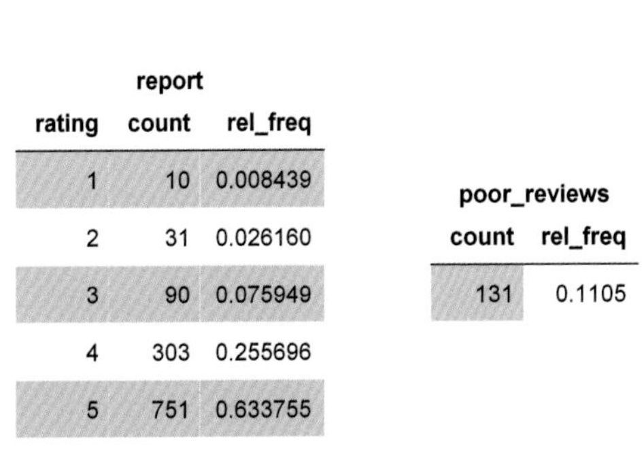

report

rating	count	rel_freq
1	10	0.008439
2	31	0.026160
3	90	0.075949
4	303	0.255696
5	751	0.633755

poor_reviews

count	rel_freq
131	0.1105

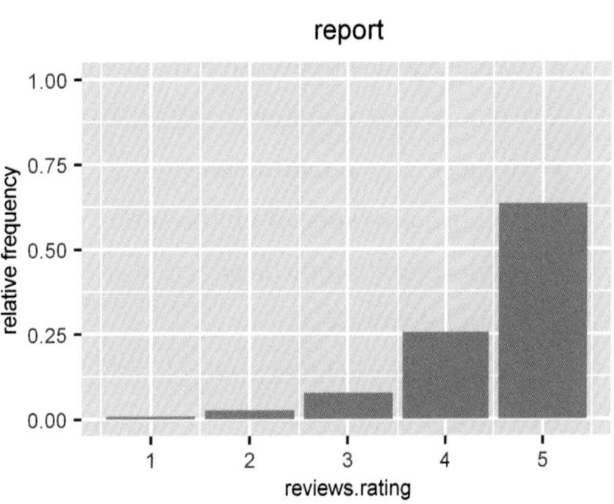

Also retrieve a reference classified hotel review dataset. This one comprises 1,600 positive and negative reviews of Chicago hotels, each known to be either truthful or deceptive. The *class* variable indicates truthful or deceptive, the *polarity* variable indicates positive or negative, and the *text* variable captures the reviewers' comments.

data.train *size 1600×3, a few observations shown*

class	polarity	text
truthful	positive	I asked for a high floor away from the elevator and that is what I got. The room was pleasantly decorated, functional and very clean. I didn't need a whole lot of service but when I did they were pleasant and prompt. I used the fitness center which was well equipped and everything was in working order. It is in a great location at one end of the Michigan Avenue shopping district.
truthful	negative	My daughter and I woke in the morning wanting to go swimming. When we arrived at the pool the water was covered by a white scum. I then attempted to use both of the phones at the pool, one white phone and one emergency red phone, to call the desk. Both were out of service!!!! I am glad there wasn't an emergency. As we were exited the pool area I ran into a hotel employee and told her about the problems and then asked her to call us when the pool was clean.... never heard back.
deceptive	positive	Recently, I traveled to Chicago for a business conference and was lucky enough to stay at the Hyatt Regency Chicago. The whole experience was wonderful! The room was spacious and beautiful, and the bed was so comfortable that I had no problem falling asleep, as I normally do at other hotels. The staff were polite and courteous, and after a delicious breakfast in the restaurant, I went to my conference with a smile on my face.
deceptive	negative	Overpriced is the best word to describe the Conrad Chicago hotel. While it may be in downtown Chicago, the room had no view. Although I asked for non-smoking, the room reeked of smoke. The elevators were very slow, and one was not working during my stay. There was a stain on the pillow, and the leg of one of the chairs in the room was broken. There was a dead bug in the bath tub. I was only given 2 towels for my 4 night stay. My credit card was billed twice, and it took 2 weeks to reverse to extra charge. I do not recommend this hotel at all!

11.6.3 Transform Reference Dataset

Transform the reference dataset to simplified text in document-term matrix representation to ready it for model construction.

Simplify the *text* variable like this:

- Replace any uppercase letters with corresponding lowercase letters.
- Remove any numbers.
- Remove any punctuation.
- Remove any special characters.
- Remove any stopwords.
- Stem all words.
- Remove any whitespace.

data.train *size 1600×3, a few observations shown*

class	polarity	text
truthful	positive	ask high floor away elev got room pleasant decor function clean didnt need whole lot servic pleasant prompt use fit center well equip everyth work order great locat one end michigan avenu shop district
truthful	negative	daughter woke morn want go swim arriv pool water cover white scum attempt use phone pool one white phone one emerg red phone call desk servic glad wasnt emerg exit pool area ran hotel employe told problem ask call us pool clean never heard back
deceptive	positive	recent travel chicago busi confer lucki enough stay hyatt regenc chicago whole experi wonder room spacious beauti bed comfort problem fall asleep normal hotel staff polit courteous delici breakfast restaur went confer smile face
deceptive	negative	overpr best word describ conrad chicago hotel may downtown chicago room view although ask nonsmok room reek smoke elev slow one work stay stain pillow leg one chair room broken dead bug bath tub given towel night stay credit card bill twice took week revers extra charg recommend hotel

Transform the *text* variable to a document-term matrix of 1-grams. Prune the matrix by removing sparse variables with more than 85% 0 values, leaving 56 variables. Replace the *text* variable with the matrix variables. In the resulting representation, each observation still corresponds to a review, but now a comment is represented by 56 binary variables rather than by 1 text variable.

data.train *size 1600×58, a few observations shown, first few variables shown*

class	polarity	also	area	arriv	back	bathroom	bed	book	busi	call	check	chicago
truthful	positive	0	0	0	0	0	0	0	0	0	0	0
truthful	negative	0	1	1	1	0	0	0	0	2	0	0
deceptive	positive	0	0	0	0	0	1	0	1	0	0	2
deceptive	negative	0	0	0	0	0	0	0	0	0	0	2

11.6.4 Model

Construct a model to predict *class* given the 56 binary variables, using the support vector machine method applied to the reference dataset in transformed representation. In-sample accuracy of the resulting model is 0.89.

insample_accuracy
0.89

data.train *size 1600×59, a few observations shown, first few variables shown*

class	class.predicted	polarity	also	area	arriv	back	bathroom	bed	book	busi	call
truthful	truthful	positive	0	0	0	0	0	0	0	0	0
truthful	truthful	negative	0	1	1	1	0	0	0	0	2
deceptive	deceptive	positive	0	0	0	0	0	1	0	1	0
deceptive	deceptive	negative	0	0	0	0	0	0	0	0	0

11.6.5 Predict

Transform the dataset of reviews about our hotel to ready it for prediction.

Simplify the *reviews.text* variable, using the same simplifications that were applied to the *text* variable of the reference dataset.

data *size 1185×3, a few observations shown*

reviews.rating	reviews.title	reviews.text
5	Outstanding Customer Service	hotel great locat room beauti clean custom servic outstand nice greet name without look credit card first
5	Wonderful	hotel great staff went beyond bring hot tea room pm charg
5	Sehr sch??nes Hotel	toll zimmer nett person
4	A pleasant stay.	friend staff good locat child pet friend great swim pool nice interest decor clean overal good hotel
2	Very Disappointing	sure call star hotel noth star disappoint hotel
1	Worst hotel I've ever visited	stay dozen upscal hotel everi year hotel renov close renov complet can exagger lousi stay

Transform the *reviews.text* variable to a document-term matrix of 1-grams. The matrix comprises 3,651 variables, 1 for each 1-gram that appears anywhere in the text. Do not prune the matrix.

dtm *size 1185×3651, a few observations shown, a few variables shown*

$day	$night	$two	abc	abd	abil	abl	abound	absolut	abut	acabou	accept	access
0	0	0	0	0	0	0	0	0	0	0	0	0
0	0	0	0	0	0	0	0	0	0	0	0	0
0	0	0	0	0	0	0	0	0	0	0	0	0
0	0	0	0	0	0	0	0	0	0	0	0	0
0	0	0	0	0	0	0	0	0	0	0	0	0
0	0	0	0	0	0	0	0	0	0	0	0	0

Reconcile variables in new document-term matrix with the 56 predictor variables expected by the model. Many variables get removed, and a few get added.

dtm *size 1185×56, a few observations shown, first few variables shown*

also	area	arriv	back	bathroom	bed	book	busi	call	check	chicago	clean	comfort
0	0	0	0	0	0	0	0	0	0	0	1	0
0	0	0	0	0	0	0	0	0	0	0	0	0
0	0	0	0	0	0	0	0	0	0	0	0	0
0	0	0	0	0	0	0	0	0	0	0	1	0
0	0	0	0	0	0	0	0	1	0	0	0	0
0	0	0	0	0	0	0	0	0	0	0	0	0

Replace the *reviews.text* variable with the matrix variables. In the resulting representation, each observation still corresponds to a review, but now a comment is represented by 56 binary variables rather than by 1 text variable.

data *size 1185×58, a few observations shown, first few variables shown*

reviews.rating	reviews.title	also	area	arriv	back	bathroom	bed	book	busi	call
5	Outstanding Customer Service	0	0	0	0	0	0	0	0	0
5	Wonderful	0	0	0	0	0	0	0	0	0
5	Sehr sch??nes Hotel	0	0	0	0	0	0	0	0	0
4	A pleasant stay.	0	0	0	0	0	0	0	0	0
2	Very Disappointing	0	0	0	0	0	0	0	0	1
1	Worst hotel I've ever visited	0	0	0	0	0	0	0	0	0

Predict the class of each review, using the model applied to the dataset in transformed representation.

data *size 1185×59, a few observations shown, first few variables shown*

class.predicted	reviews.rating	reviews.title	also	area	arriv	back	bathroom	bed	book
truthful	5	Outstanding Customer Service	0	0	0	0	0	0	0
truthful	5	Wonderful	0	0	0	0	0	0	0
truthful	5	Sehr sch??nes Hotel	0	0	0	0	0	0	0
truthful	4	A pleasant stay.	0	0	0	0	0	0	0
truthful	2	Very Disappointing	0	0	0	0	0	0	0
truthful	1	Worst hotel I've ever visited	0	0	0	0	0	0	0

Now that we have predicted class for each review, it can be useful to view the dataset with the binary variables swapped back out for the original text. The 6 reviews shown here are accepted as truthful.

data *size 1185×4, a few observations shown*

class.predicted	reviews.rating	reviews.title	reviews.text
truthful	5	Outstanding Customer Service	The hotel was in a great location. The rooms were beautiful and very clean. The customer service was outstanding!!! It was nice to be greeted by name without them having to look at my credit card first!
truthful	5	Wonderful	The hotel was great. Staff went above and beyond bringing hot tea to room at 11:30 pm at no charge!
truthful	5	Sehr sch??nes Hotel	Tolles Zimmer, nettes Personal
truthful	4	A pleasant stay.	Very friendly staff; good location. Child and pet friendly. Great swimming pool. Nice, interesting decor; clean. Overall, a very good hotel.
truthful	2	Very Disappointing	Not sure why this is called a 5 star hotel. nothing 5 star about it. was very disappointed with the hotel..
truthful	1	Worst hotel I've ever visited	I stay at dozens of upscale hotels every year. This hotel is being renovated and ought to be closed until those renovations are complete. I can not exaggerate how lousy my stay was.

These 5 reviews are suspected to be deceptive.

data *a few predicted deceptive observations shown*

class.predicted	reviews.rating	reviews.title	reviews.text
deceptive	5	Great Hotel!	This hotel was just charming. The decor was modern and eclectic and somewhat whimsical. Everything was spotlessly clean. The bed was comfortable and the linens luxurious. I would recommend this to anyone.
deceptive	5	can't wait to go back	the staff was great. it was refreshing to stay in a swanky/modern style hotel as opposed to the more traditional looks of the others. we will definately go back!
deceptive	4	Welcoming, comfortable, good location and excellent service.	The stay was good, price of the room was too expensive for the hotel. I have stayed in others in the area for less than half the price, that had more services and free parking. Don't think I will recommend or stay there again.
deceptive	3	Expected More	My experience wasn't great. There was a ton of noise, not only in the room above mine, but in the hall as well. The walls must be paper thin. And the doors of the room have a tendency to be very heavy and slam behind you if you aren't aware... RECOMMENDATION TO HOTEL: Install device to the doors to soften the blow of doors slamming in the hall. I'm trying to sleep!!!
deceptive	1	nice hotel	wrong rooms the room i booked was not the room i was placed in they then put me in another room which still was the one i paid for i was refunded the difference in the morning but of the few times ive stayed there that was the first bad experience

11.6.6 Business Result

Treating all reviews as legitimate, we saw that we received 11.05% poor ratings. However, our model predicts that some of the poor reviews are deceptive. It predicts that some of the good reviews are deceptive, too. On balance, if we treat only reviews predicted to be truthful as legitimate and ignore the rest, we see that only 10.5% of them give poor ratings. From this analysis, it looks like deceptive reviews could be distorting our view of the situation, but not by much. The 10.5% poor reviews is not quite as bad as 11.05% poor reviews, but still above 10% and cause for concern. Hotel management needs to take action to address a real customer satisfaction issue.

poor_reviews

count	rel_freq
131	0.1105

poor_reviews.truthful_only

count	rel_freq
112	0.105

report

rating	count	rel_freq
1	10	0.0084
2	31	0.0262
3	90	0.0759
4	303	0.2557
5	751	0.6338

report.truthful_only

rating	count	rel_freq
1	5	0.0047
2	26	0.0244
3	81	0.0759
4	274	0.2568
5	681	0.6382

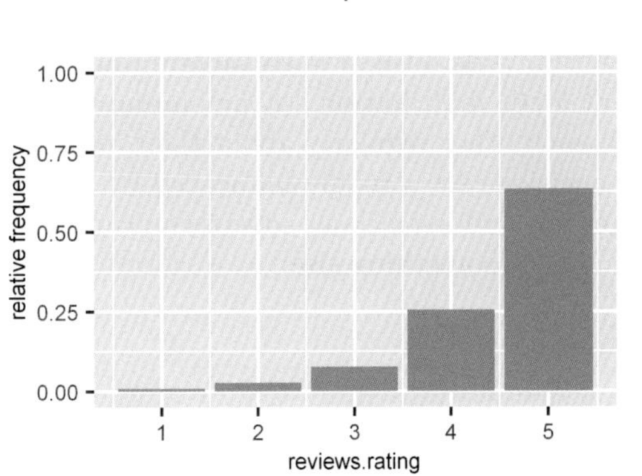

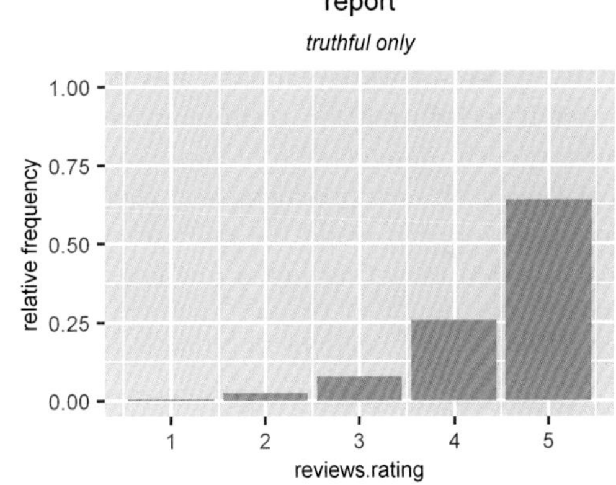

11.7 CASE | Targeted Marketing

Network analysis with descriptive statistics for network data to simulate market adoption and inform a marketing strategy in the enterprise software industry.

11.7.1 Business Situation

An enterprise software company has developed a new product and is considering how to best market it to information technology managers at large multinational conglomerates. In this industry, such managers often communicate with each other regularly about their interest and experience with new products, and their buying decisions are strongly influenced by what they hear. The company could use its marketing budget for a wide-reaching advertising campaign, or for a program targeting just a few key managers, or for something else.

- **Role:** Vice President of Sales & Marketing
- **Decision:** Which managers to market to?
- **Approach:** Treat the relationships among managers as a network. Use descriptive statistics to rank managers by importance. For various decision methods, simulate communication and influence consequences of decisions over time to predict product adoption and estimate profit.

11.7.2 Decision Model

The decision model starts with a decision method that selects which managers we market the product to. The business result is the profit measured as the revenue from product adoptions less the budget spent on marketing. We define interest in the product as the probability of adopting the product during the current time period.

Business parameters include the following:

- **budget:** total budget available to promote the product, a value set by marketing operations

- **price:** unit price of product, a value set by marketing operations
- **default interest:** a manager's pre-marketing level of interest in the product, a value derived from market research
- **referral weight:** the level of influence that relations have on a manager's level of interest in the product, a value derived from market research

business parameters

budget	price	default_interest	referral_weight
200,000	100,000	0.01	0.1

Marketing generates interest in the product based on the amounts spent marketing to individual managers, and the default level of interest that marketing builds on. The amounts spent, in turn, depend on which individual managers we market to and how the budget gets distributed among them. The number of managers who adopt the product depends on the network of relationships, managers' initial levels of interest, and the influence that relations have on each other. Revenue depends on the number of adoptions and unit price of the product.

Decision Model

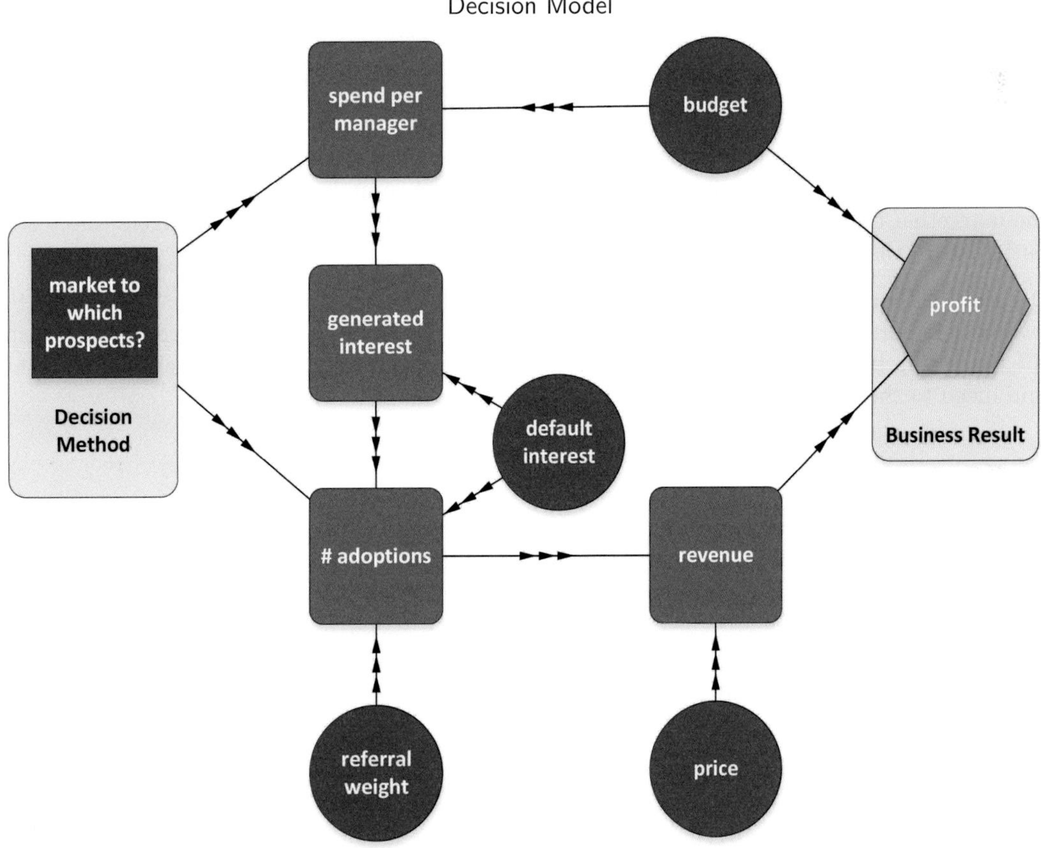

From market research, we have a formula to quantify generated interest. The relationship between interest and spend is parabolic, with default level of interest at no spend and maximum level of interest 0.82 at $100,000 spend.

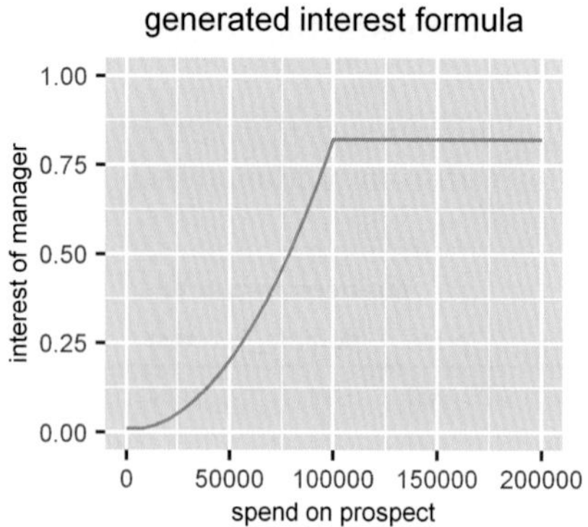

11.7.2.1 Decision Methods

We'll explore 4 decision methods:

Decision Method 1: Always do no marketing. This effectively initializes all managers' interests to the default level of interest.

Decision Method 2: Always do non-targeted marketing. This effectively initializes all managers' interests to the same level, determined by allocating the marketing budget equally across all managers.

Decision Method 3: Always do targeted marketing to a few random managers. For a few managers chosen at random, interest is initialized to the same level, determined by allocating the marketing budget equally across those managers. For the remaining managers, interest is initialized to the default level of interest.

Decision Method 4: Always do targeted marketing to the few most important managers. For the few most important managers, interest is initialized to the same level, determined by allocating the marketing budget equally across those managers. For the remaining managers, interest is initialized to the default level of interest.

11.7.3 Data

Retrieve the network data on managers and their relationships. There are 19 managers, each of whom has 1 of 4 competing products in use: A, B, C, or D. There are 32 known relationships between managers that could potentially directly influence buying decisions.

nodes

name	product
Melvin Ashe	A
Winston Allen	A
Walter Alex	A
Sam Sutter	A
Andrew O'Reilly	A
Kevin Miller	B
Mary Miller	B
Sam Albright	B
Nancy Albright	B
Hank Hanover	B
Mark Shelley	C
Francis Aguilar	C
Angela Atkins	C
Homer Atkins	C
Michelle Allen	C
Zeb Jordan	D
Arthur Ah	D
Arthur Abbot	D
Sarah Atkins	D

links *first 16 links shown*

person_1	person_2
Mary Miller	Hank Hanover
Hank Hanover	Kevin Miller
Hank Hanover	Nancy Albright
Nancy Albright	Kevin Miller
Nancy Albright	Sam Albright
Nancy Albright	Arthur Abbot
Nancy Albright	Sarah Atkins
Nancy Albright	Homer Atkins
Arthur Abbot	Sarah Atkins
Homer Atkins	Angela Atkins
Sarah Atkins	Homer Atkins
Homer Atkins	Arthur Ah
Arthur Ah	Sarah Atkins
Homer Atkins	Michelle Allen
Michelle Allen	Francis Aguilar
Arthur Ah	Zeb Jordan

links *last 16 links shown*

person_1	person_2
Francis Aguilar	Mark Shelley
Zeb Jordan	Mark Shelley
Zeb Jordan	Melvin Ashe
Mark Shelley	Melvin Ashe
Mark Shelley	Andrew O'Reilly
Andrew O'Reilly	Melvin Ashe
Andrew O'Reilly	Winston Allen
Winston Allen	Sam Sutter
Winston Allen	Walter Alex
Sam Sutter	Walter Alex
Sam Albright	Mark Shelley
Sam Albright	Zeb Jordan
Nancy Albright	Melvin Ashe
Zeb Jordan	Hank Hanover
Mark Shelley	Hank Hanover
Melvin Ashe	Hank Hanover

Here is the network data visualized as a network diagram. Nodes are color-coded by product in use. Links are bi-directional, so you can think of each one as a pair of directed links, one going from a node and another going to it.

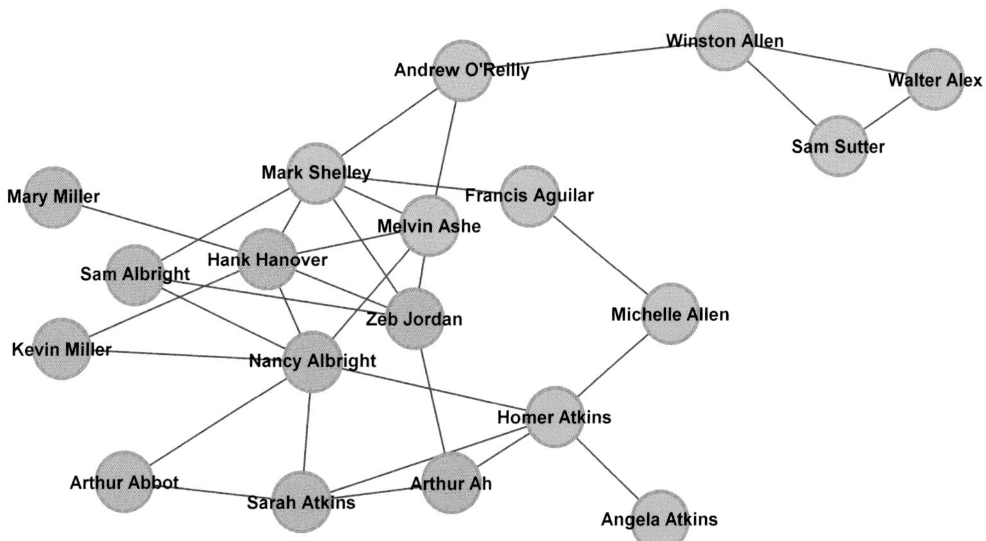

11.7.4 Descriptive Statistics

Calculate the shortest path lengths for each pair of managers.

shortest path length *first few rows shown, first few columns shown*

	Melvin Ashe	Winston Allen	Walter Alex	Sam Sutter	Andrew O'Reilly
Melvin Ashe	0	2	3	3	1
Winston Allen	2	0	1	1	1
Walter Alex	3	1	0	1	2
Sam Sutter	3	1	1	0	2
Andrew O'Reilly	1	1	2	2	0
Kevin Miller	2	4	5	5	3
Mary Miller	2	4	5	5	3
Sam Albright	2	3	4	4	2

Calculate several other node-level descriptive statistics for each manager.

node-level statistics

	indegree	outdegree	betweenness	avg_path_len	closeness	eccentricity	eigen
Melvin Ashe	5	5	33.017	1.944	0.5143	3	0.9602
Winston Allen	3	3	32.000	3.056	0.3273	5	0.1175
Walter Alex	2	2	0.000	3.944	0.2535	6	0.0341
Sam Sutter	2	2	0.000	3.944	0.2535	6	0.0341
Andrew O'Reilly	3	3	45.000	2.333	0.4286	4	0.4543
Kevin Miller	2	2	0.000	2.611	0.3830	5	0.4459
Mary Miller	1	1	0.000	3.000	0.3333	5	0.2249
Sam Albright	3	3	2.350	2.278	0.4390	4	0.6331
Nancy Albright	7	7	49.500	1.944	0.5143	4	0.9822
Hank Hanover	6	6	25.850	2.056	0.4865	4	1.0000
Mark Shelley	6	6	32.683	2.056	0.4865	4	0.9419
Francis Aguilar	2	2	7.900	2.611	0.3830	4	0.2494
Angela Atkins	1	1	0.000	3.278	0.3051	6	0.1106
Homer Atkins	5	5	27.483	2.333	0.4286	5	0.4915
Michelle Allen	2	2	4.550	2.833	0.3529	5	0.1666
Zeb Jordan	5	5	11.483	2.167	0.4615	4	0.8905
Arthur Ah	3	3	4.400	2.500	0.4000	5	0.4238
Arthur Abbot	2	2	0.000	2.778	0.3600	5	0.3338
Sarah Atkins	4	4	3.783	2.444	0.4091	5	0.5019

Calculate several network-level descriptive statistics.

network-level statistics

size	order	diameter	average_path_length	density
32	19	6	2.637	0.1871

11.7.5 Important Managers

Some managers directly and indirectly influence other managers' buying decisions more than others. Those with more influence are more important than the others, in the sense that any marketing impact on those with more influence could effectively propagate to their relations without us directly marketing to them. At least 5 statistics measure a prospect's influence: outdegree, betweenness centrality, closeness centrality, lack of eccentricity, and eigen centrality. Here are the 19 managers ranked by these statistics:

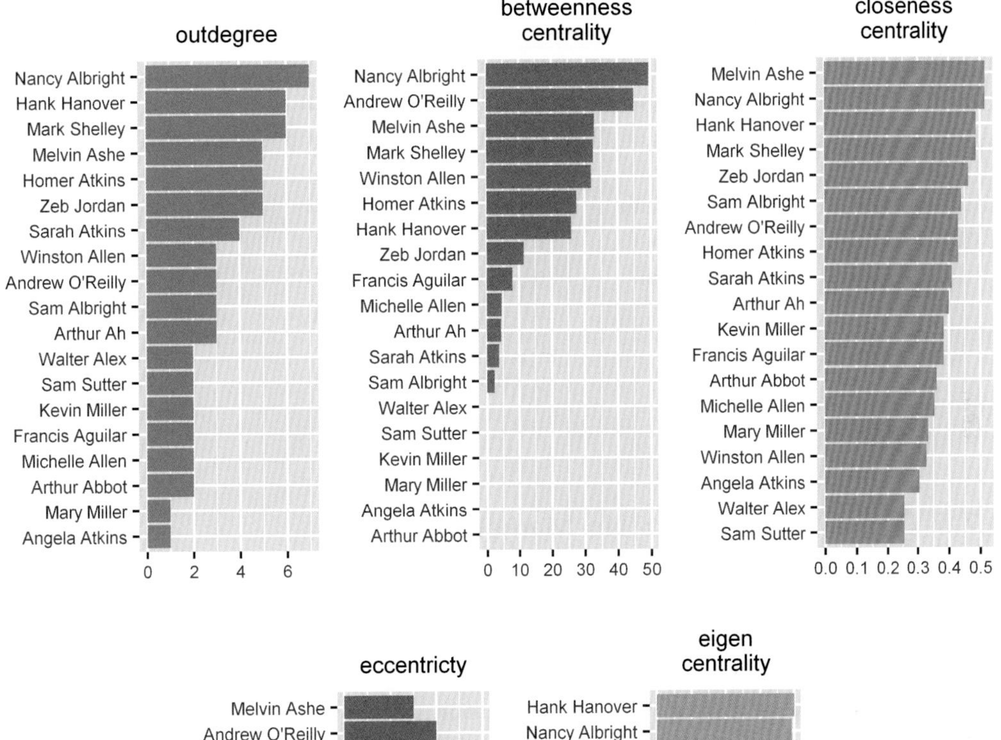

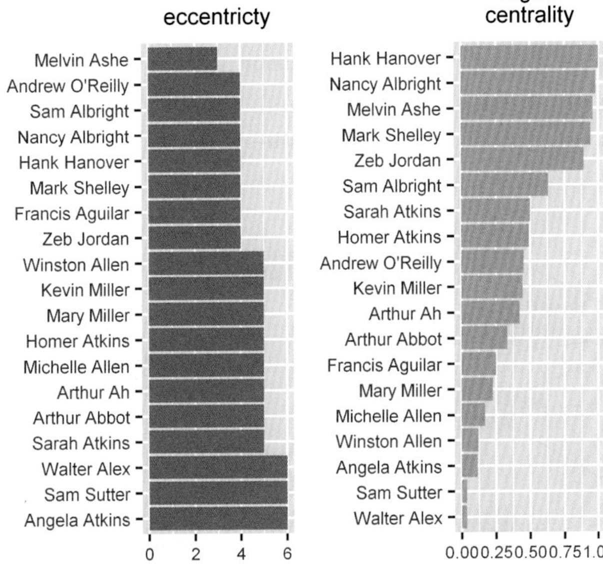

Note that some managers rank high across several measures of influence. Here are the 19 managers ranked by the number of times they appear among the top 4 managers across the 5

statistics. Melvin Ashe and Nancy Albright both appear among the top 4 across all 5 statistics. Melvin is ranked fourth by outdegree, third by betweenness centrality, first by closeness centrality, first by lack of eccentricity, and third by eigen centrality. Similarly for Nancy. Mark Shelly appears among the top 4 across 4 statistics: third by outdegree, fourth by betweenness centrality, fourth by closeness centrality, and fourth by eigen centrality. Similarly for the other managers. Let's define importance of manager as the number of times he or she appears among the top 4 managers across all 5 statistics.

in top 4

	count
Melvin Ashe	5
Nancy Albright	5
Mark Shelley	4
Hank Hanover	3
Andrew O'Reilly	2
Sam Albright	1
Winston Allen	0
Walter Alex	0
Sam Sutter	0
Kevin Miller	0

in top 4

	count
Mary Miller	0
Francis Aguilar	0
Angela Atkins	0
Homer Atkins	0
Michelle Allen	0
Zeb Jordan	0
Arthur Ah	0
Arthur Abbot	0
Sarah Atkins	0

11.7.6 Decision Method 1: No Marketing

What if the decision method produces a decision to do no marketing? What will profit be?

All managers start with the default 1% interest in the product.

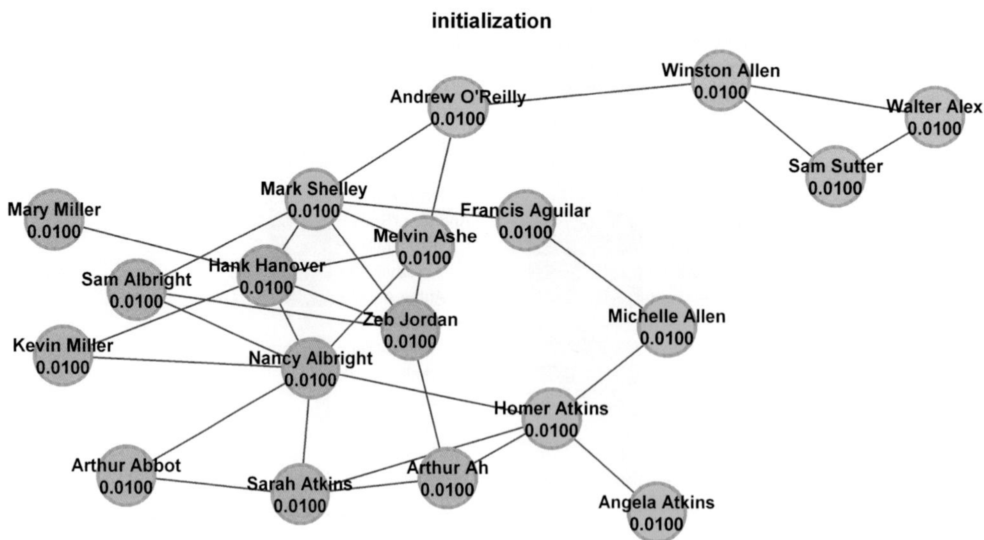

Sometime later, although probability is only 1% that any 1 manager will adopt the product, by chance Homer Atkins' interest jumps to 100% and he does adopt the product.

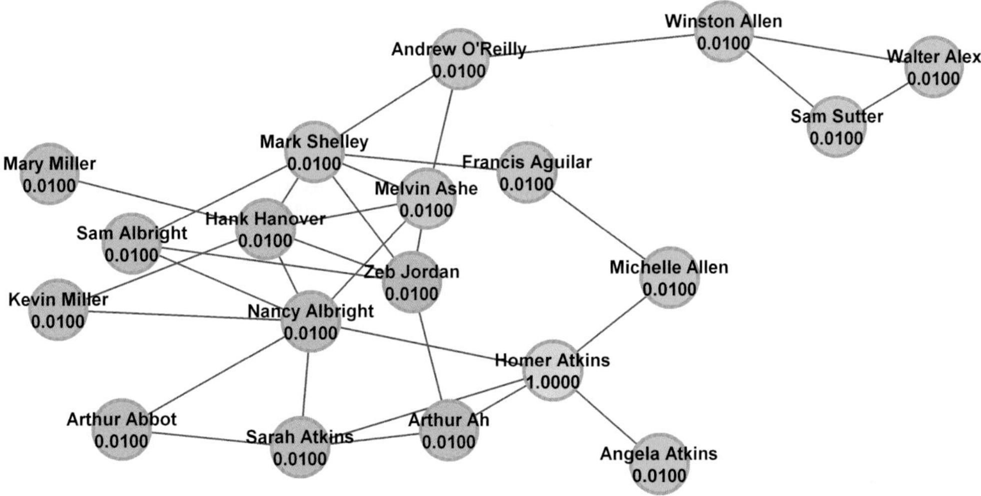

Because Homer is now fully endorsing the product, his relations Michelle Allen, Angela Atkins, Arthur Ah, Sarah Atkins, and Nancy Albright become more interested.

$$interest(v) \leftarrow \Big((1-\omega) \times interest(v)\Big) + \Big(\omega \times \underset{i}{mean}(interest(i))\Big)$$

where ...

- v is a node
- i is an arbitrary node; shortest path from v to i is 1
- ω is the referral weight

Michelle's interest is updated to
$((1.0 - 0.1) \times 0.01) + (0.10 \times mean(0.01, 1.0)) = 0.0595.$

Angela's interest is updated to
$((1.0 - 0.1) \times 0.01) + (0.10 \times mean(1.0)) = 0.1090.$

Arthur's interest is updated to
$((1.0 - 0.1) \times 0.01) + (0.10 \times mean(0.01, 0.01, 1.0)) = 0.0430.$

Sarah's interest is updated to
$((1.0 - 0.1) \times 0.01) + (0.10 \times mean(0.01, 0.01, 0.01, 1.0)) = 0.0348.$

Nancy's interest is updated to
$((1.0 - 0.1) \times 0.01) + (0.10 \times mean(0.01, 0.01, 0.01, 0.01, 0.01, 0.01, 1.0)) = 0.0241.$

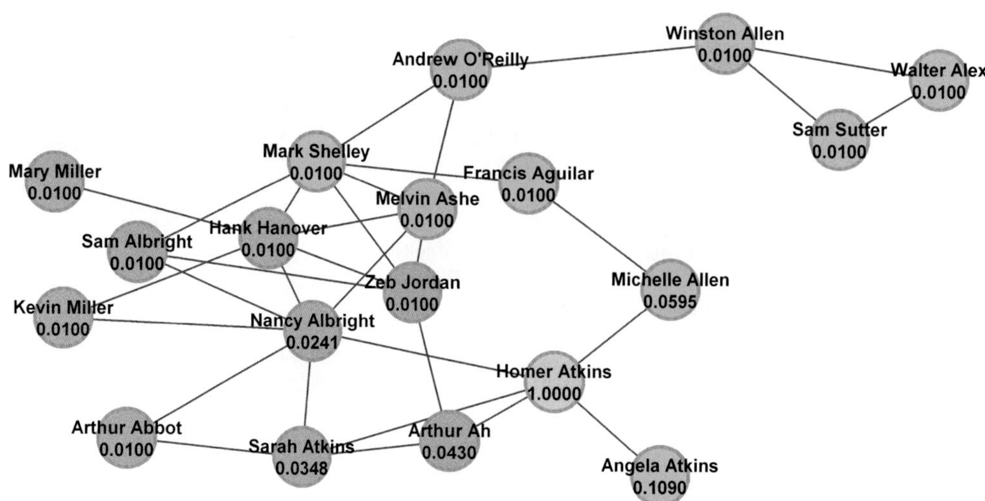

Continue on to the next timestep. Each manager might or might not adopt the product based on his or her current interest and chance occurrence. Any mangers who do adopt the product get their interests updated to 100%. Other prospects get their interests updated as influenced by their relations' interests.

After 10 timesteps, see that 6 out of the 19 managers have adopted the product.

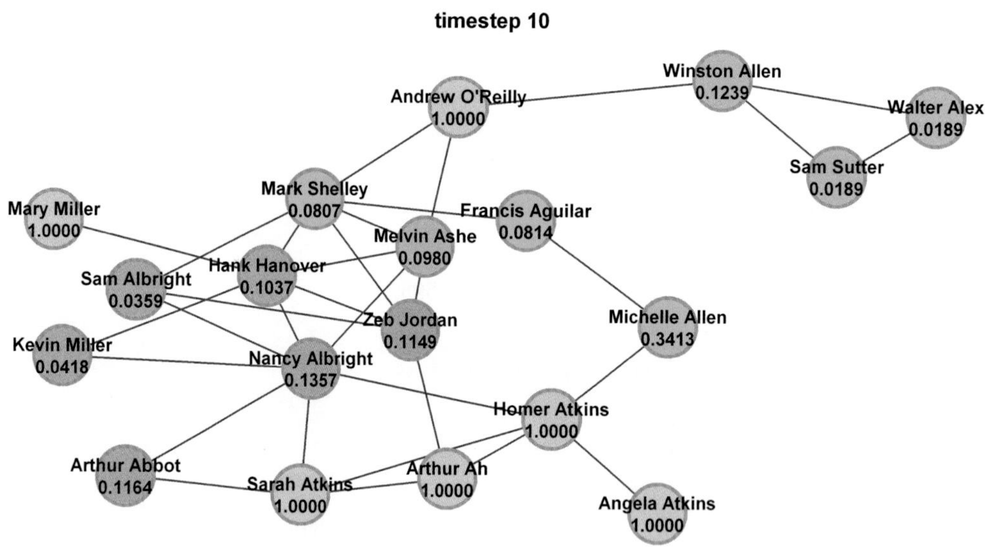

Since we do not spend any of the marketing budget, estimated profit at 10 timesteps is \$600,000.

$$\text{profit} = \text{adoptions} \times \text{price} = 6 \times 100{,}000 = 600{,}000$$

11.7.7 Decision Method 2: Non-Targeted Marketing

What if the decision method produces a decision to do non-targeted marketing? What will profit be?

Spend the marketing budget on an advertising campaign that reaches all managers, not targeting any specific managers. This effectively allocates the budget evenly across all managers.

$$\text{spend per manager} = \frac{\text{budget}}{\text{managers}} = \frac{200{,}000}{19} = 10{,}526$$

From the generated interest formula, interest generated by spend of \$10,526 is 1.47%, so all managers start with that level of interest in the product.

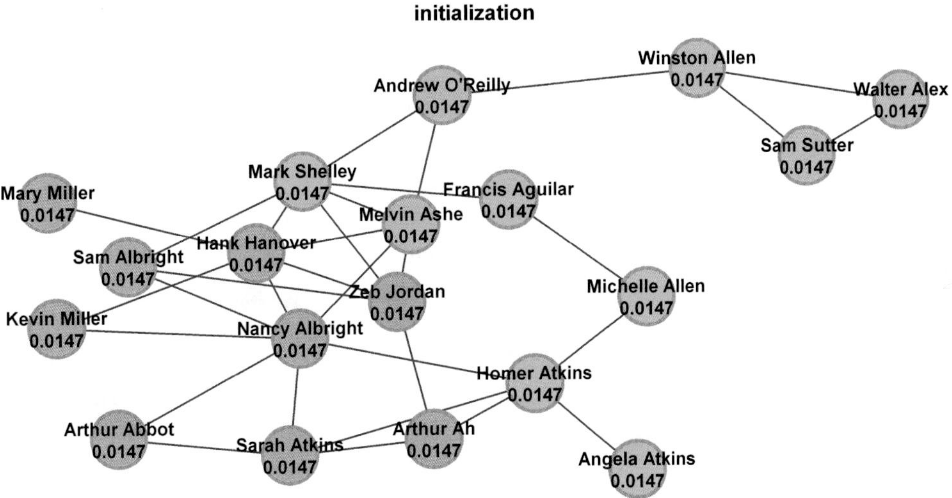

Step through product adoptions and interest updates. After 10 timesteps, see that 8 out of 19 managers have adopted the product.

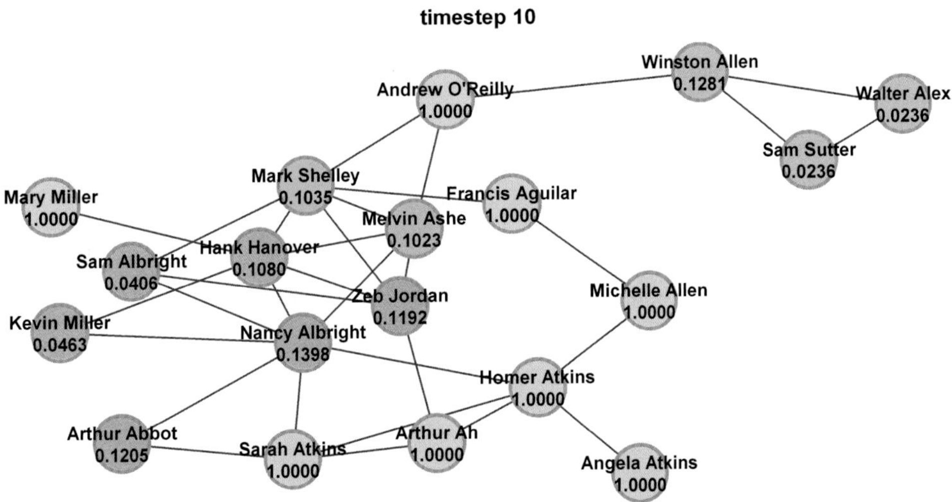

With non-targeted marketing, estimated profit at 10 timesteps is \$600,000. Non-targeted marketing produces a business result no better than no marketing does.

$$\text{profit} = (\text{adoptions} \times \text{price}) - \text{budget} = (8 \times 100{,}000) - 200{,}000 = 600{,}000$$

11.7.8 Decision Method 3: Targeted Marketing to Random Prospects

What if the decision method produces a decision to do targeted marketing to random prospects? What will profit be?

Spend the marketing budget on 2 managers, Angela Atkins and Sam Sutter, who are chosen at random.

$$\text{spend per manager} = \frac{\text{budget}}{\text{managers}} = \frac{200{,}000}{2} = 100{,}000$$

From the generated interest formula, interest generated by spend of \$100,000 is 80.20%, so Angela and Sam start with 80.20% interest in the product, and the remaining managers start with the default 1% interest in the product.

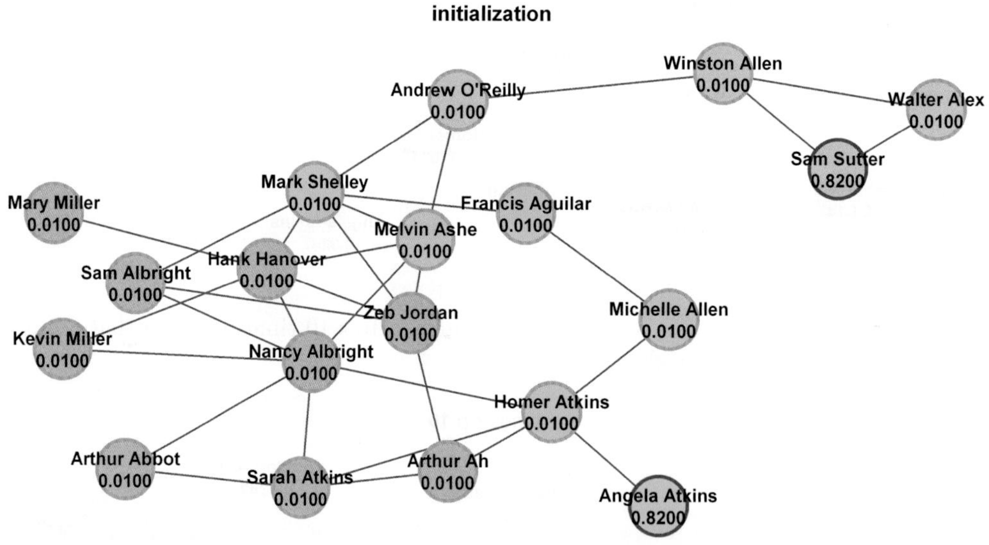

Angela and Sam immediately communicate their strong interest to their few relations. Continue to step through product adoptions and interest updates. Within a few more timesteps, Angela and Sam both adopt the product themselves, which increases their few relations' interests, and those relations communicate higher interest to the few relations of their own. After 10 timesteps, see that 8 out of 19 managers have adopted the product.

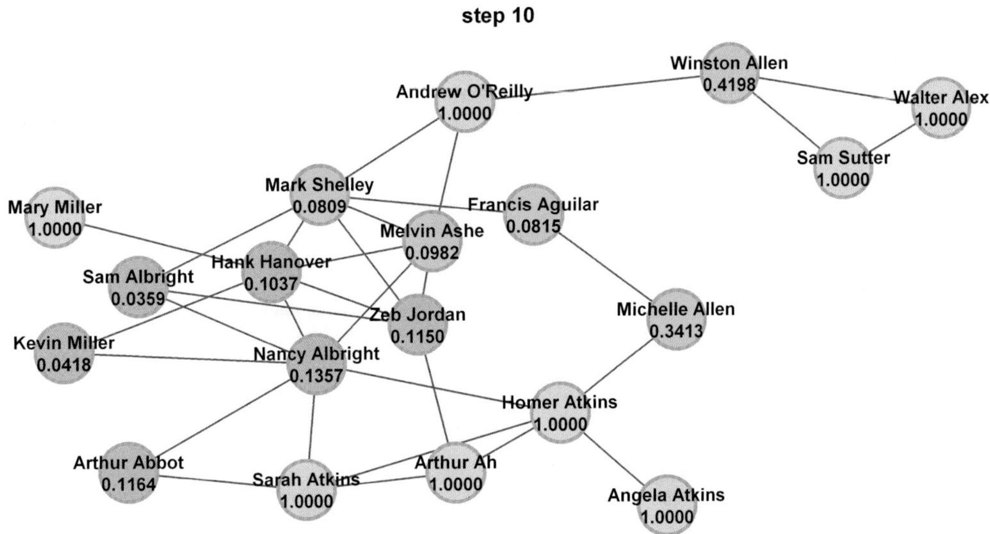

With targeted marketing, estimated profit at 10 timesteps is \$600,000. Targeted marketing produces a business result no better than non-targeted marketing does, when the targets are chosen at random.

$$\text{profit} = (\text{adoptions} \times \text{price}) - \text{budget} = (8 \times 100{,}000) - 200{,}000 = 600{,}000$$

11.7.9 Decision Method 4: Targeted Marketing to Important Prospects

What if the decision method produces a decision to do targeted marketing to important prospects? What will profit be?

From our analysis of manager importance, we determined Melvin Ashe and Nancy Albright to be the 2 most important managers. Spend the marketing budget on Melvin and Nancy.

$$\text{spend per manager} = \frac{\text{budget}}{\text{managers}} = \frac{200{,}000}{2} = 100{,}000$$

From the generated interest formula, interest generated by spend of \$100,000 is 80.20%, so Melvin and Nancy start with 80.20% interest in the product, and the remaining managers start with the default 1% interest in the product.

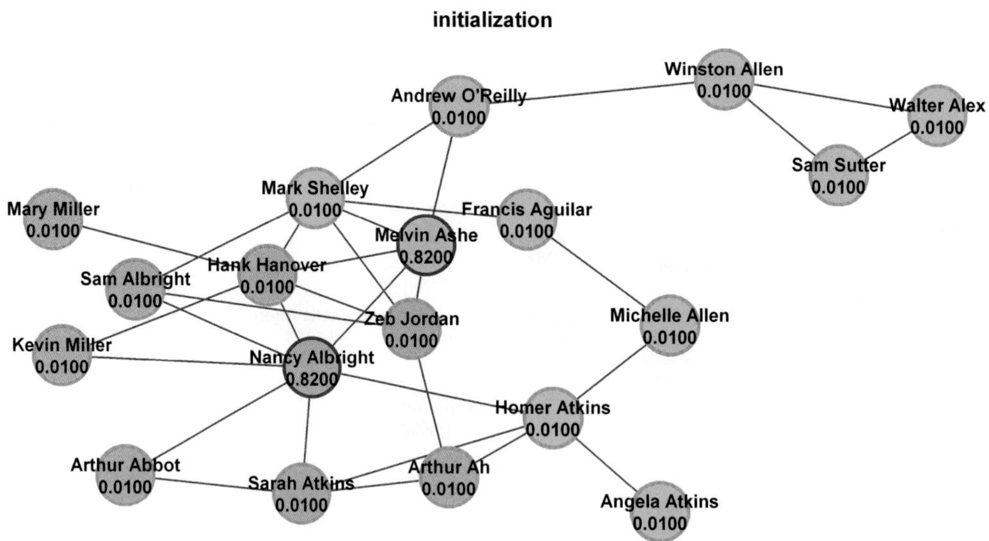

Melvin and Nancy immediately communicate their strong interest to their many relations. Some managers hear of strong interest from both Melvin and Nancy. Continue to step through product adoptions and interest updates. Within a few more timesteps, Melvin and Nancy both adopt the product themselves, which increases their many realtions' interests even more, and those relations communicate higher interest to their own many relations. After 10 timesteps, see that 13 out of 19 prospects have adopted the product.

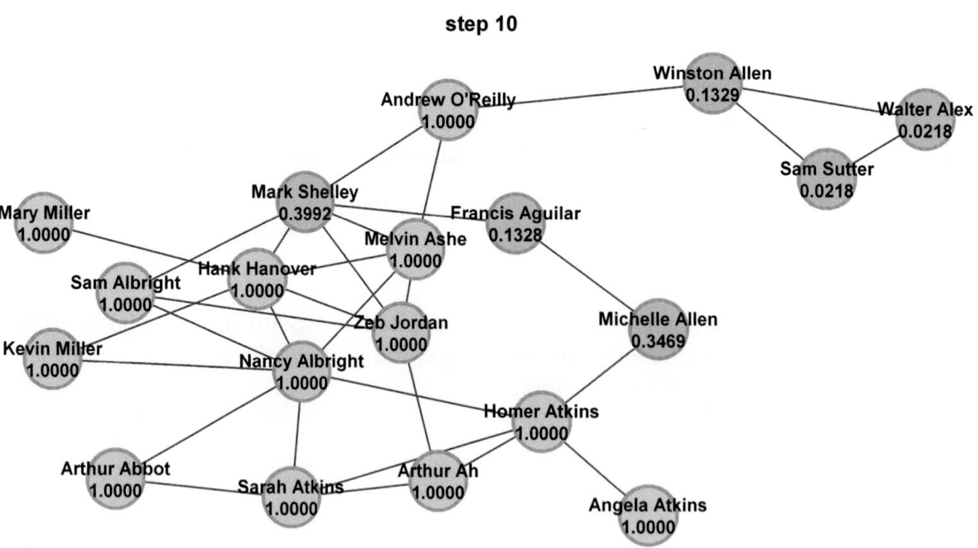

With targeted marketing to important managers, estimated profit at 10 timesteps is \$1,100,000. Targeted marketing to important managers produces a business result much better than the other strategies do.

$$\text{profit} = (\text{adoptions} \times \text{price}) - \text{budget} = (13 \times 100{,}000) - 200{,}000 = 1{,}100{,}000$$

11.7.10 Comparative Analysis

Here is a comparison of the 4 decision methods:

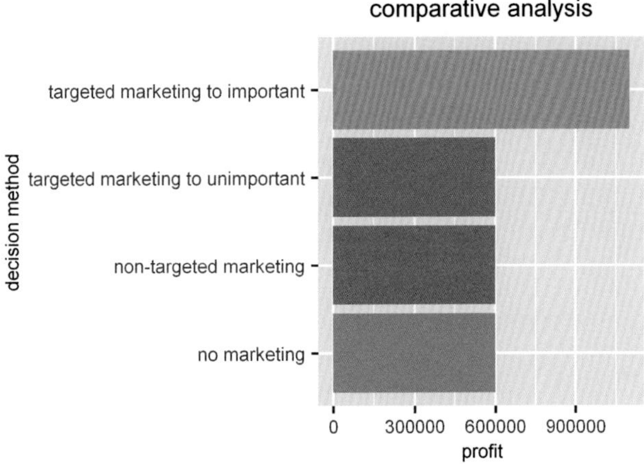

11.7.11 Reveal

The network data used here to demonstrate targeted marketing are actually based on data compiled about the 911 hijackers who attacked the United States in 2001. At the time, the organizational structure of the group was unclear. Subsequent analysis of the network of relationships, more complex but similar to our analysis here, quickly brought into focus that Mohammed Atta (Melvin Ashe) and Nawaf al-Hamzi (Nancy Albright) were the ringleaders, disseminating information efficiently to the others without directly contacting most of them.

in top 4	real_name	count
Melvin Ashe	Mohamed Atta	5
Nancy Albright	Nawaf Alhamzi	5
Mark Shelley	Marwan al-Shehhi	4
Hank Hanover	Hani Hanjour	3
Andrew O'Reilly	Abdulaziz Alomari	2
Sam Albright	Salem Alhamzi	1
Winston Allen	Waleed Alshehri	0
Walter Alex	Wail Alshari	0
Sam Sutter	Sata al-Suqami	0
Kevin Miller	Khalid al-Midhar	0

in top 4	real_name	count
Mary Miller	Majed Moqed	0
Francis Aguilar	Fayez Ahmed	0
Angela Atkins	Ahmed Alghamdi	0
Homer Atkins	Hamza Alghamdi	0
Michelle Allen	Mohald Alshehri	0
Zeb Jordan	Ziad Jarrah	0
Arthur Ah	Ahmed Alhaznawi	0
Arthur Abbot	Ahmed Alnami	0
Sarah Atkins	Saeed Alghamdi	0

I hope that posterity will judge me kindly, not only as to the things which I have explained, but also to those which I have intentionally omitted so as to leave to others the pleasure of discovery.

—René Descartes

Photo Credits

Cover

Cover | © 3dsguru / iStock via Getty Images

Executive Overview

Executive Overview | © Mehau Kulyk / Science Photo Library via Getty Images

Data & Decisions

Data-to-Decision Process Model | © Jeffrey Coolidge / Stone via Getty Images
Decision Models | © Luis Jou Garcia / Moment via Getty Images
Sensitivity Analysis | © HBSS / Corbis via Getty Images

Data Preparation

Data Objects | © onurdongel / E+ via Getty Images
Selection | © fcafotodigital / E+ via Getty Images
Amalgamation | © wasan prunglampoo / iStock via Getty Images
Synthetic Variables | © zennie / E+ via Getty Images
Normalization | © John Lamb / The Image Bank via Getty Images
Dummy Variables | © Caspar Benson / fStop via Getty Images
CASE | High-Tech Stocks | © Spencer Platt/Staff / Hulton Archive via Getty Images

Data Exploration

Descriptive Statistics | © Duncan Nicholls and Simon Webb / OJO Images via Getty Images
Similarity | © FatCamera / E+ via Getty Images
Cross-Tabulation | © ra-photos / E+ via Getty Images
Data Visualization | © Andrew Brookes / Image Source via Getty Images
Kernel Density Estimation | © Louise Heusinkveld / Photodisc via Getty Images
CASE Fundraising Strategy | © Peter Dazeley / The Image Bank via Getty Images
CASE Iowa Liquor Sales © RapidEye / iStock via Getty Images

Data Transformation

Balance | © Michal Chodyra / iStock via Getty Images
Imputation © EThamPhoto / Corbis via Getty Images
Alignment | © gui00878 / E+ via Getty Images
Principal Component Analysis | © KingWu / E+ via Getty Images
CASE Loan Portfolio | © phototechno / iStock via Getty Images

Classification I

Classification Methodology | © Federica Grassi / Moment via Getty Images
Classifier Evaluation | © choja / E+ via Getty Images
k-Nearest Neighbors | © Peter Adams / Stone via Getty Images
Logistic Regression | © wellsie82 / Moment via Getty Images
Decision Tree | © John Greim/Contributor / LightRocket via Getty Images
CASE Loan Portfolio Revisited | © phototechno / iStock via Getty Images

Classification II

Naive Bayes | © moodboard / moodboard via Getty Images
Support Vector Machine | © wenbin / Moment via Getty Images
Neural Network | © liquid kingdom-kim yusuf underwater photography / Moment via Getty Images
CASE Telecom Customer Churn | © skynesher / E+ via Getty Images
CASE Truck Fleet Maintenance | © RistoArnaudov / E+ via Getty Images

Classification III

Multinomial Classification | © Aksonov / E+ via Getty Images
CASE Facial Recognition | © Dimitri Otis / Stone via Getty Images
CASE Credit Card Fraud | © Martin Barraud / OJO Images via Getty Images

Regression

Regression Methodology | © Louisa Gouliamaki/Stringer / AFP via Getty Images
Regressor Evaluation | © South_agency / E+ via Getty Images
Linear Regression | © Bjorn Holland / Photodisc via Getty Images
Regression Versions | © Ascent/PKS Media Inc. / Stone via Getty Images
CASE Call Center Scheduling | © Marco_Piunti / iStock via Getty Images

Ensemble Assembly

Bagging | © krblokhin / iStock via Getty Images
Boosting | © GK Hart/Vikki Hart / Stone via Getty Images
Stacking | © Steve Smith / Tetra images via Getty Images

Cluster Analysis

Cluster Analysis Methodology | © Leonello Calvetti / Science Photo Library via Getty Images
Cluster Model Evaluation | © Matteo Colombo / DigitalVision via Getty Images
k-Means | © Mark Stevenson/UIG / Collection Mix: Subjects via Getty Images
Hierarchical Agglomeration | © Robert Daly / OJO Images via Getty Images
Gaussian Mixture | © Buena Vista Images / Stone via Getty Images
CASE Fortune 500 Diversity | © Flashpop / DigitalVision via Getty Images
CASE Music Market Segmentation | © Image Source / Image Source via Getty Images

Special Data Types

Text Data | © enot-poloskun / E+ via Getty Images
Time Series Data | © WPA Pool/Pool / Getty Images Entertainment via Getty Images
Network Data | © John Lund / Photodisc via Getty Images
PageRank | © Prasert Prapanoppasin / Moment via Getty Images
Collaborative Filtering | © ljubaphoto / E+ via Getty Images
CASE Deceptive Hotel Reviews | © Ziga Plahutar / E+ via Getty Images
CASE Targeted Marketing | © John M Lund Photography Inc / DigitalVision via Getty Images

Index